Authoring Tools for Advanced Technology Learning Environments

Authoring Tools for Advanced Technology Learning Environments

Toward Cost-Effective Adaptive, Interactive and Intelligent Educational Software

edited by

Tom Murray
Hampshire College, Amherst, Massachusetts, U.S.A.

Stephen Blessing
Carnegie Learning, Inc., Pittsburg, Pennsylvania, U.S.A.

and

Shaaron Ainsworth
University of Nottingham, Nottingham, U.K.

KLUWER ACADEMIC PUBLISHERS
DORDRECHT / BOSTON / LONDON

Library of Congress Cataloging-in-Publication Data

ISBN 978-90-481-6499-8

Published by Kluwer Academic Publishers,
P.O. Box 17, 3300 AA Dordrecht, The Netherlands.

Sold and distributed in North, Central and South America
by Kluwer Academic Publishers,
101 Philip Drive, Norwell, MA 02061, U.S.A.

In all other countries, sold and distributed
by Kluwer Academic Publishers,
P.O. Box 322, 3300 AH Dordrecht, The Netherlands.

Printed on acid-free paper

All Rights Reserved
© 2010 Kluwer Academic Publishers
No part of this work may be reproduced, stored in a retrieval system, or transmitted
in any form or by any means, electronic, mechanical, photocopying, microfilming,
recording
or otherwise, without written permission from the Publisher, with the exception
of any material supplied specifically for the purpose of being entered
and executed on a computer system, for exclusive use by the purchaser of the work.

Printed in the Netherlands.

Table of Contents

Preface ix

Contributors xiii

Acknowledgements xvii

SECTION I: AUTHORING TUTORS FOR DEVICE AND PROCESS SIMULATIONS

1. SIMQUEST: Authoring Educational Simulations 1
   Wouter R. van Joolingen & Ton de Jong

2. Requiem for a Development System: Reflections on Knowledge-Based, Generative Instruction 33
   Henry M. Halff, Pattricia Y. Hsieh, Brenda M. Wenzel, Tom J. Chudanov, Mary T. Dirnberger, Elizabeth G. Gibson & Carol L. Redfield

3. Authoring Simulation-Centered Learning Environments with Rides and Vivids 61
   Allen Munro

SECTION II: AUTHORING TUTORS THAT ENCODE HUMAN EXPERTISE

4. A Programming by Demonstration Authoring Tool for Model-Tracing Tutors 93
   Stephen B. Blessing

5. Automated Knowledge Acquisition for Intelligent Support of Diagnostic Reasoning 121
   Douglas Towne

6. Formative Evaluation of an Automated Knowledge Elicitation and Organization Tool 149
   Valerie J. Shute & Lisa A. Torreano

7. Using Knowledge Objects to Design Instructional
   Learning Environments   181
   M. David Merrill

SECTION III: AUTHORING TUTORS THAT INCLUDE INSTRUCTIONAL STRATEGIES

8. REDEEM: Simple Intelligent Tutoring Systems from
   Usable Tools   205
   *Shaaron Ainsworth, Nigel Major, Shirley Grimshaw,
   Mary Hayes, Jean Underwood, Ben Williams &
   David Wood*

9. The IRIS Authoring Tool   233
   *Ana Arruarte, Begoña Ferrero, Isabel Fernández-Castro,
   Maite Urretavizcaya, Ainhoa Álvarez & Jim Greer*

10. CREAM-Tools : An Authoring Environment for
    Knowledge Engineering in Intelligent Tutoring
    Systems   269
    Roger Nkambou, Claude Frasson & Gilles Gauthier

11. Eon: Authoring Tools for Content, Instructional
    Strategy, Student Model, and Interface Design   309
    Tom Murray

SECTION IV: SPECIAL PURPOSE AUTHORING TOOLS

12. Supporting Educational Software Design With
    Knowledge-Rich Tools   341
    Benjamin Bell

13. Developing Adaptive Educational Hypermedia
    Systems: From Design Models to Authoring Tools   377
    Peter Brusilovsky

CONTENTS

14. The Leap Authoring Tool: Supporting complex courseware authoring through reuse, rapid prototyping, and interactive visualizations 411
Randall Sparks, Scott Dooley, Lori Meiskey & Rick Blumenthal

SECTION V: GENERAL THEORIES AND DESIGNS

15. Principles for Pedagogy-oriented Knowledge Based Tutor Authoring Systems: Lessons Learned and a Design Meta-Model 439
Tom Murray

16. Authoring Tools for Component–Based Learning Environments 467
Steven Ritter, Stephen B. Blessingg & Leslie Wheeler

17. An Overview of Intelligent Tutoring System Authoring Tools: Updated analysis of the state of the art 491
Tom Murray

Author Index 545

Subject Index 553

Preface

Researchers and educational software developers have talked about building authoring tools for intelligent tutoring systems (ITSs), adaptive and knowledge-based instructional systems, and other forms of advanced-technology learning environments (ATLEs) ever since these forms of educational software were introduced in the 1970s. The technical complexity and high development costs of these systems contrasts sharply with the common picture of education as a "home grown" activity performed by individual teachers and trainers who craft lessons tailored for each situation. There have been two primary reasons to create authoring tools for ATLEs: to reduce development cost, and to allow practicing educators to become more involved in their creation. The goal of creating usable authoring tools dovetails with the recent trend toward interoperability and reusability among these systems.

We use the phrase "advanced-technology learning environment" to refer to educational software on the leading edge of practice and research. These systems go beyond traditional computer-based instruction or educational simulations by providing one or more of the following benefits:

- Providing rich, or even "immersive" interfaces so that students can "learn by doing" in realistic and meaningful contexts.
- Dynamically adapting the interface or content to the student's goals, skill level, or learning style.
- Providing expert hints, explanations, or problem solving guidance.
- Allowing "mixed-initiative" tutorial interactions, where students can ask questions and have more control over their learning.
- Incorporating instructional models that base interactions on proven educational theories, or that allow the interactions to more closely approach the benefits of individualized instruction by a competent pedagogue.

The ATLE authoring tools field has advanced significantly since the first conference workshop on the subject in 1995. Since then there have been a number of international workshops dealing with the subject (including workshops at the AI in Education international conferences in 1995, 1997, 1999; the Intelligent Tutoring Systems international conference in1996; and the American Association of Artificial Intelligence Fall Symposium in 1997). In addition there have been several special issues of research journals on this topic (including the International Journal of AI in Education Vol. 8. No. 3, 1998, and Vol. 10 No. 1, 1999; J. of the Learning Sciences Vol. 7 No. 1 1998; and J. of Instructional Science Vol. 26 Nos. 3-4 1998). This volume, which is the first book on the subject, contains chapters providing updated reports on all of these workshops and publications. It provides a comprehensive picture of the state of the art in ATLE authoring systems, with representative chapters from almost every major researcher in the field. Contributions to this volume come from an international cadre of researchers from

Canada, the Netherlands, Spain, the United Kingdom, and the United States. Significant work in authoring tools is ongoing in several other countries as well (including Japan and Germany).

This volume should appeal to many readers interested in the use and/or development of ATLEs. To quote from the overview chapter by Murray:

> I imagine two types of readers. First are academic or industry personnel in the field of instructional software research or development. They might ask the question "what methods and designs have been used, and how successful have they been?" in their efforts to build the next generation of systems. The second type of reader is the user, developer, or purchaser of instructional software (advanced, intelligent, or otherwise) who might ask the question: "what is really available, or soon to be available, to make ITS authoring cost effective?"

The reader will note the word "toward" in the title of the volume. The field is still very much in a formative stage. The systems described in the 17 chapters to follow are predominantly R&D efforts or local success stories. That is, few have been used to produce numerous tutoring systems nor have they been used by people not closely associated with a research team (with some notable exceptions, as discussed in the Overview chapter). This state of affairs with ATLE authoring tools reflects the state of ATLEs in general, which have shown some successes but have been slow to enter the main-stream commercial education and training markets. However, despite its formative nature, the importance of making ATLEs more cost effective and authorable warrants the publication of a book such as this that describes the state of the art. The design issues are complex and the implemented solutions are quite diverse. Much progress has been made in articulating the issues and fleshing out solutions, and a number of projects have completed empirical studies demonstrating usability and cost-effectiveness. A few of the chapters describe projects that were completed some years ago, and these were included because their research results and design innovations still represent the state of the art on certain issues.

The chapters in this volume are organized based on an analysis of authoring systems given in the Overview chapter which distinguishes authoring tools according to the following categories: Authoring Tutors for Device and Process Simulations, Authoring Tutors that Encode Human Expertise, Authoring Tutors that Include Instructional Strategies, and Special Purpose Authoring Tools. Some readers may wish to read the final Chapter first, an overview of ITS authoring tools, and authoring tools issues.

Chapter 1 describes SimQuest, an authoring tool for creating simulation-based learning environments that focus on science concepts and principles. Chapter 2 describes XAIDA, an authoring tool that has been used to develop simple simulations that can address a variety of knowledge types, including facts, concepts, procedures, and principles. Chapter 3 describes RIDES, a tool for authoring tutorials bases on sophisticated device simulations. Chapter 4 describes Demonstr8, a prototype authoring tool that explores authoring domain content by having authors providing examples and demonstrations, and then intelligently creating generalizations based on these example cases. Chapter 5 describes DIAG, a system for authoring tutors in electronic fault diagnosis that significantly simplifies the process of defining and providing instruction for complex devices and the numerous fault conditions that can occur in these devices. Chapter 6 describes DNA, a knowledge elicitation tool that simulates a semi-structured interview process for eliciting factual, conceptual, and procedural domain knowledge for an ITS. Chapter 7 describes Instructional Simulator, one of a set of commercially available authoring tools that simplify authoring for simple device simulations and conceptual knowledge. Chapter 8 describes REDEEM, an authoring tool that converts traditional computer-based instructional content into an intelligent tutor by allowing teachers to specify multiple teaching strategies, each of which is defined for a particular type of student. Chapters 9 and 10 describe the IRIS authoring tool and CREAM-tools. These systems incorporate different methods for building ITSs that incorporate complex instructional design principles that utilize the instructional theories of Gagne, Bloom, and Merrill. Chapter 11 described the Eon system, which includes highly interactive authoring tools, for authoring subject matter, tutoring strategies, interfaces, and student models. Chapter 12 describes IDLE-tools, which are used to create "investigate and decide goal-based learning environments." Chapter 13 gives an overview of authoring tools for adaptive hypermedia systems, with a more detailed description of the InterBook. Chapter 14 describes LAT, an authoring tool for creating tutors that use conversational grammars to simulate product sales representative phone conversations with customers. Chapter 15 presents contains a general design "meta-model" for ITS authoring tools (this material in this chapter was part of the originally published paper on the Eon system, Chapter 11, but was separated into a different paper and extended for this volume). Chapter 16 contains a general discussion on interoperability and component-based architectures for authoring tools, and includes examples from tools used to author model tracing tutors. Chapter 17 is an overview of the state of the art in ITS authoring, including an analysis and comparison of 31 authoring tools.

Related workshops and symposia

- ED-MEDIA-94 conference: "Teaching Strategies and Intelligent Tutoring Systems." Vancouver Canada, July, 1994. Organizing Committee: N. Major, T. Murray, K. VanMarcke.
- AI&ED-95 conference: "Authoring Shells for Intelligent Tutoring Systems, " August, 1995, Washington, D.C. Organizing Committee: N. Major, T. Murray, C. Bloom.
- ITS-96 conference workshop: "Architectures and Methods for Designing Cost-Effective and Reusable ITSs," June 1996, Montreal, Canada. Organizing committee: B. Cheikes, D. Suthers, T. Murray, N. Jacobstein.
- AAAI Fall-97 Symposium "Intelligent Tutoring System Authoring Tools," Cambridge, MA, Nov. 1997. (C. Redfield, B. Bell, H. Halff, A. Munro, T. Murray, (Organizing Committee)

- AI-ED-97 conference, "Issues in Achieving Cost-Effective and Reusable Intelligent Learning Environments," August, 1997, Kobe, Japan. Organizing Committee: D. Suthers, C. Bloom, M. Dobson, T. Murray, A. M. Paiva.
- AI-ED-99 workshop, Ontologies for Intelligent Educational Systems," LeMans France. Chairs: Riichiro Mizoguchi & Tom Murray

Journal Special Issues

- International Journal of Artificial Intelligence in Education, Special Issues on Authoring Systems for Intelligent Tutoring Systems, Vol. 8. No. 3-4, 1997; and Vol. 10 No. 1, 1999, guest editors Tom Murray and Stephen Blessing.
- Journal of the Learning Sciences, Special Issue on authoring tools for interactive learning environments, Vol. 7 No. 1 1998, guest editors Benjamin Bell and Carol Redfield.

Contributors

Shaaron Ainsworth
ESRC Centre for Research in Development, Instruction & Training, School of Psychology, University of Nottingham, Nottingham, NG7 2RD, UK. sea@psychology.nottingham.ac.uk

Ainhoa Álvarez
Department of Computer Languages and Systems, Computer Science Faculty, University of the Basque Country UPV/EHU, 649 Postakutxa, 20080 Donostia, Spain. jipalara@si.ehu.es

Ana Arruarte
Department of Computer Languages and Systems, Computer Science Faculty, University of the Basque Country UPV/EHU, 649 Postakutxa, 20080 Donostia, Spain. arruarte@si.ehu.es

Benjamin Bell
Principal Cognitive Engineer, CHI Systems, Inc. , CHI Systems, Inc., 1035 Virginia Drive, Suite 300, Fort Washington, PA 19034. BBell@chisystems.com

Stephen B. Blessing
Carnegie Learning, Inc., 1200 Penn Avenue, Suite 150, Pittsburgh, PA, 15222. blessing@carnegielearning.com

Rick Blumenthal
Regis University, 3333 Regis Blvd., L-12, Denver, CO 80221; 303-458-4304, rblument@regis.edu, www.regis.edu.

Peter Brusilovsky
School of Information Sciences, Pittsburgh PA 15260, USA. peterb@mail.sis.pitt.edu

Isabel Fernández-Castro
Department of Computer Languages and Systems, Computer Science Faculty, University of the Basque Country UPV/EHU, 649 Postakutxa, 20080 Donostia, Spain. isabelfc@si.ehu.es

Tom Chudanov
I/T Lead Systems Analyst, USAA Information Technology, 9800 Fredericksburg Road, San Antonio, Texas 78288,; 210-913-8992, tom.chudanov@usaa.com.

Mary Dirnberger
PSC 482 Box 2547 , FPO AP 96362; dirnberg@konnect.net.

Scott Dooley
Knowledge Analysis Technologies, 4940 Pearl East Circle, Suite 200, Boulder, CO 80301; 303-545-9092, dooley@k-a-t.com, www.k-a-t.com.

CONTRIBUTORS

Begoña Ferrero
Department of Computer Languages and Systems, Computer Science Faculty, University of the Basque Country UPV/EHU, 649 Postakutxa, 20080 Donostia, Spain. jipfemab@si.ehu.es

Claude Frasson
Département d'informatique et de recherche opérationnelle, Université de Montréal, Case postale 6128, succursale Centre-ville, Montréal (Québec), H3C 3J7, Canada. frasson@iro.umontreal.ca

Gilles Gauthier
Département d'informatique, Université du Québec à Montréal, Case postale 8888, succursale Centre-ville, Montréal (Québec), H3C 3P8, Canada. gauthier.gilles@uqam.ca

Elizabeth G. Gibson
SBC Online Strategy and Integration, 9505 Arboretum Blvd. - 7th Floor, Austin, TX 78759-6337; 512-372-5785; Fax: 512-241-5785, elizabeth.gibson.1@sbc.com.

Jim Greer
Department of Computer Science, University of Saskatchewan, Saskatoon, Canada S7N 5A9. greer@cs.usask.ca

Shirley Grimshaw
ESRC Centre for Research in Development, Instruction & Training, School of Psychology, University of Nottingham, Nottingham, NG7 2RD, UK.

Henry M. Halff
Halff Resources, 9 Villa Verde, San Antonio, TX 78230-2709; 210-493-7501; Fax: 760-495-6395, henry@halffresources.com, http://www.halffresources.com.

Mary Hayes
Faculty of Education, Ada Byron King Building, The Nottingham Trent University, Clifton Campus Clifton Lane, Nottingham NG11 8NS UK. Mary.Hayes@ntu.ac.uk

Patricia Yee Hsieh
System Human Resources Office, The Texas A&M University System, John B. Connally Bldg., 5th floor, 301 Tarrow, College Station, TX 77840-7896; 979-458-6166; Fax: 979-845-5281, phsieh@tamu.edu http://sago.tamu.edu/shro/pagetraining.htm.

Ton de Jong
Faculty of Behavioral Sciences, University of Twente, P.O. box 217, 7500 AE Enschede, The Netherlands. A.J.M.deJong@edte.utwente.nl

Wouter van Joolingen
Graduate School of Teaching and Learning, University of Amsterdam, Wibautstraat 2-4, 1091 GM Amsterdam, The Netherlands. wouter@ilo.uva.nl

Nigel Major
ESRC Centre for Research in Development, Instruction & Training, School of Psychology, University of Nottingham, Nottingham, NG7 2RD, UK.

Lori Meiskey
CreekPath Systems, 7420 E. Dry Creek Parkway, #100, Longmont, CO 80503; lmeiskey@creekpath.com, www.creekpath.com.

Alan Munro
University of Southern California, Behavioral Technology Lab, 250 No. Harbor Drive, Suite, 309, Redondo Beach, CA 90277. munro@usc.edu

Tom Murray
Hampshire College School of Cognitive Science, Amherst, MA, USA. tmurray@hampshire.edu, http://helios.hampshire.edu/~tjmCCS/

Roger Nkambou
Département d'informatique, Université du Québec à Montréal, Case postale 8888, succursale Centre-ville, Montréal (Québec), H3C 3P8, Canada. nkambou.roger@uqam.ca

Carol Luckhardt Redfield
St. Mary's University, Computer Science Department, 1 Camino Santa Maria, San Antonio, Texas 78228-8524; 210-346-3298, credfield@stmarytx.edu.

Steven Ritter
Carnegie Learning, Inc., 1200 Penn Avenue, Suite 150, Pittsburgh, PA 15222. steve@carnegielearning.com

Valerie J. Shute
Principal Research Scientist, Educational Testing Service, Rosedale Rd., MS-01R, Princeton, NJ 08541 USA. vshute@ets.org

Randall Sparks
Knowledge Analysis Technologies, 4940 Pearl East Circle, Suite 200, Boulder, CO 80301,;303-545-9092, rsparks@k-a-t.com, www.k-a-t.com.

Lisa A. Torreano
Product Development Manager, Bright Brains, Inc. , 2121 Sage Rd., Suite 385, Houston, TX 77056 USA. ltorreano@brightbrains.com

Douglas M. Towne
Behavioral Technology Laboratories, University of Southern California, 1120 Pope St., Suite 201C, St. Helena, CA 94574 USA. dtowne@usc.edu

Jean Underwood
Division of Psychology, Nottingham Trent University, Burton Street, Nottingham, NG1 4BU, UK. Jean.Underwood@ntu.ac.uk

Maite Urretavizcaya,
Department of Computer Languages and Systems, Computer Science Faculty, University of the Basque Country UPV/EHU, 649 Postakutxa, 20080 Donostia, Spain. maite@si.ehu.es

Brenda M Wenzel
Senior Engineering Psychologist, TRADOC Analysis Center, ATRC-WSMR-WGA,Systems Training, White Sands Missile Range, NM 88002-5502, 505-678-4661 (phone); 505-678-6887 (FAX). wenzelbm@trac.wsmr.army.mil.

Leslie Wheeler
Carnegie Learning, Inc., 1200 Penn Avenue, Suite 150, Pittsburgh, PA 15222. leslie@carnegielearning.com

Ben Williams
ESRC Centre for Research in Development, Instruction & Training, School of Psychology, University of Nottingham, Nottingham, NG7 2RD, UK.

David Wood
ESRC Centre for Research in Development, Instruction & Training, School of Psychology, University of Nottingham, Nottingham, NG7 2RD, UK. djw@psychology.nottingham.ac.uk

Acknowledgements

The following chapters contain updated versions of papers that originally appeared in the International Journal of Artificial Intelligence in Education, Special Issues on Authoring Systems for Intelligent Tutoring Systems, Vol. 8. No. 3-4, 1997; and Vol. 10 No. 1, 1999, guest editors Tom Murray and Stephen Blessing:
>Chapters 2, 3, 4, 5, 8, 14, 17.

Chapter 6 was originally published as part of a special issue of International Journal of Artificial Intelligence in Education (1999) that focused on a selection of research first presented at ITS '98.

The following chapters contain updated versions of papers that originally appeared in the Journal of the Learning Sciences, Special Issue on Authoring Tools for Interactive Learning Environments, Vol. 7 No. 1 1998, guest editors Benjamin Bell and Carol Redfield:
>Chapters 11, 12, 15, 16.

An earlier version of Chapter 9 appeared in the International Journal of Computers in Education, 1997, Vol. 8(3/4), 341-381.

WOUTER R. VAN JOOLINGEN AND TON DE JONG

Chapter 1

SIMQUEST

Authoring Educational Simulations

Abstract. SIMQUEST is an authoring system for creating computer simulations embedded in an instructional environment. A typical learning environment created with SIMQUEST allows learners to engage in an activity of discovery learning with a simulation, supported by instructional measures from within the environment. Some of these instructional measures adapt themselves to the interaction of the learner with the simulation.

SIMQUEST allows the author to create various kinds of instructional support for the learner. *Assignments* provide the learner with short term goals for the learning process, *explanations* offer additional information, a *monitoring tool* allows the learner to record and replay experiments, and, moreover, the domain can be arranged according to different levels of *model progression*. Recent developments are a *hypothesis scratchpad*, *intelligent feedback*, a *modelling tool*, and facilities for *collaborative learning* in SIMQUEST.

SIMQUEST supports the full process of authoring simulation based learning environments, from creating the simulation model to defining the instructional interaction of the learning environment with the learner. Authoring a SIMQUEST learning environment is done in an object oriented way. The author selects templates from a library to create building blocks of the learning environment, which are then edited to match the author's requirements. The SIMQUEST architecture, with a *simulation context* as central element takes care of the interaction between the various building blocks. The author is supported by the contents of the library, on-line help, on-line pedagogical advice, and a wizard that can automate part of the authoring process.

SIMQUEST has been used to create about twenty learning environments, some of which have been evaluated extensively with students. Currently SIMQUEST is used by a group of teachers to create learning material for use in their classrooms. A number of SIMQUEST learning environments are now published by commercial publishers.

1. INTRODUCTION

1.1 Scientific discovery learning

Scientific discovery learning or inquiry learning is a type of learning that has gained much interest in recent years (De Jong & Van Joolingen, 1998). In (scientific) discovery learning learners are in control over the learning process, doing experiments, stating hypotheses and in such a way constructing their own

Murray, Ainsworth, & Blessing (eds.), Authoring Tools for Adv. Tech. Learning Env.,
© *2003 Kluwer Academic Publishers. Printed in the Netherlands, pp. 1–31.*

knowledge of the domain at hand. This implies that for discovery learning, learners need to have access to an environment providing means for defining and performing experiments which provide the information needed to construct knowledge. Such an environment is of course can be found in nature itself. For several centuries doing experiments on natural systems has been the single most important source of information for the construction of scientific knowledge, within and outside the context of learning. Performing experiments on real systems still plays an important role in science education in schools and universities.

However, there may be specific reasons why doing experiments on natural systems is not preferred in education (Allessi & Trollip, 1985; De Jong, 1991). First of all, the natural system may not be available in the school, because the system itself or the measuring equipment required is too expensive or otherwise unavailable. Second, the natural system may be unsafe to use in a classroom. This is for instance the case with radioactive samples, toxic chemical substances or populations of certain bacteria. Third, doing experiments may be unethical, as is the case with livestock. Fourth, the time scale of experiments on natural phenomena may not fit with the classroom situation. Some experiments take days, months or even years to complete, others happen so fast that it is hard to visualize the processes that learners should learn about. Finally, experiments may consume resources that are rare, for instance use substances or energy, making it unattractive to let learners perform a reasonable number of experiments to see the trends and effects that are interesting in the domain under study.

To overcome the obstacles mentioned above, replacing natural experiments by computer simulations may be a fruitful enterprise (De Jong, 1991; Carlsen & Andre, 1992). Simulations are computer programs containing an executable model of a natural or other system, capable of computing the behavior of the modeled system by means of dedicated algorithms and presenting the results of these computations to the user. Simulations can overcome the above drawbacks of some natural systems. Once a model is available, it can be spread and copied as much as we like. Simulations are safe to use, as accidents or other harmful events only take place in the simulated world. Use of simulations also overcomes problems of ethical nature, as no real animals or humans will be involved. Simulations can also adapt their time scale, speeding up or slowing down processes in such a way that processes take a reasonable time to observe. Finally, simulations can be performed as much as we like, taking only resources necessary to run a computer program. We do not plea for a total replacement of experiments on natural systems, doing real experiments has its own value for learning. However, simulations can offer complementary benefits.

Apart from overcoming drawbacks of natural systems, simulations have something extra to offer to instruction. Simulations can visualize processes that are invisible in natural systems, for instance, they can create graphs of quantities like energy or impulse, or state vectors of quantum systems, and allow the learner to manipulate the representations available. This allows for multiple views and multiple representations of the simulated system (e.g. Ainsworth, 1999). More than natural systems, simulations offer a wealth of possibilities to integrate different representations and animate these representations, using data of the simulated system. For instance, a simulation of a harmonic oscillator such a mass suspended from a spring can show the basic animated movement of the mass, but also graphically represent this motion in several ways, in time-based graphs or phase diagrams. The graph and the animations can be built simultaneously showing the interrelation between the two representations.

Simulations can also increase the instructional value of a system, because there is more control over the kinds of events that occur and the frequency with which they occur. For instance, a in a driving simulation, accidents and near accidents can be simulated and explored, which would be impossible with a real system. Also events that can occur but are rare, such as entering a busy motorway, can be induced and practiced as often as is deemed necessary.

Notwithstanding all these alleged advantages of learning with simulations we see that learners have considerable difficulties with simulation based discovery learning. In de Jong and van Joolingen (1998) we have provided an extensive overview of these problems and indicated how simulations can be extended to help prevent or overcome these problems. Basically, we stated that simulations offer anchor points to integrate discovery learning with instructional support. Simulations encapsulate an explicit model of the simulated system, which can be used to interpret actions by the learner in order to provide tailored instruction. Also, instructional interventions, such as presenting exercises, or explaining observed phenomena in the simulation can benefit from interacting with the simulation model. Exercises can set the simulation in a predefined state and monitor the learner's behavior while carrying out the exercise. Explanations can be displayed whenever a state in the simulation occurs demanding for an explanation. In this way a simulation embedded in instructional interventions is created. These kinds of interventions are more difficult if not impossible to create with natural systems, even if the system is observed and controlled through a computer interface.

1.2 Authoring simulations for learning

Listing the features of computer simulations, and their use for discovery learning, one sees that they can (and actually do) provide a useful instrument in instruction. However, creating computer simulations embedded in instruction is a task that is not within reach of most teachers. Creating instructional simulations takes a number of steps, each requiring specific skills for its successful completion. In order to create an instructional computer simulation, one must

- create a *simulation model*. The model driving the simulation must be specified in a dedicated language, either a programming language or a special simulation language. For completing this part one must be an expert in the domain simulated and have knowledge of the target language. In the case of a general purpose programming language one must also create the algorithm to simulate the model;
- create a *learner interface* to the simulation. The simulation results must be visually represented to the learner, using graphics representing domain elements, graphs, numbers, etc. In order to be able to do this one must know

how to create interfaces with available tools, and be able to create the domain specific graphics in the interface. Also, knowledge of proper user interface design is very useful here;
- create an *instructional design* of the environment. The learning environment should be perceived from the side of the learner. What will be the activities that will be performed? What is their goal? What information is needed and at what moment for the learner, apart from the output generated by the simulation model? For this step, one must have knowledge of instructional design;
- create *instructional interventions*. Exercises, explanations, and other kinds of instructional interventions should be part of a good instructional simulation. Part of the information needed for a good exercise can of course be presented off-line, but in order to make full use of the simulation interaction, instructional interventions should be able to interact with the simulation. This step requires both instructional design skills, as well as domain knowledge, especially didactical knowledge, such as knowing frequently occurring misconceptions;
- *integrate the parts of the environment* to a complete system. For the learner, the instructional simulation should appear as an integrated coherent system. This means that all parts need to co-operate and that the interactions between simulation model, learner interface and all instructional interventions should be smooth and stable. This step requires programming skills in order to create an efficient and transparent environment.

This list of tasks involved in creating simulation-based learning environments for discovery learning shows, on the one hand, that most teachers lack expertise and time for creating these environments themselves. On the other hand, off-the-shelf simulations often do not match the requirements of a specific teacher.

1.3 The SIMQUEST approach

SIMQUEST was created to serve teachers and learners involved in discovery learning. SIMQUEST is an authoring system dedicated to simulations for discovery learning. It has the following two goals:
- To provide *learners* with supportive environments for discovery learning, in the form of simulations, instructional measures, and cognitive tools directed at scaffolding the processes of discovery leaning.
- To provide *authors* with a flexible tool for creating simulation-based discovery learning environments, containing both technical and conceptual support for the authoring process.

SIMQUEST was planned as an open system for the design and implementation of simulation-based learning environments for discovery learning. The SIMQUEST system is an object-oriented system, meaning that a large number of predefined objects are present which can be used to compose a learning environment. Object types include: simulation models, interface elements, instructional measures, and test elements. The object orientation of SIMQUEST means that each element in this library acts according to a specific interface protocol, making it possible to extend the library with relatively little extra effort. The protocols include functionality for editing, copying, and linking elements. These design characteristics allow for the following characteristics of SIMQUEST:

- *Openness*. SIMQUEST is an open system, allowing additional instructional measures, simulation widgets, or modeling components to be easily added as long as they respond to the protocols defined in the documented specification. This, coupled with the notion of libraries and their specific interfaces, provide the authors with a powerful, customizable environment. SIMQUEST has the ability to interface not only with simulations created using the tools provided in SIMQUEST but also to external simulations.
- *Flexibility*. There is no strict order of work defined for the author. For instance, the author can start with building a simulation interface and progress with the simulation model in an iterative manner. Using this structure, the author can also co-operate with other authors and delegate parts of the work to specialists, for instance creating a simulation model.

These two principles allow that authors can follow their preferred way of working in creating learning environments, and that authors can tailor their work to their specific needs. In the next sections we describe SIMQUEST from the viewpoints of learners and authors, and we conclude with a description of the SIMQUEST architecture.

2. LEARNING WITH SIMQUEST

Though SIMQUEST learning environments (these are simulation environments created with the SIMQUEST authoring system) may differ considerably with respect to the domains for which they were created, all learning environment share a common structure. The nature of the activities that the learner can undertake in each of the learning environments is basically the same. The current section describes these activities and presents the tools that SIMQUEST offers.

2.1 Basic learning activities

The basic learning goal of any discovery-learning environment, including those created by SIMQUEST is to construct knowledge of the investigated domain. This does not necessarily imply that the learner must learn to know the model underlying the simulation in all detail, but the goal is to understand the principles of the domain that account for the observed behavior and/or the effects of actions performed within the domain.

In order to discover the properties of the domain and to build understanding, the learner needs to perform a number of learning processes. Several authors (Njoo & de Jong, 1993; Klahr & Dunbar, 1988; Van Joolingen & de Jong, 1997; de Jong & van Joolingen, 1998) have investigated the nature of these learning processes involved in scientific discovery learning. For instance, the learning processes identified by Njoo & de Jong (1993) include orientation, hypothesis formation, experiment design, prediction, and data analysis, as well as planning and monitoring. The activities that the learner undertakes in the learning environment should facilitate these learning processes in order to result in effective learning. SIMQUEST offers tools that enable and support these activities. We discuss the main components of a SIMQUEST learning environment and show how these components support the different learning processes. These main components are a computer simulation and instructional measures of different kinds. Figure 1 shows an example of a learning environment created with SIMQUEST. The learning environment is composed of one or more windows to watch and control the simulation, windows representing *instructional measures* to support the discovery learning processes and a *learner view* for the learner to control the environment.

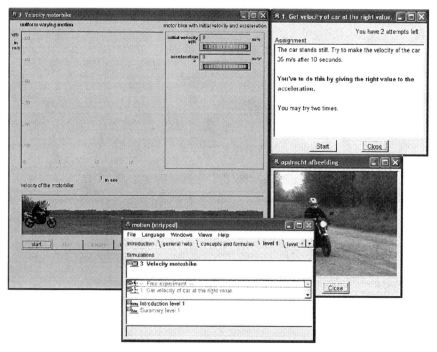

Figure 1. An example of a SIMQUEST learning environment. Shown are the learner view (bottom) providing control over all instructional measures, a simulation interface (right), and an assignment window (top right) as example of an instructional measure.

Learners working in a SIMQUEST learning environment will have to divide their attention between the simulation and the instructional measures. At any time the learner sees the simulation interface(s), a list of instructional measures in the learner view that can be opened, as well as windows representing active instructional measures. The learner can be involved in any of the following activities:
- Free interaction with the simulation;
- Interaction with an instructional measure;

- Interaction with the simulation within the context of an instructional measure;
- Planning and selecting which interaction with the simulation or instructional measure to perform next.

The first three of these activities can be associated with the basic process of discovery or the transformative learning processes; the fourth activity is concerned with planning and monitoring the learning process (Njoo & de Jong, 1993).

Operating the computer simulation

The computer simulation is present as a computational model of some system, for instance motion of a vehicle as is shown Figure 1. The computer simulation is operated by the learner through one or more *simulation interfaces*. With the interface, the learner can identify variables, modify variables, control the simulation (for instance starting and stopping it), and watch the change of variable values under influence of changes of other variables or of the progress of time.

The simulation interfaces provide the main view on the domain. All actions that the learner performs on the simulation take place through these interfaces. The interfaces, therefore, determine the view the learner will take on the domain, and hence play a role in orientation learning processes. The presence of variables as well as their position on the interface helps the learner in orientation, but also adds a bias to this process. Also, the simulation interfaces provide the main source of information and data that cater for learning processes that generate or use domain information, such as experiment design and data analysis.

The computer simulation can be operated in the context of free experimentation, or within the context of a specific instructional measure. In the latter case the instructional measure may constrain the control the learner has over the simulation interface.

Accessing instructional support

Instructional support is accessed through the learner view on the application. A window shows which *instructional measures* are available to the learner at a given point in time. The learner may then choose to activate one of the instructional measures.

The learner view also provides access to the *model progression* in the SIMQUEST application. The model progression is defined by the author as a series of models representing aspects of the domain, in the spirit of model progression as introduced by White and Frederiksen (1990). Model progressions can yield sequences of models going from simple to complex, showing different parts of a system or representing different views on the same model. Model progression is visually represented by different pages in the learner view (labeled "level 1", level 2",..., in Figure 1), where each page represents a progression level. Each progression page displays the simulation interfaces and instructional measures that are available on the corresponding level. Model progression can be seen as an instructional measure in itself, as it helps the learner to structure the domain, make a planning and monitor progress in learning.

The learner view provides the learner with information on the status of instructional measures: which measures are available, which are open, which have been opened and were completed and also which are not available but will be during the session.

2.2 Instructional measures

Instructional support to the learner is provided by *instructional measures*. Instructional measures represent different kinds of intervention in the learning process. Currently available instructional measures include assignments (exercises that the learner has to perform), explanations, and several supportive tools for specific learning processes.

Assignments

Assignments basically present support for regulative learning processes, by providing learners with short-term goals in the learning progress. The type of goal offered by the assignment differs with the assignment type. Assignments may also foster transformative processes, for example by suggesting the learner hypotheses for testing. Whenever the learner activates an assignment, it takes over some of the control over the learning environment: it *presents* itself to the learner, using text, sound or graphics, optionally it enables or disables access to variables in the simulation (blocking or hiding elements on all simulation interfaces) and defines one or more initial states, as starting points for achieving the goals presented in the assignments. For instance, an assignment that asks the learner to investigate the properties of a specific situation may set the stage for this by defining the initial states of the variables. Some assignments can offer multiple initial states with the goal of asking the learner to compare different situations.

SIMQUEST offers several types of assignments:
- *Do It/Do Them assignments* present their goal as such to the learner. This means that any goal can be given to the learner, but that no implicit support on achieving this goal is given from within the environment. The two versions (do it/do them) differ in the number of initial states that can be offered.
- *Investigation/explicitation assignments* ask the learner to inquire the relation between two or more variables. The assignments offer a range of possible hypotheses that can explain the observed phenomena, from which the learner can select one or more suitable descriptions. The assignments can trigger specific feedback based on the answer(s) chosen. The assignments differ in the sense that investigation assignments offer one initial state of the simulation, putting the burden of designing experiments on the learner, whereas explicitation assignments offer multiple initial states that can be seen as predefined experiments.

- *Specification assignments* ask the learner to predict the values of certain variables when the associated simulation reaches a state specified by the author (typically a certain time). The values predicted by the learner are allowed a deviation from the simulation's values as specified by the author in either absolute or relative terms.
- *Optimization assignments* require the learner to perform a task within given constraints and with a set target. The learner has to vary the simulation's variables' values so that the constraints specified by the author are not broken and a target specified by the author is reached.

The evaluation of the answer on the assignment is performed by SIMQUEST. An assignment can *succeed* or *fail*, the latter meaning that the learner could not reach the goal within a specified number of attempts.

Explanations

Explanations present the learner with additional information. Explanations are classified by their content type: *text, sound, image, video, html,* or *canvas* (a collection of graphics painted on a window).

Explanations can be presented at different moments in the learning environment. First of all, they can be available on request for the learner, in the overview of available instructional measures. Second, they can be used as feedback to actions of the learner within assignments such as feedback to answer alternative for assignments that present a question in multiple-choice format, or as within optimization assignments when the learner reaches the goal or breaks a constraint. Finally, they can be used to explain simulation phenomena as they occur. In this case the explanation automatically pops up as the specific event takes place in the simulation.

Specific support tools

In discovery learning it is important that the learner can plan and monitor the actions needed for constructing knowledge on the domain. This means monitoring the actions in *hypothesis* space (what are the ideas developed on the domain) and in *experiment* space (which experiments have been done to test these ideas. For keeping track of moves in hypothesis space SIMQUEST offers a *hypothesis scratchpad* and a *modeling tool*. The hypothesis scratchpad is for stating single, qualitative ideas within the learning environment, such as: when the force is great, velocity will increase rapidly. The hypothesis scratchpad was based on research by Van Joolingen and De Jong, 1991). The modeling tool offers learners the opportunity to shape hypotheses into integrated, graphical, models. Learners can specify qualitative and quantitative models that can be fed into the simulation as an alternative model to the one provided by the author. Learners can compare their model with the original model in order to test their hypotheses (Löhner, Van Joolingen & Savelsbergh, in press).

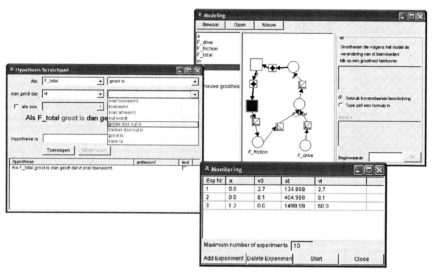

Figure 2. Three specific support tools in SIMQUEST: the hypothesis scratchpad *(left), the* modeling tool *(top right) and the* monitoring tool, *(bottom right).*

For keeping track of their moves in hypotheses, the SIMQUEST *monitoring tool* allows the learner to save experiments that were performed with the simulation, to sort them, and to replay them later onto allow, for instance, for comparison between experiments. The monitoring tool is especially useful in combination with investigation assignments, allowing the learner to keep track of the experiments performed. Figure 2 shows the three tools as they are presented to the learner. Each of the tools operates in close integration with the simulation and other tools present. Also, the tool design reflects the learning processes involved in the various stages of discovery learning.

2.3 Learner control vs. system control

As noted above, learners are free to choose any from the available instructional measures. This may suggest that learners are completely free in the way they progress through the learning environment. In practice there is a mixed initiative situation: the learner chooses the next step, but does so from a set of options offered by the learning environment. The size of this set determines the amount of freedom that a learner has. If there is only one choice available at any time, the learner has no freedom. If everything is available from the start, the initiative is completely with the learner.

During a session, the learner view shows these available instructional measures. Instructional measures can be activated by the learner (by selecting them in the learner view) or by the application. The learner may see that previously disabled instructional measures become enabled, instructional measures may become active without explicit request from the learner or new, previously invisible instructional measures, may appear in the learner view. This is controlled by the SIMQUEST instructional control system, based on author-generated specifications. These changes can be triggered by changes in state of instructional measure, for instance the successful or unsuccessful completion of an assignment, but also the occurrence of a certain event in the simulation, like a collision, passing a certain threshold, or when an otherwise interesting phenomenon takes place.

3. AUTHORING IN SIMQUEST

The learner is only one of the target users of SIMQUEST. The basic SIMQUEST functionality aims at authors creating SIMQUEST applications for their learners. Typically, there may be three kinds of authors: professional developers of instructional software, teachers and learners, creating instructional material as part of their learning process. SIMQUEST can be used by all three; however, teachers are the primary target group.

3.1 Basic authoring principles

SIMQUEST primarily focuses on teachers who are no programmers and who have limited experience with the use of simulations for discovery learning. This means that users should not be required to write any kind of programming code, and that they should be well-supported, both on technical issues and on the design and use of simulation-based learning environments. These principles are met by the following principles that guide the design of the SIMQUEST system:
- SIMQUEST uses an object-oriented method for creating learning environments. Authoring in SIMQUEST consists of selecting, modifying, and linking pre-existing building blocks;
- SIMQUEST offers a library of building blocks for creating simulations, simulation interfaces as well as several kinds of instructional measures;
- SIMQUEST offers dedicated advice on ways of composing sensible simulation-based discovery environments;
- SIMQUEST offers context-sensitive help on the technical issues involved in creating a learning environment;
- SIMQUEST offers an intelligent wizard, taking a beginning author through all stages of the authoring process.

These five principles ensure that the authoring process is both simple for the author and powerful enough to create challenging and instructionally valid learning environments.

3.2 The authoring cycle

The authoring process is the sequence of actions that an author who works with SIMQUEST has to perform in order to build a complete learning environment. This authoring process reflects the basic principles of the SIMQUEST system. De Jong and Van Joolingen (1995) describe authoring process as: *selecting* a building block from a library, *instantiating,* and *specializing* it, and using it in a learning environment. This notion is implemented in SIMQUEST to the full extent.

In SIMQUEST an author *selects* building blocks to work with from a central resource, called the *library*. Once an author has selected a library element it can be *instantiated*, meaning that a copy of the building block is created, that can be edited by an appropriate editor. The copy is stored in the application the author is working on. *Specializing* the building block is done by opening the appropriate editor on the element. The term specializing will be replaced by 'editing' in the remainder of this chapter. SIMQUEST consists of a set of tools enabling this authoring process and a library containing templates for the elements on which the tools can operate. The authoring process is illustrated in Figure 3.

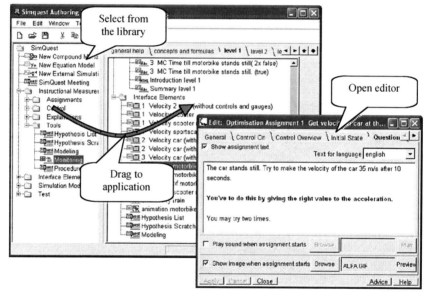

Figure 3. The authoring process in SIMQUEST, illustrated using screen shots from the actual authoring environment. Dragging a template to the application instantiates it into a building block. The author uses the editor to specializes the building block to his or her need.

The library consists of generic templates for simulation models, instructional measures, and simulation interfaces, as well as of specialized elements, suitable for use only in a limited range of domains. As a rule, generic templates are provided by SIMQUEST, but authors may add their own – specialized – library elements too for reuse in different applications.

3.3 Authoring building blocks

For each of the building blocks in the learning environment the basic way to author is to create it from the library of templates and to open the appropriate editor to modify the building block in order to specify its behavior in the learning environment and the interaction with other elements, for instance in executing instructional control. We discuss editing the three main categories of building blocks: simulation models, simulation interfaces and instructional measures. A separate section is dedicated to creating instructional control.

Creating and editing simulation models

The behavior of simulations is determined by simulation models. Simulation models specify how the values of output variables depend on the values of inputs entered by the learner and how the state of the simulation evolves over time. Simulation models are created in the same way as any other element of learning environments. However, due to the central role of simulation models in applications, the models define the structure of the application.

By creating a new model a new *model progression level* is created. Each model progression level is characterized by one underlying simulation model and the assignments and explanations for the learner that are associated with this level. For instance an author can enter models of simple harmonic oscillation, damped oscillation and oscillation controlled by an external force into one learning environment. These simulations will be visible to the learner as three different model progression levels. For each of the model progression levels, the author can create simulation interfaces and instructional measures. Model progression is a kind of instructional measure, but is technically different from the others in the sense that there is no building block in the library for defining it. It is defined by the presence of multiple models.

The author specifies the model behavior by writing equations, algebraic equations, of the form $y = a*x + b$, to compute outputs (y) from inputs (a, x, b) as well as differential equations of the form $dx/dt = - k * y$ to specify the dynamic evolution of the system. These equations are entered in the editor of the equation model, one of the available building blocks in the SIMQUEST library, as shown in Figure 4.

Apart from the equation model, there are two other ways of creating models. One, used to form complex models consisting of large numbers of equations, is the functional block method. Smaller models are combined into larger constructs by feeding output values from one model as inputs into another. For instance a model that computes (say) a velocity of a moving body can be combined with another model that computes the body's kinetic energy from this velocity. The two models are combined into a single construct. SIMQUEST offers a number of models that can be used as basic material for these models. Also, authors can create their own basic model ingredients using the equation editor. The mechanism is hierarchical: functional block models can be reused in even larger structures. The functional block mechanism enables structured modeling and reuse of model components. Figure 5 displays the functional block editor.

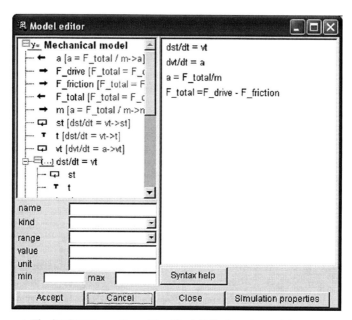

Figure 4. The SIMQUEST equation editor. The left displays the model structure and its variables, the right displays the equations.

Yet another way of creating simulation models is to use an existing, external simulation with SimQuest instruction. Currently, SimQuest provides interfaces to C++ (Borland and Microsoft), Visual Basic and Delphi. Simulations written in any of these programming languages can communicate with SimQuest. SimQuest treats these simulations in the same way as internal simulations, meaning it is possible to create SimQuest instructional measures around these simulations.

The simulation is a central resource in the learning environment. Almost any other component depends on the properties of the model and, at any moment, the current state of the simulation. The architecture of SIMQUEST has been designed in such a way that any component can have access to the simulation at any time, without being dependent on the internal properties of the model, for instance which type of editor was used to create it. In the section on the SIMQUEST architecture this is elaborated in detail.

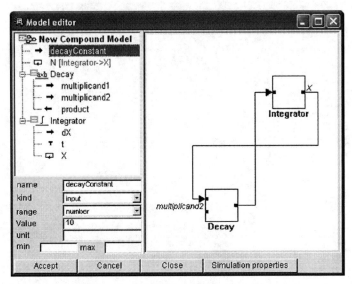

Figure 5. The functional block model editor. On the left the model structure and variables are displayed as a tree on the right as a graph.

Creating and editing simulation interfaces

The simulation model can compute the behavior of the simulation; the simulation interface is used to interact with the model. It displays the values of variables, allows learners to change values of input variables and provides control over the simulation, like starting and stopping the simulation. Creating a simulation interface is done by drawing the interface on a *canvas,* as is shown in Figure 6. The components of the interface, the *widgets,* are taken from the SIMQUEST library and dropped on the canvas. The widget set available includes graphs, sliders, buttons, dials, gauges etc. Each of the widgets can be edited with a *properties editor* (Figure 7).

The interface editor can be used to create and edit simulation interfaces or to create and edit new, more sophisticated, widgets which can then be saved in a learning environment and then transferred to a library allowing it to be reused.

A special kind of interface widget is animations. Animations allow for a dynamic display of the evolution of the simulation state. Animations consist of a number of dynamic objects. Each object, like a rectangle or circle, has properties that can be connected to model variables. For instance, an object's position can be linked to a variable calculating the position of an object, an object's color can be linked to a variable representing, for instance, temperature.

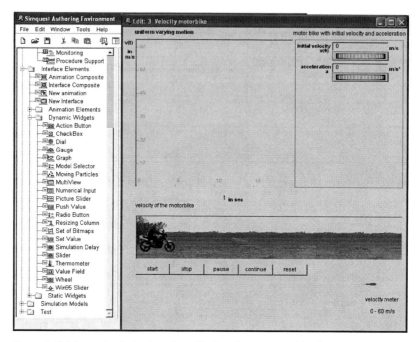

Figure 6. Editing a simulation interface. The interface is created by dragging components from the library to a "canvas". Each component can be linked to a variable in the simulation model, or with a specific action (e.g., run, pause etc.).

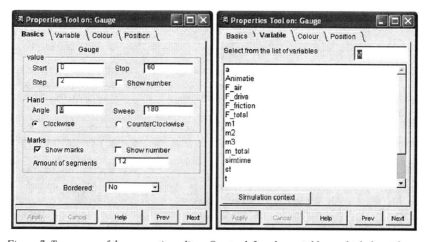

Figure 7. Two pages of the properties editor. One to define the variable to which the widget is linked, one to define the basic properties. The names of the variables are extracted from the model automatically, at run time the value of the variable will be displayed in the selected widget.

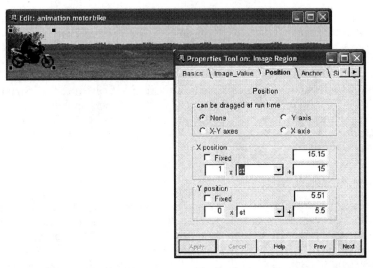

Figure 8. Creation of animations. The way of working with this tool is very much like creating an interface. On the right side, a properties tool is shown which can be used to link attributes of the objects, like size, position, and color to variables in the simulation model.

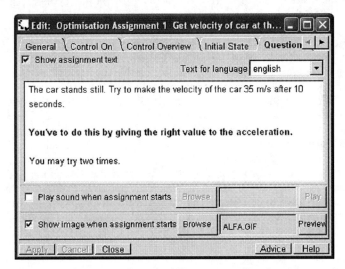

Figure 9. Instructional measure editor, the different pages allow the author to edit several aspects of the instructional measure.

Creating and editing instructional measures

Like simulation interfaces, instructional measures require close co-operation with the simulation model, and belong to the associated model progression level.

Control over the simulation is needed for assignments, for instance to control access to variables or to set an initial state for the model. Once created from the library and linked to a simulation model, and the associated model progression level (by dropping the building on the relevant page) the author can open the editor for the instructional measure (Figure 9). For the case of explanations, this usually means defining the information to be displayed, like text or a media file, for assignments this means specifying the assignment goal to the learner, and determining the expected learner behavior during the assignment's activity. Other kinds of instructional measures are edited in a similar fashion, depending on the nature of the instructional measure.

3.4 Authoring instructional control

The SIMQUEST instructional control system defines which instructional measures are available to the learner at a specific moment, based on specifications by the authors. This is done with the use of *control states* that are part of the definition of any instructional measure. Different control states are: *activated*, *enabled*, *disabled*, and *invisible*. These terms apply to the kind of visibility in the learning environment. Activated means that the instructional measure is active, i.e., it displays its window so that the learner can interact with the instructional measure. Enabled and disabled mean that the instructional measure is visible on a list for the learner, where in the case of enabled the learner can select it, view the description, and activate it. Invisible means that the instructional measure is not shown to the learner. Also for each instructional measure a number of *events* are defined, for instance *activated*, *succeeded*, *failed*, and *exited* for an assignment. Events can change states of instructional measures. For instance it is possible to specify that when one assignment succeeds, a second should be activated.

For defining transitions between instructional measure states, the system uses control events generated by the instructional measures. For each instructional measure and every simulation interface, the author can define what should happen, i.e., which transitions in states of instructional measures should occur as an effect of a control event. A drag and drop interface allows the author to specify constructs such as: "when this assignment succeeds, then stop the simulation and enable assignment xyz123", as shown in Figure 10. For the purpose of control, a simulation interface is considered to be just another kind of instructional measure, meaning that they generate events on opening and closure, and that they can be activated and terminated by other control events.

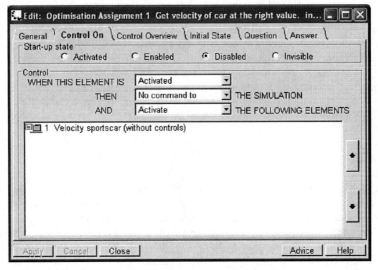

Figure 10. Instructional measure editor, the page to edit instructional control.

Because the change of state of an instructional measure itself is again a control event, a chain of events may be triggered (Van Joolingen & de Jong, 1996a). SIMQUEST offers a graphical overview over the control structure of the application.

In order to allow for more refined control over the application, SIMQUEST contains dedicated library elements that can generate control events other than the standard ones associated with instructional measures. The simplest of these elements is a *timer* that executes its control event when time specified by the author is reached. This element can for instance be used to specify that a learner should freely explore the simulation for 10 minutes before any assignments become available. A more complex control element is the *simulation daemon* that monitors the simulation's variables and executes its event when its constraints are broken. This can be used to attach instruction to events in the simulation. For instance an explanation may appear at the moment a critical value on one of the variables in the simulation model (e.g., a certain temperature level) is reached. This explanation may indicate why this situation is critical and what the learner can do to handle such a situation.

Finally, *composites* allow the author to group together a number of assignments in order to give them common control behavior. This behavior can specify control events attached to individual elements or subsets in the composite. This is useful if the author wants, for example, to specify complex control conditions, for example, to attach an event to the success of four out of six assignments.

4. EXTENDED SUPPORT FOR THE AUTHOR

In the SimQuest authoring process, conceptual support for the author is available in the form of templates offered in the building blocks. For example authors, as explained before, do not need to design assignments from scratch but are offered templates for the design of different types of assignment. In addition, we provide authors with explicit support in the authoring process. For designing this support, our target user was a domain expert, not necessarily an expert in programming and/or in the didactics of discovery learning. In the process of authoring the learning environment, we distinguished three main aspects: design, implementation, and methodology. For these, SimQuest offers three types of support for the author: advice, help, and a wizard (see also de Jong, Limbach et al., 1999).

4.1 Advice

Apart from help on the technical properties of library elements, SIMQUEST also offers advice to authors. Authors working with SIMQUEST quite often have no direct experience with the design of discovery learning environments. Advice tries to support authors in this area and consists of a large hypertext like organized database of knowledge on discovery learning and its support. Advice can be accessed through the main menu, or in a context sensitive way, directly, through the editing window of an instructional measure. By pressing the advice button on an instructional measure editor, the author is taken directly to the relevant page of advice.

The advice tool consists of a two-dimensional card-tray. Different topics on which information is available are presented on the vertical dimension, and four content categories on the horizontal axis. These four content categories are:

1. "What is?" provides information of a definition or explanation of a design aspect;
2. "Example": provides (a) textual or visual example(s) of a design aspect;
3. "Considerations": the author is provided with useful considerations about a design aspect;
4. "Background" provides all kinds of background knowledge e.g., information from the literature.

Figure 11 presents an example of the advice tool interface. Through this interface and through hyperlinks within each text block authors have flexible access to the whole information system. More information on the advice tool can be found in Limbach (2000), in de Jong, Limbach et al. (1999) and Limbach, de Jong, Pieters, and Rowland (1999).

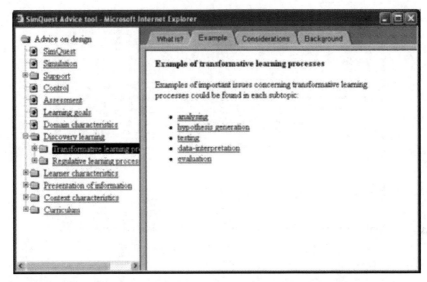

Figure 11 Example screen from the advice tool. In the example the content concerns the transformative learning process "Analyzing" and the category is "What is?"

4.2 Help

Operational support offers the user detailed steps to implement the design of the learning environment in SIMQUEST. Operational support in SIMQUEST consists of two products: online help and a manual. Both types of support follow the principles and heuristics for designing minimal documentation (Van der Meij & Carroll, 1995). This means that the help is action driven, that the tool is anchored in the task domain, that error recognition and recovery is supported, and that a principle of learning by doing is used. Figure 12 gives an example screen from the on-line manual. More information on the SIMQUEST help can be found in Gellevij (1998).

4.3 Wizard

Methodological support in SIMQUEST focuses on novice authors. By means of a wizard-like tool, these authors can generate step by step the basic structure of a SIMQUEST learning environment. This structure can later be modified and extended in the full authoring environment. Wizard support helps the author in the production process:

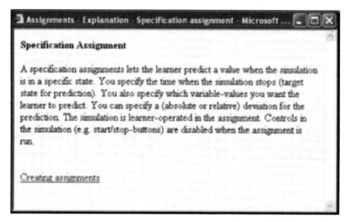

Figure 12. Example window from the on-line help

- in selecting the right template from the library at the right time;
- in providing the minimally required subject matter knowledge at the right time;
- by establishing default component links, providing default computation values, and by generating default test interfaces automatically.

The wizard support also helps the author in the design process:
- in organizing the building blocks of the application in an integrated part-whole structure, that reflects the didactical decomposition of the application;
- by providing didactical decision alternatives that govern the choice of assignments.

In this last respect, the SIMQUEST wizard is different from known wizards. It provides the author with design knowledge and also takes over part of the instructional design process. This is illustrated in Figure 13 where the wizard, based on the selected variables, provides the author with the design of assignments and interfaces for a model progression level.

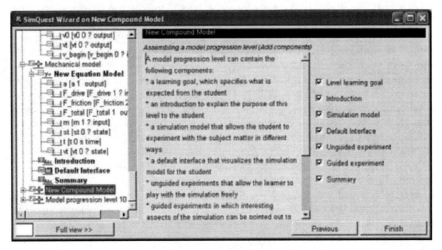

Figure 13. Example from the SIMQUEST wizard

5. SIMQUEST ARCHITECTURE

From the view of the author, creating a SIMQUEST application consists of creating and editing independent single building blocks. The only glue the author puts between these blocks is the control structure. All other dependencies between different building blocks, for instance, for retrieving variable values, are generated by the SIMQUEST system. This is made possible by the SIMQUEST architecture. Two aspects of the architecture are essential for a proper operation of the system: a strict separation between author-time elements and run-time elements, and a strict separation between the model and the instructional elements.

Each tool in the SIMQUEST authoring environment produces *specifications* of an element of a learning environment. For instance, the model editor generates a specification of the components of a simulation model in terms of variables and equations; an assignment editor will generate a specification of an assignment, etc. Once the learning environment is started, or when the author wants to test a part of the learning environment, these specifications are used to construct the actual run time elements. converted into run time objects.

Since the instructional measures interact with the simulation, a protocol has been defined for this interaction. This protocol ensures that though there may be a strong interdependency between the simulation and instructional measures at *run time*, at *author time* instructional measures and the simulation can be specified independently of each other and in any desired order. One central element in the protocol is the *simulation context*. This simulation context contains information on the variables present in the simulation model, as well as on the actions that can be performed on the simulation. This information can be created before the simulation itself. The format of information is independent of the internal model characteristics.

Instructional measures and simulation interfaces can interrogate the simulation context for the names and properties of the variables present. Also they can send a request to create a new variable. There is one simulation context for every simulation model and model progression level in the learning environment.

The simulation context is a platform of communication between all kinds of elements in a learning environment. Also, it can be a platform for communication between different co-operating authors. For instance, one author can create a model to suit a description stored in a simulation context, another author can use the same simulation context to design an interface. The common description stored in the simulation context ensures that, eventually, the interface and the model will co-operate. The strict separation between models and instructional measures, created by the introduction of the simulation context, ensures that the authoring process can be flexible which means that an author can use any order in creating the elemenst of the learning environment, that multiple authors can co-operate, and that elements can be reused over applications. The simulation context also allows the author to provide meaningful names for variables. Syntactical conventions in naming variables in the underlying model can be hidden from the learner. E.g., a variable oscillator1.energy.kinetic can be shown to the learner as "Kinetic energy of spring 1".

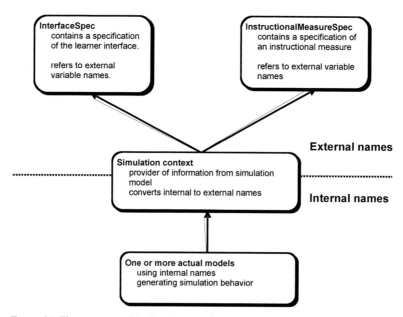

Figure 14. The structure of the SIMQUEST authoring system. Arrows indicate information flow. In a SIMQUEST application, any number of simulation contexts may be present. There is one for each model present in the application.

During run time, a specialized version of the simulation context manages the interaction between the model, the simulation interface, and the instructional measures. This runnable simulation context contains a number of so-called value holders, one for each variable in the model. These value holders communicate the value for the variable they hold to all elements dependent of it, for instance, a graph displaying the value of a certain variable will be notified each time this value changes. Also, if from the interface a learner wants to change the value of a variable, this is done through the appropriate value holder, to which the interface is linked.

6. DISCUSSION AND CONCLUSIONS

In this contribution we described SIMQUEST as a system supporting authors, typically teachers or domain experts, in the process of creating simulation based learning environments, and learners in the processes of discovery learning. SIMQUEST is the successor of the SMISLE system (de Jong & van Joolingen, 1995; van Joolingen, & de Jong, 1996b) and adds to that system flexibility, extensibility and author support. Authors are supported in the creation of challenging interactive learning environments based on computer simulations. They can create these environments without the need for programming, and can concentrate on the domain. Learners are supported in the processes of discovery by means of dedicated instructional measures that aim at scaffolding the discovery learning processes. In this sense SIMQUEST is both a tool and a body of knowledge on discovery learning. This knowledge is present explicitly, in the advice support for the author, and implicitly, in the design of the library and its elements.

SIMQUEST focuses on discovery learning of conceptual domains. This was a choice made in the design that propagates in various aspects of the system. In order to illustrate the effects of this choice, we compare SIMQUEST with RIDES (Munro, this volume), a tool for simulation-based learning that aims at the teaching and learning of operational skills. The first, and main, difference is found in the way the domain is modeled in both systems. SIMQUEST models the domain as a self standing entity describing the conceptual relations at an abstract level. A modeler in RIDES starts from the interface and adds behavior to interface elements, defined as effects of interface actions that represent the atoms of the procedure to be learned. Second, the interface in SIMQUEST is not seen as part of the model, but as a *view* on it. This strict separation allows for different views on the domain model, as well as views that can be adapted by the learner. Implicit in the RIDES method for specifying a model is that this separation between interface and model is not possible. Finally, the collection of instructional measures in SIMQUEST is aimed at supporting the processes of discovery. Typical examples are the investigation assignment and the monitoring tool. RIDES' teaching is directed at modeling and supporting the procedure to be learned.

In its focus on discovery learning SIMQUEST has a strong basis in theory. The available instructional measures, as well as the way SIMQUEST deals with the balance between freedom and guidance for the learner, by means of the instructional control, finds is basis in theoretical work and experiments done with previous versions of the system (see for an overview de Jong & van Joolingen, 1998).

6.1 SIMQUEST as an authoring system

In this section we measure SIMQUEST along the lines indicated by Murray (this volume), and hence allow for comparison with other authoring systems. In his review the Murray mentions several classifications and measures in order to be able to compare authoring systems. We think it is most useful to position SIMQUEST on the level of authoring methods that is subdivided by Murray into authoring tool goals and general authoring features. This comparison allows us to position SIMQUEST as an *authoring system*.

Murray (this volume) lists five general goals for authoring tools. In SIMQUEST we aim to support these goals in various ways, as indicated in Table 1. In a footnote Murray (this volume) also mentions as a possible goal that the author learns something about pedagogy and instructional design. The SIMQUEST advice tool was designed with that purpose. The possible missing factor is that SIMQUEST does not *explicitly* support or enforce specific teaching strategies. The author can learn about pedagogical design with the advice module, but the author cannot pick such a strategy and use this as a template for a whole learning environment (or a significant part of it). Templates are offered on the level of instructional measures, not on their sequence. Authors have to construct the pedagogical strategy from these basic building blocks.

A second set of dimensions identified by Murray (this volume) is that of authoring features. Here the focus is on what the author can actually do with the authoring tool. Table 2 provides an overview of how several SIMQUEST features match against this list. As can be seen, SIMQUEST provides a reasonable portion of these features. Two features stand out. First, the highly modular design of SIMQUEST that helps the author in reusing parts of applications in others. Second, the turnaround time of editing and testing (parts of) a learning environment is short. In this way SIMQUEST provides authors with a flexible, supportive, working environment.

Table 1. SIMQUEST classified on the five goals for authoring tools as indicated by Murray (this volume)

Authoring tool goal according to Murray (this volume).	SIMQUEST's attempt to support this goal.
Decrease the effort for making intelligent tutors.	SIMQUEST tries to achieve this by reducing the effort in programming by offering standard templates, and automating the integration of modules within the system.
Decrease the skill threshold for building intelligent tutors.	SIMQUEST decreases the skill threshold by completely hiding the level of programming from the author. An author with a reasonable experience with general computing tools will be able to learn to work with SIMQUEST on the technical level. The help module and wizard are complementary measures on this point.
Help the author articulate or organize pedagogical knowledge	The overall design of the system and of the target applications helps authors to organize their pedagogical knowledge of the domain. Instructional measures are organized according to model progression levels.
Support good design principles	The SIMQUEST advice module provides authors with support for choosing instructional measures and instructional strategies.
Enable rapid prototyping	Every part of the design of a learning environment can be prototyped rapidly. Simulation interfaces and instructional measures can be run from within the authoring environment and be displayed in the form they will take in the learning environment. Also the sequence of instructional measures can be tested in this way.

Authoring feature (Murray, this volume)	SIMQUEST Implementation
WYSIWIG editing and rapid testing.	Present in SIMQUEST. Simulation interfaces can be created with a WYSIWIG editor and tested from within the editor. Instructional measures can be tested from within the authoring environment.
Flexible opportunistic design	The design of the environment can be adapted on the fly. The wizard provides a top-down design, but the author can also start with basic components and screen designs.
Visual reification	The instructional control structure can be visualized as a graph.
Content modularity and re-usability	Modularity is high. Each instructional measure, model or simulation interface operates as a separate component. Authors can save applications as libraries in order to reuse components in other applications.
Customization, extensibility and scriptability	The library function is one kind of extensibility, author created components become available as building blocks for a new application. Due to its component-based design SIMQUEST itself can be extended relatively simple by a knowledgeable programmer. The team that maintains SIMQUEST honors requests from users.
Undo	Unfortunately SIMQUEST does not provide an undo function.
Administrative features	SIMQUEST allows generating a summary description of the learning environment created for administrative purposes. Also SIMQUEST can keep log files of the interaction with a learner that can be summarized as a web page.
Include customizable representational formalisms	For creating models two representational formalisms are available. It is not possible for the author to introduce a new representational formalism.
Anchor usability on familiar authoring paradigms	With the event-based formalism to structure sequencing of instruction, the author can use various algorithms. The wizard offers a few more traditional and more advanced paradigms, and the author is free to add his or her own.
Facilitate design at pedagogical relevant level of abstraction	We believe that the level of "instructional measure" and its instantiations like "assignment", "explanation" are the relevant level of abstraction.

Table 2. SIMQUEST authoring features following Murray's taxonomy.

6.2 Use and evaluation of SIMQUEST

SIMQUEST has been used to create approximately twenty applications so far. The domains in which these applications were made vary from physics (collisions, electricity) via biology and chemistry, to economics and geography. The subject matters in the latter domains include a simulation to explore a model of economic development of countries in Africa. Using the SIMQUEST animation tool a dynamic colored map of Africa shows the consequences of manipulating parameters in this model. This range of applications shows that simulation based learning is not limited to technical and natural science domains, but can also be applied in the humanities. Important to notice is that the role of "model" may differ for various domains. An economic model has a different status than a model of physics. The latter is directed more towards explanation, the first more towards understanding of observed phenomena.

Several of the environments created have been evaluated in empirical studies. The environment *Collisions* about two colliding particles under different conditions (de Jong, Martin, et al, 1999) has been used as a source material for several empirical studies (Swaak, van Joolingen, & de Jong, 1998; Swaak & de Jong, 2001; Veermans, van Joolingen & de Jong, 2000; Veermans 2003). In these studies various aspects of learning environments (configurations of model progression and assignments, intelligent feedback on experimentation behavior) were varied. An overall result of these studies is that the SIMQUEST instructional measures seem to be able to make a difference on the behavior of learners and in some cases also on the results on domain related knowledge tests. Other learning environments have been used to test out the modeling tool (Löhner, Van Joolingen, & Savelsbergh, in press), the hypothesis scratchpad and SIMQUEST's role in collaborative simulation-based learning (Gijlers & de Jong, submitted; Saab & Van Joolingen, 2003). This work is as yet more premature, as the relation between collaborative learning and simulation-based learning is still open for exploration. Veermans, van Joolingen and de Jong (2000) added a new type of explanation to the system that provided feedback on the experimental behavior of the learners. This type of explanation appeared to have a strong effect on the learner's behavior, indicating a more reflective way of working with the simulation. Veermans (2003) took this further by building in *heuristics* in the monitoring tool. The tool advises and constrains learners according to given heuristics ("vary one variable at a time" or "use canonical values for input variables"). The result of offering heuristics is that in particular weak learners profit from the structure imposed by the explicit heuristics. They are making the larger gains from pretest to posttest.

SIMQUEST as an authoring system has been evaluated on different aspects. Especially the measures for supporting the author in the process of creating simulation based learning environments, the help advice and wizard have been evaluated in empirical studies (Gellevij, 1998; Gellevij, van der Meij, de Jong, & Pieters, 1999; Kuyper, de Hoog & de Jong, 2001; Limbach, 2000; Limbach de Jong, Pieters, & Rowland, 1999). A main lesson learned from these studies is that, though SIMQUEST can take away much of the burden of the authoring process, the conceptual part of authoring in itself requires considerable training for the author.

So, while bringing authoring simulation based learning within the reach of a new group, SIMQUEST also introduces the need for extensive support for these authors. The built-in support can only partly fulfill this need, training and support by experienced users is necessary. A new approach with SIMQUEST is adopted by Vreman- de Olde and De Jong (submitted), who use simulation-based authoring as a learning tool for students. Learners learn by creating SIMQUEST assignments around a given model. By constructing the assignment they learn to understand the model.

Currently SIMQUEST is used by teachers at secondary schools in the Netherlands within the context of various projects and as regular part of a science method. Teachers act as authors and test their applications with their learners. Some SIMQUEST applications have found their way to educational practice. In middle vocational education and on high school level applications in physics and chemistry are shipped by educational publishers as part of their methods. Future developments of SIMQUEST are foreseen in the Co-Lab (Collaborative Laboratory) system that is currently under development. This will include dedicated support for learners collaborating on a discovery learning task, support for learners creating executable models of phenomena they observe, and integration with on-line measurements.

7. REFERENCES

Ainsworth, S. (1999). The functions of multiple representations. *Computers and Education, 33*, 131-152.

Alessi S.M., & Trollip, S.R. (1985). *Computer based instruction, methods and development.* Englewood Cliffs, NY: Prentice-Hall.

Carlsen, D.D., & Andre, T. (1992). Use of a microcomputer simulation and conceptual change text to overcome students preconceptions about electric circuits. *Journal of Computer-Based Instruction, 19*, 105-109.

Gellevij, M. (1998). Operational support in SIMQUEST. In T. de Jong & W.R. van Joolingen (Eds.) *SIMQUEST: an authoring system for integrated simulation learning environments* (pp. 95-113). Internal report. Enschede: University of Twente.

Gellevij, M., van der Meij, H., de Jong, T., & Pieters, J. (1999). The effects of screen captures in manuals: A textual and two visual manuals compared. *IEEE Transactions on Professional Communication, 42*, 77-92.

Gijlers, H. & de Jong, T. (submitted). The influence of prior knowledge on students' dialogue during a kinematics scientific discovery learning task.

Jong, T. de (1991). Learning and instruction with computer simulations. *Education & Computing, 6*, 217-230.

Jong, T. de, Limbach, R., Gellevij, M., Kuyper, M., Pieters, J., & Joolingen, W.R. van (1999). Cognitive tools to support the instructional design of simulation-based discovery learning environments: The SIMQUEST authoring system. In J. van den Akker, R.M. Branch, K. Gustafson N. Nieveen & T. Plomp (Eds.), *Design approaches and tools in education and training* (pp. 215-225). Dordrecht: Kluwer Academic Publishers.

Jong, T. de, Martin, E., Zamarro J-M., Esquiembre, F., Swaak, J., & Joolingen, W.R.van (1999). The integration of computer simulation and learning support; an example from the physics domain of collisions. *Journal of Research in Science Teaching, 36*, 597-615.

Jong, T. de, & Joolingen, W.R. van (1995). The SMISLE environment: Learning with and design of integrated simulation learning environments. In P. Held & W.F. Kugemann (Eds.) *Telematics for education and training* (pp. 173-187). Amsterdam: IOS Press.

Jong, T. de, & Joolingen, W.R. van (1998). Scientific discovery learning with computer simulations of conceptual domains. *Review of Educational Research, 68*, 179-202.

Joolingen, W.R. van, & de Jong, T. (1996a). Design and implementation of simulation-based discovery environments: the SMISLE solution. *Journal of Artificial Intelligence and Education, 7*, 253-277.

Joolingen, W.R. van, & Jong, T. de (1996b). Supporting the authoring process for simulation-based discovery learning. In P. Brna, A. Paiva & J. Self (Eds.), Proceedings of the European conference on Artificial Intelligence and Education (pp. 66-73). Lisbon, Portugal: Edições Colibri.

Joolingen, W.R. van, & Jong, T. de (1997). An extended dual search space model of learning with computer simulations. *Instructional Science*, 25, 307-346.

Klahr, D., & Dunbar, K. (1988). Dual space search during scientific reasoning. *Cognitive Science*, 12, 1-48.

Kuyper, M., de Hoog, R., & de Jong, T. (2001). Modeling and supporting the authoring process of multimedia simulation based educational software: a knowledge engineering approach. *Instructional Science, 29.* 337-259.

Limbach, R. (2000). *Supporting Instructional Designers, Towards an information system for the design of instructional discovery learning environments.* (PhD Thesis). Enschede: University of Twente.

Limbach, R., de Jong, T., Pieters, J., & Rowland, G. (1999). Supporting instructional design with an information system. In J. van den Akker, R.M. Branch, K. Gustafson N. Nieveen & T. Plomp (Eds.), *Design approaches and tools in education and training* (pp. 113-125). Dordrecht: Kluwer Academic Publishers.

Löhner S., & Joolingen, W.R. van, & Savelsbergh, E.R. (in press). The effect of external representation on constructing computer models. *Instructional Science.*

Meij, H. van der & Carroll, J. M. (1995). Principles and heuristics for designing minimalist instruction. *Technical Documentation, 42,* 243-261.

Munro, A. (this volume). Authoring Simulation-Centered Learning Environments With Rides And Vivids.

Murray (this volume). Authoring Intelligent Tutoring Systems: An analysis of the state of the art.

Njoo, M., & de Jong, T. (1993). Exploratory learning with a computer simulation for control theory: Learning processes and instructional support. *Journal of Research in Science Teaching*, 30, 821-844.

Saab, N., & Joolingen, W.R. van (2003). Effects of Communication Processes in Collaborative Discovery, paper to be presented at the AERA conference, Chicago, April 21-25, 2003

Swaak, J., van Joolingen, W.R., & de Jong, T. (1998). Supporting simulation-based learning; the effects of model progression and assignments on definitional and intuitive knowledge. *Learning and Instruction*, 8, 235-253.

Swaak, J. & Jong T. de (2001). System vs. learner control in using on-line support for simulation-based discovery learning; effects on knowledge tests, interaction measures, and a subjective measure of cognitive load. *Learning Environments Research 4,*217-241.

Veermans, K. H. (2003). Intelligent support for discovery learning. PhD. Thesis. Enschede, The Netherlands: Twente University Press.

Veermans, K.H., Joolingen, W.R. van & Jong, T. de (2000). Promoting self directed learning in simulation based discovery learning environments through intelligent support. *Interactive Learning Environments*, 8, 229-255.

Vreman- de Olde, C. & de Jong, T. (submitted). Student-generated assignments about electrical circuits in a computer simulation.

White, B.Y., & Frederiksen, J.R. (1990). Causal model progressions as a foundation for intelligent learning environments. *Artificial Intelligence*, 42, 99-157.

ACKNOWLEDGEMENTS

SIMQUEST was developed in the EU-funded project SERVIVE under contract ET1020. We would like to thank the many people that contributed to the system: Andre Alusse, Miguel Celdran, Francesco Esquiembre, Thomas Gamradt, Mark Gellevij, Hannie Gijlers, Daniel Gureghian, Hermann Härtel, Robert de Hoog, Simon King, Michiel Kuyper, Renate Limbach, Simone Löhner, Ernesto Martin, Humberto Martinez, Jan van der Meij, Sven-Ole Paulsen, Jules Pieters, Elwin Savelsbergh, David Scott, Janine Swaak, Koen Veermans, Paul Weustink and José-Miguel Zamaro.

HENRY M. HALFF, PATRICIA Y. HSIEH, BRENDA M.
WENZEL, TOM J. CHUDANOV, MARY T. DIRNBERGER,
ELIZABETH G. GIBSON & CAROL L. REDFIELD

Chapter 2

REQUIEM FOR A DEVELOPMENT SYSTEM:

Reflections on Knowledge-Based, Generative Instruction

Abstract. Over 10 years ago, the U. S. Air Force undertook a project to make it easier and less costly to develop interactive courseware. The 10-year span of this effort saw the development and field testing of a prototype, known as XAIDA, that makes it easy for subject-matter experts to develop interactive courseware. XAIDA uses a generative, knowledge-based approach. A developer uses a computer program known as Develop to make a Knowledge Base representing the target subject matter. Another program, Deliver, manages a student's interactions with the knowledge base thereby generating instruction suited to the student's individual needs. XAIDA was oriented towards maintenance training and provided, in particular, training in identifying a device's physical characteristics, and making inferences about its behavior. In a wide-ranging series of field tests, XAIDA proved to be easily accessible to developers and effective in training students. XAIDA represents the use of computers to generate instructional interactions directly from information structures that make up knowledge. It therefore requires developers to think about knowledge rather than instructional procedures, and it requires designers to think in terms of generally applicable instructional methods rather than individual instructional designs. XAIDA offered sufficient support for the conceptual support of developers, but more work is needed on the mechanisms needed to support conceptual change in the design process.

1. INTRODUCTION

In the Fall of 1989, one of us (Halff) was asked by the U. S. Air Force Armstrong Laboratory to participate in a series of meetings devoted to a new project then known as the Automated Instructional Design Assistant (AIDA[1]). One result of those meetings was an 10-year exploration of development systems for generative, knowledge-based, computerized instruction—that is, systems that generate instruction directly and automatically from content knowledge. The vehicle for this exploration was a prototype known as the Experimental Advanced Instructional Design Advisor[2] (XAIDA). This paper is an account of XAIDA, a description of the tools and research produced by the project, and reflections on her significance for other efforts devoted to the automation of instructional design and development.
Before beginning, we need to note that the paper is not a complete and detailed description of XAIDA itself or the results of associated research. For the former, we

recommend Hsieh, Halff, and Redfield (1999). For the latter, consult Wenzel, Dirnberger, and Ellis (1998); Wenzel, Dirnberger, Hsieh, Chudanov, and Halff (1998); and Wenzel and Rivas (1999).

2. HISTORY

Hermann Ebbinghaus, one of the greatest students of human learning, once remarked that "psychology has a short history, but a long past" (cited in Boring 1957, p. ix). The same can be said of XAIDA. In this section, we concentrate on her short history. What can be learned from this history and from XAIDA's long past is treated in the conclusion (Section 5) of this paper.

The terms "short" and "long" are, of course, relative. Although AIDA's 10 year history is short compared to the age of the field, it is long compared to the age of the typical research project of its kind. That the Air Force could sustain its commitment to the project over this time span is largely due to the Herculean efforts of the project's scientific director, Michael Spector, and project manager, Dan Muraida. What follows would not have been possible without their own significant technical contributions and their ability to sustain support for the project in the face of numerous unanticipated events. Not the least of these were several unannounced changes in direction on the part of the investigators.

2.1 AIDA, Phase I.

As is mentioned above, XAIDA's roots lie in a series of meetings sponsored by the Air Force Armstrong Laboratory, starting in the fall of 1989. Those meetings, whose results are presented in Spector, Polson, and Muraida (1993), were devoted to determining how computers might "assist in the instructional design process, with the objective of producing consistently effective instructional materials with reduced course development time" (Gagné, 1993). The Air Force, and indeed, the instructional-technology community in general, were facing a situation in which they could see the tremendous potential of Interactive Courseware (ICW) but were also confronted, as they still are, with tremendous development costs. Bandied about at these early meetings were figures of 300–1000 hours of development time to produce one hour of finished courseware. We doubt that these figures have changed much in the intervening years.

What emerged from the Phase I meetings was a general agreement that the instructional technology community desperately needed tools to make courseware development easier and courseware more effective. The conferees also agreed that any subsequent work on a development system should focus on maintenance training. Other fields were not excluded from consideration, but the Air Force took the position that further developments should address the needs of the maintenance training community, at the very least.

There was, however, nothing like a consensus on the form that such tools should take. From the great diversity of approaches to be found in Spector, Polson, and Muraida (1993), one distinction appears to be critical in hindsight. Halff (1993) refers to this distinction as that between *advisory* and *generative* functions of an automated development system.

An advisory system offers performance support in that it directs an instructional designer on what tasks need to be performed and how to perform them. Thus, advisory systems function as supervisors, and instructional designers function as their assistants, taking on the legwork required to build a design. The courseware produced by advisory systems does not differ in nature from that produced by unaided instructional designers. This courseware can, however be produced more efficiently and more consistently, and it can be more effective than that produced by an unaided instructional designer.

With generative systems, roles are reversed. The instructional designer specifies the design at a high level, and the computer fills in the lower levels of the design. Like advisory systems, generative systems can make instructional designs more efficient, consistent, and effective. Unlike advisory systems, generative systems can produce courseware that is radically different than that produced by any manual method. They can, for example, assemble the design at the time of delivery, modifying it, as instruction proceeds, to fit the needs of individual students.

The Air Force, faced with this fork in the road, took both paths. They initiated a project entitled the *Guided Approach to Instructional Design Advising* (GAIDA[3]) (Gettman, McNelly, and Muraida, 1999). GAIDA helps designers apply a framework known as the Nine Events of Instruction (Gagné, 1985) to development of interactive courseware using conventional authoring tools such as Click2Learn's ToolBook (2001). More important for this account, however, was the Air Force's investment in XAIDA, an approach that adhered to generative, knowledge-based techniques.

2.2 AIDA, Phases II and III

Before embarking on the development of a prototype, the AIDA project made an effort to develop a specification for this prototype. Although this specification was never developed except in a most rudimentary form, the effort itself—AIDA, Phase II—produced a trio of proposals on how the project should proceed. These proposals—by Doug Towne, David Merrill, and one of us (Halff)—are described in Hickey, Spector, and Muraida (1991). Many of the ideas in these early proposals are manifest in XAIDA's latest version.

XAIDA started as a partnership between David Merrill's research team at Utah State University and the Mei Technology Corporation, the former providing design guidance, and the latter providing development services. Although the partnership was dissolved in mid-project, Merrill's influence on XAIDA cannot be understated. His approach, then known as ID_2 (Merrill, 1993), formed the basis for every subsequent version of XAIDA.

To be specific, XAIDA was grounded in Merrill's notions of instructional *transactions* and *transaction shells* (Merrill and ID2 Research Team, 1996). A transaction is an instructional procedure for meeting a particular instructional objective such as being able to tie one's shoe or answer questions about the characteristics of an automobile engine. A transaction shell is a generic form of a transaction. It might, for example, describe a method for instruction in step-by-step procedures in general or for associative learning in general. Transactions are produced by configuring a transaction shell with particular subject-matter knowledge (e.g., the steps in tying one's shoe or the characteristics of an automobile engine).

The tangible results of Mei Technology's initial work on the project were two prototypes, only the second of which provided anything like the functionality envisioned for the system. This second prototype—known as XAIDA, Version 2—had the fundamental elements of a knowledge-based, generative, instructional development system. These elements included a database structure or *Knowledge Base* that could be used to house instructional content, a development system, called *Develop* that instructional developers could use to populate the knowledge base with content, and a delivery system, called *Deliver,* that managed instructional interactions between the student and the knowledge base.

XAIDA, Version 2 supported two transaction shells. An *Identify* shell addressed the physical structure of a device (in keeping with the high priority of maintenance training), that is, its parts, their locations, and their characteristics. An *Interpret* shell addressed the functional characteristics of a device, that is, the behavior of its components and their functional interdependencies.

Perhaps the most significant aspect of Mei's work on this early prototype was a series of field tryouts at an Air Force Technical Training Center at Sheppard Air Force Base in 1992–1993. The prototoype was put in the hands of two instructors and an instructional designer at the Center with a view to determining how it could be improved. One of the most remarkable results of these field tryouts was the enthusiastic reception accorded the prototype by the instructors themselves, who were, significantly, subject-matter experts. Also significant, in hindsight, was the fact that the prototype never became accessible to the instructional designer, who was not a subject-matter expert, despite considerable effort on her part.

The different roles of subject-matter experts and instructional designers were important determinants in their different reactions to XAIDA. These different roles are therefore worth brief descriptions at this point in the story. Subject matter experts are, as the term implies, masters of the content to be conveyed in instruction. In training environments they can play many roles. They can develop training materials (including interactive courseware); they can serve as instructors; they can provide input to professional instructional designers. These designers themselves need not be subject-matter experts. Their role is to integrate input from subject-matter experts, management, and other sources to produce and maintain a training system that meets the organization's needs. Instructional designers' expertise lies in the fields of instructional theory and practice. Only coincidentally do they have expertise in the fields for which they design instruction. In the course of their work, they need only learn enough about the field to fill the schemata used to design instruction.

2.3 AIDA Phase IV

The Air Force undertook a planned fourth research phase for AIDA at the beginning of 1994. Their ambitions for this phase were to build a serviceable prototype of XAIDA and subject it to controlled field evaluations. The contract to undertake this work was given to Mei Technology's San Antonio office. It is that prototype and research that is described below in Sections 3 and 4. We summarize here some of the more important milestones in the Phase IV effort.

Among the first issues that the Phase IV design team faced were serious usability problems in the Phase III prototype. Develop, in this prototype, was a form-based data-entry system like those found in order-entry or employee records applications. Developers using the system had little or no sense of how their instruction would appear to students. The design team's response to this problem was a move to a What-You-See-Is-What-You-Get (WYSIWYG) development environment. Developers populated the Knowledge Base using the very displays that students used to browse that Knowledge Base at run time. This move was motivated by observations of the subject-matter-expert instructors mentioned above, and, as expected, it was remarkably successful in making development more accessible to the subject-matter-expert instructor population. What we did not expect was that the change may have made development *less* accessible to other populations, including non-subject-matter-expert instructional designers (see Section 2.2).

A second major design decision was that of adopting instructional methods not (necessarily) from instructional *design* theory and practice (e.g., Reigeluth, 1983), but from successful instructional *practices* found "in the wild" and on the job. XAIDA's instructional methods were gleaned from observations of Air Force technical trainers and from the design team's instructional expertise.

We made this move to a design-free system based on the project's commitment to maintenance training and the conjecture that all maintenance training followed the same pattern (described in Polson, Polson, Kieras, and Halff, 1992). We felt that if XAIDA could instantiate the pattern, then we could shortcut the burdensome requirements of a front-end analysis and design.

The most significant outcome of our approach was the incorporation into XAIDA of practice environments that afford students the opportunity to practice answering questions of the sort asked in technical training classrooms. The questions presented for practice in these environments were not "canned," but rather were generated directly from the knowledge base. This combination of a naturalistic approach and generative technique puts the prototype's operation outside of any paradigm of conventional instructional systems design (e.g., Tennyson, 1993).

Also worth mention in connection with the Phase IV effort was a change in the names of the transaction shells from Identify to *Physical Characteristics* and from Interpret to *Theory of Operation*. The change was a move away from Merrill's (1993) designspeak to the language of maintenance technicians and subject matter experts.

These and other changes were incorporated into a fully functional two-shell development and delivery system known as XAIDA, Version 5. One of these shells,

Physical Characteristics, is described below in Section 3. The other shell, Theory of Operations, is described in Hsieh, Halff, and Redfield (1999).

The last design products of the Phase IV effort were functional designs and Deliver prototypes for two new shells intended to round out XAIDA's coverage of maintenance training. One shell, *Procedures*, provided instruction on the kinds of step-by-step procedures required for operation and maintenance of most equipment. The other shell, *Troubleshooting*, taught students how to follow and interpret troubleshooting procedures like those found in technical documentation. These designs are not treated further here. Table 1 presents an overview of each of XAIDA's four shells. Greater detail can be found in Hsieh, Halff, and Redfield (1999).

Phase IV was also responsible for perhaps the most extensive research programs ever conducted on an instructional development system. XAIDA was given field tryouts by 63 developers in a series of six studies. Much of the research (Wenzel and Rivas, 1999; Wenzel and Garcia, 1999; Hsieh and Wheeler, 1999) was conducted in community colleges in cooperation with the Alamo Community College District (ACCD), and this collaborative work lasted well into 1999 when Phase IV had long-since ended. The results of the ACCD work and other research are described below in Section 4.

2.4 The Last Days

Near the end of Phase IV, Armstrong Laboratory developed a set of goals for the next phase of the project. These goals included a wide-ranging research effort aimed at identifying the needs of all Air Force professionals involved in instructional design and development and an advanced prototype designed to meet those needs. Mei Technology won the contract for this work with a proposal calling for iterative cycles of research, development, and formative evaluation.

One of the most significant features of the follow-on effort was a commitment to use an open architecture for XAIDA's successor (XAIDA, The Next Generation or XTNG) in order to provide extensibility in two directions. First, XTNG would have a mechanism for incorporating additional shells reflecting different instructional methods and instructional development schemes. In fact, Develop was reconceived as simply another shell, along with Deliver. Second, XTNG's new architecture would provide for access to non-native knowledge bases. For example, it might allow a troubleshooting shell to generate instruction from an appropriately tagged Interactive Electronic Technical Manual (IETM).

Before this project started, Michael Spector, the project's scientific director, decided to explore the possibility of combining AIDA with the work of Gilbert Paquette at Téléuniversité, Université du Quebec. Paquette had been working on a system known as *L'Atelier de Genie Didactique* (AGD) (Paquette, Crevier, and Aubin, 1994; Paquette and Girard, 1996) that offered automated support to *professional instructional designers.* Spector discerned that AGD and XAIDA shared certain fundamental knowledge-representation techniques (namely, semantic networks) and that Paquette's group had conducted much of the research called for in the Air Force project. Spector therefore felt that the Air Force could move more quickly to development by using Paquette's existing research results, and could build a more capable product by combining XTNG with AGD.

Table 1. XAIDA 5's Transaction Shells

Transaction Shell	**Physical Characteristics**
Nature of Knowledge	The structure of the system (its modules and components), their locations, and other characteristics of the system
Instructional Objective	Recall and recognition of system characteristics in a variety of contexts
Knowledge Representation	Semantic network based on the structure of the system
Instructional Method	Structure-directed presentation of system characteristics and memory practice using diverse exercise formats
Transaction Shell	**Theory of Operation**
Nature of Knowledge	Variables characterizing system behavior, their possible values and their functional relations
Instructional Objective	Infer the values of some variables from knowledge of the values of others
Knowledge Representation	Causal reasoning scheme
Instructional Method	Presentation of salient cases (both student- and instructor-generated) about system behavior along with exercises requiring inferences about system behavior
Transaction Shell	**Procedures**
Nature of Knowledge	The steps of a procedure, characteristics of the procedure and of each step including potential mistakes and mishaps.
Instructional Objective	Memory for the steps of a procedure, the fundamental characteristics of the procedure and of each step, including potential mistakes and mishaps. Mastery of methods for error avoidance and recovery.
Knowledge Representation	Semantic network based on the steps of the procedure.
Instructional Method	Stepwise presentation of the procedure; stepwise practice of recall; practice in error recognition and recovery; global recall practice.
Transaction Shell	**Troubleshooting**
Nature of Knowledge	Successive partitions of the system used to progressively isolate a fault, observations and inferences used in the isolation process
Instructional Objective	Comprehend existing troubleshooting procedures as space-splitting fault isolation strategies.
Knowledge Representation	Discrimination net (called a *fault tree*) with regions at its nodes, observations at its branches and faults at its leaves.
Instructional Method	Troubleshooting practice -- faults are progressively added to the practice environment in the order dictated by the fault tree.

The proposed collaboration was never initiated, but the process of setting it up strikes us, in retrospect, as being informative about the instructional community's reaction to systems like XAIDA and AGD.

To begin with, we find it significant that Spector deemed XAIDA and AGD to be compatible, based not on what they did and for whom, but rather on how they did what they did, that is, on how they represented knowledge. Neither he nor anyone else saw any difficulties in the functional integration of the two systems, especially in view of XTNG's commitment to extensibility. However, had we viewed XAIDA as a tool that SMEs use to make generative instructional systems and AGD as a system that supported professional instructional designers in developing a design, we might have been less sanguine about prospects for their combination.

Also significant was a review of XAIDA by the AGD design team. Paquette had an interesting insight about the WYSIWYG nature of the development interface. He noted that the WYSIWYG interface obscured just what an instructional designer needed to see, namely the high-level structure of the subject matter. His team also mentioned the complete absence of any provisions for instructional objectives in XAIDA. These remarks illustrate how far removed XAIDA had become from an instructional design tool. Instructional designers do need to have a high-level view of the subject matter, but subject-matter experts already have such a view. Likewise, instructional designers do need to be explicit about instructional objectives. XAIDA allows subject-matter experts to bypass this step by directly mapping knowledge to instruction.

Before the shape of XTNG's future could be settled, the project fell victim to the intense competition for research funding that beset the Armstrong Laboratory. Some of the critical features of XTNG were preserved briefly in a short-lived project known as the High-level Simulator with Instructional Design Expert (HISIDE). In addition, XAIDA, Version 5 has been, and continues to be used in occasional projects outside the scope of the initial project, for example, Hsieh and Hsieh (2001, 2002, 2003). In addition, two of the us, Halff and Hsieh, are involved in an effort, sponsored by the U. S. Department of Defense, to bring many of XAIDA's main features to bear on simulation-based training for medical procedures.

XAIDA itself fulfilled virtually all of her designer's expectations and deserves the attention of the research community if only as a source of effective methods for developing instruction and evaluating instructional development systems. It is to these ideas that we now turn.

3. XAIDA, VERSION 5

This section illustrates XAIDA's core ideas by describing one shell, Physical Characteristics, in XAIDA's last fully functional incarnation, Version 5. This shell is the most refined and most extensively evaluated of the four, and an understanding of its design is all that is needed for a grasp of the significance of XAIDA. The reader seeking a fuller description of the other shells should consult Hsieh, et al. (1999).

As is mentioned above, XAIDA is based on Merrill's transaction shell theory (Merrill and ID2 Research Group, 1996). Each XAIDA transaction shell consists of two computer programs and a corpus of associated data. *Develop* is a knowledge acquisition system used by a subject-matter expert to specify the knowledge and materials making up the subject matter of instruction. The output of Develop is an XAIDA *Knowledge Base*. This Knowledge Base specifies the structure of knowledge in the domain and the materials used in interactions with students. *Deliver* is an instructional delivery program that uses transaction shells to manage the interaction between a student and the Knowledge Base.

The functionality of a shell can be approached in terms of four topics: (a) the representation of subject-matter knowledge, (b) the instructional materials associated with knowledge structures, (c) the instructional procedures embodied in Deliver, and (d) the knowledge acquisition procedures embodied in Develop. Each shell handles these topics in a different fashion. The representation of a system's physical characteristics, for example, is quite different than that of its theory of operation. Hence, what students need to learn about these two aspects of a system is different. The instructional techniques and materials differ as well.

In spite of these differences, there is much in common among shells. For example, each of the shells brings two basic modules or capabilities to the task of instruction: a *browser* that is used to present (and to acquire) knowledge, and a *practice* environment that promotes skill acquisition under the direction of an intelligent tutoring system. Our aim in this section is to convey enough about these commonalities to give the reader an understanding of XAIDA's overall philosophy and approach, and, in particular, to distinguish her approach from others. To this end it is sufficient to present a brief glimpse of XAIDA's simplest, most developed, and most extensively studied shell, the Physical Characteristics Shell.

3.1 Instructional Objectives of the Physical Characteristics Shell

Maintenance training typically provides for extensive treatment of the physical characteristics of the systems addressed in the training. Students must learn the structure of the system, that is, its modules and components. They must learn where these parts are located. They must master their salient characteristics such as their functions, capacities, and limitations. In conventional instruction students must exhibit mastery of these facts by passing tests consisting of questions about the system.

XAIDA's Physical Characteristics shell is designed to instill this knowledge in students. The type of knowledge is fundamentally associative, and we therefore use semantic networks for knowledge representation. Instructional capabilities include both a browser used to present instructional materials and an intelligent tutoring system (ITS) that can be used to practice recall of the characteristics.

3.2 Knowledge Representation: Semantic Networks

XAIDA uses *semantic networks* to represent the physical characteristics of a device. A semantic network (Collins & Quillian, 1969; Collins & Loftus, 1975) is a set of triples, called *facts* in XAIDA, of the form (*subject, attribute, object*), for example, (filter basket, part of, coffee pot). Figure 1 depicts a fragment of a Physical

Characteristics semantic network. Several points about this network are worth mention.

Central to XAIDA's knowledge representation for Physical Characteristics is the part structure of the device being represented. This structure is represented in the semantic network through the attribute "is part of". We use the term "part" to refer to any element of the part structure, including the top-level element. In a Physical Characteristics semantic network the subject of a fact is always a part.

The network contains location information. Associated with each part is a background graphic in which all of its subparts are visible. Associated with each subpart is a region of the background called a *locator* that denotes the location of the subpart. Such a locator is shown in Figure 1 for the Crew Drain Valve.

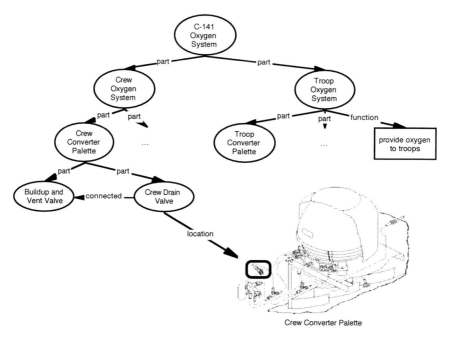

Figure 1. Semantic Network Fragment.

The developer can create any number of attributes deemed important for device understanding and create facts for those attributes. The objects in these facts can either be other parts (e.g., (Crew Drain Valve, connected, Buildup and Vent Valve) as shown in Figure 1) or text (e.g., (Troop Oxygen System, function, "provide oxygen to troops") as shown in Figure 1).

3.3 Instructional Materials

As is mentioned above, each of the elements of the knowledge representation described here has associated instructional resources that are used to convey information about the element to the student. These materials can take on several forms. *Names* of parts, attributes, and values are used by the student and system to refer to the corresponding objects. These names are fitted to *templates* to display facts and questions about facts. *Descriptions* and *resources* provided detailed information on parts and facts. Resources can be graphics, web pages, or any file with an associated executable reader.

3.4 Instructional Delivery

In providing instruction on a device's physical characteristics, XAIDA constructs a lesson outline based on the part structure of the device. A browser is used to present the materials related to each part in outline order. In addition, a practice session is inserted after all parts of any part with subparts have been covered. Thus, the first few topics covered in connection with Figure 1 are

> C-141 Oxygen System,
> > Crew Oxygen System,
> > > Crew Converter Palette,
> > > > Buildup and Vent Valve,
> > > > Crew Drain Valve,
> > > **Practice**,
> > > remaining parts of the Crew Oxygen System,
> > > ... .

The following sections describe the operation of the browser and practice capability.

The Physical Characteristics Browser.

The Physical Characteristics Browser has three functions. First, it presents an overview of the part by showing it both in the context of its enclosing part and close up. Second, it displays all of the instructional content (facts, descriptions, and resources) associated with the part (see Figure 2). Third, it supports review of any previously presented material. (A browse-forward option is also available.)

Physical Characteristics Practice.

The student is given practice on fact recall after coverage of all of the subparts of any part with subparts. The scope of the practice includes all previously presented facts. XAIDA's practice capability is an Intelligent Tutoring System (ITS) that helps students learn these facts. The ITS has three important design features. First, it provides for recall practice in a variety of contexts. Second, it is adaptive in that it concentrates practice on students' weaknesses. Third, it is complemented by a full support environment with access to hints and reference materials.

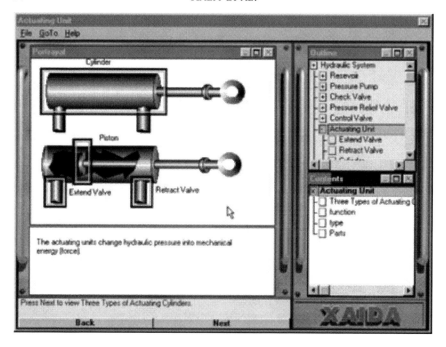

Figure 2. The Physical Characteristics Browser.

The practice module presents the student with a series of exercises like the one shown in Figure 3. Each exercise is constructed by configuring one of eleven exercise templates with a subset of the facts in the semantic network. Some templates, such as the one in Figure 3, are configured with an attribute-value combination, (function, store hydraulic fluid for the system). Others rely on part-attribute combinations, for example, "Enter the function(s) of the reservoir." Thus, in general, each exercise addresses multiple facts, and each fact can be addressed in multiple ways.

The particular part-attribute or attribute-value combination used to configure an exercise is chosen on the basis of a student model. The model tracks performance on a fact-by-fact basis, classifying each fact as either mastered or unmastered. It also tracks misconceptions, facts found in student responses that are not in the knowledge base; Figure 3 shows such a misconception, (pressure relief valve, function, store hydraulic fluid for the system).[4] The system selects part-attribute or attribute-value combinations using a random procedure biased towards unmastered facts and misconceptions. The process is therefore adaptive to the student's strengths and weaknesses.

The practice module comes with a number of support mechanisms. Students can use the browser to look up answers. They can ask for one of the answers to a multiple-answer exercise. They can skip exercises. As Figure 3 shows, feedback is extensive to the point of being annoying.

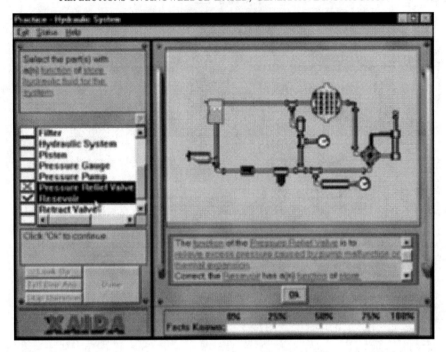

Figure 3. Physical Characteristics Exercise.

3.5 Physical Characteristics Lesson Development

As is noted above, instructional development in XAIDA is a matter of using a program called Develop to populate an XAIDA Knowledge Base. Instead of describing the functional characteristics of Develop, we can better serve the purposes of this paper by describing the main steps in lesson development. This approach should give the reader a reasonable idea of how XAIDA differs from other development tools and environments.

A developer prepares materials for XAIDA by organizing the subject matter, that is, her knowledge of some device, say the ignition system of a 1964 VW Beetle. The main elements of this organization consist of names, descriptions, and graphics of each parts (e.g., battery, plugs) and each of its subparts (e.g., contacts, gap), along with a list of part characteristics (e.g., the voltage of the battery is 12V) that serve as the basis for facts. She may also assemble other media (video, Web pages, etc.) to be used in the courseware.

After assembling materials, she opens Develop and calls for a new lesson. Because Develop is WYSIWYG, it first constructs an empty Physical Characteristics browser (see Section 3.4) for the developer. She uses this browser in conjunction with several editors (see Figure 4) to enter information into the

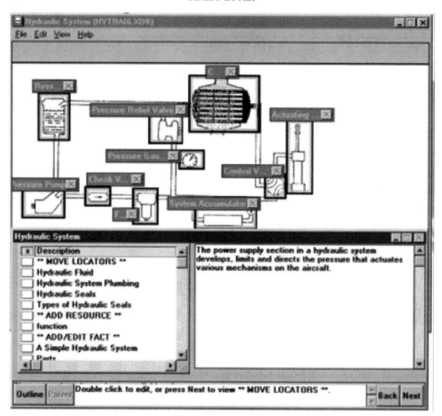

Figure 4. XAIDA WYSIWYG Develop Interface.

Knowledge Base. Using an Outline Editor, she enters the part-subpart structure of the device into the knowledge base. She uses a Portrayal Editor to associate graphics with each part and indicate the locations of their subparts. She then uses a collection of content editors to provide a description for each part, enter the facts pertinent to the part, and add any resources required for instruction in the part.

After completing a first draft of the Knowledge Base, the developer runs Deliver as a student and immediately notices that some of the wording in the exercises is awkward, for example, "Enter the parts with an access of hood." Other exercises don't make sense, for example, "Select the polarity of the positive battery contact." She returns to Develop and invokes a question editor that allows her to fine-tune the design of exercises. She selectively previews the exercises that seem to be causing problems. She customizes the wording used in the exercise templates for some attributes to make the questions less awkward, and she disables certain types of exercises for some of the attributes.

As a final editing step, she builds a slide-show like introduction to the lesson that provides an orientation and some motivating material. This step is as close as she comes to authoring traditional computer-based instruction (CBI).

She reviews the revised draft as a student and bundles it for distribution. The lesson itself provides about two hours of instruction. Since the developer is a skilled XAIDA user, it only took four hours of work with Develop to construct the Knowledge Base. An additional 20 hours were required to prepare the graphics and other resources for the lesson.

It is important to note what the developer does not do in the course of constructing a knowledge base. She does not specify instructional objectives. These objectives are implicit in the instructional schema used by the shell. She does not specify a list of target skills that might be tracked by some student model. Opaque target skills are not a feature of XAIDA, although it might be said that XAIDA derives target skills based on its Knowledge Base. She does not design anything like CBI frames, branching strategies, remediation, interactions, or test items. All of this instructional and diagnostic material is generated on-line by Deliver at run time.

3.6 XAIDA and Other Physical Characteristics Tutors

XAIDA provides a more thoroughgoing instructional treatment of physical characteristics information than any other knowledge-based system for maintenance instruction we know of (Hsieh, 1997). Most other ITSs for maintenance instruction have simulation as their centerpiece; physical characteristics instruction, if available at all, is a lagniappe. RIDES (Munro, this volume), for example, is a powerful and well-designed system for developing equipment simulations which includes a facility for easy development of various types of exercises. However, these exercises are non-adaptive, and their inclusion with the meat of the instruction (i.e., manipulation and exploration of the simulation) is left to the discretion of the developer.[5]

IDXcelerator (Merrill and Thompson, 1999) is the only other system we know of for which factual information is bread-and-butter. IDXcelerator also generates questions from developer input. However, XAIDA's knowledge representation is more fine-grained and open-ended than IDXcelerator's, so that XAIDA can ask about more kinds of information (anything that can be expressed as a part-attribute-value triplet) and can use a greater variety of questioning schema (eleven for XAIDA versus three for IDXcelerator). In addition, XAIDA provides adaptive practice.

The teaching of associative knowledge has not been a hot area for ITS research and development, possibly because it is considered to be well mapped out. However, the need to teach factual information is clear and widespread, in maintenance training and in many other domains as well. An easy-to-use authoring tool for associative knowledge would certainly both fill a gap and be very handy to have around, as our own experiences fielding XAIDA have borne out. We turn now to the research that supports this claim and provides additional information on how XAIDA was received by the instructional community.

4. RESEARCH

AIDA was a research project, and therefore not only served as a platform for theoretical exploration of generative, knowledge-based instruction, but also as a vehicle for perhaps the most extensive study of an instructional development system of its type to date. This section summarizes that program of study.

The XAIDA research program consisted of 6 separate studies of developers (Wenzel & Dirnberger, 1996; Wenzel, Dirnberger, and Halff, 1997; Wenzel, Dirnberger, Hsieh, Chudanov, and Halff, 1998; Wenzel & Garcia, 1999; Wenzel & Rivas, 1999; Wenzel, Rivas, and Hearn, 1997, 1998) and 27 instructional tryouts (Casaus, Gibson, Wenzel, & Halff, 1997; Hsieh and Garcia, 1999; Hsieh and Hsieh, in press; Richardson, Wenzel, & Halff, 1997; Wenzel, Dirnberger & Ellis, 1998; Wenzel, Dirnberger, Fox, Hearne, Licklider, Keeney, Reyna, Roberts, Strebeck, and Halff, 1997; Wenzel, Halff, and Gibson, 1996; Wenzel, Richardson, and Gibson, 1996).

These studies varied widely in their objectives and approaches, but they all employed all or part of a common schema to provide data on both the development process and instructional effectiveness of the courseware developed. The schema called for a development phase and a courseware tryout. In the development phase, novice developers learned how to use XAIDA by creating a lesson during training. The lesson was refined over the course of a week or so. Its effectiveness was then evaluated in the courseware tryout. For many of the studies, the courseware tryouts were conducted in actual classes. In some studies, the courseware was developed by the investigators to answer questions about instructional effectiveness. In other cases, when courseware tryouts were infeasible, only the development phase of the schema was employed. Despite this variability, it is most meaningful to discuss separately results bearing on XAIDA's development and delivery capabilities.

4.1 Studies of Courseware Developers

Studies of developers were mainly concerned with the ease with which new developers could master Develop and produce usable courseware. We studied the process of mastering Develop using a method that intertwined evaluation and classroom training in the use of Develop. The method provided a wealth of data on the usability and learnability of XAIDA as well as on changes in attitude toward the technology.

Development Research Methodology

XAIDA Develop training was conducted in a classroom setting over the span of 3–5 days. Three days were required for Physical Characteristics training only, and an additional two days were required for Theory of Operation training. Training typically consisted of the following steps.

1. Prior to training, developers were sent a form that they could use to identify a topic for their courseware, organize their thinking about the topic, and assemble instructional materials such as descriptions and illustrations.
2. Training began with a standup presentation, and sometimes a video, introducing developers to XAIDA.
3. Developers used a written tutorial in conjunction with an existing XAIDA Physical Characteristics lesson to become familiar with Deliver.
4. After a short presentation on Develop, developers worked through a Develop tutorial in which they recreated the courseware employed in Step 3.
5. Developers were coached through a generic tutorial to develop Physical Characteristics courseware on the topic selected in Step 1.
6. Steps 4 and 5 were repeated for the Theory of Operation shell in some studies.
7. Developers refined their courseware with production assistance and telephone support over the course of a week or so.

Evaluation instruments were designed to measure developers' competence at using Deliver. These included self reports of competence, relatedness ratings of key XAIDA concepts, and a special XAIDA-hosted set of tasks that provided a behavioral measure of competence. Successfully completed courseware served as the most direct measure of developer competence. The evaluation instruments were administered at various points throughout training.

Equally important to the research were measures of developers' attitudes towards XAIDA. These included solicited comments and responses to open ended questions and an organizational climate survey that assessed developers' perceptions of the fit of XAIDA to their organization. Finally, usability questionnaires assessed overall satisfaction with Develop's interface and perceptions of particular aspects of that interface.

Developers' Backgrounds

Studies of XAIDA developers involved some 63 participants in 6 separate studies. Developers varied in their backgrounds, attitudes, and subject-matter expertise. Most of the participants were involved in a three-year series of studies (Wenzel, Dirnberger, and Halff, 1997; Wenzel & Garcia, 1999; Wenzel & Rivas, 1999; Wenzel, Rivas, and Hearn, 1997, 1998) of Texas community college teachers. This work was conducted in collaboration with the Alamo Community College District (ACCD). Participants taught a variety of courses including oil-well maintenance, algebra, welding, nursing, computer literacy, and a number of other subjects. Many of the participants had little or no exposure to computers prior to their participation in the studies. Participants in these studies were expected not only to produce an XAIDA lesson but also to try out their lessons in their own classes.

Other studies (Wenzel & Dirnberger, 1996; Wenzel, Dirnberger, and Halff, 1997; Wenzel, Dirnberger, Hsieh, Chudanov, and Halff, 1998) involved developers from military organizations. This population was more diverse since they did not participate under the umbrella of a single research project. Thus, one study involved an Air Force medical training squadron. Another involved an aircraft maintenance training squadron, and a third involved a collection of individuals from diverse defense organizations.

Results and Conclusions

The results of these studies provided information bearing on several questions. Among the most important are the following.

Learning XAIDA. Virtually all developers learned how to use XAIDA within the time allotted. Across all studies, only two developers failed to produce a lesson within the allotted time frame (owing to commitments that took them away from training). Developers' self-ratings of competence with XAIDA increased monotonically with time in training. We used relatedness ratings of XAIDA concepts in conjunction with the Pathfinder Network Scaling technique (Schvaneveldt, 1990) to measure the correspondence of developers conceptual structure to that of expert XAIDA developers. With the exception noted below, as training progressed, developers' conceptual structures increased in similarity to that of an expert developer. Developers also exhibited overall competence in a performance test of various Develop functions.

More interesting than the course of learning were the sources of difficulty in mastering Develop. Although there were some usability problems, the main source of difficulty was conceptual. Developers initially approached the development task as one of designing a curriculum or instructional sequence. Develop is a knowledge-based development system with a browser interface, and it requires developers not to enter an instructional sequence but rather to enter data representing their knowledge of the subject matter. One developer compared this requirement to "wearing tight underwear."

Attitudes towards XAIDA. Data pertinent to attitudes consisted mainly of comments solicited at several points during developer training. These data were analyzed in two ways. First, we assigned a valence—positive, negative, or neutral—to each comment. Second, we categorized each comment in terms of the type or level of concern expressed. We used seven categories, ranging from low-level comments reflecting awareness of XAIDA ("Seems like a good product.") to high level comments reflecting need for revision ("Portrayal window needs to be larger"). Details of the method can be found in Hall (1979), Hall, George, & Rutherford (1986), and Bailey & Palsha (1992).

The valence of comments was generally positive, but this overall result was marked by two significant patterns. First, the proportion of positive comments was lower at the end of the second day of training than after either the first or third days. This U-shaped pattern was the result of the sequence of activities in developer training. The first day consisted mainly of demonstration and highly constrained practice with XAIDA, all fairly "safe" activities. On the second day, developers were more on their own, working with their own materials. The difficulties that developers encountered with their first hands-on experiences during the second day tempered the positive feelings engendered by the first-day's demonstrations. Increasing mastery led to more positive feelings on the third day of training.

Second, we found that negative comments were far more prevalent among organizations that had not had the opportunity to build some commitment to the program before training. Developers who received an orientation and were expected to develop usable courseware had more positive feelings than those who showed up for training with nothing in the way of expectations about the use of XAIDA in their organizations. Worth noting is that developers in these latter organizations also showed less well developed conceptual structures of XAIDA than those in the former types of organizations.

The level of concern evidenced by developers comments rose steadily during training. Initial comments focused on the tool itself. Later comments focused on its role in the developers' organizations and suggestions for improvements. Furthermore, developers from organizations that had established expectations for XAIDA moved more quickly to higher-order concerns than developers from organizations that had not set expectations for use of XAIDA.

4.2 Courseware Field Tryouts

A total of 27 studies (cited in Section 4) were conducted on students taking XAIDA lessons. These field studies investigated not only XAIDA's overall instructional effectiveness, but also the effectiveness of various elements of XAIDA's instructional presentation, such as the browser and the adaptive practice; the relative benefits of taking an XAIDA lesson individually or within a team of two; and the benefits of audio multimedia. These studies were also important in helping us refine XAIDA's Deliver interface.

Our results point to two conclusions. First, XAIDA is successful in almost any context at promoting mastery of typical performance standards. The results of 21 separate tryouts of the lessons created in the ACCD studies mentioned above provide the most informative data in this regard, because each of the 21 lessons was an initial effort created by a novice XAIDA developer. In spite of the developers' lack of experience, virtually every one of their lessons produced a significant gain in test performance. The median gain was 50%; the 25th and 75th percentiles were 16% gain and 103% gain, respectively. Many of the lower gains occurred in the presence of ceiling effects.

Some data bear on XAIDA instruction as compared to conventional methods. Seven of the ACCD lessons were designed to replace classroom instruction of known duration (a single class period). In these cases, average completion times of the XAIDA lessons were about half of the time required for standup instruction. Only one study, the Odessa Community College study described in Wenzel, Dirnberger, Fox, et al. (1997), employed a conventional-instruction control group. In that study the XAIDA students and their classroom counterparts performed almost identically.

Second, if students are intrinsically motivated to master the material, XAIDA promotes the development of the deeper cognitive structures typical of experts in the subject. However, these deeper structures do not appear to emerge if students are not intrinsically motivated to master the material. The data to support this conclusion is drawn mainly from analyses of students' relatedness ratings of the concepts addressed in XAIDA lessons. In some of our studies, these lessons addressed topics of concern to students in their ongoing coursework. Other studies were decontextualized instructional experiments in which the participants' only mission was to provide data on instructional effectiveness. XAIDA was effective at teaching the "facts" associated with the subject matter in both types of studies. However, when we examined relatedness ratings using Pathfinder (Schvaneveldt, 1990), we found that students who had a stake in learning had a better understanding of the relationships among concepts than those who did not have such a stake.

5. CONCLUSIONS

That XAIDA has run her course as a project, gives us the opportunity to reflect on her position in the field of advanced authoring systems, her contributions to that field and lessons for the future of the field.

5.1 What Kind of Thing Was XAIDA?

In the introduction to XAIDA's history (Section 2), we mentioned that her short history drags a long past. Her origins lie in the earliest work on the application of artificial intelligence to instruction, and, in particular, in the work of Jaime Carbonell (1970a, 1970b). Indeed, a quote from the abstract of Carbonell's (1970b) thesis could pass as a description of XAIDA's Deliver.

> ..., the present approach to CAI [Computer Assisted Instruction] can be defined as being information-structure-oriented (ISO) because it is based on the utilization of a symbolic information network of facts, concepts, and procedures. SCHOLAR [the instructional system described in the thesis] is capable to [sic] generate out of its information network the material to be presented to the student, the questions to be asked to [sic] him, and the corresponding expected answers. SCHOLAR can also utilize its information network to answer questions formulated by the student.

What differentiates XAIDA from SCHOLAR (apart from the modern student interface) is support for development, although Carbonell (1970a) did envision such support. SCHOLAR's knowledge base was nothing more than a gigantic LISP expression. The field that Carbonell invented, now known as Intelligent Tutoring Systems, has met with some success since his work was published, and some ISO systems are in widespread use today. However, tools that make it easy to develop these systems have not enjoyed the same popularity as instructional delivery systems.

The few development systems known to us include XAIDA, the Computer-Based Memorization System (Halff, Hollan, and Hutchins, 1986), and, to a certain extent, the IDXcelerator (Merrill and Thompson, 1999). IDXcelerator is discussed above in Section 3.6.

The Computer-Based Memorization System (CBMS) was a system developed in the early eighties at the Navy Personnel R&D Center. Like SCHOLAR and XAIDA, it drew upon factual knowledge (originally Naval intelligence data) represented in a semantic network. Students studied this information using a collection of quiz-like games, each of which generated questions or rounds from the semantic network. The CBMS is relevant to our purposes in two respects. First, it demonstrated the generality of ISO systems across domains. In addition to its initial Naval intelligence knowledge base, the CBMS was fitted to an Army intelligence knowledge base (which operated in conjunction with a videodisc), a knowledge base describing the solar system, a knowledge base on Civil War history, a knowledge base for office-machine sales training, and the South American geography knowledge base used in SCHOLAR. Second, the CBMS' great variety of instructional methods was a direct inspiration and source of ideas for XAIDA's practice module.

Systems like XAIDA have not attracted a great deal of attention in the literature. This may be partly due to their utter simplicity in comparison to more sophisticated intelligent tutoring systems. Their simple nature however should be taken as a source of power, not of weakness. Tools that make it easy to develop generative, knowledge-based instruction can, and should, make for radical changes in instructional design and development methods. Some of these changes are for the good. Others are less acceptable to the instructional design community.

5.2 Benefits of ISO Development Systems

XAIDA was intended to make the design and development of interactive courseware more efficient. Its approach to this goal is twofold. First, it relies on an implicit model of maintenance training (that found in Polson et al. (1992)) rather than an explicit model of instructional design such as that found in, say, Tennyson (1993). The implicit model is one derived directly from existing maintenance training practices (e.g., using a semantic network to structure presentation and practice) as they are found "in the wild." The instructional design of the model is implicit in that the objectives and the rules mapping those objectives to instructional strategies are not part of the model. Conventional explicit design procedures call for analyzing the job to determine performance requirements, using these performance requirements to formulate training objectives, further analyzing the training objectives to derive learning objectives, developing a media analysis, etc. By relying on existing practice, XAIDA can short-cut the usual extensive front-end analysis required by conventional design methods.

Second, XAIDA relieves designers and developers of the burden of specifying instructional interactions during development since these interactions are generated, SCHOLAR-style, at the time of instruction. The result of these two measures is a direct connection between a subject-matter expert and a machine. The division of labor between these two is one in which the subject-matter expert specifies knowledge (not instruction) and the machine takes on the burden of converting that knowledge to instruction. As is mentioned above in Section 4.1, this division of labor entails a change of mindset on the part of developers. At first blush, it may seem that XAIDA asks developers to relinquish control of the instructional process. However, this conclusion is unwarranted for several reasons. First, much of what passes for control of instruction is embedded in the knowledge base. A part-attribute pair (see Section 3.2) with only one value is given different treatment than one with multiple values. Developers quickly learn to structure the database is ways that provide the types of instructional control that they want. Second, XAIDA provides for significant developer control of XAIDA's behavior at delivery time, allowing her, for example, to screen out certain types of questions about certain topics. Third, XAIDA is based on the very instructional procedures that instructors use in natural conditions, thus mitigating the need for tailoring instructional control. Fourth, and most important, XAIDA's instructional procedures provide a broader range of instructional events, a higher volume of instruction, and a greater degree of dynamic individualization than could ever be achieved with manually prefabricated control structures. It does not take long for the developers to appreciate the potential of this tradeoff of control for power.

The benefits of this approach are not limited to gains in development efficiency. Accessibility is another important feature of XAIDA's approach. Murray (1999) has argued, in effect, that the complexity of developing intelligent tutoring systems requires a certain amount of training and expertise on the part of developers. XAIDA runs counter to this recommendation by making interactive courseware development accessible to just about anyone. While we share Murray's concern for the quality of courseware, we argue that any judgments should be made by evaluating that courseware directly, and not on the basis of any artificial barriers to creating that courseware. Making word processors difficult to use is not an appropriate way to improve the quality of writing.

In addition to greater efficiency and accessibility, XAIDA's approach offers greater flexibility in instructional (and development) interactions. This flexibility is the direct consequence of Carbonell's ISO approach and its ability to query a single knowledge base in many different ways. In XAIDA, Version 5, this was manifest in different modes of use (browse and practice) and in the practice module's many-many mapping of facts to exercises.

Taking full advantage of the ISO approach was a primary objective of XTNG (see Section 2.4). XTNG was meant to be two families of development systems. It would have offered to subject-matter experts the same capabilities of XAIDA, Version 5, namely the ability to populate a knowledge base without having to specify instructional designs or procedures. In addition XTNG would have offered to instructional designers, the capability to implement a variety of instructional approaches and methods each of which could deliver instruction on any knowledge base conforming to XTNG's open architecture.

5.3 Problems with ISO-Based Development Systems

We have taken a less technical and more historical approach in this paper because many of the more interesting problems that we encountered in XAIDA research and development were not technical in nature. Rather they had to do with the conceptual interface between XAIDA's approach and her users. These conceptual issues are better understood in the light of XAIDA's trajectory as a project than in terms of her status as a product.

Despite her "long" past, XAIDA was something of an innovation in that she required her users to think differently about instruction. XAIDA spoke to two different user communities, instructional designers, who were often not subject-matter experts, and instructors, who most often were subject matter experts. XAIDA called upon each of these communities to think differently about instruction, but she had a different message for each community.

When thinking about instruction, instructors generally consider what they want to say to students, what they want to show students, and what they require of students. XAIDA's Develop requires them to think about what they know and how it is structured. XAIDA offers considerable support for this change in thinking. This support, along with the developer training described in Section 4.1, enabled virtually all the developers that we studied to make the conceptual jump. One instructor, when prevented (by a flood) from delivering her XAIDA lesson, gave a stand-up presentation that she consciously structured as XAIDA did.

XAIDA turned a far less friendly face to the instructional design community. That community (at least in the military) thinks about instruction in terms of learning objectives and the instruments used to satisfy those objectives. Design is the process of making objectives explicit. Knowledge, however, to an instructional designer is usually a black box, to be pried out of a subject-matter expert's head and transcribed at appropriate points in the design. XAIDA works in exactly the opposite fashion. Learning objectives are implicit, while knowledge is made explicit. XAIDA sidesteps the design process by relying on existing instructional procedures.

It is no surprise, then, that when we presented XAIDA to subject-matter experts and instructors, the project met with considerable enthusiasm. When we presented XAIDA to instructional designers, reactions ranged from boredom to hostility and incredulity. XAIDA, Version 5 left instructional designers, their methods and their theories, out in the cold.

It is, however, important to avoid taking a too superficial view of the rough interface between XAIDA and instructional designers. The problem arises not because XAIDA's ISO approach is incompatible with instructional design practices, but rather because XAIDA, in its Version 5 incarnation, did not support the changes in thinking required to meld instructional design to ISO instructional development. These changes require designers to divorce themselves from the design of particular courses or instructional objects and to reconceptualize design as the codification of instructional methods that map many-many to content. That is, XAIDA, and more properly, XTNG, invites instructional designers to undertake the design of methods that can apply to diverse content and the design of diverse instructional approaches to the same content. For example, XAIDA, Version 5, was designed as a system that could address training in small-engine repair, medicine, aircraft maintenance, and other maintenance skills. At the same time, we could also envision expanding the instructional approaches to these objectives to include not just XAIDA's browser and practice, but also such methods as the mixed-initiative dialogs employed by Carbonell (1970a, 1970b) and the memorization games employed by the CBMS (Halff, Hollan, and Hutchins, 1986).

5.4 The Future of ISO-Based Development Systems

As is mentioned above, those working on ISO-based development systems, have, in the past, been bit players on the computer-based instruction scene. We do not see that situation changing for some time (Halff, 1999). The military itself, through its Advanced Distributed Learning (ADL) initiative (Dodds, 2001) is backing an approach based on the notion of a Self-Contained Object (SCO). An SCO is a black box that delivers a self-contained (of course) unit of instruction. The SCO is marked with certain features so that a Learning Management System (LMS) can select and assemble SCOs as needed, even dynamically at delivery time. We view this development as relevant to the concerns of this section because *the ADL initiative represents an important class of approaches to extending conventional courseware design, and that class does not include ISO approaches.* We can refer to the class as *LMS-SCO* approaches mainly in order to divorce it from the particular ADL initiative.

The overall space of design practices that concern us, then, are as follows.

Conventional design approaches, described in Section 2.2, result in integrated, opaque units of courseware. The knowledge conveyed by the unit is not explicit, nor are the general principles governing instructional sequences. It is not possible to reconfigure these courseware units to use a different instructional strategy or to deliver instruction on different content.

LMS-SCO approaches provide for some flexibility in instructional control. Courseware is still delivered in integrated, opaque units, but these units are marked with a set of context-free features (e.g., difficulty level), and these features are available to an LMS that can customize instructional sequence by matching features to instructional requirements. Thus, the ADL's approach is an automated version of conventional ISD as described in Section 2.2. The LMS plays the role of an instructional designer, and the SCO plays the role of a subject-matter expert.

ISO approaches completely divorce content and instruction. Content is delivered in the form of an information structure which, by itself, is instructionally inert. Nonetheless, the structure conforms to a grammar (semantic networks in the examples described here) that one or more general purpose instructional procedures can read to fashion instructional interactions. Any such procedure, although cognizant of the grammar governing the information structure is itself empty of content. Instructional control in ISO systems is achieved, neither by a "canned" branching strategy or by application of a procedure to a set of context-free features, but rather by the application of context-free procedures to the content of instruction.

An ISO-based approach provides for a much wider use of content than either the conventional or LMS-SCO approaches since different instructional mechanisms can manipulate an instructional knowledge base in different ways and the same instructional mechanism can be brought to bear on different knowledge bases. Even LMS-SCO approaches, in their attempt to promote reusability of *courseware*, preclude reusability of *knowledge* and reusability of *instructional strategies.* As a hypothetical, suppose that SCHOLAR, a CBMS lesson on characteristics of Russian cruisers, and an XAIDA lesson on neuroanatomy of the auditory system were each converted to SCOs. It would be impossible within any conventional or LMS-SCO system to use SCHOLAR's mixed initiative methods to converse with students about Russian cruisers, or to update Carbonell's lessons on South American Geography so that they are available to students using XAIDA's graphical browser. XAIDA's short history and long past convince us that the failure of LMS-SCO approaches to support this kind of interoperability is a critical and inherent shortcoming of the LMS-SCO systems.

If ISO approaches are to have any future whatsoever, the community interested in developing them must be more attentive to the conceptual changes required on the part of instructional designers. These conceptual changes are those involved in divorcing oneself from the particulars of an individual course, lesson, or SCO, and attending to the abstract instructional methods that can be brought to bear on kinds of courses, lessons, or SCOs involved. Thinking in more abstract terms about instructional designs is a more challenging but far more rewarding pursuit than thinking about individual instructional interactions. Not the least of these rewards is the power to use a machine to generate a range of adaptive instructional interactions that is well beyond that possible with existing design methods or even SCO-LMS approaches.

6. REFERENCES

Bailey, D. B., & Palsha, S. A. (1992). Qualities of stages of concern questionnaire and implications for educational innovations. *The Journal of Educational Research*, 85, 226-232.

Boring, E. G. (1957). *A history of experimental psychology* (2nd ed.). New York: Appleton-Century-Crofts.

Carbonell, J. R. (1970a). AI in CAI. An artificial intelligence approach to computer-assisted instruction. *IEEE Transactions on Man-Machine Systems, 11*, 190–202.

Carbonell, J. R. (1970b). *Mixed-initiative man-computer instructional dialogues* (BBN Report No. 1971). Cambridge, MA: Bolt Beranek and Newman Inc.

Casaus, M.G., Gibson, E.G., Wenzel, B.M., & Halff, H.M. (1997). *Effectiveness of adaptive practice in the Experimental Advanced Instructional Design Advisor (XAIDA)*. Unpublished manuscript, Mei Technology Corporation, San Antonio, TX.

Collins, A. M., & Loftus, E. F. (1975). A spreading-activation theory of semantic processing. *Psychological Review, 82*(6), 407-428.

Collins, A. M., & Quillian, M. R. (1969). How to make a language user. In E. Tulving and W. Donaldson (Eds.), *Organization and memory*. New York, New York: Academic Press.

Dodds, P. (2001) *SCORM 1.1* [On-line]. Alexandria, VA: ADL. Available http://www.adlnet.org/.

Gagné, R. (1985). *The Conditions of Learning* (4th ed.). New York: Holt, Rinehart & Winston

Gagné, R. (1993). Preface. In J. M. Spector, M. C. Polson, and D. J. Muraida (Eds.) *Automating Instructional Design: Concepts and Issues* (pp. v–vii). Englewood Cliffs, NJ: Educational Technology Publications..

Gettman, D. J., McNelly, T., & Muraida, D. J. (1999). The Guided Approach to Instructional Design Advising (GAIDA): A case-based approach to developing instructional design expertise. In J. van den Akker, R. M. Branch, K. Gustafson, N. Nieveen & T. Plomp (Eds.), *Design approaches and tools in education and training*. Dordrecht, NE: Kluwer Academic.

Halff, H. M. (1993). Prospects for automating instructional design. In J. M. Spector, M. C. Polson, & D. J. Muraida (Eds.), *Automating instructional design: Concepts and issues* (pp. 67–132). Englewood Cliffs, NJ: Educational Technology Publications.

Halff, H. M. (1999). ITSs into the sunset: A radio play for four actors and announcer [On-line]. *International Journal of Artificial Intelligence, 10*, 1100–1109. Available http://cbl.leeds.ac.uk/ijaied/abstracts/Vol_10/Halff.html.

Halff, H. M., Hollan, J. D., & Hutchins, E. L. (1986). Cognitive Science and Military Training. *American Psychologist, 41*, 1131–1139.

Hall, G. E. (1979). The concerns-based approach to facilitating change. *Educational Horizons, 4*, 202-208.

Hall, G. E., George, A. A., & Rutherford, W. L. (1986). *Measuring stages of concern about the innovation: A manual for the user of SoC Questionnaire.* Austin, TX: Southwest Educational Development Laboratory.

Hickey, A. E., Spector, J. M., & Muraida, D. J. (1991). *Design specifications for the Advanced Instructional Design Advisor (AIDA)* (Tech. Rep. AL-TR-1991-0085). Brooks AFB, TX: Air Force Armstrong Laboratory.

Hsieh, P. Y. (1997). *A review of knowledge-based systems for maintenance training.* Unpublished manuscript, Mei Technology Corporation, San Antonio, TX.

Hsieh, P.Y., Halff, H.M. and Redfield, C.L. (1999). Four easy pieces: Development systems for knowledge-based generative instruction, *International Journal of Artificial Intelligence in Education. 10*, 1-45. Available http://cbl.leeds.ac.uk/ijaied/abstracts/Vol_10/hsieh.html.

Hsieh, P. Y. & Wheeler, J. (1999). Using instructor-developed courseware: Part II of a demonstration professional development project. San Antonio, TX: Mei Technology Company.

Hsieh, S. & Hsieh, P.Y. (2001). Intelligent tutoring system authoring tool for manufacturing engineering education, *International Journal of Engineering Education*, 17(6), 569-579.

Hsieh, S. & Hsieh, P.Y. (2002). Web-based programmable logic controller learning system, *Frontiers in Education Conference Proceedings*, Boston, MA, November 6-9, 2002. Available http://fie.engrng.pitt.edu/fie2002/papers/1176.pdf

Hsieh, S. & Hsieh, P.Y. (2003). Animations and intelligent tutoring systems for programmable logic controller education. To appear in *International Journal of Engineering Education*, 19(2).

Merrill, M. D. (1993). An integrated model for automating instructional design and delivery. In J. M. Spector, M. C. Polson, and D. J. Muraida (Eds.) *Automating Instructional Design: Concepts and Issues* (pp. 147-190). Englewood Cliffs, NJ: Educational Technology Publications.

Merrill, M. D. & ID2 Research Team (1996). Instructional Transaction Theory: Instructional Design based on Knowledge Objects. *Educational Technology, 36* (3), 30-37.

Merrill, M. D., & Thompson, B. M. (1999). The IDXelerator: Learning-centered instructional design. In Jan van den Akker, Robert Maribe Branch, Kent Gustafson, Nienke Nieveen & Tjeerd Plomp (Eds.) *Design approaches and tools in education and training.* Dordrecht, NE: Kluwer Academic.

Murray, T. (1999). Authoring intelligent tutoring systems: an analysis of the state of the art. *International Journal of Artificial Intelligence in Education, 10*, 98–129.

Paquette, G., Crevier, F., & Aubin, C. (1994). ID Knowledge in a Course Design Workbench. *Educational Technology, 34* (9), 50–57.

Paquette, G., & Girard, J. (June, 1996) AGD: A course engineering support system, Montreal: ITS-96.

Polson, M. C., Polson, P. G., Kieras, D., & Halff, H. M. (1992). *Functional requirements of an Advanced Instructional Design Advisor: Task analysis and troubleshooting* (Interim Technical Paper AL-TP-1992-0035-Vol-2). Brooks AFB, TX: Armstrong Laboratory.

Reigeluth, C. M. (1983) *Instructional design theories: An overview of their current status.* Hillsdale, NJ: Lawrence Erbaum Associates.

Richardson, K.H., Wenzel, B.M., Halff, H.M., & Gibson, E.G. (1996). *The transfer of mental models in computer-based training.* Poster presented at the Eighth Annual Association for Research in Memory, Attention, Decision-making, Imagery, Language, Learning, and Organizational Perception Conference, University of Texas, Austin, Texas.

Schvaneveldt, R. W. (Ed.). (1990). *Pathfinder associative networks: Studies in knowledge organization.* Norwood, NJ: Ablex.

Spector, J. M., Polson, M., & Muraida, D. (1993). *Automating instructional design: Concepts and issues.* Englewood Cliffs, NJ: Lawrence Erlbaum Associates.

Tennyson, R. (1993). A framework for automating instructional design. In J. M. Spector, M. C. Polson, & D. J. Muraida (Eds.), *Automating instructional design: Concepts and issues* (pp. 191–212). Englewood Cliffs, NJ: Lawrence Erlbaum Associates.

ToolBook [Computer Software] (2001). Bellevue, WA: Click2Learn.

Wenzel, B.M. and Garcia, V. (1999). *Empowering Community College Instructors with Instructional Technology: A Demonstration Professional Development Project.* Unpublished manuscript, Mei Technology Corporation. San Antonio, TX.

Wenzel, B. M., & Dirnberger, M. T. (1996). *The Experimental Advanced Instructional Design Advisor Training (XAIDA): A multidimensional approach to training evaluation.* Paper presented at the annual meeting of the International Military Testing Association, San Antonio, TX.

Wenzel, B. M., & Rivas, L. (1999). A model professional development project: Intentional and incidental benefits for faculty and students. *Proceedings from the Society for Information Technology and Teacher Education International Conference* (CD-ROM). San Antonio, TX.

Wenzel, B. M., Dirnberger, M. T., Hsieh, P. Y., Chudanov, T. J., & Halff, H. M. (1998). Evaluating subject matter experts' learning and use of an ITS authoring tool. In B. Goettl, H. Halff, C. Redfield, and V. Shute (Eds.), *Intelligent Tutoring Systems: 4th International Conference, ITS '98, San Antonio, TX* (pp. 156-165). Berlin: Springer (Lecture Notes in Computer Science, Vol. 1452).

Wenzel, B. M., Dirnberger, M. T., & Halff, H. M. (1997). *Evaluating a courseware generation system designed for subject matter experts.* Unpublished manuscript, Mei Technology Corporation, San Antonio, TX

Wenzel, B. M., Dirnberger, M.T., and Ellis, R. (1998). Evaluation of the instructional effectiveness of distributed interactive multimedia courseware for emergency medical technician training. *Proceedings from the 16th Biennial Applied Behavioral Sciences Symposium,* USAF Academy Department of Behavioral Sciences and Leadership. Colorado Springs, CO.

Wenzel, B. M., Keeney, C., Licklider, J., Roberts, J. D., & Reyna, H. (1997). *Evaluation of the courseware developed and delivered using the Experimental Advanced Instructional Design Advisor.* Presentation at the annual meeting of the Texas Association of College Technical Educators, Austin, Texas.

Wenzel, B. M., Richardson, K. H., Halff, H. M., & Gibson, E. G. (1996). *Assessing the instructional effectiveness of the Experimental Advanced Instructional Design Advisor (XAIDA).* Unpublished manuscript, Mei Technology Corporation, San Antonio, TX.

Wenzel, B. M., Rivas, L, & Hearn, R. (1998). *Texas State Leadership Consortium for Professional Development: Computer-Based Instruction Component.* Presentation at the annual meeting of the Texas Association of College Technical Educators, Austin, Texas.

Wenzel, B. M., Rivas, L., & Hearn, R. (1999). Introducing community college campuses to the benefits of instructional technology. *The Texas Technology Connection,* Spring, 20-23.

Wenzel, B.M., Dirnberger, M.T., Fox, H., Hearne, R., Keeney, C., Licklider, J., Reyna, H., Roberts, J.D., Strebeck, N., & Halff, H.M. (1997). *Field tests of an interactive courseware development system.* Unpublished manuscript, Mei Technology Corporation, San Antonio, TX.

ACKNOWLEDGEMENTS

All authors were in the Training Research Division of the Mei Technology Program at the time of the study. Henry M. Halff is now the principle of Halff Resources, San Antonio, TX. Patricia Y. Hsieh is now in the Human Systems Resources Office, Texas A&M University, College Station, TX. Brenda M. Wenzel is now at the U. S. Army's TRADOC Analysis Center at the White Sands Missile Range, NM. Thomas J. Chudanov is now at USAA, San Antonio, TX. Mary T. Dirnberger is now in Okinawa, Japan. Elizabeth G. Gibson is now at SBC Southwestern Bell, Austin, TX. Carol L. Redfield is now in the Computer Science Department, St. Marys University, San Antonio, TX.

---

[1] The project name itself, but not its acroynm, changed several times in the course of the project. "Automated" became "Advanced." "Assistant" became "Associate," and then "Advisor." Thus, the last official project name was the Advanced Instructional Design Advisor. However, as the result of its many changes, AIDA, in some circles, stands for Acronym Indicating Damn-near Anything.

[2] The term "Advisor" is a complete misnomer, reflecting more the sponsor's expectations than reality. XAIDA took advice but never gave it. See Note 1.

ALLEN MUNRO

Chapter 3

AUTHORING SIMULATION-CENTERED LEARNING ENVIRONMENTS WITH RIDES AND VIVIDS

Abstract. *RIDES* and *VIVIDS* are applications for authoring and delivering interactive graphical simulations and tutorials in the context of those simulations. Some types of instruction can be generated automatically by exploiting structured simulation data. RIDES technology plays an important part in a number of related research and development projects. RIDES introduces innovations in the human-computer interface (HCI) of simulation-centered tutorial authoring systems, including support for constraint and event authoring, enforcing the primacy of reference, and permitting the authoring of procedure tutorials by interactive demonstration. RIDES simulations provide low level automatic support for detecting student operations and observations and are well-suited for teaching procedures. Authoring use has revealed a number of additional design considerations that should be taken into account in the development of future tutor authoring systems. Foremost among these is the need for an open architecture that supports collaboration among tutor components, including collaboration with types of tutor components that have not yet been developed.

1. INTRODUCTION

Intelligent tutoring systems (ITSs) often include interactive graphical simulations. For many types of tutoring, the use of an interactive graphical simulation helps to assure that what students learn is relevant to actual tasks that they must learn to perform, in a way that a primarily textual approach to learning interactions cannot. Interactive simulations can help to ensure that performance skills—as opposed to mere test-taking skills—are acquired as a result of tutoring. To date, most research projects on intelligent tutoring systems that have incorporated simulations have relied on low level tools (i.e., programming languages) to develop both the ITSs and the simulations. Reliance on such low-level development techniques naturally makes simulation-centered tutoring extremely expensive. It can also make it very difficult to determine what features of a particular tutor are responsible for its efficacy (or lack thereof). The details of the craft of low-level development using programming languages can overwhelm the effects of the general principles that are followed in a particular tutor. An authoring system, by ensuring a uniform quality of low-level instructional interaction and by providing easily edited and modifiable tutorials (and simulations), can make it possible for developers to experiment with different high-level approaches to tutoring in a given domain.

    RIDES is an X-Windows-based Unix application for interactively authoring graphical simulations and simulation-centered tutorials. RIDES (and a version of

RIDES that lacks authoring features, called *sRides*—for *Student RIDES*) delivers simulation-centered tutoring to students. Because the simulation authoring system is designed to support tutorials, many types of instruction can be very rapidly authored, and many high quality instructional interactions are generated automatically.

Many tutors have now been built using RIDES, including two large tutors (and many smaller ones) that have been produced in our lab. Many more tutors have been developed at other sites. Developers at Armstrong Laboratory have created a large number of RIDES tutors, covering a wide range of subjects, including the operation of medical devices, the nomenclature and theory of orbital mechanics, the human circulatory system, and a wide range of tutors on the operation or maintenance of particular devices. RIDES has also played a role in a number of other research projects, as described below. Our experiences in collaboration with other tutoring projects lead us to believe that a more componential approach to tutorial delivery would significantly enhance the value of authored components such as RIDES simulations and RIDES procedure tutorials.

Background

The field of simulation in intelligent tutoring systems (ITS) research is a large and rapidly growing one, and this paper would be much larger if it were to review all the widely relevant work. On the other hand, the field of simulation-based tutor *authoring systems* is a very much smaller one. In this section, we briefly discuss several authoring systems for the development of simulations for learning.
In the past, many ITS research projects developed isolated intelligent tutors that were created using a variety of general-purpose tools, especially programming environments. There are several reasons why there are few exemplars of simulation-based tutor authoring systems. One of these is that the development of a usable authoring system for simulation-based tutors is a very large task. A good authoring system must have a very large number of quite different, easy-to-use authoring interfaces, or editors. It must be possible to draw (or import) and edit graphic objects, to specify the behavior of the objects, to enter tutorial information about the objects, to build complete lessons in the context of simulations, to build courses, to search for authored data, to debug simulations and lessons, and so on. The development effort is similar to that required to produce several different types of commercial software applications, such as a word processor, a spreadsheet, and a presentation system, and bind them all together in an integrated application suite. It is simply too arduous and expensive an undertaking to be undertaken casually as a part of a project to produce a tutor. It can only be justified if it can then be used to produce scores or thousands of different tutors at significantly lower cost than would be possible using less task-specific tools, such as programming languages.

STEAMER (Williams, Hollan, and Stevens, 1981; Hollan, Hutchins, and Weitzman, 1984) provided a direct manipulation simulation for students learning about a steam propulsion plant. The STEAMER project is an important spiritual ancestor of RIDES. It offered a discovery world for students and a demonstration platform for instructors, but it did not provide authoring tools for the development and delivery of instruction to the learner. Furthermore, simulations had to be written developed as conventional computer programs. An authoring tool was then used to link simulation values to STEAMER graphic objects. As the simulation values changed, so did the states of the STEAMER graphics.

Forbus (1984) developed an extension of STEAMER called the *feedback minilab*, which could be used to produce interactive graphical simulations without first writing separate simulation programs. This early authoring system provided a set of predefined components (such as valves and switches). Composing a device of these components determined the behavior of the simulated system as a whole.

IMTS (Towne and Munro, 1988, 1992) provided tools for authoring interactive graphical simulations of electrical and hydraulic systems, but the model authoring approach was limited. A library of graphic behaving objects could be composed, but the external effects of these objects had to be either electrical, mechanical, or hydraulic in nature. IMTS supported troubleshooting assistance by a generic expert called Profile (Towne, 1984), but it could not be used to develop or deliver other kinds of instruction.

An early approach to direct manipulation instructional authoring was Dominie (Spensley and Elsom-Cook, 1989). That system, however, did not support the independent specification of object behaviors; the specification of simulation effects was confounded with the specification of instruction.

RAPIDS (Towne and Munro, 1991) and RAPIDS II (Coller, Pizzini, Wogulis, Munro, and Towne, 1991) were descendants of IMTS that supported direct manipulation authoring of instructional content in the context of graphical simulations. These systems provided a much more constrained simulation authoring system than is found in RIDES, and they did not offer authors low level control over instructional presentations. Like IMTS, these programs were available only on specialized AI workstations.

RIDES provides much more robust simulation authoring tools (described below) and instructional editing facilities than were to be found in RAPIDS and RAPIDS II. The RIDES system has some features in common with the SMISLE system (de Jong, van Joolingen, Scott, deHoog, Lapied, and Valent, 1994; Van Joolingen and De Jong, 1996) developed by a consortium of European academic and industrial research groups, but is less restrictive about how simulations can be structured. SMISLE authors must separately specify an inner, 'real' level of behavior and one or more surface depictions of the behaving system. Similar effects can be achieved using RIDES, but they are not required. The SMISLE system also contains facilities for supporting student hypothesis formation, but lacks the unconstrained simulation authoring and instruction authoring capabilities of RIDES.

2. RIDES: A TUTOR DELIVERY AND DEVELOPMENT SYSTEM

RIDES is an integrated software environment for developing and delivering computer based tutorial instruction and practice that is based on graphical simulations. Using RIDES, authors can build interactive graphical models of devices or other complex systems and then swiftly build interactive lessons in the context of those graphical models. Students use RIDES to interact with the authored tutorials. If the author chooses, students can be allowed to explore graphical simulations in a free play mode, but, in addition, many types of structured tutorials can also be productively authored and delivered using RIDES.

2.1 Model Based Instruction

One of the key concepts in RIDES is that instruction takes place in the context of an authored graphical model of the particular domain. For example, if the domain is the operation of a certain item of medical equipment, then the appearance, behavior, and proper usage of that equipment is the domain to be learned. Figure 1 shows a student environment with two windows open. The lower window is the student instruction window, where instructional text and remedial directions are displayed. The upper window is one of several windows in this simulation that contain depictions of the domain of interest—here, a pulse oximeter. Simulation scenes, such as the one with the title "Pulse Oximeter" in the figure, consist of a set of graphical objects in a window. Such scenes provide the context for all instruction in RIDES. Many elements of instruction can be automatically generated by RIDES because they are developed in the context of a structured domain model.

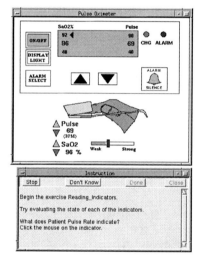

Figure 1. A Student View of Instruction in the Context of a Graphical Model[1]

Authors can build complex graphical models by copying library objects and pasting them into their scenes. They can also draw objects directly onto the scenes, using a palette of drawing tools, and can specify rules that control the values of object attributes. The finger in the figure above is one such object. Authors can open an *object data view* of the object, such as the one shown in the figure below. An object data view of an object shows its name, together with a list of its attributes with their values and their rules, if they have any. In this figure, there is a rule for

---

[1] Developed by Tim Miller and Carol Horwitz at Armstrong Laboratory, Brooks AFB, San Antonio Texas.

the attribute named *pulse*. The present value of this attribute is determined by the rule, which refers to the attribute of another object.

Figure 2. Object Data View for a Graphical Object

Some attributes directly control the appearance of graphical objects. When the values of such attributes are changed, objects may disappear, move, stretch, rotate, or undergo other visible changes.

RIDES has lesson-building tools that can exploit the information in a graphical model. For example, students can be taught the names of objects, because the simulation author gave the objects names that can be used by RIDES lessons. More interestingly, an instruction author can 'record' a procedure that students must learn, simply by carrying out the procedure. During tutoring, the student will be prompted to carry out the correct sequence of actions.

Because RIDES is an integrated development system for producing simulations and instruction presented in the context of those simulations, many aspects of the lesson-authoring process have been automated or streamlined.

2.2 Development with RIDES

RIDES offers a number of advantages to authors, to students, and to managers in comparison with other technologies for developing interactive graphical tutoring systems.

Simulation Based on Behaving Graphical Objects

At the simulation level, students don't merely interact with 'hot spots' on a screen, but rather with objects. This has several advantages. Students have access to more robust and more realistic simulations than would otherwise be the case. Where the experience would be appropriate, the student can be allowed to work freely with an immersive free play simulation. For developers, graphical objects support the reuse of these simulation components in multiple simulations. Authors find it easier to develop simulations that are flexible and realistic than would be the case with a 'hot spot' approach to simulation actions.

RIDES provides a range of graphic primitives, including lines, ellipses, rectangles, poly-lines, text, splines, and colored bitmaps. The inclusion of structured graphic types (as opposed to a bitmap-only approach found in some CBT authoring systems) makes it computationally practical to carry out operations such as scaling or stretching objects and rotation under simulation control. Such operations would be slower, jerkier, and visually less appealing if only bitmap objects were supported. In addition to encouraging the development of responsive and flexible simulations, non-bitmap graphical objects often have smaller memory requirements than bitmaps of the same size.

A number of aspects of the RIDES implementation of graphical objects enhance the authoring and maintenance of simulation behavior. In most cases, for example, an author can find out why an object behaves as it does by selecting the object, opening its data view, and looking at its rules. The binding of behavior to objects makes it easy for authors to debug and/or modify behavior in a simulation.

Instruction Grounded in Simulation

The experience of simply using an interactive graphical simulation is not ordinarily sufficient to learn how to correctly carry out tasks or how to perform procedures. Students can easily learn incorrect models of the systems they are using (Self, 1995). Most students need guidance to attain learning goals in the context of a simulation. The instruction-authoring features of RIDES exploit the structure of simulations to make the authoring of certain types of lessons fast, accurate, and easily maintainable. Authors cannot direct students to put the simulation model into 'impossible' or internally inconsistent states, for example. Procedure training can be authored simply by carrying out a procedure.

Textual information can be entered in *knowledge units* that can be associated with model objects. Some types of lessons can be generated from textual discussions and from other types of information stored in these knowledge units.

Lessons can be played to students in three modes with differing levels of user responsibility. In *demo mode*, students only pace the progress of a lesson. In *practice mode*, students are required to carry out the actions of the lesson, but are given remediation when they fail to perform an action correctly. In *test mode*, students are not given remediation when they mis-perform a step during a learning sequence. It is not necessary to author these three types of lessons separately; all of them are created at once when the lesson is authored.

A number of highly structured kinds of instruction—called *patterned exercises* in RIDES—are authored quickly and directly from simulation data and a few specifications from instructional authors. The generated lessons can be customized and new, innovative lesson types can be built using more detailed instruction authoring tools that also interact directly with the authored simulation.

Courses Based on Objectives

A RIDES course is a set of learning objectives that must be realized by a student. Each objective is associated with a lesson for teaching that objective. A model of the knowledge of each student is based on the objectives of the course. Decisions about what lesson to present next are controlled by the relationships that hold among course objectives and by the state of the student model.

A Supportive, Highly Integrated Authoring Interface

The RIDES simulation-development environment is very natural for most authors with previous experience using window-based application software. To find out why an object is behaving in a certain way, the author can select the object and open a view that displays the rules that govern the object's behavior. (This can be done while the simulation is running or when it is paused.) An author can modify simulations on-the-fly, even as the simulations are running. Authored changes in attribute values, relations, and events are reflected immediately in a running simulation. Similarly, direct manipulations of simulation objects that modify those objects' values are immediately reflected in data views of those objects. The authoring system is designed to be highly transparent and consistent.

Authoring mistakes can be easily remedied by using the Undo feature, which supports multiple levels of *undo* and *redo*.

Behavior rules are automatically formatted in ways that help authors to immediately pick out object and attribute references, and that highlight any errors in such references.

Copying and pasting is well supported. In addition to conventional copy-and-paste capabilities, RIDES lets an author copy a named graphic object and paste it in a textual context, such as a behavior rule; the name of the copied object is placed at the insertion point in the text.

Two approaches for creating instruction are integrated in the RIDES authoring application: one for rapidly creating certain kinds of structured lessons, called *patterned exercises*, and one for building custom lessons. Both permit the author to carry out many aspects of lesson authoring by directly manipulating the interactive simulation in the same ways that students will be required to do.

Supplementary Utilities

These include:
- An integrated debugger lets the author step through simulation execution, evaluating simulation expressions at the time of rule executions.
- A list of any 'erroneous rules' that have not yet been repaired is maintained, and authors can directly access the data views for those rules from that list.
- A 'find' utility lets authors search for named entities or text strings in RIDES, either unrestrictedly, or searching only in certain types of data.
- A 'consistency checker' can be used to report on the presence of certain commonly observed possible problems in the RIDES document.

On-line Reporting to the Instructor Console

RIDES reports student progress to an instructor console program, called RADMIN. Instructors can observe which networked student stations are currently delivering RIDES instruction, what students are using those computers, which course and course objective each student is working on, and how long the student has been on that objective. The RADMIN program also provides instructor facilities for enrolling students at a tutoring site, and for setting up classes. The details of

RIDES course administration are described in the *RIDES Administration Manual* (Munro and Surmon, 1996)

2.3 Overview of the Tutor Development Process

A model of development for RIDES authoring is shown in the figure below.

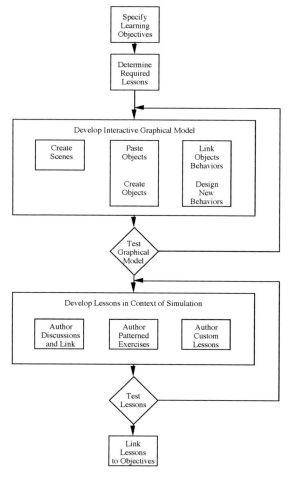

Figure 3. The Tutor Development Process in RIDES

Authors must specify the objectives of a tutor, must relate those objectives to particular elements of instruction, and must develop a model of the domain of interest that can be used to author the lessons that will meet the instructional objectives. After the interactive simulation (the graphical model of the subject matter domain) is developed, the needed lessons must be built and linked to the objectives of the tutor. One or more prototype student models must then be built and the tutor can be tested for effectiveness with students. RIDES provides an integrated set of editors for carrying out all of the tasks shown in Figure 3.

Using the Course Editor, an author can design the objectives that are to be met by the tutor. Then the author can build an interactive simulation. This is often accomplished by a combination of pasting library objects and drawing and giving behavior to new objects. There are scene editors, object editors, attribute and event editors, simulation debuggers and other views and tools that can be used to develop and test simulations. The RIDES simulation authoring environment is so powerful and interactive that some users employ it not to produce tutors, but rather as an application prototyper or as an application development system. Once a simulation has been built, the author can construct lessons, using either the patterned exercise authoring tools, which require only very simple choices, or using the custom authoring tools, which permit greater control over the instruction process. A combination of both patterned exercises and custom lessons is often used, and generated patterned exercises are sometimes edited using the custom instructional editing tools. Finally, the objectives that were designed in the first step of the tutor authoring process are linked to the authored lessons. RIDES can then present the complete authored course to students.

For a step-by-step account of how a simple simulation is authored and how simple lessons are developed in the context of such a simulation, see the RIDES QuickStart manual, which is available on-line at http://btl.usc.edu/rides/documntn/qsMan/.

Human-Computer Interface Issues for Interactive Tutor Development

The RIDES project has addressed two fundamental research issues for human-computer interfaces (HCI). The first is, "Which HCI features can help in the development of behaving interactive graphical simulations?" The second is, "Which HCI features will best support an author's development of performance-oriented tutors in the context of interactive graphical simulations?"

2.4 HCI for Authoring Behaving Graphical Simulations

Figure 4 shows the RIDES graphic tool palette and examples of the nine primitive graphic types, together with a grouped object. Any graphical object can be given a name and *attributes*. In RIDES, attributes are used to store values associated with objects. Values can be of six types: number, logical (boolean), text, point, color, and pattern.

Some object attributes are created automatically, while others are created by authors. For example, an author can add a new number attribute to an object, give the attribute a name, specify its current value, and, if desired, write a constraint (see also Borning, 1979, 1981) that prescribes the attribute's value in terms of the values of other attributes. Attributes that are explicitly created by the commands of authors are called *authored attributes*. Attributes that are created automatically are called *intrinsic attributes*.

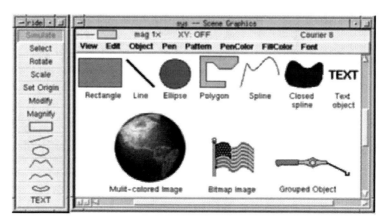

Figure 4. The RIDES Drawing Environment with Example Primitives (at top of the scene window)

Most intrinsic attributes control aspects of the appearance of objects. Every graphical object has the attributes Visibility, Location, Scale, and Rotation. Each of these attributes controls some aspect of the appearance of an object. If Visibility is false, the object is not shown on its scene. Location is a point type value that prescribes the Cartesian coordinates of the object on the 'page' that is shown in a scene window. Changing the value of an object's Location will cause it to move to a different spot on its scene. The Scale attribute is also of type point; it specifies scaling factors that should be applied to the X and Y dimensions of the object. (Scaling is with respect to the size that the object had when it was originally drawn or otherwise created.) Rotation is a number attribute that controls the orientation of the object. Rotation values express the extent of an object's counter-clockwise rotation from its original orientation.

In addition to these four universal attributes, objects of particular graphic types have other intrinsic attributes. For example, lines have the additional attributes PenColor, PenStyle, and PenWidth. Filled graphic primitives, such as rectangles, ellipses, polygons, and splines, have these plus FillColor and FillPattern. Text primitives have a TextValue attribute that determines what text is actually displayed by the graphic, and so on.

Simulation authors can view an object's attributes by selecting the object and then opening its object data view, such as the one shown below in Figure 5. This is a grouped graphical object. (An author creates a grouped object by selecting a number of graphical objects and then issuing the Group command.) The PenColor and FillColor attributes of its component graphics can be observed by opening their object data views.

Attribute values can be changed in any of four ways: an author can manipulate the object with a tool in a way that changes an attribute value; a value can be typed into an attribute value cell in a data view; a relational constraint may change the value of the attribute; or an event statement that sets the value of the attribute may be executed.

(1) Tool Manipulation. If an author manipulates an object with graphical tools or commands, corresponding attributes will be changed.

(2) Value Editing. An object data view (shown in Figure 5, below) lists all the attributes of an object. Here the author can change the names of attributes and can enter new values. Changes to *intrinsic* attributes, such as Location or Rotation, have immediate graphic effects.

(3) Constraint Evaluation. To the right of the value cell on each attribute line is a *constraint expression cell*. An author can enter a relation here that determines the value of the attribute. Figure 5, below, shows an object data view in which the Rotation attribute has a constraint. This constraint specifies that if the user holds the mouse button down while pointing to this object (named SpringLever) then its rotation will be 16 degrees; otherwise, its rotation will be 0.

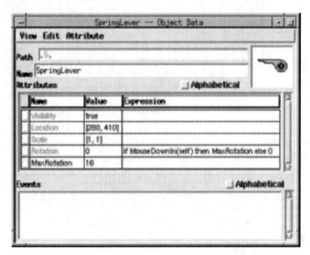

Figure 5. An Object Data View with a Constraint on the Value of the Rotation Attribute

The value of attributes can be expressed by relations. For example, in

`.S.MainSpring.Rotation * 2`

the value of an attribute with this constraint will be twice the Rotation of the MainSpring object on scene S.

Constraints are written as expressions. Whenever any value that is referred to in a constraint expression changes, the expression is evaluated and a new value for the attribute is determined. It is not necessary to explicitly state that the expression above must be re-evaluated whenever the Rotation of the SpringLever on scene S changes. Authors need not concern themselves with when a value needs to be recomputed if that value is determined by a constraint.

There is an alternative way of viewing relational constraints in RIDES. An author can select an attribute row in an object data view, such as those shown in Figure 5, and can then open a more detailed *attribute data view*. Figure 6 shows the attribute data view for the Rotation attribute in Figure 5. This view includes a *code editor* sub-window—the frame labeled 'Rule Expression' in Figure 6. In code editor views, relational expressions are displayed with reserved words in bold and with automatic indenting. Object references (such as the *self* in this expression) are shown in a special object reference font and color. References to attributes are also shown in a distinctive color and font.

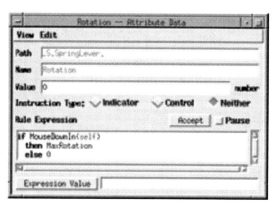

Figure 6. An Attribute Data View

(4) *Event Definition.* An alternative way of prescribing behavior is to write events that set attribute values and carry out other actions when triggered by some condition. In RIDES, an event consists of such a conditional expression, together with a delay expression, and an event body, which is a list of statements. When an

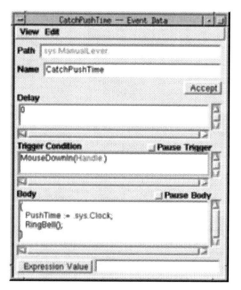

Figure 7. An Event Data View

event's conditional expression is evaluated and found to be true, the delay expression is evaluated to determine when the event statements should be carried out. In most cases the delay expression of an event is *0*, so the event body is carried out as soon as the event is triggered. Figure 7 shows a simple event data view. It is possible to create events that belong to certain objects. Other events are global in nature and are simply stored in a list of unattached events.

Both types of behavior specification, constraints and events, have their uses. Constraint-based specifications promote a focus on *results* or *effects*. Event-based specifications promote a focus on *causes*. Constraint-based behavior specifications do not require expertise in controlling the flow of effects, and are therefore easier for many authors to make use of. Certain simulation effects, however, can only be achieved through event specifications.

2.5 HCI for Authoring Procedure Tutorials

Authoring by Doing. RIDES provides a very simple interface for creating instructional vignettes that have one of a number of constrained structures, or patterns. Instructional units created using this interface are called patterned exercises. Figure 8 and Figure 9, below, show a patterned exercise being created. In Figure 8, the window at the left displays a simulation scene, while the window at the right shows the patterned exercise editor when the author has specified that a new exercise about operational setup (called "Procedure") should be created.

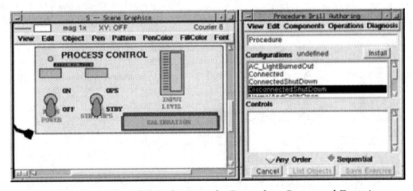

Figure 8. Beginning the Authoring of a Procedure Patterned Exercise

In Figure 9, the author has carried out several operations by clicking on the mouse-sensitive graphical objects, such as the power cord and switches. As each such control object is clicked, its name appears in the Controls list in the patterned exercise editor. At the same time that the actions are being recorded in the patterned exercise editor, they are generating graphical simulation effects in the simulation scene—switches change position, lights change colors or begin flashing, and so on. These graphical effects are brought about by the execution of previously authored simulation rules that determine the values of attributes of the graphical objects.

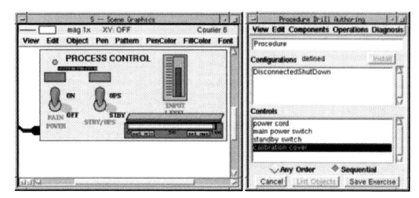

Figure 9. During the Authoring of a Procedure Patterned Exercise

By carrying out the sequence of actions that a student will be required to carry out, an author creates a *specification* of the exercise. When the author clicks the "Save Exercise" button, then a detailed instructional vignette is actually built and can be stored for later presentation to students.

Tutorial Modes. Instructional vignettes, such as the operational setup exercise (named "Procedure") specified in Figure 9, can be presented to students in any of three modes: a demonstration mode, a practice mode, and a test mode. This feature is an extension of a similar approach in our earlier RAPIDS II system (Towne and Munro, 1991). In each of these modes, essentially the same sequence of steps is undertaken, but with different levels of required student interaction and with different prompts presented to students. In the demonstration mode, each control action such as throwing a switch is taken automatically by RIDES. The student merely paces the presentation of text and actions by clicking a mouse button. See Figure 10.

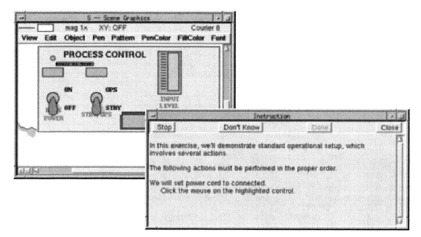

Figure 10. Instructional Presentation in Demonstrate Mode

In the practice mode, students are prompted to carry out certain actions. If a student fails to perform correctly, the simulation is reset to its prior state and the student is given another chance. After a specified number of attempts, the object that must be manipulated is highlighted and the student clicks the mouse to perform the action. The exercise then continues to the next required action. See Figure 11.

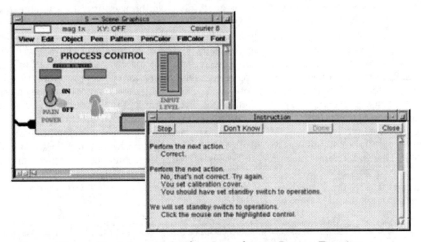

Figure 11. Automatic Student Remediation During Tutoring

In the test mode of a procedure instructional vignette, students are told to carry out the next action in a sequence. If an action is not done correctly, then the correct action is carried out by RIDES and the student is told to carry out the next action. Student performance measures are recorded in the perform and test modes of instructional presentation.

Customizing Generated Tutorials. A good deal of instructional presentation can be easily generated using the procedure patterned exercise authoring interface. Exercises that can be presented in all three modes are generated in about the same amount of time that it takes to simply *do* the procedure. This is a highly productive approach to generating computer-based tutorials. In addition to being fast, the patterned exercise interface to procedure authoring has the advantage that it does not require extensive training for authors. Any subject matter expert who knows how a procedure should be performed can build an exercise. The author simply starts the procedure mode of the patterned exercise authoring tool by issuing the Procedure command from the Operations menu (see Figure 8) and then carries out the actions of the procedure.

The reason that so little instructional presentation authoring needs to be carried out is that the patterned exercise authoring tool exploits data that were created during prior simulation authoring. During the simulation authoring process, authors give names to objects. These names are used in composing text presentations to the student. In addition, if an object is one that the student can manipulate (by clicking or by dragging in it, for example), then the simulation author will mark one of its attributes as a Control attribute. The instructional presentations can then describe the state or 'value' of a control in terms of the values of the Control attribute. If the

Control attribute of an on-off switch takes on the values "on" and "off" under the control of simulation rules, then the automatically generated instruction will tell the author to set the switch to "on" or to "off".

Another interface is also available for authoring instruction about procedures. This interface—which is called the *instructional unit editor*—can be used to build a complete instructional vignette from scratch, or it can be used to edit a lesson that was built using the patterned exercise editor.

Figure 12 shows the instructional unit editor being used to edit the procedure lesson that was generated in Figure 8 (using the patterned exercise authoring tool). In this view of the instructional unit, a tree structure displays the elements of the lesson. Two main types of nodes are found in an instructional tree: group nodes (the colored rectangles) and terminal nodes. The terminal nodes represent elementary instructional presentations of different types. For example, the first terminal node in the tree—the one labeled "text_explanation", at the top of the window—is a generated text presentation. This element contains the first text presentation that is shown in Figure 10, above. An instructional author can customize this instructional item. Double-clicking on this node opens a dialog in which the message can be customized, as in Figure 13, below. (In that figure, the author has already replaced canned text of the form "we will demonstrate Procedure" with "we'll demonstrate standard operational setup, which....")

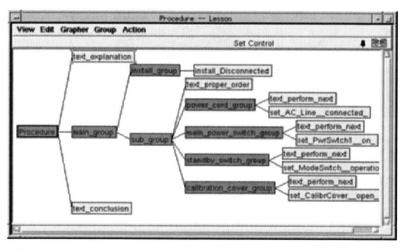

Figure 12. Viewing a Generated Lesson in the Instructional Unit Editor

Many instructional items specify more than textual presentations. The nodes that specify the control actions that a student is to take in carrying out a procedure are called Control instructional items. They, too, can be edited. Figure 14 shows a view of one of the control items in Figure 12, the one named "set_PwrSwtch1_on". In this dialog, an author can specify not only the textual prompts that should be given to students, but also what attribute value is the goal of the control item and even what object is the control.

AUTHORING SIMULATION-CENTERED LEARNING ENVIRONMENTS 77

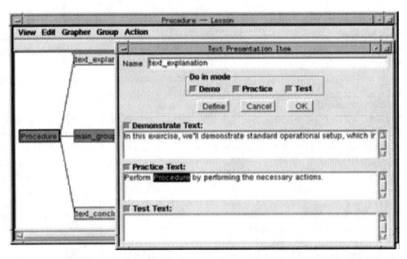

Figure 13. Editing an Instructional Text Presentation

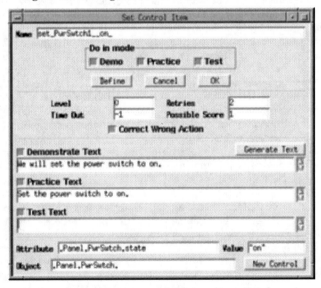

Figure 14. Editing a Control Item Specification

A number of other instructional control aspects are also available to authors in these and other instructional item dialogs. These include whether and when an instructional item should time-out, how many attempts should be permitted before the answer is presented, how to weight the item's score, and whether to present the item in various lesson presentation modes. These are described fully by Munro and Pizzini (1996).

In addition to being able to edit the instructional items of a lesson, authors can delete, cut, copy, and paste these items. Their order can be altered by dragging them to new positions. Whole groups, as well as individual item nodes can be subjected to these operations.

New instructional items can be added to a lesson in the instructional item editor. Some types of items can be specified by issuing menu commands. Many of these commands automatically open dialogs such as those shown in Figure 13 and Figure 14 where authors can provide detailed item specifications. Other types of instructional items are created by choosing a 'tool' and carrying out an action (such as clicking on an object) in the simulation scenes. The instructional authoring tools are Perform Control, Read Indicator, and Find Object. If a graphical object is manipulated with the Set Control tool, then a Control instructional item is created. Clicking with the Read Indicator tool creates a type of instructional item that requires that a student tell what value an object is displaying. If the Find Object tool is used on an object, it generates an item that requires students to click on the object when its name is presented.

Just as in the case of the procedure patterned exercise editor, using the Set Control tool in the instructional unit editor can automatically create a series of steps in a procedure that students will be required to perform. As the instructional author carries out the actions, the simulation scenes update and new Control item nodes appear in the tree displayed in the instructional unit editor.

A glance at the custom authoring environment, shown in Figures 12-14 above, suggests that its use is significantly more complex than the use of the patterned exercise authoring environment, which is shown in Figure 8 and Figure 9. In fact, this is so. Instructional authors cannot make productive use of the custom instructional authoring interfaces unless they have a fairly robust understanding of the uses of the three instructional modes—demonstrate, practice, and test—and of the nature of the different types of elementary instructional presentations. (There are twenty-five such elementary instructional item types, including the text presentation type—shown in Figure 13—and the control item type—shown in Figure 14.) Full productivity with the custom authoring of certain types of items even requires an understanding of the same kinds of authored rule expressions that are used to build simulations.

In summary, one RIDES instructional authoring environment, the patterned exercise editor, requires no understanding of the structure of instructional specification. It can be used by authors with almost no technical understanding of the RIDES authoring system. A second instruction authoring environment, the instructional unit editor and its item dialogs, requires that authors understand more about the structure of simulations and simulation-based training specifications, but it offers customizable instruction authoring. In the RIDES instruction authoring environment, the tradeoff between ease of use and power has been resolved by providing two different kinds of instructional authoring tools. Because the data generated by the easy-to-use tool can be edited with the custom authoring tool, authors who choose to begin an instructional specification using the easier approach are not restricted from enhancing their specifications later in an environment that offers them more control.

3. VIVIDS

VIVIDS is an extended version of RIDES that can work with 3D views as well as with 2D graphics. The 3D views are presented by a collaborating application, such as Vista, a research product developed under the direction of R. Stiles at Lockheed-Martin. Horwitz, et al., have also developed collaborating 3D applications that present simulation views under the control of VIVIDS. In addition, VIVIDS can communicate with an *autonomous agent* that can observe and critique student actions and play a role in simulated team tasks. Figure 15, below, shows a typical environment with a VIVIDS simulation rendered by the Vista 3D browser, inhabited by two instances of an autonomous agent.

Figure 15. A Simulation Environment Inhabitted by Autonomous Agents

The autonomous agent *Steve* (Johnson, Rickel, Stiles & Munro, 1998) works with VIVIDS and Vista to deliver engaging artificial participant simulation, student monitoring, and student advising.

Figure 16, below, schematically presents the authoring process for building a VE-based tutor using VIVIDS. First (starting at the upper right in the figure), the author builds a prototype 2D simulation in VIVIDS. The purpose of this step is to come to understand the behavior of the system that is to be simulated, and to determine the correct level of detail that must be simulated in order to achieve the instructional objectives for this tutor. Conventional 2D simulation development is described in *VIVIDS Quickstart* (Munro, 1997) and in chapters 1-14 of the *VIVIDS Reference Manual* (Munro and Pizzini, 1998.)

Simulated behaviors are then tested and refined. If a Vista 3D model for the domain is ready at this point, the VIVIDS simulation can be enhanced to coordinate with Vista. This process is described in the following section of this document.

Alternatively, an author can begin to prototype tutorial lessons for the tutor, testing them only in the 2D simulation. The processes of integrating with the Vista 3D model and of tutorial development usually reveal the need to revise the simulation, refining the authored behaviors.

Typically, authors evaluate the VIVIDS/Vista simulation environment in advance of fully developing and evaluating authored lessons in VE. This helps to isolate pure simulation issues from tutorial issues. (This does *not* mean that no further simulation authoring will be required during the tutorial development process. It is often the case that additional behavioral features need to be added to make the tutorials work as the author desires.)

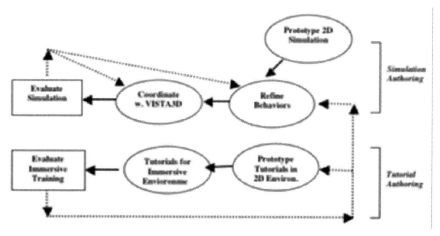

Figure 16. Cyclical Development of Simulation Behavior and Instruction

The Vista application and VIVIDS communicate using Tooltalk, an interapplication messaging system developed for SunOS Unix originally, and since ported to other Unix environments, including the Silicon Graphics systems used in the VET project. Vista implements a scripting language called T-Script. VIVIDS provides support for sending and receiving TScript messages via Tooltalk. Sending is straightforward. A **TScriptSend** VIVIDS function call is used to send a TScript message. The first parameter of **TScriptSend** specifies the TScript type of the message; the second parameter specifies the content of the message. For example,

```
TScriptSend ("vrTranslateGO", "cyl1ptr 0 -0.75 -0.1");
```

sends a message of the vrTranslateGO type that has the effect of moving the virtual environment graphical object *cyl1ptr* to the location [0, -0.75, -0.1]. If the object was previously at [0, -0.75, 0], then it moves down (in the Z dimension) 0.1 meter. To make a VIVIDS simulation receive TScript messages, an author must ensure that an event establishes what VIVIDS *text attribute* is to receive messages of a particular TScript type. When a new Tooltalk message that has been linked to an attribute is received, the attribute's value contains the name of the message type plus the contents of the message. For example,

> "vrPick cyl1ptr_grf_dcs allen 0.010958 - 0.246440 0.253525"

specifies that there was a vrPick event on the *cyl1ptr* object at the point identified by the three numbers (in the coordinate system of the object). To specify that a particular VIVIDS attribute (say, one named *vrPickInfo*) should get vrPick messages, the author would use this function call in an event:

> TScriptLink ("vrPick", .Stage.vrPickInfo)

where the *vrPickInfo* VIVIDS attribute belongs to a scene object named *Stage*.

Note that once a VIVIDS attribute has been *linked* to a particular message type it will automatically receive all broadcast messages of that type. It is not necessary that the author write an event to monitor for Tooltalk messages of interest. The act of establishing the link using TScriptLink() is enough to ensure that VIVIDS will catch the message and direct it to the appropriate VIVIDS attribute.

It is possible to make more than one message type 'report to' the same VIVIDS attribute. Therefore, an author could arrange to have all messages of interest sent to one attribute, and could then respond to these messages using VIVIDS events and relation rules. The message type of a message is included in the value placed in the receiving attribute in order to support this approach. Alternatively, of course, an author can assign each message type of interest its own VIVIDS attribute, in which case the author's rules can simply ignore the first field (the message type field) in received messages.

In many respects the Vista objects are passive; they only change their appearance when instructed by VIVIDS to do so. This is accomplished by a set of TScript messages; when a VIVIDS object changes some aspect of its appearance, it can instruct the corresponding Vista object to change in a similar manner. For example, if a VIVIDS object rotates 45 degrees, the corresponding Vista object must also rotate 45 degrees. However, since the Vista object is in three-dimensional space, the author needs to be concerned with which axis the rotation is to take place around. Similarly, translation in the two-dimensional world of VIVIDS must be converted to a three-dimensional translation for Vista. TScript messages which cause changes in Vista must include specification of the type of change, e.g. vrTranslateGO for a translation (or movement), the name of the Vista object (not necessarily the same as the name of the VIVIDS object), and one or more parameters, depending on the type of change. A possible message to effect a translation is:

> TScriptSend ("vrTranslateGO", "hndl 0 0.2 0");

The effect of this rule would be to move the Vista object 'hndl' to the 0 position on the x-axis, the 0.2 position on the y-axis, and the 0 position on the y_axis.

The most frequently used object modifications can be dealt with using the following:

> **vrTranslateGO <obj_name> <x> <y> <z>**

Translate named object to a given point. Translation is local to frame of reference, and not in world coordinates. Translation values are in meters.

> **vrRotateGO <obj_name> <yaw> <pitch> <roll>**

Rotate named object. Angles are in degrees.

> **vrScaleGO <obj_name> <scale_num>**

Scale named object. Range is 0.0 to 100.0.
> `vrSetMaterial <obj_name> <materialType> <red> <green> <blue>`

'materialType' is usually "diffuse", but it could instead be "ambient", "specular", or "emission". The values of <red>, <green>, and <blue> can range from 0.0 to 1.0.
> `vrSwitchGO <obj_name> <switch_num>`

if <switch_num> is 0, the named object will be invisible; if it is 1, the object will be visible.

In order to have VIVIDS interface with external sound, speech, and three-dimensional components, the VIVIDS code has been modified to interact with a number of special simulation objects. These special objects are not required for 2D graphical tutoring environments. For 3D environments, some of these objects are required so that VIVIDS can correctly collaborate with other applications to deliver simulation and instruction.

All of the special objects are saved as library objects. The library object names are composed of the object name with the suffix ".lib", for example, "gui_object.lib". A typical interaction is that the simulation assigns values to one or more attributes of one of the special objects, and then waits until some attribute has been changed due to a student action or a model state change.

A major learning support feature of VIVIDS is that *content-based Help* presentations in VE are supported. In RIDES, authors can give students access to ancillary information associated with objects. In the VIVIDS 2D simulation environment, a student holds down the Control key and mouses on an object to bring up a pop-up menu of available information. This menu can contain the name of the object, its control and/or indicator state, and its failure state (if it is a failable object). If the author has created a knowledge unit (a bundle of textual discussions and links to other knowledge units or to lessons) for the object, then the popup menu also gives the student access to the authored discussions and linked lessons. Most of these features are also available in the 3D view, as well. Figure 17 displays the VIVIDS version of the help menu in the 3D environment.

In VE, especially when immersed, a student does not have access to a keyboard control key. VIVIDS therefore provides an option for going into a new *Help Mode*. The student does this by pressing the "Show Information" choice on the student's command interface. When he or she does this, the pointer becomes a tool for inquiring about objects instead of a tool for manipulating control objects. While in the Help mode, the "Show Information" choice is green. To get out of the Help mode, the student presses on the "Show Information" choice again. The symbol is gray when the Help mode is no longer active.

The available content-based help features include the name of the object, its indicator and/or control values, and a "Replace" command if the object is one that can fail. In addition, if there are authored knowledge unit discussions for the object and if speech is available, a list of the discussion topics will be included in this menu. Selecting one of these topics causes the discussion to be read aloud by a speech output module. In Figure 17 above, the VE popup menu shows that the name of the selected object is "first stage failure light" and that it has an indicator attribute named "state" that currently has the value "off". The object is failable—hence the *replace* menu item. A discussion on the topic "Function" is available; if this menu item is chosen, the discussion will be read to the student.

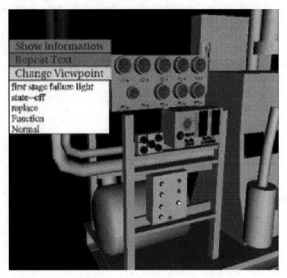

Figure 17. A Content-Based Help Menu

3.1 Opportunistic Instruction

VIVIDS provides an opportunistic instruction feature. Authors can write events that can present instruction. These instructional presentations can take place even if another lesson is currently being delivered, replacing or suspending the current lesson.

The VIVIDS language function PlayInstruction is used to present instruction under the control of an event. Authors can write events that deliver all or only a portion of a previously authored lesson to students when a particular condition occurs. The event condition that triggers the presentation of instruction may refer to some state of the simulation, or it may refer to student model attribute value changes or instructional item attributes.

The PlayInstruction function can only be used in event bodies. The function takes either three or four parameters. (The last parameter, a number, is optional.)
```
PlayInstruction (<text>, <text>, <text>, <number>)
```
The first text parameter is the name of the instructional item to play. An example is
```
"I:HandlePowerError.We_will_reset."
```

The second text parameter is one of "Demonstrate", "Practice", and "Test". This parameter prescribes the mode in which the lesson or lesson fragment should be presented. The third parameter is either "Resume" or "Stop". The "Resume" option means that if opportunistic instruction occurs during a lesson, then that lesson should resume when the opportunistic lesson or lesson fragment is finished. The "Stop" option means that the lesson that had been playing will end right away. The fourth, optional, parameter is a number that specifies the number of seconds that the opportunistic instruction should be allowed before it times out.

3.2 Coordinating instructional control with Steve, the autonomous agent

VIVIDS and Steve need to communicate at several levels. At a deep level, VIVIDS tells Steve when attributes that are of interest to Steve have changed. It also tells Steve when a set of changes is (however briefly) complete, so that the 'world picture' conveyed by that set of attribute values is correct. These and other collaborations take place automatically when VIVIDS and Steve are working together. The sequence of structured VIVIDS lessons and Steve-based procedural practice sessions requires explicit coordination through VIVIDS authoring.

Instructional cooperation between VIVIDS and Steve is necessary so that VIVIDS can present a course of instruction that includes sessions in which Steve demonstrates procedures or monitors student performance. Messages of the *vrSteveGoal* type are used to bring about this coordination.

vrSteveGoal *nameOfGoal* Monitor *score*

VIVIDS asks Steve to monitor and advise the student during a procedure by sending the above message. An example lesson that hands off control to Steve is found in the latest *vrhpac* files. In the current implementation, the *score* parameter is meaningless when VIVIDS asks Steve to monitor the student.

vrSteveGoal *nameOfGoal* Done *score*

Steve informs VIVIDS that its session of monitoring a student's procedure is over. The *score* parameter can be used by VIVIDS to determine what lesson to present next.

4. INTEGRATION OF RIDES AND VIVIDS WITH OTHER RESEARCH EFFORTS

RIDES has played a major role in a number of other research efforts. Several such efforts are briefly described in this section.

4.1 REACT[2]

In the REACT project, members of the research staff at the Jet Propulsion Laboratory collaborated with USC researchers in our lab to integrate RIDES with software developed at JPL. The JPL staff showed that RIDES could be used to carry

---

[2] This project was funded by the Jet Propulsion Laboratory supported by the National Aeronautic and Space Administration, under Contract No. 959893. Dr. Randall Hill led the collaborating JPL research team.

out knowledge acquisition for complex domains (Hill, Fayyad, Santos, and Sturdevant, 1994; Hill, Chien, Smyth, Fayyad, and Santos, 1994). Their work studied the use of RIDES for knowledge acquisition about complex domains in the context of a simulation of Deep Space Network (DSN) subsystems. A special SunOS version of RIDES was developed that permits communication with the DSN monitor and control system. This made it possible to develop RIDES behavioral simulations for testing the advanced monitor and control system knowledge base.

4.2 Tactical Decision Making Simulation and Research[3]

Using RIDES, Towne (1995) developed a system that provides a simulation of a shipboard radar that is tracking surrounding aircraft and ships. The simulation includes an authoring system for rapidly producing real-time tactical exercises. It has been utilized as a research tool capable of generating exercises and recording detailed performance data. Several features of this system specifically address learning research objectives, including the automatic generation of exercises, the automatic recording of the operator's decisions (and their consequences) throughout a scenario, and an option for substituting a computer model for the human operator (in order to support research in machine learning).

4.3 DIAG[4]

DIAG is a system for authoring and delivering instruction on device and system troubleshooting and maintenance (Towne, 1996, 1997, this Volume). It was developed entirely in RIDES/VIVIDS. DIAG supports the development of a hierarchical model of a complex system. It will provide all the necessary functions for moving about in that model, for conducting tests, replacing suspected elements, and for consulting with a built-in diagnostic expert. During exercises, expert advisement is provided about the normality of indications, the significance of symptoms, and the implications of the test outcomes seen by the learner. After exercises, the learner can ask for 1) a debriefing in which DIAG points out the inferences that were possible from the learner's testing sequence, and 2) a demonstration of an expert troubleshooting strategy for the fault.

4.4 IETMs and RIDES[5]

The Department of Defense Integrated Electronic Training Manual (IETM) specification prescribes an application of standard generalized markup language for the delivery of interactive technical manuals by computer(Fuller, Holloway, Jorgensen, and Brission, 1992; Jorgensen, 1994; Jorgensen and Bullard, 1994; Rainey and Fuller, 1994). This project seeks to integrate RIDES with markup-

---

[3]   This project was funded by the Office of Naval Research under ONR Contract No. N00014-93-1-1150.
[4]   The DIAG project is funded by the Office of Naval Research under Air Force Contract No. F33615-90-C-0001.
[5]   This project is funded by the Office of Naval Research under Air Force Contract No. F33615-90-C-0001.

language-based presentation systems, such as IETMs. One outcome of this work has been the development of a facility to direct Netscape Navigator to present web pages to students, either under the control of RIDES simulation rules, or under the control of a tutorial. A second product of this work is a Java-based approach to presenting RIDES instruction in the Netscape Navigator world wide web browser. RIDES collaborates with an applet running in Netscape: the applet and Netscape together provide an instructional interface that is an improved version of the RIDES instructional text window.

5. FUTURE DIRECTIONS: COLLABORATING COMPONENTS

Two lessons that we have learned as a result of implementing RIDES and VIVIDS is that they are too monolithic and that it is too restricted as to delivery platform (Unix/Linux). These restrictions have, in some cases, made it difficult for colleagues in the intelligent tutoring systems research community to take advantage of RIDES or VIVIDS in their own research projects. For example, some researchers have expressed an interest in making use of the RIDES simulation development and delivery system, in coordination with a different tutor delivery system from the one provided by RIDES. Others would like to use our instructional components with their own, previously developed, simulations.

Our work on interacting tutor components has been influenced by continuing discussions with colleagues in the ITS community, especially at the ITS 96 workshops on *architectures and methods for designing cost-effective and reusable ITSs* and on s*imulation-based learning technology*, as well as at the workshop on *architectures for intelligent simulation-based learning* environments at AI-ED '97. Ritter and Koedinger (1996) have described a architecture for plug-in tutor agents that permits tutors to collaborate with applications that were not originally designed to provide services to tutors. Our focus is somewhat different, in that we hope to develop a set of standard services that simulations should be able to provide in order to support the widest range of useful tutoring interactions.

We envision an open architecture for simulation-centered tutors. Figure 18 shows a simplified schema for one such tutor based on five collaborating components. The components communicate and provide services to each other. (Some tutors would have more or fewer components. Only a subset of the required communication links is displayed in the figure.)

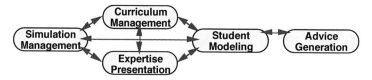

Figure 18. Collaborating Components in a Simulation Based Tutor

In this architecture, there can be many tutor components, including a simulation and interaction engine, one or more student modelers, expert advisors, procedure presenters, explainers, and so on. No one research or development group could be expected to produce leading edge versions of all these tutorial components without the use of higher-level tools. When every aspect of a tutor is developed using low-level tools by a single group, it is likely to have some strong and some weak components. This, together with the (for most practical purposes) monolithic nature of most experimental tutors, can make it very difficult to judge claims about the efficacy of the features of a particular type of tutor. The collaborating components approach would make it possible for a single simulation to be used with many other tutor components in order to compare the efficacy of a variety of tutorial approaches.

Student operations and observations. In a simulation environment, students carry out operations that change the state of the simulation. Certain changes that take place can be observed by students. In contrast with a generic simulation composition tool, one designed for use in tutorial systems will be able to report student operations and observations in a way that is useful to pedagogical components. The simulation authoring system will provide easy-to-use mechanisms for identifying simulation attributes and events that indicate that operations and observations have been conducted. Simulations built in this fashion will also be able to provide instructional interventions (at the direction of tutorial components) that require the students to make observations or to carry out operations, and they will be able to automatically generate useful textual directives or commentary.

Of course a wide range of other services—in addition to operation- and observation-based services—must also be provided by a simulation component for the other components of a tutor. These include putting the simulation into specified states, freezing and resuming simulation, making objects visually salient, hiding and displaying objects, and so on. Group learning support should be provided, so that several students can interact with the same simulation and yet receive appropriate individual tutoring.

Authoring tools and collaborating delivery components. In the collaborative components approach to tutor development, a series of authoring tools could be developed for producing the data required for each type of tutor component. See Figure 19.

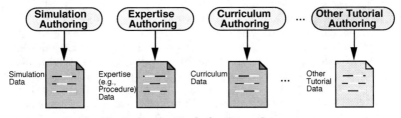

Figure 19. Authoring Tools for Tutor Components

The tools used to develop data required by simulation components may or may not be themselves multi-platform, but robust authoring tools will typically be larger executables than the multi-platform (typically Java-based) tutor components that deliver the authored simulations, expertise, curricula, etc. Figure 20 presents the notion that the authored data will be used by tutor components to deliver useful presentations or interactions to students.

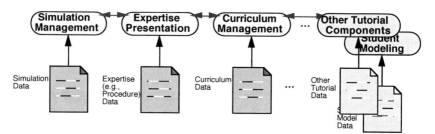

Figure 20. Tutor Components Are Responsible for Tutorial Delivery

Communications infrastructure. The current focus of our collaborating components research is to define what services components should be able to render to each other, rather than what communications infrastructure should be employed. In fact, once the appropriate service sets have been determined, the interaction infrastructure should require only a straightforward development process. Using appropriate wrappers, many different communications platforms could be supported.

6. SUMMARY

RIDES and VIVIDS are robust applications for authoring highly interactive graphical simulations and tutorials that are delivered in the context of those simulations. They supports the composition and delivery of instruction centered about a detailed model of a device or system of interest. The authoring system incorporates several innovative advances in human-computer interfaces (HCI) for tutor authoring systems. These include HCI features in support of simulation behavior specification and authoring-by-doing features for the development of instruction. RIDES has played an important role in several other research projects. The REACT project at JPL made use of RIDES in a project on knowledge acquisition for complex domains. The Tactical Decision Making Simulation project utilized RIDES to create a scenario authoring system in support of research on machine and human learning. The DIAG project developed an intelligent aiding and action evaluation system using the RIDES/VIVIDS development environment.

VIVIDS has been employed in the VET project (Virtual Environments for Training) to support the development of interactive behaving simulations in immersive 3D environments, and to support the delivery of RIDES-authored and autonomous-agent monitored instruction. It has also been utilized by researchers at the Air Force Research Laboratory to develop virtual environments for training that incorporate guided practice and opportunistic instruction features provided by VIVIDS.

For Further Information

Three major documents on RIDES and VIVIDS authoring and administration are available at
> `http://btl.usc.edu/rides/documentn/`

Many simulations and tutors have been developed using RIDES. Information about some of these tutors is available on the internet at our site:
http://btl.usc.edu/rides/examples/
Additional information about the special features of VIVIDS for virtual environments training can be found at:
http://btl.usc.edu/VET/

7. REFERENCES

Borning, A. (1979). Thinglab: A constraint-oriented simulation laboratory. Xerox Parc technical report SSL-79-3. Palo Alto, CA: Xerox Palo Alto Research Laboratory.

A. Borning. (1981). The programming language aspects of ThingLab, a constraint-oriented simulation laboratory. ACM Transactions on Programming Languages and Systems, 3(4):353–387.

Coller, L. D., Pizzini, Q. A., Wogulis, J., Munro, A. & Towne, D. M. (1991). Direct manipulation authoring of instruction in a model-based graphical environment. In L. Birnbaum (Ed.), *The international conference on the learning sciences: Proceedings of the 1991 conference*, Evanston, Illinois: Association for the Advancement of Computing in Education.

de Jong, T., van Joolingen, W., Scott, D., deHoog, R., Lapied, L., Valent, R. (1994). SMILSLE: System for multimedia integrated simulation learning environments. In T. de Jong and L. Sarti (Eds.) *Design and production of multimedia and simulation based learning material*, Dordrecht: Kluwer Academic Publishers.

Forbus, K. (1984). *An interactive laboratory for teaching control system concepts.* (Tech. Report 5511). Cambridge, Massachusetts: Bolt Beranek and Newman Inc.

Fuller, J. J., Holloway, S., Jorgensen, E. L., and Brisson, J. B. (1992). *Military Specification MIL-D-87269 Data Base, Revisable: Interactive Electronic Technical Manuals, For the Support of*, MIL-D-87269, Bethesda, Maryland: Tri-Service Working Group for Interactive Electronic Technical Manuals, 20.

Hill, R., Chien, S., Smyth, C., Fayyad, K., and Santos, P. (1994). *Planning for deep space network operations*, Pasadena: Jet Propulsion Laboratory.

Hill, R., Fayyad, K., Santos, P., and Sturdevant, K. (1994). Knowledge acquisition and reactive planning for the deep space network. In *Working notes of the 1994 fall symposium on planning and learning: On to real applications*, New Orleans: AAAI Press.

Hollan, J. D., Hutchins, E. L., and Weitzman, L. (1984). STEAMER: An interactive inspectable simulation-based training system, *The AI Magazine*, **2**.

Johnson, W. L., Rickle, J., Stiles, R. and Munro, A. (1998). Integrating Pedagogical Agents into Virtual Environments. *Presence: Teleoperators and Virtual Environments* 7(6):523-546.

Jorgensen, E. L. (1994). *DoD Classes of Electronic Technical Manuals*, CDNSWC/TM-18-94/11, Bethesda, Maryland: Carderock Division, Naval Surface Warfare Center.

Jorgensen, E. L., and Bullard, L. (1994). *Metafile for Interactive Documents (MID)*, Bethesda, Maryland: Carderock Division, Naval Surface Warfare Center.

Munro, A. (1994). Authoring interactive graphical models. In T. de Jong, D. M. Towne, and H. Spada (Eds.), *The Use of Computer Models for Explication, Analysis and Experiential Learning*. Springer Verlag.

Munro, A. (1995). *RIDES QuickStart*, Los Angeles: Behavioral Technology Laboratories, University of Southern California.

Munro, A., Johnson, M. C., Pizzini, Q. A., Surmon, D. S., and Wogulis, J. L. (1996), A Tool for Building Simulation-Based Learning Environments, in *Simulation-Based Learning Technology Workshop Proceedings, ITS'96*, Montreal, Québec, Canada.

Munro, A., Johnson, M. C., Surmon, D. S., and Wogulis, J. L. (1993). Attribute-centered simulation authoring for instruction. In the *Proceedings of AI-ED '93*—World Conference on Artificial Intelligence in Education.

Munro, A. and Pizzini, Q. A. (1996). *RIDES Reference Manual*, Los Angeles: Behavioral Technology Laboratories, University of Southern California.

Munro, A. and Surmon, D. S. (1996). *RIDES Administration Manual*, Los Angeles: Behavioral Technology Laboratories, University of Southern California.

Northrop Corporation. (1994). *Technical manual general system on-equipment maintenance: Landing gear B-2A aircraft*, TO 1B-2A-2-32GS-00-1, Los Angeles: Northrop Corporation.

Pizzini, Q. A., Munro, A., Wogulis, J. L., and Towne, D. M. (1996). The Cost-Effective Authoring of Procedural Training, in *Architectures and Methods for Designing Cost-Effective and Reusable ITSs Workshop Proceedings, ITS'96*, Montreal, Québec, Canada.

Rainey, S. C., and Fuller, J. J. (1994). *Navy Interactive Electronic Technical Manual (IETM) Acquisition Guide, Initial Draft*, CDNSWC/TM-18-95/01, Bethesda, Maryland: Carderock Division, Naval Surface Warfare Center.

Rigney, J. W., Towne, D. M., King, C. A., and Moran, P. J. (1978). *Field Evaluation of the Generalized Maintenance Trainer-Simulator: I. Fleet Communications System.* (Technical Report 89) Los Angeles: Behavioral Technology Laboratories, University of Southern California.

Ritter, S. and Koedinger, K.R. (1996). An architecture for plug-in tutor agents, *International Journal of Artificial Intelligence in Education,*, 7, 315-348.

Self, J. (1995). Problems with Unguided Learning, Proceedings of the International Conference on Computers in Education (ICCE '95).

Spensley, F. and Elsom-Cook, M. (1989). Generating domain representations for ITS. In D. Bierman, J. Breuker, and J. Sandberg (Eds.), *The proceedings of the fourth international conference on artificial Intelligence in Education*. Amsterdam: IOS, 276-280.

Stiles, R., McCarthy, L., Munro, A., Pizzini, Q., Johnson, L., Rickel, J. (1996). *Virtual Environments for Shipboard Training*, Intelligent Ship Symposium, American Society of Naval Engineers, Pittsburgh PA.

Towne, D. M. (1984). A generalized model of fault-isolation performance. In *Proceedings, Artificial Intelligence in Maintenance: Joint Services Workshop*.

Towne, D. M. (1995). *ONR final report: A configurable task environment for learning research*. Los Angeles: Behavioral Technology Laboratories, University of Southern California.

Towne, D. M. (1996). *DIAG: Diagnostic instruction and guidance—application guide*. Los Angeles: Behavioral Technology Laboratories, University of Southern California.

Towne, D. M. (1997). Approximate Reasoning Techniques for Intelligent Diagnostic Instruction, *International Journal of Artificial Intelligence in Education* 8, 262-283.

Towne, D. M. & Munro, A. (1981) *Generalized maintenance trainer simulator: Development of hardware and software*. (Technical Report No. 81-9) San Diego: Navy Personnel Research and Development Center.

Towne, D. M. & Munro, A. (1984). *Preliminary design of the advanced ESAS System*. (Technical Report No. 105) Los Angeles: Behavioral Technology Laboratories, University of Southern California, December.

Towne, D. M. & Munro, A. (1988). The intelligent maintenance training system. In J. Psotka, L. D. Massey, and S. A. Mutter (Eds.), *Intelligent tutoring systems: Lessons learned* (479-530). Hillsdale, NJ: Erlbaum.

Towne, D. M. & Munro, A.(1991) Simulation-based instruction of technical skills. *Human Factors*, 33, 325-341.

Towne, D. M. & Munro, A. (1992). Two approaches to simulation composition for training. In M. Farr and J. Psotka (Eds.), *Intelligent instruction by computer: Theory and practice*. London: Taylor and Francis.

Towne, D. M., Munro, A., Johnson, M. C. (1982). *Generalized maintenance trainer simulator: Test and evaluation*. (Technical Report No. 98) Los Angeles: Behavioral Technology Laboratories, University of Southern California.

Towne, D. M., Munro, A., Pizzini, Q. A., Surmon, D. S., Coller, L. D., & Wogulis, J. L. (1990). Model-building tools for simulation-based training. *Interactive Learning Environments*, 1, 33-50.

Van Joolingen, W.R. and De Jong, T. (1996). Design and implementation of simulation-based discovery environments: the SMISLE solution, *International Journal of Artificial Intelligence in Education*, 7, 253-276.

Williams, M. D., Hollan, J. D., and Stevens, A. L. (1981). An overview of STEAMER: an advanced computer-assisted instruction system for propulsion engineering. *Behavior Research methods and Instrumentation*, 13, 85-90.

ACKNOWLEDGMENTS

Major funding for this research was provided by the United States Air Force and the Office of Naval Research under contract F33615-90-C-0001. Additional support was provided by the Office of Naval Research and the Air Force under contracts N00014-93-1-1150, F33615-90-C-0001. My colleagues Mark Johnson, Quentin Pizzini, David Surmon, and Douglas Towne co-designed and implemented RIDES, and the first three collaborated in the design and development of VIVDS. James Wogulis designed and implemented many significant portions of RIDES which have survived in VIVIDS. Lee Coller made design and implementation contributions to early versions of RIDES. Donna Darling provided web page development and administrative support for these projects. We thank the following people for helpful feedback on RIDES and VIVIDS: Susan Chipman, Albert Corbett, Michael Crumm, Zuzanna Dobes, Jim Fleming, Randall Hill, Carol Horwitz, Ken Koedinger, Len Mackie, Tim Miller, Wes Regian, Trish Santos, Chuck Swanberg, and Rusty Trainor. Special thanks go to our collaborators on the VET project: Lewis Johnson, Laurie McCarthy, Jeff Rickel, Randy Stiles, and Sandeep Tewari. Many other researchers, developers, authors, and students have also made helpful comments and suggestions that contributed to these projects.

STEPHEN B. BLESSING

Chapter 4

A PROGRAMMING BY DEMONSTRATION AUTHORING TOOL FOR MODEL–TRACING TUTORS

Abstract. Model–tracing tutors have consistently been among the most effective class of intelligent learning environments. Across a number of empirical studies, these tutors have shown students can learn the tutored domain better or in a shorter amount of time than traditionally taught students (Anderson, Boyle, Corbett, & Lewis, 1990). Unfortunately, the creation of these tutors, particularly the production system component, is a time–intensive task, requiring knowledge that lies outside the tutored domain. This outside knowledge—knowledge of programming and cognitive science—prohibits domain experts from being able to construct effective, model–tracing tutors for their domain of expertise. This paper reports on a system, referred to as Demonstr8 (pronounced "demonstrate"), which attempts to reduce the outside knowledge required to construct a model–tracing tutor, within the domain of arithmetic. By utilizing programming by demonstration techniques (Cypher, 1993; Myers, McDaniel, & Kosbie, 1993) coupled with a mechanism for abstracting the underlying productions (the procedures to be used by the tutor and learned by the student), the author can interact with the interface the student will use, and the productions will be inferred by the system. In such a way, a domain expert can create in a short time a model–tracing tutor with the full capabilities implied by such a tutor—a production system that monitors the student's progress at each step in solving the problem and gives feedback when requested or necessary, in either an immediate or delayed manner.

1. INTRODUCTION

Model–tracing tutors have proven extremely effective in the classroom, with the most promising efforts demonstrating more than a standard deviation's improvement over traditional instruction (Anderson, Boyle, Corbett, & Lewis, 1990; Koedinger & Anderson, 1993a; Koedinger, Anderson, Hadley, & Mark, 1997). They are referred to as model–tracing tutors because they contain an expert model that is used to trace the student's responses to ensure that the student's responses are part of an acceptable solution path. The creation of such tutors, particularly the expert models that underlie them, is a time–intensive task, requiring much knowledge outside of the domain being tutored. Anderson (1992) estimated that 100 hours of development time yields about 1 hour of instruction, with others estimating even more (Woolf & Cunningham, 1987; Murray, 1999; Halff, this volume). The goal of the authoring tool described in this paper is to drastically reduce the amount of time and knowledge needed to create a model–tracing tutor. Since this authoring tool produces a tutor which is functionally equivalent to one of Anderson's ACT tutors, what follows is a description of those tutors, and then a discussion of how an ACT tutor is actually created (see Anderson, Corbett, Koedinger, & Pelletier, 1995, for a more complete discussion of the ACT tutors).

1.1. A Description of the ACT Tutors

The ACT Tutors developed by Anderson and his colleagues (Anderson, Corbett, Koedinger, & Pelletier, 1995; Corbett & Anderson, 1990; Anderson, Conrad, & Corbett, 1989) all operate by the same basic mechanism. What forms the backbone of the system is an expert model, realized as a set of production rules, that contains all the knowledge needed to solve problems within the domain being tutored. A production rule is a statement with a condition and an action, and a set of such statements can specify the procedural knowledge needed to perform a task. Within the algebra equation solving tutor, for example, this expert module is a set of around 150 productions (S. Ritter, personal communication, December 10, 1996). The tutors use this expert model to check the student's answers. In all of the ACT Tutors, this production set is general enough to be able to solve novel problems. That is, a programmer, a teacher, or even a student can enter a new problem into the system, and then the tutor will be able to solve it and to provide tutoring on it. This generality is part of what makes the architecture of the ACT Tutors so powerful.

Another feature of the ACT Tutors that is consistent across the tutors is the student model. The student model is the assessment by the tutor of the student's current knowledge state. As the student interacts with the system, getting some of the answers right and others wrong, this student model is updated. The ACT Tutors contain a list of skills that make up the tutored domain. Skills correspond to a sequence of production rules that result in a student action. Each skill is considered to be in either a learned or unlearned state, with a probability assigned to it that it is currently in the learned state. As students demonstrate proficiency (or a lack of proficiency) in a skill by corresponding to (or not corresponding to) a set of productions, this probability is adjusted according to a Bayesian algorithm. When this probability gets above a certain level, generally 95%, that skill is assumed to be in the learned state. Many of the tutors have an external realization of this student model, referred to as the Skillometer. This Skillometer is essentially a bar chart, with each bar representing a skill, and each bar displaying the current probability that the skill is in the learned state. When the bar gets above the criterion level for that skill to be assumed to be in the learned state, a little checkmark is placed next to it.

The third main feature of the ACT Tutors is the student's interface, which must vary across the different tutored domains. The interface that the student interacts with in the geometry proof tutor is very much like a typical computer drawing program, whereas the interface used by the programming tutors is a structured text editor. However, no matter the specifics of an interface, for each student action within the interface (clicking a button, typing in a text field, selecting a menu option, etc.), that action can be checked against the expert model. This process of checking student actions using the expert model is referred to as model tracing. The outcome of this checking can either be displayed immediately, right after the student does the action, or it can be delayed until the student requests the feedback. Also, in the case that the tutor displays the feedback right away, the tutor can either not allow the action or somehow indicate within the interface that the action is not correct (perhaps by displaying the student's incorrect response in red italics). Depending on what skill the student's action corresponded to, the student model is also updated, in a process called knowledge tracing. Once all the skills that make up the current lesson are assumed to be in the learned state (i.e., all the skills in the Skillometer are "checked"), the student is graduated to the next lesson, which will add skills to be mastered.

1.2. Creating an ACT Tutor

Anderson and Pelletier (1991) described a development tool for the creation of the ACT Tutors. This tool is referred to as the Tutor Development Kit, or TDK. The TDK is based in Common LISP, and provides a working memory manager, a production interpreter, and several utilities to make the creation of a tutor easier. While this is better than starting to program a tutor from scratch, a fair amount of non–domain knowledge is needed to create even the simplest tutor. The student's interface needs to be constructed, the appropriate representation of that interface needs to be encoded within the tutor's working memory, and the production rules for the task need to coded. All of this requires not only a good knowledge of the TDK's syntax, but also a decent familiarity with LISP and how to create graphic interfaces.

As an example of what it takes to program a tutor using the TDK, consider the code displayed in Table 1. This is part of the code one might write for a tutor whose domain is multi–column addition. The actual syntax is not important, but rather the general feel for the overall complexity involved in creating a tutor for a seemingly easy task like multi–column addition. The top four lines define the types of objects that can be in working memory (WME is short for Working Memory Element). The first word after "defwme" is the name of the type of object, and then the following words are attributes, or slots, of that object. The next two statements, the "make–wme's" actually create elements within the tutor's working memory. A column is made, and then a cell. The values of the slots are assigned upon the WME's creation, and they can change as the student interacts with the tutor. These lines are necessary, the defwmes and make–wmes, because the ACT Tutors must maintain within their working memory a representation of the current state of the problem—what appears onscreen to the student. As the student works on the problem, this representation is changed to reflect what the student has done. Help messages and hints are partially based upon this representation. Many more make–wme statements would be required in the complete definition of this tutor.

The last several lines of Table 1 contain one of the actual TDK productions needed by the expert model. The full model for multi–column addition would contain on the order of 10 such productions. This production is responsible for figuring out the sum of the two digits in a particular column. Other productions would figure out which column is important and what exactly to write down. The words with equal signs in front of them are variables. This production will match to the two numbers in the current column of interest. Once it finds the sum, it sets a subgoal to actually write the answer in the column, which will be handled by another production. The last couple of lines contain some help text (which will use the current numbers in the problem) that will be used when the student asks for help.

Table 1. TDK code segment for a multi-column addition tutor

```
(defwme addition-goal column)
(defwme addition-column rows part-of english)
(defwme cell text row column parent part-of note)
(defwme write-answer column object)
(make-wme column1 isa addition-column rows (c03 c02 c01 c00)
          part-of root english (name tens))
(make-wme c00 isa cell text "2" part-of column1 row 0 column 3)

(defproduction process-column model (=goal)
  =goal>
     isa addition-goal
     column =column
  =column>
     isa addition-column
     rows ($ =cell1 =cell2 =cell3)
  =cell1>
     isa cell
     text =num1
  =cell2>
     isa cell
     text =num2
 ==>
     !eval! =sum (princ-to-string (+ (convert-to-digit =num1)
                                    (convert-to-digit =num2))
     =subgoal>
        isa write-answer
        column =column
        object =sum
     !chain! model (=subgoal)
     :help '("Add " ,=num1 " and " ,=num2 "." ~n)
           '(,=num1 " + " ,=num2 " = "
             ,(princ-to-string (+ (convert-to-digit =num1)
                                  (convert-to-digit =num2)) "." ~n)
```

Table 1 contains much less than 10% of the code needed for an addition tutor. The author of such a tutor would need to type all of the code into a blank document, run it, and then debug it. No provision is made within the TDK for the automatic generation of working memory elements or productions. For these things, authors simply have a clean slate they must fill in. The TDK does do the knowledge tracing automatically, provided that the necessary hooks are in place. In general, a lot of programming "glue" is needed to get everything—model and knowledge tracing, and the student interface—running correctly. It would probably take a competent LISP and TDK programmer a half-day or more to program a basic addition tutor.

1.3. Going Beyond the TDK

Based on the short example above, one can easily see that the creation of a tutor that would be used throughout an entire course, like the ACT Tutors for programming and algebra that have been constructed, would require many, many hours worth of work. Additionally, it requires close collaboration between the educators, the research scientists, and the programmers. An educator or other domain expert could not sit down and create a model–tracing tutor, nor could they easily modify an existing tutor for their individual needs. Existing tutors do have ways for educators to create new problems for the tutors (in one of the geometry tutors, it's as easy as using drawing package), but this is a far cry from being able to create a tutor which teaches a new skill—something that would be advantageous for educators and curriculum designers to be able to do. What is needed is a system that drastically reduces or eliminates the non–domain knowledge needed to create a model–tracing tutor.

By allowing the author to simply manipulate the actual interface that the student is going to use for the creation of working memory elements and productions, it becomes much more feasible for non–cognitive scientists to create intelligent, model–tracing tutors. The main mechanism which allows the tool described in this paper, Demonstr8, to infer the production rules, the heart of a model–tracing tutor, is similar to ACT–R's analogy mechanism (Anderson, 1993; Salvucci & Anderson, 1998)[1] to be explained in the following paragraphs.

An important distinction within the ACT–R architecture is between declarative knowledge, one's knowledge of facts (e.g., "Washington DC is the capital of the United States") and procedural knowledge, one's knowledge of how to perform actions (e.g., adding numbers together). One of the claims of the ACT–R theory is that all knowledge has declarative origins. That is, the only way new procedural knowledge, in the form of production rules, enters the system is by the process of analogizing from the current goal to some previous declarative knowledge. This mechanism operates by forming an analogy from examples stored in declarative memory to the current goal. The current authoring tool uses this idea, since the items on the screen can be represented by declarative knowledge structures, and as the author interacts with them, the procedural knowledge of what to do with them (i.e., what will become the expert model of the tutor) can be inferred. Demonstr8 translates the actions of the domain expert (i.e., their interactions with the objects in the interface) into the knowledge needed by the tool to successfully tutor students.

To provide an example of ACT–R's analogy mechanism, assume that an ACT–R model of a person learning LISP has the declarative knowledge that the command to multiply 5 by 7 is (* 5 7). This model has a goal to add 132 and 254. The situation can be diagrammed as:

Current Goal: *Previous Example:*
Add 132 and 254   Multiply 5 and 7
                        ↓
                     (* 5 7)

The arrow shown connecting the two pieces of declarative information in the Previous Example simply indicates that the goal of multiplying 5 by 7 can be realized by typing (* 5 7), as illustrated by the example. Two additional pieces of declarative information that the system has stored are that the symbol for multiplication is '*' and the symbol for addition is '+.' By analogizing from the Previous Example in order to solve the Current Goal, and using the additional knowledge of which operator is indicated by which English word, ACT–R can construct the following production:

IF the current goal is a LISP operation with two arguments
    AND *op* is the symbol corresponding to the operation
    AND *arg1* and *arg2* are the two arguments
THEN the LISP call should be: *(op arg1 arg2)*

As can be seen, the analogy mechanism has generalized across the different numbers, and has linked the knowledge that '*' is the operator for multiplication with '+' is the operator for multiplication to construct the generalization that when the goal is to do some LISP operation, use the associated operator in the front position of the LISP call.

The rest of this paper describes Demonstr8, a system that begins to address the ability of non–cognitive scientists being able to program a model–tracing tutor by using something like this analogy mechanism. Using Demonstr8, both the time and knowledge required to produce a model–tracing tutor is drastically reduced. With limited training, a non–cognitive scientist can produce a model–tracing tutor for arithmetic in less than 20 minutes (an estimate based on informal observations).

2. DEMONSTR8 DESCRIPTION

Using Demonstr8, an author can create a model–tracing tutor for some specific application within arithmetic—multi–column addition or subtraction, for example. What follows is a description of the authoring process for a simple subtraction tutor (and section 2.4 discusses the output of that process). While Demonstr8 has been implemented for the construction of a particular class of tutors, parts of it are general enough to apply to any domain, and the ideas behind the parts that are not can be modified to work within almost any setting. Throughout the description of Demonstr8, these generalizable features will be highlighted, and the General Discussion addresses this specific point of which features are readily generalized and which require additional effort.

Within Demonstr8 the author has available three things:

- a palette of MacDraw–like tools used to create the student interface

- a method for creating higher–order declarative representations for these student interface elements (e.g., making a column of numbers)
- a programming by demonstration method for creating productions.

There is also a way of inputting new abstract, declarative knowledge into the system, such as subtraction facts, which aids in the induction of the production rules. However, the system has a number of built–in facts for doing arithmetic, so an author may never have to use this feature. The above three items are all that are necessary to create a model–tracing tutor for some aspect of arithmetic.

When the system first starts, three windows, a menu titled Author, and the Author Palette appear. The three windows are:

- Student Interface: The author will create the student's interface within this window, using the available tools. (Shown in Figure 1)
- Working Memory Elements: This window contains a list of the current working memory elements of the tutor. At startup, the only item is a list of predefined memory elements, which are the numbers 0 through 18 (sufficient for arithmetic tasks through multi–column subtraction), a blank, and a slash character.
- Productions: This window contains a list of current productions, which is empty at startup. At the bottom of this window is a checkbox which indicates if the system is in recording mode. When the box is checked, the system is in recording mode, and is recording the author's actions and trying to induce the productions behind them (more on that in the Demonstrating Productions section below).

Both of the last two windows are scrolling, hierarchical lists from which items can be selected, edited, and deleted. The Author menu contains options for creating working memory elements, new productions, a problem generator, and other authoring activities. These will be discussed as they arise in the creation of a tutor. The Author Palette will be described in the next section. The rest of this section discusses designing an interface, creating the working memory elements, and programming the productions within the context of creating a multi–column subtraction tutor.

2.1. Designing the Student Interface

The tools available to the author for creating the student's interface are basic, but complete enough to provide all the functionality needed for an arithmetic tutor. All the tools are contained in the Author Palette, as seen in Figure 1. The tools work like the tools in a drawing program. They are, from left–to–right:

- Selection Tool: Used to select any object within the student's interface. Multiple objects can be selected, which is useful when creating working memory elements (see next section).

- Cell Tool: Used to place cells within the student's interface. Cells are the place holders for numbers, and authors create them simply by clicking where they want the cell to be.
- Line Tool: The author can draw lines in the student interface, to make it look more like an arithmetic problem.
- Worksheet Tool: This is the grid onto which the cells get placed. While it is possible to have more than one worksheet per tutor, it probably is not necessary (though another class of tutors for a different domain could make use of this feature).

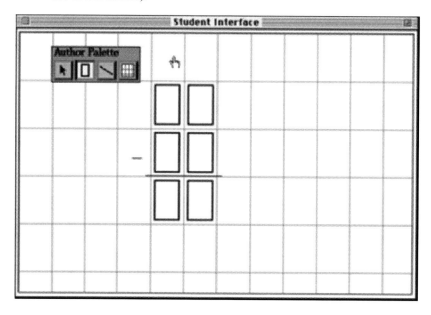

Figure 1. Designing the interface.

Figure 1 displays a student interface an author has just created. On the worksheet, the author has created six cells arranged in two columns of three, and has drawn two lines so that the interface resembles a simple subtraction problem. When cells are placed on the worksheet, they automatically become available as WMEs. Designing a student interface in such a way, using a set of drawing tools, can easily be applied to any domain. Domain specific tools, like the Cell Tool, could be supplied as plug–in packages available to the author. These domain specific tools, as will be seen with the Cell Tool, can contain specialized knowledge for operating correctly in the authored domain (e.g., cells know how to display numbers and that numbers can have slashes through them).

At this point, the author has created the interface that he or she will use to demonstrate the skills, and this interface will also be the one students will ultimately use. The actions the author has performed are:

- Selecting the Cell Tool from the Author Palette
- Placing six cells on the provided worksheet grid
- Selecting the Line Tool from the Author Palette
- Drawing two lines so that the interface looks like a subtraction problem

2.2. Creating Working Memory Elements

After the author has created the basic layout of the student's interface, he or she must next define any higher–order working memory elements that are part of this interface. For the simple subtraction tutor, the six cells that have been placed correspond to two columns, and these two columns correspond to one problem. These two columns and one problem must be defined in order for the correct productions to be induced. One could imagine a system, particularly a system devoted to arithmetic, already knowing about columns (i.e., cells that are aligned vertically) and problems (i.e., columns that are aligned horizontally), but this feature of Demonstr8 was provided for two reasons. First, it allows the system to be more extensible by allowing the author to define novel arrangements of cells (e.g., a tutor for long division might make use of this feature). Second, and more importantly, it demonstrates the generality of the way in which working memory elements based on primitives (like cells in an arithmetic domain, or any of the other items directly available from the Author Palette) could be authored, based on the student interface and employing end–user programming techniques (Smith, Cypher, & Spohrer, 1994; Nardi, 1993). The following description shows how the cells can be grouped into columns, and then the columns into a problem.

2.2.1. Grouping cells into columns

To group the three cells to the right into a column, the author selects all three cells using the Selection Tool. With all three cells selected, he or she must next select Name WMEs from the Author menu. A dialog box similar to what is depicted in Figure 2 appears, which has been filled out. Since this is the first time a column has been created, the author must leave the New radio button checked, and fill in what the classname (*defwme* in TDK parlance) should be, "Column." Next, the author must give a new instance name to this particular column, for example, "Column1."

The middle of the dialog contains a scrolling, two–column table that lists the properties (or "slots") of this classname on the left, and their current values for this instance on the right. Since three cells were selected in the student's interface, the system assumes there are three properties, one for each cell. That was the proper guess in this instance, since columns are composed of a Top, Bottom, and Answer cell. The author can rename the property names, as the author is currently doing in Figure 2. If the values of the properties are wrong, they can be edited by double–clicking them and obtaining an editing box, or values can be dragged–and–dropped from the Working Memory Elements window.

Below the properties table is an edit box labeled "Help Tag." The author can input here a word or short phrase that will be used by the help system when the system generates a help message. Since this is the ones column, the author can type "ones column" or "ones" in the box. When the author clicks the Okay button, the

Figure 2. Creating working memory elements.

WME type Column appears in the Working Memory Elements Window, with its one instantiation, Column1.

Defining the second column, the tens columns, is considerably easier, since the column type has already been defined. After the author has selected the three cells in the other column and selected Name WMEs from the Author menu, the author can select "Column" from the pop–up menu under classname (this pop–up menu contains the name of the WME types the author has already created), which automatically fills in the correct property names. All that is left for the author to do is to give this particular column a name ("Column2"), provide a help tag ("tens"), and click the Okay button.

At this point, two columns have been created based on the six initial cells the author placed in the interface. The actions the author had to perform were:

- Selecting the Selection Tool from the Author Palette and selecting the three leftmost cells.
- Choosing "Name WMEs..." from the Author Menu
- Completing the resulting working memory dialog box:
- Creating a new classname ("Column") for the selected object, and naming this particular instance ("Column1")
- Providing names for the attributes of this class ("Top," "Bottom," and "Answer" cells)
- Indicating a piece of help text to be associated with this instance
- Selecting the three rightmost cells and choosing "Name WMEs..." from the Author Menu
- Completing the dialog box for this column ("Column2"), which is greatly simplified since the class Column has already been defined

2.2.2. Grouping columns into a problem

The last WME the author defines is the problem. This demonstrates the way a WME can be created that has no direct objects on the screen that represent them. A problem is composed of the two columns, and whereas the cells that make up the columns are objects on screen that can be selected, the columns themselves cannot (though one could imagine an authoring interface which could make apparent some of these higher–order WMEs). Therefore, the author cannot have anything selected when the Name WMEs item is selected from the Author menu. Once the Name WMEs dialog appears, and the new classname of "Problem" and an instance name of "Problem1" has been entered, the author fills in the Properties table, which is currently empty, since nothing was selected. Using the New Property button, the author can either create two new properties, one for each column ("OnesColumn" and "TensColumn"), or one property ("Columns") which has list of columns as its value. Based on the way the author has decided to create the production system, the latter option is selected since it will allow for the easier creation of the rest of the system. To create the list of values, the names of the columns are dragged over from the Working Memory Elements Window and dropped on the Properties table. Once more than one value has been dropped, a list is automatically created for that property's value. The author decided to use this method because Demonstr8 has special features to reason about lists (e.g., finding the rightmost element in a list, or an item which is to the immediate left of another item). This feature will be highlighted in the next section, which describes how the author demonstrates the procedural knowledge of a task.

The author has now defined all the necessary WMEs needed for this tutor. To define the Problem WME, the actions the author had to perform were:

- With nothing selected in the interface, choosing "Name WMEs..." from the Author Menu
- Completing the resulting working memory dialog box:
- Creating a new classname for the selected object ("Problem", and naming this particular instance ("Problem1")
- Providing a name for the attribute of this class ("Columns")
- Dragging the values for this attribute from the WMEs window into the row named above

The structures that are perhaps most key to inducing the productions behind the actions of the author are Knowledge Functions, which can be thought of (and depicted as) ACT–R working memory elements which represent a table of values. These structures represent declarative knowledge not depicted directly in the interface. In the current implementation, Knowledge Functions take one or two values and return a single result. In this respect, they are similar to look–up tables, and as such enable many WMEs to be depicted in an easy–to–read, easy–to–enter manner. While they are limited to only two–dimensions in the current application, n–dimensional Knowledge Functions are possible (and indeed, the ACT–R analogy mechanism is meant to deal with such structures). Demonstr8 has built–in the Knowledge Functions for the standard arithmetic operations (e.g., addition, subtraction, and decrementing). Figure 3 shows part of the Subtraction Knowledge

Function. An easy interface exists within Demonstr8 to create new, novel Knowledge Functions. After selecting New Knowledge Function... from the Author menu, and indicating the size and name of the table, the author can simply drag and drop keys (the inputs to the table, which can be any WME in the system) and values (the result to be returned—again, these can be any WME) onto the table. In such a way, an author could create a subtraction function for octal arithmetic, and have it automatically available to the system from which to infer productions.

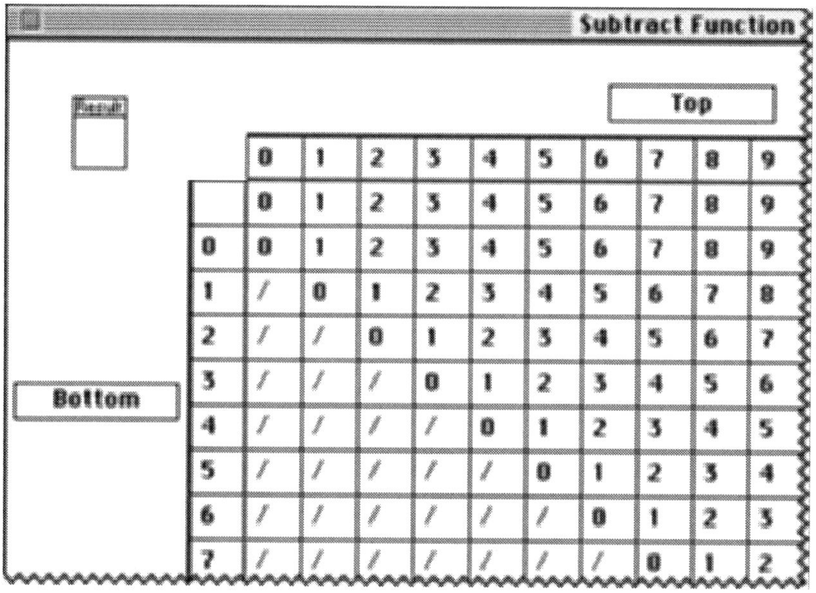

Figure 3. The Subtract Knowledge Function.

This method of creating new working memory elements—grouping items in the interface or creating tables of values—is general to any domain. Since almost all working memory elements correspond to things a person can point to (or at least has an easy–to–generate representation that could be pointed to), having a visual method of placing and creating WMEs should be natural and easy–to–do in any domain.

2.3. Demonstrating Productions

With all the necessary working memory elements constructed, the author is now ready to demonstrate the skill to be tutored, and have Demonstr8 induce the underlying production rules. First, however, the author will want to create a problem within the student's interface to be solved. The author can drag the predefined numbers from the Working Memory list and drop them onto the cells that represent the problem. The cells will then display those numbers. Alternatively, the author can use one of the options under the Author menu, Define Problem Generator. Selecting this option displays a dialog that lists all the cells in the student interface. The author can indicate which cells should contain a number, and what range that number should fall. In such a way, the author can prohibit, if desired, the system from generating problems that would involve borrowing. While the description to follow is specific to demonstrating the productions needed for subtraction, the general approach (essentially presenting the system with before and after shots and having it infer the underlying action) can be applied to almost any domain, and is the basic way ACT–R's analogy mechanism works.

Once the problem is in place, the author can begin to solve the problem. To indicate to the system that it should now start recording what the author is doing, the author checks a box marked "Recording" at the bottom of the Production List. The system will now take note and will attempt to induce the productions behind the author's actions, recording the results within the currently highlighted production in the Production List.

Two ways exist for the author to define a production using Demonstr8. The first is to interact directly with the Knowledge Functions. With the proper Knowledge Function on the screen, the author can drag and drop the items of interest from the problem displayed in the student's interface onto the table, and then drag the function's result onto the proper cell in the problem. Dragging and dropping a result from a Knowledge Function onto the student interface indicates a student action, and the system constructs a production based on the actions of the author from the creation of the last production (or the start of recording) to the use of some function's result. Having the author define the production in this way directly specifies to Demonstr8 the relevant WMEs and Knowledge Function needed to construct the production.

The other method that Demonstr8 has for creating productions is much more powerful and flexible, and is based on ACT–R's analogy mechanism. The author enters a value directly into a cell. When that happens, the system attempts to induce why the author entered that value into that cell. In trying to induce the production, Demonstr8 has available its Knowledge Functions and the Working Memory Elements which the author defined. For example, in the present case the author has arranged three cells into a column of numbers, and has created the appropriate WMEs. The top two cells on the right have numbers in them (say a "7" with a "2" below). The author indicates that the bottom–most cell should have a "5" in it. Since these three cells have been arranged in working memory as a column, the system has access to the "7" and "2" in order to figure out where the "5" comes from (i.e., this cell that should contain a "5" is part of this column, and so the other cells of this column may contain useful information; this column is also part of this problem, and if necessary, the system may reason about that as well). By using the "7" and "2" in various combinations with the available Knowledge Functions in order to figure out the appearance of the "5," it will find that a "7" and a "2" with the Subtract Function will produce a "5." In such a way, the system has induced a rule that the Top number of a column and the Bottom number of a column can be used to produce the Answer of that column. If the indicated number (the "5" in the above example) could have come about from multiple ways (e.g., by using different Knowledge Functions with the WMEs that are related in some way to the "5"), the system displays a Discrimination Dialog, asking the author to pick the proper interpretation of the action.

After the system has either gone through the above process, or the author has chosen to interact directly with the Knowledge Functions, a dialog box similar to the one displayed in Figure 4 appears. Using this dialog, the author can fine–tune the production that was just created. If the author used the second method of production creation, probably very little, if any, fine–tuning will be needed, since the system has had to infer much more about the production than it would if the first method had been used. Specifically, using the first method, the system would not know that the representation of column needs to be invoked in order to properly use this rule (i.e., what was important about putting the "5" in that cell was because that cells containing a "7" and a "2" were also part of that column).

2.3.1. Condition and Action

The dialog box in Figure 4 has three parts, accessed by the radio buttons in the upper right. These parts appear in the thick rectangle that takes up most of the dialog, and parts that have not been accessed are italicized. The production's name appears in the upper left, and can be edited easily. The first part that comes up, and the one displayed in the figure, is the part that actually shows the form of the production that has been induced. This is the way the dialog would look if the act of entering a "5" after the option–click had been done, as discussed above. Many of the pop–up menus are a consequence of how the working memory elements were initially created. While it may look complicated, the interpretation is easy, and as previously stated, the author will probably not have to make many, if any, changes.

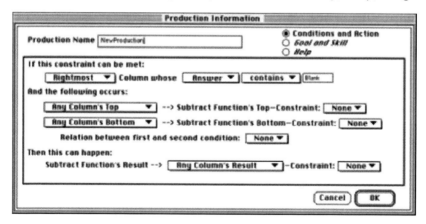

Figure 4. Fine–tuning a production.

The dialog as shown in Figure 4 is the correctly specified production, and only two related changes had to be made from the default (which are mentioned at the end of this subsection).

Let us first consider the lines which follow the statement "And the following occurs:" in the middle part of the dialog. This is the production's condition statement. The way this condition should be thought of is, "If the top and bottom number of a column is used with the Subtract Function..." The menu options for the pop–up menu currently set to "Any Column's Top" contains the full container hierarchy of how to refer to the top–most cell of that column (e.g., Cell1 —> Any Cell —> Column1's Top —> Any Column's Top), and one can generalize the production to any of those levels. This refers to the cell that contained the "7" in the problem. Since the Column1 working memory element needed to be invoked in order to access this "7" (because the "5" is in the same column), the pop–up menu is automatically set to a one higher level of generality (just as a rule of thumb, which turns out to be correct in most instances in the arithmetic domain). The arrow can be translated as "is placed on," and then after it appears the Knowledge Function which was used. The pop–up menu set to "None" contains a list of comparison functions (e.g., "<," "=," ">=," "contains," etc.). When one of these comparison functions is selected, a box appears to the right of the pop–up. A value can then be entered into the box in order to place a constraint on the possible values which whatever cell is indicated can have. For example, you may want one action to occur when borrowing from a zero occurs and another action to occur when borrowing from a non–zero. In the first case, you can set the pop–up to "=" and put a "0" in the box that appears.

The second line, which starts "Any Column's Bottom" has the same interpretation, and came about the same way as the first line. The line below it, which starts off "Relation between first and second condition:" and ends with a pop–up menu gives the author the opportunity to input a constraint (the pop–up contains a list of comparison operators) between whatever the values the first and second conditions are instantiated as. For example, in multi–column subtraction with borrow, one rule may apply when the top number is equal to or greater than the bottom, and a different would apply when the bottom number is bigger. That relation can be specified with this pop–up.

Demonstr8 is currently limited to having only two of these conditions, primarily because the Knowledge Functions are limited to two dimensions. While this may seem a detriment (though it would scale up easily—the ACT–R analogy mechanism can create arbitrarily complex productions, if needed and correctly specified), there is a movement within the ACT–R community to create simpler productions, those in which only one, or at most two, memory retrievals are performed. Larger productions are harder to understand and debug, and given the purpose of this tool (allowing non–programmers and non–cognitive scientists to create ITSs), forcing an upper limit on the complexity of the authored productions is a desirable attribute.

The line after the phrase, "Then this can happen:" is the production's action, and is arrived at much the same way was as both of the conditions. In this particular instance, it can be thought of as "...then the result from the Subtract Function can be placed in the column's result cell." Constraints can also be placed on the values that this result can have. Again, Demonstr8 is limited to creating productions with only one action. This action corresponds to a change being made within the tutor's interface. If multiple actions are possible at any one point in solving a problem (e.g., different strategies can be followed), then multiple productions which correspond to each of the individual actions will need to be authored.

Given just the above information (what is specified under "And the following occurs" and "Then this can happen"), the system does not know which column is being referenced. The information under "If this constraint can be met:" gives this information. This roughly corresponds to setting the goal of the production (i.e., it's "range of influence"). Since the system has induced that columns are important for this production, it continues up the WME container hierarchy looking for a slot value that contains a list of columns. The Problem WME has such a list, and this is the list it will use. (If the author was not having Demonstr8 induce the rules, he or she could drag the WME that contains such a list and drop it in the box below where it says, "If this constraint can be met:" and the system will generate the line shown.) In the last section it was mentioned that Demonstr8 has knowledge about how to reason with lists—what it means to be rightmost or left of an item in a list. The first pop–up menu under "If this constraint can be met:" contains such relations. The word after the pop–up is the Classname of interest (in this case, Column). The second pop–up is a list of the slot names associate with the Classname of interest (Top, Bottom, and Answer for the present example). The third pop–up of comparison operators and its accompanying text box operate like they do in the other lines. The interpretation given to this line in Figure 4, which has been set to the right selections, would be, "This production will match to: The rightmost column whose answer property contains a blank." (The default is to set the first pop–up to 'rightmost,' since arithmetic strategies usually go from right to left, the second pop–up to the first item in the list—Top, in this case—and to leave the box empty. This is where the two changes had to be made from the default assumptions—change Top to Answer, and put Blank in the box). Wherever "Any Column" appears in the following "If" and "Then" parts of the parts of the production, it will take on the value of that column.

2.3.2. Goal and Skill

When the Goal and Skill radio button is selected, the main part of the Production Dialog changes to two simple sections. The top section contains two checkboxes and one text box and states what the topmost goal of the system currently is (Demonstr8 defaults to "Do Arithmetic" as the topmost goal). As the author demonstrates the actions that make up a skill, subgoals may have to be set and satisfied. The top checkbox states: "I am now going to do this:" and the text box follows. When the author is going to start some specialized procedure, like borrowing in subtraction, after the just–specified action, a subgoal may need to be set. This indicates to the system to place the indicated subgoal on top of the goalstack, and subsequent productions will be in service to that subgoal. Once the author has demonstrated an action that accomplishes this subgoal, the second checkbox can be checked, which states, "I have completed this subgoal." This will remove the topmost goal from the goalstack. Subgoaling and keeping a goalstack is necessary for when the same action occurs in different contexts (e.g., crossing out a number to add ten to it versus crossing out a number to decrement it). A current research aim is the automatic detection of subgoals and subgoal completion.

The second part of the dialog allows the author to indicate which skill this production supports. As mentioned in the Introduction, one of the features of the

ACT Tutors is the Skillometer, a list of skills that are being taught and the probabilities that the skills are in a learned state. This tool supports such a Skillometer. The author can indicate if the current production supports a skill that has already been identified (via a pop–up menu listing skills previous productions have supported), or if this production supports a new skill (by typing the skill's name in a text box).

2.3.3. Help

Selecting the last radio button allows the author to enter help text specific to the current production. When selected, the main part of the dialog will display four text boxes, labeled Levels 1 through 4. Each level corresponds to a more specific hint that the tutor will provide when the student asks for help repeatedly at the same spot (the ACT Tutors generally provides three levels of help). The help text can contain variables in order to provide context–sensitive help. The values of the variables will either be a specific number (when the variable refers to a slot name whose value contains a cell) or the text of a WME's help tag (when the variable refers to a specific WME). The variable names are preceded by an equal sign, and the actual name must refer to a name from the Conditions and Action part of the dialog (these names are listed at the bottom of the Help part to aid the author). In the current instance, =top, =bottom, =answer, and =column are valid variable names, generated by Demonstr8 based on the slot names of the appropriate classnames. The value of the first three would be the value of a cell, and the value of =column would be its help tag text. An example of explicit help message would be, "You must subtract =bottom from =top in the =column column," which might be instantiated as "You must subtract 2 from 7 in the ones column," if a student asked for help.

While the preceding section has been long, the author has had to perform very few actions in demonstrating this production. The author had to simply do the action, and then largely confirm that the induced production looked correct, makring very few edits. The actions were:

- Entering "5" into a worksheet cell
- Completing the resulting production dialog box:
- In the Condition and Actions part, changing the second pop–up menu to read "Answer" and dragging "Blank" from the WMEs window to the box in the first line
- In the Goal and Skills part, typing a new skill name ("Subtract") in the bottom box
- In the Help part, typing in the help text

The author continues demonstrating how the problem should be solved, specifying the productions as needed. For a subtraction tutor that does not handle borrowing, the production just specified is sufficient for the task. For subtraction with borrow, six productions are needed. An easy way exists to specify when the problem is solved. One could imagine writing a specific Done production (realizing when a problem is solved is a skill that students need to learn), but for most problems in the domain of arithmetic, problems are done with then leftmost cell is filled. The system has an implicit Done production, whose condition is satisfied when that cell is filled (the author indicates that cell by selecting it and then choosing a menu command). Once the productions and the Done Cell have been specified, the author can have the system Auto–Solve a problem by simply generating a new problem and selecting "Auto–Solve" from the Author Menu. The system will work through the problem, filling in the appropriate cells as it goes along. This provides the author an opportunity to see if the specified productions are sufficient for the desired curriculum. If a mistake is encountered, the author can fine–tune the faulty production (double–clicking on a production's name will bring up the Production Dialog), or it may be necessary to record additional actions if they were not demonstrated. In general, knowing when enough example solutions have been demonstrated is difficult, particularly as the domain gets more complex. For those complex domains, the best recourse is to simply test the tutor in the real world and see where the deficiencies lie. When some are found, the missing productions can easily be demonstrated and added to the system.

The preceding description of how to create productions could also apply to the creation of what are termed "buggy" productions as well (Brown & Burton, 1978). In the course learning a domain, a student may develop a misconception about a particular step in the problem solving process. These misconceptions are "buggy" pieces of knowledge that the student has. There is a set of common misconceptions for any domain, and the author may want to target instruction for when a student apparently possesses one of these misconceptions. A common misconception in subtraction is that one always takes the larger number from the smaller, even if the larger one is on bottom (thereby eliminating the need for borrowing). While Demonstr8 does not currently have this feature (though having buggy productions with specific remediation is a feature of the ACT Tutors), one could easily imagine a menu toggle indicating that the next action that the author is going to demonstrate is a buggy production (however many there might need to be for a domain), and so should not be considered a correct step. When the student is using the tutor, if he or she performs one of the buggy productions the proper help text could be displayed.

2.4. Using the Tutor

Once the author is satisfied with the productions that have demonstrated, the system can be put into "Student Mode" by selecting that option from the Author Menu. The screen will then appear as in Figure 5. The authoring windows have disappeared, and the Author Menu is replaced with the Student Menu, which has three options: Help, Done, and New Problem. The Student Interface has been modified to be more presentable to a student, and two windows have been created: Skillometer, which contains a list of all the skills the author specified, and the Student Palette, which contains the numbers 0 – 18 and a slash. Next to each skill in the Skillometer is a bar graph indicating the probability that the skill is in the learned state. The numbers and slash of the Student Palette can be dragged from the palette and dropped onto the problem in the appropriate (or not appropriate) places. In operation, this tutor behaves essentially like one of the ACT Tutors. The student can ask for help at any time, and the tutor will respond with an appropriate, context–sensitive help message. When the student performs an action, the tutor will check that action against the productions specified by the author. If the action is correct, the appropriate skill is incremented. If incorrect, the action is not allowed and the appropriate skill decremented. Once all of the skills have more than a 95%

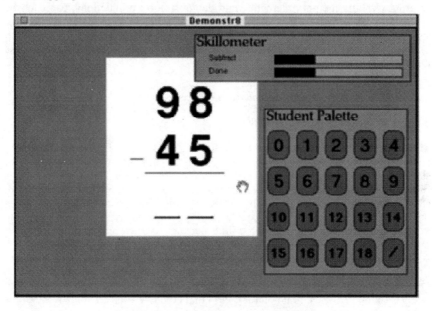

Figure 5. The finished tutor's interface.

chance being in the learned state, a dialog box appears congratulating the student on mastering the tutored domain. While the domain is simple and the model–tracing perhaps straight–forward here, this example begins to show the power of the approach. With the addition of bug rules, coupled with the generative help messages that can be authored, this simple tutor rises above the level of drill and practice software that merely indicates right and wrong answers. The simple cognitive model behaves like cognitive models in more sophisticated tutors.

2.5. Summary

This section has described how Demonstr8 can be used to create a simple model–tracing tutor for multi–column subtraction without borrowing. The total time the author spent creating the tutor was less than 10 minutes. To extend the tutor to problems with borrowing, the author would need to demonstrate 5 more productions, embodied in a single example, which would add no more than 10 minutes to the tutor creation time. Creation of the tutor involved using a set of MacDraw–like tools to design the student interface, defining working memory elements through a simple–to–use dialog, and finally demonstrating the underlying rules of the domain by working with the student's interface, with only minor additions by the author.

3. GENERAL DISCUSSION

The three parts of creating a tutor in Demonstr8, designing the student interface, creating working memory elements, and demonstrating productions, can each be evaluated with respect to two questions: 1) How easy is it to do in the current system, and 2) How general is the technique? The following sections consider each of these parts and the questions in turn, followed by a discussion of making these three parts separate tools.

3.1. General Principles within Demonstr8

3.1.1. Designing the student interface

The tools in Demonstr8 to design the interface the student will use are extremely simple (essentially containing widgets only for drawing lines and cells), but they are sufficient to create any kind of arithmetic interface. Any person familiar with using a computer drawing package could create a student interface within Demonstr8. (Remember, the alternative in the TDK would be to code LISP statements describing lines and cells—a task doable only by programmers.) Being able to create a student interface using a drawing–like package creates a situation in which designing the interface is not only easy to do, but it is also quite general. A sophisticated interface can be easily created using such methods. Several off–the–shelf, commercial packages (e.g., Apple's Hypercard or Macromedia's Director programs) allow designers to easily create interfaces with sophisticated widgets (pop–up menus, radio buttons, etc.) that could be used as student interfaces in tutors. Some even allow for plug–in widgets, so that a programmer could create something like the cell tool, which an educator could then have available in designing a tutor.

However, designing an interface that maximizes the time spent by the student in learning the domain, and not in learning the interface, is not trivial. There are human–computer interface design issues that need to be taken into consideration, but that the average educator could not be expected to have. There are a few courses of action that could be taken. First, packages of plain interfaces could be made available, and the domain experts could modify them to suit their needs. Lewis, Milson and Anderson (1987) described an algebra tutor that allowed teachers to slightly modify the interface and the tutoring method (though no provision was made for the teachers to actually augment the underlying production rules). Alternatively, the application used by the educator to create the interface could offer suggestions about the interface (e.g., such as SimQuest's author advice, van Joolingen & de Jong, this volume), or maybe even not allow some interface choices. Finally, either an interface designer could work with the educator in creating the interface, or perhaps the educator could be given some instruction beforehand in proper interface construction.

3.1.2. Creating working memory elements

This is arguably the most important step in creating a tutor using Demonstr8, since the working memory elements as defined by the author serve as a major determiner the format of the resulting productions. It is important to use the right representation for the WMEs, so that the induction method can successfully produce the right productions. As realized within Demonstr8, this process isn't much more difficult than using a drawing package like discussed above, but to do it correctly still requires more knowledge of cognitive science and production systems than a typical educator would have. To take the example of creating the subtraction tutor, why was it important that each column be identified and segmented into the three cells (Top, Bottom, and Answer)? Why did those columns need to be grouped into a problem? The answer to both questions is so that productions could be created that would sufficiently solve the problem. The realization that such WMEs would be needed comes from introspection as to how the problem is segmented in order to solve it, as well as experience in designing such systems. It may also come from listening to people solve such problems, and finding out what sorts of things they mention in the course of the solving. To make this task doable by educators, some instruction in designing WMEs may inevitably have to be given. However, things could be done within the tool to make this process easier, such as having it ask questions or make intelligent guesses as to the correct way of parsing the interface as drawn. Also, the method itself could be made easier, perhaps by doing away with the dialog and having the author construct and group the WMEs on the interface itself.

In terms of the generality of this method of designing WMEs, that of visually defining them as opposed to typing out statements in a LISP document, it can be quite general. Most WMEs represent things that can be pointed to, like a column of numbers or the symbols that make up an algebraic equation. That being the case, they can be selected, grouped, and named, and their parts can be separably identified. For WMEs that have no on–screen counterpart, perhaps a representation can be created to allow them to be done so. In Demonstr8, the addition and subtraction facts are represented as tables, and these tables can be easily created and modified. A table format can perhaps represent many such abstract WMEs. For WMEs that represent goals and other declarative information without an easily represented form, the best representation may be something akin to the currently used list form in the TDK.

3.1.3. Demonstrating Productions

Once an adequate set of WMEs have been defined, actually generating the productions is relatively easy within ACT–R's analogy mechanism. However, these productions are obviously the most important thing in creating a model–tracing tutor . The author merely has to perform the task, and for each intended student action, make sure that the created production is at the right level of specificity, assign it to a skill, and write help text for it. With Demonstr8 inducing the structure of the production (i.e., what WMEs are being referred to), little or no fine–tuning of these productions should be needed, though the author will need some training in understanding the induced production, in case a slight modification is needed. Creating a production without the induction method (as in the tool described in Blessing, 1995) is moderately difficult and requires an adequate understanding of production systems. Also, if the skill requires subgoaling, those have to be indicated at this point as well. Similar to WME creation, instruction on when to use subgoals may have to be given to the educator –author as well.

Given that the induction method employed by Demonstr8 is based on the analogy mechanism of ACT–R, it should be as general as that mechanism is. As stated in the Introduction, one of the strong claims of the ACT–R theory is that all productions are created by this mechanism, based on the contents of declarative memory (i.e., existing WMEs). By embodying such a mechanism within a tool like Demonstr8, a strict test of that claim can be made.

3.2. Component Architectures

As described, Demonstr8 is an all–inclusive system. It contains the components necessary to design the student interface, create working memory elements, demonstrate the productions, and tutor the student. However, other researchers have argued for a component–system approach to tutor design (e.g., Ritter & Koedinger, 1995). The pieces of Demonstr8 are amenable to such a view.

In a component architecture system, the different parts are actually separate applications that communicate by sending messages back and forth (e.g., by using AppleEvents on a Macintosh). This allows for the student interface to actually be a piece of off–the–shelf software like Microsoft Excel, which would report the student's interface actions to a tutoring agent (a separate application, designed apart from Excel, and usable in the context of other spreadsheet applications). This agent then judges the correctness of the student's actions, which it would then report back to Excel.

Applying such a model to Demonstr8, the component that creates the student's interface could be anything—something simple like what exists now in Demonstr8, a program like Macromedia's Director, or some other off–the–shelf solution. The only restriction is that the component must be able to tell other applications what the student is doing (in AppleEvents nomenclature, be recordable), and also other applications must be able to tell it what to do (i.e., be scriptable) and be able to request information from it, so that when the student is using the interface, the interface can be updated correctly if the student makes a mistake.

A second tool, essentially the guts of Demonstr8, would be needed that aided the author in creating WMEs and productions. This tool would be able to parse the student interface in order to create WMEs, and also allow the author to create higher–order WMEs (e.g., columns for multi–column subtraction) by grouping the existing WMEs in the interface. Furthermore, this tool would also need to support the creation of more abstract WMEs, such as addition and subtraction facts, and any goal structures needed to solve the problems. Once those are in place, the author could create the productions by putting the interface application in "before" and "after" states (in the course of solving an actual problem), and the tool would induce the production needed to get from the "before" state to the "after" state. The output of the tool would be a set of productions usable by a tutoring agent in a component architecture system.

3.3. Beyond Demonstr8

With the current tool only arithmetic tutors can be created. What about other domains? I have argued that the techniques embodied within Demonstr8 are usable to design other systems with which other tutors could be created. This section considers the form of those other systems could take in different domains.

The main requirement for a tool like Demonstr8 to work is that successive states in the problem solving process be concretely represented. Let us consider what this means in algebra—a domain similar to arithmetic, but different and complex enough to be worthwhile creating another authoring tool for. Within algebra, representing the successive states of the problem solution is quite natural. An author should be able to demonstrate the following problem:

$$3x + 5 = 14$$
$$3x = 9$$
$$x = 3$$

and have the system infer the productions needed to solve such problems (i.e., first subtracting from both sides and then dividing by the coefficient in order to solve for x). Neves (1978) actually developed a system, called Alex, for doing just this, and in a manner similar to Demonstr8. Neves' concern in constructing Alex was how a system could learn from textbook examples, similar in most respects to the main concern of Demonstr8. Alex implemented Newell and Simon's (1972) GPS approach to problem solving. It had available knowledge of simple arithmetic, and when given an example like the one above, could infer the rules behind it by seeing what had changed between pairs of lines in the example (i.e., what has been removed or transformed between the left and right sides of the equation).

Using manipulations like those described in creating the subtraction tutor, one could imagine the author indicating to the system the general form of equations by placing cells that could contain numbers, variables, or operators onto the worksheet, and then grouping those cells into terms, the terms into sides, and the sides into an equation. Having created the necessary working memory types and elements, the author could demonstrate how the problems should be solved by dragging and dropping those elements to the next line on the worksheet. In going from Line 1 to Line 2 in the example presented above, the 3x stays the same on the left–hand side, and the 5 and the 14 get combined (the result of applying a Knowledge Function) to generate the 9. Likewise, in getting the solution, the x stays on the left–hand side, but the 3 and 9 are used to generate the answer, 3.

However, not all domains are equally amenable to having tutors constructed in them using Demonstr8–like tools. Successful ACT Tutors have been built for algebra word problem solving and algebra equation solving, and, as shown above, versions of these tutors could be authored using programming by demonstration methods. Even the tutors for programming languages could be demonstrable (Neves had Alex learn LISP by example). However, programming a geometry proof tutor (Koedinger & Anderson, 1993b; Anderson, Boyle, & Yost, 1985) by demonstration may not be straight–forward. These tutors taught how to do geometry proofs, and the student could work on the proof either forwards or backwards, by applying the requisite theorems and axioms necessary to do the proof. The problem in trying to induce the productions necessary lies in the fact that there is much knowledge between successive states of the problem solving process that is not directly observable in the interface—much of the reasoning behind why certain theorems were applied when is not represented in the interface, but rather is inside the solver's head (Koedinger & Anderson, 1989). This indicates that it may be necessary in some domains to create the production rule set in an interface different than that the student will use—perhaps one that has been augmented to indicate the overall plan that is being implemented to solve the current problem.

In general, the challenge in using the techniques discussed in this paper to create an authoring tool lies in finding the correct representations to use. For arithmetic the challenge was perhaps simpler than it would be for other tasks, but above I have argued that it would be just as straight–forward for some (algebra and even programming) and more difficult for others (geometry). For any task, the difficulty in applying these techniques arises when whatever is implicit in performing the task must be made explicit. In Demonstr8 this was satisfied by the use of Knowledge Functions, and I believe these would generalize to many domains. However, it will only be constructing authoring tools for other domains that we will be able to see what techniques truly are general and which are specific for a particular task.

The next generation of a Demonstr8-like system is being developed by Koedinger, Aleven, and Heffernan (2003). It shares many features with Demonstr8, such as providing a GUI with which to construct the student interface and the way in which the author creates the cognitive model by constructing the successive states of the problem solving process. The main backbone is still the TDK, but it does provide assistance in writing the wmes and productions.

4. LESSONS LEARNED

The main contribution of Demonstr8 to the field of ITS authoring tools is its application of ACT–R's analogy mechanism. This analogy mechanism provides a general way in which the productions of a model–tracing ITS, the backbone of such an ITS, could be authored. Moreover, the way in which these productions are authored, essentially by having the tool "look over the shoulder" of the author and inducing the productions, opens up this part of the authoring process to domain experts, not just cognitive scientists. In essence, all authors have to do to create these productions is to do what they would do anyway—solve problems within a standard interface. The tool then uses ACT–R's analogy mechanism to create the set of productions (the cognitive model for the task), which may require, hopefully very little, fine–tuning. In order to test the completeness and correctness of the authored production system, the tool can be placed in "Auto–Solve" mode, whereby the author can observe the tutor solving novel problems. This again is a straight–forward skill doable by domain experts and not just cognitive scientists.

I have argued that this method is a general way to author model–tracing tutors. Demonstr8, however, comes with a fair amount of domain knowledge concerning arithmetic. While this domain knowledge is authorable using the current system, design decisions will need to be made regarding who the true target audience is (as is true for any of the systems discussed in this book), and what support is necessary for that audience. For even a determined classroom teacher, requiring them to learn techniques above and beyond their domain of expertise will serve as a barrier to wider dissemination of the tool. As Bell (this volume) argues with regards to IDLE–Tool, the kind of teacher who would use such a tool still probably requires a high level of support. While making such choices may limit the generality of any tool created on these principles, the level of training needed in order to use the tool will decrease. Of course, if one relaxes the constraint on the level of the author, then the tool can be more general.

As described in this chapter, Demonstr8 itself provides everything the author needs to create an arithmetic tutor—a way to construct the interface, a way to define the necessary declarative knowledge, and the part that induces the rules as the author solves problems (and provides a run–time engine for the student as well). As discussed above, however, using another tool to construct the interface may be preferable. Or, perhaps using an interface that has already been created (e.g., Excel) would be better. In a like manner, other tools may also be preferable for defining the declarative knowledge. Many tools described in this volume have methods to collect and organize such knowledge. All that is needed is a way to parse the environment into meaningful chunks, and a way to describe other useful declarative information that exists outside of the environment (e.g., subtraction facts). This is the information that the ACT–R analogy mechanism takes as input to induce productions. This chapter describes one method to do this, one quite amenable to ACT–R's analogy mechanism, but other ways exist as well. As stated above, what Demonstr8 brings to the table is the ability to take this description of knowledge, observe an author acting on the environment (interface), and induce the productions that underlie those actions.

Evaluation

Currently, Demonstr8 is a prototype system. Only members of the lab have used it. As has been mentioned, authoring any sort of arithmetic tutor with it takes a very short amount of time—much less than an hour (but, keep in mind that these are Ph.D. cognitive scientists using it). However, a tutor like the ones authored have been deployed in second grade classrooms and have provided over five hours of instruction (Blessing & Gregoire, unpublished)—potentially a very healthy return on the investment in time to develop the tutor.

An obvious evaluation of the current tool would be to have a small group of teachers attempt to author an arithmetic tutor, and see what difficulties are encountered. In general, though, future goals of evaluation are twofold: 1) to see how general this method is, and 2) to compare the fidelity of tutors authored using this method versus tutors that were more traditionally authored (in a manner similar to Shute, this volume). The reason for the first evaluation goal should be obvious—if this method is to succeed, it needs to be applicable to a variety of domains. The second evaluation goal is to ensure that tutors constructed using this method are as instructionally effective as their more labor–intensive cousins. It could be the case that authoring by demonstration does not provide the range of expression as allowed by programmatically creating a tutor, and that this hurts its fidelity. If this does happen, then the extra effort required to program a tutor may be called for if it results in better student learning.

5. CONCLUSION

This paper has described a tool which makes the creation of model–tracing tutors much easier than currently realized (e.g., by the Tutor Development Kit). The goal of the research is to empower any domain expert, even an educator in a classroom, to be able to create an intelligent tutor in the domain in which they are expert. The current tool, Demonstr8, falls somewhat short of that goal, since some training is still required, but contains some techniques, such as using ACT–R's analogy mechanism to induce the production rules, that places us closer to that ideal.

NOTES

[1] The ACT Tutors do not use ACT–R, the most recent version of Anderson's ACT Theory. The TDK, and most of the ACT Tutors, were created before ACT–R. They do share a common heritage.

6. REFERENCES

Anderson, J. R. (1992). Intelligent tutoring and high school mathematics. In C. Fasson, G. Gauthier, & G. I. McCalla (Eds.). *Proceedings of the Second International Conference on Intelligent Tutoring Systems.* Spring–Verlag: Berlin, Germany.
Anderson, J. R. (1993). *Rules of the Mind.* Hillsdale, NJ: Lawrence Erlbaum Associates.
Anderson, J. R., Boyle, C. F., Corbett, A. T., & Lewis, M. W. (1990). Cognitive modelling and intelligent tutoring. *Artificial Intelligence, 42,* 7–49.
Anderson, J. R., Boyle, C. F., & Yost, G. (1985). The geometry tutor. In *Proceedings of the International Joint Conference on Artificial Intelligence—85.* Los Angeles: IJCAI.
Anderson, J. R., Conrad, F. G., & Corbett, A. T. (1989). Skill acquisition and the LISP Tutor. *Cognitive Science, 13,* 467–506.
Anderson, J. R., Corbett, A. T., Koedinger, K. R., & Pelletier, R. (1995). The cognitive tutors: lessons learned. Journal of the Learning Sciences, Vol. 4(2), 167–207.
Anderson, J. R., & Pelletier, R. (1991). A development system for model–tracing tutors. In *Proceedings of the International Conference of the Learning Sciences* (pp. 1–8). Evanston, IL.
Blessing, S. B. (1995). ITS authoring tools: The next generation. In J. Greer (Ed.), *Proceedings of AI–ED 95–7th World Conference on Artificial Intelligence and Education* (p. 567). Charlottesville, VA: Association for the Advancement of Computing in Education.
Blessing, S. B., & Gregoire, M. (1997). *A pen–based intelligent tutor for subtraction.* Unpublished manuscript.
Brown, J. S., & Burton, R. (1978). Diagnostic models for procedural bugs in basic mathematical skills. *Cognitive Science, 2,* 155–192.
Corbett, A. T., & Anderson, J. R. (1990). The effect of feedback control on learning to program with the LISP tutor. In *Proceedings of the Twelfth Annual Conference of the Cognitive Science Society.* Hillsdale, NJ: Lawrence Erlbaum Associates.
Cypher, A. (1993). *Watch What I Do: Programming by Demonstration.* MIT Press, Cambridge, MA.
Koedinger, K. R. & Anderson, J. R. (1989). Perceptual chunks in gemoetry problem solving: A challenge to theories of skill acquisition. In *Proceedings of the Eleventh Annual Conference of the Cognitive Science Society.* Hillsdale, NJ: Lawrence Erlbaum Associates.
Koedinger, K. R., & Anderson, J. R. (1993a). Effective use of intelligent software in high school math classrooms. In *Proceedings of the World Conference on Artificial Intelligence in Education,* 1993. Charlottesville, VA: AACE.
Koedinger, K. R. & Anderson, J. R. (1993b). Reifying implicit planning in geometry: Guidelines for model–based intelligent tutoring system design. In S.P. Lajoie and S.J. Derry (Eds.) *Computers as Cognitive Tools.* Hillsdale, NJ: Lawrence Erlbaum Associates.
Koedinger, K. R., Aleven, V., & Heffernan, N. (2003). Toward a rapid development environment for Cognitive Tutors. Submitted to Artificial Intelligence in Education conference.
Koedinger, K. R., Anderson, J. R., Hadley, W. H. & Mark, M. A. (1997). Intelligent tutoring goes to school in the big city. *International Journal of Artificial Intelligence in Education, 8,* 30-43

Lewis, M. W., Milson, R., & Anderson, J. R. (1987). The Teacher's Apprentice: Designing an intelligent authoring system for high school mathematics. In G.P. Kearsley (Ed.) *Artificial Intelligence and Instruction: Applications and Methods* (pp. 269–301). Addison–Wesley Publishing Company: Reading, MA.

Murray, T. (1999). Authoring Intelligent Tutoring Systems: Analysis of the state of the art. *International Journal of Artificial Intelligence in Education.* Vol. 10(1), pp. 98-129.

Myers, B. A., McDaniel, R. G., & Kosbie, D. S. (1993). Marquise: Creating Complete User Interfaces by Demonstration. In *Proceedings of INTERCHI '93: Human Factors in Computing Systems*, April 24–29, 1993.

Nardi, B. A. (1993). *A small matter of programming: Perspectives on end–user computing.* Cambridge, MA: MIT Press.

Neves, D. M. (1978). A computer program that learns algebraic procedures by examining examples and by working test problems in a textbook. *Proceedings of the Second National Conference of the Canadian Society for Computational Studies of Intelligence.*

Newell, A., & Simon, H. A. (1972). *Human problem solving.* Englewood Cliffs, NJ: Prentice–Hall.

Ritter, S., & Koedinger, K. R. (1995). Towards lightweight tutoring agents. In J. Greer (Ed.), *Proceedings of AI–ED 95–7th World Conference on Artificial Intelligence and Education* (p. 567). Charlottesville, VA: Association for the Advancement of Computing in Education.

Salvucci, D. D., & Anderson, J. R. (1998). Analogy. In J. R. Andersion & C. Lebiere (Eds.), *The Atomic Components of Thought* (pp. 343–383). Mahwah, NJ: Erlbaum.

Smith, D. C., Cypher, A., & Spohrer, J. (1994). KidSim: Programming agents without a programming language. *Communications of the ACM, 37*(7), 55–67.

Woolf, B.P. & Cunningham, P.A. (1987) Multiple knowledge sources in intelligent teaching systems. *IEEE Expert*, Summer 1987.

ACKNOWLEDGEMENTS

The work presented in this paper is based upon work supported by the National Science Foundation and the Advanced Research Projects Agency under Cooperative Agreement No. CDA–940860. I would like to thank Marsha Lovett, Steven Ritter, and three anonymous reviewers for their comments on earlier drafts of this paper, and also John Anderson and Jim Spohrer for their help and suggestions with this work.

DOUGLAS TOWNE

Chapter 5

AUTOMATED KNOWLEDGE ACQUISITION FOR INTELLIGENT SUPPORT OF DIAGNOSTIC REASONING

Abstract. An intelligent simulation-based system for presenting and supporting diagnostic exercises can resolve many of the constraints that currently limit the value of troubleshooting practice in the training setting. By focusing on highly contextualized and domain-specific reasoning issues rather than upon general troubleshooting principles, such a system can reveal gaps in system understanding and can address shortcomings in applied diagnostic reasoning. Moreover, by providing expert guidance in choosing and interpreting tests, such a system can essentially eliminate the impasses that so often typify troubleshooting exercises.

Authoring such systems via conventional expert systems has proven to be exceedingly expensive. A more robust approach automatically inspects a domain-specific model of the target system to produce fault effect information capable of supporting diagnostic reasoning and hence intelligent support of diagnostic practice. Because the diagnostic reasoning processes are general rather than domain specific, only the model of the target system must be developed to support this process. The authoring process involves 1) representing the behaviors of the operational units of a system in terms of inputs received from functionally adjacent elements, 2) representing controls and indicators graphically, so that the learner may operate and inspect them during practice problems, and 3) invoking an automated function that generates fault effect information by executing the device simulation.

1. INTRODUCTION

While there have been a number of intelligent tutoring systems (ITSs) that have demonstrated excellent instructional capabilities in the domain of fault diagnosis, the cost of authoring a tutor for a new target system increases dramatically with the complexity of that system. This is not to say that existing methods in diagnostic training systems have failed to achieve the instructional objectives their developers established, but rather that the current methodologies are proving to impose very high development costs in the face of increasing complexity in the diagnostic environment. As with all ITSs, therefore, those in the realm of fault diagnosis must be judged both by their ultimate instructional power and by the cost of authoring new applications. A brief examination of the existing methodologies will establish the problem.

The approaches that have been taken to author and deliver intelligent instruction in fault diagnosis tasks may be considered under two major categories: 1) knowledge engineering approaches and 2) model-based approaches.

1.1 Knowledge Engineering (KE) Approaches

Knowledge engineering (KE) approaches, such as Sherlock (Lesgold, Eggan, Katz, and Rao, 1992; Lajoie and Lesgold, 1992), capture and operate upon experts' strategic and tactical knowledge about diagnosing particular faults in a particular target system. In Sherlock, the underlying domain expertise is a hierarchy of sub goals, each representing a problem solving method for some problem area. Upon this structure, and a graphical simulation of the target system, computer-coached practice is supported.

While very impressive instructional dialogues can be authored and delivered via the KE approach, that result comes at an extremely high price. KE methodology requires specialized skills and time-consuming effort to acquire the rules that experts use in diagnosing specific systems. The developers face the daunting task of making explicit that which is often implicit and subconscious. One appeal of this approach is that the expert system, once acquired, represents both the diagnostic reasoning and the domain-specific system knowledge required to troubleshoot a system.

The workload upon the author increases dramatically, however, with increased system complexity, leading to very high costs and unknown reliability of the captured expertise. Furthermore, the captured strategic expertise is necessarily couched in some assumed maintenance environment, such as depot level, intermediate level, or flight line maintenance. Thus, the expert system must be reworked to accommodate a different maintenance environment or to respond to engineering modifications of the target system.

1.2 Model-based Approaches

Model-based approaches represent the target system via a computer model that informs an artificial diagnostic expert about the normal and abnormal behaviors of the target system. Unlike the KE approach, model-based approaches require both domain-specific functional information and some kind of domain-free expression of diagnostic reasoning expertise, or Artificial Diagnostic Intelligence (ADI). Typically, the learner operates upon a graphical representation of the target system, and the instructional functions are kept advised of the tests performed by the learner on that presentation. A great advantage to the model based approaches is that the ADI component can serve any device model that provides the necessary behavioral information. Thus, the device model serves both to inform the ADI functions and to provide the vehicle upon which the learner performs troubleshooting exercises.

The model-based approaches can be further differentiated by the manner in which the actual device is modeled. Existing approaches range from very superficial device models to deep models that represent the physical processes that govern the system's operation. These differences produce markedly different levels and types of diagnostic reasoning processes that can be conducted by the ITS as well is distinct implications for development. Three categories of device models will now be examined in order of increasing model depth: 1) signal-tracing models, 2) device simulation models, and 3) physical process models.

1.2.1 Signal–tracing Models

Systems such as MITT (Johnson, Duncan, and Hunt, 1988; Wiederholt, Norton, Johnson, and Browning, 1992) represent a particular device in terms of its normal (unfailed) connectivity. The basic elements of a MITT-type model are blocks, which may be functionally defined or physically defined, and inputs to and outputs of those blocks. Test outcomes are then interpreted in terms of the system units that are, or are not, connected to the observed indication in some way, i.e., a normal test outcome absolves the blocks that are 'upstream' from the observation, while an abnormal outcome implicates the predecessors as possibly faulty.

The signal-tracing model approach is certainly the easiest methodology to apply, for there is no requirement to express the functional operation of the system elements. Additionally, in the face of extremely complex target systems, the ITS author may elect to limit the level of detail reflected in the connectivity model, thereby keeping development cost well within reason. Moreover, the diagnostic reasoning is easily expressed in terms of system blocks implicated or exonerated from suspicion, based upon normal and abnormal symptoms observed along the connection paths of the model.

The fatal flaw of the approach is that its diagnostic inferences are based upon the assumption that fault effects propagate along the connections expressed in the static and fault-free connectivity representation. In the real world, however, this assumption is rarely true, since many faults propagate in directions not related to normal signal flow, while others change the very connectivity of the system itself.

This form of system representation can represent *normal* system operation in an instructionally useful manner, but lacking a behavioral model of the target system, it cannot reliably support diagnostic instruction.

1.2.2 Device Simulation Models

Systems such as ReAct (Towne, 2000) and IMTS (Towne and Munro, 1988; Towne, Munro, Pizzini, Surmon, and Wogulis, 1990) represent the target system via a connected composition of graphical objects, each of which carries rules stating how that object behaves normally and abnormally. The graphical objects correspond to physical entities within the target system, whether individual components or subassemblies of any size. Typically, the rules within an object are expressed in terms of the states or outputs of functionally adjacent objects. This system model can then be automatically interrogated under a wide range of modes and failure conditions to produce symptom information suitable for generating expert and highly contextualized interactions with the learner.

The graphical/behavioral device model therefore serves both as the medium upon which the learner practices troubleshooting and the vehicle for specifying the behavior of the device to the built-in diagnostic expert.

The serious weakness of simulation-based diagnostic trainers such as IMTS is that the quality of the diagnostic reasoning is highly dependent upon the completeness of the fault conditions represented. This is not to say that a great many faults must be provided as *exercises*, for a very modest pool of faults can expose the learner to a surprising wealth of diagnostic experiences. Similarly, minor gaps in simulating fault possibilities do not seriously impact test selection recommendations, since there is no need (and little chance) to generate optimal testing strategies. Rather, fault conditions that are not expressed within the device simulation ultimately reveal themselves in faulty interpretation of symptoms and imperfections in generated explanations about the wisdom of performing various candidate tests. These errors can impair the accuracy of the reasoning, leading to a significant and well-deserved loss of credibility of the training intelligence.

1.2.3 Physical Process Models

Physical process models represent a device or system via the underlying physical principles that govern its operation. For example, the processes might be chemical, biological, electronic, or thermodynamic. One such system, CyclePad (Forbus and Whalley, 1994), supports the learner in both analyzing a complex thermodynamic system and experimenting with design alternatives. Because the physical process being modeled is well defined and stable, the instruction can deal with a learner in qualitative terms as well as quantitative ones. Such models have the capacity to support intelligent diagnostic reasoning as well.

The physical process models can deliver very effective instruction, but at an extremely high initial development cost. The problem with this approach is simply that each application is limited to one fully analyzed domain, thus it cannot address particular devices unless their underlying first principles have been fully modeled and the device is expressed in very high detail.

1.3 Addressing the Weakness of Simulation Models for Diagnostic Instruction

The remainder of this paper will describe DIAG (Towne, 1997a, 1997b), a system developed specifically to resolve the weaknesses found in such systems as IMTS while maintaining its strengths. The objective was to produce an ITS authoring and delivery system that would support learners working fault diagnosis exercises. The dialogues generated by DIAG respond to learners' inquiries during or after an exercise. These dialogues can enable learners to continue with an exercise that would otherwise be ruined by an impasse, they can clarify domain-specific concepts evoked by the exercise, and they can demonstrate and explain expert diagnostic performance in the context of specific problems. Thus, the intent of DIAG is to act like an instructor who is monitoring students undertaking fault diagnosis exercises on real equipment.

2. SYSTEM OVERVIEW

The functions involved in producing and delivering a DIAG application are depicted in Figure 1.

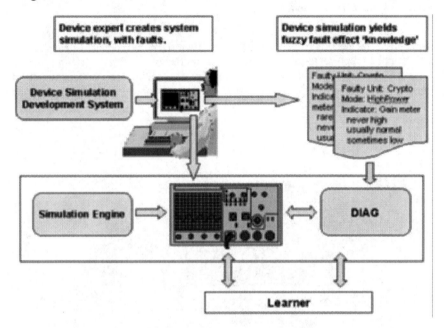

Figure 1. Producing and Delivering a DIAG Application.

The DIAG author employs a *device simulation development system* to produce a *working model* of the target system and commands DIAG to produce a body of *fault effect information*. The device model is then presented to the learner under various fault conditions as selected by DIAG. A *simulation engine* maintains the presentation of the simulated device as the learner manipulates it. For each exercise, the learner operates and tests the simulated device as DIAG maintains records of tests performed and provides assistance as needed. When required, DIAG provides guidance, as generated by its built-in diagnostic expert (Towne & Johnson, 1987).

The application development process will now be elaborated, followed by the instructional delivery process.

3. APPLICATION DEVELOPMENT

A DIAG application consists of a model of the physical system, an optional functional system model, automatically generated fault effect information, ancillary maintenance information about each replaceable/repairable unit, and a textual problem report that initiates each exercise.

3.1 The Physical Device Model

Using tools within DIAG, the author sets up one or more screens, each dedicated to displaying some section of the target system. Then the author populates each screen with graphical representations of functioning entities of the target system. Figure 2 illustrates a sample screen displaying a model of a radio receiver constructed of working front panel controls, indicators, test points, input jacks and background graphics[1].

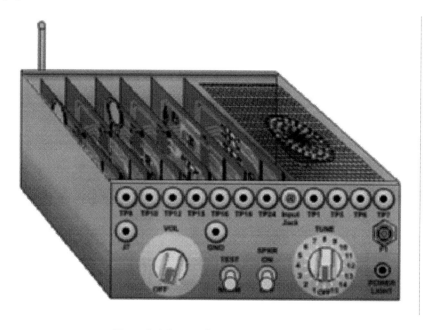

Figure 2. A Screen of a DIAG Device Model.

Device models developed in one application can also be used as objects in other applications. For example, the user may employ a model multimeter, oscilloscope, or signal generator as shown in Figure 3 to test signal characteristics at test points of other device models.

---

[1] The DIAG applications of Figures 2 and 3 were developed by Jennifer Little, Bruce Liu, Scott Nash, Thang Nguyen, and Alpha Thiam of Instructional Science and Development, Inc., Pensacola, FL. Graphics were produced by Chris Taylor of that firm.

INTELLIGENT SUPPORT OF DIAGNOSTIC REASONING 127

Figure 3. Operable Test Equipment Models.

3.1.1. Device Simulation Development Systems

The original version of DIAG was developed specifically to operate upon device models developed in the RIDES system (Munro, Johnson, Pizzini, Surmon, Towne, & Wogulis, 1997), running under Linux. The more recent version of DIAG operates upon models developed in the ReAct (Towne, 2000) simulation system. This latest version supports both Windows and Macintosh platforms and can be presented either in stand-alone configurations or within common Web browsers.

The primary components of ReAct are: 1) graphical editing tools for producing representations of system elements, 2) a programming language for expressing object behaviors, and 3) a simulation engine that maintains the graphical device model as a user operates it. The latest version of ReAct uses Flash MX graphical editing tools to achieve high-quality vector graphic representations.

3.1.2. Object Behavior Rules

After producing the graphical representation of the target system, the author enters rules for each object, specifying how the object behaves in response to its immediate environment. These rules are typically expressed as if-then statements within the various graphical objects.

For operable controls, the rules include the specification of how the object changes its graphical appearance and how it changes its outputs when the user manipulates it (with the mouse). For indicators, such as panel lights or test points, the rules specify how the object changes appearance as a function of its inputs. Thus, a meter sets the rotation of the needle according to the value of the input to the meter.

For all failable objects, including controls and indicators, the rules indicate how the object's outputs are affected by the different *kinds* of abnormalities that can occur in the object. This does not require exhaustive enumeration of all the different faults that can occur. For a circuit board, for example, there may be a few outputs that would be affected by failures in the board. The numerous possible abnormalities typically collapse to a very modest number of cases, e.g., "no output", "low output", and "wrong frequency". The objects that receive inputs from that circuit board would then express their behaviors in terms of these possible cases, as well as their own failure possibilities.

Note that the use here of the terms *input* and *output* do not restrict the device model to systems in which there is only electrical or electronic connectivity. The effects of hydraulic, mechanical, and other phenomena can be specified in terms of object *states* rather than using the terms input and output.

To avoid an explosion of possibilities, the device model is built under the assumption that there is at most one fault in the system at any time. While multiple faults occur in complex systems with irritating frequency, particularly when one fault causes another, the diagnostic process of experts seems to involve identification and resolution of one fault at a time. Thus, mastering the single fault condition is the critical necessary condition to coping with multiple faults, and it is sufficient once the learner appreciates the need to verify system restoration following each repair or replacement action.

Upon completion of this phase of development, the author can operate the device model and observe the correct indications in either a non-failed condition or any of the possible failure conditions. The author then defines any number of device *modes*, each a combination of switch settings, cable connections, or other configuration details. Each mode represents a condition in which DIAG will simulate faults, record the symptoms produced, and converse with the learner. Typical modes represent conditions such as 1) power on, normal operating mode, 2) standby mode, or 3) transmit mode.

3.2 Specifying the Functional Architecture of the Target System

Optionally, the author may employ ReAct's simulation authoring tools to produce a model that represents the *functional* organization and behavior of the target system, as exemplified in Figure 4.

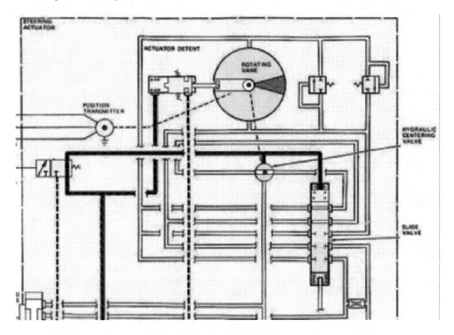

Figure 4. A Functional Representation.

In this representation each screen presents more abstract functional diagrams, such as block diagrams or signal flow diagrams. If desired, the author may also signify correspondences that exist between physical entities and functional entities so that the learner can alternate between physical views and functional views of comparable sections of the target system. Whether these identifying linkages are provided or not, the physical and functional models are linked internally so that actions taken upon one of the two forms are automatically reflected in the other, when viewed.

The functional views have been found to be particularly instructive, as the learner can observe internal conditions not normally apparent in the real world. Alternatively, if a device model is developed only to assist field technicians in troubleshooting, the applicator might choose to forego developing functional views.

3.3 Generating Fuzzy Fault Effect Knowledge

Human technicians gain fault effect knowledge primarily through experience. Like chess players, they appear to recognize a modest set of fault-specific symptom complexes that result from the most common faults in a specific system. When a symptom complex is familiar, the source is relatively easily identified from that prior experience. When a fault exhibits symptoms that differ markedly from any of the known symptom complexes, the technician must resort to a deeper analysis of system organization and operation. In many maintenance environments the small number of unusual faults account for the great majority of the diagnostic workload.

DIAG acquires similar fault effect 'knowledge' by stimulating the device simulation in each specified failure condition and operating mode and recording the readings or observable states of all the indicators in the target system. Here, indicators are not limited to objects intended to convey system state information. They also include any object whose condition provides information, such as smoking brake pads or a frayed cable (temperatures and smells are valid symptoms, too, but these must be conveyed via text or graphics on standard PC platforms).

The computational process carried out by DIAG is as follows:
1. Insert the first defined fault into the device model.
2. Set each control in the device model to establish the first defined mode.
3. Invoke ReAct's simulation engine to set the states of indicators and test points.
4. Record the states of indicators and test points in the device model.
5. Repeat steps 2 through 4 for all modes.
6. Repeat steps 1 through 5 for all faults.
7. Repeat steps 1 through 5 for the no-fault condition (to get normal readings)

DIAG stores the raw symptom information so produced in a three-dimensional array (mode x indicator x fault), as shown in Figure 5.

Figure 5. Raw Fault Effect Data.

Thus, at one corner of this cube lies the symptom for mode 1, indicator 1, fault 1, which could be mode "Power on, normal operating conditions", indicator "Power Light", fault "relay K10 open". The value at this cell would be "ON" if the light is normally on in this mode and the fault in relay K10 does not affect it in this mode, and it would be "OFF" otherwise.

Now, the object rules that collectively produced this datum would be in quite a different form. The rule for the Power Light might simply say "if my input is 'high' then I'm "ON", else I'm "OFF", and the value of input is determined by other objects, including switches and other parts.

DIAG then makes a second pass through the detailed data, 'compiling' the symptom information into fuzzy sets related to the replaceable or repairable units (RUs) in the system. For example, the fine-detail symptom data may reveal that faults in a particular RU produce one kind of symptom most often, but a few other faults produce another symptom with a much-reduced frequency.

Each fuzzy set reflects one of seven likelihoods with which a particular symptom (indicator reading) is found to occur as a result of faults in a particular RU in a particular mode.

Likelihood	Meaning
Always	All faults in this RU produce this symptom
Usually	Most faults in this RU produce this symptom
Often	Many faults in this RU produce this symptom
Often as not	About half of the faults in this RU produce this symptom
Sometimes	Some faults in this RU produce this symptom
Rarely	Few faults in this RU produce this symptom
Never	No faults in this RU produce this symptom

The process of producing this fuzzy fault effect knowledge is illustrated in Figure 6. The author clicks a button in DIAG labeled *Generate* and observes as the simulation is automatically exercised. This process normally requires from one to ten minutes. Upon completion, DIAG writes the fuzzy fault effect information to file for use during instruction.

The meaning of the first fuzzy symptom compilation shown in Figure 6 is that *few* faults in the Crypto unit cause the Gain meter to read higher than normal in Low Power mode, *none* allow it to read normal, and *most* cause the Gain meter to read *low*. Note that this information was derived from a statistical analysis of the detailed fault data shown in Figure 5, which in turn resulted from executing the specification of the system model. The developers of the device model do not ever see the data of Figure 5 or Figure 6, unless they choose to explore the data files DIAG builds for its own purposes.

The basic approach employed to create the fuzzy sets adapts methodology from a body of work usually called 'fuzzy set theory' (Zadeh and Kacprzyk, 1992, Kosko 1993).

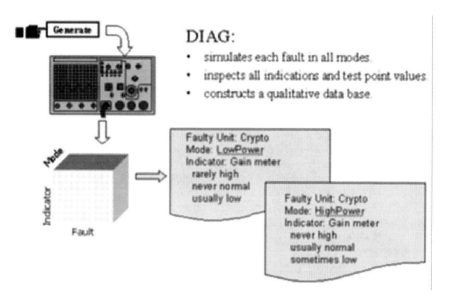

Figure 6. Generation of Fuzzy Fault Effect Knowledge

We have found that the automatic fault effect generation process produces a behavioral representation far richer than even the most experienced technicians embrace, and would have not been captured in a conventional expert system. Furthermore, the fuzzy form in which the data are retained permit the instructional functions to work effectively with novices, since the unusual and rare symptoms that could be produced by failures do not appear as significant considerations for most exercises.

3.4 *RU Information*

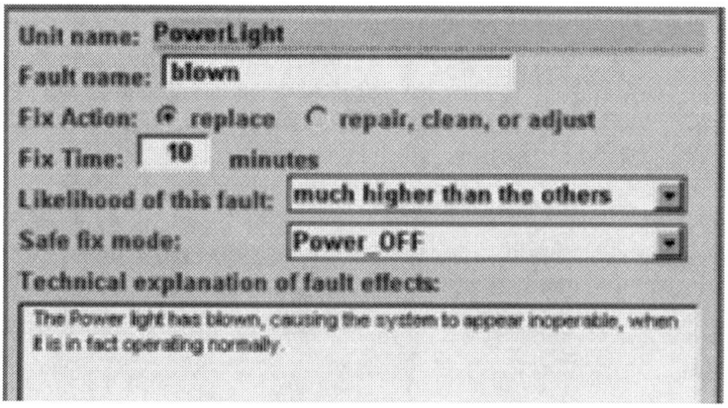

Figure 7. RU Specification Dialog Box.

To support effective troubleshooting decisions by DIAG, the domain expert also estimates the reliability and repair time of each RU, along with the repair action and safe fix mode, as shown in Figure 7.

3.4.1 RU Reliabilities

The reliability of each unit is specified relative to the other units in the target system, via one of the following five categories. The likelihood of any specified fault is:
- much higher than the others;
- somewhat higher than the others;
- about the same as the others;
- somewhat less than the others;
- much less than the others.

As elaborated below, DIAG rank orders its suspicions of each unit at the start of each problem. As symptom information is obtained by the learner, it updates its suspicions of the units. Consequently, the units are initially sorted into at most five levels of suspicion, according to relative reliability, and then they disperse into many more levels of suspicion as symptom information is received and processed.

3.4.2 RU Repair/Replacement Times

The RU replacement times impact the decision to conduct further testing, versus replacing the most suspected RU. Sometimes two equally suspected RUs cannot be discriminated from the test opportunities that the design of the target system affords, thus the learner (as well as an expert technician) must replace one of them. The repair/replacement times affect the recommendations of the artificial diagnostic reasoner at this stage.

3.4.3. Technical Recap

For each fault in the exercise pool, the domain expert prepares a brief technical explanation of its impact upon the target system. This recap is presented to the learner at the conclusion of each exercise, as shown here.

> The failure in the Optical Fan Sensor A14 caused it to cut off the fan and raise the alarm condition.

3.5 Exercise Specifications

For each exercise, the domain expert specifies the fault to be simulated, the mode in which the target system will be presented at the start of the exercise, a time limit if desired, and a problem report that is issued at the start of the exercise. Figure 8 presents the dialog box used.

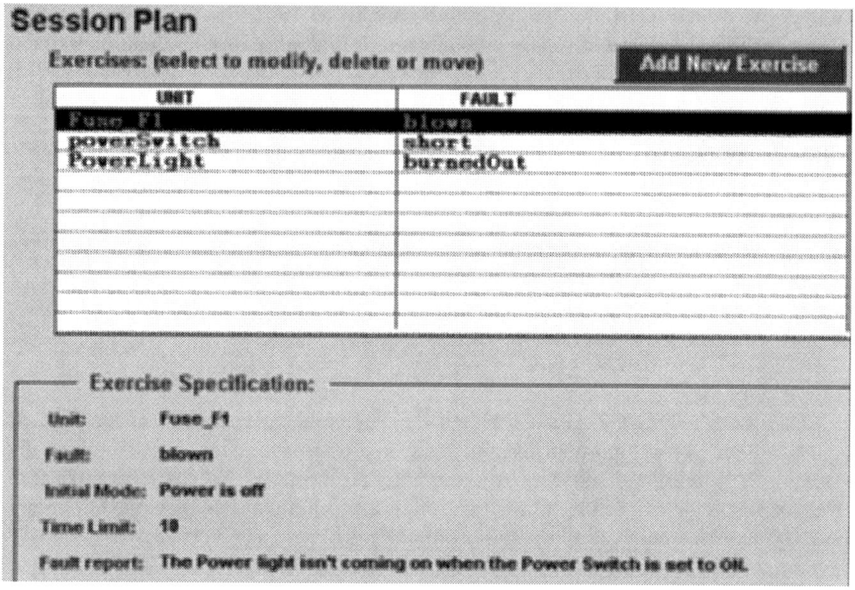

134   D. TOWNE

Figure 8. Exercise Specification.

When the authoring phase described above is complete, DIAG will deliver guided exercises in fault isolation, administering all aspects of the interactions. The next section will describe the interactions and processes.

4. INTELLIGENT GUIDANCE DURING PRACTICE

This section will outline the processes that DIAG performs as it interacts with a learner. The primary functions performed are 1) problem selection, 2) recording and interpreting learner performance, 3) providing assistance during the exercise, and 4) debriefing the learner following an exercise.

4.1 Problem Selection and Fault Introduction

The course developer can specify either of two problem selection techniques: 1) a fixed sequence of problems, or 2) problems selected according to difficulty and individual ability. The first of these approaches is useful if a class of students should experience particular faults prior to scheduled classroom discussions. The second approach attempts to select problems that present an appropriate level of difficulty for the individual learner. Problem difficulty is computed by automatically examining the symptoms produced by each candidate fault.

Consider the fault effects represented in Figure 9. Here are shown the effects of faults in three RUs upon two indicators. Indicator A has just one abnormal symptom value (such as an unlit light), and indicator B has two abnormal symptom values (such as 'no signal' and 'garbled signal').

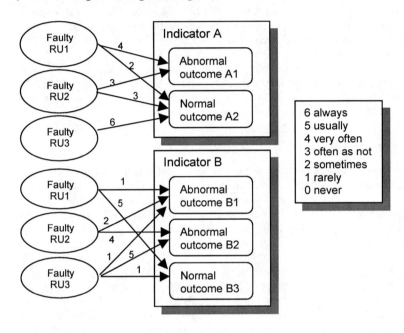

Figure 9. Fault Effects of Three RUs on Two Indicators.

According to the diagram, faults in RU1 *very often* (4) produce abnormal outcome A1 at indicator A and *sometimes* (2) produce normal outcome A2. Suppose we have two candidate faults in RU1 that produce the following symptoms:

Fault	Indication at A	Indication at B
Fault x in RU 1	A1	B3
Fault y in RU 1	A2	B1

From Figure 9 we see that each fault produces one abnormal symptom and one normal symptom. Therefore there is no difference in the difficulty of detecting the presence of the two faults. All other factors being equal, faults that produce very few abnormalities are more difficult to resolve than those that provide more evidence of their existence.

Secondly, note that fault x corresponds well with the approximate symptoms of RU1; both outcomes A1 and B3 are representative of faults in RU1 (A1 occurs very often; B3 occurs usually). Fault y, however, will be much more difficult to identify, since its symptoms do not correspond well with the population of faults that typically occur in RU1 (outcome A2 occurs sometimes; outcome B1 occurs rarely). Thus, fault y will be much more difficult to diagnose than will be fault x.

It is also important to realize that a particular fault might even exhibit symptoms that are more representative of *a different RU than its true host RU*. For example, a fault in RU1 that gives symptoms A2 and B2 looks more like a faulty RU3 than a faulty RU1. An expert troubleshooter would rationally suspect RU3 over RU1 after observing these symptoms.

After analyzing and rank ordering the faults that are available for exercises, DIAG attempts to select a fault that presents an appropriate level of difficulty for the individual. Upon selecting the fault to be presented, DIAG introduces it into the simulation of the target system and issues the problem report for that exercise.

4.2 Recording and Interpreting Learner Performance

In order to provide assistance when requested, DIAG maintains suspicions about the faults based upon the learner's work. It initializes its suspicions at the start of each problem by rank ordering the RUs according to their relative reliabilities. As the learner performs tests, DIAG interprets each symptom displayed according to its internal fault effect knowledge, and it revises its suspicion rankings.

Suppose, for example, that indicator B in Figure 9 is a Power Meter with a normal reading of 12 VDC, and that RU3 is a Low Voltage Power Supply (LVPS). If a learner observes 12 VDC at the meter, the diagnostic expert would significantly reduce its suspicion of the LVPS, as this normal reading is rarely observed when the LVPS fails. Likewise, it would drastically reduce its suspicion of RU2, since failures in this unit always produce some abnormal reading at the meter. Thus, after this indication is observed, the ITS would greatly increase its suspicion ranking of RU1, compared to the other two RUs. Alternatively, if the learner observes outcome B2 at the meter, DIAG would drastically reduce its suspicion of RU1, since this outcome is never produced by faults in RU1. As the learner works, the RUs that could produce the observed symptoms move toward the top of DIAG's internal suspect list.

At any time in an exercise, the learner can replace any RU that he or she suspects, given that the simulated device is in a safe replacement mode. The learner is then advised that the selected part has been replaced with a known good spare, and is advised to continue with the exercise. Internally, DIAG notes whether the correct RU was replaced. If so, it invisibly removes the failure condition from the simulation so that any subsequent tests produce normal indications. The instructional system does not advise the learner whether or not the replacement was correct, since a critical skill to be learned is judging when the system has been repaired. In addition to recording what RU was replaced, DIAG refers to its own suspicion rankings to determine if the replacement was rational or not, based upon the evidence obtained up to that point by the learner's own tests.

4.3 Providing Assistance During the Exercise

Unlike the IMTS before it, DIAG does not intercede during the course of an exercise unless the learner asks for assistance. Previous attempts to intercede when the learner performed apparently unproductive tests were found to be ineffective, as they seemed to question the learner's wisdom in double-checking results or performing tests that confirm theories. Instead, DIAG provides a *Consult* button, which when pressed displays the list of options shown in Figure 10.

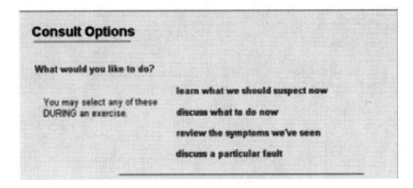

Figure 10. Within-Exercise Consultation Options.

4.3.1. Learn What We Should Suspect Now

When the learner selects this consultation option, DIAG lists the faults that it suspects, based upon the symptoms that the learner has seen, as shown in Figure 11.

Note that the elements listed may be individual faults, RUs, or higher-level elements. When there are many faults suspected, DIAG automatically collapses the listing of suspected faults into RUs or higher-level elements, until the list presents ten or less elements, or until no further collapsing is possible. In this way, the discussion about suspected elements progresses from high-level entities early in exercises down to low-level failure instances late in the exercise.

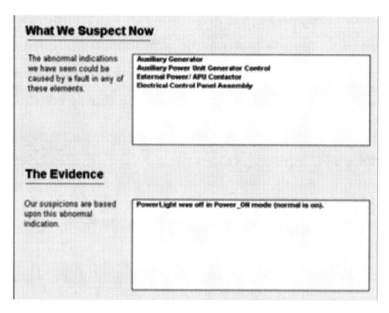

Figure 11. Listing of Suspected System Elements.

4.3.2. Discuss What to Do Now

Often a learner will reach an impasse during troubleshooting practice in which he or she is not clear about what should be done next. Usually, this condition is related to errors in reasoning that lead to an empty suspicion set or insufficient domain knowledge to select a useful test to further discriminate the failure area. Alternatively, the learner may simply wish to compare his or her intended action to that of an expert. This illustrates the rationale for presenting the intelligent interactions as *consultations*, rather than *help*. When the learner selects this consult option, DIAG determines what test will best discriminate from the currently suspected elements. Alternatively, it will recommend that the learner perform a replacement, if the symptoms point clearly to a particular RU or there are no tests that will further discriminate from among the suspected elements. Figure 12 illustrates the recommendation provided, which includes what test to perform, and a justification for performing that test.

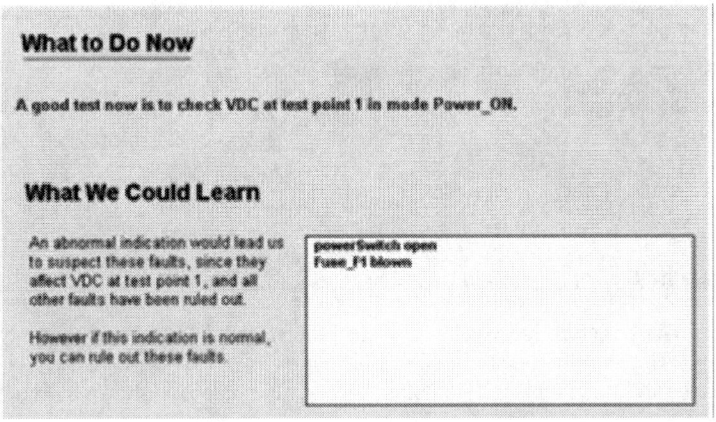

INTELLIGENT SUPPORT OF DIAGNOSTIC REASONING 139

Figure 12. Testing Recommendation and Justification.

Section 4.4.1 presents the computational process employed to generate next test recommendations.

4.3.3. Review the Symptoms We've Seen

The learner selects this consultation type to reflect on the implications of the symptoms that have been seen so far in the exercise. As shown in Figure 13, DIAG first lists the significant indications (those that impacted suspicions) along with an assessment of whether each indication was normal or not, in the particular mode.

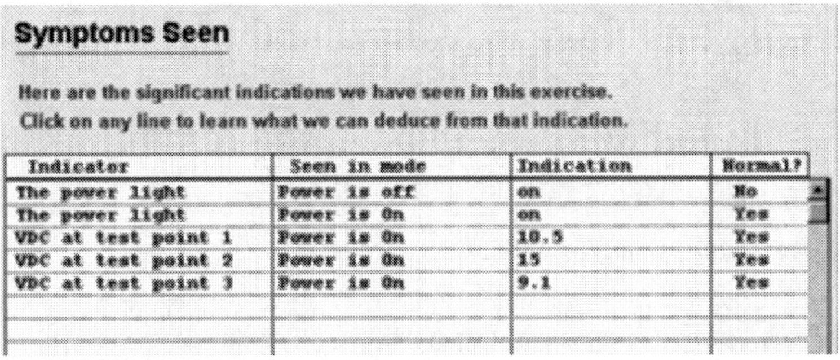

Figure 13. Listing of Symptoms Seen.

The learner may select any of the listed symptoms, to learn more about the inferences that could be drawn from that observation. In Figure 14 the learner has selected a reading obtained by use of (simulated) test equipment, and learns that this normal symptom can be used to eliminate two fault hypotheses.

> VDC at test point 2 was 15 in Power is On mode, which is NORMAL.
>
> Therefore, we can eliminate the following fault possibilities:
>   The power switch : open
>   Fuse_F1 : blown

Figure 14. Elaboration of a Selected Symptom.

4.3.4. Discuss a Particular Fault

The learner may determine what a good technician would surmise about any fault, based upon the symptoms exhibited during the exercise. DIAG constructs a dialog that reviews and interprets the symptoms that were exhibited, as shown in Figure 15.

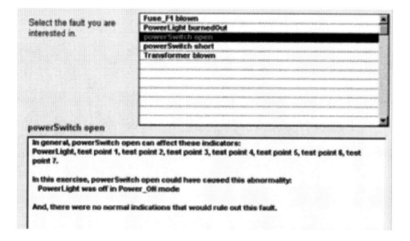

Figure 15. Contextualized Discussion of a Selected Fault.

4.3.5. Exercise Completion

When the learner brings an exercise to a close, by either correctly claiming that the fault has been resolved or giving up, DIAG records:
- the time taken to complete the problem;
- whether or not the fault was resolved;
- the number of replacements that were made;
- whether or not the learner incorrectly claimed the system was fixed; and
- the number of times the learner invoked the Consult options.

4.4. After-Exercise Debriefings

DIAG then offers the choice of moving on to the next exercise, or going back over the completed exercise via the options shown in Figure 16.

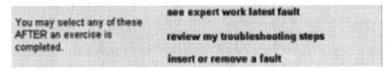

Figure 16. After-Exercise Debriefing Options.

4.4.1. See Expert Work Latest Fault

For this consultation type DIAG re-inserts the fault into the device simulation and demonstrates an expert approach to the problem, as shown in Figure 17.

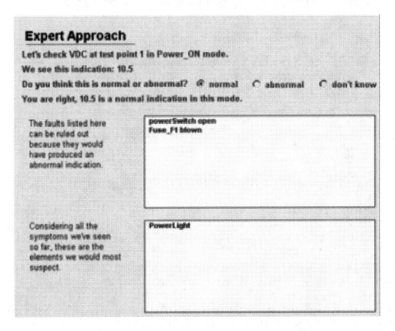

Figure 17. A Step in the Expert Diagnostic Demonstration.

In the process, it justifies each selected test, it lists the resulting symptom, and the units that should be most suspected at each stage. As seen in Figure 17, the learner participates by assessing the symptoms as they are noted.

At each stage of a diagnostic problem the ADI component determines the extent to which each candidate test is likely to change the current RU suspicion rankings. The most productive tests are those promising the greatest expected impact upon suspicion rankings. An ideal test would be one that has many possible equally likely outcomes, each of which clearly eliminates some of the more highly suspected RUs from suspicion. Note that this is in harmony with, and is a refined instantiation of, the 'half–split' concept often taught in the classroom.

Surprisingly, this relatively simple test selection algorithm exhibits additional expert meta-strategies that are not explicitly expressed in the system. That is, early in a diagnostic problem, the ADI functions prefer tests that are very likely to yield abnormal symptoms, even though the theoretical information value of such tests is relatively low. This corresponds to an expert performing an initial operational check, to determine the normalcy of the system. Early in problems, the preferred tests naturally partition the system into major subsets, as reflected by the functional architecture of the system. This corresponds to the "fault localization" phase taught in the classroom. Late in problems, the tests selected are those that relate directly to just a few RUs, which is termed the "fault isolation" phase of troubleshooting.

4.4.2. Review My Troubleshooting Steps

This debriefing process is identical to that shown for expert diagnosis, except now the learner's own steps are reiterated and discussed.

4.4.3. Insert or Remove Fault

The final after-exercise option allows the learner to insert any faults of interest, in order to observe their effects and compare the indications to normal ones.

5. INTELLIGENT GUIDANCE DURING FIELD MAINTENANCE

The functions of DIAG were implemented within an advanced technical performance aiding system (Towne 2001, 2002) under sponsorship of NAVAIR Orlando TSD. The prototype application demonstrated the ability of DIAG to interact with field technicians working to resolve faults in an S3B aircraft nose wheel steering system. In this use, DIAG presents step-by-step troubleshooting guidance. Each step in the fault isolation process appears as shown in Figure 18.

Upon reporting a symptom observed on the actual failed unit, the maintainer sees DIAG's evaluation of that symptom, and a summary of all that DIAG has inferred up through the just-completed test, as shown in Figure 19.

This process continues until DIAG has isolated the fault to a single replaceable unit, as shown above, or to the minimum set of possibly failed units that can be identified from the tests available.

6. APPLICATIONS AND EVALUATIONS

To date, eight DIAG applications have been developed. The first three applications were produced primarily to evaluate the usability and sufficiency of the authoring tools and to determine the technical quality of the guided practice; four applications were subsequently developed for use in the Navy's simulation-based course in basic electricity and electronics (BEESIM); and the S3B application just described was developed for use as a field diagnostic aid.

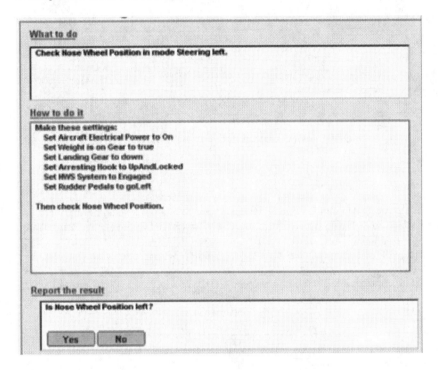

Figure 18. A Step in DIAG Guided Troubleshooting.

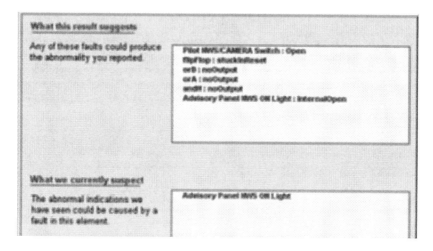

Figure 19. DIAG Summary Following Each Guided Test.

6.1 Evaluation Applications

The first three DIAG applications were developed to evaluate the authoring tools, as summarized in Table 1. Although the Aircraft Power Distribution System involved the most replaceable units, the majority of those units were simple connectors and switches, whereas the replaceable units in the other two systems were considerably more complex. The times to work problems in these systems ranged from a few minutes to approximately ten minutes each.

Table 1. Evaluation Applications

Target System	Replaceable Units	Screens	Controls	Weeks to Develop†
Shipboard Radar Transmitter	86	17	31	5 + 4
Aircraft Power Distribution System	148	28	10	3 + 1
Home Heating System	13	15	5	4 + 2

† authoring person-weeks + subject-matter expert person-weeks

A formal evaluation of DIAG diagnostic aiding dialogs was conducted in the context of the home heating system application (Di Eugenio & Trolio, 2000). Two major weaknesses found by this study were:

1. The listings of suspected units, all referring to faults in specific RUs, obscured the successive localization from high-level units to RUs to faults in RUs.

2. The dialogs reflected little continuity across tests, and tended to be test-specific.

As a result of this evaluation, DIAG was made to maintain a more structured view of the system. Thus, early in exercises, DIAG was made to refer to high-level suspected units, only mentioning specific faults when the number of possibilities became more narrowed.

The second criticism was largely address by extending the Consult functions. For example, the Discuss Fault function was extended to describe the general effects of a fault first, followed by the specific effects that have been observed in the particular exercise. Similarly, the Symptoms Seen, What We Suspect Now, and What to Do Now functions were all extended to tie recommendations or evaluations to prior results as well as the latest observation.

6.2 Basic Electricity and Electronics (BEESIM) Applications

Four DIAG applications have been developed for use in the Navy's simulation-based course in basic electricity and electronics (BEESIM) by Instructional Science and Development, Inc., (ISD) of Pensacola, FL. The applications are 1) basic power supply, 2) basic radio receiver, 3) an electronic warning system, and 4) a digital ring counter. This work has provided the opportunity to evaluate the usability of the authoring tools and the resulting diagnostic guidance in the context of a large course covering technical fundamentals along with DIAG-guided troubleshooting practice.

Many improvements and extensions to DIAG have been implemented as a result of the BEESIM development program, primarily 1) the technical content available to the user during diagnostic exercises has been greatly extended, 2) DIAG exercises and other technical resources such as ReAct simulations of multimeters and oscilloscopes have been made fully modularized, and 3) the student performance data recorded by DIAG has been extended and linked to a higher level student management function developed by ISD.

7. CONCLUSIONS

The current version of DIAG is a product of two previous generations, starting with IMTS, progressing to the Linux-based version of DIAG, and finally to the current Windows/Mac system. Each version of DIAG has involved modifications based upon previous findings, prototype application, and evaluation of the authoring process and the intelligent diagnostic guidance functions.

7.1 Findings and Lessons Learned

Among the most fundamental findings and lessons learned via the BEESIM development and evaluation program are these:

- Computer programmers, working with subject matter (electronics) experts, effectively employed ReAct and DIAG to develop the device models. These applicators had no prior experience in computer-based instruction, fault diagnosis, or development of intelligent tutors.

- The most difficult of the four applications was the warning system, which involved equipment states that depended upon the performance of a sequence of actions by the operator. The other three systems were more easily modeled, as their behaviors depended only upon mode of operation and failure conditions.

- Little heavy-duty computer programming was involved in constructing the device models in ReAct. The only intensive programming involved the simulation of test equipment (oscilloscope and multimeter).

7.2 The Future

DIAG achieves an end we have long sought: Hand a computer model of a device to a simulator combined with domain-independent diagnostic intelligence, and receive effective and rationalized troubleshooting strategies applicable to either instructional purposes or performance aiding purposes. There may come a time when DIAG models can be generated directly from the design documentation, as CAD technology continues to evolve.

8. REFERENCES

Di Eugenio, B. & Trolio, M.J. (2000). Simple aggregation rules make a difference: an application to intelligent tutoring systems, Proceeding, International Conference on Natural Language Generation.

Forbus, K.D., & Whalley, P.B. (1994). Using qualitative physics to build articulate software for thermodynamics education, *Proceedings of AAAI-94*, August, 1994, 1175-1182.

Johnson, W.B., Norton, J. E., Duncan, P.E., & Hunt, R.M. (1988). *Development and demonstration of an intelligent tutoring system for technical training* (MITT) (AFHRL-TP-88-8). Brooks AFB, TX: The Air Force Human Resources Laboratory.

Kosko B. (1993). *Fuzzy thinking: The new science of fuzzy logic.* New York: Hyperion.

Lesgold, A., Eggan, G., Katz, S., & Rao, G. (1992). Possibilities for assessment using computer-based apprenticeship environments. In J. Regian & V. Shute (Eds.*), Cognitive approaches to automated instruction* (pp 49-80). Hillsdale, NJ: Erlbaum.

Lajoie, S.P. & Lesgold, A. (1992). Apprenticeship training in the workplace: Computer-coached practice environment as a new form of apprenticeship. In M. Farr and J. Psotka (Eds.), *Intelligent instruction by computer: Theory and practice*. London: Taylor & Francis.

Munro, A., Johnson, M.C., Pizzini, Q.A., Surmon, D.S., Towne, D.M., & Wogulis, J.L. (1997). Authoring simulation-centered tutors with RIDES. International J. of Artificial Intelligence in Education, Vol. 8, No. 3-4, pp. 284-316.

Towne, D.M. & Johnson, M.C. (1987). *Research on computer-aided design for maintainability.* (Technical Report No. 109) Los Angeles: Behavioral Technology Laboratories, University of Southern California.

Towne, D.M. & Munro, A. (1988). The intelligent maintenance training system. In J. Psotka, L.D. Massey, and S. A. Mutter (Eds.), *Intelligent tutoring systems: Lessons learned* (479-530). Hillsdale, NJ: Erlbaum.

Towne, D.M., Munro, A., Pizzini, Q.A., Surmon, D.S., & Wogulis, J.L. (1990). *Intelligent maintenance training technology.* (Technical Report No. 110) Los Angeles: Behavioral Technology Laboratories, University of Southern California.

Towne, D.M. (1997a). Intelligent diagnostic tutoring using qualitative symptom information, Proceedings, *American Institute of Artificial Intelligence*, Intelligent Tutoring Systems Authoring Tools, Nov., 1997.

Towne, D.M. (1997b). Approximate reasoning techniques for intelligent diagnostic instruction, *International Journal of Artificial Intelligence and Education*, Vol. 8, No. 3-4, pp. 262-283.

Towne, D.M. (2000). *ReAct Users Manual*. General Analysis, Inc., St. Helena, CA., 94574.

Towne, D.M. (2001). *An Integrated Environment for Technical Training and Aiding: Annual Technical Report, Year Two*. Naval Air Weapons Center, Training Systems Division, Orlando, FL., 32826.

Towne, D.M. (2002). Use of device models to support learning and performing maintenance tasks: Final Report, Los Angeles, CA: Behavioral Technology Laboratories, University of Southern California.

Towne, D.M. (2002). Advanced Techniques for IETM Development and Delivery, Proceedings Human Factors and Ergonomics Society, 46th Annual Meeting, Baltimore, MD, October 3, 2002.

Wiederholt, B.J., Norton, J. E., Johnson, W. B., & Browning, E.J. (1992). MITT Writer and MITT Writer Advanced Development: Developing Authoring and Training Systems for Complex Technical Domains, Final Technical Report AL-TR-1991-0122, Armstrong Laboratory, Brooks Air Force Base, TX.

Zadeh, L. & Kacprzyk, J. (1992). *Fuzzy logic for the management of uncertainty* (Eds.). New York: John Wiley & Sons, Inc.

ACKNOWLEDGEMENTS

The DIAG system was initially developed under sponsorship of the Office of Naval Research. ReAct and the current version of DIAG were developed under the Dual Use Science and Technology Program (DUAP). Susan Chipman, Ph.D. was the technical point of contact for both.

These systems have been further refined, applied, and evaluated under funding from NAVAIR Orlando TSD (formerly NAWCTSD), Katrina Ricci, Ph.D. technical point of contact. The BEESIM project was performed by Instructional Science and Development, Inc., Pensacola, FL, Dewey Kribs, Ph.D., President. The contract was directed by Steven Parchman of what is now NAVAIR Orlando TSD. Les Wetherington of NAVAIR Orlando TSD conducted informal evaluations of DIAG reasoning for the S3B nose wheel steering system.

VALERIE J. SHUTE & LISA A. TORREANO

Chapter 6

FORMATIVE EVALUATION OF AN AUTOMATED KNOWLEDGE ELICITATION AND ORGANIZATION TOOL

Abstract. This chapter serves three purposes. First, we briefly review knowledge representations to stress the implications of different knowledge types on instruction and assessment. Second, we describe a novel cognitive tool, DNA (Decompose, Network, Assess), designed to aid knowledge elicitation and organization for instruction – specifically geared to increase the efficiency of creating the domain model used within intelligent instructional systems. Third, we present an exploratory test of the tool's efficacy. Three statistical experts used DNA to explicate their knowledge related to measures of central tendency in statistics. DNA was able to effectively elicit relevant information, commensurate with a benchmark system, generating a starting curriculum upon which to build instruction, and did so in hours compared to months for conventional elicitation procedures.

1. INTRODUCTION

The face of teaching and training is changing—from classroom-based, teacher-led instruction to electronic learning (e-learning) with a focus on individual or small groups of students and their knowledge and skill acquisition. Along the same lines, e-learning is shifting from developing infrastructures and delivering information online to improving learning and performance (see Shute & Towle, in press, for more on this topic). One large obstacle in this envisioned path concerns obtaining relevant content that will underlie these new student-based systems to support learning and performance. In the best case, relevant content is derived from the results of cognitive or behavioral task analyses. The downside of these approaches relates to their exorbitant price tag—i.e., a very high cost in terms of both time and money, with no guarantees as to effectiveness.

The aim of knowledge-elicitation tools (KETs), in general, is to increase the efficiency of collecting and using content; but current KETs are limited in utility, typically focusing on just one specific purpose (e.g., eliciting variables and their relations for a student model) and one type of knowledge (e.g., conceptual) (e.g., Chipman, Shalin, & Schraagen, 2000). Yet, education and training courses are substantially richer in scope. Furthermore, there is a wide range of purposes for e-learning systems. Where do we start?

Murray, Ainsworth, & Blessing (eds.), Authoring Tools for Adv. Tech. Learning Env.
© 2003 *Kluwer Academic Publishers. Printed in the Netherlands, pp. 149-180.*

Anyone who has attempted to design effective instruction or training knows that it begins with sound curriculum. In all cases, whether instructing karate beginners, nuclear physicists, network administrators, or aircraft mechanics, what information to include in the curriculum and how to ensure learners' mastery of the material must be determined. Good teachers and trainers make these determinations intuitively; the computer's insight, however, must be programmed. Therefore, resolving and specifying these "what to teach" and "how to teach" issues is critically important in forthcoming computer- or Internet-based instructional systems. New tools are needed to aid elicitation and organization of knowledge and skills for both assessment and instructional purposes. Specifically, KETs need to be designed to facilitate the development of future e-learning courses.

To render such instructional systems intelligent—or *responsibly adaptive*—three components must be specified: (a) a domain model, (b) a student model, and (c) an instructor model (e.g., Lajoie & Derry, 1993; Polson & Richardson, 1988; Shute & Psotka, 1996; Sleeman & Brown, 1982). The domain model represents the material to be instructed. This includes domain-related elements of knowledge, as well as the associated structure or interdependencies of those elements. In essence, the domain model is a knowledge map of what is to be taught. The student model represents the student's knowledge and progress in relation to the knowledge map. Finally, the instructor model, also known as the "tutor," manages the course of instructional material based on discrepancies between the student and domain models. Thus, the instructor model determines how to ensure learner mastery by monitoring the student model in relation to the domain model and addressing discrepancies in a principled manner. In short, these three models jointly specify "what to teach and how to teach it."

There are three main aims of this chapter, which was originally published in a special issue of International Journal of Artificial Intelligence in Education (1999). First, we briefly overview knowledge representations, focusing on those that can support student and domain modeling across different types of knowledge and skill. Specifically, we describe three categories of knowledge: (a) declarative (what), (b) procedural (how), and (c) conceptual (why). Our contention is that each knowledge type, best captured by different representations (i.e., knowledge maps), implies slightly different instructional and assessment techniques. For instance, assessing a person's factual knowledge of some topic requires a different approach than assessing how well someone can actually execute a procedure. By attending to knowledge type distinctions, and their representations, we hope to be better able to specify the component models of adaptive instructional systems for a broad range of content.

Second, we describe a novel cognitive tool that has been designed to aid elicitation and organization of knowledge for both assessment and instructional purposes. Specifically, it was originally designed to facilitate the development of intelligent tutoring system (ITS) curricula, while maintaining sensitivity to the knowledge type distinctions we discuss in the representation section of the paper. The same tool can be used in adaptive e-learning systems. Our primary aim for this tool, embodied in a program called DNA (Decompose, Network, Assess), is to increase the efficiency of developing the domain model—often referred to as the backbone of intelligent instructional systems (Anderson, 1988) and sometimes called a "proficiency model" in assessment circles (e.g., Almond, Steinberg, & Mislevy, in press; Mislevy, Almond, Yan, & Steinberg, 2000; Mislevy, Steinberg, & Almond, 1999; Mislevy, Steinberg, Almond, Haertel, & Penuel, 2001). The tool attempts to automate portions of the cognitive task analysis process, often viewed as a bottleneck in system development. We will summarize its interface and functionality, but refer the reader to a more detailed description of the program (Shute, Torreano, & Willis, 2000).

The third and primary purpose of this paper is to present the results of an exploratory test of the tool's efficacy, or design feasibility. We outline the results from an empirical validation of the tool that examined how efficiently and effectively DNA works in the extraction of knowledge elements related to statistics. Specifically, we used DNA with three statistical "experts" to explicate their knowledge related to measures of central tendency. (Note: These were not technically "experts" but volunteers who were quite knowledgeable in the area of statistics, thus we use the term "experts" for economy).

1.1 Knowledge Representation

A variety of knowledge representation schemes have been developed that can be used to support student (and domain) modeling across diverse types of knowledge and skill (e.g., Merrill, 1994; 2000). For instance, Merrill (1994) presents four types of knowledge: facts, concepts, procedures, and principles. We simplify the issue by describing three broad categories of knowledge, conjoining Merrill's first two types into our single knowledge type: (a) declarative (what), (b) procedural (how), and (c) conceptual (why). Each has implications for instruction and assessment.

Declarative knowledge is factual information – propositions in the form of relations between two or more bits of knowledge that are either true or false. A formal distinction is often made between declarative knowledge that is autobiographical (episodic), and that representing general world (semantic) knowledge. Episodic knowledge entails information about specific experiences or episodes (e.g., *I inadvertently chewed a chili pepper hidden in my entrée - and it was hot! My mouth burned for twenty minutes and I was unable to taste the rest of my dinner*). Semantic knowledge (i.e., the meaning of information) is not tied to particular events, but rather entails information that is independent of when it is experienced, such as category membership and properties (e.g., habañero, tabasco, and jalapeño are kinds of chili peppers – habañero being one of the hottest). Episodic knowledge is thought to precede and underlie semantic knowledge. For example, after the experience of biting a habañero, one would likely be able to recognize novel examples of the pepper as being members of the same category – and of being hot.

Declarative (specifically semantic) knowledge can be functionally represented as a network of nodes and links, often called a semantic network (originally coined by Collins & Quillian, 1969). Alternatively, it may assume the form of a Bayesian inference network (e.g., Mislevy, et al., 2000). Although initially developed as an efficient means of storing information in a computer, semantic networks have been shown to be cognitively plausible by studies that reveal that the hypothesized organization of the network structure is predictive of human performance on a variety of tasks. For example, response time to verify category and property statements (e.g., "A habañero is a chili pepper" or "Chili peppers contain capsaicinoids)" as well as to answer questions (e.g., "Is a habañero a pepper?") are predicted by features of the structure. Some of these features include the number of hierarchical levels to be crossed and whether stored features must be retrieved. Collins and Loftus (1975) proposed more general semantic network models along with the concept of spreading activation. These more general models do not strictly entail hierarchical relations.

For adaptive or intelligent instruction in declarative domains, semantic networks have been used as student models by instantiating the network with the knowledge to be taught, and then tagging nodes as to whether the student has learned it or not. These networks are an economical way to represent large amounts of interrelated information, are easily inspected, and support mixed-initiative dialogs between user and tutoring system. They are considerably less effective, however, for representing procedural information (i.e., knowledge or skill related to doing things).

Procedural knowledge is the knowledge of how to do something, and *procedural skill* is the demonstrable capability of doing so. For example, one may know how to remove the skin of a chili before cooking by roasting, but not do it very well. Or one may know how to preserve chilies, and also be able to do so quite well. In the former case (skinning), one may be said to have procedural knowledge but not procedural skill. In the latter case (preserving), one would have both procedural knowledge and skill. While there may be some cases where it is possible to have skill and not knowledge (or at least be unable to articulate that knowledge, such as when knowledge has become automated), more commonly having the skill logically entails having the knowledge.

Current theories of knowledge representation hold that procedural knowledge/skill can be functionally represented using a rule-based formalism, often called a production system (Anderson, 1993). These rules, or productions, consist of two parts – an action to be taken and the conditions under which to do so. An example might be, "if the goal is to alleviate a burning mouth that results from chewing a chili pepper, then drink milk." Thus, production systems combine step-by-step procedures (actions) with propositions (conditions), described previously as being represented by semantic networks. Production systems have been shown to be cognitively plausible by studies showing that the hypothesized structure of the rule-base is predictive of the kinds of errors people make in solving problems.

For intelligent instruction in procedural domains, production systems have been used as student models in several ways. One way is to instantiate an expert (production) system with the knowledge/skill to be taught, and then teach the knowledge/skill to the student, keeping track of what is and is not learned by tagging productions appropriately (e.g., Anderson, 1987). In another approach, expertise is modeled through negation by matching student errors to previously identified common patterns of errors that are associated with incorrect productions, or procedural "bugs" (e.g., VanLehn, 1990). Production systems are a fine-grained way to represent procedural knowledge or skill, are easily implemented in most programming languages, and support a variety of straightforward ways to automate instruction because they directly represent the performance steps to be taught. They are sub-optimal, however, for representing declarative information. Additionally, the level of feedback that is most easily obtained may be too elemental for efficient instruction. Finally, the "bug library" approach to teaching procedural knowledge/skill is limited in that it is not possible to anticipate all possible procedural errors that students might manifest, and procedural bugs tend to be transient before disappearing altogether.

Conceptual Knowledge supports qualitative reasoning and constitutes a specialized category of knowledge not well handled by either semantic networks or production systems alone. Conceptual knowledge stems from the organization, or structure, of one's knowledge of a domain and the intuitive theory developed from what one has experienced in order to explain *why* things are as they are. For example, reasoning about principles of electricity, complex weather systems, or even why chili peppers are hot seems to involve internalized mental models that contain both declarative information (e.g., knowledge about electrical components) and procedural information (e.g., knowledge about how electrical systems behave). Conceptual knowledge allows humans to reason about how a system will behave under changing input conditions, either accurately or inaccurately. Regarding misconceptions, students who think that electricity flows through wires analogous to water flowing through pipes, will make predictable errors in reasoning about electricity. Conceptual knowledge also allows humans to generalize domain-specific knowledge and apply it in novel situations. In the words of Friedrich Nietzche, "*He who has a why can endure any how.*"

Conceptual knowledge can be functionally represented by mental models, which are representations that support imagined states of affairs reflecting one's understanding of a domain. Pragmatic reasoning schemas, reflecting a generalized form of a specific rule, may also be used to represent conceptual knowledge. In general, conceptual knowledge is built on declarative and procedural knowledge, and thus can be partially represented by semantic networks in that certain cognitive processes considered "conceptual" in nature—such as similarity comparisons or generalization across domains—could be predicted by these formalisms. Thus, semantic networks account, in part, for conceptual knowledge by providing organization, or the structural glue, for category membership and property/feature information.

These networks primarily describe storage structure of knowledge units and predict patterns of retrieval of information. Mental models, in contrast, apply to semantic representations of complex scenarios allowing for reasoning about situations. Consequently, one's conceptual knowledge may be faulty either because it is built on unsound declarative or procedural knowledge or, when based on a sound foundation, because the intuitive theory is inaccurate. For example, if unaware of capsaicinoid compounds found in chilies, one may erroneously deduce from experience that color or size is the cause of a chili's heat. Indeed, this theory may prevail even with the knowledge that capsaicinoids are contained in chilies if it is not understood how they affect nerve pain receptors (i.e., they release a molecule that sits on the pain fiber of the nerve, thus sending a message of pain to the brain). Having a rich mental model of chilies and their compounds' biological effects may lead to hypotheses about medicinal uses of peppers, such as treating chronic pain or mouth sores (i.e., understanding causes of pain may suggest ways to prevent or manage pain via related chemical processes).

A variety of reasoning studies support the cognitive plausibility of mental models by showing that mental model theory can predict the types of errors that people are likely to make and can explain individual differences in reasoning capacity in that better reasoners create more complete models (Johnson-Laird, 1983; Minstrell, 2000). For purposes of adaptive instruction, certain kinds of qualitative reasoning can be modeled by matching the student's beliefs and predictions to the beliefs and predictions associated with mental models that have been previously identified as characteristic of various levels of understanding or expertise. It is possible to infer what conceptualization the student currently holds, and contrive a way to show the student situations in which the model is wrong, thus pushing the student toward a more accurate conceptualization. This "progression of mental models" approach (White & Frederiksen, 1987) or "failure-driven learning environments" (Schank, 1999) teach reasoning skills that are ideal for remediating misconceptions, but cannot easily address other kinds of declarative knowledge or procedural knowledge/skill.

Our interest in knowledge representations is that we would like to outline the parameters for deriving, representing, and utilizing valid knowledge and skill elements for automated instructional and/or assessment systems. For example, in an adaptive e-learning system, the design of instruction may best be driven by a clear understanding of the representational nature of the knowledge or skill to be taught or assessed, subsequently tailored to address specific knowledge/skill deficiencies per learner. One key to optimizing the predictive utility of an assessment instrument is a careful mapping between the knowledge and skill tapped by the instrument and the knowledge and skill required in the classroom or on the job. The knowledge representation and student modeling techniques being developed by the intelligent tutoring, e-learning, psychometric, and assessment communities provide the basis of a formal system for accomplishing that mapping.

Assessment of declarative knowledge is fairly ubiquitous, particularly in classroom environments. Furthermore, the most common formats for such assessments include multiple-choice and fill in the blank items. For these item types, predictive validity is often limited (i.e., successful solution of these types of items does not guarantee successful performance on tasks that require procedural skill). With an understanding of the task requirements, in conjunction with the underlying knowledge representation, we believe probes can be designed to assess not only declarative knowledge, but also procedural knowledge/skills and conceptual understanding. The exception is certain procedural skills (especially those requiring specialized motor skills), which are more challenging to assess without technologies that provide psychomotor fidelity.

Presenting various scenarios may be used to assess a learner's misconception(s) of some phenomenon. For example, the computer could provide a series of questions concerning DC circuits. This would be in the form of: "What would happen if ..." questions (e.g., *If you measure the current in each of the branches of a parallel net and sum those measurements, would the total be higher, lower, or equal to the current in the entire net?*). Solutions to these types of items would provide information about the presence and nature of the current conceptualization (pun intended) of the domain.

The program focused on in this chapter was originally designed to operate with a particular student modeling approach to obtain and manage the critical knowledge required by an intelligent instructional system. That is, DNA (Shute, et al., 2000) is a knowledge elicitation and organization tool that was designed to operate with SMART (Student Modeling Approach for Responsive Tutoring; Shute, 1995), a student modeling paradigm based on a series of regression equations diagnosing mastery at the element level (i.e., particular knowledge or skill). Furthermore, SMART is an instructor modeling paradigm that determines a pathway of instruction based on mastery diagnosis. Thus, DNA relates to the "what" to teach, while SMART addresses the "when" and "how" to teach it. Both programs divide the universe of learning outcomes into three types: basic (or declarative), procedural, and conceptual.

In general, SMART engages in the following activities: (a) calculates probabilistic mastery levels via a set of regression equations, (b) evaluates what a learner knows in relation to individual bits of knowledge and skill (curriculum elements), (c) tailors instruction and assessment for the learner by combining both micro-and macro-adaptive modeling techniques (see Shute, 1995), and, (d) adapts to both domain-specific knowledge/skills as well as general aptitudes.

More specifically, SMART consists of curriculum elements (CEs—units of instruction and assessment) that represent the complete set of knowledge and skill elements comprising the curriculum. These are arranged in an inheritance hierarchy. Each new piece of instruction introduces the next set of CE(s), which in turn are assessed while students solve problems in the tutor. Each question within a problem set posed by the tutor is associated with a specific CE, so blame assignment (and consequent remediation) is precise and timely.

A value, which represents the learner's probable mastery of the CE (p[CE]), is maintained for each CE. The program allows for continuous representation of the learner's probable mastery values, employing regression equations to compute new p[CE] values. SMART's specific regression equations are shown, below. Each of the four equations is linked with the level of assistance required by the learner in the solution of a problem involving one of more of the CEs. In other words, the equation invoked is tied to the actual number of hints (i.e., level of feedback) provided by the system to the learner, from no feedback (level 0) to most explicit (level 3).

$$\_{(Level\ 0)} = 0.3026 + 1.4377X - 0.7207X^2$$
$$\_{(Level\ 1)} = 0.3316 + 0.2946X + 1.1543X^2 - 0.9507X^3$$
$$\_{(Level\ 2)} = -0.0117 + 0.566X + 0.3518X^2$$
$$\_{(Level\ 3)} = 0.0071 - 0.6001X + 2.5574X^2 - 1.4676X^3$$

SMART is initialized based on pretest performance data, where each pretest item is scored, in real-time, from 0 to 1, with partial credit given where appropriate (note:

the pretest contains items assessing all CEs, but adaptive testing is also possible). This provides the potential for pre-assessed abilities (per CE) which influences tutor delivery. A learner is thus placed in the curriculum (relative to the CE hierarchy) and presented with the CE(s) having a p[CE] value below some pre-established mastery criterion (e.g., < .70). The hints given are progressively more explicit (ranging from level 1, vague, to 3, specific). Moreover, the feedback is specific to the particular problem, and sensitive to the number of retries. It is provided in response to erroneous inputs, not explicitly requested by the student.

SMART has been incorporated into an experiential learning environment called Stat Lady (Shute & Gluck, 1994) and has undergone a series of controlled evaluation studies where the main components (e.g., diagnostic updating routines, and mastery and remediation control structures) have been systematically evaluated. Two studies have been completed and are discussed in more detail in Shute (1995). Results show dramatic (i.e., 2.2 standard deviation) learning gains in the normal Stat Lady environment, and even greater improvement with SMART active. The efficacy of the program's diagnostic capabilities was shown to be quite accurate, accounting for 54% of the unique outcome variance on the basis of just the computed student model values, and 67% of the outcome variance when aptitude and pretest data entered the equation.

We believe that the SMART approach to student modeling, used in conjunction with DNA to obtain the CEs for instruction and assessment, can provide for a diagnostically valid system that can assist with both micro- and macroadaptation decisions (i.e., what to teach, as well as when and how to teach it). We now present an overview of DNA.

1.2 General Description of DNA

DNA (Decompose, Network, Assess) is a novel cognitive tool designed to help expedite, without sacrificing accuracy, the cognitive task analysis (CTA) phase of developing adaptive assessment or tutoring systems. In addition, our goal is to create a tool that is broadly applicable across domains. That is, our goal is for the tool to be able to help map out constituent knowledge and skill elements for a variety of potential domains. Specifically, DNA should be equally capable of analyzing task performance (e.g., how to interpret radar signals), as well as domains more conceptual in nature (e.g., understanding the factors that influence stock market fluctuations). For a more detailed description of the program, see Shute, et al. (2000).

In short, DNA is intended to Decompose a domain, Network the knowledge into comprehensive structures, and employ other experts in the given domain to Assess the validity, completeness, and reliability of the knowledge representations. The program embodies a semi-structured series of questions aimed at extracting and organizing knowledge structures from experts. These questions, in general, map on to the three main types of knowledge that DNA attempts to elicit—basic (AKA declarative or symbolic), procedural, and conceptual knowledge. These knowledge types make DNA compatible with SMART, described earlier.

1.3 Modules of DNA

There are four "modules" comprising DNA. In addition to the expert-centered modules—Decompose, Network, and Assess—there is a Customize module that is used by the person requiring curriculum elements and structures for training or assessment purposes. Each will be discussed in turn.

Customize. The Customize module allows the instructional designer to provide information about the domain that is to be analyzed, characteristics of the intended learner population, as well as a list of the goals for the training session, assessment, or instructional course. Additionally, by adjusting "what, how, and why" gauges, the instructional designer indicates what is desired from the expert's decomposition of the domain in terms of the intended relative instructional emphasis or flavor for the curriculum. For instance, the instructional designer may want experts to focus primarily on providing procedural knowledge (75%) for some training regime, with less basic (20%) and conceptual (5%) knowledge delineation. Altogether, the instructional designer's input is intended to guide experts in their task of conveying knowledge so that it will be suitable for the instructor's purposes. After obtaining all of this information from the instructional designer, the Customize module generates a brief introductory letter addressed to prospective experts and a set of floppy diskettes that contain all the necessary program files to execute DNA (note: the next version of DNA is intended to reside online). This letter may be printed, as is, or edited within the preferred word processing software. The introductory letter and diskettes are forwarded to one or more experts who will use DNA to delineate the curriculum. See Figure 1 for an example letter generated by the Customize module that requests the delineation of measures of central tendency in the field of statistics.

Decompose. The Decompose module does the bulk of the work in eliciting the subject-matter expert's explicit domain knowledge. This module functions as an interactive, semi-structured interview that is similar to the "What, How, Why" questioning procedure that has been shown in the past to successfully elicit knowledge from experts (e.g., Gordon, Schmierer, & Gill, 1993; Hyperknowledge, at http://www.hyperknowledge.com). In particular, each of these general questions has been transformed into a path of interrogation. The "what" path elicits basic knowledge, the "how" path focuses on procedural knowledge, and the "why" path is aimed at obtaining conceptual knowledge. These paths result in three different interfaces that attempt to obtain information corresponding to the different representations discussed earlier.

The first screen the expert sees upon opening the Decompose module appears with the items ("ultimate goals") that were articulated in the Customize letter, restated as questions. These comprise the general learning objectives that will be further fleshed out during the decomposition process. The first two queries (see Figure 2, below) relate to basic knowledge and thus would invoke the "what" path, upon selection. The third query requests procedural knowledge and relates to the "how" path. And the last question seeks to obtain more conceptual information from the expert—bringing up the "why" path when it is selected.

Figure 1. An example letter generated by the Customize module requesting delineation of measures of central tendency.

Dear [Insert Expert's Name Here],

We're writing today to get your help in designing a course teaching *measures of central tendency*. Before you begin working with the enclosed program, please sit down and think about the critical things that help you understand various measures of central tendency.

As you go through the enclosed program and respond to our questions, try to respond in terms of how you currently think about the particular domain. Please don't respond with your original knowledge of measures of central tendency; you have probably developed more complex ways of thinking about the domain since then.

The ultimate goals of the course are for our students to:

Identify the main measures of central tendency
Specify relevant formulas
Know how to compute or derive each measure
Understand the functional relationship(s) between each measure and different underlying distributions

How specific should you get? You can presume that our students will have the following knowledge and skills:

Basic math abilities (including algebra skills)
Familiarity with PCs (e.g., Windows 98, 2000, XP environments)
Basic reading skills

Therefore, you will not need to define knowledge or skills at a detailed level in relation to these elements.

When answering questions during the program, please adjust your responses to fit the following guidelines:

What box: 55%
How box: 35%
Why box: 10%

Thanks very much for your time.

Sincerely,
[Signature]

Figure 1. An example letter generated by the Customize module requesting delineation of measures of central tendency.

AUTOMATED KNOWLEDGE ELICITATION AND ORGANIZATION TOOL 159

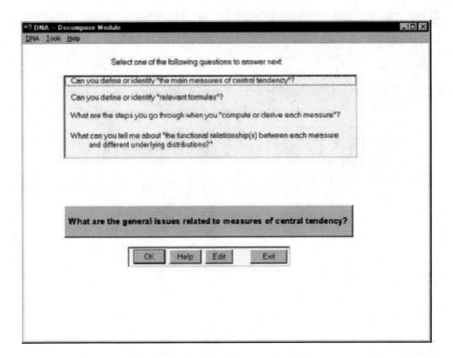

Figure 2. First screen of the Decompose Module

Given the domain of *measures of central tendency*, for example, suppose an expert proceeded down the basic knowledge (i.e., "what") path. The expert would select a question, then be guided through a series of questions that aim to elicit terms and definitions related to the curriculum element (CE) in focus. Further suppose that the expert began with the first question relating to defining the main measures of central tendency and elected to start with the Mean. At some point during the expert's definition of the Mean, the issue of distributions of data would arise, spawning a new line of questions (e.g., "Define or identify a normal distribution"). The expert can choose to decompose an area either breadth-first (e.g., specifying Mean, Median, and Mode as the three main types of central tendency). Alternatively, the expert may decompose in a depth-first manner—specifying the Mean, then within that context, discussing distributions, which may give rise to normal and skewed distributions, and so forth. In any case, responses are typed directly into a text box that can hold up to 16,000 characters. Multimedia files may be explicitly associated (via the "Link This" button) with a curriculum element to further embellish it. See Figure 3, below, for an example of the kinds of things that may be associated with a particular CE as part of the "Link This" option.

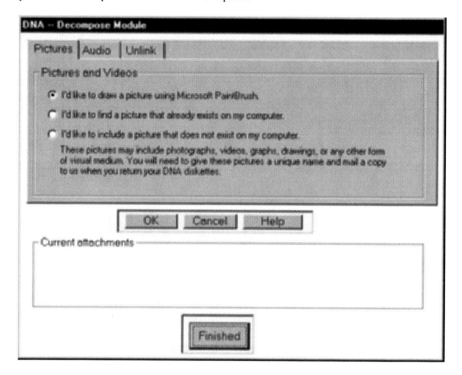

Figure 3. Screen from the "What" path of the Decompose Module in response to choosing the "Link This" option.

If a graphic were desired to supplement the definition, the expert would choose the "Link This" option, then either elect to draw a picture or associate the CE with an existing graphic. As shown in Figure 3, the expert chose to draw a picture.

Figure 4 shows an example of some output produced using the option to draw and label a "normal distribution." That file then becomes part of the particular CE record.

When decomposing procedural knowledge, the expert uses the "how" path, which presents a series of screens that allow the expert to construct procedures in the "step editor." In this process the expert delineates the steps of, and any conditional statements embodied within, the procedure. An expert's procedure for finding the Median in a data set with an odd number of values might be represented as the following:

(1) Sort the data in the distribution
(2) Determine the midpoint: (N+1)/2
(3) Find the corresponding X value

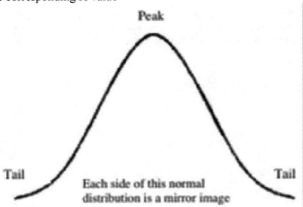

Figure 4. Example resulting from the option to draw and label a "normal distribution"

Any of the steps in a procedure could potentially be further decomposed into a sub-procedure. For instance, step 1 (sort the data in the distribution) may be broken into a sub-procedure detailing how to sort data in either ascending or descending order.

During the delineation of a procedure, the expert has a number of options to clarify and enrich the explanation of the task. The expert can add if-then statements, re-arrange steps, insert new ones, or delete any that are deemed unnecessary. In addition, and at any point, the expert may define terms that may otherwise be ambiguous to novices, thus providing additional basic knowledge. Figure 5 illustrates the step editor interface that shows one way an expert might summarize the steps underlying the computation of the Mean.

To decompose conceptual knowledge, the expert is guided through the "why" path, which is a series of questions that attempt to elicit as much information about complex concepts as possible. To illustrate using our example domain of measures of central tendency, suppose the expert chose to characterize the relationship between the Mean and its underlying distribution. The first question that DNA would present is: "What are the important issues that relate to the Mean and its underlying distribution?" This question is intended to obtain an initial listing of important elements associated with the Mean, such as: (a) "The Mean is affected by each value and its associated frequency within some distribution" and (b) "There are various types of distributions (e.g., normal, skewed, bimodal)."

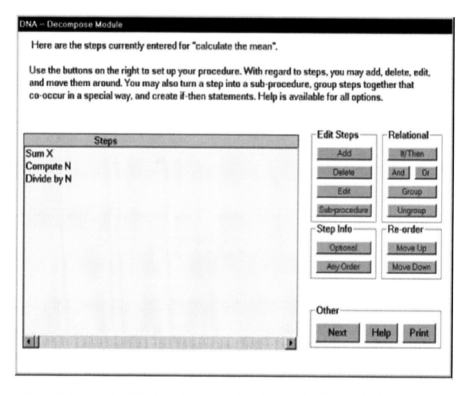

Figure 5. An example of the step-editor screen, from the procedural knowledge (PK) path, with the steps for calculating the Mean.

The second question in this path of inquiry is: "How are these elements functionally related?" This question is designed to elicit conceptual knowledge concerning how the important components (cited in the previous response) function together. A representative answer to this query might be, "The Mean is located in the center of a normal distribution, along with the Median and Mode. However, because the Mean is the only measure of central tendency affected by extreme scores, it will shift away from the center of skewed distributions and fall closer to the tail—where the extreme scores reside—than either the Median or Mode. For bimodal distributions, the Mean is located between the two humps."

The third question of the conceptual path asks: "Why is knowing about the relationship between the Mean and its underlying distribution important in understanding measures of central tendency?" This question attempts to link the current element being decomposed (Mean and its underlying distribution) to the general topic of instruction (measures of central tendency). Each of these questions, residing along this path, aims to provide a database of rich conceptual knowledge. A reasonable response would be: "Knowing the type of distribution of some data can influence your decision as to which measure of central tendency to use. For a skewed distribution (e.g., salaries in a small business where most are in the lower range and one or two in the very high region), the Mean would not be as good a summary of the central tendency of these data as the Median. Rather, it would be artificially inflated."

Finally, the expert is asked to describe typical and atypical situations in which knowing or understanding the relationship(s) between the Mean and different underlying distributions, is useful. An exemplar response would be: "A typical situation related to understanding the relationship between the Mean and various distributions is if you need to determine which measure of central tendency you should use to summarize some data. An atypical situation involving use of this knowledge would be if you wanted to purposefully distort a conclusion. For instance, if you wanted to impress some friends about the average salary of the small business (described above), you could report the Mean, knowing that the more typical salary was far less."

A particular path (what, how, why) is completed when its series of questions has been answered and the expert clicks the "Finished" button to indicate that no elaboration or additional elements warrant explanation at that point. How does the expert know when the domain is finally decomposed? The instructional designer specified the "ultimate learning goals" of the curriculum in the letter generated by the Customize module. This indicates the starting point for the expert's decomposition of the domain. The stopping point is also indicated in the letter by the statements of knowledge and skill that the learner population is presumed to possess. For instance, in the letter shown in Figure 1, learners are presumed to have basic math skills, thus the expert need not decompose the curriculum below that point. That is, if the expert delineated the procedure of computing the Mean (sum all numbers and divide by the sample size), no additional steps would have to be decomposed relating to the arithmetic operations embodied by those steps. In addition, the stopping point occurs when the expert believes that sufficient information has been specified for each of the ultimate learning goals indicated in the Customize letter.

All information given by experts is stored in a MS Access database record of CEs. These CEs serve as the guidelines for developing assessment or instruction in the domain. Multiple fields are listed with each CE record, e.g., name, number, description, relationships to other CEs, learning objective tapped, format, and so on. By storing this type of information in each CE record, it was hoped that restructuring DNA's output into teachable curriculum units would be more easily accomplished compared to traditional cognitive task analysis interview methods. Figure 6 illustrates DNA's object model.

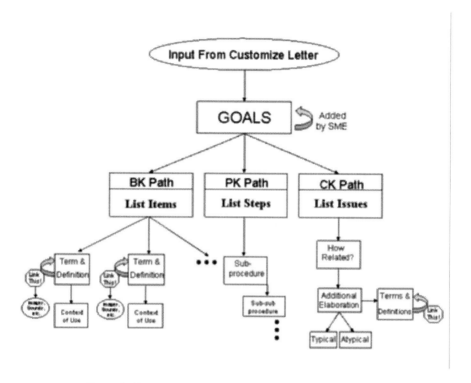

Figure 6. Object model representing DNA's Decompose Module.

Network. This module is currently under redevelopment. Ultimately, it is intended to transform CEs elicited during the Decompose module into graphical nodes that experts spatially arrange and link to form knowledge hierarchies, conceptual graphs, or production rules. Each node assumes the name of the CE and its contents that were defined during the Decompose module. To simplify viewing, only main-level CEs and their first-level "children" nodes appear upon the initial screen. "Pregnant" CEs are those that have elements embedded within them, such as sub-procedures within procedures. They appear in bold font. Any pregnant element can be unpacked to reveal its components by right clicking on the node and choosing the option "unpack."

To compose a meaningful hierarchy, nodes and their links are designed to differ along certain dimensions. Node shapes indicate the various knowledge types used by the SMART framework—rectangles reflect basic knowledge, ovals are procedural elements, and rounded rectangles denote conceptual knowledge. Links differ along three dimensions: type, direction, and strength of association. Some links are already in place when the subject matter expert (SME) arrives at the Network module. These come from information provided during the Decompose module (e.g., IF-THEN relationships from the step editor window). Other links must be created and labeled by the SME.

The first kind of link relationship is "type." This denotes the specific kind of relationship(s) between nodes (e.g., is a, causes, fixed serial order, child of). DNA's link types can relate to both semantic and procedural knowledge elements. Semantic links enable the SME to specify the relationships among curriculum elements, allowing for the conceptual structure of the domain to be specified. Procedural links enable the SME to specify the relationships among procedural steps and sub-steps, similar to a production-system representation. In addition to the semantic and procedural links available, there is a user-definable link that allows the SME to type in a label for a relationship not already defined.

The second link-label option is "directionality." This refers to the flow of control or causation between curriculum elements. Three options exist for this: uni-directional, bi-directional, and no direction. These relationships are established via arrowheads that are attached to the end of a line. For instance, the formula for the Mean ($\Sigma X/N$) could have arrows emanating from it to the individual elements comprising the formula (i.e., to each of Σ, X, and N and with a "parent of" label assigned to each node).

Finally, links can differ in terms of the "strength" of association. There are three values for this trait: weak, moderate, and strong. This indicates the degree to which the items are related. The information on strength is accomplished by varying the width of the link line (fine, medium, and bold).

This module is intended to be functionally similar to conceptual graph analysis (e.g., Gordon, et al., 1993) except that with DNA experts generate the conceptual graphs instead of the instructional designers. We believe that the use of a graphical representation will make relationships among knowledge units salient, which could also highlight missing knowledge components. Thus, we speculate that the network module of DNA will enable experts to recognize gaps in the knowledge and skills they provided in their decomposition. Moreover, they have a chance to readily correct inadequacies as they can return to the Decompose module and update the curriculum element record by adding or editing information.

After experts complete the Network module, data are stored on floppy diskettes and returned to the instructional designer who reviews the curriculum element record and conceptual graphs for any glaring omissions in content. If any omissions are present, the instructional designer can ask the expert to expand the inadequate curriculum elements to encompass, in full, the intended scope of instruction.

Assess. The final module, which is actually more a process, will be used to validate the CE records and conceptual graphs generated by experts. This will be accomplished by having other experts in the domain review the data and conceptual graphs generated by the first expert or group of experts. That is, multiple experts will be employed to review and edit one another's conceptual graphs as a method of validating externalized knowledge structures.

Before describing the results from the preliminary examination of DNA's efficacy, we first present DNA in the context of (a) the Field of AI and education, in general; followed by (b) its relation to other ITS authoring systems, specifically.

2. DNA'S NICHE IN THE FIELD OF AI AND EDUCATION

We are creating DNA in response to the charge that conventional cognitive task analysis (CTA) methods are often inefficient, laborious to translate into usable instruction, limited to procedural tasks, and difficult to use (see Shraagen, et al., 1997). These shortcomings identify areas to be improved in the intelligent tutoring, or adaptive e-learning system arenas. To help alleviate the impediment of the CTA process, we are attempting to address some of these limitations in the design of DNA.

Efficiency. Traditional CTA methods typically involve extensive interviews with experts, transcription of ensuing protocols, and organization of knowledge and skill units. This process normally requires many months of work and many person-hours to achieve. These traditional methods often employ knowledge engineers to interview and observe experts, others to transcribe sessions, and cognitive psychologists to summarize the data into a hierarchical representation. In contrast, DNA attempts to streamline the bulk of the interview, transcription, and organization process which is intended to significantly decrease both time and personnel resources required for the cognitive task analysis.

Instructional design framework. A common limitation of traditional CTA methods is that it is often difficult to translate the pages of interview transcriptions and conceptual graphs into a usable curriculum. DNA is designed such that its output is compatible with an existing instructional system framework (i.e., SMART; Shute, 1995), which should further enable efficient, adaptive systems development. In short, both the goal and the format of instruction are considered in the information sought. DNA's database record of CEs contains rich and useful information at the individual CE level – the unit base for structuring usable curriculum. CEs are classified according to knowledge types that are compatible with the SMART framework (i.e., basic, procedural, or conceptual knowledge). In addition, each CE includes a unique number, detailed description, and hierarchical information relating it to other CEs in the knowledge structure of the domain. The hierarchical structure represents dependency relations among knowledge elements that inform curriculum design.

In the near future, DNA will include expert-supplied embellishments such as: typical points of difficulty (impasses) in understanding the domain, good examples and counter-examples of concepts and procedures, along with more specific questions assessing conceptual and/or functional understanding of the particular domain or individual CE. All of this information is well suited for subsequently developing principled instruction.

An additional improvement to DNA, already begun, is to align it with the evidence-centered design (ECD) approach (e.g., Mislevy, et al., 1999). This is intended to enhance its capability to aid in the design of valid assessments. ECD involves: (1) defining the general proficiencies and particular claims to be made about the students (i.e., the knowledge, skills, and abilities to be measured), (2) establishing and delineating relevant evidence, per claim (i.e., student performance data demonstrating varying levels of mastery), and (3) determining the nature and format of tasks that will generate or elicit that evidence. Evidence, in the center, ties the tasks directly back to the underlying claims and proficiencies. As part of the original program, DNA already elicits the first part of the ECD requirements (i.e., the claims). We plan to expand it to also elicit associated evidences, per CE. Incorporating a content model will ensure that the associated instruction/assessment is tied to the desired proficiencies. Conforming to current industry standards (e.g., IMS, SCORM) will allow these diagnostic assessments and instructional units to be recycled in many different learning environments.

Broad applicability. Another common limitation of traditional CTA methods is that many are only applicable to procedural domains. DNA's specific purpose is to support intelligent tutoring system or adaptive e-learning development, applicable across a range of domain topics, both procedural and conceptual in nature. It attempts to achieve this broad applicability by eliciting CEs ranging in knowledge types compatible with the SMART framework. In addition, this applicability is to be achieved via its underlying hybrid representational structure of knowledge and skill elements, functionally a cross between a semantic net and production system (see Shute, et al., 2000).

User-friendly. As indicated previously, traditional CTA methods often rely on several individuals trained in knowledge elicitation techniques. In contrast, DNA was designed to be usable by those without CTA expertise. The interface offers context-sensitive examples and the interview questions were written at a fifth-grade reading level. Thus any instructional designer who wants to develop a curriculum will be able to use this tool, with a variety of experts, to elicit knowledge.

We now examine the question of how DNA fits in the field of ITS authoring systems.

DNA and Other ITS Authoring Systems

Although DNA was designed with the goal of facilitating ITS development, it is not an ITS authoring tool, per sé. As mentioned, DNA serves the development of intelligent instructional systems by attempting to streamline the process of interviewing subject matter experts (i.e., individuals with expertise about the domain to be instructed). This interview process is laborious but necessary, as the author of a course (or the instructional designer) does not always have the expertise of the domain to be taught, nor does the SME necessarily have the inclination or ability to instruct. Foremost a cognitive task analysis tool, DNA uses a semi-structured automated dialogue to elicit and structure the elements of knowledge of a domain from the SME that will be used by the instructional designer to create instruction. More precisely, rather than helping to "author" or output instruction, DNA helps to produce the input of the "authoring." Thus, relative to other authoring tools, DNA is decidedly limited in scope to producing the elements that go into the content or domain model – it does not produce complete tutors.

As is the trend for authoring tools, DNA divorces the knowledge base from the instructional strategy (Murray, 1998). Adherence to this divorce is intrinsic in the fact that DNA's scope is limited to the content or domain model. In addition, although DNA was designed with SMART in mind, it is not committed to any particular instructional strategy. In fact, the output of DNA would require a bit of transformation before being able to be used by SMART.

First, by producing a representation of the knowledge (not the instruction) that underpins a domain, DNA provides for designing at the pedagogical level, not the media level. The content or domain model in SMART, however, encapsulates the actual material to be presented to the learner during an instructional session. Thus, there would be some transition work (wording, arranging the graphics, etc.) to take DNA's output to the point of being a full domain model on which SMART can operate. The degree of effort required to transform DNA's output into an instructional format to be presented to the learner will vary, depending on the SME's direct responses and the goals of the tutor.

Second, while DNA's output identifies curriculum elements—the crux of the content—and implicitly represents the relationship among CEs (and will do so explicitly when the Network module is re-coded), this representation does not strictly specify an order of instruction. Rather, the output provides a map of the underlying knowledge domain, but the sequencing of instruction is left to the instructional designer's choice of instructional strategies. For example, the relationship between a procedure, its sub-procedures, and the conceptual knowledge supporting decisions and reasons for the process would be mapped out in the output. From that representation, the instructional designer could choose to take a part or whole task approach, or provide conceptual support for the procedure before or after requiring practice. Thus, additional specifications of sequencing DNA's output would be required before taking shape as a domain model for SMART, or other systems.

The tradeoff of DNA's output not being plug 'n play with SMART is that DNA's output is not restricted to use with SMART; it is not committed to a particular ordering of instruction, nor is it committed to a particular instructional theory. Thus, with a narrow focus towards the content or domain model, DNA's applicability is widened both in terms of content addressed and instructional strategies incorporated. Theoretically, with the aforementioned transitions, DNA's output should be usable with any number of intelligent instructional systems—whether the pedagogy is "learn by reading and thinking" or "learn by doing" simulation-basedsystems – a distinction made by Murray (1998).

Finally, given that DNA seeks out and identifies multiple knowledge and skills types (fact, process, concept), its output can be used with systems that are predicated on the belief that different knowledge/skill types should be instructed in different manners (e.g., Gagné, 1985; Merrill, 1994). Differentiation of knowledge types and their corresponding components, intra-relations, and inter-relations is done with DNA. However, facilitating the production in these types of tutors, the rules specifying feedback, hints, explanations, content as presented to learner, sequencing of instruction, and so forth is not done by DNA.

In general, our goal for DNA is that of decreasing the overall effort for making intelligent instructional or assessment systems by supporting the acquisition and organization of the knowledge base of the domain to be assessed and/or taught. Although DNA is an incomplete authoring tool prototype, initial evaluation supports the feasibility of the approach, as will be addressed in the next section. Further research remains in order to determine the full effort required to transition the material DNA produces to a domain model functioning in a tutor. By focusing on the cognitive task analyses phase of development and not specifying the pedagogical model, authors require instructional design skill, as they are not guided in how to finalize the domain model to fit whichever instructional strategy they would like to follow. The person actually using the system, however, needs no special training or knowledge base, and can use the DNA system with a minimal learning curve.

We now turn our attention to a formative investigation testing the Decompose module of the DNA system. In general, the different evaluation issues relate to the efficiency of the system and the validity of the output.

3. PRELIMINARY DNA EVALUATION

3.1 Design

DNA promises a great deal in its potential to uncork the cognitive task analysis (CTA) bottleneck. However, because DNA has been designed to be broadly applicable across domains, it is an open-ended and flexible system. The downside of this design feature is that the system may sometimes fail to keep SMEs grounded in their explication of domain expertise. Therefore, before relative benefits of DNA can be assessed, the more fundamental issue of whether DNA's general design is functionally feasible must be determined. As a stand-alone program and with only minimal direction to the SME via an introductory letter, can DNA actually extract *any* knowledge that can serve as the basis for curriculum development?

In order to address this basic feasibility question, we tested the degree to which our SMEs' data agreed with a benchmark representation of a topic. Williams (1993) conducted a similar analysis using a production system representing cutting and pasting text with a word processor. We extended this evaluation technique beyond its previous use with a simple procedural task by using it with a more complex domain containing a variety of knowledge types (i.e., measures of central tendency). Thus, we used the curriculum from an existing tutor, the second descriptive statistics module (DS-2) from Stat Lady (Shute, Gawlick, & Lefort, 1996) that focuses on the topic "measures of central tendency," as the benchmark. The curriculum for this module of Stat Lady was derived from a traditional cognitive task analysis involving document analysis as well as interviews with two SMEs. Although no formal records were kept regarding development time, we estimated that the CEs in the Stat Lady curriculum required approximately five months to obtain, structure, and outline.

Using a domain that has already been decomposed and transposed into an effective curriculum provides a way to gauge DNA's potential efficiency and validity. The Stat Lady curriculum provides a benchmark as to (a) the time and cost of eliciting the curriculum elements of the domain (i.e., an efficiency measure), and (b) the qualitative characteristics of curriculum elements of the domain (i.e., exemplar elements that constitute a valid, effective curriculum).

The degree to which the knowledge elements derived by DNA from experts map onto the elements of the Stat Lady curriculum, already embodied in an existing tutor, will shed light on the potential effectiveness of DNA's output. If the obtained output is close to the "idealized" extant domain structure of a tutor that has already been shown to improve learning, we can infer that the output is valid—or that it could be the basis for developing an effective curriculum.

3.2 Participants

Three volunteer subject-matter experts participated in this preliminary study. While none were formally "statisticians," all had graduate degrees in psychology and a minimum of 10 years experience conducting statistical analyses. Further, all reported that they were quite familiar with the measures of central tendency. None had prior, formal interactions with Stat Lady.

To assess incoming levels of expertise, the SMEs completed a computer-based test of measures of central tendency that is typically used in conjunction with Stat Lady. The test assessed knowledge and skills related to all CEs contained within the Stat Lady curriculum (i.e., a total of 127 CEs). While no time limits were imposed, our experts required between 1-1.5 hours to complete the test. Scores ranged from 71.3% to 87.5% (M = 79.2, SD = 8). Following the test, each expert completed the Decompose portion of DNA.

Before the experts' sessions with the program, the authors of this chapter completed the Customize module of DNA to produce a letter, similar to the one shown in Figure 1, informing the experts of the curriculum goals for some hypothetical students to achieve. In addition, this letter informed the SMEs of the intended learner population's expected skills and abilities. This provided the SMEs with parameters for their decomposition of the domain. Experts interacted with DNA in individual sessions, during which at least one of the authors was present to answer only general questions.

3.3 Benchmark

The Stat Lady DS-2 (Shute, et al., 1996) database consists of 127 curriculum elements. However, of those, only a subset of 78 CEs served as the benchmark against the output of DNA's Decompose module. This benchmark was used as the basis for assessing completeness and validity of the SMEs output. Some Stat Lady CEs were not included in the benchmark because they were deemed as not applicable, for a variety of reasons, to our current purpose. For instance, most of the first 37 CEs of the tutor constitute a stand-alone review module extracted from the first descriptive statistics module of Stat Lady. The review module included CEs related to organizing data (e.g., sorting data, identifying the minimum or maximum value, etc.) and manipulating frequency distribution tables. Since most of these items were not our experts' focus, all but 7 of these CEs were excluded from analysis. The CEs from the review module that *were* judged as relevant to the experts' task, and therefore kept in the benchmark, include knowing: (a) definitions for distribution, frequency distribution, and variable, (b) notations for variable, frequency, and sample size, and (c) the steps needed to create a frequency distribution.

Five additional CEs from the benchmark were removed because they were deemed as somewhat idiosyncratic to the Stat Lady tutor. That is, three conceptual knowledge (CK) elements were eliminated since they related to the instruction of measures of central tendency via analogy to a seesaw (not a standard practice, but helpful to learners, nonetheless). The remaining two CEs included basic knowledge (BK) elements that were concerned with identifying tutor-specific notation for the Median (i.e., Mdn) and the Mode (i.e., Mo). It is unrealistic to expect "experts" to outline these curriculum elements, given that these particular abbreviations for Median and Mode were specific to the Stat Lady curriculum, and not standard in Statistics instruction. Finally, an additional 14 Stat Lady CEs were excluded due to a subtle difference between procedural knowledge (PK) and procedural skill (PS). That is, Stat Lady CEs are coded either as BK, CK or PS elements depending upon how they are instructed and assessed. For instance, if a learner's knowledge of how to calculate the Mean was assessed by identifying steps of the procedure from a multiple-choice list, the element would be coded BK (which includes "knowledge of rules" or PK). In contrast, if the learner's knowledge was assessed by having them actually calculate the Mean of a set of data, the element would be coded PS. In short, coding of knowledge is context sensitive. In DNA, however, when decomposing their knowledge, experts describe procedures of a domain (i.e., knowledge of procedures – PK); they do not perform their "procedural skill" of these elements. Because elements coded as PS in the tutor context track the learner's ability (or success) in doing various tasks or procedures, they are not appropriate to serve as a comparison benchmark. Therefore all of Stat Lady's PS elements were excluded from the benchmark. Some of these PS elements that were removed include computing: the sum of values, N, cross products, midpoint, Mean, Median, and Mode (and doing so in a variety of contexts).

In general, Stat Lady's "measures of central tendency" curriculum concentrates on basic, procedural, and conceptual knowledge relating to the Mean, Median, and Mode. Basic elements include definitions, formulas, and notations for each measure and their components (e.g., sample size $N = \Box f$; Mean $= \Box X/N$; cross product $= Xf$). Procedural elements describe the steps of how to calculate each measure of central tendency from both data sets and frequency distribution tables. In addition, alternative methods for these calculations are detailed, where appropriate. For example, the curriculum includes differences in the procedure for calculating the Mean when all frequencies equal one ($f = 1$) and for when they do not (i.e., some $f > 1$). Conceptual elements emphasize understanding which central tendency measures are appropriate within different circumstances, and why.

For sufficient instruction of the domain, additional BK, PK, and CK elements cover various types of distributions (e.g., normal, flat, symmetric, bimodal, platykurtic, leptokurtic, mesokurtic, postively and negatively skewed), as well as issues of symmetry, kurtosis and skewness. To bolster concept integration, many elements highlight the relationship between the three measures of central tendency and the underlying distribution. Specifically, they instruct and assess on each measure's location, and relationship(s) to one another, within different types of distributions. The sum of this information supports understanding of the guidelines for using each of the three measures.

In total, 78 CEs from the Stat Lady DS-2 curriculum remained as the final benchmark for analysis. The distribution of knowledge types in the benchmark was as follows: 74% BK elements, 18% PK elements, and 8% CK elements. This was not substantially different from the distribution of the original 127 CEs for the entire tutor (79% basic, 13% procedural, and 8% conceptual elements).

4. RESULTS AND DISCUSSION

The output from DNA exists in two forms: (a) a Microsoft Access database of CEs and (b) a graphical array of the hierarchical knowledge structure (future design). The focus of this DNA assessment was on the Decompose module therefore the CE databases were analyzed in this formative evaluation.

The analysis involved assessing the content of each SME's database relative to the benchmark described above. For each CE we assigned either a "1" to indicate that the SME included it in the decomposition, or a "0" to denote its absence. In some instances, we assigned partial credit if we judged that a portion of a CE was decomposed (e.g., .67 if 2 out of 3 steps of a procedure were listed). There were a couple of cases where a SME delineated a CE that was not present in the benchmark listing. Those instances were noted, but not included in the current analysis. For example, one expert delineated and defined "data" (i.e., *a set of observations about the world; within statistics, data commonly refers to a set of numbers that are collected or observed*). This CE was not in the original Stat Lady database as it was presumed to be part of incoming knowledge.

How well do the experts capture the benchmark curriculum? Our three SMEs' output captured 25%, 49% and 23% of the Stat Lady benchmark database. Furthermore, each required 285, 170, and 100 minutes to complete DNA, respectively. One expert (SME-2) was clearly more in line with Stat Lady than the others, producing the array of CEs most consistent with the benchmark in less than 3 hours of decomposition time.

When developing a curriculum for a domain, an instructional designer aggregates information from several sources. Likewise, we combined the outputs produced by all three experts, however we did not have to deal with the issue of potentially contradictory data from multiple SMEs in this case. This issue of aggregating data across SMEs, consistent and otherwise, will be examined further in an upcoming study by the first author. Specifically, the utility of a statistical approach called combinatorial data analysis (Hubert, Arabie, & Meulman, 2001) will be examined as a possible solution to combining potentially disparate data.

Table 1 presents the comparison between (a) the CEs elicited by DNA from our three SMEs combined, and (b) the CEs that compose the benchmark. The data in the table show the total count of CEs, overall and by knowledge type. Results showed that the distribution of knowledge types derived by DNA in our combined SME data

(71% BK, 23% PK, and 6% CK) is similar to the distribution seen in the benchmark data (74% BK, 18% PK, and 8% CK). This seems to suggest that DNA addresses the different knowledge types adequately.

	Total	BK	PK	CK
Combined SMEs' CE output	48	34	11	3
Stat Lady Benchmark CEs	78	58	14	6

Table 1. Comparison of curriculum elements (CEs) elicited from our experts by DNA to those of the Stat Lady benchmark, overall and by knowledge type (basic, procedural, and conceptual).

With regard to the SMEs' collective capture of the benchmark, results show that 62% (i.e., 48/78) of the Stat Lady CEs were delineated by at least one of our three experts. For this domain, DNA was relatively more successful at eliciting a match of the benchmark's *procedural* knowledge, capturing 11/14 (79%) of the benchmark, than at eliciting *basic* 34/58 (59%) or *conceptual* knowledge 3/6 (50%).

Which elements were extracted and which were not? Some benchmark CEs were reported by all of our experts, some by only a subset of the SMEs, while other elements were omitted completely. In the following paragraphs, we discuss the nature of the CEs produced by the decomposition and those omitted.

Results indicated that nine (i.e., 12%) benchmark CEs were outlined by all three experts (5 BK and 4 PK). These included definitions of the Mean, Median, and Mode. To illustrate, one of the SMEs outlined the definition of the Mean shown in Figure 7; the other definitions were comparable. Other CEs that were reported by all experts included the basic steps required to determine the values of each measure of central tendency. For instance, each expert delineated the steps to (a) calculate the Mean when $f = 1$, (b) determine the Median when N is odd and when it is even, and (c) identify the Mode. See Figure 5 in the General Description of DNA section for a SME's outline of the procedure to calculate the Mean. Finally, all SMEs conveyed that in a normal distribution, the three measures of central tendency have the same value.

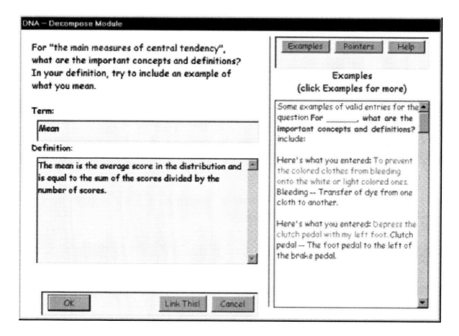

Figure 7. SME's output defining the Mean in the basic knowledge (BK) path.

Next, 39 (i.e., 50%) benchmark CEs were reported by a subset of our experts: 29 BK, 7 PK, and 3 CK (Note: SME-2, who individually matched the benchmark 49%, provided the bulk of these elements, while the other two experts contributed only 8 additional unique CEs). Some of these elements included: definitions of normal distribution, tail, and skewness, notations for sample size (N) and variable (X), and the formula for computing cross products (X * f). Other examples of elements reported by a subset of experts included the guidelines for using different measures of central tendency and the relationship among them within a skewed distribution (e.g., the Mode is used with categorical data; the Median is better for representing quantitative data within a skewed distribution). A number of CEs were reported that relate to distributions (e.g., normal, positively and negatively skewed) and their particular relationship(s) with the measures of central tendency. For example, the functional relationship of each of the three measures within a normal distribution was described, and the Mean was further discussed within skewed distributions. Figure 8 shows an excerpt of one SME's response to DNA's conceptual path query regarding the important aspects of the relationship between a measure of central tendency and its underlying distribution.

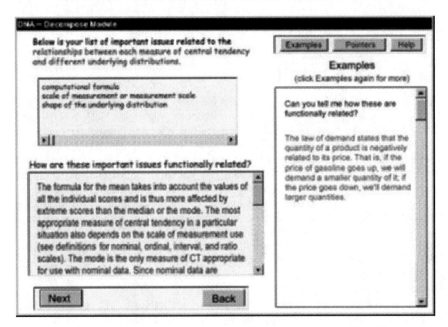

Figure 8. A response along the conceptual knowledge (CK) path representing an excerpt of a SME's output on the functional relationship between measures of central tendency and underlying distribution types. The vertical scrollbar indicates additional text.

Finally, there were 30 (i.e., 38%) benchmark elements omitted by all three experts (24 BK, 3 PK, 3 CK). Some of these omissions included low-level information that related to formulas (e.g., the sum of cross products, $\Sigma[X * f]$), definitions (e.g., variable), and notations (e.g., f for frequency). Thus, either (a) the stopping point for the decomposition of knowledge was not communicated well by the Customize letter, or (b) what was outlined as the goal of the tutor did not match exactly with the benchmark domain model. Additional omissions included the specification of alternative formulations (e.g., computing the Mean when $f > 1$, and use of midpoint formula as a step to determine the Median). Other elements not reported by any of our SMEs were some conceptually complex ones. For instance, no expert described the Median and Mode in relation to skewed or flat distributions. Finally, the last set of elements omitted were those fairly peripheral to the curriculum emphasized by the Customize module letter. Some of these included defining platykurtic, mesokurtic, and leptokurtic distributions.

In sum, the agreement between the aggregate and benchmark data showed that DNA was able to elicit 62% of the CEs present in an existing database, and was able to do so in a reasonable amount of time (i.e., approximately 9 hours, the total time required by all 3 experts). In relation to simple counts of CE types, our SMEs produced more BK elements than either PK or CK ones. But in relation to the benchmark, our SMEs' output matched a greater percentage of PK elements than either BK or CK elements.

Limitations

How do we interpret these data? Why did we not see 100% overlap? We suspect there is an interaction of at least three factors contributing to this "less than perfect" capturing of the benchmark: (1) idiosyncrasy of the Stat Lady curriculum, (2) issues related to our specific "experts," and (3) inadequacies within the DNA program.

First, with regard to the Stat Lady curriculum, the elements selected for inclusion represent "measures of central tendency" as culled from extensive document analysis on the topic, as well as interviews with two subject-matter experts. Some of the items our current (DNA using) experts omitted included definitions of leptokurtic, platykurtic, and mesokurtic distributions, possibly deeming these items as not central to (or too esoteric for) the scope or goals of the decomposition. Further, other elements that were not articulated by our experts included very low-level CEs such as defining the summation notation (Σ). Thus, the Stat Lady curriculum contained many items that our experts may have considered to be only tangentially related to the decomposition task.

The second factor we suspect contributed to our failure to get perfect overlap involved the nature of our experts. As mentioned earlier, we solicited local participants who are not formally statisticians, but rather experimental psychologists who are familiar with statistics. Their knowledge structure of the field, while no doubt solid, may not have reflected the knowledge structures of true statisticians. This was further indicated by their test data; we suspect that statisticians would have scored in the 90th percentile on that test. Recall that the mean pretest score from our group was 79%. Thus, it appears that the experts participating in the current evaluation had areas of deficient knowledge.

The third factor contributing to our obtained degree of overlap relates to possible shortcomings of the DNA program itself. The data from the present study made apparent several places where DNA could be enhanced. First, the data showed that our experts provided fewer CK elements than PK or BK elements in relation to the benchmark. This finding could be an indicator that the conceptual path in DNA was simply not effective in eliciting CK structures. We are currently addressing this problem by adding some follow-up questions at the end of important junctures within DNA. For instance, at the end of the entire Decompose module, the expert will be asked a series of thought-provoking questions designed to capture an overview of the domain/field (e.g., themes and principles). We believe that this information will further aid the instructional designer in generating curriculum and provide more illuminating conceptual knowledge to the curriculum. Some example global follow-up questions include: (a) What are some difficult areas you've encountered in the acquisition of [domain being decomposed]? (b) What has worked for you in surmounting these obstacles? (c) Can you describe a good analogy that can help learners understand aspects of the domain?

In addition, we are planning to elicit more CK information in conjunction with explicated procedures. That is, at the conclusion of each "how path," the experts will be specifically probed to flesh out the procedures in terms of their underlying rationales. Thus, besides obtaining a listing of steps comprising some procedure, we also want to elicit the reasons *why* they chose to do it that particular way.

Another important revision to the Decompose module was motivated by our findings. That is, on occasion, our experts would input procedural specifications that were ambiguous (e.g., Do A or B and C). DNA is now becoming sensitive and responsive to instances of ambiguity. As a result, the new version of DNA will require the expert to specify "groupings" to render any potentially ambiguous procedure or statement more precise (e.g., Do (A or B) and C). Furthermore, DNA will also request that the expert think about alternative methods to accomplish the same goal. For example, if the expert has specified some conditional statements in a procedure, the Decompose module will probe for additional, logical antecedents and consequences (e.g., When A does not hold, should one still do B? Are there other conditions that can trigger B?).

In summary, these data provide preliminary information about the efficacy of DNA as a knowledge elicitation tool. That is, given limited direction via one introductory letter of expectations for the decomposition of the domain and minimal guidance in use of the DNA program, experts appear to be able to use the tool efficiently to explicate components of their knowledge structures. Moreover, the obtained data are, for the most part, consistent with an existing curriculum. Thus we are gaining confidence that our tool has potential value as an aid to ITS and adaptive e-learning system development. Rather than being discouraged that our overlap was "only 62%", we are encouraged that the results suggest the basic design of DNA is feasible.

5. SUMMARY AND CONCLUSIONS

This paper describes an ongoing effort to develop DNA, a knowledge-elicitation tool to be used by subject-matter experts across a variety of domains. We also describe an exploratory test of the effectiveness and efficiency of the program. Preliminary results show that DNA can produce reasonably valid and reliable data within an acceptable amount of time. This has a direct implication for streamlining the intelligent assessment and instructional system development process, often viewed as a major obstacle in developing adaptive instructional systems. In addition, given these data were obtained from individuals who are not "statisticians" suggests that DNA can be used by persons varying in levels of expertise. This also suggests a potential avenue for DNA as a research tool investigating knowledge structures of people with varying levels of competence in a domain, as well as changes in those structures over time.

There are several key features of DNA that, we believe, make this a viable alternative to current, costly knowledge-elicitation techniques. Because DNA supports streamlining portions of the interview, transcription, and organization processes, it allowed us to obtain data simply by giving each expert the program along with a short letter explaining the goals of the curriculum. The program obviates the need for transcribing lengthy interviews. Additionally, experts are able to explicate and organize their knowledge within the same elicitation session, which translates into expected savings of time and money without sacrificing accuracy. This will be examined in future studies.

DNA's applicability is enhanced because it elicits, and then allows SMEs to represent graphically, a range of knowledge types. Specifically, the Decompose module focuses on eliciting *three* knowledge types: basic, procedural, and conceptual (what, how, and why). Additionally, the Network module will ultimately be able to produce a conceptual graph that incorporates information from the three types of representations mentioned earlier. The result is that the representational scheme enables DNA to obtain declarative, procedural, and conceptual information, promoting applicability across multiple topics. Heretofore, intelligent instructional systems have been built for single outcome types (e.g., production systems for procedural knowledge), thus varied knowledge types have been forced into a one-scheme-fits-all representation. In contrast, typical courses or curricula contain rich mixtures of knowledge types. For example, one can know the formula of the statistical Mean (BK) but not know how to compute it (PK), or one can be unfamiliar with the formula, but know how to compute it. In any case, it makes sense to be sensitive to representation differences when initially gathering curriculum elements for any course (during the CTA). That is what we are attempting to do with DNA via the three interfaces or paths reflecting the three main knowledge types.

Another design feature of DNA is its compatibility with an empirically validated instructional framework (i.e., SMART). SMART relies on information present in hierarchical-knowledge structures (e.g., parent/child relations) to manage instruction and remediation. DNA's Network module provides the SME with tools to create such a hierarchical knowledge structure. In addition, the Decompose module's what, how, and why questions map onto the instructional framework of basic, procedural, and conceptual knowledge types embodied by SMART, which relies on these knowledge types to provide differential instruction, remediation, and assessment. For instance, procedural knowledge is instructed within a problem-solving context, while conceptual knowledge may use analogies for instruction. Therefore, DNA's capacity to identify different knowledge types facilitates SMART's management of more customized instruction.

Our initial question underlying DNA's design feasibility concerned whether, indeed, DNA can extract comprehensive and reasonable knowledge from experts. Results from this preliminary evaluation are encouraging. In a relatively short amount of time and with minimal resource cost, the Decompose module of DNA was able to elicit 62% of the curriculum elements that are in place in an extant tutor. This suggests that the general approach implemented by DNA (with all of its limitations) works to produce valid data that could potentially serve as the basis for curriculum development. Future studies will examine DNA's efficiency relative to standard knowledge elicitation techniques. Additional questions we plan to explore include, among others: (a) Can DNA be used to elicit knowledge across a broad range of domains? (b) Is it differentially effective in eliciting basic, procedural, and conceptual knowledge elements? and (c) Do differing levels of expertise result in data structures that vary in kind, rather than quantity? In short, future research and development will focus on identifying where we have and have not succeeded in our aim to expedite development of intelligent instructional systems.

6. REFERENCES

Almond, R., Steinberg, L. & Mislevy, R. (in press). A four-process architecture for assessment delivery, with connections to assessment design. *Journal of Technology, Learning, and Assessment.*

Anderson, J. R. (1987). Skill acquisition: Compilation of weak-method problem solutions. *Psychological Review, 94*, 192-210.

Anderson, J. R. (1988). The expert module. In M. C. Polson & J. J. Richardson (Eds.), *Foundations of intelligent tutoring systems* (pp. 21-50). Hillsdale, NJ: Lawrence Erlbaum Associates.

Anderson, J. R. (1993). *Rules of the mind.* Hillsdale, NJ: Lawrence Erlbaum Associates.

Chipman, S., Shalin, V., & Schraagen, J. (Eds.) (2000). *Cognitive Task Analysis.* Hillsdale, NJ: Erlbaum Associates.

Collins, A. M., & Loftus, E. F. (1975). A spreading activation theory of semantic processing. *Psychological Review, 82*, 407-428.

Collins, A. M., & Quillian, M. R. (1969). Retrieval time from semantic memory. *Journal of Verbal Learning and Verbal Behavior, 8*, 240-248.

Gagné, R. (1985). *The Conditions of Learning and Theory of Instruction.* Holt, Rinehart, and Winston. New York.

Gordon, S. E., Schmierer, K. A., & Gill, R. T. (1993). Conceptual graph analysis: Knowledge acquisition for instructional system design. *Human Factors, 35*, 459-481.

Hubert, L., Arabie, P. & Meulman, J. (2001). *Combinatorial data analysis: Optimization by dynamic programming* (Vol. 1). Philadelphia, PA: SIAM/ Monograph on Discrete mathematics and applications.

Johnson-Laird, P., N. (1983). *Mental models.* Cambridge, MA: Harvard University Press.

Lajoie, S. P., & Derry, S. J. (1993). *Computers as cognitive tools.* Hillsdale, NJ: Lawrence Erlbaum Associates.

Merrill, M. D. (1994). *Instructional Design Theory.* Englewood Cliffs: Educational Technology Publications.

Merrill, M. D. (2000). Knowledge objects and mental models. In D. A. Wiley (Ed.), *The Instructional Use of Learning Objects: Online Version.* Retrieved March 6, 2002, from the World Wide Web: *http://reusability.org/read/chapters/merrill.doc*

Minstrell, J. (2000). Student thinking and related instruction: Creating a facet-based learning environment. In J. Pellegrino, L. Jones, & K. Mitchell (Eds.) *Grading the Nation's Report Card: Research for the Evaluation of NAEP.* Committee on the Evaluation of NAEP, Board on Testing and Assessment. Washington, DC: National Academy Press.

Mislevy, R. J., Almond, R. G., Yan, D., & Steinberg, L. S. (2000, March). *Bayes nets in educational assessment: Where do the numbers come from?* (CSE Technical Report 518). Retrieved from *http://www.cse.ucla.edu/CRESST/Reports/TECH518.pdf*

Mislevy, R. J., Steinberg, L. S., & Almond, R. G. (1999, January). *On the roles of task model variables in assessment design* (CSE Technical Report 500). Retrieved from *http://www.cse.ucla.edu/CRESST/Reports/TECH500.pdf*

Mislevy, R. J., Steinberg, L. S., Almond, R. G., Haertel, G. D., & Penuel, W. R. (2001, February). *Leverage points for improving educational assessment* (CSE Technical Report 534). Retrieved from *http://www.cse.ucla.edu/CRESST/Reports/newTR534.pdf*

Murray, T. (1998). Authoring Knowledge Based Tutors: Tools for Content, Instructional Strategy, Student Model, and Interface Design. *Journal of the Learning Sciences* (Special Issue on Authoring Tools for Interactive Learning Environments), 7, No.1, pp. 5-64.

Polson, M. C., & Richardson, J. J. (1988). *Foundations of Intelligent Tutoring Systems.* Hillsdale, NJ: Lawrence Erlbaum Associates.

Schank, R. (1999). *Dynamic memory revisited.* Cambridge, England: Cambridge University Press.

Shraagen, J. M. C., Chipman, S. E., Shute, V. J., Annett, J., Strub, M., Sheppard, C., Ruisseau, J. Y., & Graff, N. (1997). *State-of-the-art review of cognitive task analysis techniques.* Deliverable Report of RSG.27 on Cognitive Task Analysis NATO Defense Research Group (Panel 8/RSG.27). TNO Human Factors Research Institute Group: Information Processing.

Shute, V. J. (1995). SMART: Student modeling approach for responsive tutoring. *User Modeling and User-Adapted Interaction, 5,* 1-44.

Shute, V. J., & Gluck, K. A. (1994). *Stat Lady: Descriptive Statistics Module.* [Unpublished computer program]. Brooks Air Force Base, TX: Armstrong Laboratory.

Shute, V. J., & Psotka, J. (1996). Intelligent tutoring systems: Past, present, and future. In D. Jonassen (Ed.), *Handbook of Research on Educational Communications and Technology,* (pp. 570-600). New York, NY: Macmillan.

Shute, V. J. & Towle, B. (in press). Adaptive e-Learning. Paper to appear in special issue of *Educational Psychologist,* in honor of Dr. Richard Snow.

Shute, V. J., Gawlick, L. A., & Lefort, N. K. (1996). Stat Lady (DS-2 module) [Unpublished computer program]. Brooks Air Force Base, TX: Armstrong Laboratory.

Shute, V. J., Torreano, L. A., and Willis, R. E. (1999). Exploratory test of an automated knowledge elicitation and organization tool. *International Journal of AI and Education, 10*(3-4), 365-384.

Shute, V. J. & Torreano, L., & Willis, R. (2000). DNA: Towards an automated knowledge elicitation and organization tool. In S. P. Lajoie (Ed.) *Computers as Cognitive Tools, Volume 2.* Hillsdale, NJ: Lawrence Erlbaum Associates, pp. 309-335.

Sleeman, D. H., & Brown, J. S. (1982). *Intelligent tutoring systems.* London, England: Academic Press.

VanLehn, K. (1990). *Mind bugs: The origins of procedural misconceptions.* Cambridge, MA: MIT Press.

White, B. Y. & J. R. Frederiksen (1987). Qualitative models and intelligent learning environments. In R. Lawler & M. Yazdani (Eds.), *AI and education,* (pp. 281-305). Norwood, NJ: Ablex Publishing.

Williams, K. E. (1993). *The development of an automated cognitive task analysis and modeling process for intelligent tutoring system development.* Contract final report on N00014-97-J-5-1500. Manpower Personnel and Training Program, Office of Naval Research.

ACKNOWLEDGEMENTS

This work was done while that authors worked for Armstrong Laboratory Human Resources Directorate. The research was supported by the USAF Armstrong Laboratory, and also, in part, by a National Research Council (USAF) Research Associateship Award granted to the second author (1997-1999). We would like to acknowledge the invaluable contributions to this research (from concept design to development) by our colleague Ross Willis, and to thank Tom Murray and two anonymous reviewers for their sage comments on an earlier draft of this chapter. Finally, we thank Irv Katz for his assistance specifying DNA's object model.

M. DAVID MERRILL

Chapter 7

USING KNOWLEDGE OBJECTS TO DESIGN INSTRUCTIONAL LEARNING ENVIRONMENTS

ABSTRACT. The primary purpose of this paper is to describe and illustrate a PEAnet knowledge structure and its use in designing instructional learning environments. The ID_2 Research Group at Utah State University used this architecture to design a prototype authoring system, the Instructional Simulator. The knowledge object architecture described has implications for the design of instructional systems beyond the prototype system. The emphasis of this paper is on the underlying architecture rather than on the Instructional Simulator prototype itself. The importance of our contribution is in defining knowledge objects, knowledge structures, knowledge bases, and how these content representations can be used with appropriate instructional strategy objects to provide a variety of instructional interactions, including learning environments and direct instruction, to a student. The detailed implementation of this architecture in the Instructional Simulator and subsequently in the IDVisualizer™ is only one possible implementation of this architecture.

1. ID EXPERT AND SUBSEQUENT DEVELOPMENTS

ID Expert™ (Merrill et al, 1998) was a prototype system that implemented multiple knowledge types (Murray, 1999). This system was in the process of commercialization when the sponsoring company fell into financial difficulty and the development of this authoring system was discontinued. The ID_2 Research Group at Utah State University subsequently continued the development of the ideas in ID Expert in two separate products: The Electronic Textbook[1], which continued as a multiple knowledge type template system (Merrill & Thompson, 1999) and the Instructional Simulator[2] which more completely implemented our work on knowledge representation in a device simulation system (Merrill, 1999). Merrill and Thompson (1999) describe the Electronic Textbook in detail elsewhere. This report emphasizes the knowledge representation system underlying the Instructional Simulator prototype and its successor the IDVisualizer.

2. A LEARNING ENVIRONMENT

The ID$_2$ Research Group built a prototype learning environment authoring system, the Instructional Simulator, that included both simulation and direct instruction capabilities. This demonstration system was built using Toolbook™. Utah State University subsequently licensed this product to Mindware Creative Inc. for marketing and further development. Mindware Creative named the tool the IDVisualizer™. The learning environment described in this paper and Instructional Simulator prototype tool used to build this learning environment was the forerunner of the IDVisualizer. Readers should contact Mindware Creative at www.mindware1.com for the latest versions of the product.

This paper first describes a demonstration learning environment constructed using knowledge objects as implemented in the Instructional Simulator. After the description of this learning environment the paper will describe how these knowledge objects were used to construct this learning environment.

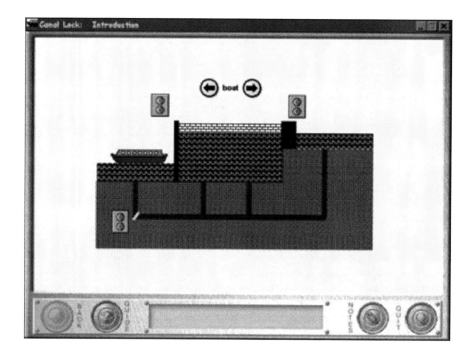

Figure 1 A Learning Environment for a Canal Lock

Figure 1 illustrates a learning environment for teaching students how a canal lock works. This is an interactive environment that allows the learner to manipulate the elements of the environment to see how they work. This environment consists of the following entities (parts): a canal boat that can move up and down the canal by use of the two arrow buttons at the top of the diagram. An upper and lower gate that can be opened and closed using the push buttons above either gate. An outlet valve that can be opened and closed using the push buttons adjacent to the valve in the lower left corner of the diagram.

Moving the canal boat through the lock would involve the following actions on the part of the learner. As the diagram appears in Figure 1 the upper gate must first be closed by clicking on the lower button in of the upper right control. The water must then be lowered by opening the outlet valve by clicking on the lower button of the control in the lower left. The lower gate must then be opened by clicking upper button of the upper left control. The canal boat is then moved into the lock by clicking on the right boat arrow. The lower gate must then be closed by clicking on the lower button of the upper left control. The water must then be raised by closing the outlet valve by clicking on the upper button of the lower left control. The upper gate must then be opened by clicking on the upper button of the upper right control. The canal boat must then be moved up the canal by again clicking on the right boat arrow. The upper gate should then be closed by clicking on the lower button of the upper right control.

The simulation is not linear. The learner can click on any button at any time. The resulting consequence may not occur if it is not allowed by the function of the lock. For example, the learner may first try to open the outlet valve. But the outlet valve cannot be opened until the upper gate is closed so nothing happens.

This visualization is more than just an interactive environment, it is an instructional learning environment. This means that in addition to being able to interact with the simulation the student can also obtain information and guidance.

Moving the cursor over any part of the lock displays the name of this part in the panel at the bottom of the screen. Right clicking on any of the parts of the lock provides a description of this part. For example, right clicking on the canal boat pops up the following message: "A flat bottomed boat used to transport people and goods through a canal waterway." Right clicking on the boat down control button pops up the following message: "This control is used to move the canal boat down through the canal lock."

At the bottom of the diagram are several navigation buttons. The *BACK* button takes the student back to the introductory information or instruction that precedes the visualization. The *NOTES* button allows the student to make and save their own notes about their experience. The *GUIDE* button provides a number of instructional functions described in the following paragraphs.

Clicking on the *GUIDE* button displays the following menu items: *Tell me about, Identify, demonstrate, Practice, Perform.* Clicking on *Tell me about* displays one or more "lectures" about the system. In this case there is only a single lecture on *lock controls*. A lecture is a systematic presentation of the descriptions for each of the parts of the system. In this case the lecture highlights each of the lock controls in turn and pops up its function description. The student controls the pace of the lecture by clicking the mouse button.

Clicking on *Identify* displays two options: *control locations, control names.* Selecting the *control locations* option causes the system to display the names of each of the controls in a pop-up window. The names are presented in random order. The student is directed to click on the control associated with the name. Students are given immediate feedback on their response. If the response is incorrect then the system highlights the correct control for the student. The student's score in identifying the locations of the controls is recorded in the student file. The location quiz uses a sampling with replacement strategy so that if a student misses a given control it is put back into the list for a second try later. The student can abort the quiz at any time. Selecting the *control names* option causes the system to highlight each of the controls in turn and directs the student to select the name of the control from a pop-up window displaying the names for all of the controls. Immediate feedback is provided. If the student' response is incorrect the correct name is highlighted for the student. The naming quiz also uses sampling with replacement and missed items are retained in the pool for another try later in the quiz. Student scores are recorded in the student file. The student can abort the quiz at any time.

Clicking on the *Demonstrate* item displays two options: *move boat up, move boat down.* The visualization knows where the boat is at any time so selecting either option demonstrates only those steps necessary to complete its journey through the lock. If the boat is below the lock and the *move boat up* option is selected then all of the steps necessary to move the boat to above the lock will be demonstrated. However, if the boat is already in the lock, the lock water is high, and the move boat up option is selected then only the last steps, open the upper gate, move the boat up, and close the upper gate will be demonstrated. A "Simon Says"[4] approach is used for the demonstration. A pop-up window directs the student in the next action to take. For example, "First, push "upper gate closer". After the student completes the action the next direction is given. If the student does not do the directed action a message indicates "that is not the upper gate closer" and the student is directed to try again. After the action is completed the next direction is given, e.g., "Next, push the outlet valve opener." This demonstration is continued until the student has completed the travel of the boat through the lock or until the student aborts the demonstration. The student is given the option to see an explanation during the demonstration. An explanation describes for each action taken what happened and why. For example, "When you push the upper gate closer the gate position of the upper gate is set to closed. This happens because the gate position of upper gate is open."

Selecting the *Practice* option also displays two options: *move boat up, move boat down.* The student is first given the goal for the practice: "Goals: lock position of canal boat is above and gate position of upper gate is closed." The student is directed "Do the first step of the procedure now." If the student does the correct action the next direction is given, "Do the next step of the procedure now." If the student performs the wrong action a feedback message is displayed, "This is not the outlet valve opener. Try again." No score is kept for the demonstration, however, for practice the number of incorrect actions performed by the student is saved in the student file. The student also has the option of selecting explanation during the practice. This operates the same as demonstration. Following each action the explanation indicates what happened and why: "When you push the outlet valve opener ... First, the valve position of the outlet valve is set to open. This happens because the valve position of the outlet valve is closed, and the gate position of the upper gate is closed. Second, the water level of the lock water is set to low. This happens because the water level of the lock water is high, and the gate position of the upper gate is closed. Third, nothing happens because the lock position of the canal boat is not in." Note that when a number of processes are triggered in succession the explanation system explains each of these processes in turn. The third explanation above results from the third process in the sequence to move the canal boat down with the water if it is in the lock. Since the canal boat is not in the lock the explanation indicates that nothing happens to the canal boat. These explanations may seem a bit awkward in syntax. This is because all of these explanations are generated automatically by the system using the components of knowledge objects rather than being written by the developer. This process will be explained later in this paper.

Selecting the *Perform* option also displays two options: *move boat up, move boat down.* For the *Performance* option there is very little guidance for the student. The goal is presented "The goals for this practice are: 1) lock position of canal boat is above, 2) gate position of upper gate is closed." The student is directed: "When you think you have accomplished the goal(s) push the FINISHED button." The student can also select the explanation during this performance. The student can then push the controls in any order they want. If a button is pushed that causes nothing to happen because the conditions are not met the only indication to the student is in the explanation indicating that nothing happens. For example, "When you push the boat down control nothing happens because the lock position of the canal boat is not above, and the gate position of the upper gate is not open." The student can play with the visualization as long as they want. When they think they have finished the task they push the *FINISHED* button. If the task in not complete they receive the following message: "This is incorrect. You have not accomplished the goals. Let me show you one way to do it." The student is then given his scoring: "Steps in path: 7 Deviations: 6" A table is presented showing each of the correct steps in the left column and the students actions in the right column. The incorrect steps taken by the student are highlighted in red allowing the students to compare their performance with a correct path through the visualization. The deviations scores are recorded in the student record. It should be noted that there may be several correct paths through the simulation. Any acceptable path is scored as correct. This is a not a lock step simulation like so many of the so-called simulations often used to teach software applications.

3. KNOWLEDGE OBJECTS

Knowledge objects identify the components of knowledge required by a learning environment. Knowledge objects are containers consisting of compartments for different related components of knowledge. The framework of a knowledge object is the same for a wide variety of different topics. The contents of a given knowledge component differ, but the components stay the same. A knowledge object is only content as contrasted with learning objects which are often defined as a small segment of instruction including an objective, presentation, and practice. (See Merrill, et.al., 1993, 1996; Merrill, 1998, 1999, 2001a, 2001b, 2002 for a more detailed discussion on knowledge objects.).

A knowledge object for a learning environment contains the following components:

- A set of entities (things) or parts of these entities.
- Portrayals (graphic, auditory, text representations) for each of these entities or parts of entities.
- Properties (qualities or quantities) of these entities or parts that can assume different values
- Portrayals for each value assumed by these properties
- Activities (actions taken by the learner) that trigger processes
- Processes consisting of consequences (changes in property values with subsequent changes in the portrayal of the property and conditions (values on one or more properties) and triggers for subsequent processes

The first step in designing a learning environment using knowledge objects is to identify both the static and dynamic entities (parts) involved. Static entities are those that do not change. Dynamic entities are those for which properties are defined with two or more values for each property. Each of the properties is associated with a portrayal that indicates a change in the entity (part). Controllers are also defined. Controllers are parts that when acted upon by the participant cause a process to be triggered and thus a change in one or more property values to occur. For each of these entities a name, a description, and a graphic portrayal is stored in a knowledge base (database). The name for each property, the values that can be assumed for each property, and the graphic portrayal associated with each property value is also stored in the knowledge base.

Figure 2 indicates the dynamic entities for the canal lock. The table includes the part name, the propert(ies) associated with the part, the values that the property can assume, and the portrayal for each of these property values. The static entities of the lock, those parts that do not change as part of the visualization, are not indicated in this table. For example, the canal above and below the lock, and the pipes allowing water to flow except for the outlet valve. The descriptions that are stored in the knowledge base for each part are not shown in the table.

There is a controller associated with each of these dynamic entities that allow a given property value to be selected by the participant in the visualization. Each of the gates has a controller that sets the property position to a value of either open or closed. The outlet value has a controller that sets its property position to either open or closed. The boat has two controllers: the up controller increments the boat property canal position from down, in, up. The other increments the boat property canal position from up, in, down. Changing a property value by means of the controllers also causes the visualization to change the portrayal of the entity (part) to the graphic corresponding to a given property value.

Entity (part)	Property	Legal Values	Portrayal
outlet valve	position	open, closed	
upper gate	position	open, closed	
lower gate	position	open, closed	
lock water	level	high, low	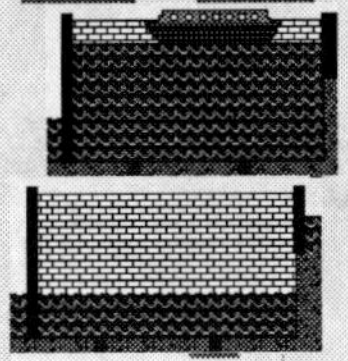
canal boat	canal position	below, in, above	
	lock position	up, down	

Figure 2 Canal Lock Entities, Properties, Values, and Portrayals

Processes, entities, and activities are related to each other via a knowledge structure called a PEAnet (process entity activity network). These PEAnet relationships are illustrated in Figure 3. The participant executes some activity by clicking on a controller. This action triggers a process. If the conditions for the process are true, then the process changes the value of the property to a new value. When the value of the property changes, the portrayal for the property changes to the portrayal corresponding to the new value. This change in value is the consequence of the action and appears to the participant as a change in the visualization. In this diagram the same property is involved as a condition and then as a consequence. In many situations different properties are involved as conditions for a consequence. (See Figure 4).

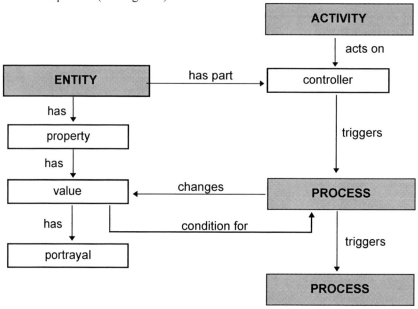

Figure 3 PEAnet relationships among processes, entities, and activities

Figure 4 illustrates a portion of the knowledge structure or PEAnet for one action in the Canal Lock visualization. The participant clicks on the inlet valve opener. This action triggers the process inlet valve opens which causes a change in the value of the property position of inlet valve to change to open with a corresponding change in the visualization for the inlet valve. The process inlet valve opens also triggers the process water flows in which changes the property level of lock water to a value of high with a corresponding change in the portrayal of the lock water in the lock. Note however that the process water flows in will only execute if the property position of outlet valve has a value closed and the level of the water is low, and the position of the lower gate is closed. The process water flows in triggers yet another process canal boat rises which changes the lock position of the canal boat to a value of up with a corresponding change in the portrayal of the canal boat if the property location of canal boat has a value of in.

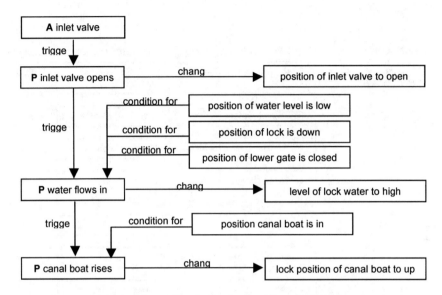

Figure 4 PEAnet relationships for the Activity (A) push inlet valve control.

Figure 5 shows a complete knowledge base or PEAnet structure for the canal lock visualization. In Figure 5 the first column represents each of the actions that the participant can make. The arrows indicate the name of the process(es) triggered by these actions. Column 4 indicates the consequence of each process, i.e., the change in property value that is caused by the execution of the process. Column 5 indicates the conditions that must be true for the process to execute. These conditions are the consequences of other actions that are indicated by the letter corresponding to the consequence that must be true. By finding a given action the reader can determine the corresponding consequence and the conditions that must be true for this consequence to occur. The change in portrayal resulting from the change in property value can be determined from Figure 2.

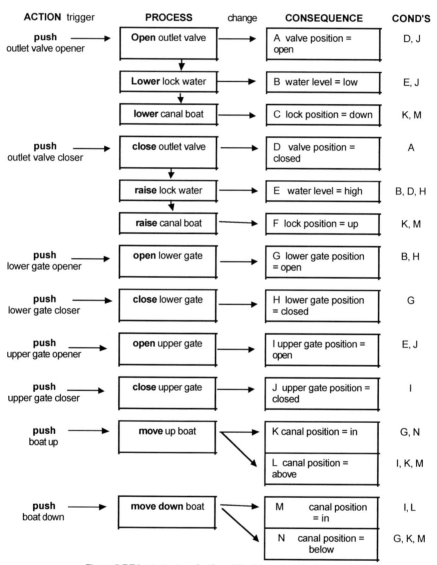

Figure 5 PEAnet structure for Canal Boat Learning Environment

4. USING KNOWLEDGE OBJECTS FOR INSTRUCTION

The Instructional Simulator implementation of a learning environment involves the following functions: more information, lecture, identify names or locations, a simulation engine, explain, an inference engine, Simon says demonstration, next step practice, free play performance, prediction, and trouble shooting. Each of these instructional functions will be described indicating the way in which knowledge objects are used to perform these instructional functions.

More information

When the mouse moves over an active part (entity) in the diagram the system retrieves the name of that part from the knowledge base and displays the name. When the student right clicks on the part the system retrieves the description of the part from the knowledge base and displays the description.

It should be noted that the program for retrieving and displaying the name, like all of the functions to be described, is a general program that is part of the system. The system does not care what parts are included making it a general-purpose engine that can teach more information about any device or graphic display.

Lecture

When authoring the system the developer indicates what lectures to include. A lecture is defined by a lecture name, a list of the parts to be included in the lecture, and the order in which these parts should be presented. When the student selects a lecture the system goes to the lecture list, highlights the graphic for the part, retrieves the name and description for the part, and displays them in a pop-up window. When the student clicks the mouse the system retrieves and displays the information for the next part. There can be as many different lectures as required. Each lecture can include the same or different entities. Each lecture can include the same or different information types. More than a single description can be stored for a given part and different lectures can call upon this different information.

Identify names

During authoring the developer can specify an identify function by providing a list of entity names that are to be included in the exercise. When the student selects *Identify Control Names* from the guide the system randomly selects a name from the list, highlights the part corresponding to the name, provides a list of all the part names, and directs the student to select the correct name from the list. If the student is correct the system repeats the algorithm for next randomly selected name from the list. IF the student is incorrect the system puts the name back into the list and highlights the correct name for the student before highlighting the next part.

Locate parts

During authoring the developer can specify a location function by providing a list of entity names. When the student selects Identify Control *Locations* from the guide the system randomly selects a name from the list, displays the name, and directs the student to click on the location of the part. If the student is correct the system repeats the algorithm for the next randomly selected name from the list. If the student is incorrect the system puts the name back into the list and highlights the correct part for the student before presenting the name of the next part.

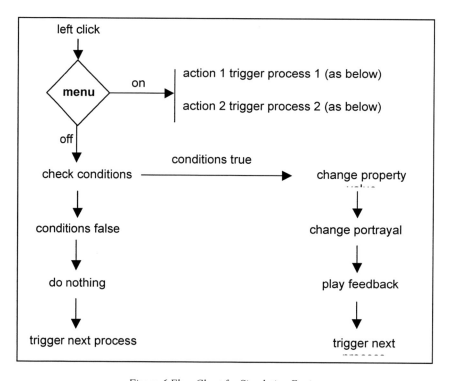

Figure 6 Flow Chart for Simulation Engine

Simulation Engine

Figure 6 illustrates the simulation engine that drives the visualization. When authoring the system the developer associates the rules from the PEAnet with the controllers represented by the actions in Figure 5. When a student clicks on the controller the simulation engine is invoked and the associated processes (rules) are executed as per the flow chart. The simulation engine is merely code that implements the relationships illustrated in Figures 3 and 4 and implemented by the rules (processes) stored in the knowledge base as represented by Figure 5. At the time of authoring the system also allows the developer to store a feedback item with the execution of any process. This feedback can be a text message, an audio message, a graphic message, or a piece of video. The flowchart indicates that if this feedback message has been specified it is displayed immediately after the portrayal is changed.

Explain

The explain system attempts to provide a what-happened and why statement related to every action taken by the participant. The explain system consists of a set of text templates that are instantiated with information from the knowledge base. One of the text templates is the following: "When you push the <controller name> (action) the <property > of the <entity> is set to <property value>. (what?) This happens because the <property> of <entity> is <property value> (why?)" The values for the explanation come from the knowledge base as represented in Figure 5. So filling in the values when the participant clicks on the upper gate closer control: "When you push the <upper gate closer> the <gate position> of the <upper gate> is set to <closed>. This happens because the <gate position> of the <upper gate> is <open>." The what part of the explanation is the consequence, a change in property value. The why part of the explanation is one or more conditions, a value of a property.

This explanation system is one of the powerful algorithms made possible by the careful specification of knowledge components appropriately identified, carefully named, and stored in a knowledge base. As with the other algorithms of the Instructional Simulator, this explanation function can be used with almost any content. Storing the PEAnet rules in the knowledge base provides the information necessary for the explanation system to operate. It should be noted that naming of the properties and values becomes important if the explanation system is to approximate normal syntax.

Inference engine

How does the system know what steps are left to take for any given starting conditions of the system? How does the system know what steps are required to complete the visualization? How does the system know whether the student took the correct steps? The system uses a simple artificial intelligence inference engine for this part of the system.

Consider the following diagram indicating the location of the canal boat in the lock. The initial conditions are indicated in the Figure 7.

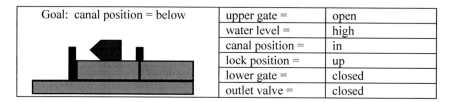

Goal: canal position = below	upper gate =	open
	water level =	high
	canal position =	in
	lock position =	up
	lower gate =	closed
	outlet valve =	closed

Figure 7 Initial Conditions for Canal Boat

The inference engine then generates the correct sequence of actions and then uses them for the demonstration or practice or as the solution against which to compare the student's actions in performance. For the above situation the inference engine would generate the following sequence of actions. Note the list is in the order used by the inference engine to determine the sequence whereas the order for the application of the actions is in the reverse order as indicated by the numbers.

- Is canal position below? no, then push boat down [4].
- Is lower gate open? no, then push lower gate opener [3].
- Is canal position in? yes
- Is water level low? no, then push outlet valve opener [2].
- Is lower gate closed? yes
- Is valve position closed? yes
- Is upper gate closed? no, then push upper gate closer [1].
- Is upper gate open? yes

When the participant starts a demonstration, practice, or performance the inference engine is invoked. It looks first at the goal and checks to see if the boat is below. It is not. It then scans the PEAnet structure or rulebase (Figure 5) to determine what action is necessary to change the canal position of the boat to below. From the rule base it determines that the action associated with this goal is push boat down. It then checks to see if the conditions for process are true. In this case the lower gate position is not open but the canal position is in. It looks to see how to open the lower gate. It finds push lower gate opener and checks to see if the conditions for this process have been met. It finds that the water level is not low. It scans for an action to lower the water level and finds push outlet valve opener. It checks its conditions and finds that the outlet valve is closed but that the upper gate is open. It then checks the conditions for close the upper gate and finds push upper gate closer. It checks the conditions and finds that the upper gate is open. This action is then ready for execution and becomes the first step in the process. The order for the steps is to move back up through the stack as shown by the numbers in the list above.

Note that there is no action on the part of the author except to store the PEAnet rules in the knowledge base. The inference engine can then use the rules in the knowledge base to infer a correct path through the visualization.

Simon Says Demonstration

When a participant selects the Simon says demonstration the inference engine is invoked to determine the location of the canal boat and infer the sequence of steps necessary to complete the demonstration for either moving the boat up or moving the boat down. The system then displays the first step: "Push the upper gate closer." If the participant does the step the system displays the next step: "Push outlet valve opener." If the participant does not do the correct step (click on the correct controller) then the system displays a message "That is not the <name of controller>" i.e., "That is not the upper gate closer."

Note that for the developer of the system the Simon says demonstration is ready as soon as PEAnet rules have been put in the knowledge base. Also note that the Simon says demonstration like all of the other functions in this system doesn't care what rules or what portrayals are in the system. Therefore this is a general system that will run any visualization for which graphic portrayals of entities and properties is possible.

Next Step Practice

Next step practice works the same as the Simon Says Demonstration except rather than naming the next step the initial display merely indicates "Do the next step". If the participant does not do the next step then the system displays the same message for the step as for Simon Says, i.e., "That is not the <name of the controller> i.e., "That is not the upper gate closer."

Free Play Performance

When a participant selects the *Performance* option the system invokes the inference engine to determine the appropriate sequence of steps for completing either the task move the boat up or move the boat down. The simulation engine is enabled and the participant is free to take any action in the system. The system will respond to any action within the limitations of the conditions in the system. A record system records each action taken by the participant. When the participant clicks *FINISHED* the system compares the students list of steps with the steps generated by the inference engine. The participant is shown the steps determined by the inference engine and the steps performed by the student. Incorrect steps, those not on the inference engine list, or redundant steps, those performed unnecessarily even if they are on the inference engine list are highlighted in red for the student. The students discrepancy (number of wrong or redundant steps) is recorded in the student's file.

Predication

The canal demonstration did not include prediction but predication is also possible in the Instructional Simulator. For prediction the system sets up a problem, i.e., the canal boat is positioned in a given position and the participant is directed to continue its progress up or down the canal. A problem is an initial set of conditions such as those indicated in Figure 7. The participant is asked to predict whether a given action or series of actions will execute. The participant is asked to indicate why a given process will execute. The reader should realize by now that the why? Question is asking the participant to identify the conditions that are true (why?) or the conditions that are not true (why not?). One implementation of the why function is to present the conditions in a pop-up window and have the participant click on all that are true and all that are false.

Troubleshooting

The canal visualization also did not include troubleshooting but troubleshooting is also possible in the IDVisualizer ¯. The system sets up a problem by setting the initial conditions and inserting one or more failed conditions. A failed condition is one that is not true or missing. The participant runs the simulation. The consequence is then unexpected, either the process fails to execute or the consequence is different than the desired consequence. The participant is then asked to find the failed or faulted condition. This is similar to indicating why or why not for prediction.

The explanation system is used to generate predication and trouble shooting explanations for the student. The explanation system is modified indicate what happened (the consequence) and then rather than listing the why (the conditions that were satisfied or not satisfied) the system lists several conditions and asks the participant to identify the correct condition(s). Note again that prediction or troubleshooting requires no additional authoring on the part of the developer but can be built into the system.

5. AUTHORING A LEARNING ENVIRONMENT USING KNOWLEDGE OBJECTS

The first step in authoring is to identify the entities involved in the visualization and a portrayal for each of these entities. For our demonstration we will identify two entities: a light switch and a lamp. These portrayals are illustrated in Figure 8. For each entity we identify some dynamic properties. For the light switch we identify the property of *position* with two values *up* and *down*. For the lamp we identify the property *lighted* with two values *on* and *off*. For each value of each property we identify an appropriate portrayal. Figure 8 illustrates portrayals for each of our entities. Each entity has two portrayals one for each of the values its property can assume.

The use of knowledge objects as described in this paper could be implemented in many ways to create an effective authoring system. The following paragraphs describe the implementation in the Instructional Simulator ToolBook prototype or the IDVisualizer™.

First, to create this learning environment use the ToolBook drawing tools to place a rectangle on the screen for the switch and another for the lamp. Select one of the

Figure 8 Portrayals for Switch position (down/up) and Lamp lighted (off/on)

rectangles and then click on *make selection an object* from the *ISAuthor* menu on the ToolBook menu bar. Type in the name of the object, *switch*. Click on *add properties*. A dialog box appears. Select *add properties*. Type in the name of the property, *switch position*. In the dialog box click *enumerated* from the list of property types: *enumerated, numeric, list, string*. Next type in the legal values that this property can assume, *up, down*. Select the property, *switch position*. In the dialog box click *multiple graphic* from the list of indicators (portrayals): *horizontal groove, vertical groove, diagonal groove, multi graphic, register, custom*. Click on a value for the property, *up*. From the pop-up file menu select the file corresponding to the value, *swup.bmp*. The graphic corresponding to the value appears on the screen. Repeat for the other value, *down*, the image is replaced with the other image.

Repeat all of the above for the lamp. You have now completed the identification of the entities involved, an associated property, the values of this property, and the portrayal for each of the values. Arrange the images so that the rectangle corresponding to the switch is on top over the portrayal of the switch and the rectangle for the lamp is on top over the portrayal of the lamp.

The second step in authoring is to identify processes associated with the entities. These processes are as follows:

Toggle switch: If switch position = up (condition), then set switch position to down (consequence) trigger lamp lighted (process). If switch position = down (condition), then set switch position to up (consequence) trigger lamp lighted (process).

Light lamp: If switch position = down (condition), then set lamp lighted to off (consequence). If switch position = up (condition), then set lamp lighted to on (consequence).

Select *define processes* from the *ISAuthor* menu. Select an entity from the list in the simulation object box, *switch*. Select *add Process.* Type the name of the process,

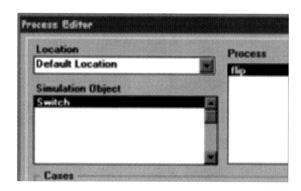

Figure 9 Process Editor from Instructional Simulator Prototype

flip. Select first case from cases box. Click *Edit* Cases. Select *add condition*. Click on property, *switch position*. Click on value, *down*. Select *add consequence*. Click on property, *switch position*. Click on value, *up*. Click on *add trigger*. Click on process, *light lamp*.

Click on *add case*. Click on edit button. Click on *add condition*. Click on property, *switch position*. Click on value, *up*. Click on *add consequence*. Click on property, *switch position*. Click on value, *up*. Click on *add trigger*. Click on process, *light lamp*. By all of these clicks you have created two rules of the form: If switch position = down (condition) set switch position to up (consequence) trigger light lamp (trigger). If switch position = up (condition) set switch position to down (consequence) trigger light lamp (trigger).

Repeat this authoring to create a second process, *light lamp*. Select entity, *lamp*. Click *add process*. Type name, *light lamp*. Click on add case. Click on edit button. Click on *add condition*. Click on property, *switch position*. Click on value, *up*. Click on *add consequence*. Click on property, *lamp lighted*. Click on value, *on*. Click on condition. Click on property, *switch position*. Click on value, *down*. Click on consequence. Click on property, *lamp lighted*. Click on value, *off*. By all of these clicks you have created a rule of the form: If switch position = up(condition), set lamp lighted to on (consequence). If switch position = down(condition), set lamp lighted to off(consequence).

The third step in authoring this learning environment is to identify the action that will be performed by the participant in the visualization. In our case the action is to *flip switch* done by clicking on the light switch. Select *define actions* from the *IS Author* menu. In the dialog box click on add action. Type in name of action, *flip switch*. Select an action type: change location, select location, pick up object, drop object, move object, custom, or converse with. Click on *custom*. Click *add process to trigger*. Click on name of process to be triggered, *flip*.

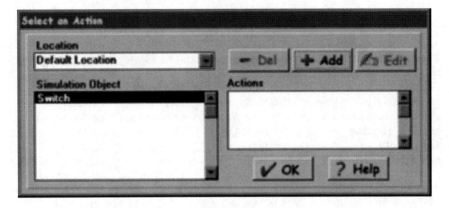

Figure 10 Select Action Dialog box

Given the graphics the authoring of this simple simulation takes less time than it does to read about it. This simulation can be authored in 2 or 3 minutes at most. Once these values have all been entered into the knowledge base the visualization is ready to go.

When the participant clicks on the switch, the lamp lights. When the participant clicks on the switch a second time, the lamp turns off.

We can make this visualization more interesting by adding a second property to the lamp called *burned out*. We will give this property two values: *true and false*. The light lamp process is modified as follows:

Light lamp: If switch position = down (condition), then set lamp lighted to off (consequence). If switch position = up (condition) and burned out = false (condition), then set lamp lighted to on (consequence). If switch position = up (condition) and burned out = true (condition), then set lamp lighted to off.

Authoring is the same as described above except that another condition is added to the light lamp process as stated in the above rule.

Now when the switch is flipped to up if the value of *burned out* is true the lamp will not light.

More extensive visualizations using knowledge objects are merely an extension of this process. First, identify entities, properties, values, and portrayals for these properties. Second, identify the processes (conditions and consequences) triggered by these actions. Third, identify the actions to be taken by the participants. To implement all of the instructional functions there are only a couple of additional required authoring steps. For the more information the author adds a description or other information associated with each entity. For the lecture the author adds a list of the parts to be included in each lecture. For the identify names and locate parts the author adds a list of the parts to be included in each of several exercises. An author can turn on or off the other functions like demonstration, practice, performance, predication and troubleshooting from a menu, but no additional authoring is necessary.

6. HOW HAS THE INSTRUCTIONAL SIMULATOR PROTOTYPE BEEN USED?

The Instructional Simulator prototype has proved to be an easy to use tool that can be used for the development of a wide variety of different learning environments. The first major learning environment designed by the USU ID$_2$ Research Group was a simulation of an ethnographic study of an African Village. The entities were villagers, the properties were their attitudes, and the activity of the participant was to question or make statements to the villagers. The processes were the change in villager attitudes and actions triggered by the questions or statements of the participant. The participant could either learn a great deal about the village or could eventually be asked to leave depending on their interactions with the villagers. This simulation was never formally evaluated but the initial reaction of ethnographers who reviewed the simulation was very favorable. They felt that even though the number of properties assigned to the villagers was small that the simulation still approximated a realistic experience for the ethnographer in training. Since this simulation was built simultaneously with the development of the simulation tool we did not get a good feel for how long it would take to create such a simulation with a more finished tool. However, the majority of the time involved was in the analysis of the subject matter to figure out the properties, values, and processes involved in ethnography rather than in programming the simulation. One important lesson learned from this product was to include dialog as an action to trigger processes.

A second learning environment was for training users of the Hewlett Packard 5SI printer. The visualization gave the participant a printing problem and asked the participant to configure the printer to provide the type of output appropriate for the problem. The entities were the controls of the printer. The consequence was the output of the printer and the sorting of the output into appropriate mail boxes. This was a complex visualization with many entities since it emulated the entire control system of the printer. The rules were the processes that happened as a result of setting a certain configuration on the control panel. One of the challenges of this system was the extensive number of simultaneous events that were possible. We wanted to avoid a Simon Says simulation that allows only one response at a time, rather we wanted the simulation of the system to work as close to the actual system as possible. We learned that the PEAnet structure and the ToolBook implementation were able to handle a relatively large number of simultaneous events without a significant loss in system performance. This product was distributed as a training CDROM with the 5SI printer. It worked well in the field. As a result of this product development the Toolbook prototype of the Instructional Simulator was considerably fine tuned.

Another commercial product using the Instructional Simulator prototype was for training customer service representatives (CSR) in the telecommunications industry. The learning environment included a typical customer that called in with a problem. The participant played the role of the CSR and selected statements (actions) to make to the simulated customer. The property of the customer was attitude. The portrayals of a change in attitude were the comments made by the customer back to the CSR. The CSR used a database to attempt to find an answer to the customer's problem. If the problem was solved and the CSR maintained a pleasant conversation the customer was satisfied and made positive comments about the CSR at the end of the conversation. If the CSR was unable to solve the problem, or made inappropriate comments to the customer, the customer replied with angry comments or threats to discontinue the service. There was not a formal evaluation of this product but the product is still in use by the customer, NRTC, for training CSRs in rural communities. The Instructional Simulator prototype was in a much more advanced stage of development for this product. The major part of the effort was in defining the role of the CSR with the customer. Once the role of the CSR was defined the content analysis required and the programming of the simulation was completed in a matter of couple of weeks. This simulation was only one part of a much more extensive package all built for the customer using the Instructional Simulator. The total cost of the entire package was far less than a similar development effort using a conventional authoring tool.

7. EXPERIMENTAL RESEARCH USING THE CANAL BOAT SIMULATION

We conducted a series of studies (Mills, Lawless, Drake, and Merrill, in press) with elementary students using the canal boat simulation. In the first study, students explored moving a boat up through the lock under one of three conditions. In the first treatment students received an explanation after every step. In the second treatment students received an explanation only when nothing happened. In the third treatment students received no explanation. The students were then tested by asking them to move a boat down through the lock. A fourth treatment was a control consisting only of the test. The score was the number of moves made by the student. All three groups did better than the control immediately after the training but were not significantly different from each other. However, a month later the group who received an explanation after every step performed significantly better than all of the other groups.

In a second study three different types of demonstration were compared. The first treatment consisted of demonstrating how to move the boat through the lock but with no interaction on the part of the student. In the second group the students received a Simon Says demonstration where they were directed to perform each step. A third group engaged in a free explore situation until they were able to move the boat up through the lock. The test was moving the boat down through the lock. The Simon Says group performed significantly better than either of the other two groups and took significantly less time than either of the other two groups.

Both of these studies indicate that direct instruction promotes more effective and efficient performance in learning environments. Knowledge objects enable direct instruction within a learning environment.

8. HOW DOES A LEARNING ENVIRONMENT BASED ON KNOWLEDGE OBJECTS COMPARE WITH OTHER AUTHORING SYSTEMS?

Using Murray's categories, IDExpert was a multiple knowledge type system. Our subsequent tool following this tradition was the Electronic Textbook commercialized as IDXelerator™ (Merrill & Thompson, 1999). The Instructional Simulator attempted to implement a second generation IDExpert that combined device simulation with multiple knowledge types. The term *Instructional Simulator* was chosen to indicate that this system included both device simulation and direct instruction related to this simulation.

As indicated in Halff's paper in this volume, Xaida was originally based on our work with IDExpert using a multiple knowledge type approach. The ID_2 research team at USU were involved in the first phase of the Xaida project and provided the original designs for this system. The Instructional Simulator was designed to include some of the same functions as the Electronic Textbook (IDXelerator) and consequently as Xaida, especially the part identification functions. In the Instructional Simulator these functions are integrated with device simulation.

The Instructional Simulator (IDVisualizer) has more in common with RIDES (see Monroe chapter in this volume) in that it is a state simulator in which interaction with the system changes the state and consequently the visualization of the system. RIDES, however, is much more sophisticated in that the dynamic objects are given more complete methods than is the case in our tool. Our goal was ease of authoring and we traded off sophistication of the simulation involved for a simpler representation of the underlying knowledge. The word *simulation* is really inappropriate for the Instructional Simulator or IDVisualizer since there is really no actual simulation of the device or events involved. Consequently the name Visualizer was chosen to more accurately represent what is being portrayed to the student.

In our opinion the importance of our work is not in the implementation of the Instructional Simulator or IDVisualizer as particular tools but in the underlying knowledge object conceptualization as a way of representing knowledge. We have found this knowledge representation structure to have considerable value in performing knowledge analysis for instructional design regardless of the authoring system involved in the implementation. The IDVisualizer was our attempt to build a prototype system that was a direct implementation of this knowledge representation system.

9. WHAT ARE THE ADVANTAGES OF AN AUTHORING TOOL BASED ON KNOWLEDGE OBJECTS?

The Instructional Simulator prototype, and subsequently the IDVisualizer, essentially eliminates the programming required to build instructional simulations while at the same time providing important direct instruction additions to learning environments. The only requirement for development is subject matter analysis to determine an appropriate PEAnet and graphic production to develop the required dynamic and static portrayals for the properties involved.

Our productivity goal for this project was to reduce the programming time for creating instructional simulations by an order of magnitude. When we started the project simulation authoring using conventional tools by experienced programmers often required from 300 to 400 hours of programming for even a rather simple simulation. The Instructional Simulator accomplished this goal by reducing the programming time to only a few hours for rather complex simulations. We often demonstrated the Instructional Simulator at conventions by building simple simulations in a matter of 5 to 10 minutes in real time in front of an audience.

The Instructional Simulator and the IDVisualizer still requires a significant amount of time to analyze the subject matter and determine the knowledge structure (PEAnet) involved. However, the knowledge analysis process is much more efficient than is usually the case because of the predefined format for knowledge objects and knowledge base underlying the tool. The system also does not reduce the time required to create and store the graphics required for the portrayals of the dynamic and static objects involved. However, subject matter analysis and media production is a requirement for any system. Because of the significant reduction in the time required for knowledge analysis and the dramatic reduction in programming time, the The Instructional Simulator and IDVisualizer have reduced building simulations to a much simplified subject matter analysis process and a graphic production activity rather than an undefined knowledge analysis process and intensive programming activity.

We have demonstrated that PEAnet knowledge structures are robust and can be used to represent a wide variety of different processes including device simulation and the simulation of human interactions. PEAnet knowledge structures greatly simplify the analysis of complex processes by providing a rather simple vocabulary to be used in the analysis of complex content. PEAnet structures are able to support simulations that involve the possibility of multiple actions and the appropriate consequence following such actions. This is in contrast to the many so-called Simon Says simulations that allow only a single action at any given point in time. The result is much more realistic simulations.

Our own experimental research demonstrated that representing processes as consequences and conditions defined in terms of properties and property values, as implemented by the Instructional Simulator explanation system, facilitates student's comprehension of procedures and processes and their subsequent performance in a simulated system (reference).

10. CONCLUSION

Using knowledge objects to create interactive learning environments enables the design and development of tools that make the creation of interactive environments much more efficient and effective. The Instructional Simulator and its successor the IDVisualizer are such tools and have proved to be very capable for developing complex visualizations that are not just simulations but instructional simulations.

11. REFERENCES

Merrill, M. D. & ID2 Research Team. (1993). Instructional Transaction Theory: knowledge relationships among processes, entities, and activities. *Educational Technology*, 33(4), 5-16.

Merrill, M. D. & ID$_2$ Research Team (1996). Instructional Transaction Theory: Instructional Design based on Knowledge Objects. *Educational Technology, 36 (3), 30-37*.

Merrill, M. D. (1998). Knowledge Objects. *CBT Solutions*, March/April issue, pages 1, 6-11.

Merrill, M. D. & ID$_2$ Research Group (1998). ID Expert: a second generation instructional development system. *Instructional Science*, 26(3-4), 243-262.

Merrill, M. D. (1999). Instructional Transaction Theory (ITT): Instructional Design based on Knowledge Objects. In C. M. Reigeluth (Ed.). Instructional Design Theories and Models, Volume 2, LEA Publishers.

Merrill, M. D. & Thompson, B. (1999). The IDXelerator: learning-centered instructional design. In J. van den Akker, R. M. Branch, K. Gustafson, N. Nieveen & t. Plomp (Eds.). *Design Approaches and Tools in Education and Training*. Dordrecht: Kluwer Academic Publishers.

Merrill, M. D. (2001a). A knowledge object and mental model approach to a physics lesson. *Educational Technology*, 41(1), 36-47.

Merrill, M. D. (2001b). Components of instruction: toward a theoretical tool for instructional design. *Instructional Science*. 29(4/5), 291-310.

Merrill, M. D. (2002). Knowledge objects and mental models. In David A. Wiley (Ed.) *Instructional Use of Learning Objects*. Agency for Educational Technology and Association for Educational Communications and Technology.

Mills, R. J., Lawless, K. A., Drake, L., & Merrill, M. D. (in press). Procedural knowledge in a computerized learning environment.

Murray, T. (1999). Authoring intelligent tutoring systems: an analysis of the state of the art. *International J. of Artificial Intelligence in Education*, 10, 98-129.

---

[1] Mark Lacey was the primary architect of the Electronic Textbook. Subsequent modifications were made by Ben Thompson.

[2] Leston Drake was the primary architect of the Instructional Simulator which he built as part of his dissertation project for his PhD.

NOTES

1. The IDVisualizer ¯ is a commercial tool available from Mindware Creative. See their web site at www.mindware1.com. While students at USU Mark Lacey developed the content for the canal lock and Leston Drake programmed the Instructional Simulator (IDVisualizer).

[4] Simon Says is the children's game where the child acting as Simon says "take a baby step" and then if the child attempt some other move Simon says "no that's not a baby step" and the child must return to the original position.

SHAARON AINSWORTH, NIGEL MAJOR, SHIRLEY
GRIMSHAW, MARY HAYES, JEAN UNDERWOOD,
BEN WILLIAMS & DAVID WOOD

Chapter 8

REDEEM: SIMPLE INTELLIGENT TUTORING SYSTEMS FROM USABLE TOOLS

ABSTRACT. REDEEM allows teachers and instructors with little technological knowledge to create simple Intelligent Tutoring Systems. Unlike the other authoring tools described in this book, REDEEM does not support the construction of domain material. Instead, authors import existing computer-based material as a domain model and then use the REDEEM tools to overlay their teaching expertise. The REDEEM shell uses this knowledge, together with its own default teaching knowledge, to deliver the courseware adaptively to meet the needs of different learners. In this chapter, we first explain how the REDEEM tools capture this knowledge and how the REDEEM Shell uses it. Then, we describe four different studies with REDEEM aimed at answering questions concerning the effectiveness of this approach to ITS development. We conclude by reflecting on the experiences of the last six years and the lessons that we have learned by using REDEEM in a variety of real world contexts.

1. INTRODUCTION

Intelligent Tutoring Systems (ITSs) have long promised significant improvements in learning outcomes. Their ability to model student behavior offers the chance to give individualized instruction to students when a teacher is not available. Research has shown that individual training significantly improves student performance over classroom learning. Bloom (1984) famously agues that one-to-one tutoring by expert tutors produced an average gain in test scores of two standard deviations (a 2 sigma effect) compared to traditional whole class teaching. Non-experts are not quite as effective but can still improve tutoring by around 0.4 sigmas (Cohen, Kulik, & Kulik, 1982). During the 1980 and 1990s a number of important ITSs were developed (*e.g.* PROUST; Soloway & Johnson, 1984; SHERLOCK; Lesgold, Lajoie, Bunzo, & Eggan, 1992; the LISP tutor; Anderson & Reiser, 1995; PAT; Koedinger, Anderson, Hadley & Mark, 1997) which have delivered impressive performance. These individualized computer tutors are beginning to produce similar effects as human tutors (Shute, 1990). For example, evaluations of ITSs reveal effect sizes of between 0.4 and 1 sigmas compared to classroom teaching (*e.g.* AUTOTUTOR, Graesser *et al*, 2002, CMU algebra tutors, Koedinger *et al*, 1997).

However, ITSs have not yet achieved widespread application in schools, colleges or workplaces. One potential reason for this has been the difficulty in developing an ITS even in a relatively limited domain - creating an ITS is estimated to take more than 300-1000 hours to produce an hour of instructional material (*e.g.* Woolf & Cunningham, 1987; Murray, 1999; Halff, in this volume). Consequently, to cover any reasonable school curriculum with ITS-based teaching would take many years of development effort. Even if this were possible, there has been concern amongst teachers that ITSs would not reflect their own pedagogic concern, embodying rather the beliefs of the system designers (Major, 1995).

A partial panacea to the difficulties of ITS development began to emerge with the advent of authoring environments. These allowed appropriate domain material to be constructed together with the ability to have teachers create their own teaching strategies. The early authoring environments included the Instructional Design Environment (Russell, Moran, & Jordan. 1988), KAFITS (Murray & Woolf, 1992) and COCA (Major, 1995). An evaluation of the authoring tools in COCA (Major, 1994) showed that despite offering considerable power to teachers, there remained a gap between the kinds of interfaces teachers would be prepared to use and the AI-based representations that authoring tools required them to manipulate. Even when expressed in pseudo natural language, the language of artificial intelligence did not match or overlap with the language of teaching. For example, a simple rule in COCA might be expressed as "IF summarized next concept AND taught next concept THEN next activity of session is test". A simple matter for AI researchers used to representing knowledge in production rules, but abstract and artificial for most teachers. REDEEM (Reusable Educational Design Environment and Engineering Methodology) was developed as a response to this evaluation. REDEEM reduces the teacher's opportunities to modify low level instructional behavior in favor of improving the ease of authoring in order to allow classroom teachers the opportunities to be seriously involved in ITS development.

REDEEM is one of the new generation ITS authoring tools aimed at creating ITSs in ways that are less effortful, require less training and knowledge, provide help for authors to articulate their knowledge, support good practice or enable rapid prototyping (Murray, 1999). REDEEM's main goals are to: a) allow classroom teachers and trainers to construct ITSs in a reasonable timeframe; b) support reuse of existing material; c) focus on the authoring of pedagogy; and d) exploit the symbiotic relationship between psychology and reusable ITSs – using research to inform the design of ITSs, which can then be used to test the theories embedded within it, which in turn can inform developing theories of instruction and learning (Major, Ainsworth & Wood, 1997).

REDEEM represents one end of the continuum of the authoring environments described in other chapters in this book. REDEEM generated ITSs are among the least sophisticated of such systems. For example, they have little domain knowledge compared to systems such as Demonstr8 (Blessing, in this volume), which has a detailed production system account of the domain or Diag's knowledge of fault finding and diagnosis (Towne, in this volume). They rarely include complex simulations of the sort that RIDES and SIMQUEST support (Munro, in this volume; Van Joolingen & de Jong, in this volume). The REDEEM tools themselves are generic in terms of the domains to which they can be applied and so we have sacrificed the advantages that come with knowledge rich tools like LEAP (Bell, in this volume). REDEEM is classified by Murray (1999) as one of the authoring tools primarily concerned with development of Tutoring Strategies (other examples being Eon (Murray, in this volume) and GTE (Van Marcke, 1992). Indeed, and in contrast to the other ITS authoring environments described in this book, REDEEM does not support the construction of domain material. Instead, REDEEM focuses on the authoring of pedagogy. Authors (who need not have any programming knowledge) import pre-existing domain material and then authoring tools capture their knowledge of how they want to teach this material, this allows the REDEEM shell to teach students in a way that is adapted to each learner's individual needs. In the next section, we will describe how this is achieved.

2. THE REDEEM SOFTWARE SUITE

The REDEEM suite was developed in Click2Learn ToolBook Instructor and runs on Windows 95+. It consists of three main pieces of software - the courseware catalogues, the authoring tools and the ITS shell (see Figure 1). Teachers and trainers use the REDEEM authoring tools to describe these existing courses, supplement them with additional learning activities, construct teaching strategies and identify particular types of students. The REDEEM ITS shell uses this knowledge, together with its own default teaching knowledge, to interpret the courseware in such a way as to deliver adaptive, interactive instruction. The shell's role is to sequence this material for different users, provide a number of teaching strategies, supplement the course material with additional questions and feedback, support integration into classroom teaching by the use of non-computer based tasks and reflection points and provide teachers with detailed feedback on students' performance. However, it is limited to the content of the pre-existing course. Each of these components will now be described in turn.

2.1 Courseware Catalogues

Domain material in REDEEM is based on the idea of a courseware catalogue. It consists of pages from computer-based training developed in a standard authoring package, Click2Learn ToolBook or downloaded from the Internet to provide the basic pre-prepared subject content. Consequently, this limits the flexibility of the resulting ITS. However, it does allow greater reusability, and, of course, significantly reduces the time to create an ITS compared to creating the domain material from scratch. The ideal courseware for REDEEM presents discrete pages of material showing different aspects of the domain at varying levels of difficulty. Pages can contain multi-media displays, simulations, animations, questions and exercises. However, REDEEM does not model the learners' actions on these pedagogical objects. If the course has pre-existing control knowledge hard-coded into a page, this information will have to be manually removed before authoring and, if required, re-represented using the authoring tools.

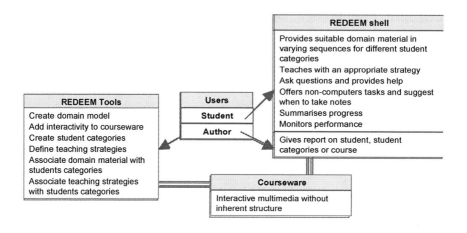

Figure 1. REDEEM schematic

Two types of courseware can be used with REDEEM: those created specifically for the purposes of authoring and delivery by REDEEM; and those created for other purposes and subsequently adapted to use in REDEEM. Those created for REDEEM (*e.g.* the Genetics course and the Primary Shapes course) do not look like typical CBT courses. They have no control knowledge, only limited learner interaction and contain a certain amount of repetition as various topics are treated at different levels of difficulty. They have only weak underlying prerequisite structure so multiple alternative structures can be easily imposed upon them (see Section 3.3). Alternatively, the existing CBT reused in REDEEM does tend to have existing control knowledge (which needs to be removed), often has existing exercises and questions (which are left or recreated in REDEEM depending upon authors' preferences), and can have a strong prerequisite structure. This does tend to limit the flexibility of the resulting ITSs, though as we shall see later, it does not necessarily invalidate the approach.

2.2 Authoring Tools

REDEEM's authoring tools decompose the teaching process into a number of separate components. Essentially authors are asked to describe what they are teaching, whom they are teaching and how they would like to teach these students.. This information is then combined by assigning particular teaching strategies and types of material to different learner groups. This can be seen in Figure 2.

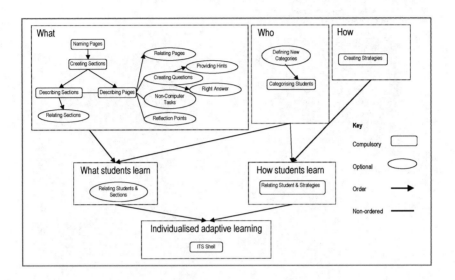

Figure 2. The REDEEM authoring process

2.2.1 What to Teach

One of the most important stages in the authoring process involves the description of the course material. The first task is to give each page a learner appropriate name; other tasks can then be performed in an order that authors find compatible with their teaching preferences. Pages that are not named are not delivered by the ITS shell, providing authors with a very simple means to exclude material they consider inappropriate.

Pages are combined into sections (see Figure 3). Pages can be placed in multiple sections and sections need not consist of contiguous pages in the underlying CBT. Sections can be created with alternative conceptions of the course, (*e.g.* the course could be organized to promote depth or alternatively breadth of understanding) or different sections on the same topic could be created that vary in the difficulty of the language or concepts. One section is marked as the introduction; this is always shown to all students at the beginning of the course irrespective of the teaching strategy dimensions.

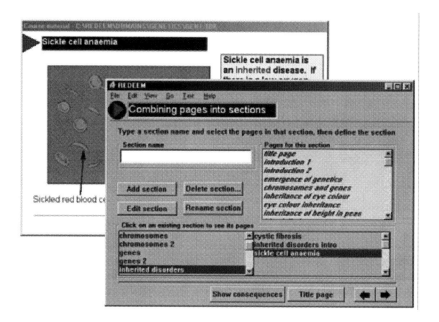

Figure 3. Creating sections

Sections are then described upon a number of dimensional ratings, *i.e.* they describe how familiar, easy, general or introductory a section is likely to be to their students. This is done by graphical manipulation of sliders. The positions of the sliders do not take into account any changes that may occur during the lesson itself. In addition, authors may describe relations between sections, such as "Genetic engineering" is an application of "Biological Techniques". The most commonly used relation is the prerequisite relation, which ensures that a section is not offered to students until prerequisite sections have been completed. Creating sections and describing sections is one of the key ways that authors impose their own views of the appropriate structure of the course (see Section 3.3)

Pages themselves are then described in terms of the same dimensional ratings and relations (Figure 4). Normally, these descriptions are considered in relation to other pages in the same section rather than in comparison to pages across the whole course. Accordingly, a relatively complex page in an early easier section would still be marked as difficult. Relations between pages are only supported within a section.

These tools provide information that the system uses as a semantic network describing the structure (rather than the content) of the teaching material. This network expresses syntactic information about the properties of page and section contents and relations between these pages and sections. There are only three levels to this network, which represents a compromise between additional flexibility

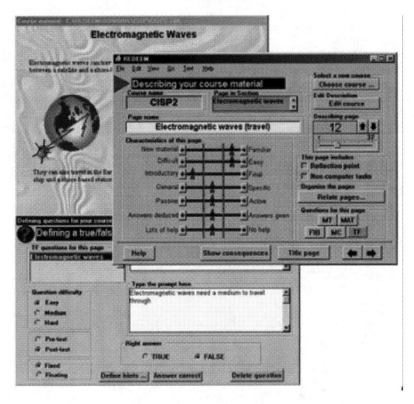

Figure 4. Describing a page of course material in REDEEM

and ease of authoring. This network enables the shell to make default decisions about adapting content and to implement teachers' preferred routes through material.

The next stage is to add interactivity to what may otherwise be a fairly static course. This can be achieved in a number of ways. Firstly, authors can associate reflection points with a page. This means that when students reach this page in the ITS shell, it will suggest that they should consider taking notes and displays an on-line note page. Secondly, authors can associate a non-computer task with the page. This ensures that students are directed to leave the system and perform the indicated learning activity. Thirdly, authors can create a number of types of questions. Five types of question are currently supported – multiple choice, fill in the blank, multiple true, true-false and matching questions. Each type of question is authored in a similar way. For example, when creating a multiple choice question, the teacher begins by providing the question prompt, "Cats are members of the same species because they" and up to five answers such as "are the same size", one of which should be the correct answer "are able to breed and produce fertile offspring". They provide feedback which will explain to the student why that answer is correct "Well done - scientists define a species as a group of living things that can breed and produce fertile offspring". In addition, an important aspect of the REDEEM approach is the ability to offer learners multiple levels of help in way that is similar to contingent help (Wood, Bruner & Ross, 1972). The author can create up to five different hints for each question, ranging from very general hints such as "think about the differences between Siamese and Burmese cats" to very specific hints such as "When cats breed they produce kittens which can produce kittens of their own". Finally, authors describe a number of characteristics of the question which the ITS shell uses to decide how to use the question given a specific teaching strategy. They assign a difficulty level to the question, decide whether it should be offered before or after the page (pre-test or post-test) and whether its position is held constant with respect to the page or whether it can vary with respect to the teaching strategy.

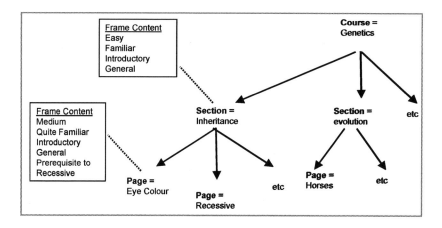

Figure 5. A specimen semantic network

2.2.2 Who to Teach

Students can be described as belonging to one of a set of teacher-defined categories. The teachers can specify these at any degree of granularity ranging from the whole class to an individual child (see Figure 6). Commonly, teachers have tended to use performance-based measures (*e.g.* high flyer, struggler) or task-based measures (*e.g.* revising) or have combined these (*e.g.* high reviser). Primary school teachers also have tended to use categories based on the UK's National Curriculum levels. However, it is possible to use any dimension that authors find appropriate, so far teachers have suggested learning styles or level of literacy or numeracy.

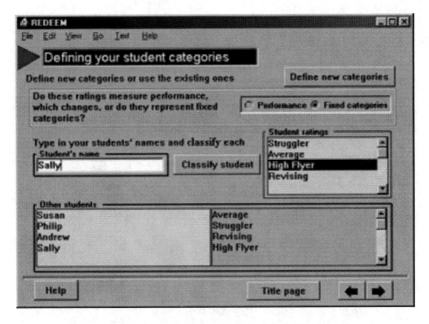

Figure 6. Describing students

If the teacher wishes, the validity of (performance-based) categories can be evaluated against students' question performance. If this is the case, then the shell will automatically change the category as the overall standard of the student (as defined in the student model) changes. This often results in a new teaching strategy.

2.2.3 How to teach

The third important aspect of the authoring task is the definition of a number of teaching strategies as the basic repertoire of the ITS shell. Figure 7 shows the teacher defining a strategy that has been called practice. A graphical interface allows teachers to create a number of teaching and testing styles. Thus the process of constructing teaching strategies is a very simple enterprise in terms of the interface. The simpler authoring necessitates a certain loss of control for the teacher that is transferred to the teaching shell, but there is still considerable control available.

Different instructional principles can be embodied in various strategies by manipulating the sliders. Each slider in Figure 7 has three discrete positions that result in different instruction. Consequently teachers are free to create as many strategies as can be composed from the various instructional attributes. Table 1 provides a brief summary of the effects of the different slider positions. Questions are also associated with teaching strategies in terms of their difficulty (*e.g.* include easy and medium questions) or their type (exclude matching questions). Teachers can create as many strategies as they wish. In fact, REDEEM can offer nearly 20000 different teaching strategies each subtly different to each other, although to date no author has created more than seven.

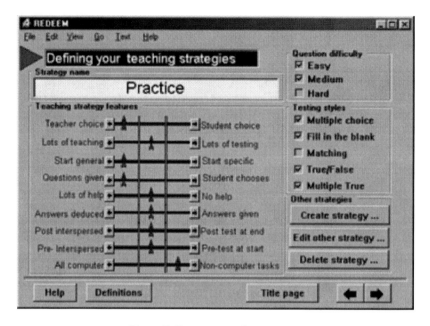

Figure 7. Creating a teaching strategy

Sometimes, authors might wish to have an overall teaching strategy but override for specific occasions. REDEEM supports this for dimensions of teaching strategies concerned with questions. Firstly, as described above, questions can be "fixed" and then their position is not determined by the teaching strategy but is tied to the page. In addition, on individual pages (see Figure 4) questions parameters such as on the amount of help and attempts per question dimensions can be altered. Thus, teachers could set a general strategy for "hint on request and error" but for a question such as "Do you know how to use a mouse?" they could override this preference to "single attempt".

Table 1. The effects of the slider positions on teaching behavior

Slider Position	Slider Left	Slider Center	Slider Right
Student control	No student choice	Choice of order of sections	Free choice of all pages
Lots of teaching	Offer no questions	One questions limit per page	All questions available
Start general	Prefer general		Prefer specific

	pages first		pages first
Questions given	Questions given according to teaching strategy	Choice of when questions appear	Choice of when and which questions appear
Lots of help	Help on request and error	Help on error	No help
Post-question position	Questions after a each page	Questions after each section	Questions at end
Pre-question position	Questions before each page	Questions before each section	Questions at start
Answers deduced	Right answer given if no further options available	Right answer given on second error	Right answer given on error
Non-computer tasks	No non-computer tasks	Non-computer tasks after each section	Non-computer tasks after each page

2.2.4 What Students Learn

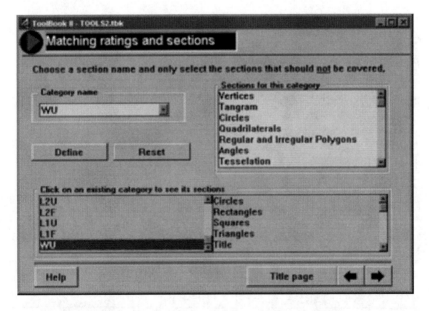

Figure 8. Assigning section to different students categories

Authors differentiate material for different groups of learners by associating sections of the course with different student groups. By default, all categories of learners see all the material, but if the teacher wishes they can choose to remove sections from a particular category. This is frequently used by authors to focus on introductory material for learners who need more help whereas another group may have these sections removed and difficult sections added to allow them to spend more time on more complex aspects of the course. This can either be achieved by the use of alternative sections that cover roughly the same material but at different levels of difficulty (this was commonly in the authoring of the Genetics Course) or through selecting completely different aspects of the course (which was very frequently seen in the Primary Shapes course). For example, Figure 8 shows one of the authors selecting just five sections for her lowest National Curriculum level group.

2.2.5 How Students Learn

The final necessary stage of authoring is to relate the different student categories to alternative teaching strategies (Figure 9). In our research to date, authors have varied from creating a single preferred teaching strategy to creating a unique strategy for each of seven groups. Authors have tended to focus either on the perceived knowledge of their students, their perceived abilities or their role (first time versus reviser).

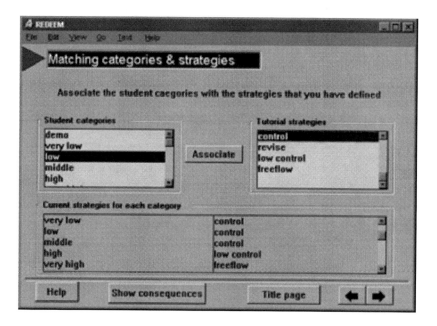

Figure 9. Assigning strategies to different students categories

In addition to overall teaching strategy changes as students move between categories (Section 2.2.2), the REDEEM tools include the facility for strategy refinement which can lead the teacher through a number of multiple-choice questions, eliciting information about the circumstances in which particular aspects of the current strategy might change (see Figure 10). Adapting the form (macro-adaptation) as well as the content (micro-adaptation) of teaching has been identified as crucial for successful tutoring systems (Ohlsson, 1986). Certainly, human teachers often subtly alter their strategies in response to student behavior (Major, 1993; Wood et al., 1976).

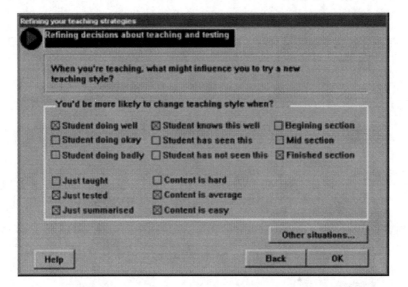

Figure 10. REDEEM tools eliciting knowledge about strategy refinement

In REDEEM's case the teacher may decide, for example, that if the student's performance improves to a certain level, then the strategy should offer more learner control. Figure 10 shows one of the interview screens. The strategy refinement tools were developed by analyzing the original model of teaching employed in COCA. The interview tools are intended to ask questions of the teacher that enables the shell to select the appropriate model at any given time, somewhat analogous to traversing a decision tree. More details of the approach taken in this tool are given in Major & O'Hara (1995). An interviewing tool has been implemented, but to date, we have not used it in any of our studies and there is only limited functionality in the shell to exploit the results of the interview. For this reason, it remains an open question as to how the additional refinements provided by such a tool would be used by authors.

2.3 ITS Shell

The ITS shell delivers the courseware according to the instructions generated by teachers using the authoring tools in combination with its predetermined defaults. To do so it includes a limited student model, which also serves the basis of reports given to teachers.

2.3.1 Delivering adaptive instruction

The main role for the ITS shell is to deliver the course material to each student in the manner that the teacher has specified using the authoring tools. The shell is given the teacher's strategy description contained in the dimensional ratings, and the semantic network created from the teacher's descriptions of the course material which provides a powerful engine for achieving adaptive behavior in the final ITS. The tutorial actions available to the shell (depending upon the teaching strategy) are: to teach new material; offer a question (and help if appropriate); suggest that students make notes on the on-line tool; offer a non-computer based task and by means of password protection check that is has been completed; or summarize students' progress. The two most complex actions are teaching and questioning.

If the shell is teaching, it computes a weighted array of choices using the semantic network of pages and its default assumptions. Such assumptions include prefer easy material before difficult material, introductory before final or familiar before unfamiliar. This is done both at the section and page level. Other rules check that pages in the same section are presented close together and that pre-requisite pages are taught in the correct order. The way that this weighted array is used depends on the level of student control. If the teaching strategy dimension for student control is set to full, the student is presented with the shell's view of the most appropriate page. If set to partial student control, the learner is presented either with a choice of sections or if mid section, the next appropriate page. If set to full student control, then learners are presented with a hierarchically presented menu of the complete course organized according to the weighted array and they may chose any of the pages.

Questions are selected and offered to learners in a way that depends on the many interacting factors of the teaching strategy, *i.e.* question choice, amount of questions, pre-test position, post-test position, level of difficulty and type of appropriate question. If question choice is set to low student control, then the ITS shell must determine if there is an appropriate question it should ask before entering the course, section or page, after exiting the page, section or course, whether it should ask none, one or all questions associated with the page. If the student has more control over questions, then some of this responsibility for making this decision is passed from the shell to the students. For example, they can choose when to answer post-test questions associated with any of the material they have seen. The support the ITS shell offers to students for answering questions also differs depending on the strategy. Hence, to decide upon a response to a student's wrong answer, the shell computes the number of attempts per questions a learner is allowed and whether to offer help either on request or error.

2.3.2 Student modeling and history

REDEEM employs a basic overlay model that records the system's understanding of the students' knowledge of an area. The values of the model change over the course of a session both as the student sees new material and answers questions. The basic course material unit being modeled is the page. This student model is used primarily to ensure material is presented appropriately and to determine whether the student's performance indicates that they should change (performance-related) category.

An important role for the shell is to maintain a student history in addition to the student model. This is used to offer reports to the author either on an individual student's progress, a student category progress or to give a report on the course. To do this, the shell keeps a trace of all modules taken, including pages visited, questions that were asked and their answers, number of hints offered, scores and time on tasks. Teachers can use this information to monitor the progress of learners, for example to see if they require multiple attempts to get question right, using help appropriately, *etc*. Student category reports allow teachers to compare performance of a group of students, for example, to determine if one student is falling behind. The course report allows teachers to see an overall picture of how their class is progressing. It may also provide a way to see how particular questions are being answered. For example, since the 'mitosis true false' question is being answered at chance level (the average score is 0.4/1; Figure 11), there may a problem with that particular question.

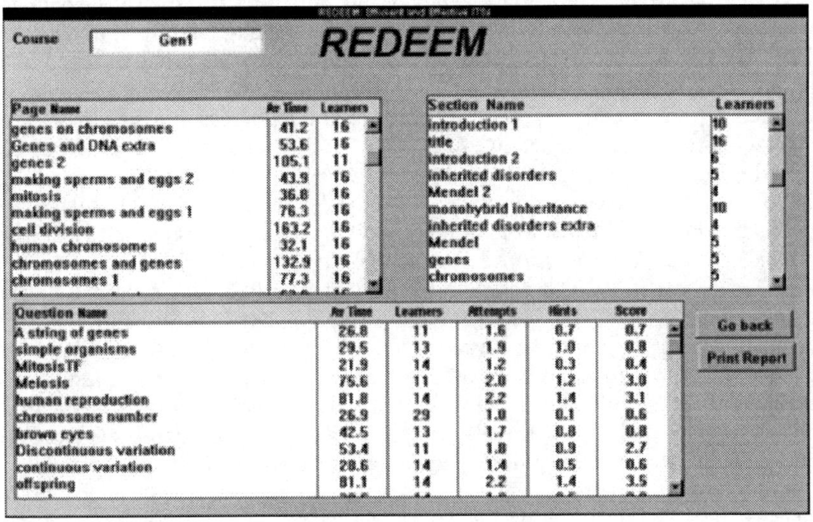

Figure 11. A course report

3. EVALUATING REDEEM

3.1 Evaluation Criteria and Studies

Over the last few years, we have conducted a number of studies with REDEEM aimed at answering a number of questions about its effectiveness and usability. First, we introduce the four main studies.

Study One (the Primary Shapes Study) focused on the authoring phase of ITS deployment. Four educators were recruited, one subject matter expert (SME) and three teacher practitioners (TPs). The SME was a teacher trainer with over twenty years experience in teaching primary mathematics. The TPs were classroom teachers who had not previously developed computer-based environments. All authors were asked to create an ITS from a course "'Understanding Shapes" that is designed for 7-11 year-old children and focuses on mathematical concepts such as angles, vertices, and symmetry. The material covers around eight hours of teaching and includes a range of multimedia presentations, with text, graphics, sound, and animation. As we wished to make comparisons between the different ITSs created by the teachers, a technique based on a virtual class was developed. Vignettes were created describing seven different girls performance in mathematics over the last year. Authors were presented with this class and asked to create ITSs for them.

Study Two (the Genetics Studies) involved secondary school teachers creating two ITSs from genetics material developed at the University of Nottingham for classes of 15-year-old students. The aim of this study was to compare the effectiveness of REDEEM ITSs compared to the underlying CBT. The material is based on the UK National Curriculum and includes text, graphics, sound, animation and simulations. It would normally take around 12 hours of teaching time to cover in normal classroom-based teaching. One version of the study took place at the University and a second study was conducted in school.

Study Three (the Navy Studies) is funded by the Office of Naval Research and explores the utility of REDEEM in military training. Two authors created ITSs from the same material; one for full time personnel at a Naval College and one for a Naval Reservist Center. The course material that was REDEEMed was a seven-chapter course on Communication and Information Systems Principles (CISP) previously written by the Royal Navy School of Educational Training Technology. It presents linearly structured declarative material with the occasional question and contains high-quality video, animation, *etc*. We are comparing the effectiveness of CISP v REDEEMed CISP. In related work, two of these chapters have been evaluated with both an undergraduate population and a Royal Air force cohort.

Study Four (the Trainee Teacher Study) again involves the Understanding Shapes course. The authors were 26 trainee teachers either in their first or fourth year of training. They were presented with a partially authored course (the "what to teach" had been completed) and a virtual class of 30 boys and girls. They were asked to customize the course by creating student categories and teaching strategies for this class. This study focused on whether REDEEM can act as a way of exploring authors' conceptions of teaching.

We had a number of different evaluation goals for these studies. Evaluations of ITSs tend to focus on usability and effectiveness. In typical ITSs these criteria focus on learners' responses to the system - can they 'operate' the package and do learning outcomes occur? To establish successful outcomes on either of these criteria is not trivial. Identifying causal relations between aspects of the ITS design and positive learning gains is yet a further complication. To be done successfully, large-scale experiments are often needed. Furthermore, the effectiveness of any learning environment is influenced by its context of use (*e.g.* Wood, Underwood & Avis, 1999). For authoring tools, these methodological and philosophical issues are multiplied because the resulting ITS is a combination of the authors' decisions and the systems' interpretation and delivery of those decisions. For REDEEM the problem is compounded still further as any ITS not only depends on author, authoring tools and ITS shell, it also involves externally imported domain material.

Murray (1997) proposes that appropriate metrics for determining the success of an authoring environment include: (a) the diversity of the subject matter and teaching styles that an authoring environment supports; (b) the cost effectiveness of those tools; (c) the depth and sophistication of the ITSs that result from the authoring process and (d) the ease with which the tools can be used. The metrics we have used to evaluate REDEEM are not dissimilar and emphasize the experiences of users and learners. We have focused on the following four criteria.

1) REDEEM should be usable

One key characteristic of a successful authoring tool is whether users find it simple to understand and use. Ideally, it should be easy to learn, requiring only a short training period. Interfaces should be matched to authors' needs, providing simple to use tools and providing appropriate feedback on the consequences of their authoring decisions. It should be time efficient allowing authors to create ITSs in a time that they consider appropriate. REDEEM, because its intended users are classroom teacher, lecturers and trainers with little or no previous computing knowledge, requires higher usability standards than is necessary in ITS authoring tools aimed at more specialized authors.

2) REDEEM should be functional

Usability of authoring tools is a necessary condition for their successful application beyond the research laboratory, but it is not a sufficient condition. In addition, authoring tools should provide authors with appropriate functionality. So one important criterion is that authors should be able to create ITSs that reflect their own pedagogic principles and that meet the learning needs of their learners. However, it is equally important to limit the functionality that authors do not require. For example, if all authors make very similar decisions about a teaching strategy, then choice in this dimension is redundant and should become hard-coded into future systems. This should allow the development of systems that are quicker and simpler to use. Or it could be used to 'free up' time so allowing the authoring environment to expand its repertoire of other pedagogical functions.

3) REDEEM ITSs should be effective

We hope that ITSs created and delivered by REDEEM will lead to more efficient or to effective learning. Ideally, learners will come to understand the subject matter more completely, will have found the experience of learning motivating and should reach the desired outcome in a more time efficient way. The nature of the control in such an evaluation is very important. Often, an ITS may be compared against a human teacher (*e.g.* Shute, 1993). We believe that such a comparison is not useful for our purposes as the differences between the two are so large that little sensible can be said about why any difference in learning processes or outcomes occurred. Alternatively, within system evaluations can be used to identify what aspects of the design lead to positive learning outcomes (*e.g.* Ainsworth, Wood & O'Malley, 1998). In REDEEM's case, there is a further alternative that provides a very strict but appropriate control – the original CBT. Hence, Studies Two and Three have compared learning outcomes of students using REDEEM ITSs to the original Genetics and CISP material.

4) REDEEM should expand the teaching knowledge base.

This is the least clearly operationalised of our evaluations goals. However, there are a number of positive indicators that we could use to assess if REDEEM has met this requirement. Firstly, we hope that REDEEM can act as tool for encouraging practioners to reflect upon the nature of their professional practice and expertise. Hence, it should encourage authors to externalize their potentially implicit assumptions about teaching and then represent this in a way that encourages reflection. Secondly, in so doing authors may be provided with ways of comparing and sharing their expertise. For example, they may interact with the authoring (either in the tools or by acting as a student in the ITS) of other more experienced teachers, or compare alternative ways of teaching the same course with colleagues either remotely or face to face. Finally, we hope that REDEEM can act as a research laboratory for researchers interested in comparing the effectiveness of teaching strategies. REDEEM has the advantage that different teaching styles can be applied consistently and to the same course material, thus eliminating many sources of variance. In addition, REDEEM provides control over specific elements of strategies. Consequently, evaluation studies can be much more focused than broad comparisons between strategies. The same course can be taught with the same strategy but with only a single variable altered, such as the ration of teaching to testing. Thus, we will be in a position to examine the effectiveness of teaching strategies in a fine-grained manner with respect to particular learners in particular domains. Of course, evaluation of ITSs to inform psychological theory will remain costly and time-consuming. REDEEM does not offer a solution to the time taken to run experiments, but it does substantially reduce the time needed for ITS re-implementation.

3.2 Is REDEEM usable?

The Primary Shapes and Navy studies primarily addressed the usability of the REDEEM tools (*e.g.* Ainsworth, Underwood & Grimshaw, 1999; Ainsworth, Williams & Wood, 2001). Overall, we have found that it is possible for teachers with no prior experience with computer-based learning to use the tools to express, represent and assess their teaching knowledge to create an ITS within a feasible time scale. Initial training in the use of the REDEEM tools requires between one and two hours. No author has found the overall decomposition of teaching process incompatible with his or her approach. REDEEM's reliance on graphical manipulation of sliders and form-fill style interview tools has proved simple and easy for authors to use (see the one exception below). REDEEM has been described as one of the most usable ITS authoring tools (Murray, 1999) and for the most part we are happy to agree with that evaluation.

Unsurprisingly, a number of small changes to the REDEEM interface have been made over the last four years based on author feedback (*e.g.* more undo functions, clearer labeling of features), and in addition, two aspects of REDEEM design that deserve further reconsideration have been identified. The first issue is how effectively the REDEEM tools support authors in understanding the consequences of their decisions. In the first version of the REDEEM tools, the only way to check the consequences of an authoring decision was to swap to the ITS shell and run the environment as a student. This is easily achieved and we have found that though this remains an excellent way to check the consequences of adjusting macro-features such as teaching strategy changes, it is a poor way of checking micro-structural issues such as position of questions and page order. Consequently, and in agreement with Murray (1999) calls for debugging tools, we have begun to develop more integrated visualization tools so that authors can more easily see the consequences of their actions (*e.g.* Williams, 2001). However, as any visualization will remain an abstraction from what might actually occur in the ITS shell (given that an ITS responds to a student's performance) this raises a host of other design problems. The second issue concerns the way that teachers describe the features of page and sections in order to create the semantic network that the REDEEM shell uses to structure routes through the course. Currently, authors describe characteristics of the page (such as the page's likely familiarity and complexity) and then the shell computes a route. This accords with the call in the mid 1990s for the shift from story boarding to knowledge-based authoring (*e.g.* Major, 1995; Murray, 1996). The experience of the evaluation studies has convinced us that this call is over stated. No author liked this aspect of REDEEM, it proved to be the most time-consuming aspect of authoring and it was hard for authors to visualize the consequences of their decisions. Furthermore, if we provided visualizations these were used in such a way as to undermine the syntactic features of the sliders. We have become convinced that this approach ignores the important role that narrative plays for authors and for learners when they are interacting with new material. In future developments of REDEEM style authoring environments, we are likely to return to the story-boarding metaphor for overall domain structuring reserving knowledge-based approaches for aspects such as strategies and exercises.

Finally, to stand a realistic chance of use in the classroom, authoring tools must also be efficient of teachers' time. In Study One, authors took between six and eleven hours to author the six course - a ratio of around two hours per hour of instruction. In Study Two, the teacher took less than 25 hours to create the two ITSs (around eight hours of instruction) and in Study Three, the Navy authors began by requiring 10 hours per chapter (around 6:1) that dropped to six hours by the end of authoring (around 3:1). Furthermore, the time consuming aspects of the ITS development lies in the domain authoring. In Study Four, trainee teachers were presented with a previously authored course that they just had to invidualize to their students needs. After training, these authors only required 90 minutes to customize the six-hour course.

This timescale makes it a feasible option for teachers to be involved in the development of ITSs. Of course, this does not include the time taken to develop the course material, nor the time to develop the non-computer based tasks. So it might be suggested than this measure is not appropriate. However, we believe that as there is much CBT material that can be reused in this way, it is a useful metric.

3.3 Does REDEEM provide appropriate functionality

This question was again most directly addressed in the Primary Shapes and Navy studies. Essentially, we asked if teachers wanted the functionality that REDEEM provides and whether they could use it to create ITSs that reflect their own pedagogic preferences? We found that authors particularly appreciated:

- the tools that allowed creation of sections of differing complexity that covered the same material allowing teachers to differentiate course material for different groups of learners;
- the opportunity to place pages in multiple sections;
- the ways in to increase interactivity by adding questions and reflection points (even the Navy authors whose courseware already included significant numbers of questions);
- the opportunity to structure the domain material in ways that reflect their own beliefs (primary and secondary school teachers only) and;
- the creation of different teaching strategies that either reflected the author's own preferred strategy rather than the courseware designers (Navy study) or multiple teaching strategies to meet different learners' needs (school studies).

Furthermore, if we had found that all authors viewed the same course and students in a similar way then it could be argued that tools such as REDEEM are redundant. Rather than provide teachers with tools that they can use to customize their own ITSs, we should instead give the 'right' ITS. This is not what was observed. Analysis of the Primary Shapes ITSs revealed strong inter-author differences in their creation of the domain model (*e.g.* Ainsworth, Grimshaw & Underwood, 1999). To take one example, the authors did not identify the same number of sections in the course, nor the order in which these sections should be taught, and nor even pages within sections. Each author's semantic network of course structure was unique. These differences in course structure can be quantified using a variation of the Levenshtein difference algorithm for assessing course similarity (see Ainsworth, Clarke & Gaizauskas, 2002 for more details).

There were also very substantial differences in the way that the sections were assigned to student categories. For example, "Alison" a typical student in the virtual class saw between 45% and 80% of the course depending upon the author. The teachers created different questions from each other, and if given previously authored questions tended to edit both the expression of question and the help provided. The authors also differed in their teaching strategies (Ainsworth, Underwood & Grimshaw, 2000). The authors created between two and six teaching strategies, which were produced from combinations of the eight strategy dimensions. In total the four authors created 17 unique strategies. Authors tended to agree on how some dimensions of the teaching strategy should be used (*e.g.* teach general concepts before specific). The striking degree of similarity for "when to summarize progress" provided evidence that this be hard-coded into the REDEEM architecture to reduce unnecessary decision-making. But for other dimensions, such as degree of student control and whether answers to questions should be deduced or given, there were marked disparities between the authors. Essentially, there was little doubt from this study that the primary school teachers did not share a single view of the 'right' way to teach this course for these children.

However, in the Navy study we found much less inter-author disagreement (Ainsworth, Williams & Wood, 2001; Ainsworth, Clarke & Gaizauskas, 2002). The ITSs created were structured similarly to the CBT, there was much less use of use of REDEEM differentiation features, with one author creating only a single teaching strategy and student category and assigning all the available material to that category. The reasons for this were, in the main, more practical than pedagogical. Nevertheless, REDEEM did provide useful functionality: the authors imposed their own teaching strategy on the implicit one in the original courseware; they added significantly more interactivity to the course; and there were differences between the authors with the reservist trainer finding more of the differentiation features useful for his population. REDEEM was not used to its fullest extent in the Navy, but it did meet the needs of trainers in these situations.

The designs of the ITSs were recognized by all the authors as closely related to their instructional approach. They expressed more satisfaction with the ITS course upon completion of authoring than with the original CBT, and felt they would be more likely to accept their REDEEM ITS in their classroom than the CBT alone or another author's ITS. Of course, this does not tell us if the authors' decisions would have lead to more successful learning outcomes for their students, this was the goal of the next studies.

3.4 Is REDEEM effective?

This question was addressed in the Navy and Genetics studies. In total five separate evaluation studies have been conducted, four have been analyzed at the present time (see Table 2). All studies compared REDEEM delivered ITSs to the original courseware using a similar experimental design. We will describe the method in detail for one experiment (Ainsworth & Grimshaw, 2002a) and then summarize the results of all four experiments.

A secondary (high) schoolteacher authored two courses on Genetics (Gen1, Gen2). She created alternative routes through the courseware differentiated to five different learner categories, multiple teaching strategies were used, significant interaction added with nearly 75% of pages having an associated question and up to five hints per question, reflection points assigned, and non-computer tasks created and associated with pages in the course. The only feature she chose not to use was the opportunity to validate student categories automatically. For the control condition, a vanilla CBT was created by the teacher from the original courseware by selecting an order for the pages and providing a booklet that contains the same non-computer based tasks as those in the REDEEM study.

The potential added value of the REDEEM features was examined using a crossover design with 86 15-yr-old students. Half the students used REDEEM for Gen1 and then CBT alone for Gen2 and the other half saw CBT Gen1 and then REDEEM Gen2. Students came to the local University computing laboratory with their class teacher for up to four sessions (eight hours maximum). Before and after the intervention they completed a 60 item multi-choice test on Genetics. These tests contained 20 questions that were directly asked by REDEEM, 20 that were surface transformation of REDEEM questions and 20 questions that could be answered using material presented by REDEEM and CBT but was not directly questioned.

The results of this study showed that whilst pupils in all conditions improved their knowledge of genetics, there was no differential impact of REDEEM on learning outcomes. Subjects' scores with REDEEM only improved by 2% more than they did with CBT. This was true for learners in all student categories. We also examined learners' performance according to their assigned student category. It was evident that the teacher had good knowledge of the likely performance of her students as the relationship between pre-test scores and student category was significant. However, there was no evidence of differential improvement for the student categories; both high and low performers learned the same amount.

However, as we were unhappy with motivational consequences of removing students from their classroom to come to the University we repeated the study, but this time in a local school (Ainsworth & Grimshaw, 2002b). The basic material was the same as Study One. However, this school followed a different syllabus and so the courseware was modified to take this into account. A class teacher recruited from the participating school then used the REDEEM tools to create his ITSs. He was provided with the ITSs from the Study One and maintained many of the features. This teacher chose a coarser-grained description of learners than in Study One. Three different categories of learners were created that corresponded to different sets (classes differentiate by ability) at the school. He made limited use of the REDEEM macro-adaptation features as the three ITSs created with REDEEM had only similar material and questions and used the same teaching strategy. This time learning with REDEEM did lead to significantly greater improvement than learning with the CBT - REDEEM scores improved by 16% whereas CBT scores improved by 8%.

Two further studies were conducted with the CISP material (Study 3) with both University students and RAF trainees (Ainsworth, William & Wood, submitted). In these cases, a researcher created the REDEM ITSs (on the topics of personal computing and networking). As he had no personal knowledge of the students, REDEEM was used to create one ITS for each class. In these studies, REDEEM again was significantly more effective than CBT.

Table 1 Summary of Four Learning Outcomes Studies

Study	Subjects	ITSs	Gain	Effect size
Genetics at Uni.	86, 14-16yrs	5 ITSs: different content & strategies	RED = 10% CBT = 8%	0.21
Genetics in School	15, 14-16 yrs	3 ITSs: different content	RED = 16% CBT = 8%	0.82 *
Undergrad	35, 20-28 yrs	1 ITS	RED = 52% CBT = 44%	0.83 *
RAF	33, 20-45 yrs	1 ITSs	RED = 47% CBT = 32%	0.81 *

Note * = statistically significant difference.

Overall, REDEEM led to 32% improvement from pre-test to post-test, whereas the same CBT increased scores by 19%. This advantage for REDEEM ITSs translates into an average effect size of 0.76. This compares well to non-expert human individual tutors and is in the same region as other ITSs when compared to classroom teaching.

Current analysis is focusing on determining what aspects of the REDEEM, author, courseware and learner interaction leads REDEEM to differentially improve learning in some circumstances and not others. Preliminary analysis suggests that REDEEM promotes learning by increasing interactivity rather than by macro-adapting teaching strategy and content to learners' needs. It is those students whose student histories identifies them as taking most opportunity to participate in REDEEM interaction who were subsequently revealed on the post-tests to have learnt the most.

3.5 Does REDEEM expand the knowledge base?

One goal for REDEEM is that it should provide opportunities for authors to reflect upon their professional practice. We have observed this at a number of points in the studies and particularly in the Primary Shapes study (Ainsworth, Underwood & Grimshaw, 1999). Firstly, as authors were required to become more explicit about their views while authoring, it could result in reflection upon their underlying conceptual model of the domain. Secondly, authors experienced the consequences of their own teaching decisions, which prompted reflection upon teaching strategies. For example, one author upon reviewing the course began to change her views from "questions as tests" to "questions for prompts for engagement". Thirdly, teachers can compare views of the course provided by different authors. The participants in Primary Shapes study were shown the other authors' decisions in REDEEM tools after the study was completed. They expressed interest in the approaches to the extent that they wanted to (sometimes strongly) query other authors on the grounds for some of their decisions. REDEEM, by providing an external representation of teachers' views of course structure, can prompt these sorts of discussions.

In the Trainee Teacher study, we have asked whether REDEEM can be used as a way of capturing trainees' implicit teaching models (*e.g.* Hayes, Underwood, Ainsworth & Grimshaw, 2001). Analysis is on-going but interesting results include the way that REDEEM has revealed that first year students are more varied in their approach to student categorization than fourth year students. It would appear that as trainee teachers moves from the raw recruit stage to the initiate stage in their apprenticeship, they discard idiosyncratic strategies and conform to a normalized model. It will be interesting to see if this pattern continues through their early years practicing as teachers in classroom. Furthermore, not all features of teaching strategies were equally likely to differentiate the trainee populations. For example, a dimension such as student control was more likely to prompt disagreement amongst authors. Studies such as this could be used to identify dimensions of teaching strategies that cause most dissention. These dimensions could then be subjected to systematic experimentation.

4. LESSONS LEARNED

The studies with REDEEM authoring environment have offered us a number of valuable lessons and raised still further questions.

The first lesson is a reminder of the importance of iterative development for usability. Like any complex piece of software, designers are unlikely to achieve usable tools by relying on their intuitions alone. Using the REDEEM tool 'in the wild' with real authors revealed many ways that the tools could easily be made more usable and has led to many small but significant improvements. It has also revealed that even tools as relatively simple as REDEEM still require authors to engage in complex information processing. More effective debugging environments where authors can see the consequences of their decisions will provide more support for working memory and reduce the complex inferencing required. Adding expert systems such as the Instructor Modeling component of WEAR (Virvou &Mondriou

2001) which feedback the way that students are using the resulting ITSs may also facilitate this goal.

Time is crucial. Authors need to create learning environments that meet their pedagogic needs in a time-efficient way. REDEEM achieves a ratio of around 3 hour of authoring to 1 hour of instruction when a trained author, familiar with the domain and with teaching, creates a full blown REDEEM ITS from imported domain material. This ratio substantially undercuts the majority of ITS authoring tools. A lesson from our authors was "this is still not fast enough!"

Another question, raised by Murray (1999), is who should be doing the authoring, with his answer being a relatively experienced computer-literate specialist authors. This is not REDEEM's intended user population, and in our experience, classroom teachers can create ITSs with REDEEM. This result may be due to REDEEM's approach. We agree that most teachers don't write textbooks. However all teachers do customize these textbooks to use in their classroom by suggesting an order to read chapters to their students, explaining difficult terms, providing exercises and worksheets, *etc*. REDEEM supports the teaching and learning process in the same way - the domain material is not created by teachers but its pedagogical functionality is. Furthermore, we have become increasingly convinced that authoring teams are the long-term answer to this question: no one person is likely to have the skills, knowledge or time necessary. Thus, REDEEM ITSs could come with domain authoring completed and a variety of pre-existing teaching strategies leaving teachers to customize it to the particular needs of their classes by describing students and differentiating to these students by strategy and material - a task that can take as little as 30 minutes. Then, as their experience with a course grows, teachers may wish to change the domain authoring to support additional flexibility or match their needs more closely. We agree with Sparks *et al* (in this volume) that authoring tools will be more useful if they easily support progressive authoring. In our experience, this requires even more explicit visualizations of the resultant ITS to be provided in the authoring tools.

A final question, still unanswered in our case, is whether we design authoring tools to provide authors with just what they tell us they want. Much has been written (*e.g.* Murray, 1996) on the need to encourage authors to shift from a storyboarding to knowledge-based metaphor for ITS construction. However, we have suggested that this call may have been over-stated for content authoring. The majority of authors in our studies not only would have preferred story boarding, they would also have been more comfortable using REDEEM to create customized CBT rather than adaptive ITSs. Indeed, in the Navy study, arguably that is what has been created. For example, authors often wanted control over the order of presentation of material, like CBT, and felt uncomfortable at releasing this role to the machine like an ITS requires. This is not an uncommon finding (*e.g.* Underwood & Brown, 1997). Hence, we acknowledge the problem but remain unsure as to how to answer it. Should teachers be encouraged to envisage a future where they work in collaboration with more intelligent software or instead should we provide them with tools to create software to fulfill their needs today? Perhaps one answer lies in determining when full-blown ITSs support learning requirements more effectively than CBT. Relevant dimensions to explore include what types of knowledge (*e.g.*

procedural, declarative) for what types of learners (children, adults, experts, novices, high or low performers, *etc*) and with what desired outcome (more quickly, more robustly, *etc*) will most benefit from adaptive instruction. Experiments such as those we are performing comparing REDEEM to non-adaptive courseware should help with this goal.

5. CONCLUSIONS

The REDEEM authoring environment was developed as a response to a desire for teachers and trainers to be involved in the development of adaptive learning environments for their classroom. Its design is predicated on the belief that if teachers are given usable tools that allow them to overlay their pedagogical expertise on existing course content, the learning experience for their students will be more supportive of their requirements and hence more successful. The evaluation studies we have conducted over the last three years suggest that we are making some progress towards that goal. We have shown that the REDEEM tools are usable by non-programmers and have identified ways to improve them. Authoring has been found to be time-efficient. The way that REDEEM decomposes the authoring process is generally effective and the functionality it provides has been appreciated by authors as a way to support learners and to share their expertise with colleagues. The studies have revealed that teachers have complex models of teaching and learning which underpin their work. They do not adhere to simple one-dimensional accounts of learning. The flexibility that REDEEM provides for adapting courseware should allow such courseware to be used in ways that are appropriate to each teacher's methods. Comparisons with similar but non-adaptive CBT suggest that REDEEM ITSs can deliver significant improvements in learning outcomes compared to CBT. Although we do not consider that the REDEEM approach is the suitable in all circumstances and the results of the empirical studies suggest that REDEEM ITSs fall short of the 2-sigma effect, we propose that much can be gained by providing classroom teachers with simple ITS authoring tools.

6. REFERENCES

Ainsworth, S. E., Clarke, D., & Gaizauskas, R. J. (2002). Using edit distance algorithms to compare alternative approaches to ITS authoring. In S. A. Cerri & G. Gouardères & F. Paraguaçu (Eds.), *Proceedings of the 6th International Intelligent Tutoring Systems Conference* (pp. 873-882). Berlin: Springer-Verlag.

Ainsworth, S.E., Grimshaw, S.K. & Underwood, D.J. (1999) Teachers as designers: Using REDEEM to create ITSs for the classroom. *Computers and Education,* 33(2/3),171-188.

Ainsworth, S. E., & Grimshaw, S. K. (2002a). Are ITSs created with the REDEEM authoring tool more effective than "dumb" courseware? In S. A. Cerri & G. Gouardères & F. Paraguaçu (Eds.), *Proceedings of the 6th International Intelligent Tutoring Systems Conference* (pp. 883-892). Berlin: Springer-Verlag.

Ainsworth, S. E., & Grimshaw, S. K. (2002b). Evaluating the effectiveness of REDEEM Authoring Environment. Technical report number 69, ESRC Centre for Research in Development, Instruction and Training, School of Psychology, University of Nottingham.

Ainsworth, S.E., Underwood, J.D. & Grimshaw, S.K. (1999) Formatively Evaluating REDEEM: An authoring environment for Intelligent Tutoring Systems. In S. Lajoi, & M. Vivet, (Eds.) *Proceedings of Artificial Intelligence in Education Conference,* pp93 - 100. Amsterdam: IOS Press.

Ainsworth, S.E. Underwood, J.D. & Grimshaw, S.K. (2000) Using an ITS authoring tool to explore educators' use of instructional strategies. In G. Gauthier, C. Frasson & K. VanLehn (Eds.) *Proceedings of the 5th International Conference Intelligent Tutoring Systems Conference:*. pp 182-191. Berlin: Springer-Verlag.

Ainsworth, S.E., Williams, B.C & Wood, D.J. (2001) Using the REDEEM ITS authoring environment in naval training. In T. Okamoto, R. Hartley, Kinshuk, & J.P. Klus (Eds.) *Proceedings of the IEEE International Conference on Advanced Learning Technologies*, pp 189-192. IEEE Computer Society, Los Alamitos, CA.

Ainsworth, S.E., Williams, B.C & Wood, D.J. (submitted) Comparing the learning effectiveness of REDEEM and CBT.

Ainsworth, S.E., Wood, D.J. & O'Malley, C. (1998) There's more than one way to solve a problem: Evaluating a learning environment to support the development of children's multiplication skills. *Learning and Instruction*, 8(2), 141-157.

Anderson, J.R. & Reiser, B.J. (1985) The LISP tutor. *BYTE, 10(4),* 159-175.

Bloom, B.S. (1984) The 2 sigma problem: The search for methods of group instruction as effective as one-to-one tutoring. *Educational Researcher, 13(6),* 4-16.

Cohen, P.A., J.A. Kulik, and C.C. Kulik, (1982) Educational outcomes of tutoring: A metaanalysis of findings. *American Educational Research Journal*, 19, 237-248.

Graesser, A.C., et al., Teaching Tactics and Dialog in AutoTutor. *International Journal of Artificial Intelligence in Education*, 2001. 12: p. 257-279.

Koedinger, K. R., Anderson, J. R., Hadley, W. H., & Mark, M. A. (1997). Intelligent tutoring goes to school in the big city. *International Journal of Artificial Intelligence in Education*, 8, 30-43.

Lesgold, A., Lajoie, S., Bunzo, M. & Eggan, G. (1992) Sherlock: A coached practice environment for an electronics troubleshooting job. In J. Larkin & R. Chabay (Eds.), *Computer Based Learning and Intelligent Tutoring* (pp. 202-274). Hillsdale, NJ: LEA.

Major, N.P. (1993) Teachers and Teaching Strategies. *Proceedings of the Seventh International PEG Conference*, Heriot-Watt University, Edinburgh.

Major, N.P. (1994) Evaluating COCA - What do teachers think? *Proceedings of the World Conference on Educational Multimedia and Hypermedia - EDMEDIA 94*. AACE Press.

Major, N.P. (1995) Modelling Teaching Strategies. *Journal of Artificial Intelligence in Education*, 6, 117-152.

Major, N., Ainsworth, S.E., & Wood, D.J. (1997) REDEEM: Exploiting symbiosis between psychology and authoring environments, *International Journal of Artificial Intelligence in Education 8(3/4)*, 317-340.

Major, N.P. & O'Hara, K. (1995) Grounding DTMs: An interview tool for acquiring meta-strategic teaching knowledge. In J. Hallam (Ed.) *Hybrid Problems, Hybrid Solutions*. Amsterdam: IOS Press.

Murray, T. (1996). From story boards to knowledge bases, the first step in making CAI 'intelligent'. In Carlson & Makedon (Eds.) *Proceedings of Educational Multimedia and Hypermedia 1996*, pp. 509-514. AACE, Charlottesville, VA.

Murray, T. (1997). Expanding the knowledge acquisition bottleneck for intelligent tutoring systems. *International Journal of Artificial Intelligence in Education, 8(3*-4), 222-232.

Murray, T. (1999). Authoring Intelligent Tutoring Systems: Analysis of the state of the art. *International Journal of Artificial Intelligence in Education. 10(1)*, 98-129.

Murray, T. & Woolf, B. (1992) Tools for teacher participation in ITS design. In C. Frasson, G. Gauthier & G.I McCalla. (Eds.) *Proceedings of Intelligent Tutoring Systems 92*. Berlin: Springer-Verlag.

Ohlsson, S. (1986) Some principles of intelligent tutoring. *Instructional Science*, 14, 293-326.

Russell, D.M., Moran, T.P. & Jordan, D.S. (1988) The instructional design environment. In J., J. Psotka, S.A Massey,. & A. Mutter. (Eds.) *Intelligent tutoring systems: Lessons learned*. Hillsdale, NJ: LEA.

Shute, V.J. (1990) Rose garden promises of intelligent tutoring systems: Blossom or thorn *Presented at the Space Operations, Applications and Research Symposium,*

Shute, V. (1993). A comparison of learning environments: All that glitters is not gold. In S. J. Derry & S. P. Lajoi (Eds.), *Computers As Cognitive Tools* (pp. 47-73). Hillsdale, NJ: LEA.

Soloway, E.M. & Johnson, W.L. (1984) Remembrance of blunders past: a retrospective on the development of PROUST. *Proceedings of the Sixth Cognitive Science Society Conference*. Boulder, Colorado.

Underwood, J & Brown, J (1997) Integrated Learning Systems: Potential into Practice London: Heinemann,

Virvou, M., & Moundridou, M. (2001). Adding an instructor modelling component to the architecture of ITS authoring tools. *International Journal of Artificial Intelligence in Education*, 12, 185-211.
Van Marcke, K. (1992) Instructional Expertise. In In G. Gauthier, C. Frasson & G.I. McCalla, (Eds.) *Proceedings of Intelligent Tutoring Systems 92*. Berlin: Springer Verlag.
Williams, BC. (2001). The role of external representations in intelligent tutoring system authoring. In S. Ainsworth & R. Cox (Eds*.) External representations in AIED: AIED'2001* Workshop, San Antonio Texas.
Wood, D.J., Bruner, J.S. & Ross, G. (1976) The role of tutoring in problem solving. *Journal of Child Psychology and Psychiatry, 17*, 2, 89-100.
Woolf, B.P. & Cunningham, P.A. (1987) Multiple knowledge sources in intelligent teaching systems. *IEEE Expert*, Summer 1987.

ACKNOWLEDGEMENTS

This work was supported by the ESRC at the ESRC Centre for Research in Development, Instruction and Training and by the Office of Naval Research under grant no N000 14-99-1-0777. Iona Bradley, Sue Cavendish, Wendy Crossland, Ruth Guy-Clarke, Sue Hewes, CPO Pete Skyrme at HMS Collingwood, and CRS JJ O'Neil at HMS Sherwood were invaluable as the authors in these studies, as was the help of Royal Navy School of Education and Training Technology and John Allison at RAF Waddington in facilitating the military studies.

ANA ARRUARTE, BEGOÑA FERRERO,
ISABEL FERNÁNDEZ-CASTRO, MAITE URRETAVIZCAYA,
AINHOA ÁLVAREZ & JIM GREER

Chapter 9

THE IRIS AUTHORING TOOL

Abstract. IRIS is an authoring tool developed to help human instructors to build intelligent teaching-learning systems in a wide variety of domains. The instructor/designer is required to produce a set of pedagogical requisites, which, in turn, are used to automatically configure a generic tutor architecture and produce an intelligent tutoring system. In order to provide IRIS with a sound basis for producing systems, a theory of instruction that integrates *cognitive processes, instructional events* and *instructional actions* has been considered. In this chapter we explain, through the analysis of the cognitive theory, the generic architecture. We present several system components, the requirements of the different components, and show how we integrate these components in IRIS. Moreover, we embed requirements, cognitive principles, and design requisites in an authoring tool in order that human instructors can follow them easily. Various design issues, an example of building a tutor for mathematical differentiation by using IRIS, and some experiences of use and evaluation are also presented.

1. INTRODUCTION

Intelligent Tutoring Systems (ITSs) define an active and still promising area in computer-aided education. However, it is demonstrable that the really hard and complex task of ITS construction has impeded their wide-scale use. Thus, a new research line has arisen with the aim of facilitating the construction of ITSs in a variety of domains. Up to now, several authoring tools have been produced. They take as basis different orientations and perspectives (Murray, 1999; Chapter 17 in this volume) and so provide different characteristics both in their utilization and in the final systems they generate.

In recent years, while our research group has been working in the area of ITSs, our goals have evolved toward the development of ITS authoring tools. First, we developed a generic ITS architecture derived from two applications: TUTOR (Fernández-Castro *et al.*, 1993), which focused on conceptual domains, and INTZA (Gutiérrez, 1994), which focused on conceptual and procedural domains. Then we tried to include this architecture in a set of tools valid for building ITSs and Intelligent Learning Environments (ILEs) in a wide variety of domains. In order to give the final systems a sound formal basis they should integrate several requisites, from pedagogical theories to architectural characteristics (Figure 1). Thus, the pedagogical requisites were derived from a cognitive theory of instruction, the CLAI

Model (Arruarte *et al.*, 1996a), developed specially to cover the pragmatic construction of ITSs.

The CLAI Model: *Cognitive Learning from Automatic Instruction* integrates *cognitive processes, instructional events* and *instructional actions* within a three level framework. It addresses two main aspects of tutoring. On the one hand it is suitable for integrating into an instructional plan various educational imperatives such as using multiple teaching styles (Srisetamil & Baker, 1995-1996; Graesser *et al., 2001*), generating flexible tutorial responses (Reye, 1995), and adapting the tutor's performance to changing situations (Van Marcke & Vedelaar, 1995; Vassileva, 1995a-1995b). On the other hand the CLAI model's generality makes it valid for multiple domains (Khuwaja *et al.,* 1996) involving conceptual and/or procedural contents.

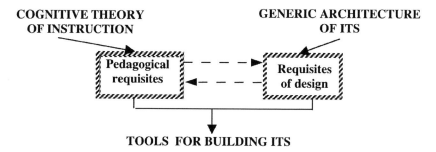

Figure 1. Underlying basis involved in the design of tools for building ITSs

Using as a basis the CLAI model and a generic ITS architecture we developed the IRIS authoring tool. It was created with the aim of facilitating teachers' attempts to build ITS for those domains in which they are experts. Starting from the first prototype (Arruarte *et al.,* 1997a), it has followed a continuous development, increasing its functionalities for both the teacher (or ITS designer) and the student (or ITS user). We have concentrated on mechanisms to overcome the diagnosis problem. Diagnosis of erroneous knowledge is a crucial matter for both the student and the teacher, but in different ways. A good or bad diagnosis will affect the effectiveness of the student's learning process, while the teacher will be worried about the kind of assessment tests that the ITS will use with each particular teaching domain or student.

This chapter is organized as follows. First the characteristics and general functionalities of IRIS are described. They involve the requirements associated with the main tutor components: domain and learner model, pedagogic component and diagnostic process. The general behaviour of the IRIS-tutors is described as well. Next, the IRIS architectural and design issues are described and justified. Then, a comparative analysis of IRIS against related systems helps us to put IRIS in perspective. A section devoted to our experiences of use and evaluation of IRIS together with some lessons learned follows. The chapter concludes with a reflection and discussion on future perspectives.

2. CHARACTERISTICS AND FUNCTIONALITIES OF IRIS: GENERAL DESCRIPTION.

2.1. How a tutor is built with IRIS: An overview.

The process of building a new tutor by using IRIS consists of two phases (Figure 2). During Phase 1 the general requirements of the tutor are specified by the designer and a skeletal architecture of the target tutor is generated. The requirements are used to customize a generic ITS architecture, named INTZIRI. They are grouped around three basic aspects: behaviour of the *tutor*, description of the teaching-learning *domain,* and *learner* characteristics. In Phase 2 the skeletal architecture is filled with content and the final tutoring system is produced. Some of this content is authored by the teacher (*e.g. learning units instances, specific presentation forms, etc.*) and some is generated automatically by IRIS (*e.g. rules for refining the instructional plan*). Subsection 3.1 (Architecture of IRIS) includes a detailed description of the major tasks in each phase.

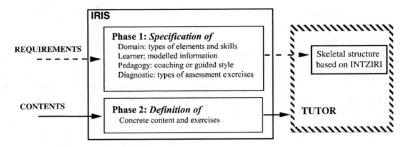

Figure 2. Phases in building a tutor with IRIS

In summary, IRIS provides the following functionalities:

- it assists with data acquisition related to the semantics of the teaching domain, the nature of the desired tutoring system, and its final users;
- it determines a tutor architecture derived from the previously specified properties;
- it creates the final tutoring system by selecting or generating the necessary set of rules and objects in terms of the already defined properties of the tutor, domain and final users;

In the next sections the requirements associated with each main aspect of an IRIS-generated tutor are explained together with their general characteristics. In order to illustrate some of the important ideas, along the paper we will build a specific ITS, called *"Maisu"*, which operates in the small domain of a subset of the mathematical symbolic differentiation. This domain was chosen just as a first experimental benchmark to prove the performance, utility and ergonomy of IRIS. We think that a tiny-domain containing, more or less, 22 contents is enough to give us a first evaluation measure. In this case we adopted the role of designer, and developed an ad hoc and simple interface.

2.2. Specification of the target tutor: Requirements

In this section we will discuss the *Maisu's* requirements associated with the *Domain*, the *Learner*, the *Tutor* and the *Diagnosis Process* that must be known in order to fully specify the desired target tutor. These requirements are the *responsibility* of the designer and are listed below:

Domain (mathematical symbolic differentiation)
- The student must learn *concepts* and *procedures*.
- In general, the student will be able to *know* all domain concepts and *apply* correctly the derivation rules.
- *Maisu* should use several types of presentations, such as *texts* and *examples*, and several evaluation forms, such as *multiple-choice test, fill-in-gaps* and *procedural exercises*.
- In the usual teaching of this domain, it is known that there are some concepts that must be taught after the student has acquired previous knowledge. In addition, there is a consensus about the teaching order (as commonly illustrated by textbooks in the domain). Therefore, some order among concepts must guide the *Maisu* tutor performance.

Learner (assuming an adult learner of mathematical symbolic differentiation).
- The adaptability of the system will be based on the following learner characteristics: *type* (novice or expert in the teaching-learning domain), *motivation* for learning that domain (high, medium or low), *preferred learning method* (guided learning or free exploration), and *preferred session duration*.
- The learners' interventions will refer to the control of the session *(sleep, follow, finish)* and to the session development *(ask for explanations, solve exercises, agree, disagree, repeat explanations, repeat exercises, ask for an exercise)*.

Pedagogy (assuming a coaching style of instruction)
- It is required that the tutor leads the learning session, although the student must be allowed to interrupt the normal development with questions or requests.
- Besides, the student must be provided with some auxiliary learning tools such as *summary window* or *underlining* capabilities.

- The tutor must use motivation resources according to the general type of user, for example *beep, attention/alert message, provide congratulation* and *give encouragement.*

Diagnosis
Concerning the diagnosis, certain assessment exercises are very common in the classroom: simple test, filling gaps and solving derivatives exercises. So, Maisu should consider them.

2.2.1. Domain knowledge requirements for IRIS

Instructional Design Theories study in detail knowledge representation paradigms from an educational perspective. They are primarily concerned with prescribing optimal methods of instruction to bring about desired changes in learner knowledge and skills. In particular, these optimal methods must specify what must be learned (Scandura, 1983) and some way to represent knowledge. There are three basic features relating to ITS design that are taken into account in different Instructional Design Theories: 1) learning units or kinds of teaching-learning contents, 2) relationships among contents, and 3) skills to be achieved. All of these are represented in IRIS.

Basic Learning Units. IRIS is based on Merrill's (1983) 'Component Display Theory'. It presents *facts, concepts, procedures* and *principles* as the basic units to be learned (BLUs). From this perspective it is possible to determine a complete schema of knowledge representation organized from three different views: *conceptually*, when a conceptual structure (taxonomy of parts or types) is used to organize the concepts and the facts, e.g. in the TUTOR system (Fernández-Castro *et al.*, 1993); *procedurally*, when a procedure based structure is used for the domain organization, e.g. in the INTZA system (Gutiérrez, 1994); and, *theoretically*, when a structure based on principles or theories is used for this organization, e.g. in the WHY system (Stevens, 1982).

Thus, once a particular domain is chosen, the immediate task is to determine the kind of characterization required to describe the contents to be conveyed to the student. For instance, *Maisu* uses the mathematical symbolic differentiation domain for practicing differentiation rules, so two types of BLUs, namely concepts and procedures, are sufficient to represent its domain. Each kind of BLU is supported by a specific set of attributes that will be determined by the kind of skill to be mastered. For example, if the student must learn a concept, its representation will have to include several associated texts, a difficulty level, and assessment items. On the other hand, a procedure will need to include its steps or actions, some application examples, and practice-tests. Figure 3 shows the specification of the Concept BLU in the *Maisu* domain; the selected characteristics are those shadowed, specifically the skill to be mastered for concepts is *knowledge* (see next subsection) and we want the final tutor to also consider the difficulty level of each concept. The rest of the concept specification is shown in Figure 4 where presentation and evaluation forms are defined for the skill *knowledge*.

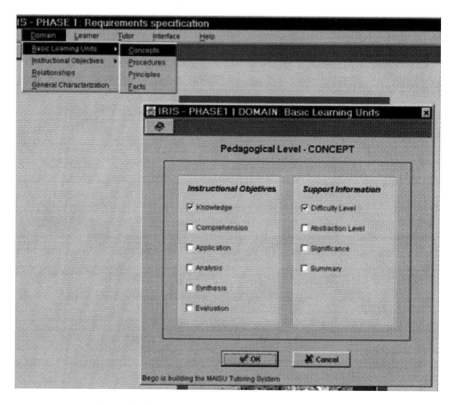

Figure 3. Specification of the BLU Concept in Maisu tutor

Instructional Objectives (IOs). These refer to the application of particular skills over BLUs and form a useful part both in planning the teaching process and in creating didactic activities. Traditionally the IOs have been hierarchically organized. The *taxonomy of teaching objectives* (Bloom *et al.*, 1956) and the *taxonomy of learning objectives* (Gagné *et al.*, 1988) are the most accepted classifications in the psycho-educational field. Bloom identifies three different learning categories: *cognitive*, *affective*, and *psychomotor*. Inside the *cognitive* category, six IOs have been defined: *knowledge, comprehension, application, analysis, synthesis* and *evaluation*. Gagné identifies five categories of learning: *intellectual skills, cognitive strategies, verbal information, motor skills,* and *attitudes*; only the first three are valid for acquiring static knowledge and problem-solving skills.

IRIS needs to complete each BLU in the domain by adding the skills (*i.e.* IOs) to be developed in the learner. For instance, a BLU procedure can be shallow learned just by knowing its associated steps (*knowledge*), or learned in a deeper way by knowing how to execute it (*application*).

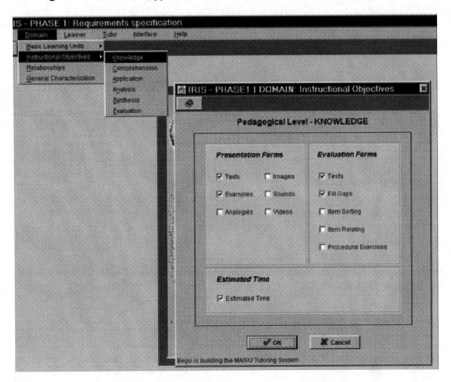

Figure 4. Specification of the Knowledge Instructional Objective

In Maisu we specify two of Bloom's IOs: knowledge or remembering of ideas or phenomena (e.g. the learner knows the definition of the procedural differentiation rule for a product expression) and application or correct use of the procedure (e.g. the learner is able to differentiate a product). Both kinds of objectives need a set of presentation forms (techniques which can be used to introduce the domain BLUs to the learner –text and example in Maisu, Figure 4), evaluation forms (techniques for assessing domain concepts –tests and fill gaps in Maisu), difficulty level (a refinement of the difficulty level property associated to the corresponding BLU) and estimated-time for acquiring that IO. Figure 4 shows the selection of characteristics for the knowledge instructional objective for Maisu.

Relationships between contents. In order to establish a pedagogical view useful for selecting and/or sequencing the learning units, Reigeluth (Reigeluth *et al.*, 1978) identifies four kinds of relationships:

- *Requisite relationships*. E.g.: "The learner must know X (or must be able to do X) before learning Y (or be able to do Y)". They appear in the TUTOR (Fernández *et al.,* 1993) and INTZA (Gutiérrez, 1994) systems.
- *Conceptual relationships*. E.g.: "X is Y-type ", "X is part of Y". These appear in TUTOR and INTZA as well.
- *Procedural relationships*. These are either *order relationships*, e.g.: "The learner must do X before doing Y" (INTZA) or *decision relationships*, e.g.: "Given a condition A, the learner must do X rather than Y or Z".
- *Theoretical* or *principles-based relationships*. These can be *cause-effect relationships*, *e.g.:* "Y is the effect of X" as in the WHY system (Stevens, 1982), or *prescriptive relationships e.g.:* "In order to achieve Z it is necessary that X and Y happen in a specified order".
- So, IRIS includes in BLU representations some attributes that relate them to one another. Some relationships we use in *Maisu* are *is-a, part-of, next* and *prerequisite.*

As a summary, the three main domain knowledge features (*basic learning units, instructional objectives* and *relationships between elements)* are fundamental to many Instructional Design Theories, and also are needed by IRIS for generating the domain model related to each new tutor. Unlike other systems, IRIS requires an explicit representation of these features and so provides the instructor with tools for specifying their actual values.

2.2.2. Learner Requirements in IRIS

Although the Learner or Student Model is a widely recognized component of ITSs, there is no consensus about the information it should include. Moreover, there is a debate about whether or not it is an essential component in order to achieve an effective and efficient instructional system (Holt *et al.*, 1994; Self, 1999).

From a pragmatic point of view we consider the learner model as a needed component whose information is a basis for the Pedagogic Module of a tutor to make individualized planning decisions and thus to produce a more efficient instructional process. Even though "learner models by themselves achieve nothing" they do provide other components with useful data for diagnosis, sequencing content, determining the level of explanations, and so forth (Self, 1990).

Different criteria have been used to classify learner models. Kok (1991) classifies these criteria on the basis of several parameters: *why are users modelled, who is modelled, what is modelled,* and *how are users modelled.* Verdejo (1992) classifies them along six dimensions, valid also for constructing and defining them; they are: *the use of the model, the extent of the user's domain knowledge to be represented, shallow* or *deep model, generic* or *individual model, permanent* or *temporal model,* and *predefined* or *inferred model.*

The ideal learner model should include all the aspects related to behaviour and knowledge that influence the learning process (Wenger, 1987). In spite of this assumption, IRIS generates a pragmatic learner model that, in the sense of Evertsz &

Elsom-Cook (1990, pp. 216), is "accurate enough as it is necessary for guiding the tutorial actions of the teaching-learning system"; and so its attributes depend on the behaviour of the target tutor.

The learner is modelled in IRIS following a successfully tested classical approach. Based on the characteristics identified in the learner model of INTZA, a passive-descriptive model that represents the acquired knowledge by means of the overlay and genetic graph techniques is created (Carr & Goldstein, 1977; Goldstein, 1982). It is a shallow, individual, system-inferred student model containing a combination of temporal and permanent information. The model, which is built up during the teaching-learning process, defines the individual learning characteristics and the evolution of each student. It includes learning preferences exhibited by the learner, supporting actions the learner has used, knowledge the learner has acquired, and teaching materials such as texts, tests, etc. the learner has accessed (see Figure 5).

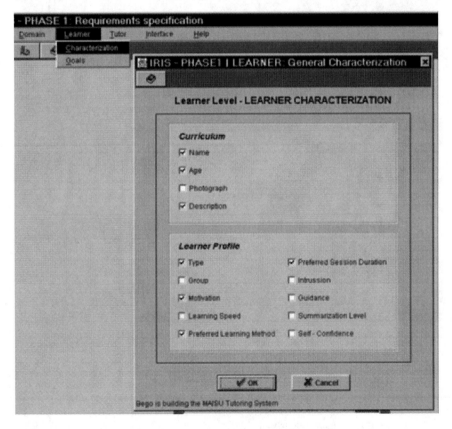

Figure 5. Learner Characterization for Maisu

IRIS also takes into account the grain-size of the learner model representation. As a consequence, the level of adaptability in tutors generated with IRIS can vary; the more fine and specific representation of the learner specified by the instructor, the more adaptation is obtained.

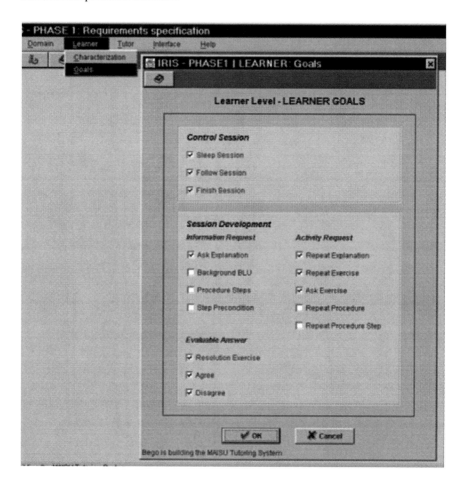

Figure 6. Specification of the Learner Goals

Besides modelling the state of knowledge of the learner, it is necessary for an intelligent tutor to be able to react appropriately to various student interventions. The best tutor ought to recognize every possible learner's goal in order to compare it to the tutor's goals and re-plan the activities when a conflict is detected. Since IRIS is defined as a generic domain-independent tool, it is not possible, or really complex, to create an interface which allows us to obtain this exigent functionality. So, the designer is required to describe the learner's goals that the target tutor will be able to solve. Learner's goals have been split into two groups (Figure 6) according to their functionality: *control* and *development* of the session. Together they collect the set of main learner goals identified in the literature (Barnard & Sandberg, 1994; Breuker *et al.*, 1987;Diaz de Ilarraza, 1990; Vadillo *et al.*, 1994).

Figures 5 and 6 show the properties used in IRIS for characterizing the learner and his or her goals in *Maisu*. Learner characteristics are separated into two groups: *curriculum* and *learner profile* (Figure 5). The former refers to the physical and professional aspects of the learner; the latter refer to characteristics that influence the learning process. The selection of one or more of the learner profile characteristics implies that the final tutor will consider it in its pedagogical decision process. For instance in Figure 5 several characteristics have been selected: *type, motivation, preferred learning method* and *preferred session duration*. As the *type* attribute has been selected, the final tutor will consider three possible types of students: novice, medium, expert; so, *type* refers to the student's knowledge background on the domain. These characteristics are the basis for tutorial decisions about Cognitive Processes, Instructional Actions and communication acts between the tutor and the learner. Learner goals are selected directly by the instructor from a predefined set (Figure 6). For example, taking into account the selection showed to control the session *Sleep, Follow*, the final tutor will let the student to develop a learning session in an non-continuous way. On the other hand, during the session development the tutor will be able to provide an asked explanation about a content *Ask Explanation*, but not able to explain the preconditions of a procedure step *Step precondition* is not selected.

2.2.3. Pedagogic Requirements for IRIS

Pedagogic knowledge is the core of any tutoring system. It is responsible for planning and executing instructional activities adapted to each individual learner considering curriculum needs and learning characteristics. Specifying the pedagogic knowledge for planning instructional sessions is one of the most difficult aspects that instructors face in the process of building ITSs by using shells or authoring tools. This becomes even more difficult if the knowledge has to be represented by the designer in a rule-based mode (Major, 1995).

Several planning approaches supported by decisions about various pedagogical aspects give rise to a range of tutoring styles. In particular, tutors generated by IRIS share an incremental planning schema of minimum commitment. They integrate a pragmatic cognitive theory of instruction, the CLAI Model (Arruarte *et al.*, 1996) and are based on a minimum agreement instructional planning process where, a priori, the tutor only plans the initial content or BLU. IRIS is completely *opportunistic*, which in this context means the student's request can be accepted at any time. A rule-based planner performs the process of building the Instructional Plan (IP), which in turn determines the activities of the tutor.

The general planner integrated in IRIS incorporates a complete set of decision rules for all levels of the instructional plan (see section 2.4). The term "complete", in this context, means that it is valid for every tutor whose specification includes any sub-set of all possible non-conflict requisites. In this way, the planner can be adapted for each particular tutor according to the specified requirements. For example, if the instructor chooses the property *prerequisite* as a requisite relation in the pedagogical domain, only the rules corresponding to *prerequisite* will be included in the corresponding rule set to be used for selection of BLUs in the new tutor. Therefore the instructor is not obliged to explicitly define the different sets of refinement rules needed for planning. Thus, the specification of the planning knowledge is an easy task for the designer as it is indirectly done by selecting the other requisites of the target system. Figure 7 shows that in IRIS it is enough to indicate the kind of instructional method used by the target tutor, in the sense that a *guided learning* method necessitates the existence of a planner component (following the characteristics above mentioned) while *free exploration* eliminates this component from the skeletal architecture being generated.

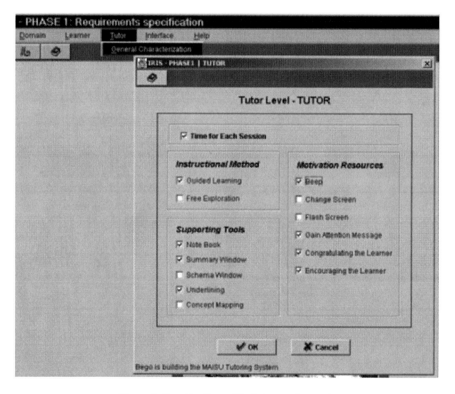

Figure 7. Specification of the tutor requirements

IRIS also allows us to specify *supporting tools* and *motivation resources* (see Figure 7). Supporting tools (Arruarte et al., 1996) provide the learner with a set of additional learning tools that enable the learner to perform a group of specific tasks. *Supporting tools* assist the learner to make a *summary,* create a *schema,* create a *conceptual map* (Arruarte *et al.,* 2001), etc.

2.2.4. Diagnostic requirements

Diagnosis of correct and erroneous knowledge acquired by the student is difficult, yet it is a key issue to consider in order to obtain suitable and successful tutor behaviour. This task is usually tackled by analysing deeply the answers of the student to several assessment tests. The kind of domain and skills the learner is hoping to acquire may make it necessary to use different types of exercises. For instance, in declarative domains, where the ability to be tested is *knowledge* (Bloom *et al.,* 1956), most interactions with the student are limited to *multiple choice, fill-gaps* or similar tests. However, these methods are inadequate for procedural domains, where the system has to infer the student's knowledge from the sequence of steps executed to reach an objective. This is due to the necessity of diagnosing other skills, such as *application* or *synthesis*.

In declarative domains the diagnostic module of a tutor directly profits from the static domain description. Some parts of this representation can be used as correct matching models to compare against the student's answers. However, in procedural domains the instructor must define explicitly the functional objects, procedural exercises, and their most significant solving models.

The problem of diagnosis is even bigger if we try to build a generic diagnostic tool to be included in IRIS. Our approach must be pragmatic in the sense of allowing the designer to choose among a collection of predefined general test forms applicable and adaptable to each domain.

DETECTive carries out the diagnostic process in IRIS. It is a generic and customisable diagnostic tool (Ferrero *et al.,* 1999a; 1999b) capable of diagnosing conceptual and procedural knowledge, as well as guiding and assessing the users. DETECTive can be used autonomously or integrated in an authoring tool or instructional system to monitor the student's actions. Its diagnostic process combines several techniques: model-tracing paradigm, error libraries, order deviations and direct pattern-matching against domain knowledge; the system selects the most appropriate one according to the kind of exercise and characteristics of the domain:

- *model-tracing* (Anderson *et al.,* 1990; Corbett *et al.,* 1990; Urretavizcaya & Verdejo, 1992) is based on a set of predefined problem solving models corresponding to procedural exercises;
- *order deviations* (Ohlsson, 1994; Mitrovic, 1998) are described as rules that applied to the established problem solving models generate a set of non-optimum or deviated solutions which allow the system to diagnose a first category of errors;
- *declarative representation* (Ferrero *et al.,* 1999a) of the domain procedures, including their pre- and post-conditions, allows the system to check the correctness or incorrectness of certain actions.

In the first phase, the designer is required just to select the kinds of assessments tests used for each Instructional Objective (IO). This will set up the corresponding component of DETECTive to be incorporated to the skeletal architecture. While defining the requirements of *Maisu*, the evaluation forms test, fill-gap and procedural exercises have been selected for the IO Application.

2.3. Filling content: second phase

Once finished the specification phase, the designer has made several choices about the four main issues above discussed. All together these define the behaviour of the future tutor. In summary these choices are:

- On the Domain: basic learning units, instructional objectives, presentation and evaluation forms, and relationships between contents, i.e. the *pedagogical level* of the domain.
- About the Learner: learner characteristics that will be taken into account in developing the instructional plan and learner goals that will be considered by the tutor.
- With respect to the Pedagogic: instructional method, supporting tools and motivation resources.
- About the Diagnosis: the kind of tests to be used to assess the learner knowledge, i.e. fill-gaps, procedural exercises, etc.

In the second phase, the concrete contents of the domain must be defined. Observing the characteristics of the requirements and their functionality and utility in the final tutor, it is easy to deduce that the task of defining the teaching domain and diagnostic exercises is complex. The Learner Model is pretty much defined in the first phase by a small set of attributes (Figure 5), which will be directly demanded by a suitable interface in the second phase (Learner Characterisation). On the other hand, learner goals are already completely fixed in the first phase as well as the Pedagogical characteristics, so these parts are not reflected in the second phase (Figures 6 and 7).

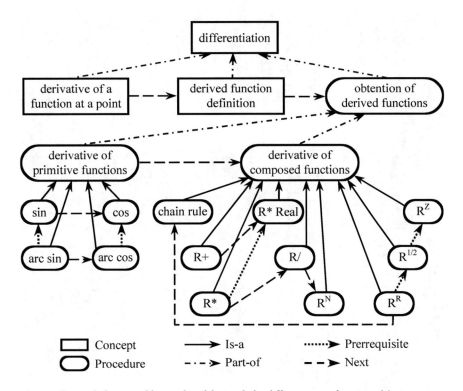

Figure 8. Structural hierarchy of the symbolic differentiation domain in Maisu

Concerning the teaching domain the process is different. First the designer must carry out a deep analysis in order to identify all the elements that must be conveyed to the learner together with the skills to be reached for every one, in concrete, the whole set of basic learning units, the structural and pedagogical relationships among them and the instructional objectives. Figure 8 shows the structural hierarchy of the *Maisu* domain. Once this is done, IRIS provides an adapted window to create the elements and a guided process to request the values for their attributes. In some cases the values correspond to plain text or images, so several graphical and text external editors are also provided. In other cases the attributes describe the specific exercises for evaluating each domain element. So, a specialized interface for acquiring several kind of assessment test has been integrated in IRIS. Figure 9 shows the mechanism to define a multiple answer test.

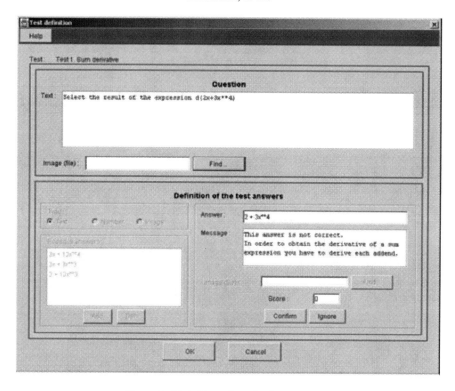

Figure 9. Definition of a multiple answer test

2.4. General characterization of IRIS-tutors

This section briefly describes the common structural characteristics shared by the tutors based on the generic architecture INTZIRI, as it involves all the aspects previously described (see Figure 10).

The *Domain* of these tutors contains the explicit representation of the content to be taught organized from a pedagogical point of view. It represents the basic contents or elements associated with the teaching-learning process *(i.e. basic learning units)*, the skills to be mastered by the learner *(i.e. instructional objectives)*, the necessary pedagogical resources, and the relationships between these elements in order to get an effective teaching-learning process. Two different levels are used to represent it (Arruarte & Fernández, 1995): *Concrete* or *Performance Level* and *Pedagogical Level*. The first focuses on the performance properties of the basic contents to be conveyed in the teaching-learning process *(i.e.* basic learning units) and their didactic resources (instances of presentation and evaluation forms). This level will be more or less complex depending on the kind of diagnosis to be realised: a target tutor which specifies to assess the application of procedures will require to define a rich domain involving the objects to be manipulated, the solution models and the possible deviations. The *Pedagogical Level* focuses on the skills to be mastered by the learner (*i.e.* instructional objectives) and the relationships between contents in order to get an effective teaching-learning process. Similar pedagogical relationships between *learning units* or contents to be learned by the students are also represented in the ECSAI system (Gavignet, 1994).

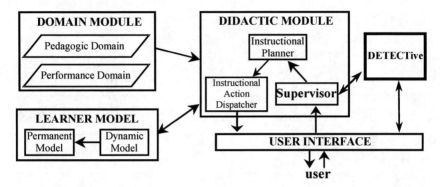

Figure 10. INTZIRI general architecture

The *Learner Model*, based on an overlay approach (Goldstein, 1982), defines the individual learning characteristics and the knowledge evolution of each student; it is built up during the teaching-learning process. The model is organised in two parts, i) the *Permanent Model*, which is maintained during all the teaching-learning process, contains the personal and learning characteristics of the student, the acquired knowledge, the errors made and also the collection of the most important events of the whole process; and ii) the *Dynamic Model* reflects those events occurring up to the current moment in the session, this model exits just during the current session and it is used for updating the Permanent Model.

Regarding the pedagogic knowledge, the *Didactic Module* is responsible for deciding *what to do next* at each point of the teaching-learning process (Wasson, 1996). It integrates a rule-based instructional planner, which dynamically plans the instructional activities to be developed by the tutor or the student. The Instructional Plan (IP) has a stratified structure in which each level solves a main tutor objective (see Figure 11):

- to determine the next Basic Learning Unit (BLUs) to teach.
- to determine the Instructional Objective (IO), or cognitive skill, that the tutor wants the student to acquire.
- to select the Cognitive Processes (CP) or mental activities in which the student must be engaged for reaching the previously chosen instructional objective.

- to refine the cognitive processes into a sequence of Instructional Events (IE) that the system must carry out in order to activate the required cognitive processes in the student's mind.
- to select the most suitable Instructional Actions (IA) for applying these instructional events. Instructional actions include didactic activities and also activities for guiding and motivating the student.

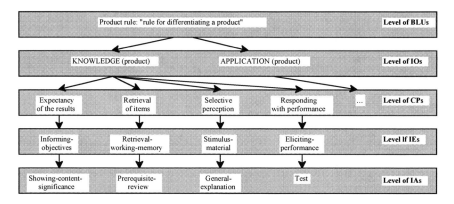

Figure 11. Structure of the instructional plan

Each level of activity involves a set of rules to refine it in terms of the subsequent level. Figure 11 shows an example based on the differentiation domain of *Maisu* and illustrates a possible refinement of the IP for teaching a particular content, specifically a procedural rule for differentiating a product expression.

Finally, the treatment of the student's interventions must be considered. The Supervisor Module (Fernández-Castro *et al.,* 1993) has the primary responsibility of treating these interventions by determining the kind of interaction, *i.e.* some of the previously specified student's goals, and by proposing suitable partial changes on the instructional plan that will be later realized by the Didactic Module. The Supervisor module activates DETECTive when a student's assessment intervention is detected. The diagnostic process itself is tightly linked to the domain performance level, but its approach is generic enough to form a domain independent core implemented separately in the DETECTive system. Its process (Ferrero *et al.,* 1999) is able to diagnose declarative and procedural domains. Diagnosis in declarative domains is realised in a simple way by means of a pattern matching process. However a more sophisticated technique based on an adapted model tracing diagnostic process is carried out for procedural domains (see figure 12). It encompasses three approaches and selects and applies the most suitable one according to both the kind of user's task and the domain characteristics.

First the Model-Tracing technique, using a set of previously defined solution models, monitors each step of the student's activity carrying out *a Model-Directed Diagnosis.* As it is not possible to assure a complete set of solution models, actions not included in any model are treated in a different way. In these cases the defined deviations are used to adapt the existing models to the student's answer. If an adapted model matching the user's answer exists, the system continues performing the same *Model-Directed Diagnosis*.

In the other case the system gives up the directed diagnosis for the current problem, and starts to perform a *Domain-based Diagnosis*. In this situation the performance level of the domain and, in particular, the articulation of the procedures (pre and post conditions and defined errors) allows the system to determine the correctness of the student's step according to the current state of the problem-solving process. This monitoring mode cannot assure an exact diagnosis/assessment in all cases, as it is possible to reach an incorrect solution or to fall into an infinite cycling process even when all preconditions are true. Both of these problematic cases are due to incorrect or incomplete domain definitions.

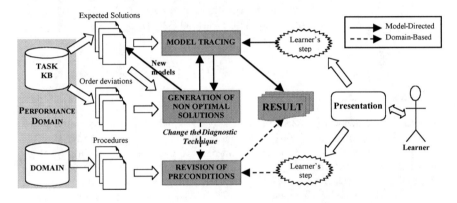

Figure 12. Detection and diagnostic generic process

Taking into account that the instructor has previously described the errors included both in the Expected Solutions models and in the Order Deviations, all of them are considered *Defined Errors*. They can immediately identify student lacks and facilitate the score computation. On the contrary, the *Deduced Errors* correspond to infringement of procedure preconditions and are dynamically identified by the system.

With the mentioned diagnosis results, a *Result* element is generated (see Figure 12). This element is related to a concrete task and stores the executed learner's steps, the errors made and the elapsed time. It can be later checked by the instructor who can use it to improve the domain definition.

Table 1 summarizes the diagnostic mechanism described above. Its process analyses each step the student carries out to obtain the final solution for a proposed task.

Table 1. Diagnostic mechanism

If	the complete student's answer matches an *Expected Solution*
Then,	as it provides all the available information about the diagnosis and assessment, including the errors identified by the designer, the system is able to produce an early diagnosis of the student's errors.
Else,	the system tries to adapt dynamically the closest expected solution to the student's one using the set of *Order Deviations*.
If	the adaptation is possible,
Then,	the adapted model lets the system to provide the errors identified by the designer as well as the order deviations used.
Else,	the concrete descriptive representation of the task, based on its pre-conditions and post-conditions, is used by the system to detect erroneous applications of the learner actions.

3. ARCHITECTURAL AND DESIGN ISSUES

3.1. Architecture of IRIS

As mentioned in section 2, IRIS works in two phases, which run sequentially. In the first phase, the tutor structure (skeletal architecture) is generated on the basis of the target tutor requirements, and in the second phase the skeletal architecture is filled with contents. So, the IRIS design must reflect this incremental construction. We have defined an architecture that includes four main components that carry out different activities for each phase (Figure 13): *Generator of the Tutor Structure*, *Object Generator*, *Rules Generator* and *Interface*.

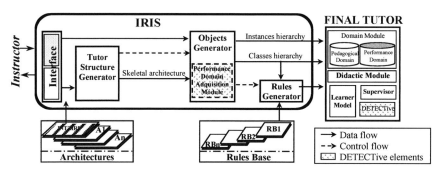

Figure 13. Architecture of the IRIS authoring tool

The Generator of the Tutor Structure has a twofold function in the first phase. It customizes the modules of the architecture INTZIRI and checks its creation preconditions; for example, it will be illegal to specify a tutor without any Basic Learning Unit ⟩ as it would mean an empty teaching domain!. Once the skeletal architecture of the tutor has been produced, the Object Generator completes and saves the declarative knowledge associated to each component of the new tutor (its classes and instances). In the first phase this module identifies the classes of objects corresponding to the components of the selected skeletal architecture. In the second phase it generates the corresponding attribute values to create pertinent instances from the previously defined classes (Figure 14). It also verifies the completeness of the contents; for instance, in principle, every concept must be provided with, at least, one presentation form.

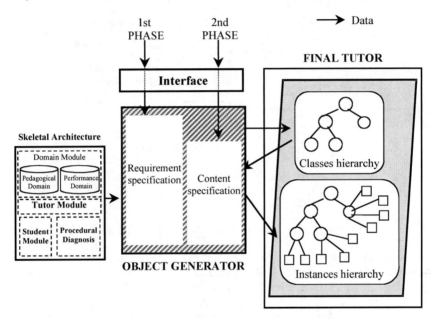

Figure 14. *Partial schema related to the Object Generator*

The Rules Generator works after the skeletal architecture of the tutor and the first phase of the Object Generator have been completed. Its function is to generate and/or select the necessary sets of instructional decision rules in order to get operative components for the tutor. This module is composed of a *Selector* and a *Generator*. If we select predefined values in the first phase, as it was shown at the subsection 2.2, the *Selector* sub-module will be the activated. If, on the other hand, we introduce new slot values, the *Generator* will be activated instead.

The current IRIS prototype includes only the *Selector* sub-component while the Generator will be approached in our future research. The *Selector* customizes the whole set of rules existing in the initial rule hierarchy, taking into account the requirements specified by the instructor (Figure 15). For example, if we select only two requisite relationships (*prerequisite* and *next*) from the four possible ones, the set of BLU selection rules (in the *Pedagogic Planner*) will be composed of rules related to only those two relationships.

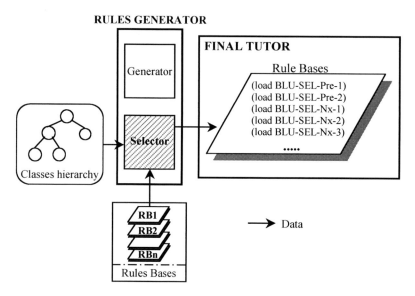

Figure 15. Partial schema related to the Selector module

The initial hierarchy groups five sets of rules related to each level of the instructional plan: contents (BLU-SEL), instructional objectives (IO-SEL), cognitive processes (CP-SEL), instructional events (IE-SEL) and instructional actions (IA-SEL).

The Interface maintains the interaction process with the human instructor by means of several graphical windows, some of which were shown earlier in the paper to illustrate the construction of the *Maisu* tutor. The current IRIS prototype interface is implemented in Java and is being extended with the graphical conceptual map editor CM-ED. It is a Concept Map Editor developed with the aim of being useful in different contexts and uses of the educational agenda. CM-ED is used inside IRIS to specify in a graphical way the domain knowledge of an ITS (Rueda *et al.*, 2002).

There are some advantages in using Concept Maps to design such a complex structure, for instance: it allows the designer to have all the information directly accessible; it makes it easier for the designer to see information in different ways or from different points of view; and the designer always knows the development stage of the domain, where she is, i.e. what she has already done and what remains to do.

3.2. Design issues: knowledge reusability

IRIS is an authoring tool developed with the aim of facilitating the efficient production of ITSs through *software reuse*. The main reason for taking reusability issues into account in the ITS field stems from the fact that building ITSs necessitates large and costly knowledge based system development environments and significant amounts of time. These development environments tend to require sizeable computing resources and are seldom suited for developing both experimental research prototypes and practical teaching-learning systems. Taking into account that prototype ITSs are built incrementally through successive enhancements and refinements, the time and cost of development is reduced if existing software and knowledge is reused.

Concerning the construction of ITSs, IRIS considers knowledge reusability at different levels (Arruarte *et al.*, 1996b; Arruarte *et al.*, 1997b), *knowledge bases/data structures, libraries of teaching resources, libraries of teaching strategies, reusability of modules* and *reusability of architectures*. Tutors built by using IRIS, *e.g. Maisu*, reflect all these levels of knowledge reusability. *Maisu* reuses knowledge and rule bases, uses some of the teaching resources and strategies defined in previously developed tutors and reuses the modules of the architecture of INTZIRI. *Reusability of architectures* is achieved when capturing the whole architecture of a previously developed system and using it for organizing new systems (Krueger, 1992). In this sense, IRIS facilitates the development of new tutors by reusing and customizing the whole architecture INTZIRI.

Building any system from scratch, even an ITS, requires three main phases: *analysis, design* and *implementation*. The utilization of a high level tool like IRIS greatly facilitates the system development process by virtually eliminating the implementation phase and significantly reducing the design phase.

When using IRIS to develop a tutor, the analysis phase involves high-level decisions about each main component of the tutor *(i.e.* domain module, learner model and pedagogic component). The domain analysis can be supported by textbooks, by previous teaching experience, and also by user help provided by IRIS. The outcome of the domain analysis will result in the necessary Basic Learning Units (BLUs) for representing the domain, the Instructional Objectives, and the selection and/or sequencing relationships between BLUs.

Analysis involving the desired style of tutoring determines both the learner model and the pedagogic module. The same basic type of learner model is maintained in all tutors developed by using IRIS, but the analysis phase will determine the grain size of the learner model representation, *i.e.* representations range from coarse to fine representation of acquired knowledge. This analysis leads also to specify the learner's goals that the tutor must be able to recognize and interpret. Concerning the pedagogic module, the instructor must define the instructional method for the new tutor, the supporting tools that the tutor will be able to offer to the learner, and the motivation resources that the tutor will use.

The design of a tutor constructed by IRIS is implicitly conducted by the instructor through selecting the different requisites and characteristics offered by

IRIS for each component. The implementation phase vanishes as IRIS takes charge of generating the new tutor's code automatically.

Let us suppose that we want to develop a new tutor for, say, symbolic integration. This domain is very similar to that of differentiation in *Maisu* tutor, therefore we may presume many similarities with *Maisu*. In fact, we can generate similar learner and pedagogic modules, but a different domain component would be required. The requirements for the new domain can be represented using the same types of Basic Learning Units (concepts, procedures), the same Instructional Objectives (knowledge, application) and the same requisite relationships (prerequisite, next). The difference arises in the content definition phase as integration contents must be defined instead of differentiation contents.

In conclusion, a reflection on the process of building a new tutor based on IRIS shows that the analysis phase is always required (to plan the structure of the tutor), the design phase is considerably simplified (to select parameters within IRIS and to design the domain knowledge and interface), and the implementation phase is mostly automated (with the exception of the interface).

4. RELATED SYSTEMS. A COMPARATIVE STUDY

The goal of developing authoring tools for building ITSs has been considered as a main focus by the ITS community. Murray's survey (Murray, 1999; Chapter 17 in this volume) forms a good basis that we will take as a common reference to briefly describe and compare some existing systems relevant to our work.

The first version of IRIS (Arruarte *et al.*, 1997) was classified under the *pedagogy oriented systems* which, according to Murray's description, focus on how to sequence and teach relatively canned content. Some other systems under this title are IDE, GTE and COCA. However, the new extensions of IRIS described here include the diagnostic process as a primary and basic aspect for building an intelligent tutor. So, this comparative study will be centred also on what Murray catalogues as *performance oriented systems*, as only these make substantial references to their diagnostic processes. In this group RIDES –device simulation–, and Demonstr8 –expert system– are classified.

IDE –Instructional Design Environment– (Russell *et al.*, 1990) is a hypertext-based tool whose aim is to provide assistance to the designer in creating courses, so falls in the group valid for providing assistance for sequencing curriculum. For this purpose, the knowledge describing the course content and structure, and the set of rules corresponding to the instructional method must be supplied. Due to the great amount of knowledge needed the initial course construction is a very complex task for the designer. Nevertheless once a course is generated, it can be reused or modified. The knowledge structures produced by IDE are used as knowledge sources for IDE-Interpreter (Russell, 1988).

IDE-Interpreter is the core of tutors built by using IDE in the same way that INTZIRI is the core of tutors built by using IRIS. However, while INTZIRI is adapted according to the tutor requirements, IDE-Interpreter carries out a pre-determined behaviour. Although both, IRIS and IDE, require the specification of the content of the course (teaching-learning domain), in IRIS is neither necessary to specify the course structure, nor the set of rules associated with the instructional planner. The first is obtained by applying the selected relationships between domain elements. The latter is automatically obtained by customising the initial predefined set of rules existing in INTZIRI. The requirements specified by the designer are taken into account for this task. Like IDE, IRIS also produces ITSs.

GTE and COCA excel at representing diverse teaching strategies. GTE –Generic Tutoring Environment– (Van Marcke, 1992) defines a formalism for representing the instructional expertise of experienced human teachers in terms of instructional tasks, methods and objects. The underlying assumption of GTE is that this knowledge is not specific to any individual situation, and can be generally re-applied in a variety of situations or in completely new domains. *Instructional tasks* are the building blocks of an instructional process; the great majority of which are very general (test, teach, etc). An *instructional method* is a knowledge-based description of a procedure for carrying out an instructional plan. It includes context-dependent knowledge in order to execute tasks. The *objects* are instructional primitives manipulated directly by the knowledge sources and the instructional methods. GTE provides a library of instructional tasks, methods and objects that can be used to author a new teaching strategy. It collects the knowledge that human teachers use during the instructional process but lacks a formal theoretical basis. The author argues that existing theories are so weak that they are largely irrelevant for computational purposes.

Although we absolutely agree with GTE developers in their generic view of the instructional expertise and in the possibilities it offers to create ITSs, the current IRIS prototype does not support that functionality. Nevertheless, the idea of a generic instructional process constituted an initial and basic hypothesis in the development of IRIS. The *instructional tasks* in GTE correspond to *instructional actions* in IRIS (Arruarte, 1998), with the same generic and wide perspective. The adaptation of the tutor is obtained in IRIS by using the instructional plan context, formed by the BLUs, IOs and the student model. Contrary to GTE, we have considered it necessary to link computational and educative efforts, so we proposed the CLAI Model, a theory for guiding the development of instructional plans.

COCA -CO-operative Classroom Assistant- is a system developed to allow for authoring ITSs. It makes a clear distinction between three types of knowledge relevant to the design of an ITS (Major & Reichgelt, 1991): material to be taught or domain knowledge, teaching strategies, and meta-strategic knowledge. COCA uses a simple object-oriented representation language to represent each fragment of domain knowledge as a frame with a number of user-defined attributes and attribute values. The teaching strategies concern the way in which the material is to be taught and the meta-strategic knowledge determines the conditions under which to apply a certain teaching strategy as well as to revise a teaching strategy in the light of previous results. For representing both strategic and meta-strategic knowledge COCA uses production rules that must be constructed by teachers. The difficulty of specifying a large amount of knowledge with rules is one of the bigger weaknesses attributed to COCA (Major, 1995). Trying to solve this problem and using COCA as a kernel, REDEEM (Reusable Educational Design Environment and Engineering

Methodology) (Major *et al.*, 1997; Chapter 8 in this volume) offers graphical windows to assist teachers with the task of authoring.

While the strategic knowledge in IRIS is fixed and formed by the instructional actions, the meta-strategy knowledge (in the sense of selection of instructional actions) is automatically generated by adapting a set of instructional decision rules according to the designer's specifications. So, although it is obvious that the general decisions in IRIS are established in advance, it will be interesting to extend IRIS with a mechanism that allows designers to adapt or create new instructional and meta-strategic rules.

FITS –Framework for ITSs– (Ikeda & Mizoguchi, 1994) is another system that deserves our attention. Murray classifies it as a shell, so it was not included in his survey, which is restricted to authoring tools. Murray's distinction between shells and authoring tools lies with the final designer-users. While authoring tools are intended for non-computer-specialized users, shells are environments built for knowledge engineers. This distinction seems to rely more heavily on the interfaces provided by the system rather than the essential nature of the system. The distinction is really a reflection of the complexity of using the many features of the authoring tools 〉 IRIS included.

FITS was developed to examine what functions can be realized as a domain-independent framework among those which are needed in ITSs. Its final goal is to identify those generic instructional functions and provide a set of *building blocks* useful to cover essential tasks for teaching; in a sense, is similar to the basic hypothesis of GTE. Following expert system technologies, each building block is designed as a domain-independent problem solver for its corresponding generic task. FITS is totally oriented to knowledge engineers and does not offer any suitable interface for human teachers who may be non-experts in the computational area.

Regarding most of the authoring tools introduced above, one aspect that deserves special mention is the difficulty instructional designers find when they confront the interfaces necessary for developing the different components of an ITS. First, many instructional designers are non-experts in the computational field; moreover, building even the most simple tutor requires such a large amount of data that is very hard for the instructor to specify the system requirements. Another weakness of these tools is that, although some of them include or observe various pedagogical principles, none of them incorporates a whole teaching-learning theory.

Many others ITS authoring systems have been and are now being developed, but they are less relevant for our work. In some of them, for example in the Eon system (Murray, 1996; 1998; Chapter 11 in this volume), the initial approach is quite different. Although Eon excels at representing several teaching strategies, it has been designed under the assumptions of a user base line similar to typical users of commercially available authoring systems for traditional computer-based teaching. As such, many of the tools supported in standard CBT authoring systems are included as basic tools in Eon. In other cases, for example CREAM-Tools (Nkambou *et al.*, 1996; Chapter 10 in this volume), they are focused on only one of the components associated with the architecture of an ITS. The main goal of

CREAM-Tools is to facilitate instructional designers to generate curricula by representing instruction differentially based on knowledge type.

An aspect not considered (or described) in the above referenced systems is that of diagnosing and testing the student's errors. We have to inspect another group of systems, what Murray names *performance oriented systems*. These are systems focused on providing rich learning environments in which students can learn skills by practicing them, receiving feedback, and obtaining explicit descriptions of diagnostic processes.

The diagnosis of student knowledge is a main basis for obtaining an adapted teaching or learning process. The more accurate the diagnosis, the better adapted is the teaching. So, this is an initial guarantee for obtaining successful learning experiences for the student. The tools developed to help in the construction of ITS face this problem in different ways depending on the particular domain and the teaching objectives of the final tutor.

Some of these tools generate systems whose interactions with the student are limited to 'multiple choice', 'fill-gaps' or similar types of exercises. These include REEDEM (Major *et al.*, 1997; Chapter 8 in this volume) and early versions of IRIS (Arruarte *et al.*, 1997a). They deduce the student's cognitive state from the simple analysis of responses. These methods can be valid for declarative domains but not for procedural ones, where the sequence of the student's actions is a reflection of the state of knowledge and, therefore, needs a deep analysis supported by more specific knowledge. Thus, these instructional systems require powerful tools that enable them to propose the student procedural exercises to deduce both skills and knowledge level.

Instructional simulation is the main approach taken for building skill-diagnosis systems. These authoring tools generate *learning-by-doing* tutors in which "introductory or conceptual instruction is absent or limited, assuming that the students have a basic familiarity with important concepts and procedures in the domain before using the tutor" (Murray, 1999 pp. 103). RIDES (Munro *et al.*, 1997; Chapter 3 in this volume) is a representative example.

RIDES generates tutoring and practice systems based on graphic simulations, which enable diagnosis of a student's skills. A RIDES course is composed of a set of learning objectives that must be achieved by the student. Each objective is associated with a lesson that can be played in three different modes with different user responsibility. In *demo mode*, students only observe the progress of a lesson. In *practice mode*, students are required to carry out the actions of the lesson, and are given remediation when they fail to perform them correctly. In *test mode*, students do not obtain any error feedback but several trials are allowed and the correct action is shown at the end. The tutor also keeps the student's performance in the *practice* and *test* modes to report it to the instructor.

RIDES is very useful to build systems to practice tasks that involves the execution of a fixed set of actions, as occurs with some hydraulic, mechanical or electrical systems. However, there is no reference to tasks that can be attained with more flexible sets of actions. The diagnosis of incorrect procedure execution is determined by following the prescribed order among its steps, and only simple feedback is offered to the student (e.g. "you have not pressed the right switch", "you should have checked the pressure", etc). However, other relevant knowledge associated with a procedure may be missing, such as the reasons why every steps is executed, the effects of that step (including those not shown in the simulation) and the circumstances in which the step can be carried out.

IRIS associates both pedagogic knowledge (IO knowledge and IO application) and functional knowledge (pre-conditions, actions and post-conditions) to the procedures. In addition it enables us to define alternative step sequences to perform the same procedure and to identify typical errors (incorrect step sequences and deviations).

Finally as a different approach, it is worth mentioning model-tracing tutors (Anderson *et al.*, 1990) as they also diagnose procedural skills. DEMONSTR8 (Blessing, 1997; Chapter 4 in this volume) is an authoring tool that builds model-tracing tutors for arithmetic applications. They contain an expert model, which trace the student's response to ensure that it belongs to an acceptable solution path. The expert model is formed by a set of production rules containing the knowledge needed to solve problems within the domain being tutored. The final system deduces the student's progress by monitoring each problem-solving step and offers feedback when it is requested or when it is necessary, either immediately or in a delayed way. This system only generates tutors for arithmetic domains. However, although their authors claim that many parts of this tool are general enough to be applied to any domain or are easily modifiable, this claim has not been proved. So, even when the underlying ideas are very significant, the adaptation process of this proposal to any other kind of domain has not been demonstrated.

IRIS is based on an initial idea similar to that of a model-tracing tutor. Thus, the functionality obtained by the production rules in DEMONSTR8 is also found in DETECTive. DETECTive encodes a functional definition of the procedures together with a hierarchical structure, which enables it to express the order among the procedure steps. In addition, DETECTive provides the possibility to include other types of knowledge, i.e. deviations, as an auxiliary support, which makes it possible to carry out the diagnostic process when the solution model set is not complete.

To conclude, it can be said that IRIS not only uses all the diagnostic techniques mentioned above but it also extends them. As we pointed out in subsection 2.2.4, IRIS diagnostic process combines model-tracing paradigm, error libraries, order deviations and direct pattern matching against domain knowledge. IRIS selects the most appropriate one according to the kind of exercise and characteristics of the domain. Besides, now we are including a new set of exercises in IRIS based on Concept Maps. The more complete the set of different kind of exercises that IRIS provides, the greater the potential of the generated new tutors. Integrated in IRIS, CM-ED allows designers to create graphical exercises based on Concept Maps (Larrañaga *et al.*, 2002).

5. USES AND EVALUATION OF IRIS. LESSONS LEARNED

As this chapter has described in detail, IRIS facilitates the development of new tutors by reusing and customizing INTZIRI, which is a previously developed generic

ITS architecture. INTZIRI constitutes the central core of all tutors developed by this means, and its correctness can be considered validated for declarative domains 〉 tutor on program specification at introductory level (Fernández-Castro et al., 1993), and procedural domains 〉 operator trainer in a power plant (Gutiérrez, 1994).

Recently, this architecture has been also used to create an ITS on management of human resources, *THuman*. The domain included 58 related theoretical contents, with three presentation forms and two evaluation forms for each of them. The designer group consisted primarily of psychologist and teachers with one knowledge engineer. The creation process took two months, which were dedicated primarily to analysing and structuring the teaching / learning domain; once this was done, to authoring the system resulted in a surprisingly easy task. The tutor interface was developed in an ad hoc manner and oriented to a future use on the Web. Although the system was not proved with real students, this experience gave rise to the necessity of creating a development methodology in order to help designers both in the task of specifying the target tutor requirements and analysing the domain. On the other hand, a designer group was asked about their difficulties in the process of creating a new tutor; their answers were very positive in the sense that they found very similarities with the design of a classical course.

Although in a basic ITS architecture traditionally four main components have been identified (Wenger, 1987) 〉 *Domain component, Student module, Pedagogic module* and *Interface,* throughout this chapter we have mainly focused on three of them. The interface issues, specifically the automatic generation of new tutor's interfaces, have not been considered, so, at present, tutors built by using IRIS are not self-sufficient, i.e. it is necessary to build an *ad-hoc* interface for each tutor. This fact has restricted seriously the type of use and evaluation we have made.

Formative evaluation occurs during the design and early developments of a project and is oriented to discover the immediate needs of developers who are concerned with modifying and improving the design and behaviour of a system (Mark & Greer, 1993). It is used to obtain detailed information that can be used for these purposes. The current IRIS prototype was formatively validated in the development of *Maisu*; specifically the *expert inspection* technique (Mark & Greer, 1993) was applied to each component of the architecture[1]. The experts' 〉 *Maisu* tutor designers together with IRIS developers〉 knowledge was used as an explicit standard for judging the program correctness.

Although IRIS has been validated, the preliminary state of the designer-interfaces impedes, for the moment, a summative validation of the whole system. This will be carried out in the near future, once the designer-interface complies with minimum quality standards.

One other aspect that deserves special attention is that of diagnosis. DETECTive is the subsystem that, integrated within IRIS, carries out this task. Before its

---

[1] Now IRIS contains most of the components identified in its architecture; it runs on a PC and has been implemented in CLIPS and Java.

integration with IRIS, DETECTive was validated with different techniques including several experiences with real students. After verifying its correctness *(expert inspection)* a *pilot test* was developed. The *Pilot test* technique (Mark & Greer, 1993) is valid for identifying users' problems and concerns; investigation of use of the actual system by some members of the intended user population is often recommended as part of the formative evaluation of the systems under development. DETECTive has been used in the *Frogalan* diagnostic system to assess student's abilities in the machine tool domain, particularly in the use of a lathe. Graphical 2D and 3D interfaces were developed ad hoc for testing some of the exercises. Our intended population were 40 students from the *Machine Tool Institute of Eibar* (IMH), a private high school for vocational training, separated into an experimental group and a control group. Mainly, two aspects were considered: diagnosis accuracy and facility of use by students.

In order to determine the accuracy of diagnosis, students' solutions were diagnosed both by the system and by their own teachers. The errors detected in both cases were contrasted in order to measure the system fidelity. We identified an incorrect diagnostic process mainly caused by a bad or incomplete definition of resolution models. In addition a lack of formalizing of teacher's assessment knowledge was discovered as well as different evaluation criteria.

Students were asked about the friendliness and facility of use of the systems by means of a questionnaire. Several conclusions have been derived from this study and have led to a new, improved version of DETECTive. A significant number of students' errors were due to lack of student skill in the use of computers (what fall outside the scope of the system). An inadequate interface was the source of many detected errors. These two reasons caused us to substantially modify the interface.

In summary, we must say that until now, there has been neither wide-scale generalised use nor a complete evaluation or a validation of the IRIS authoring tool. However, several parts have been evaluated independently with satisfactory results. They encourage us to continue with the current development of IRIS. As an immediate task, we plan to test and evaluate the global authoring tool with human instructional designers from an educational and a usability perspective.

Several lessons have been learned from the IRIS experiences and, in some way, have been described along this chapter. But at this point we would like to summarize those most general that have a particular interest and relation with our current developments. They highlight three different aspects: the intricacy of immediate use of the authoring tool by teachers; the difficulty of formalizing the whole diagnostic knowledge as the main core of an accuracy diagnostic component; and the complexity of boarding a generic tool to develop the final tutor's interface.

Concerning the first aspect, intricacy of immediate use of the authoring tool, two small developments state it: *Maisu* and *THuman*. As we acted as designers and developers in performing *Maisu*, it served as a first laboratory test that let us to improve the authoring interface in several senses such as a more intuitive grouping of characteristics, several possibilities of chaining the interface windows, or partial developments of complex tutors. *THuman* was carried out by an external designer group that found difficulties not in the authoring interface, which had been improved, but in the designing process, mainly in the formalization of the domain knowledge. After a training period focusing on the analysis process that must accompany every tutor construction, they were able to develop their system without great problems. As a conclusion, we were aware of the necessity of developing adequate methodological guidelines to facilitate the use of IRIS.

The difficulty of formalizing the whole diagnostic knowledge was observed during the construction of *Frogalan*. We realized that it is a complex and hard task to build a "complete" set of possible model solutions for procedural exercises, even including typical deviations or commons errors. The solution given was to let the designers to build the domain knowledge of a final tutor by successive incremental refinements. Therefore, as the tutor can work with incomplete descriptions of the domain the diagnostic process can be unconfident, so the student's answers are recorded to be latterly evaluated by the real teacher. In this way, correct students' solutions can be incorporated to the tutor domain knowledge.

Finally, again the three very different systems created will let to presume the complexity of building a generic tool to develop the final tutor's interface. Interfaces for *Maisu* and *THuman* are similar, in the sense that all kinds of students' goals can be supported by a graphical menu-driven interface. However, as the main goal of *Frogalan* is to diagnose procedural activities related to the use of complex physical systems (mechanical tools) its interface requires a tough modelling process using 2D and 3D graphical environments and so hard to generalize. Hence, our approach to build a tutor with IRIS should allow two possibilities: either to build a simple interface directly with IRIS, or to create an *incomplete tutor (I-Tutor)* that can be later integrated with an ad hoc interface. In this last case, the I-Tutor should be seen as a software component whose connection interface would be completely defined by IRIS.

As a conclusion, we are aware of the necessity of developing adequate methodological guidelines to facilitate the use of IRIS, in addition to focussing the problem of tutor's interface. In order for authoring tools to take advantage the most from the involvement of teachers and instructors, Virvou & Moundridou (2001) discuss the need of incorporating an *instructor modelling component* in the architecture of ITS authoring tools. They argue that this inclusion may be beneficial both for the quality of the ITSs to be produced and for the instructor herself. In this way, IRIS is provided with different mechanisms. On the one hand, IRIS offers instructors a means to search for already constructed ITSs in order to make them available for future modifications. Thus, instructors can profit from the database of ITSs that have been previously created using IRIS. The ITSs stored possess various attributes such as the domain structure, the student characteristics used for adaptation, or the exercises types. On the other hand, the provision of individualised feedback and guidelines would be useful and advantageous for instructor during the ITS creation process.

6. CONCLUSION AND FUTURE LINES

The goal we have pursued in this chapter is to describe the design and implementation of IRIS, an authoring tool to aid in the construction of instructional environments integrating pedagogical principles within a general ITS architecture. We assume that a human instructor establishes the requirements of the final tutor and these requirements be used to adapt automatically a previously built generic architecture producing a new tutor.

INTZIRI is the previously developed architecture on which IRIS is modelled. It is valid for conceptual and procedural domains and provides a core for IRIS and a basic common architecture found in all IRIS-generated tutors. Thus, any new tutor built with IRIS is provided with a flexible planner and shares many characteristics of INTZIRI, including its types of domains and how it generates, executes and re-plans its Instructional Plan. Any IRIS-generated tutor will retain the representation structure and the reasoning scheme of INTZIRI with changes only in the content of its components.

With the aim of providing a sound basis for computer-based training, we have previously defined a pragmatic cognitive theory of instruction, the CLAI Model, which has been integrated into IRIS. A deep analysis of both the architecture and the theory has allowed us to extract the necessary requirements that affect the different components of a tutor. The information required for building the domain knowledge has been organized in four groups: meta-information for characterizing the domain in a general way, basic learning units, instructional objectives and requisite relationships. For modelling the learner, IRIS requires a learner profile, and learning goals. Regarding the necessary pedagogical information, it includes the specification of the instructional method that the target tutor will use, the supporting tools, and the motivation resources; all of them will be used to customise the instructional plan refinement rules. Finally, the diagnostic mechanism is specified just by identifying the types of assessment tests the tutor must use. All these requirements (which must be specified by the ITS designer) have directly influenced the design and the basic architecture of IRIS and allow us to integrate those pedagogic principles with a general ITS architecture.

An important aspect remains to be considered: the generation of interfaces. It constitutes one of our current research lines. We are also concerned about facilitating the process of knowledge acquisition, what has been pointed out as a weak point in many of the developed authoring tools.

7. REFERENCES

Anderson, J.R., Corbett, A. & Lewis, M.W. (1990). Cognitive Modelling and Intelligent Tutoring. *Artificial Intelligence, 42*, 7-49.

Arruarte, A. & Fernández, I. (1995). A two-phased development shell for Learning Environments. A design proposal. Tinsley & van Weert (Eds.), *World Conference Computer in Education VI* (pp. 53-65). Chapman & Hall.

Arruarte, A., Fernández, I. & Greer, J. (1996a). The CLAI Model. A Cognitive Theory to Guide ITS Development. *Journal of Artificial Intelligence in Education, 7*(3/4), 277-313.
Arruarte, A., Elorriaga, J.A. & Fernández-Castro, I. (1996b). Knowledge Reusability: some Experiences in Intelligent Tutoring Systems. *Proceedings of the Workshop Architectures and Methods for Designing Cost-Effective and Reusable ITSs*. Montreal.
Arruarte, A., Fernández, I., Ferrero, B., & Greer, J. (1997a). The IRIS Shell: "How to Build ITSs from Pedagogical and Design Requisites". *International Journal of Artificial Intelligence in Education 8*(3/4), 341-381.
Arruarte, A., Elorriaga, J.A. & Fernández-Castro, I. (1997b). Reutilización del Conocimiento: Experiencias en los Sistemas Tutores Inteligentes. *Journal of Informática y Automática 30*(3), 61-67.
Arruarte, A. (1998). Fundamento y Diseño de IRIS: un entorno para la generación de *Sistemas de Enseñanza Inteligentes*. Ph. Dissertation. Leioa, Euskal Herriko Unibertsitatea (University Microfilms, D.L.: B-29967/99).
Arruarte, A., Elorriaga, J.A., Rueda, U. (2001). A Template-based Concept Mapping Tool for Computer-Aided Learning. Okamoto, T., Hartley, R., Kinshuk, J.P. Klus (Eds.), *Proceedings IEEE International Conference on Advanced Learning Technologies ICALT'2001* (pp., 309-312). IEEE Computer Society.
Barnard, Y.F. & Sandberg, J.A.C. (1994). The learner in the centre: towards a methodology for open learner environments. Ph. Dissertation. Universiteit van Amsterdam, Faculteit Psychologie, Amsterdam.
Blessing, S.B. (1997). A Programming by Demonstration Authoring Tool for Model-Tracing Tutors. *International Journal of Artificial Intelligence in Education, 8*, 233 - 261.
Bloom, B.S., Engelhart, M.D., Murst, E.J., Hill, W.H. & Drathwohl,D.R. (1956). *Taxonomy of Educational Objectives*. The Cognitive Domain, Longmans.
Breuker, J., Winkels, R. & Sandberg, J. (1987). A Shell for Intelligent Help Systems. Proceedings of the 10th International Conference on Artificial Intelligence, 167-173,
Carr, B. & Goldstein, I. (1977). Overlays: A Theory of Modelling for Computer-Aided Instruction. *International Journal of Man-Machine Studies, 5*, 215-236.
Corbett, A.T., Anderson, J.R. & Patterson, E.G. (1990). Student Modelling and Tutoring Flexibility in the Lisp Intelligent Tutoring System. Frasson, C. & Gauthier, G. (Eds.), *Intelligent Tutoring Systems: At the crossroads of artificial intelligence and education* (pp. 83-106). Ablex.
Diaz de Ilarraza, A. (1990). Gestión de diálogos en Lenguaje Natural para un Sistema de Enseñanza Inteligente, Ph. Dissertation, University of the Basque Country UPV/EHU, Donostia.
Evertsz, R. & Elsom-Cook, M. (1990). Generating Critical Problems in Student Modelling. Elsom-Cook, M. (Ed.), *Guided Discovery Tutoring. A Framework for ICAI Research* (pp. 216-246). Paul Chapman.
Fernández-Castro, I., Díaz-Ilarraza, A. & Verdejo, F. (1993). Architectural and Planning Issues in Intelligent Tutoring Systems. *Journal of Artificial Intelligence in Education, 4*(4), 357-395.
Ferrero, B., Fernández-Castro, I. & Urretavizcaya, M. (1999a). Diagnostic et évaluation dans les systèmes de «training» industriel. Diagnosis and assessment in industrial training systems. *Simulation et formation professionnelle dans l'industrie, 6*(1), 189-217.
Gagné, R.M., Briggs, L.J. & Wager, W.W. (1988). *Principles of Instructional Design. Third Edition.* Holt, Rinehart & Winston.
Gavignet, E. (1994). Instructional expertise in ECSAI. Desalles, J. (Ed.), Proceedings of the International Conference on Computer Aided Learning and Instruction in Science and Engineering CALISCE'94, TELECOM, 249-257.
Golstein, I.P. (1982). The Genetic Graph: A Representation for the Evolution of Procedural Knowledge. D. Sleeman & J.S. Brown (Eds.), *Intelligent Tutoring Systems* (pp. 51-77). Academic Press.
Graesser, A.C., Person, N.K., Harter, D. and The Tutoring Research Group. Teaching Tactics and Dialog in AutoTutor. *International Journal of Artificial Intelligence in Education, 12*, 257-279.
Gutiérrez, J. (1994). INTZA: un Sistema Tutor Inteligente para Entrenamiento en Entornos Industriales. Ph Dissertation. Euskal Herriko Unibertsitatea, UPV/EHU, Donostia.
Holt, P., Dubs, D., Jones, M. & Greer, J. (1994). The State of Student Modelling. In. J. Greer & G. McCalla (Eds.), *Student Models: The Key to Individualized Educational Systems* (pp. 3-35). Springer Verlag,.
Ikeda, M. & Mizoguchi, R. (1994). FITS: a Framework for ITS - A Computational Model of Tutoring. *Journal of Artificial Intelligence in Education, 5*(3), 319-348.

Khuwaja, R., Desmarais, M., Cheng, R. (1996). Intelligent Guide: Combining User Knowledge Assessment with Pedagogical Guidance. Frasson, C., Gauthier, G., Lesgold, A. (Eds.), *Proceedings of the Third International Conference Intelligent Tutoring Systems ITS'96* (pp. 225-233). Springer-Verlag,.

Kok, A.J. (1991). A Review and Synthesis of User Modelling in Intelligent Systems. *The Knowledge Engineering Review*, 6(1), 21-47.

Krueger, C.W. (1992). Software Reuse. *ACM Computing Survey*, 24(2), 131-183.

Larrañaga, M., Rueda, U., Elorriaga, J.A., Arruarte, A. (2002). Using CM-ED for the Generation of Graphical Exercises Based on Concept Maps. Kinshik, Lewis, R., Akahori, K., Kemp, R., Okamoto, T., Henderson, L. and Lee, C.-H (Eds.), *Proceedings of International Conference of Computers in Education ICCE'2002* (pp. 173-177). IEEE Computer Society.

Major, N. & Reichgelt, H. (1991). Using COCA to build an intelligent tutoring system in simple algebra. *Intelligent Tutoring Media*, 2(3/4), 159-169.

Major, N. (1995). REEDEM: Creating Reusable Intelligent Courseware. J. Greer (Ed), *Proceedings of Seventh World Conference on Artificial Intelligence in Education AI-ED'95* (pp. 75-82). AACE.

Major, N., Ainsworth, S. & Wood, D. (1997). REEDEM: Exploiting Symbiosis Between Psychology and Authoring Environments. *International Journal of Artificial Intelligence in Education* 8(3/4), 317-340.

Merrill, M.D. (1983). Component Display Theory. Reigeluth, C.M. (Eds.), *Instructional-Design Theories and Models: an overview of their current status* (pp.279-333). Lawrence Erlbaum Associated.

Merrill, M. & the ID$_2$ Research Group (1996). Instructional Transaction Theory: Instructional Design Based on Knowledge Objects. *Educational Technology*, May-June, 30-37.

Mitrovic, A. (1998). Experience in implementing constraint-based modelling in SQL-TUTOR. B. P. Goettl, B.P., Halff, H.M., Redfield, C.L. & Shute, V.J. (Eds.) *Intelligent Tutoring Systems 1998* (pp. 414-424). Springer.

Munro,A., Johnson, M.C., Pizzini, Q.A., Surmon, D.S., Towne, D.M. & Wogulis, J.L. (1997). Authoring Simulation-Centered Tutors with RIDES. *International Journal of Artificial Intelligence in Education*, 8, 284-316.

Murray, T. (1996). Having It All, Maybe: Design Tradeoffs in ITS Authoring Tools. Frasson, C., Gauthier, G., Lesgold, A. (Eds.), *Proceedings of the Third International Conference Intelligent Tutoring Systems ITS'96* (pp. 93-101). Springer-Verlag.

Murray, T. (1998). Authoring Knowledge Based Tutors: Tools for Content, Instructional Strategy, Student Model, and Interface Design. *Journal of the Learning Sciences*, 7(1), 5-64.

Murray, T. (1999). Authoring Intelligent Tutoring Systems: An Analysis of the State of the Art. *International Journal of Artificial Intelligence in Education*, 10(1), 98-129.

Nkambou, R., Gauthier, G., Frasson, C. (1996). CREAM-Tools: An Authoring Environment for Curriculum and Course Building in an Intelligent Tutoring System. Díaz de Ilarraza Sánchez, A. & Fernández de Castro, I. (Eds.), *Computer Aided Learning and Instruction in Science and Engineering* (pp. 186-194). Springer-Verlag.

Ohlsson, S. (1994). Constraint-Based Student Modelling. Greer, J. & McCalla, G. (Eds.), *Student Modelling: The Key to Individualized Knowledge-Based Instruction.* NATO ASI Series F: Computer and Systems Sciences, Vol.25 (pp. 167-189), Springer-Verlag

Reigeluth,C.M., Merrill, M.D., & Bunderson,V. (1978). The Structure of Subject Matter Content and Its Instructional Design Implications. *Instructional Science*, 7, 107-126.

Reye, J. (1995). A Goal-Centred Architecture for Intelligent Tutoring Systems. J. Greer (Ed), *Proceedings of Seventh World Conference on Artificial Intelligence in Education AI-ED'95* (pp. 307-314), AACE.

Rueda, U., Larrañaga, M., Arruarte, A., Elorriaga, J.A. (2002). Using a Concept Mapping Tool for Representing the Domain Knowledge. V. Petrushin, P. Kommers, Kinshuk, I. Galeer (Eds.), *Proceedings of IEEE International Conference on Advanced Learning Technologies ICALT'2002* (pp. 387-391). IEEE Computer Society.

Russell, D.M. (1988). IDE: The Interpreter. In Psotka, J., Dan Massery, L., Mutter, S.A. (Eds.), *Intelligent Tutoring Systems. Lessons Learned* (pp. 323-349), Lawrence Erlbaum Associates.

Russell, D.M., Burton, R., Jordan, D.S., Jensen, A., Roger, R., Cohen, J. (1990). Creating instruction with IDE: tools for instructional designers. *Intelligent Tutoring Media*, 1(1), 3-16.

Scandura, J.M. (1983). Instructional Strategies Based on the Structural Learning Theory. Reigeluth, C.M. (Eds.), *Instructional-Design Theories and Models: An overview of their current status* (pp. 213-246), Lawrence Erlbaum Associates.
Self, J.A. (1990). Bypassing the Intractable Problem of Student Modelling. Frasson, C. & Gauthier, G. (Eds.), *Intelligent Tutoring System At the Crossroads of AI and EI* (pp. 107-123). Ablex.
Self, J.A. (1999). The defining characteristics of intelligent tutoring systems research: ITSs care, precisely. *International Journal of Artificial Intelligence in Education, 10*, 350-364.
Srisetamil, C. & Baker, N.C. (1995). Application and Development of Multiple Teaching Styles to an Engineering ITS. J. Greer (Ed), *Proceedings of Seventh World Conference on Artificial Intelligence in Education AI-ED'95* (pp. 75-82), AACE.
Srisetamil, C. & Baker, N.C. (1996). ITS-Engineering: A Domain Independent ITS for Building Engineering Tutors. Frasson, C., Gauthier, G., Lesgold, A. (Eds.), *Proceedings of the Third International Conference Intelligent Tutoring Systems ITS'96* (pp. 677-685). Springer-Verlag.
Stevens, A. (1982). Misconception in student' understanding. Sleeman, D. & Brown, J. (Eds.), *Intelligent Tutoring Systems* (pp. 13-24). Academic Press.
Urretavizcaya, M. & Verdejo, F. (1992). A cooperative system for the interactive debugging of novice programming errors. Dijkstra, S., Krammer, H.P.M. & van Merriënboer, J.J.G. (Eds.). *Instructional Models in Computer-Based Learning Environments* (pp. 421-444), Springer-Verlag.
Vadillo, J.A., Díaz de Ilarraza, A., Fernández, I., Gutiérrez, J. & Elorriaga, J.A. (1994). Explicaciones en Sistemas Tutores de Entrenamiento: Representación del Dominio y Estrategias de Explicación. Actas II Congresso Ibero-americano de Informática na Educaçao, 2, 289-309.
Van Marcke, K. (1992). A Generic Task Model for Instruction. Dijkstra, S., Krammer, H.P.M., VanMerrienboer (Eds.), *Instructional Models in Computer-Based Learning Environments* (pp. 171-194). Springer-Verlag,.
Van Marcke, K. & Vedelaar, H. (1995). Learner Adaptivity in Generic Instructional Strategies. J. Greer (Ed), *Proceedings of Seventh World Conference on Artificial Intelligence in Education AI-ED'95* (pp. 323-333). AACE.
Vassileva, J. (1995a). Dynamic Courseware Generation: At the Cross Point of CAL, ITS and Authoring. Authoring Shells for Intelligent Tutoring Systems, Workshop at AI-ED'95, Washington, AACE.
Vassileva, J. (1995b). Reactive Instructional Planning to Support Interacting Teaching Strategies. J. Greer (Ed), Proceedings of Seventh World Conference on Artificial Intelligence in Education AI-ED'95 (pp. 334-342). AACE.
Verdejo, M.F. (1992). User Modelling in Knowledge-Based Systems. Ezquerro, J. & Larrazabal, J.M. (Eds.), *Cognition, Semantics and Philosophy* (pp. 23-46). Kluwer Academic Publishers.
Virvou, M. & Moundridou, M. (2001). Adding an Instructor Modelling Component to the Architecture of ITS Authoring Tools. *International Journal of Artificial Intelligence in Education, 12*, 185-211.
Wasson, B. (1996). Instructional Planning and Contemporary Theories of Learning: Is it a Self-Contradiction?. In Brna, P., Paiva, A. & Self, J. European Conference on Artificial Intelligence in Education. Lisboa (pp. 23-30). Ediçôes Colibrí.
Wenger, E. (1987). *Artificial Intelligence and Tutoring Systems*. Morgan Kaufmann Publishing.

ACKNOWLEDGEMENTS

This work is partly supported by the University of the Basque Country UPV/EHU (1/UPV 00141.226-T-14816/2002 and 1/UPV 00141.226-T-13995/2001) and the Spanish Ministry of Science and Technology (TIC2002-03141).

An earlier version of this paper appeared in the *International Journal of Computers in Education,* 1997, Vol. 8(3/4), 341-381.

ROGER NKAMBOU, CLAUDE FRASSON & GILLES GAUTHIER

Chapter 10

CREAM-TOOLS : AN AUTHORING ENVIRONMENT FOR KNOWLEDGE ENGINEERING IN INTELLIGENT TUTORING SYSTEMS

Abstract. This chapter presents an authoring model and a system for curriculum development in Intelligent Tutoring Systems (ITSs). We first present an approach for modeling knowledge of the subject matter (the curriculum) to be taught by a large-scale ITS, and we show how it serves as the framework of the authoring process. This approach, called CREAM (*Curriculum REspresentation and Acquisition Model*), allows creation and organization of the curriculum according to three models concerning respectively the *domain*, the *pedagogy* and the *didactic* aspects. The domain is supported by the capability model (CREAM-C) which represents and organizes domain knowledge through logical links. The pedagogical view allows the definition and organization of teaching objectives by modeling skills required to achieve them and evaluating the impact of this achievement on the domain knowledge (CREAM-O and pedagogical model). The didactic component is based on a model of resources which defines and specifies different activities that are necessary to support teaching (CREAM-R). The construction of each part of CREAM is supported by specific authoring tools and methods. The overall authoring system, called CREAM-Tools, allows Instructional Designers (IDs) to produce a complete ITS curriculum based on the CREAM approach. Although this article is limited to curriculum development, we give some guidelines on how the resulting system could support the construction of other ITS components such as the planner and the student model.

1. INTRODUCTION

In education, the development of a curriculum is considered an important step in the instructional design process (Finch and Crukilton, 1986). In Intelligent Tutoring Systems (ITSs), very little research has considered the necessity of a curriculum; consequently, very few definitions and representations can be found in the literature (Lesgold, 1988; Halff, 1988; McCalla, 1990; Hartley, 1990; Derry, 1990). Halff (1988) considers that the purpose of the curriculum in an ITS is to formulate a representation of the teaching material (the activities), and to select and arrange training activities from this representation. Thus, Halff orients the representation of the curriculum toward activities. McCalla (1990) gives a more cognitive definition according to which the curriculum represents the selection and sequencing of knowledge in order to realize teaching goals adapted to the current context and the learner. He emphasizes the fact that a curriculum must be flexible, subject to evolution, and adaptable to the needs of the learner and the requirements of the teaching sequence. Jones and Wipond (1990) and Merrill (1991) approach the construction of specific environments intended for curriculum and course development by teachers. While several research efforts have focused on complete ITS authoring (Arruarte et al., 1997; Murray, 1998), we believe that we cannot optimize this process without considering problems related to the authoring of the individual ITS components, inasmuch as they involve different kinds of expertise that come from different types of users. For instance, Instructional Designers (IDs) and domain experts are more concerned with curriculum development, whereas teachers are more concerned with pedagogical or tutorial strategies. Most of the research on ITS is concerned with the latter because the intelligent behavior of the ITS emerges not out of the curriculum itself, but out of the adaptation of tutoring strategies based on the student model (Mizoguchi & Bourdeau, 2000).

While the issue of knowledge is one of the most important in an ITS, its acquisition ordinarily takes place through a variety of learning activities supported by didactic resources, so the curriculum must also take into account the didactic resources involved in the interaction with the learner. For example, the acquisition of knowledge related to solving linear equations requires the completion of a number of activities (learning certain concepts related to linear equations, solving various exercises and problems associated with linear equations). These activities are made possible by using specific available didactic resources.

A curriculum is defined as a *structured representation* of the subject matter to be taught in terms
- of capabilities,
- of objectives that contribute to the acquisition of capabilities, and
- of didactic resources (exercises, problems, demonstrations, videos, simulations, etc.) that support learning.
-

All these elements should be organized into knowledge structures that can support teaching and learning. The idea is to create and organize an environment able to support course structuring, planning, and delivery driven by a learner model. This definition is quite different from the one proposed by McCalla, but it satisfies essential characteristics needed for a good curriculum:

1. a flexible structure with declarative knowledge for learning objectives, capabilities and resources
2. a progressive structure with easy manipulation for insertion, updating and creation of knowledge
3. a structure that can be adapted to each learner with specific activities related to his or her level of knowledge.

In this paper, we present the characteristics of such a curriculum and we focus on its authoring process. After examining some approaches to curriculum representation and some existing authoring tools, we present the CREAM (*Curriculum REpresentation and Acquisition Model*) architecture. This architecture is based on three networks of knowledge that model capabilities (CREAM-C), pedagogical objectives (CREAM-O) and resources (CREAM-R). These three models combine to form a transition network structure called CKTN (Curriculum Knowledge Transition Network) that represents the pedagogical model of the curriculum. For each of these components, we present the authoring process, including tools, methods and authoring guidelines. We then describe how individualized courses (in the form of instructional plans) can be generated from CREAM, given specifications for target learners (target profile) and training requirements. The course generation kit is part of CREAM-Tools, and includes some supporting tools (coaching and critiquing systems) to provide the designer with hints based on instructional design guidelines (Gagné, 1985; Gagné, Briggs & Wager, 1992; Spector, Polson & Muraida, 1993) that can prove useful during the authoring process. Several examples of applications are described in the paper. These examples come from real curricula implemented with CREAM-Tools and used in existing ITSs.

2. RELATED WORKS

2.1 Curriculum Representation

Early work on curriculum was concerned with the representation of knowledge. Barr, Beard & Atkinson (1976) proposed a representation called CIN (Curriculum Information Network) which includes organization of tasks, abilities and themes. This representation was used in BIP I and II, two ITSs for teaching programming in BASIC. In CIN, tasks are associated with abilities in order to allow acquisition by practice. Abilities are organized into a semantic network.

Hartley (1990) assumes that a subject to be taught (called a theme) can be acquired in three levels: operational, conceptual and procedural. In the representation proposed, the main object is the theme, which is represented by a combination of these three levels. Themes are connected with one another by prerequisite links, composition links or sub-class links. Teaching objectives are selected according to the level of acquisition of the theme. Derry (1990) propose a representation called representation models knowledge, where learning objectives are represented by nodes of a graph. Links between objectives can be of three types: prerequisite, performance to realize, and behavior. An important issue associated with this representation concerns the principle of *teaching point* expressed by the competence to acquire (objective to reach) and its acquisition level. Lesgold (1988) proposes a model of ITS in which the curriculum is represented by a hierarchical goal structure (objectives) that guides the teaching of expertise represented by domain knowledge. Elements of this hierarchy are connected by prerequisite links. Lesgold's approach tries to clearly distinguish domain knowledge and teaching objectives knowledge from strategic knowledge (which is more independent from the specific domain).

These different representations are complementary rather than contradictory. Indeed, although Barr does not mention organization of resources, he nevertheless recognizes that these resources are necessary, in particular to acquire abilities by practice. Hartley's representation highlights the idea of knowledge acquisition level. Theories such as those of Gagné (1985), Klausmeier (1990) and Bloom (1969, 1978), which are integrated into CREAM, evolve along the same lines. Indeed, the pedagogical resource that is associated with an objective (in order to acquire a capability) or with a capability needs to be closely associated with the *kind of capability* and its *knowledge level*. For example, in an ITS aiming to teach nurses the practice of primary infusion, the acquisition of the perfusion concept is different from the perfusion procedure. At the conceptual level, it would be useful to present documents explaining the concept of perfusion, followed by tests for evaluation. Acquisition rules would, however, require the effective solving of exercises and problems.

The network of goals proposed by Lesgold highlights the idea that teaching goals are oriented as a function of a knowledge domain and therefore depend on the teaching content that we represent in terms of capability. However, he does not show how this representation is used in an ITS.

Our main curriculum design objectives are to provide a flexible and progressive structure that can

- Be used for various ITS components such as the learner model, the planner (in charge of distributing the sequence and nature of knowledge), and the tutor. We also believe that this component-based authoring approach will lead to more efficient ITS.
- Facilitate the authoring process, distinguishing the knowledge part and the pedagogical part, which can evolve separately (new knowledge can be added and new pedagogical approaches can be inserted).
- Facilitate course generation and student model maintenance.
- Allow insertion of different pedagogical theories and evaluation schemes.
- Support insertion of already developed didactic resources together with specific and more intelligent resources that we detail in this paper.

This involves domain expertise as well as definition of instructional objectives and creation of didactic resources to be related to the content to be taught. To provide this flexibility, we distinguish three networks of knowledge: *capabilities* or knowledge to acquire, *objectives* that represent the pedagogical goals to achieve, and *resources* that support teaching material. A general modeling approach for content is presented, and for each resulting network, we discuss its authoring process in order to provide more general guidance to developers of authoring tools.

2.2. Authoring Tools

Murray (1999) has classified existing authoring tools under two categories: those that focus on how to sequence and teach relatively canned content (pedagogy-oriented authoring tools) and those that focus on providing a rich learning environment in which students can learn skills by practicing them and receiving feedback (performance-oriented authoring tools).

REDEEM (Major et al, 1997) is an example of the first category of authoring tools. It does not explicitly generate an instructional plan, but allows the production of a representation of instructional expertise, enabling the author to categorize the didactic material, or tutorial page, according to its level of difficulty, its generality and the prerequisites that connect it to other materials. This represents an implicit sequencing of the content and learning activities.

The functionalities offered by CREAM-Tools for organizing content in terms of interconnected structures gives it the characteristics of a pedagogy-oriented authoring tool. Moreover, its organizing capabilities go beyond didactic material (as is the case with REDEEM) and are able to deal with both cognitive aspects (organization of domain knowledge) and pedagogical aspects (organization of learning objectives).

Other authoring tools which use pedagogy oriented domain modeling are: Eon (Murray, 1998), IDE (Russell et al, 1988) and GTE (Van Marcke, 1992).

CREAM-Tools also belongs to the category of performance-oriented authoring tools, since it allows the connection between skills and how to acquire them. For example, specific learning materials are linked to specific skills to cause the student to acquire them. In this way, CREAM-Tools allows automatic generation of instruction and especially of complex learning materials that provide the student with a rich learning environment.

Other authoring tools in this category include RIDES (Munro et al., 1997), an authoring system used for the construction of tutors that teach students how to operate devices through simulations. RIDES generates instruction by providing tools for building graphical representations of a device and defining the device's behavior. A system that adds capabilities to those of RIDES is DIAG (Towne, 1997), a tool that simulates equipment faults and guides students through their diagnosis and repair. DIAG is concerned with the creation of domain knowledge and performs student error diagnosis by providing a mechanism that is applicable to many domains related to diagnosing equipment failure. When problems or exercises are created using CREAM-Tools, a knowledge structure for student tracking and error diagnosis during the problem-solving phase is also generated.

2.3. Domain-Specific or Generic Authoring Tool?

Although Murray (1999) concludes that one way to have both powerful and usable authoring tools is to limit them to particular domains or knowledge types, CREAM-Tools can support the creation of instructional components in various domains. This is because it has been built upon an explicit knowledge base, based on a clear taxonomy of the domain knowledge. We have considered each type of knowledge individually and studied the way to integrate it and have it supported by the tool. We have been inspired by Gagné's taxonomy, which covers a wide variety of types of knowledge and clearly presents not only the differences between them but also the specific means to be implemented to acquire them (Gagné, 1985), and has given us ideas about the tools that should be included in CREAM-Tools (Nkambou, Gauthier & Frasson, 1996).

Even though we are particularly interested in specific domains such as simulation (the Baxter pump, biology) and the teaching of concepts (Quebec traffic regulations), CREAM-Tools can support ITS development in a variety of fields, as long as the knowledge covered can be categorized according to Gagné's taxonomy.

This is in contrast to a number of authoring tools that focus on one particular learning domain.

3. MODELING CAPABILITIES

Definition: *a capability* is knowledge that is acquired or developed, allowing a learner to succeed in an intellectual or physical activity. This information (knowledge or cognitive unit) is stored in long-term memory and allows the learner to produce a behavior when faced with a problem-solving situation. To represent capabilities, we need to know what should be learned by the student in terms of content to be acquired. Several theories of capability classification exist (Bloom, 1969, 1978; Gagné, Briggs & Wager, 1992; Merrill, 1991; Anderson, 1988). Other approaches have been defined (Balacheff, 1991; Balacheff et al., 1993). We have selected the classification of Gagné for the following reasons:

- knowledge is represented at a fine-detail level;
- most existing classifications can be included in this representation;
- most classifications disregard some of the categories of capabilities considered in Gagné;
- for each category, Gagné has developed strategies for acquiring capabilities according to the learning conditions.

According to Gagné, five categories of capabilities can produce most human activities: verbal information, intellectual skills, cognitive strategies, motor skills and attitudes. Some of these categories include several types of capabilities. In the curriculum knowledge context, we will consider only the first three categories, motor skills and attitudes being less relevant as teaching subject. Attitudes are considered in the student modeling process (see Lefebvre et al., 1997).

3.1. Representation of Capabilities

Representation of a capability depends on its type. In a general manner, we define a capability as in figure 1. We have used the BNF (Backus Naur Form) notation to support the language of curriculum representation. This is because we need a uniform declarative formalism that can support simple specification of curriculum elements. However, in our future work, we plan to develop a language for textual curriculum specification.

DomainElement represents the object of the domain on which the capability is defined. For the same subject matter element, we can define several capabilities.

For instance, capabilities *infusion(concept)* and *infusion(rule)* are defined from the same element, *infusion*.

Attributes of a capability vary with the type of capability considered. For example, for a rule, procedures have to be represented; for a concept, discriminating factors (functional and intrinsic attributes of the concept) and rules of recognition have to be represented (figure 1). Figure 2 shows examples of capability representation expressed in a pseudo-code that closely resembles Smalltalk, our initial implementation language.

```
<Capability> : := <Notation> <Description> <Attributes>
<Notation> : := <DomainElement> ( <Type> )
<Description> : := <Text>
<Attributes> : := <VIAttributes> | <DiscriminationAttributes> | <DefinedConceptAttributes>
                | <ConcreteConceptAttributes> | <ProceduralKnowledgeAttributes>
<DomainElement> : := <ID>
<Types> : := law | proposition | setOfPrositions | definedConcept |
concreteConcept | rule
            | highOrderRule | problemSolvingStrategy | learningStrategy
<ConcreteConceptAttributes> : := <BasicAttributes> [<FunctionalAttributes>]
<RecognitionRule>
                  [<Examples>] [<NonExamples>] [<Nearmisses>]
<ProceduralKnowledgeAttributes> : := <RuleAttributes> | <HighOrderRuleAttributes>
                | <CognitiveStrategyAttributes>
<DiscriminationAttributes> : := <ListOfDiscriminationFactors>
<DefinedConceptAttributes> : := <DefinitionPredicate> [<Examples>] [<NonExamples>]
[<Nearmisses>]
<RuleAttributes> : := <ListOfProcedures>
<RecognitionRules> : := <Condition> <Condition>* <Action>
<BasicAttributes> : := <Label> <Label>*
<ListOfProcedures> : := <Procedure> <Procedure>*
```

Figure 1. Capability Representation

```
ConcreteConceptClass
        Notation: #Button-ON-OFF-CHARGE(Concrete Concept)
        Description: ``Baxter pump start/stop button''
        BasicAttributes: #(color, label)
        FunctionalAttributes: #(state #(on, off))
        RecognitionRule: [(color = #yellow) and: [label = 'ON-OFF-CHARGE'].

RuleClass
        Notation: #Perfusion(Rule)
        Procedures: #((pump isTurnOff) and:
                        [turnOn(pump). TurnOn(Boutton-ON-OFF-CHARGE).
                        programming(infusionRate).
                        programming(volumeToBeInfused).
                        start.])
```

Figure 2. Sample of Capability Definition

3.2. Acquisition Level of a Capability

We need to use a specific ontology to evaluate the acquisition of a capability. For instance, we will say that a learner **knows** a rule when he is able to apply it or to transfer the application of this rule to another problem-solving context. For that purpose, the evaluation alphabet of a rule contains two values qualifying the level of performance: *apply* and *transfer*. In the case of concepts, Klausmeier's alphabet (Klausmeier, 1990) offers four possible levels of mastery: *identify, recognize, classify* and *generalize*. A simpler evaluation alphabet could also be considered for concepts: *possess, not-possess*.

The same type of knowledge can be qualified using several alphabets. In CREAM, we have included four well-known taxonomies: those of Klausmeier, Bloom, Merrill and Gagné. One of them can be selected by the ID at the beginning of the curriculum authoring process. This provides a valuable aid to the designer, who can benefit from an integrated expertise. Also, by supporting different evaluation metrics in our model, we provide a more open authoring system that is usable by IDs with different backgrounds. However, even if we pre-defined these evaluation metrics, CREAM-Tools allows the ID to define his own metrics (see figure 6). All qualitative evaluation metrics are transformed into integer-ordered sets that are used internally in CREAM.

3.3. Organization of Capabilities

We have identified five types of relations between capabilities: *analogy* (A), *generalization* (G), *abstraction* ($A.$), *aggregation* (Ag) and *deviation* (D).

Analogy: the analogy between two capabilities can be established according to their functionality, results or definition (in the last two cases, we are speaking about structural analogy). For instance consider $k1$= *primary-infusion (rule)* and $k2$= *secondary-infusion (rule)*, two capabilities related to use of the Baxter pump, a device used in intensive-care units for infusing drugs into a patient. There exists a functional analogy, represented by the notation $A(k1, k2, functional)$, between $k1$ and $k2$.

Generalization: some capabilities are more general than others. Two capabilities linked by this type of relation share attributes of the most general capability, but the more specific capability contains additional attributes. Let us consider $k1$= *primary-infusion (rule)* and $k2$= *primary-infusion-with-rate-volume (rule)*. Capability $k1$ is more general than capability $k2$, and this is represented by the notation G $(k1, k2)$.

Abstraction: when one capability is abstracted from another, it inherits some of its attributes. Generalization is a special case of abstraction.

Aggregation: this relation indicates that a capability is part of another one. If we consider capability $k1$= *rate (rule)*, $k2$= *volume (rule)* and $k3$= *time (rule)*, $k2$ and $k3$ are components of $k1$, represented by the notation Ag $(k1, k2)$ and Ag $(k1, k3)$.

Deviation (misconception): this relation (noted D) indicates that there is the possibility of confusion between two capabilities. For example, *primary-infusion-with-time-volume (concept)* can be a deviation of *primary-infusion-with-time-rate (concept)*.

3.4. Model of Capabilities.

Each relation defines a set of links between capabilities. A link can contain information describing its nature or any other necessary information about its semantics. The subset defined by each relation is a labeled graph corresponding to the organization of capabilities regarding this relation.

The model of capabilities (CREAM-C) is represented by the multigraph *(E, A, G, A., Ag, D)* where *E* is the set of capabilities and *A, G, A., Ag* and *D* are the (labeled) graphs defined by the relations described above. This model remains extensible to other types of relations.

Figure 3 shows a part of the CREAM-C model for the curriculum on the Baxter pump. The pedagogical interest of CREAM-C is emphasized by two important applications: the student modeling process and the automatic course generation process. The planner also uses this structure as a basis for making any decision concerning a lesson to be produced.

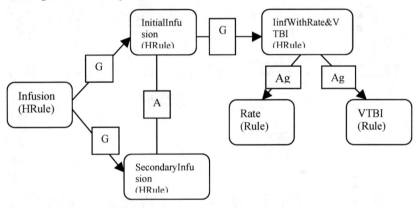

Figure 3. Part of the Baxter Pump Capability Model

Separating the domain knowledge model (CREAM-C) from pedagogical and didactic aspects of the subject matter allows the domain expert to better analyze knowledge elements and their interconnection independently of how they will be taught or what means will be used. CREAM-C as a stand-alone model is very useful in the ITS context. It serves to support student modeling (overlay, inference of new knowledge about the student, diagnosis (see Nkambou, Lefebvre & Gauthier, 1996)). We have developed a simple tutor called PSS-Tutor (Nkambou, Gauthier, Frasson & Aimeur, 1996) in which CREAM-C has been integrated to support "Polya-like" tutoring during the problem-solving process.

3.5. Authoring in CREAM-C

Modeling curriculum knowledge provides implicit guidelines for curriculum design. We have developed authoring tools based on CREAM-C that allow a domain expert to specify domain knowledge involved in the curriculum. Figure 4 shows part of CREAM-C for "Flight Simulator", an ITS built to support intelligent tutoring based on Microsoft Flight Simulator software.

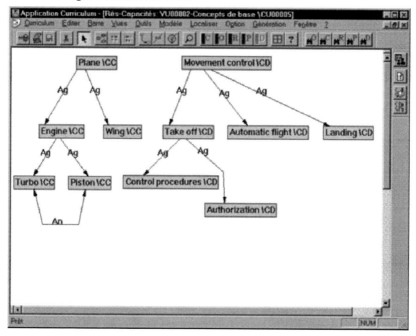

Figure 4. Part of CREAM-C for the Flight Simulator ITS Curriculum

Capabilities are linked by aggregation relations. For instance, a wing and an engine are parts of an airplane. All the capabilities and links can be entered, modified or deleted, using the toolbar elements. Each capability is displayed with its type (for instance CC, concrete concept, or CD, defined concept). We can see the buttons for defining capabilities (C), objectives (O), resources (R) and pedagogy (P). The curriculum authoring indicated above is written in C++.

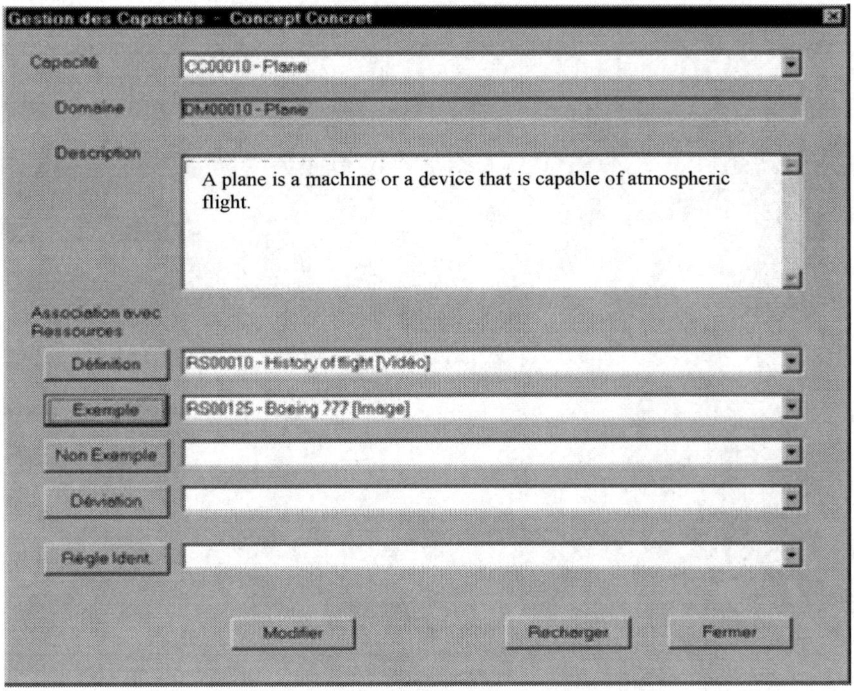

Figure 5. Concept Creation

Elements of knowledge in this domain have been identified, classified and implemented according to the CREAM approach. Links have also been defined with respect to the domain knowledge. In figure 5, we can see windows that allow definition of a concept. These windows give access to materials such as video, image and text that can be connected as examples, non-examples or near-misses of a concept. In figure 6, we present an interface in which the designer can choose an existing evaluation metric to be considered in the ITS. The metric deals with concepts, verbal information, or rules. We can see different ontologies that have been implemented: Klausmeier (for concepts), Merrill (for verbal information) and Winograd (for rules). This variety of methods is offered to the designer for two reasons: first, it is a way to inform or teach the designer about well-known methodology in the educational domain (most teachers do not know any design methodology); second, the designer can choose the methodology with which he or she is most familiar. For instance, a designer who does not agree that transfer can be used to measure the level of performance (Winograd's terminology for rules transfer) can choose another metric. Note that the designer also has the possibility of defining his or her own metric.

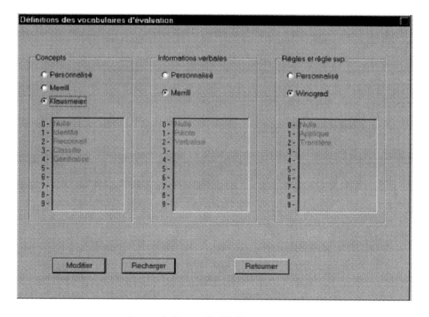

Figure 6. Setting the Evaluation Metric

4. MODELING PEDAGOGICAL OBJECTIVES

A learning *objective* is a description of a set of behaviors (or performances) that a learner should be able to produce after a learning session. It can also describe the set of capabilities to be mastered by a student after a learning activity. Thus, it describes the learning result rather than the learning process or the means involved. A number of works have demonstrated the necessity of indicating the objectives in a learning system (Webster, 1994). We have taken this dimension into account by introducing a pedagogical objectives model (CREAM-O) in which pedagogical objectives are represented and connected by didactic links.

4.1. Classification and Representation of Objectives

We chose Bloom's ontology to distinguish the different levels of objectives. Bloom's taxonomy provides a useful classification, in which action verbs are used to qualify the skill involved in an objective. It makes a distinction between affective and cognitive instructional objectives, which is useful in guiding us toward appropriate activities (Bloom, 1969; Bloom, 1978). Moreover, Bloom's classification is used widely (although sometimes with some differences) in schools and in education in general. By integrating this taxonomy into our model, we can support the designer in selecting relevant material to help achieve an objective. This support is based on guidelines from Gagné's conditions of learning (Gagné, 1985) depending on the type of skill involved in the objective. For example, our system will recommend problem-solving activities if the objective belongs to class 3 (application) in Bloom's classification. Figure 7 shows the definition of an objective.

```
<Objective> ::=
<Notation><Description><Level>[<Context>] [<AssessmentRule>]
<Notation> ::= <Ability>|<DomainElement>
<Level> ::= acquisition | comprehension | application |
            analysis | synthesis | evaluation
<Ability> ::= <AcquisitionSkill> | <ComprehensionSkill> |
              <ApplicationSkill> | <AnalysisSkill> |
              <SynthesisSkill> | <EvaluationSkill>
<AcquisitionSkill> ::= enumerate | name | identify | indicate |
                       define | recognize
<ApplicationSkill> ::= solve | apply | perform | formulate |
                       practice
<AssessmentRule> ::= <Rule>
...
...
```

Figure 7. Instructional Objective Definition Template

- *Ability* describes the skill involved in the objective. This attribute is represented by a an action in Bloom's taxonomy that expresses the behavior or performance required by the objective. Examples are acquisition, comprehension, application, analysis, synthesis and evaluation.
- *DomainElement* describes the element in the domain.
- *Description* is the textual description of the objective.
- *Level* indicates the category to which the objective belongs. Normally, this category can be deduced from the ability.
- *Context* describes the conditions in which the student will perform the task.
- *AssessmentRule* represents the selected rule when the objective is achieved.

An example of a curriculum objective (for a curriculum dealing with traffic regulations) is presented in figure 8.

```
ObjectiveClass
     Notation : #Recognize[Work-Signs]
     Description : 'Learn how to recognize road repair signs'
     Level: #acquisition
     Context: nil
     AssessmentRule : nil
```

Figure 8. An Instructional Objective for a Curriculum on Traffic Regulations

4.2. Operational Objective

To be operational, an objective must be linked to the context in which it is to be realized. Operational objectives are centered on action. We have defined two approaches for constructing operational objectives:

- We build an operational objective by indicating the context of realization and an evaluation rule (success factor) allowing measurement of its completion (Mager, 1990). In CREAM, an operational objective contains the attributes *Context* and *AssessmentRule*. A single objective can be set as operational by associating several operational objectives with it. For example, for the objective mentioned in figure 8, we can define the two operational objectives indicated in figure 9.
- Another approach to creating an operational objective is to associate a didactic resource with it. If a didactic resource is associated with an objective, the objective becomes an operational objective for which the context of realization is the same as the one defined for the associated didactic resource.

```
ObjectiveClass
    Notation : #Recognize[Work-Signs]
    Description : 'Learn how to recognize road repair signs'
    Level: #acquisition
    Context: 'The student will be able to point out and name
             work road signs between a given set of signs'
    AssessmentRule : #(2 SIT/3 + 3 DT/4) " comment : success
             on at least two simple identification tests
             (SIT) between three, and on at least three
             designation test (TD) between four"
ObjectiveClass
    Notation : #Recognize[Work-Signs]
    Description : 'Learn how to recognize road repair signs'
    Level: #acquisition
    Context: 'The student will be able to point out and name
             work road signs between a given set of signs'
    AssessmentRule : #(5 MIT / 7) "comment : success on at
             least five multiple identification tests (MIT)
             between seven"
```

Figure 9. Operational Objectives Associated with the Objective Defined in Figure 8

4.3. Organization of Objectives

CREAM allow the creation of a network of instructional objectives connected by several types of relations: *prerequisite* (P), *pretext* (P*) and *aggregation* (C).

An objective O1 is a *mandatory prerequisite* to objective O2, if the student has to reach O1 before beginning to realize O2; we indicate this fact by P(O1, O2, obligatory). A weaker form of prerequisite is the *desirable prerequisite*. Objective O1 is a desirable prerequisite to objective O2, written P(O1, O2, desirable), if the completion of O1 furthers the realization of O2. Prerequisite relations can be automatically generated or deduced by reasoning applied to the model resulting from the linkage of networks, as we will see with the pedagogical model.

An objective O2 is considered to be *pretext* to objective O1, written P*(O1, O2), if O2 can serve as support for the development of abilities specified by O1. For example, if the objective is to develop physical device manipulation abilities, then learning how to manipulate the Baxter pump could be considered a pretext objective.

An *aggregated objective* (sub-objective) is defined as one of several elements that constitute an objective. An objective can include several sub-objectives. We write C(O1, O2) if O1 is a sub-objective of O2. Just as an objective can be associated with a capability, the aggregated structure of capabilities can be mapped onto the corresponding objectives. The result is a structure of sub-objectives.

The model of objectives (CREAM-O) is represented by the multi-graph (O, P, P*, C) where O is the set of objectives and P, P* and C, are labeled graphs defined by the relations described above. It is used in the overlay part of the student model and to support propagation and control mechanisms in the student model (Nkambou, Lefebvre & Gauthier, 1996). It is also used in course planning.

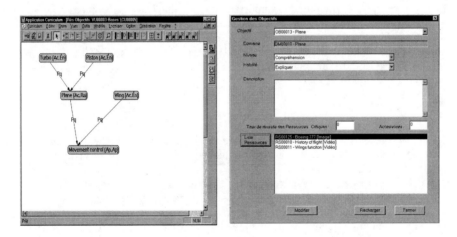

Figure 10. Part of CREAM-O for the Flight Simulator ITS Curriculum

4.4. Authoring in CREAM-O

Several tools have been included in CREAM-Tools to support CREAM-O authoring. Figure 10a shows a graphical editor for creating and linking instructional objectives. The links between objectives are prerequisite links.

For defining an objective, the authoring environment offers a dialog box with predefined information (figure 10b) to facilitate the designer's task. In this case, the level "comprehension" and the ability "explain" have been selected.

5. MODELING DIDACTIC RESOURCES

We define a didactic resource as a tactical way (exercise, problem, test, simulation, demonstration, HTML document) used by the system to support the acquisition or strengthening of capabilities by the learner, who will then be capable of performing in accordance with the objectives.

5.1. Classification and Representation of Didactic Resources

Didactic resources can play an important role in the learning process. In fact, learners can acquire most of their knowledge through interaction with didactic resources. It is important to consider the different categories of resources in order to appreciate their impact on the learning process. An analysis of the different resources has led to distinguishing three main categories: *tutoring resources, intelligent resources* and *dumb resources*.

5.1.1. Tutoring Resources

A tutoring resource is capable of handling the interaction with a learner during a learning session. Two sub-categories of tutoring resources have been identified: generic and non-generic.

Generic tutoring resources represent resources, generally integrated into the tutor, that have a certain tutoring expertise; for example, expertise in teaching concepts or in presentation of verbal information. These resources are capable of generating some intelligent actions to allow the learner to acquire certain knowledge. For example, a tutoring resource for teaching concepts knows strategies for teaching concepts that generally consist in searching for examples, non-examples, and similar concepts associated with a concept in order to generate activities to be performed by the learner: presentation of content or tests, for example.

Non-generic tutoring resources are separate from the tutor and are specialized in a tutoring strategy. They are generally equipped with a set of strategies that enable them to support interaction with a learner. The tutor can delegate tutoring functions to be performed independently. An example of this type of resource is the coach, which specializes in training a student in problem-solving situations or task execution (for instance, SOPHIE or SHERLOCK). They range from systems with low complexity, such as task demonstrators, to complex systems such as critiquing systems, simulation-based systems, etc. In general, non-generic tutoring resources focus on intelligent resources (problems, exercises).

5.1.2. Intelligent Resources

Intelligent resources are didactic resources for a specific activity to be performed by the learner. They are generally equipped with a model of knowledge that allows them to support interaction with the student and to follow the path of the student's reasoning. They are capable of self-management and self-presentation (Nkambou, Quirion, Kaltenbach & Frasson, 1995), and they can draw parallels with other resources and deal with the interaction with learners. They can be activated by any component of an ITS.

5.1.3. Dumb Resources

Dumb resources play a passive role in the learning process and are generally used in an intelligent resource and/or a tutoring resource. Two sub-categories have been defined for this type of resource: static (or atomic) and dynamic. The first have no accessible internal structure to be consulted by the learner. The second have an internal structure that, although in a black box, can be consulted by the system for the internal needs of the ITS. In both cases, these resources are not capable of managing the interaction with a learner who uses them; moreover, in contrast to tutoring resources and intelligent resources, they cannot include an evaluation of learner actions.

Although most didactic resources have to be created explicitly, we believe that some of them, such as didactic resources for the evaluation of concept acquisition, can be generated automatically from specifications. We have experimented with this question, using a system that generates multiple-choice tests (accessible through the Web) from CREAM-C and a curriculum on Quebec traffic regulations (Nkambou & Gauthier, 1996).

5.2. Organization of Didactic Resources

Once the didactic resources have been identified and represented, it is important to proceed with their organization. We have chosen six relationships among resources, based on their pedagogical interest: similarity (analogy), abstraction, particular case, utilization, assistant and equivalence. Here are some examples.

- Let us consider problem *p1: initial-infusion-with-rate-and -volume* and *p2: second-infusion-with-rate-and-volume*. We consider that *p1 **is analogous to** p2* from the point of view of their solving strategies.

- Problem *p3: initial-infusion* **is more abstract** than problem *p1*.
- Problem *p4: initial-infusion-with-rate=20m/s-and-volume=400ml* **is a particular case of** problem *p1*.
- Problem *p1* **uses** the non-generic tutoring resource *adviser*.
- A resource *r2* is considered auxiliary to a resource *r1* if the consideration of *r2* during the solving of *r1* can contribute to that of *r1*. We say that *r1* is the main resource and *r2*, the auxiliary resource. For instance, consider *p1: solve x4-13x2 + 36= 0*. If we note *that x4= (x2) 2*, then we can introduce an auxiliary variable *y= x2* and thus solve a new problem *p2: solve y2-13y + 36*. *p2* **is an auxiliary problem of** *p1*, with *y* as auxiliary variable.
- Two resources are **equivalent** if the completion of the first one implies the solution of the other. In the preceding example, problems *p1* and *p2* are equivalent because solving *p2* implies the solution of *p1*(by finding that *y=x2*).

The resource model (CREAM-R) is a multigraph defined by the preceding relationships. This model can be used to advise a learner during the interaction with a didactic resource. For example, in the event that the learner has difficulties with a problem already solved for a particular case, the system should provide the information that he or she has already solved a particular case of the problem and, if possible, should give the context.

5.3. Authoring in CREAM-R

Figure 11 shows an overview of the CREAM-R authoring interface. In this figure, each node represents an instance of a particular resource. Each node is labeled with a text indicating the resource type: Sim for Simulation, Vid for movies, Img for images and Htl for HTML files. Links between resource nodes are of several types: CP (particular case), Ax (abstraction) or An (analogy).

CREAM-Tools offers two ways of integrating didactic resources: by *creating* or *referencing*. Creating means that the instructional designer wants to create new didactic resources. The designer has to choose the type of resource to be created (figure 12a); the system then opens the specific tool for that resource. Resource creation tools are of two types: external software (HTML editors, text editors, animation creation) and tools belonging to CREAM-Tools (exercise and problem graph editor, test creation tool, demonstration creation tool). Resources can be linked together using the tool indicated in figure 12b.

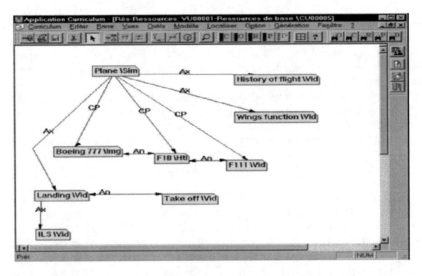

Figure 11. Part of CREAM-R for the Flight Simulator ITS Curriculum

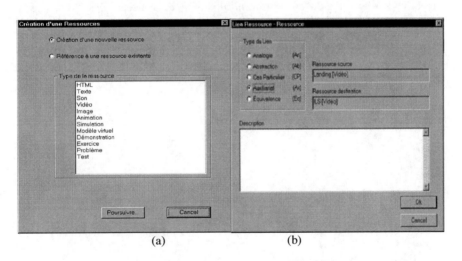

Figure 12. Some CREAM-R Tools

5.4. Representation of Links between Knowledge Elements

Links between the different elements of a curriculum generally carry information. These links are considered to be knowledge in themselves because the fact of their existence between two knowledge elements is also knowledge. For example, consider the analogy link *A(k1, k2, functional)* that indicates a link of functional analogy between *k1: initial infusion (rule) and k2:second infusion (rule)*. A learner who perceives the existence of this link knows that the procedure for an initial infusion is similar to that for a second infusion. This information has to be considered in the student model.

Given that links between knowledge elements are also knowledge, it is necessary to represent them as real objects of a curriculum. Furthermore, we think that some learning can consist essentially in establishing links between objects of a domain. Thus links, like any other knowledge in a domain, can be a subject of learning.

6. THE PEDAGOGICAL MODEL

By joining the three models (CREAM-O, CREAM-C, and CREAM-R), we bring together each objective and its associated didactic resources in an element that we call *transition* (figure 13). The resulting structure is called CKTN (Curriculum Knowledge Transition Network), or more simply, the pedagogical model. We see that a transition exists between a set of input capabilities and producing output capabilities. Figure 14 shows a portion of the pedagogical model extracted from the curriculum for the Baxter pump. For instance, we see that if learners have the capability k2 (knowing the concept of *infusion time*, the concept of *button time*, and the concept of *starting the infusion*), they will be able to acquire capability k11 (knowing the rule about *infusion time*) by using transition T2, in which a demonstration and exercises show how to program an infusion. This final structure, plus the specification of a target group, allows automatic course generation (Nkambou, Frasson & Frasson, 1996).

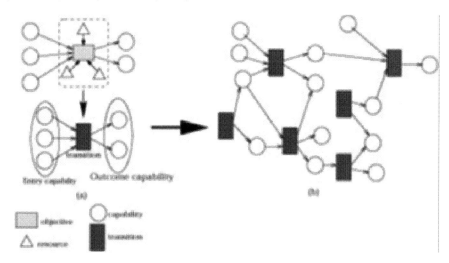

Figure 13. Construction of the Pedagogical Model

6.1. Authoring the Pedagogical Model

CREAM-Tools includes tools dedicated to authoring the pedagogical model. Figure 15 shows a part of the pedagogical model for the flight simulator curriculum. It is also possible to have an overview of the four networks related to a curriculum (figure 16).

The rectangles represent capabilities and the ovals, objectives. The links indicated are contribution and prerequisite links. For instance, the objective Wing, with the ability Acquisition and the level Enumerate, contributes (Ct) to the concrete concept Wing. This capability is a prerequisite to the objective Plane, which in turn contributes to the acquisition of the concrete concept Plane.

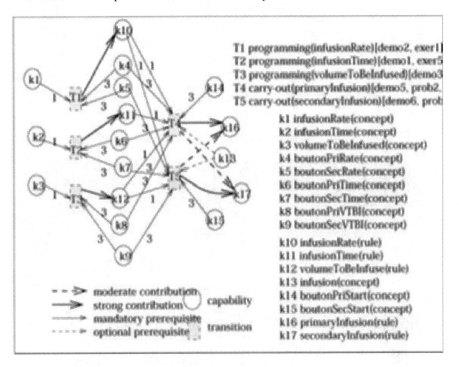

Figure 14. Part of the Baxter Pump Pedagogical Model

The pedagogical model serves as the basis of course and lesson planning (see section 10) and of some inferences in the student model (Nkambou, Lefebvre & Gauthier, 1996).

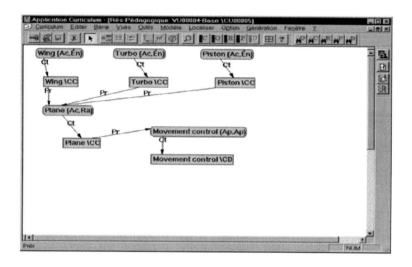

Figure 15. Part of the Pedagogical Model for the Flight Simulator Curriculum

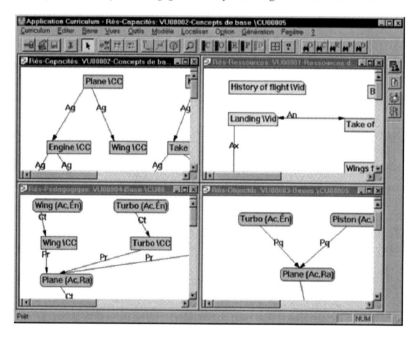

Figure 16. Overview of the Networks of the Flight Simulator Curriculum

7. CREAM: A CURRICULUM-KNOWLEDGE REPRESENTATION AND MODELING APPROACH

The model we propose (Figure 17) leads to a representation of the curriculum according to three networks: organization of capabilities (CREAM-C), organization of learning objectives (CREAM-O) and organization of didactic resources (CREAM-R). We build an additional structure representing the pedagogical model of the curriculum that links the three networks, as indicated above.

CREAM offers an interface that includes protocols allowing other components of an ITS or users (teachers, instructional designers) to access the information contained in its knowledge networks. The acquisition module (authoring environment) is composed of methodologies and toolkits. It represents the module that supports design of the curriculum according to a method that can be selected by the designer from among several instructional design methods integrated into CREAM. The module makes possible a dialogue among the different experts who contribute to the creation of the knowledge networks, including domain experts, experts in pedagogy, instructional designers and teachers. The interface with an ITS is particularly built to support student modeling and instructional planning (see section 10).

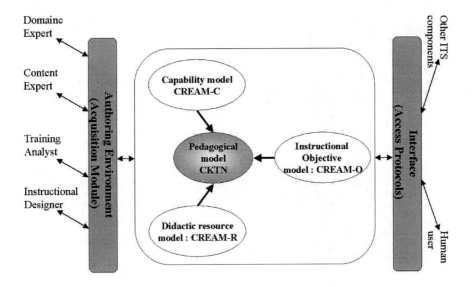

Figure 17. Architecture of CREAM

8. METHODOLOGY OF CURRICULUM CONSTRUCTION

In order to provide the designer with the capability to define, create and organize the curriculum using a methodology, we have defined three approaches to curriculum construction: **content-driven, course-driven** and **material-driven**.

8.1. CONTENT-DRIVEN APPROACH

Also called competence-oriented approach, the content-driven approach allows the user to build a curriculum by first specifying fine-grain domain knowledge in terms of capabilities. This phase is followed by the definition of instructional objectives and the specification of resources to achieve these objectives (figure 18). The main advantage of this approach is that it leads to a curriculum with a "strong cognitive content" allowing the derivation of a number of courses and pedagogical views. However, this approach is costly in development time for a large domain, since we may be constructing details that are unnecessary for a given course.

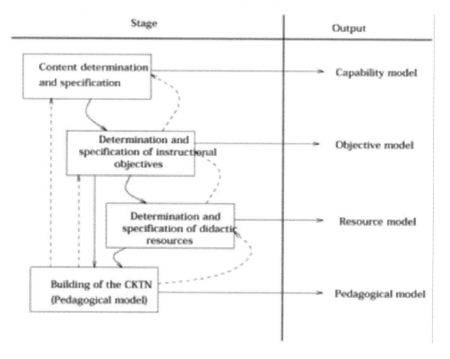

Figure 18. Content-Driven Specification Stages

8.2. COURSE-DRIVEN APPROACH

In the course-driven approach (figure 19), curriculum construction starts with a course already in the designer's mind. This means that the general instructional objectives are known. Their refinement constitutes the main part of the curriculum objectives specification stage. They in turn determine the domain knowledge to be included in the subject matter. These specifications lead to low-level objectives permitting the user to figure out the knowledge (capabilities) involved in the subject matter. The final stage is resource specification, in which the material to be used is defined.

The advantage of this approach is that it leads to a good organization of instructional objectives; however, it could lead to poor content related to the domain.

8.3. MATERIAL-DRIVEN APPROACH

The third approach (which we have not yet tried) is the material-driven approach. It consists in identifying and collecting didactic materials and defining instructional objectives that could be covered by a set of materials. This approach does not seem very efficient, however, because it might result in the acquisition of resources that are not really relevant to a specific course.

Curriculum development remains an iterative process. For instance, when the subject-matter-content phase precedes the instructional-objective-specification step, new capabilities could be identified at the latter stage and then be integrated into the subject-matter content. From our own curriculum development experience, we found that the first approach is very well adapted to small domains but that the second approach is more efficient for large domains.

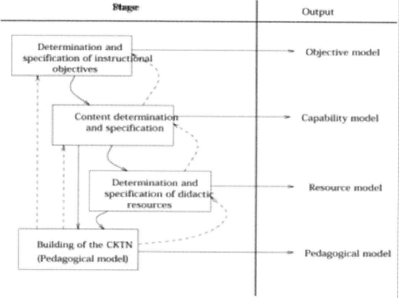

Figure 19. The Course-Driven Approach

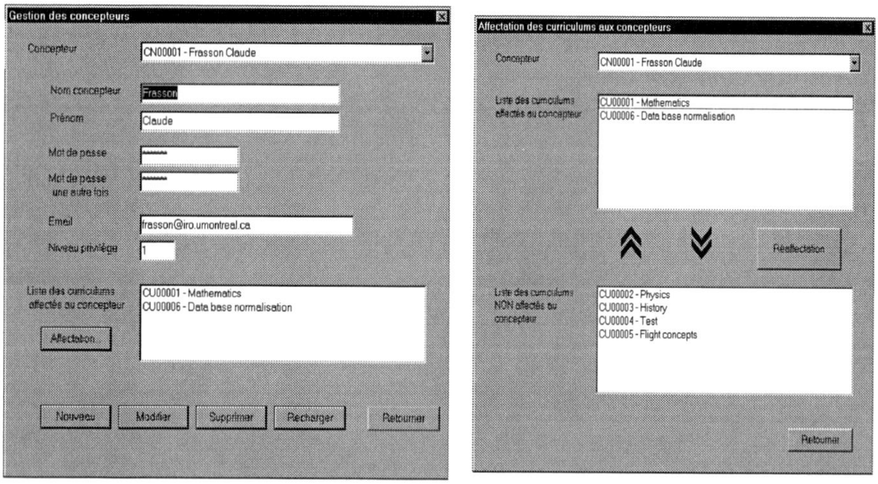

Figure 20. ID Manager Tools

9. SECURITY ISSUES IN CREAM-TOOLS

CREAM-Tools allows the system administrator to create accounts for authorized IDs. A number of curricula can be created and stored as relational databases. When creating an account, the administrator assigns the ID access rights to existing curricula in the database. An ID who creates a new curriculum is the default owner and has all the rights to that curriculum. But the owner can share some rights with other IDs by allowing them to access and copy part of the curriculum, access and modify it, etc. Figure 20 (a) shows the dialog box for ID account creation, and figure 20 (b) shows the tool for assigning curricula to an ID.

10. GENERATING ADAPTED COURSES FROM THE CURRICULUM

10.1. Definition of the Target Group

We define a target group (TG) as a grouping of students according to the state of their knowledge of various capabilities, which may be part of several subjects (curricula). For instance, the knowledge of a novice nurse on the handling of the Baxter pump will not be the same as that of an experienced nurse. A course on this topic, therefore, should not include the same objectives for the former as for the latter; otherwise, the experienced nurse would waste her time learning things she already knows. These two groups of nurses thus constitute two different student target groups, and the course generator should build a course that is well-suited to each group. Figure 21(a) presents the tool used for specification of the target group.

10.2. Definition of Training Requirements

Training requirements are expressed either as a set of objectives that the course should reach, or as set of capabilities to be acquired by the student. It is also possible to mix these two approaches. Figure 21(b) shows the tool that allows the designer to specify this element.

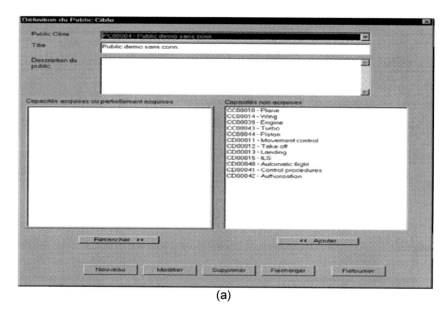

Figure 21.Target Group and Requirements Definition Tools

10.3. Course Generation Algorithms

Course generation is performed by going through the pedagogical model graph defined on the chosen curriculum. But before that, the TG's state of knowledge is assigned to the capabilities and links that constitute the pedagogical model. The resulting graph is called a *dynamic pedagogical model* (DPM), and we call this operation the *marking* of DPM. More precisely, it consists in attributing

- to each prerequisite link a value in the list {*acquired, partially acquired, not acquired*} indicating whether the minimum acquisition level for this link has been reached, according to the target group's state of knowledge
- to each capability a value in {*possessed, partially possessed, not possessed*} representing the target population's acquisition standard for this knowledge, calculated using the levels assigned to the links.

After the marking process, the generation algorithm runs through the resulting DPM to determine which objectives have to be included in the course to allow acquisition of the knowledge specified in the training requirements (for instance, specified in terms of capabilities). To do this, we start at each capability in the training requirements and perform a backward chaining passage through the subgraph whose root is at that capability in order to choose the instructional objectives judged necessary for acquisition of the capability. We first evaluate the immediate prerequisite objectives of the capability, and then, since some objectives possess mandatory prerequisite knowledge which in turn has contributing objectives, we have to trace the subgraph back until we reach an objective without any prerequisite or a capability already mastered by the student (as specified in the training requirements or seen in the marking). The choice of objectives is carried out by applying heuristic rules introduced into the system (figure 22a) which take several parameters into account: the links between capabilities and objectives (prerequisite or contribution), the knowledge in the training requirements, and the DPM. As the output of this process, a course graph is **generated** and displayed in an editor (figure 22b). The ID can then make modifications, structure the course, and store it in the database.

298   R. NKAMBOU, C. FRASSON & G. GAUTHIER

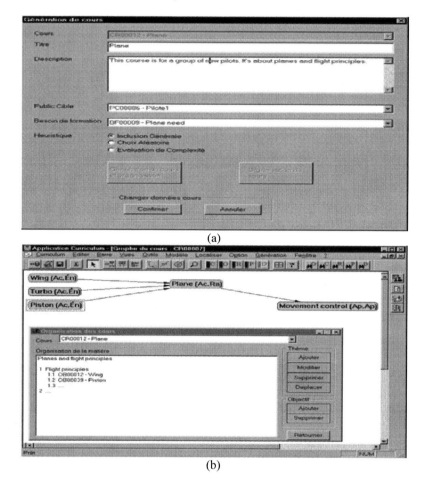

Figure 22. Course Generation Tools

11. INTELLIGENT ASSISTANT TOOL IN CREAM-TOOLS

CREAM-Tools allows the designer to make up curriculum objects (building of capability-model objects, objective-model objects and learning-material objects, definition of objectives and capabilities, creation of learning material). This part of our authoring environment takes advantage of systems such as ID Expert (Merrill, 1991, 1993), IDE (Pirolli & Russell, 1991), ISD Expert (Tennyson, 1993), the GAIDA project (Gagné, 1993), KAFITS (Murray & Woolf, 1992), AGD (Paquette et al., 1994) and other recent ITS authoring systems (Murray, 1999). Furthermore, two intelligent tools are available in CREAM-Tools.

One of these intelligent tools is concerned with automatic course generation from the curriculum. For instance, reasoning about prerequisites and contribution links in the CKTN allows the system to generate prerequisite links between objectives (see above). The other intelligent tool we have integrated into our authoring environment is an expert system for curriculum validation (Nkambou, Gauthier, Frasson & Antaki, 1995). It contains a knowledge base with about sixty rules extracted from instructional design theory (Bloom, 1969, 1978; Merrill, 1993; Tennyson, 1993; Gagné, 1993; Reigeluth, 1993). These rules support advising during the design process or critiquing of the designer's work. The system is thereby able to give hints on an ongoing basis (if the user wants to receive them) at any stage of the building process. For example, a hint could be an error signal or a suggestion. In critiquing mode, the system intervenes only after a user's request. This intervention is formulated as general comments.

12. TOWARD COLLABORATIVE AUTHORING WITH CREAM-TOOLS

Some features have been added to CREAM-Tools in order to support knowledge and expertise sharing between several authors. The three main features are: (1) an agent-based system for finding and indexing existing learning resources, (2) an XML-based storage option and (3) an ontology-based authoring to support multiple learning theories.

12.1. Finding and Indexing Existing Learning Materials

We have developed an agent-based system which is integrated into CREAM-Tools to serve as a finder of existing learning materials. When creating a new curriculum, authors can use this system to request existing resources and to index and publish the resources they create. The aim is to allow authors to share their experience with others. This is done by using a resource server based on middleware architecture with search agents implemented as servlets. The interesting point here is that the resource server can store requests without a solution, process them later and inform users the next time they connect.

12.2. Storage Option

CREAM-Tools offer two storage options: a relational database with Oracle or Access, and/or an XML database. In the case of XML, a set of metadata has been developed, each one corresponding to a curriculum object template. By using the obtained DTD or XML Schema, a whole curriculum can be stored as an XML file. Then a simple XML-based query language such as XML-QL can be used to access curriculum elements.

All these features can be considered to form a foundation for collaborative curriculum authoring, since designers can now easily access all or part of other designers' work whenever such permission is granted. What is missing is compliance with existing standards; this would consist in making our DTD correspond to existing XML-based standards for learning such as SCORM.

Encouraging the sharing of experience in curriculum resource development will lead to a cost-effective development process for Intelligent Tutoring Systems. Creation of learning materials is considered one of the most costly part of the ITS development process; sharing them will contribute to decreasing the cost.

12.3. Ontological issues: Ontology-Based Authoring

The potential of Ontologies for ITS Authoring Environments has yet to be demonstrated. In a previous paper, Bourdeau and Mizoguchi (2002) envisioned the power of Ontologies for sustaining the ITS authoring process in an ITS Authoring Environment, and explored methodologies for engineering declarative knowledge from instructional and learning sciences.

Existing ITS authoring environments aim at combining providing authoring tools and knowledge representation (Murray, 1999), but so far none of them possesses desired functionalities of an intelligent authoring system such as *Retrieve appropriate theories for selecting instructional methods* or *Provide principles for structuring a learning environment*.

Ontologies are considered a solution to the problems of indexing, assembling and aggregating Learning Objects in a coherent way (Kay & Holden, 2002; Paquette & Rosca, 2002; Aroyo, & Dicheva, 2002), either automatically, semi-automatically or done by humans.

12.3.1. The Role of Ontology in Authoring Process

Several views or theories of domain knowledge taxonomy can be found in the literature as well as how this knowledge can be represented in a knowledge-based system for learning/teaching purposes (to become possible learning outcomes). In this chapter, Gagné's theory has been presented. Merrill (1991) suggested a different view of possible learning outcomes or domain knowledge. Even if there are some intersections among existing taxonomies, it is very difficult to implement a system that can integrate those different views without an agreement on the semantics of what should be learned by the student. We believe that ontological engineering can help the domain expert agent to consider those different views in two ways: 1) by defining things associated with each taxonomy and their semantics, the domain knowledge expert can be aware of other agents of the system during their interaction. For example, if the current focus of the learning is 'define concept' according to Gagné's taxonomy, the pedagogical agent needs to know it in order to plan the appropriate learning activity to promote the learning. 2) by creating ontology for a meta-taxonomy which can include different views. We are experimenting with each of these approaches. Ontological engineering can also be instrumental for including different instructional theories into the same pedagogical agent: Gagné's learning event theory, Merill component-based theory. This could lead to the development of multi-instructional theories ITS which could switch from one instructional theory to another with respect to the current instructional goal.

Furthermore, ontology engineering is crucial for the development of distributed ITS Learning Environments in the sense that, as agents are stored in different machines with eventually different implementations, they need to agree about the definition and the semantics of the things they share during a learning session. Even if pure multi-agent platforms based on standards such as FIPA offer ontology-free ACL (Agent Communication Language), the ontological engineering is still necessary since the ontology relates to shared concepts, which are in turn sent to the other party during the communication. It should be an easy task to implement using FIPA-ACL standards in which performatives (communication acts between agents) can take a given ontology as a parameter to make it possible to the other party to understand and to interpret concepts or things included in the content of the message.

By adding intelligence to ITS authoring environments in the form of theory-aware environments, we could also obtain intelligence in the learning environments that they generated. Not only curriculum knowledge, not only instructional strategies, but also the foundations, the rationale upon which the tutoring system relies and acts. As a result of having ontology-based ITS authoring environments, we can expect that: 1) the ITS that is generated can be more coherent, well-founded, inspectable, expandable, 2) the ITS can explain and justify to learners the rationale behind an instructional strategy (based on learning theories), therefore support metacognition; can even offer some choice to learners in terms of instructional strategies, with pros and cons of each option, and therefore support development of autonomy and responsability.

Having access to multiple theories (instead of one) in an ITS authoring environment such as CREAM-tools would be an added value for: 1) the possible diversity offered to authors as well as to learners, better adequacy, and even a better chance for integrating multiple theories into a common knowledge base via an ontology 2) a curriculum planning module that would then be challenged to select among theories, and would therefore have to be more intelligent and 3) an opportunity to make it possible collaboration between authors (even with different views of instructional or learning theory) in the development of ITS modules.

12.3.2. What could be the general functionalities of a theory-aware ITS Authoring Environment?

In an Ontology-based Authoring Environment, authors (human or software) could benefit from accessing theories to: 1) make design decisions (macro, micro) after reflection and reasoning, 2) communicate about or explain their design decisions, 3) check consistency among design decisions, intra-theory and inter-theories, 4) produce scrutable learning environments, 5) have heuristical knowledge grounded in theoretical knowledge.

Useful functionalities could be queries such as: 1) ask the system what theories apply best to this or that learning situation/goal, 2) ask the system to show examples,

3) ask the system for advice on whether this element of a theory can be combined to an element from another theory, what is the risk associated to doing so, any preferable other solution, etc.

13. INDUSTRIAL APPLICATIONS AND EVALUATION: TRAINING OFFICE AND CREAM-TOOLS

Training Office™ is a well-known software package developed by Novasys Inc. which is used in industrial training. Training Office's content modeling is based on a simplified version of CREAM, and the next version of this sofware will include the CREAM in its entirety, with CREAM-Tools and its automatic course and activity generation features. Novasys Inc. is a leader in the development of cutting-edge online learning and knowledge management technologies. Training Office is being adopted by an impressive and growing list of companies and organizations, including Siemens, Canadian National, Kraft Canada, Institute of Canadian Bankers, Aluminerie Bécancour, Suncor Energy and the Quebec Department of Transportation. Novasys also has customers for Training Office in other countries, including the United States, Italy and Austria.

The Training Office extension with CREAM-Tools is also supported by the Canadian National Research Council and the Canadian Space Agency. The latter's primary interest is in having intelligent training tools for the Canadarm II, a robot manipulator for the International Space Station. The simulation-based training tools will be used for the training of astronauts who operate the arm and the ground station staff supporting them. CREAM-Tools is used for the creation of knowledge related to the Canadarm II training tasks.

CREAM-Tools is currently used at the University of Sherbrooke for the development of a tutor called Cyberscience, which is dedicated to the teaching of biology and mathematics. The tutor will be used by first-year university students, and learning activities include concept learning and procedural activities (in a math virtual laboratory). Figure 23 shows the Cyberscience learning environment. An evaluation is planned within the same environment for a third-year university biology course in which several activities on a virtual microscope are created, and CREAM-Tools is used for the development of the related curriculum. In Cyberscience project, 4 university professors have used CREAM-Tools mainly for the development of the content in terms of concept maps an of cognitive task structure related to the activities.

As we have stated early, CREAM-Tools has also been used for the development of several other ITSs in the university context: Baxter Pump Manipulation Tutor, Traffic Regulations Tutor, Problem Solving Strategies Tutor, Intensive Care Unit Tutor and Excel Tutor. In most case, the content-driven approach was used. For instance, for the traffic regulation tutor, up to 500 concepts were defined, as well as up to 300 learning materials, most of them HTML resources. Some of the materials, especially those used for knowledge assessment, were generated automatically, using CREAM-C.

At this stage, we did not have sufficient data to evaluate the usability and the effectiveness of CREAM-Tools when used by actual instructional designers. We are planning to undertake such an evaluation soon.

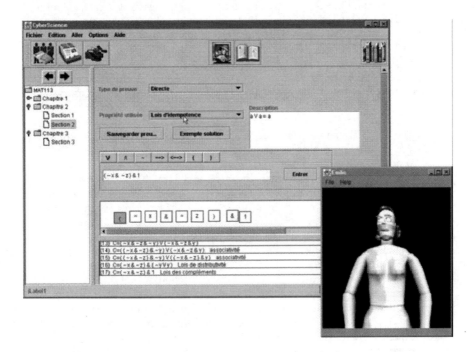

Figure 23. Cyberscience Learning Environment

14. DISCUSSIONS AND CONCLUSION

CREAM is a model of curriculum representation able to support large course teaching. Among the most original features provided by CREAM are the definition of various parts of a curriculum using graphical methods, the course generation process, the planning of learning and the support of a large course (not described here). We have experimented with integrating this model into an ITS and insuring the interaction with its other components. Several tutors using CREAM have been developed (Baxter Pump Manipulation Tutor, Traffic Regulations Tutor, Problem Solving Strategies Tutor, Intensive Care Unit Tutor and Excel Tutor). Initially prototyped in Smalltalk, CREAM is now fully implemented in C++. An industrial version of the system is currently being developed by our partner, Novasys, and should soon be on the market.

The CREAM model fulfills two fundamental characteristics of instructional design theory: the representation of the subject matter content and its organization. We have integrated these two characteristics at each level of the curriculum: at the level of instructional objectives, activities, and learning material, and at the level of the knowledge involved. Curricula built according to the CREAM approach are components that can be plugged into an ITS without modifying their internal behavior (Plug and Play). This represents a great advantage as a software engineering methodology for ITS.

CREAM-Tools takes advantage of existing authoring environments and implements new features. It can be considered a fourth-generation authoring system for several reasons:

1. The subject matter is well defined. The CREAM approach for subject-matter modeling allows the designer to specify fine-grain domain knowledge elements and to organize them into a whole.
2. Instructional design theories are integrated into the system to support designers through intelligent assistance. These theories could be easily edited to add new constraints and rules for the curriculum development process. Currently, about sixty rules have been introduced into CREAM-Tools, most of them based on Gagné's theory.
3. The authoring environment is adaptable to the designer's needs. CREAM-Tools offers a global environment specification tool allowing designers to incorporate their own vocabulary or to choose one of the default vocabularies that are already implemented in the system.
4. Automatic generation of courses and didactic resources is a feature provided by CREAM-Tools that could be very useful in the instructional design context. This feature could allow course designers to prototype and test courses quickly in order to validate them before their actual delivery.
5. Although CREAM-Tools is used to build ITS curricula and courses, we have found that it can also be a very useful tool in the area of formal teaching. Teachers in a given field can use CREAM-Tools to create the content to be taught and a broad set of varied teaching activities. The system helps the teacher create these activities according to students' profiles.

Some limitations

- Multiple spaces in CREAM increase the complexity of system architecture and realization. With CREAM-Tool, a real curriculum would consist of a number of nodes. For instances the curriculum for the traffic regulation tutor includes about 500 capability nodes. Both learners and curriculum authors are easy to lose in such large space. If the system can supplies visual navigation ability, it could enhance the usability.
- Few functional components can be shared with other intelligent tutoring system components and files containing domain knowledge is not encodes

to the format which is easy to be transferred or interpreted. If the system uses the common vocabularies with others' and the established domain knowledge is in internet-oriented file format, the workload is much less to build other curriculum if some defines nodes are used.
- The system is not suitable for running on the Internet. This restricts the range of users' locations, and further increases users' inconvenience.

Some issues

CREAM-Tools provides several features in order to assist ITS authors. However, the hints given by the system during the authoring process are based only on the instructional theories incorporated in the system. When designers define a concept, they could be prompted to specify examples, non-examples and near- misses, if this has not already been done. We think that, as Tennyson states, it could be very useful to take the designer's model into account. This could lead to more individualized authoring support.

Another issue we will examine is a way to enable collaborative curriculum and course authoring. We have developed some basis of this issue in section 12. The aim is to see how our system might allow several instructional designers to collaborate in the curriculum and course building process, even from clients with different configurations. This issue brings up the problem of interoperability with respect to data, objects and knowledge exchange between designers. We are now working on a meta-authoring language that will permit a distributed way of specifying a curriculum. An XML-based content specification could support content sharing between designers. The meta-authoring language will be compliant with standards such as the Sharable Courseware Object Reference Model (SCORM) and the Instructional Management System (IMS). These standards form the foundation for interoperability between different kinds of learning technologies, including content, learning object repositories, delivery frameworks, knowledge management tools, and learning management systems.

Another important issue is the incorporation of software agents into the design process. The intelligent software agent approach can provide a flexible solution to the interoperability problem, along with support for collaborative curriculum authoring.

15. REFERENCES

Anderson, J. R. (1988). The expert module. In M.C. Polson & J.J. Richardson (Eds.). *Foundations of Intelligent Tutoring systems;* pp. 21-53. Lawrence Erlbaum Associates, Hillsdale, NJ.

Aroyo, L. & Dicheva, D. (2002). Authoring Framework for Concept-based Web Information Systems. *Proc. of the ICCE Workshop on Concepts and Ontologies in Web-based Educational Systems.* Technische Universiteit Eindhoven, CS-Report 02-15, 41-48.

Arruarte, A., Fernández-Castro, I., Ferrero, B. & Greer J. (1997). The IRIS Shell: How to Build ITSs from Pedagogical and Design Requisites. *International Journal of Artificial Intelligence in Education.* 8, 341-381.

Balacheff N. (1991). Contribution de la didactique et de l'épistémologie aux recherches en EIAO. In: Bellissant C. (ed.) *Actes des XIII Journées francophones sur l'informatique*, pp. 9-38. Grenoble (France).

Balacheff, N., Baron, G.L., Baron, M., Dillembourg, P. Grandbastien, M., Gras, R., Madaule, F., Mendelson, P., Nguyen-Xuan, A. & Nicaud, J.F. (1993). EIAO: points de vue des disciplines. In *Actes des 3ème journées EIAO de Cachan*; pp. 7-14. Eyrolles, Paris.

Barr, A., Beard, M. & Atkinson, R.C. (1976). The Computer as a Tutorial Laboratory: The Stanford BIP project. *International Journal of Man-Machine Studies*, 8 (5), 567-596.

Bloom, B.S. (1969). *Taxonomie des objectifs pédagogiques. Tome 1: Domaine cognitif.* Education nouvelle, inc. Montreal

Bloom, B.S. (1978). *Taxonomie des objectifs pédagogiques. Tome 2: Domaine affectif.* Education nouvelle, inc. Montreal.

Bourdeau, J. and Mizoguchi, R. (2002) "Collaborative Ontological Engineering of Instructional Design Knowledge for an ITS Authoring Environment" In: S.A. Cerri, G. Gouarderes and F. Paraguacu (Eds): Intelligent Tutoring Systems, LNCS 2363, pp. 399-409. Springer-Verlag, Berlin.

Derry, S.J. (1990). Learning strategies for acquiring useful knowledge. In B.F. Jones & L. Idol (Eds.): *Dimensions of Thinking and Cognitive Instruction*; pp. 15-51. Lawrence Erlbaum Associates, Hillsdale, NJ.

Finch, C.R. & Crukilton, J.R. (1986). *Curriculum Development in Vocational and Technical Education: Planning, Content and Implementation.* Allyn and Bacon, Inc., 2nd edition.

Gagné, R. M. (1993). Computer-Based Instructional Guidance. In Spector, J.M., Polson, M.C. & Muraida, D.J. (Eds): *Automating Instructional Design: Concepts and Issues.*; pp. 133-146, ETD. Englewood Cliffs, N.J.

Gagné, R.M, Briggs, L. & Wager, W. (1992). *Principles of Instructional Design.* Harcourt Brace Jovanovich, 4th edition, Orlando, FL.

Gagné, R.M. (1985). *The Conditions of Learning* (4th Ed). New York: Holt Rinehart and Winston.

Halff, H. (1988). Curriculum and instruction in ITS. In M.C. Polson & J.J. Richardson (Eds.). *Foundations of Intelligent Tutoring Systems*; pp. 19-108. Lawrence Erlbaum Associates, Hillsdale, NJ.

Hartley, R. (1990). The curriculum and instructional tasks: Goals strategies and tactics for interactive learning. In *Adaptative Learning Environments: Foundation and Frontiers*; pp. 123-146. Springer-Verlag, Berlin.

Jones, M. & Wipond, K. (1990). Curriculum and Knowledge Representation in a Knowledge-Based System for Curriculum Development. *Educational Technology*, Mars 1990, 7-14.

Kay, J. & Holden, S. (2002). Automatic Extraction fo Ontologies from Teaching Document Metadata. *Proc. of the ICCE Workshop on Concepts and Ontologies in Web-based Educational Systems.* Technische Universiteit Eindhoven, CS-Report 02-15, 23-26.

Klausmeier, H.J. (1990). Conceptualizing. In Jones, B.F. & Idol, L (Eds): *Dimensions of Thinking and Cognitive Instruction*; pp. 93-138; Lawrence Erlbaum Associates, Hillsdale, NJ.

Lefebvre, B., Nkambou, R., Gauthier G. & Lajoie S. (1997). The student model in the SAFARI environment for the development of intelligent tutoring system development. In *Proceedings of the 1st International Congress on Electromechanical and System Engineering*, pp. 1-8, Mexico City.

Legendre, R. (1993). *Dictionnaire actuel de l'éducation.* Librairies Guérin et Eska, Montréal.

Lesgold, A. (1988). Toward a Theory of Curriculum for Use in Designing Intelligent Instructional Systems. In Mandl, H. and Lesgold, A. (Eds.), *Learning Issues for Intelligent Tutoring Systems*; pp. 114-137. Springer-Verlag, New York.

Mager, G. (1990). *Comment définir les objectifs pédagogiques.* Bordas, Paris.

Major, N., Ainsworth, S. & Wood D. (1997). REDEEM: Exploiting Symbiosis Between Psychology and Authoring Environments. *International Journal of Artificial Intelligence in Education*, 8 (3-4), 317-340.

McCalla, G.I. (1990). The search for adaptability, flexibility and individualization: Approaches to curriculum in intelligent tutoring systems. In *Adaptative Learning Environments: Foundation and Frontiers*; pp. 91-112. Springer-Verlag, Berlin.

Merrill, M. D. (1991). An Introduction to Instructional Transaction Theory. *Educational Technology*, 31, 45-53.

Merrill, M. D., (1993) An Integrated Model for Automating Instructional Design and Delivery. In Spector, J.M., Polson, M.C. & Muraida, D.J. (Eds): *Automating Instructional Design: Concepts and Issues*; pp. 147-190. ETD. Englewood Cliffs, N.J.

Mizoguchi, R. & Bourdeau, J. (2000) Using Ontological Engineering to Overcome AI-ED Problems. *International Journal of Artificial Intelligence in Education*, 11, 107-121.

Munro, A., Johnson, M.C., Pizzini, Q.A., Surmon, D.S., Towne, D.M, & Wogulis, J.L. (1997). Authoring simulation-centered tutors with RIDES. *International Journal of Artificial Intelligence in Education.*, 8 (3-4), 284-316.

Murray, T., & Woolf, B. (1992). Tools for teacher participation in ITS design. In Frasson, C., Gauthier, G. & McCalla, G. *Intelligent Tutoring Systems*; pp. 593-600. Springer-Verlag, Berlin.

Murray, T. (1998). Authoring Knowledge-Based Tutors: Tools for Content, Instructional Strategy, Student Model, and Interface Design. *Journal of the Learning Sciences*, 7 (1). Lawrence Erlbaum Associates, Hillsdale, NJ.

Murray, T. (1999). Authoring intelligent tutoring systems: an analysis of the state of the art. *International Journal of Artificial Intelligence in Education*, 10, 98-129.

Nkambou, R. & Gauthier, G. (1996). Integrating WWW resources in an intelligent tutoring system. *Journal of Network and Computer Science Applications*, 19 (4), 363-375.

Nkambou, R. Lefebvre, B. & Gauthier, G. (1996). A Curriculum-Based Student Modeling for ITS. In *Proceedings of the Fifth International Conference on User Modeling*; pp. 91-98. Kanula-Kona, Hawaii.

Nkambou, R., Frasson, M.C. & Frasson, C. (1996). Generating courses in an intelligent tutoring system. In *Proceedings of the 9th International Conference on Industrial and Engineering Applications of Artificial Intelligence and Expert Systems*; pp. 261-267. Gordon and Breach Science, New York.

Nkambou, R., Gauthier, G. & Frasson, C. (1996). CREAM-Tools: an authoring evironment for curriculum and course building in an ITS. *Proceedings of the Third International Conference on Computer-Aided Learning and Instruction in Science and Engineering, CALISCE*. Springer-Verlag, Berlin.

Nkambou, R., Gauthier, G., Frasson, C. & Aïmeur, E. (1996). PSS-Tutor: Un système tutoriel intelligent pour l'enseignement des stratégies de résolution de problèmes. In *Proceedings of the Fourth Maghrebian Conference on Software Engineering and Artificial Intelligence*, pp. 291-303. AFCET-UNESCO.

Nkambou, R., Gauthier, G., Frasson, C. & Antaki, M. (1995). Integrating Expert Systems in an Authoring System For Curriculum and Course Building. In *Proceedings of the 7th International Conference On Artificial Intelligence and Expert Systems Application*; pp. 485-490. San Francisco, CA.

Nkambou, R., Quirion, L, Kaltenbach, M., & Frasson, C. (1995). Using Multimedia In Learning about Processes; DEGREE: A Simulation-Based Authoring System For Multimedia Demonstration Building. *Multimedia Modelling: Toward Information Superhighway*; pp. 365-378. World Scientific Publishing, Singapore.

Paquette, G., Crevier, F., Aubin, C., & Frasson, C. (1994). Design of a Knowledge-Based Didactic Engineering Workbench. In *CALISCE 94*, Paris.

Paquette, G & Rosca, I. (2002). Organic Aggregation of Knowledge Objects in Educational Systems. *Canadian Journal of Learning and Technology*, 28 (3), 11-26.

Pirolli, P. & Russell, D.M. (1991). Instructional design environment: technology to support design problem solving. *Instructional Science*, 19 (2), 121-144.

Reigeluth, C. M. (1993). Functions of an Automated Instructional Design System. In J. M. Spector, M. C. Polson, & D. J. Muraida (Eds.): *Automating Instructional Design: Concepts and Issues*; pp. 43-58. ETD. Englewood Cliffs, N.J.

Russell, D., Moran, T. & Jordan, D. (1988). The Instructional Design Environment. In Psotka, Massey, & Mutter (Eds.), IntelligentTutoring Systems, Lessons Learned. Hillsdale, NJ: Lawrence Erlbaum.

Spector, J.M., Polson, M.C., & Muraida, D.J. (1993). *Automating Instructional Design: Concepts and Issues*. ETD. Englewood Cliffs, N.J.

Tennyson, R. (1993). A Framework for Automating Instructional Design. In Spector, M., Polson P. & Muraida, D., Eds., *Automating Instructional Design: Concepts and Issues*. ETD. Englewood Cliffs, N.J., pp. 191-217.

Towne, D.M. (1997). Approximate reasoning techniques for intelligent diagnostic instruction. *International Journal of Artificial Intelligence in Education*, 8 (3-4), 262-283.

Van Marcke, K. (1992). Instructional Expertise. In Frasson, C., Gauthier, G., & McCalla, G.I. (Eds.) Procs. of Intelligent Tutoring Systems '92. New York: Springer-Verlag.

Webster, J.G. (1994). Instructional Objectives and Bench Examinations in Circuits Laboratories. *IEEE Transactions on Education*, 37 (1), 111-113.

TOM MURRAY

Chapter 11

EON: AUTHORING TOOLS FOR CONTENT, INSTRUCTIONAL STRATEGY, STUDENT MODEL AND INTERFACE DESIGN

Abstract. This paper describes the Eon system, a suite of domain independent tools for authoring all aspects of a knowledge based tutor: the domain model, the teaching strategies, the student model, and the learning environment.

1. INTRODUCTION

This Chapter describes the Eon system, a suite of domain independent tools for authoring all aspects of a knowledge based tutor: the domain model, the teaching strategies, the student model, and the learning environment. Though development work on the prototype system ended several years ago, it remains the only example of an authoring tool for intelligent tutoring systems (ITSs) that contains a fully integrated set of authoring tools for all aspects of ITS design, though it is designed to meet the needs of pedagogy-oriented tutors more than performance-oriented tutors (as explained in Chapter 17, pedagogy-oriented tutors focus on representing pedagogical knowledge and teaching non-procedural tasks). This Chapter is a companion Chapter 15. This Chapter focuses on describing the Eon authoring tools. Chapter 15 discusses generic principles and lessons learned during the Eon project. The reader can start with either Chapter, depending on whether one finds it most perspicuous to learn about generalities or a particular examples first. In describing the authoring tools I use our Implementation of the Refrigerator Tutor as the main example. At the end of the paper I describe four other tutors built with Eon.

1.1 Preliminary Research

This work is an outgrowth of an earlier investigation of tools for the acquisition of ITS domain and teaching knowledge which culminated in a dissertation thesis and a system called KAFITS (Knowledge Acquisition Framework for ITS) (Murray 1991). The problem being addressed by this work was the gap between the ITS research community and the educational research and design community, as ITSs of increasing complexity were being developed without tools that would allow practicing educators to participate knowledgeably in the design process (Clancey & Joerger 1988). Several tools were created, including a semantic network editing tool for visualizing topics the their relationships, and an editor for creating instructional strategies in the form of Parameterized Action Networks (similar to ATNs but replacing states with actions to create a planning rather than parsing formalism).[1] Our sixteen month case study of three educators using the tools to build a 41 topic tutor for high school Statics (representing about six hours of on-line instruction) was reported in (Murray 1996, Murray & Woolf 1992a, and Murray & Woolf 1992b). Table 1 shows the productivity data for the domain expert (physics teacher), the "knowledge base managers" who did most of the data entry, and the knowledge engineer who did most of the knowledge representation work. The Table gives an indication of the relative amounts of time spent on different activities:

- An analysis of productivity indicated that it took about 100 person-hours of development time per hour of instruction (596 total hours for 6 hours of instruction, or about 15 hrs per topic);
- The above data was interpreted cautiously but we did note that it compared favorably with the 100 to 300 hours of development per hour of instruction often given for building traditional (non-intelligent) CAI;
- The domain expert invested significant time in designing and debugging the tutor, 47% of the total, while the knowledge based managers worked 40% of the total time, and the knowledge engineer only worked 13% of the total time;
- Design constituted about 15% of the total time, and implementation the other 85% (time spent on formative evaluation is not included in the data); and
- Training totalled about 15% of the total time (vs. 85% for development).

	Domain Expert		KB Managers		Knowl. Engineer		All	
	Train.	Devel.	Train.	Devel.	Train.	Devel.	Train.	Devel.
Design	22.7	36.8	0	0	22.7	3.7	46	40.5
Implem.	14	203	6	234	20	32	40	469
Totals	36.7	240	6	234	42.7	35.7	86	510
	277		240		79		596	

Table 1: Person-hours vs. Participant Role in building the Statics Tutor

We also studied the design process itself, as well as several usability and representational issues. We learned of the importance of 1) providing clear visual representations of the underlying concepts and structures of the system; 2) providing features which reduced cognitive load on working memory (by reifying information

---

[1] In the more recently developed Eon system, described later, a flowline paradigm was used, which maintained all of the necessary functionality of PANs.

and structure) and long term memory (by providing remindings); 3) facilitating opportunistic design by not forcing the user to make decisions in a rigid order; and 4) allowing quick movement and iteration between testing and modifying what is being built.

In sum, this work, combined with experience the author later gained using COTS (common off the shelf) authoring tools to build training systems in industry, formed the conceptual foundation for the Eon authoring tools project. The productivity data, though only from a case study of building one tutor, have given us some guidelines for estimating productivity figures on other projects, and also yielded the encouraging suggestion that intelligent tutors can be built with human resources comparable to building CAI.

1.2 Supporting Authors in a Paradigm Change

Chapter 15 begins by describing intelligent tutoring systems (ITSs) and the need for ITS authoring tools. It then describes how a shift from traditional multimedia and computer based instruction (CAI) authoring tools to ITS authoring tools involves a change from a "story board" conceptualization of instructional content to a "knowledge based" one. In the knowledge based approach tutorial content is represented as modular reusable units that are distinct form the tutoring strategies that specify how and when the content is given to the learner. The Chapter also describes how ITS authoring tools should support authoring at the "pedagogical level" as opposed to the "media level" of design by supplying basic building blocks with pedagogical meaning, such as "hint", "explanation," "summary," "prerequisite." This support authors in expressing their design ideas at an appropriately abstract and meaningful level.

As mentioned in Chapter 17, there are power/usability tradeoffs in designing authoring tools. Our goal was to give the Eon tools a usability difficulty on par with applications such as FileMaker, Excel (in advanced spreadsheet design), or AutoCAD software, rather than the lower skill level and learning curve needed for tools like PowerPoint or Email. Unlike some other ITS authoring projects (see Ainsworth et al., Halff et al., and Merrill in this Volume) we do not aim to enable the average teacher or industry trainer to create an ITS, as I think that this is an overly ambitious goal. The goal is to empower design teams who have at least one person who is trained to author ITSs.

Though there are few ITS designers, there are many CAI instructional designers. This established user population uses off the shelf software to create instructional systems. Empowering these users to build more powerful instructional systems such as ITSs requires new tools and a paradigm shift in the way many of them conceptualize instructional systems. However, this shift should be accessible, incremental, and evolutionary. Rather than starting with a laboratory-based AI tutoring system and asking how it can be generalized to produce more generic shell, as is the case in the design of some ITS authoring shells, our design base-line was commercially available and widely used authoring systems such as Authorware, Icon Author, Macromedia Director, and ToolBook. Our goal was to extend rather than replace the capabilities afforded by such systems, to preserve the level of usability and some of the authoring methods instructional designers have become familiar with, and to add additional tools, features and authoring paradigms to allow more powerful and flexible tutors to be built. For this reason, on the surface many of the Eon tools have a look and feel similar to off the shlef tools, yet allow additional levels of abstraction, modularity, and visualization necessary for producing an ITS.

Stretching off the shelf tools to the limit. Actually, many "power users" of commercial authoring tools have begun this paradigm shift. They have built layers, shells, or macros on top of the existing authoring systems that capture the repetitive or modular format of their instructional application, so they don't have to repeat the same work with every new topic or question. But these additional layers are usually large and awkward code patches that result in increased authoring efficiency, but at a loss of generality, since they are created for a specific application. The powerful features of the authoring tool are compromised, because commercial packages *allow, but do not support*, this type of abstraction. For instance Authorware has an edit-in-place feature that allows the designer to pause the tutorial, click on text or graphics, and edit right on the screen. This is extremely useful, because the screen may contain a number of text and graphic items that were brought up at different times and specified in distant portions of a large curriculum control structure. With edit-in-place the user does not have to search through this structure to find each piece. But when a shell incorporating more general procedures that access a database of questions is built on top of Authorware, the edit-in-place feature is lost. When authors pause in such an augmented system to correct, say, a spelling error in a question, the display shows a variable called "the-current-question," rather than the actual text of the question sought. To edit the actual text they have to switch to a different program (the database program), search for it in the data base, then edit it and return to the original program to see if their change resulted in the desired effect on the screen. This is one of many ways in which the powerful features of CAI authoring tools are compromised or lost when they are coerced into a form which allows separation of subject matter and instructional strategy.

2. EON ITS AUTHORING TOOLS OVERVIEW

Next I will describe the authoring tools by showing how they were used to build a tutor that teaches how a refrigerator works.

2.1 The Refrigeration Tutor

The Refrigeration Tutor was designed to be used in a new UMass course called "Engineering, the Human Enterprise," a sort of "engineering for poets" class to give non-technical students a sense for the history, concepts, processes, and wider social aspects of engineering and design. A large section of the class was be based upon the evolution of the needs for and engineering/scientific responses to societies needs for refrigeration. The instructor for this course was the domain expert for this tutor, and participated in its conceptualisation and pilot testing. Due to logistical constraints, the tutor was incorporated into the classroom activities in only a peripheral way.

The Refrigeration Tutor teaches about the operation of the refrigerator, and the relationships between temperature, pressure, volume, energy, and phase. Its goal is to allow students to understand and grapple with questions such as:

- How is it that we can cool something off by putting energy *into* it?
- Why is the refrigerant boiling in the *colder* part of its cycle?
- Why is it that if you leave the refrigerator door open in the kitchen the room gets hotter?
- Why would a fluid such as water not work as well as Freon and other materials used as refrigerants?

The Refrigerator Tutor is relatively simple (its interactions are mainly multiple choice and point-and-click interactions) and it does not fully utilize much of Eon's functionality, but it provides a good example case for introducing the tools due to this simplicity. Since our goal is to describe the authoring tools, not the tutor itself, I will only describe enough of the tutor to show all of the tools at work.

2.2 Design Steps and Authoring Tools

We will present the tutor design process in an order which best suits the tools description, but in fact the design of the tutor happened with several stages taking place in parallel, and in a much more opportunistic fashion. The Eon tools can be used in any order that is logically consistent. Top down, bottom up, and opportunistic design approaches are possible. Eon does not walk the author through a series of design steps, nor does it have "wizards" that instruct authors in certain steps (though these would be useful). The Refrigeration Tutor was authored primarily by two members of our lab, who worked closely with the domain expert, who did not have the time to learn to use many of the tools (except the Contents Editor).

Design of a tutor can start with a concrete, bottom-up orientation, designing the screens and interface the student will use, and sketching out story boards of typical interactions. However, in our description of authoring the Refrigeration Tutor I will start top-down, building the most abstract components of the tutor, i.e. the topics and the topic network. Following that I will jump down to the concrete level and describe tools for authoring the student screens and learning environment. Next I will describe how the student model is authored. Finally I will describe how instructional strategies are authored using flowlines. Figure 1 shows the relationship between the knowledge bases in Eon (domain model, teaching model, interface specification, and student model) and the authoring tools used to build them.

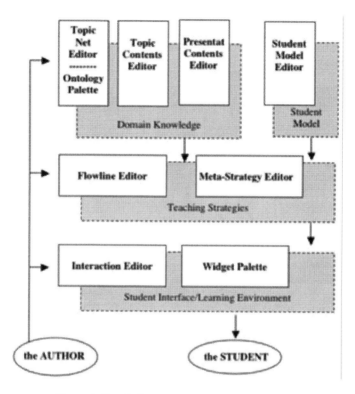

Figure 1: Eon Authoring Tools and Knowledge Bases

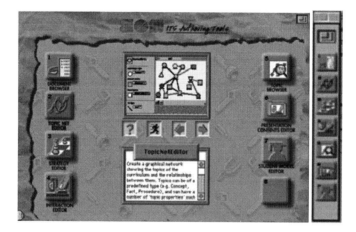

Figure 2: Tool Launcher Screen and Tool Launcher Palette

When Eon is launched it shows the screen to the left in Figure 2, which allows the author to choose among the tools, and provides brief documentation on each tool. The use can toggle between this screen and a floating palette, shown to the right in the figure--both give access to all of the tools.

3. AUTHORING THE DOMAIN MODEL

A major difference between ITSs and conventional CAI systems is that ITSs contain an inspectable model of domain expertise. This expertise can be either runnable (usually a rule-based expert system) or non-runnable. The domain model also contains two types of information: performance information, which represents knowledge about the subject matter and problem solving in the domain, and pedagogical information (information relevant to learning or teaching the content). The domain model in Eon consists of a semantic network representation of the units of knowledge (called topics) that the tutor is designed to teach. Although this semantic network may represent domain expertise such as part-whole relationships and sequences of steps, the focus is on pedagogical information, i.e. links such as part-of and prerequisite which can be used in sequencing the instruction.

Figure 3: Topic Ontology Palette

Eon tutors are fairly "curriculum driven," though they can facilitate significant student control in the selection and style of the material. do not include rule-based representation of expertise. The Eon tools are not well suited for representing complex procedures or problem solving skills, yet should excel in domains where multiple teaching strategies can be written and predicated on inferred student knowledge. Tools are under development that support other classes of ITSs. Model tracing tutors and other tutors based on runnable models of domain expertise and student knowledge are extremely powerful in the situations where they apply (i.e. where the expertise can be represented at a fine gain size), and authoring tools for these are under development (Anderson & Pelletier 1991, Koedinger, personal communication). Another class of ITSs involves teaching about the functionality of equipment and associated diagnostic procedures. Authoring shells that allow the designer to build functioning simulations of equipment and diagnostic strategies have also been built (Towne & Munro 1988).

3.1 The Topic Ontology Palette

The first step in building a tutor is to map out the learning goals or topics and their relationships in the form of a topic network, using the Topic Network Editor. However, prior to this we must define the "topic ontology," which specifies the types of nodes and links allowed, and also the types of properties topics can have. In Chapter 15 I discuss the benefits of including customisable ontologies in ITS authoring tools. Primary among these benefits is the ability to adapt the authoring tool to fit the conceptual model and pedagogical assumptions of a particular ITS project. Figure 3 shows the Topic Ontology Palette which is a visual representation of the topic ontology and is used to draw topics onto the topic network. The topic ontology defines a number of "topic types" (or knowledge types), which are shown in a pop-up menu on the palette, with each topic type having its own shape. For the Refrigeration Tutor we defined these types: Fact (square), concept (pentagon), principle (triangle), physical component (circle), and unspecified (oval). The topic ontology also defines a number of "topic properties." For the Refrigeration Tutor I defined "importance" (with allowed values one to five associated with the topic node's color) and "difficulty" (with allowed values "easy, moderate, difficult" associated with the topic node's border color). The topic ontology also defines "topic link types," and for the Refrigeration Tutor we defined "prerequisite" (red), "part-of" (black), "is-a" (blue), and "context-for" (green). The topic ontology also defines "topic levels," which I will discuss later, and which are not shown graphically on the Ontology Palette or on the topic network (the are shown in the topic level editor).

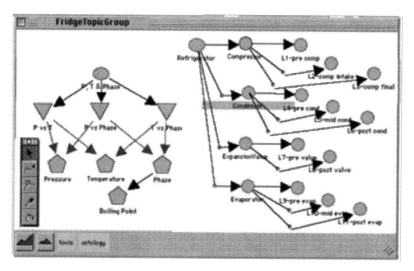

Figures 4: Topic Network Editor

Eon does not yet contain an authoring tool for defining the topic ontology itself, and this must be done via a text file that is loaded in at the beginning of the authoring session. It contains lines like these:

```
DefineTopicOntology <name>
DefineTopicLinkType <name>
DefineTopicProperty <name> <allowedvalues>
DefineTopicLevel <name>
DefineTopicType <name>
    <allowedLinkTypes><allowedProperties>
    <allowedLevels>
```

Additional information is included in the text file to define how graphic properties (shapes, colors, etc.) are associated with these semantics. As is evident from the last line of pseudo-code, each topic type has a customized set of link types, properties, and topic levels.

When the ontology file is loaded it defines a topic ontology object, and the Topic Ontology Palette (also called simply the "Topic Palette") shows a visualization of the ontology.[2] To create a new topic the author selects the desired topic type and property values in the palette. The appropriate graphic attributes are shown in the "new topic" node on the palette. The author types the desired name for the new topic to the right of this new node. Finally, to instantiate this new topic the author drags the node onto the Topic Network Editor and drops it at the desired location.

3.2 The Topic Network Editor

Once the topic ontology is defined the author can use the topic palette to draw out the topic network. Figure 3 shows the Topic Network Editor and the topic network developed by the Refrigeration Tutor domain expert. New topics are created as described above, and they can be repositioned on the screen by dragging them. To create links between the topics the author selects the link type at the bottom of the ontology palette, then clicks the "link creation tool" button on the Topic Editing Tools Palette, shown to the bottom left in the Figure, and draws a segmented line from one topic to another. In the Figure some lines are "part of" links and some lines are "prerequisite" links (they are black and red, respectively, on the computer screen).

The flow of instruction in the Refrigeration Tutor is organized around the parts of the refrigeration cycle. The student is taken on several trips around the cycle, each one having more difficult information and questions. The main components

---

[2]Note these other capabilities: 1) More than one ontology can be defined, thus the pop-up menu at the top of the palette the for selecting the ontology. 2) More than one "topic group" can be created, thus the pop-up menu near the top of the palette the for selecting the topic group. Each topic group is its own topic network, and each topic group uses one and only one topic ontology. 3) Each topic type is defined to specify which properties and links are allowed for it.

318   T. MURRAY

involved are the compressor, which compresses the gaseous refrigerant and heats it up, the condenser, which cools down the gas and turns it into liquid (fanning the heat to the outside), the expansion valve, which cools down the refrigerant, causes a drop in pressure and a partial phase change back to gas, and the evaporator, which absorbs heat from the inside of the refrigerator causing the refrigerant to boil and become completely gaseous again.

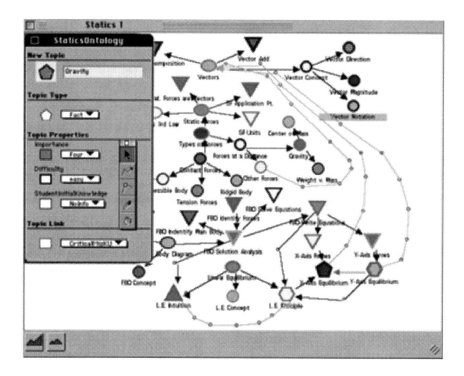

Figure 5: Topic Ontology Palette an Topic Network Editor for Statics Tutor

The domain expert has identified eleven important refrigerator components to focus on in this cycle, and these are shown in the topic network as sub-parts of each of the components (labeled Ln-XXX, to the far right in Figure 4). The main concepts being learned are also shown to the left in the topic network, including understanding the relationships between pressure, temperature, and phase. The student model (explained later) is used to infer the student's mastery of each of these topics. In the Refrigeration Tutor the eleven component locations are cycled through three times, with questions of higher difficulty given each cycle. The questions are linked to the concepts in the topic network as described later.

Figure 5 shows the ontology palette ("Statics Ontology") and the topic network defined for the Statics Tutor (described in Section 8). The ontology for this tutor was similar to the Refrigeration Tutor, but had an additional topic property: StudentInitialKnowledge, which was used to define the level of assumed initial knowledge level for the target student population for each topic (the vocabulary of topic types and link types also differed for the two tutors).

4. AUTHORING PRESENTATIONS AND CONTENTS

The aspect of most ITS authoring shells that is most sorely lacking, in relation to COTS CAI authoring systems, is student interface design, which for ITSs is also called learning environment design. Eon allows authors to completely customize the student interface to create highly interactive learning environments.

4.1 The Interaction Editor and Interface Extensibility

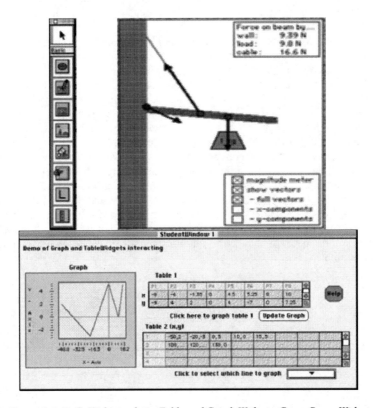

Figure 6 A, B, C: Widget palette, Table and Graph Widgets, Crane Boom Widget

Eon's Interaction Editor tool contains a hierarchical pallet of user interface components called widgets. There are simple widgets such as buttons, text, pictures, sliders, movies, and hot-spots, and more complex widgets such as multiple-choice dialogs, tables, and graphs. There are a total of 26 widgets in six categories: Basic, Controller, Geometrical, Complex, Special, and Custom. Widgets are selected for drawing onto the interaction screen using the Widget palette. Figure 6A shows the Basic widget set. The author clicks where "Basic" appears to see a a pop-up menu of the other widget categories. Figure 6B shows two tables and a graph, widgets from the Complex category.

The Widget Palette is extensible via the "Custom" category. Arbitrarily complex widgets can be programmed outside of Eon, and "dropped in" as needed for particular domains. These custom widgets can be device simulations or whole learning environments. For example, our Statics Tutor has a "crane boom" widget (see Figure 6C) which lets students manipulate positions of objects and cables and observe the resulting static forces. In order for custom widgets to inter-operate with the rest of the Eon tools, they must adhere to a simple protocol which involves specifying the "parameters" used to set a widget's properties, and the student "events" that the widget recognizes. The events can be simple as "button-pushed," or require some processing as in a multiple choice widget's "correct answer" event, and can be arbitrarily sophisticated, as in a "student has moved the load past the tension limit of the cable" event in the crane boom widget.

Widgets are selected from the Widget Palette and drawn onto the Interaction Editor (Figure 7). Figure 7 shows the screen design for the Refrigeration Tutor's multiple choice interactions. It includes a picture, text areas for the question and answer choices, a text area for hints and an "elaboration," an icon-ized map of the refrigeration cycle (lower right) onto which a "you are here" indicator is placed. This is a reusable template screen which was built using text, graphic, multiple choice, and button widgets from the widget palette. All multiple choice questions are shown using this template screen, by filling in the question-specific information each time it is shown to the student. This is a significant and unique feature in the Eon tools. The screen design shown in the Figure is not for a particular multiple choice question, but for a large set of them. As explained later, a tool called the Contents Editor is used to manage the data for the many instances that get "plugged into" the template.

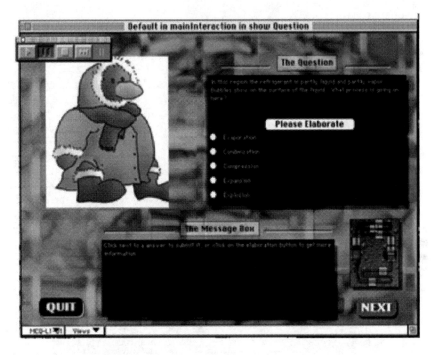

Figure 7: Interaction Editor (Refrigerator Tutor)

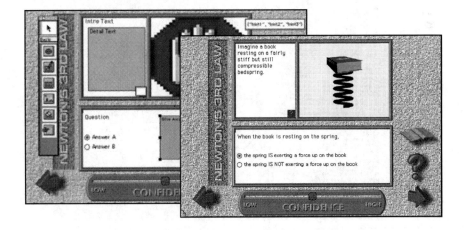

Figure 8: Interaction Editor Template and Final Screen (BA Tutor)

To the left of Figure 8 is a template interaction screen for the Bridging Analogies tutor (described in Section 8). To the right is the template filled in with data from one of its Contents objects, as the student would see it.

Eon distinguishes two types of widget attributes: "options" and "properties." Options comprise most of the widgets attributes. They are set using the widget's options dialog and will usually remain as initially set during the tutorial. Figure 9 shows the options dialog for a push-button widget, and gives an indication of the complexity of Eon's widgets. Widget *properties* are the small set of the most important widget attributes that deal with student input or instructional content, for example, the text of a text widget, and the picture in a graphic widget. If the author is using template screen a widget's properties are likely to change during the course of the tutorial. The widget properties of the multiple choice widget are: the question text, the answer choices text, the correct answer index, and the answer selected by the student (which is set at run time by the student, not the author). Both options *and* properties can be manipulated dynamically at run time (using a scripting language), allowing for dynamic screens with content generated on the fly. Properties, however, have additional flexibility as described below.

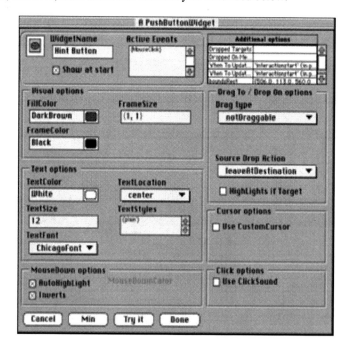

Figure 9: Options Dialog for a Push-button Widget.

A large amount of effort was put into Eon's student interface builder, in order to allow authors complete flexibility in the design of the interface. As well as the template feature, making it easy for authors to create repetitive content, all widget properties can be manipulated via scripts, allowing the screens to be composed and modified dynamically during the tutorial. Visual and semantic properties of widgets can be made to depend on each other, allowing simple simulations to be built.[3]

Still, Eon is not as facile at authoring complex learning environments and simulations as tools built specifically for this purpose. For example, the RIDES system (Munro in this Volume) allows widgets such as simulated meters, levers, faucets, and motors to be connected by wires or pipes, and represents the interactions between these components in such a way that students can inspect how the device operates. RIDES, like other special purpose authoring tools built to date, has only limited abilities to represent curriculum, content abstractions, or multiple teaching strategies

4.2 Content Generation and Re-use

Widget properties, such as text and graphics, can be set in several ways:

1. **Single value**. E.G. a graphic widget always has the same picture.
2. **Calculated value**. The value can be attached to a script. E.G. each time the picture is shown in the tutorial, the script is evaluated to produce a new value (e.g. a pointer to a new picture).
3. **Template**. Screens containing widgets can be specified as "templates" which get reused. In such cases the properties of the widgets are stored in "Contents" objects (described below).

Using templates the author can create re-usable screen formats, and then create multiple "Content" objects to fill in a template dynamically. Figure 7 shows one of the template-based interaction screens authored for the Refrigeration Tutor. The Figure shows the default contents of this template. About fifty Contents objects have been created to fill in this template, each with its own question, picture, explanation, and hints. As the author adds widgets to the screen a data base entry form called the Contents Editor is updated to show the properties of all of the widgets. Figure 10 shows the Contents Editor for the multiple choice template screen, with the contents object MCQ-L1-Q1 shown. The Contents Editor shows all of the properties of all of the widgets on the student screen. Some properties are designated "D" to use the default value (a "C" would indicated that the value is computed dynamically, i.e. attached to an author-defined script). The author can edit widget properties directly from the Interaction Editor (which is WYSIWYG), or she can edit the properties using the Contents Editor (which is like a database form).

---

[3]However, the system gets slow and cumbersome for simulations with many interacting components, and in such cases it is better to program a separate custom widget, as we did for the Crane Boom simulation

In the bottom left of the Contents Editor and the Interaction Editor is a pop-up menu listing all of the contents that have been created for this template (MCQ-L1-Q1 is one of them), an item "default" to view the default contents, and an item "New" to create a new contents item. The "Views" button to the right of this button is for easy navigation between the three tools which constitute three views of this domain content: the Interaction Editor, the Contents Editor, and the Flowline Editor (see below).

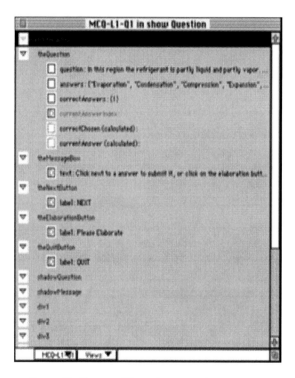

Figure 10: Contents Editor showing widget properties

To summarize, content reuse is facilitated by allowing an author to create interactive screens as templates. The widgets are drawn once using the Interaction Editor, and then numerous Contents are created using the Contents Editor. Additional flexibility is available by attaching widget properties to scripts (as opposed to canned material) so that interactive screens can be generated on the fly.

4.3 Connecting Topics to Contents

Thus far I have shown how the author works at the abstract level of the curriculum, in mapping out the topic network, and at the concrete level, designing the interactive

EON AUTHORING TOOLS   325

screens and (if they are template screens) filling in data base forms to define the Content objects that fill in the screens with domain content (the questions, hints, explanations, etc.). In this Section I will describe how the abstract level is linked to the concrete level. Basically, Content objects are assigned to the topics, but it is a bit more complex than that, and to explain how, first I must add one detail about topics left out of the earlier discussion: Topic Levels.

In Eon topics need not refer to a single monolithic entity, but have an extra level of internal structure called Topic Levels (see Chapter 15 for a discussion motivating their inclusion). Each topic has one or more Topic Levels which can specify different aspects or uses for the topic, for instance: introduction, summary, teach, test, beginning level, difficult level, etc. In the Refrigeration tutor the topics levels "Introduce," "Teach," and "Summary" were defined. A list of Content objects are assigned to each Topic Level for each topic. Thus when we want to "introduce a topic" we give the Contents in its Introduction level, and when we want to teach a beginning level of a topic we give the Contents listed in its Beginning level. The list of Contents in a Topic Level is usually thought of as a sequence of contents to present, but it can also be a *set* of applicable Content objects, and selection and sequencing of these can be left to the teaching strategy (for example choosing randomly from the set). The topic levels used in a tutorial are defined in the Topic Ontology object, described previously.

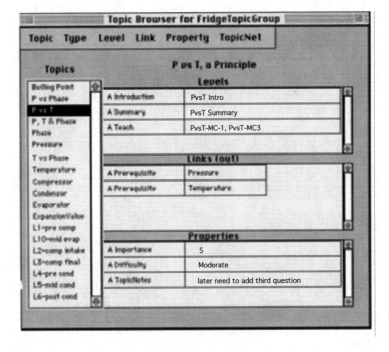

Figure 11: Topic Contents Browser

Thus far I have described the curriculum contents as it is stored in modular, declarative units: as Topic and Content objects. Later I will discuss teaching strategies, which are used to determine how this declarative information is used: i.e. how the topics are sequenced, when each topic level is given, how the Content objects are sequenced, when the interactive screens are shown, and how student behavior is responded to. For now, I will only remind the reader that all of the domain information discussed thus far is strategy-independent. It can be sequenced in arbitrary ways, as specified by teaching strategies.

The Topic Contents Browser. The Topic Contents Browser is an authoring tool that shows another view of the topic space, a tabular one as opposed to the graphic view given in the Topic Net Editor. Figure 11 shows the Topic Contents browser for the topics in the Refrigeration Tutor. The Topic Contents Browser shows a list of all of the topics, and the links and Properties of the selected topic. This is another view of the information available visually in the Topic Net Editor. In addition (unlike the Topic Network Editor) it shows the Topic Levels and the Content objects associated with each level.[4] The author used the topic contents browser to edit the values of the levels, links, and properties, either by typing into the form (topic Importance in the Figure) or by choosing from a list (selecting "PvsT Intro" from among the defined Contents for the Introduction level).

---

[4]The terms "principle," "introduction," "summary," "teach," "prerequisite," "importance," and "difficulty," seen in the Topic Contents Browser, and other terms which define the conceptual vocabulary for describing content and pedagogy in the Refrigerator Tutor, are defined in the Topic Ontology object. This illustrates how the conceptual vocabulary is customizable for each tutor.

5. AUTHORING THE STUDENT MODEL

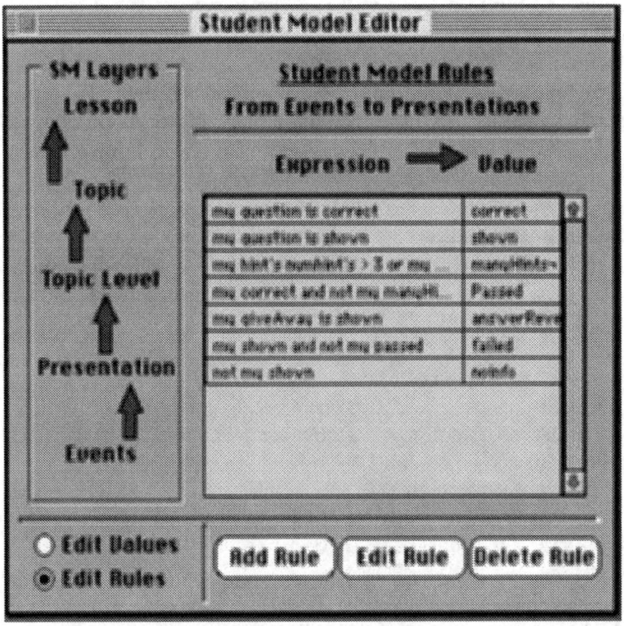

Figure 12: Student Model Editor

The student model is the component of the system that keeps track of student behaviors and makes inferences about what the student knows. Eon is the only ITS authoring tool that include the ability to customize how the student modeller works. Eon uses a variation of an "overlay student model" (Wenger 1987) in that mastery values are calculated to correspond with each topic. The Eon student model can also be used as a "bug library," since topic types for "mis-knowledge" such as misconceptions and buggy procedures can be defined to keep track of known classes of common deficiencies.[5] I call our student model a "Layered Overlay Student Model" because values are inferred at several "decision layers," as shown in Figure 12. Most overlay student models assign values to topics only. In Eon values are assigned to objects at several decision layers: Lesson, Topic, Topic Level, Presentation Contents, and Events.[6] Objects at each layer are composed of objects

---

[5]In our Statics tutor we defined a topic type called "Misconception," and a link type called "critical misconception" which was used to associate physics concepts to common related misconceptions, so that these common misconceptions could be diagnosed before the concept was taught

[6]Lessons are used to specify the top level teaching procedure and the goal topic or topics for a tutorial session. Lesson objects were not used in the Refrigeration Tutor, and they are defined in text files as no authoring tool for them has been built yet.

at the next lower layer, for example, running a lesson will invoke the teaching of a number of topics, teaching a topic will run a number of its topic levels, and each topic level consist of a number of Contents (representing student interactions or blocks of information). Within a Content, for example a multiple choice question, a number of low level student and tutor events will occur, such a selecting an answer or asking for help (a student event), or giving a hint (a tutor event). As shown in the Student Model Editor (Figure 12) objects at each level can have a value. The value of objects at any level is determined by the Student Model rules written for that level. These rules specify how the value of an object depends on the values of the objects at the next lower level.

Figure 12 shows the rules for mapping from the Events level to the Presentation Contents level for the Statics Tutor. For the Refrigeration tutor, some example rules are:

```
Topic Level to Topic:
   my Teach Level is KNOWN
       OR all of my Parts are KNOWN
   Topic value ==> KNOWN
   my Teach Level is SHOWN
       OR my Introduce Level is SHOWN
       OR my Summary Level is SHOWN
   Topic value ==> SHOWN

Presentation to Topic Levels:
   greater than 80% of my Presentation Contents are
   CORRECT
       TL value ==> KNOWN
   any of my Presentation Contents is SHOWN
    TL value ==> SHOWN
```

The student model is used to make the tutorial adaptive to the student's inferred state. This is accomplished by referring to student model values in decisions in teaching strategies (and meta strategies), for example, decision branches predicated upon whether a topic is "mastered" or whether a Contents has been already "shown". The Refrigeration Tutor uses the student model to ask fewer easy questions if a topic is near mastery, and to give more hints if the topic is far from mastered.

The vocabulary of terms used to define the student model values (e.g. "known," "mastered," "suspected misconception") is customizable for each tutorial using the student model editor. We have found the current Student Model Editor to be too restrictive however, since values and rules can only be defined on a per-decision-level basis, i.e. every item in a decision level has the same rules and the same set of allowed values. We are working on an extension to this system to allow rules to be assigned to groups of objects. We would like some topics to use different student modeling rules than others. For example, in the Refrigeration tutor we would like the topics representing the important concepts (to the left in Figure 4) to use a different rule set than the topics representing the components and locations within the refrigerator (to the right in Figure 4).

6. AUTHORING THE TEACHING MODEL

To represent teaching strategies we use a flowline paradigm, a graphically portrayed procedural representation of strategic knowledge that explicitly shows structural and contextual control information. Our Strategy Editor (also called the Flowline Editor) has a look and feel similar to commercially available authoring tools such as Authorware and Icon Author. Eon Flowlines, like procedures in programming languages, can have input parameters, local variables, and can return values.[7] All variable referencing and naming is facilitated by menus and drag and drop tools, so the author does not have to memorize or type in these terms (as one does in scripting languages).

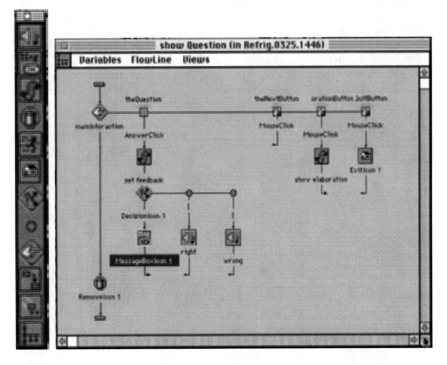

Figure 13: Icon Palette and Flowline (Refrigeration Tutor)

---

[7]Though of similar surface appearance, the Eon flowline system is actually much more powerful than those seen in commercial tools. For example, commercially available tools do not support input parameters or return variables. They are not "real" procedures that can be called recursively.

Figure 13 shows the Flowline Editor and the Icon palette used to drag and drop flowline icons onto the flowline. Flow of control travels down the flowline icons, and branches to the right for some icon types. The Run Icon invokes another flowline and the Return Icon is used to exit a flowline prematurely, or to specify a returned value. The icons in the palette are, from top to bottom:

- Sound-- to play any type of sound resource.
- Message Box -- quick way to show text to the student (without an interaction screen).
- Script -- arbitrary scripts which can refer to flowline local variables.
- Erase/Remove -- hide or show widgets.
- Run -- invoke another flowline, passing input parameters if needed.
- Home -- return from a flowline, returning a value if needed.
- Decision -- repeat loops, branching, If-Thens, etc.
- Branch -- individual decision branches.
- Interaction -- bring up an interaction screen and respond to student-generated widget events.
- Copy Data-- transfer data from one location to another (e.g. from a Content object to a local variable).
- Animate -- animate widgets or graphics along an arbitrary path.
- Composite -- a call to a sub-flowline.

The Flowline shown in the Figure 13 brings up the main multiple choice screen interaction, then branches are defined for giving feedback on student answer selections, for pushing the Next or Quit buttons, and for selecting the Elaborate button.

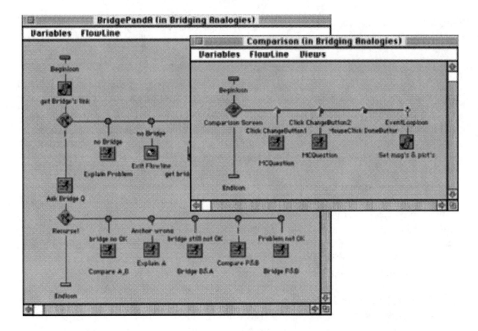

Figure 14: Flowlines for BA Tutor

Figure 14 shows two Flowlines from the Bridging Analogies tutor. The "BridgePandA" flowline is a "doubly recursive" procedure that calls itself twice at the second decision icon. The Comparison Flowline is one of the sub-flowlines called in the first Flowline. The "Ask Bridge Q" icon in the BridgePandA flowline calls a flowline that brings up the screen in Figure 8, and the Comparison Screen icon in the Comparison Flowline brings up the screen in Figure 17.

A variety of representational formalisms have been used for control and strategic knowledge in ITS shells and authoring tools. Some employ relatively sophisticated AI techniques such goal-based planning (Russell et al. 1988), black board architectures (W. Murray 1990), agents (Cheikes 1995), task decomposition (Van Marcke 1992), and production rules (Anderson & Pelletier 1991, Major & Reichgelt 1992). No framework or visual editor has yet been devised for any of these formalism which lowers the complexity level sufficiently for our intended user audience. These formalisms are highly modular, but control information elicited from human experts often has clearly defined structure (Gruber 1987), and high modularity can hide the structure of strategic knowledge, obfuscate the context of strategy decisions, and make strategy design unwieldy (Lesser 1984).

Strategy representation in Eon is based on a flowline paradigm for visual authoring, which has proven to be highly understandable and usable. It is not as powerful as the more AI-intensive methods mentioned above, because it does not allow a tutor to search a large space of potential instructional actions, or to reason about what it could do further along in the session.

Meta-strategies

Ohlsson (1987, pg. 220) points out that "in order to provide adaptive instruction, a tutor must have a wide range of instructional actions to choose from." Human tutors have more than one teaching method or style available to them, and likewise, intelligent computer tutors should be able to change teaching style dynamically depending on student characteristics. Spensley et al. (1990) describe a shell which allows meta-strategies to choose among pre-defined general strategies, including cognitive apprenticeship, successive refinement, discovery learning, abstraction, practice, and Socratic diagnosis. The strategies themselves are fixed however, and fine grained decisions can not be modified. REDEEM (see Ainsworth et al in this volume) is a highly usable authoring tool that allows teachers to set a number of teaching strategy parameters to customize and select applicability conditions for teaching actions. In this system some flexibility is traded for usability, since the underlying instructional strategies are pre-defined (though parameterized). Van Marcke's (1992) GTE system uses multiple alternative rule sets to carry out the actions of a given tutorial goal. This system is more flexible but difficult to author.

As a method for representing multiple strategies in Eon we considered implementing multiple flowlines with the same purpose (e.g. multiple "Give a Hint" flowlines) as in the GTE system, but this seemed too confusing for users. Eon uses a parameterized approach similar to REDEEM, but is more flexible since the strategies can be built from scratch.

Eon strategy parameters are like global variables that can be used in decision points in flowlines. Authors can define a number of strategy parameters, for example, "degree of hinting," "degree of interruption," "preference for general vs. specific information," and "amount of information." A parameter called "number of hints" can be defined and used in a flowline to specify whether one, two, or three hints are given. A "student control" parameter can be defined and used in a flowline to decide whether to allow students to choose to skip topics. Strategy parameters values are set through meta-strategies, and are defined using the MetaStrategy Editor (Figure 15). Each meta-strategy includes a set of strategy parameters, and a setting for each of those parameters. Also, each meta-strategy has an "applicability condition" that defines when the MetaStrategy is triggered. For example, in the "High Feedback" MetaStrategy shown in Figure 15, the applicability condition is "Recent Wrong" (a variable in the student model) is greater than 50%. When this is true, the High Feedback strategy is triggered. When it is triggered it sets the values of several strategy parameters: number of hints, student control, auto-explanations, and difficulty level. Since these strategy parameters are used in branch and decision icons in flowlines, the behavior of the tutor will be changed accordingly.

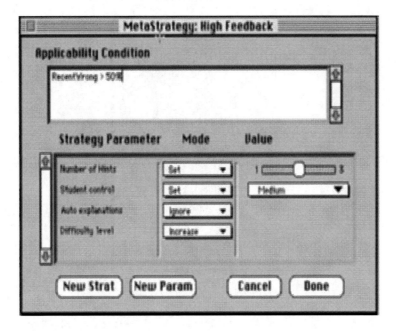

Figure 15: MetaStrategy Editor

Though the Meta-Strategy Editor is functional, it was not used in the Refrigeration Tutor before.

7. OTHER TOOLS, MISCELLANEOUS CAPABILITIES, AND IMPLEMENTATION DETAILS

The authoring tools have a WYSIWYG pause-and-edit feature, which allows the author to test run a tutorial, pause it at any point, and easily access the Interaction Editor, Contents Editor, or Flowline Editor, to modify the data bases of teaching strategies. Eon has a number of other tools not described above, including tracing and debugging tools, and a Document Browser which gives a hierarchical view of every object in a tutorial document. The Document Browser is shown in Figure 16. The document browser is an alternate way to view, access, and edit any object or object attribute in the system. Double clicking on an object in the document browser brings up the appropriate editor (e.g. the Flowline Editor if a flowline name is double-clicked).

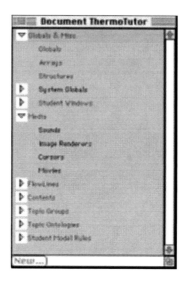

Figure 16: Document Browser

Eon is implemented in a high level programming language called SK8, developed by Apple Computer's Advanced Technology Group (see http://SK8.research.apple.com). SK8 is a very powerful high level language that was designed not only to build applications, but to build custom application builders. SK8 has the programming power of LISP, a graphics engine comparable to Photoshop, a visual programming paradigm analogous to Visual Basic, and a number of artificial intelligence information processing features. All of this allowed us to build the Eon prototype in a fraction (we estimate one fifth to one quarter) of the time it would have taken to build Eon in C++ (or, alternatively, given fixed resources we able to add four to five tiems as much functionality). Unfortunately SK8 development and support was discontinued while the language was still in an alpha stage and SK8, though a powerful programming environment, was still not optimised and was slow, not bug-free, and took up an inordinate amount of run time memory.[8] As a result, the Eon authoring tools are relatively slow, run only on Quadra-generation Macintoshes in an obsolete version of the Mac OS, and experience occasional crashes (all of these problems were to be fixed at the SK8 language level, had it continued as an Apple product). As a consequence the Eon tools are alpha prototypes, useful for demonstrating ITS authoring and capable of producing ITSs given certain restrictive hardware limitations on the runtime environment.[9] Despite these hindsight problems with using the SK8 development environment, we have been able to build a very large and complex proof-of-concept system, with a high degree of interactivity and usability, in a fraction of the time it

---

[8] SK8 source code it is now available in the public domain.

[9] The Eon software is not publicly available, nor would the code run on modern computers.

would have taken to build in a more traditional programming environment (we estimate 3 person-years vs. 10 to 12). Thus, from a research perspective we made the right choice in using SK8, but in order for the Eon to be a viable ITS development platform, the system would need to be re-implemented in another environment (C++ or Java, for example) at considerable cost. Though development on the Eon system stopped several years ago, we no of no other ITS development environment to date that matches the level of functionality, generality, and usability that it provided.

8. OTHER TUTORS BUILT WITH EON

Eon was used to build four other tutors, which I describe briefly below. The tutors are all prototypes that were not used in actual classroom situations. While most were designed to demonstrate and test specific Eon capabilities, the Keigo, Statics, and Refrigerator Tutors were designed to address real educational needs. Due to the above mentioned problems with SK8 these systems were later redesigned (in some cases removing some of the more intelligent features) in another language (Macromedia Director) so that they could be used for their intended purposes (the descriptions given below apply only to the Eon-built tutors).

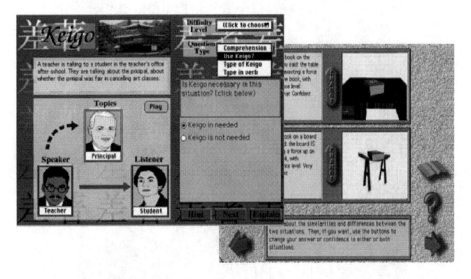

Figure 17 & 18: Keigo Tutor & Bridging Analogies Tutor

The **Keigo Tutor** (Figure 17) teaches a part of Japanese language called "honorifics," dealing with the complicated rules used to determine verb conjugations which appropriately honor the listener and topic of a conversation. For this tutor Eon is interfaced with a rule based expert system encoding rules about how to map from surface level features of the conversational situation to linguistically relevant properties of the situation (the expert system was written in the SK8 language). Students are presented with a variety of situations involving people of varying levels of status and formality, and are asked what types of verb conjugations are needed. Feedback is given based on which rules are applicable. This tutor has been used and evaluated in a Japanese Language class (Miyama working paper).

The **Bridging Analogies Tutor** (Figure 18) incorporates a Socratic teaching strategy developed and tested by cognitive scientists to remediate common persistent misconceptions in science (Murray et al. 1990). This tutor demonstrates the implementation of a recursive teaching strategy which was researched in human one-on-one tutoring and classroom teaching. The student is presented with a sequence of analogous situations in an attempt to bridge the conceptual distance between their current understanding of the phenomena ("does a flat surface push back up on something that sits on that surface?" in this case) and the correct physics interpretation. Occasionally students are presented with screens that encourage them to compare and contrast previous answers and they are given the option of changing a previous answer in light of new conceptual connections.

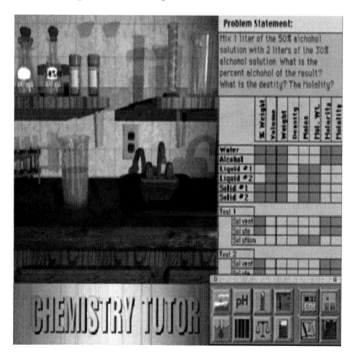

Figure 19: Chemistry Workbench

The **Chemistry Workbench** (Figure 19) is the tutor which demonstrates the most open-ended learning-by-doing environment of the tutors built with Eon. Students can mix chemicals from the shelf by dragging and dropping them on beakers. Color and precipitates of the resulting solutions are shown visually in the beakers, and the instruments in the tool palette at the bottom right can be used to measure the volume, pH, etc. of the results. Unlike the Cane Boom simulation widget mentioned above (see Figure 6C), all of the graphical interactions in the Chemistry Tutor were created using Eon's built-in widgets. The goal of the tutorial is to learn about solvency and chemical reactions by interactively mixing chemicals and measuring the results. The student fills in the table as he accumulates data to answer the chemistry questions posed (see table widget above). This tutor was designed as an open-ended learning environment without feedback or analysis of student tasks. The knowledge engineer for this tutor was a University of Massachusetts Chemistry professor.

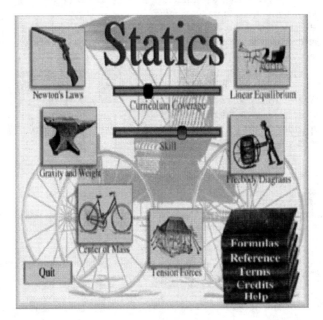

Figure 20: Statics Tutor

The **Statics Tutor** (Figure 20) teaches introductory Statics concepts, and includes the "crane boom" simulation widget (Figure 6C). This tutor has the largest topic network and curriculum knowledge base, comprising 40 topic and misconception nodes (see Figure 5), and hundreds of presentations with multiple-choice questions. Using topic levels called "Summary," "Teach Easy," "Teach Moderate," and "Teach Difficult," in conjunction with topic link types "Familiarity Prerequisite," "Easy Level Prerequisite," and "Moderate Level Prerequisite," simulates a "spiral teaching" strategy, in which the same set of topics are taught several times, but at a higher level of difficulty each time. Most of the knowledge engineering for this tutor was done as done in the precursor project to Eon, KAFITS, discussed in Section 1.1. This content was re-authored and extended using the Eon tools. The domain expert for the Statics Tutor was a "master" teacher in high school physics fro a local high school.

9. CONCLUSION

We have tried to produce a suite of highly usable tools that have enough similarity to off-the-shelf CAI/multimedia authoring tools to support users of these existing tools in making the transition to authoring knowledge based tutors. After using the tools for several tutors and several authors I believe that the authoring system, though fairly large (the user documentation is several hundred pages long), is composed of tools which are quite learnable and usable.

Though, for reasons described above, the Eon tools did not progress past alpha software, I believe that the project contributes to the field by uniquely exemplifying a full-featured, integrated set of tools for authoring all aspects of an ITS. In a companion Chapter to this one (Chapter 15) I describe an generalization of Eon's representational framework, and describe lesson learned under the following issue headings: "Who Are the Users of ITS Authoring Tools?" "From Story Boards To Knowledge Bases," "How Generic Can Teaching Strategies Be?" "Topic Modularity and Interdependence," "Knowledge Structure and Complexity," and "Non-Independence of Content and Strategies."

10. REFERENCES

Anderson, J. R. & Pelletier, R. (1991). A development system for model-tracing tutors. In Proc. of the International Conference on the Learning Sciences, (pp. 1-8), Evanston, IL.

Cheikes, B. (1995). Should ITS Designers be Looking for a Few Good Agents? In AIED-95 workshop papers for Authoring Shells for Intelligent Tutoring Systems.

Clancey, W. & Joerger, K. (1988). "A Practical Authoring Shell for Apprenticeship Learning." *Proceedings of ITS-88*, pp. 67-74. June 1988, Montreal.

Gruber, T. (1987). "A Method for Acquiring Strategic Knowledge from Experts." University of Massachusetts Dissertation.

Lesser, V. (1984). Control in Complex Knowledge-based Systems. Tutorial at the IEEE Computer Society AI Conference.

Major, N. P., (1993). Teachers and Teaching Strategies. *Proc. of the Seventh International PEG Conference*, Heriot-Watt Univ., Edinburgh.

Major, N.P. & Reichgelt, H (1992). COCA - A shell for intelligent tutoring systems. In Frasson, C., Gauthier, G., & McCalla, G.I. (Eds.) *Procs. of Intelligent Tutoring Systems '92*. Springer Verlag, Berlin.

Murray, T. (1993). Formative Qualitative Evaluation for "Exploratory" ITS research. *J. of AI and Education*. V. 4. No. 2.

Murray, T. (1991). *Facilitating Teacher Participation in Intelligent Computer Tutor Design: Tools and Design Methods*. Ed.D. Dissertation, Univ. of Massachusetts, Computer Science Tech. Report 91-95.

Murray, T. (1996a). Special Purpose Ontologies and the Representation of Pedagogical Knowledge. *In Proceedings of the International Conference on the Learning Scieces*, (ICLS-96), Evanston, IL, 1996. AACE: Charlottesville, VA.

Murray, T., Schultz, K., Brown, D., & Clement, J. (1990). An Analogy-Based Computer Tutor for Remediating Physics Misconceptions. *J. of Interactive Learning Environments*, Vol. 1 No. 2, pp. 79-101.

Murray, T. & Woolf, B. (1992a). Results of Encoding Knowledge with Tutor Construction Tools. *Proceedings of AAAI-92*. San Jose, CA., July, 1992.

Murray, T. & Woolf, B. (1992b). Tools for Teacher Participation in ITS Design. In Frasson, Gauthier, & McCalla (Eds.) Intelligent Tutoring Systems, Second Int. Conf. , Springer Verlag, New York, pp. 593-600.

Murray, W.R. (1990). A Blackboard-based Dynamic Instructional Planner. In *Proc. of AAAI-90*.

Ohlsson, S. (1987). Some Principles of Intelligent Tutoring. In Lawler & Yazdani (Eds.), *Artificial Intelligence and Education,* Volume 1. Ablex: Norwood, NJ.

Russell, D., Moran, T. & Jordan, D. (1988). The Instructional Design Environment. In Psotka, Massey, & Mutter (Eds.), *Intelligent Tutoring Systems, Lessons Learned,* Hillsdale, NJ: Lawrence Erlbaum.

Spensley, F., Elsom-Cook, M., Byerley, P., Brooks, P., Federici, M. and Scaroni, C. (1990). "Using multiple teaching strategies in an ITS," in Frasson, C. and Gauthier, G. (eds.), *Intelligent Tutoring Systems: At the crossroads of Artificial Intelligence and Education.* Norwood, NJ: Ablex.

Towne, D.M., Munro, A., (1988). The Intelligent Maintenance Training System. In Psotka, Massey, & Mutter (Eds.), *Intelligent Tutoring Systems, Lessons Learned,* Hillsdale, NJ: Lawrence Erlbaum.

VanLehn, K. (1988). "Toward a Theory of Impasse-Driven Learning." In Mandl, H. & Lesgold, A. (Eds.), *Learning Issues for Intelligent Tutoring Systems.* New York: Springer-Verlag.

Van Marcke, K. (1992). Instructional Expertise. In Frasson, C., Gauthier, G., & McCalla, G.I. (Eds.) Procs. of Intelligent Tutoring Systems '92. New York: Springer-Verlag pp. 234-243.

Wenger, E. (1987). *Artificial Intelligence and Tutoring Systems.* Los Altos, CA: Morgan Kaufmann.

ACKNOWLEDGMENTS

Many thanks to the following people who were crucial in developing the Eon system: Matt Cornell for realizing the ideas in a gazilllion lines of pristine code; Kate Cremer for early versions of the Topic Net Editor; Erik Eide for widget dialogs and the student model editor; Erik Haugsjaa for continued code maintenance and numerous feature enhancements; Ryan Moore for tutor construction and enthusiasm. This material is based upon work supported by the National Science Foundation and the Advance Research Projects Agency under Cooperative Agreement No. CDA-940860.

BENJAMIN BELL

Chapter 12

SUPPORTING EDUCATIONAL SOFTWARE DESIGN WITH KNOWLEDGE-RICH TOOLS

Abstract. Several questions have emerged surrounding the design of authoring tools for instructional software that have helped frame an on-going dialog within the community. One such question is how specific or customized an authoring tool should be with respect to the range of applications it can support. One project that comes down on the side of specificity is IDLE-Tool, which guides authors through the process of creating an Investigate and Decide Learning Environment. Despite the narrow focus, though, the original instantiation of this tool lacked any real knowledge of the investigation process and its components. An add-on to this tool supplies an Investigation Map (IMap) that brings a richer representational scheme to the underlying tool. This chapter summarizes the IDLE-Tool work and introduces a set of primitives that capture the structure of a simplified form of investigation. The functioning of the tool after being enhanced with IMap is presented in detail, and a limited knowledge base of investigation components is described.

1. LIFE WITH A KNOWLEDGE-RICH AUTHORING TOOL

The process of creating sophisticated instructional applications is costly, complex and tedious and relies on expertise from multiple disciplines. Authoring tools are applications that aim to reduce the effort needed to produce software, by assuming responsibility for mechanical aspects of the task, by guiding the author, and by offering predefined elements that an author can package together to suit a particular need.

Ideally, such a tool would have some understanding of what the author wishes to create and could then offer more useful and specific support. Consider a category of learning environments in which the student conducts an investigation and makes some decision on the basis of his findings. To author such a learning environment requires some understanding of the structure the investigation (as a learning environment) should follow, so that students could potentially develop appropriate decisions based on information derived by applying some testing, measuring, or analytic procedures. The author would also need to possess some understanding of the domain, so that appropriate materials, apparatus, and so on would populate the investigating and deciding activities.

Consider an Earth Sciences teacher designing a simulation in which the student must determine the source of a contaminant that is polluting a lake. Where to begin? To generate a cohesive environment requires that the author systematically consider all the relevant variables that could enter into the student's inquiry and what predictions the student might make based on the values that these variables assume.

Alternatively, the authoring tool could itself could offer a template that lays out the appropriate parameters that the author needs to define. For instance, it is important to consider what the student will be deciding (what caused the change in the ecosystem?) and how the student will make this determination (measuring dissolved gases? pH?). Suppose the Earth Sciences teacher in this example wanted to browse around for suggestions as to how students could measure the level of oxygen in the lake water. We would then want a tool that allows the author to view hierarchically the relevant portions of the knowledge (Figure 1).

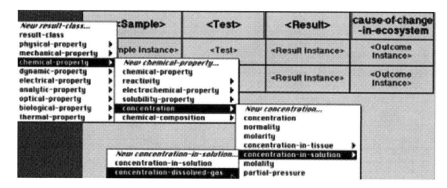

Figure 1. Selecting a result from the knowledge base during investigation design

To enhance the power of this tool it should also be equipped to recommend some appropriate testing procedures (Figure 2).

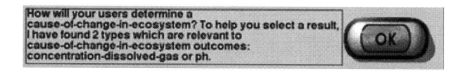

Figure 2. Suggestions from the knowledge base offered by tool

To help the author maintain orientation, the tool should also present a summary view of the investigation that the author has specified thus far (top row of Figure 3).

Water Sample	Dissolved Oxygen Test	Concentration Dissolved Gas	Cause Of Change in Ecosystem
Southeast Region Sample	Dissolved Oxygen Test	3.8 Ppm	Critical Concentration
Southwest Region Sample	Dissolved Oxygen Test	4.3 Ppm	Low Concentration
Northwest Region Sample	Dissolved Oxygen Test	5.0 Ppm	Moderate Concentration
Northeast Region Sample	Dissolved Oxygen Test	6.5 Ppm	Normal Concentration

Figure 3. Example design template for lake pollution example

In addition the author must instantiate specific paths or scenarios. To accommodate the case in which a specific region of the lake possesses a low level of dissolved oxygen, for example, the author might define the scenario shown in the second row of the table in Figure 3.

This brief example is a preview of what a tool with limited but specific knowledge of the author's task can offer in the way of design support. But what knowledge must an authoring tool possess in order to offer such guidance? The issues of what (and how much) knowledge is required, how it should be represented, and how it can brought to bear on the authoring process are the questions addressed in this chapter. The first part of this chapter summarizes an authoring tool that *lacks* knowledge of the task semantics and the domain, but instead relies on a syntactic model. The remainder of the chapter introduces an extension to this tool that supports the author with specific structural and domain-level knowledge, and provides detailed examples of how this knowledge contributes operationally during the authoring process.

2. INVESTIGATE & DECIDE LEARNING ENVIRONMENTS

This chapter presents a knowledge-rich extension to an authoring tool created to aid in the construction of *Goal-Based Scenarios* (Schank, Berman, & Macpherson, 1999; Schank, Fano, Bell, & Jona 1994). Goal-Based Scenarios (GBS) is a framework for simulation-based learn-by-doing instruction, in which the learner is engaged in pursuing a goal, within a simulated environment, in order to master a set of target skills.

There is a potentially wide range of programs that could be designed in accordance with GBS principles: programs that allow students to build artifacts; programs in which the student controls a device or participates in a process; programs in which the student conducts investigations, and so on. Because we are interested in creating tools that help designers create GBSs, it is important to design the right sort of tool for each class of GBS, of which Schank & Korcuska (1996) have identified eight.

A class of GBS called Investigate & Decide Learning Environments (Bell, 1998; Dobson, 1998; Qiu, Riesbeck, & Parsek, 2003) describes applications in which the principal focus is on conducting investigations to gather information in support of a decision the student is asked to make. Investigate & Decide Learning Environments (IDLE) is a model for instruction aimed at teaching the conceptual and causal elements of a specific domain or set of related phenomena, in which the learner is engaged in an inquiry process based in analysis (investigation) and synthesis (decision-making).

The IDLE model not only helps guide the designer but also influences the end-user's experience. For instance, in the first GBS built on the IDLE model, Sickle Cell Counselor (Bell, Bariess, & Beckwith, 1994), the user assumes the role of genetic counselor and is confronted with clients whose offspring might be at risk for Sickle Cell Disease or to carry the Sickle Cell gene. The *investigate* activities engage the user in taking blood samples, running multiple laboratory tests, and asking questions of experts. The *decide* activities involve interpreting the results and determining what to tell the clients.

Specializing the GBS model for Investigate & Decide learning is useful in two ways. First, it allows an instructional model to be defined that adheres closely to teaching principles and strategies. Second, an authoring tool that embodies this model can become a more powerful design assistant, since it can "know" more about the objectives and constraints that characterize the author's design activities (Bell, 1995; Riesbeck & Dobson, 1998). In other words, the design constraints the tool is meant to enforce become easier to operationalize when they are expressed in more specific terms. Categories like IDLE thus represent abstractions useful for developing a suite of specialized GBS tools.

3. IDLE-TOOL: A NOT-SO-KNOWLEDGE-RICH AUTHORING TOOL

3.1 Summary

IDLE-Tool is a prototype GBS construction tool built collaboratively by a team of researchers and developers at the Institute for the Learning Sciences [1]. The purpose of the tool is to allow a domain expert or teacher to create an IDLE application, without requiring expertise in programming and instructional design. The tool employs the underlying model to govern the interaction, so that the design process is carried out in a manner consistent with the organization of the model.

IDLE-Tool steps the author through the design process in a protocol described as Guided Case Adaptation (Bell, 1998), which blends case-based design, hierarchical refinement, and generate-and-test modes of interaction. A guided case adaptation session allows an author to incrementally alter an exemplar application until it becomes a new IDLE application that satisfies the author's original design criteria (Qiu & Riesbeck, 2002).

The interface includes a workspace, in which the designer's emerging GBS is shown and in which the example program, Sickle Cell Counselor (Bell, Bariess, & Beckwith, 1994) is also displayed on request. A graphic representation of the GBS model highlights the part of the model that the designer is currently working on, and serves also as control buttons that can be used to jump to a desired part of the model. The tool operates in three modes. Build mode carries out the guided case-based adaptation. The GBS designer creates the basic framework of the application - providing text labels and selecting images - in Build mode during which the example case is available as a reference. Run mode allows the designer to try out the current GBS as defined thus far in the interaction; switching to Run mode alters the interface from an application design environment to an application execution environment. Design mode enables Investigation Mapping, that is, defining the investigation and decision processes that govern the overall task structure.

3.2 Field Testing

Preliminary studies were conducted with three groups of authors who used IDLE-Tool to create Investigate & Decide Learning Environments (Bell, 1998). During the early implementation phase of this work, twenty-one first-year graduate students participating in a seminar were assigned the task of creating GBSs using the tool, and were instructed to build an application that would provide roughly thirty minutes of instruction. The objective was to collect early user data to help guide the design of the tool. Ten GBSs were created using IDLE-Tool by students working in pairs (one tuple) for ten weeks. Topics of study were diverse (see Table 1); Figure 4 shows the initial display from one of the GBSs from this trial.

In general, students reported that they liked the basic structure of the tool and that using it yielded a speedup during the initial design phase. A common suggestion (50%) was that the tool needed to provide guidance that was more conceptually-oriented and less interface-oriented. The tool used in the experiment guided a step-by-step adaptation of the exemplar GBS, but did not attempt to explain the overarching concepts governing these steps. This interface guidance fell short of the kind of conceptual guidance the subjects said they wanted to see, with the reported consequences including losing focus on content design, and losing track of the overall flow because editing proceeds one screen at a time.

A second formative evaluation was performed with classroom teachers, several months after the conclusion of the first. Eight primary school teachers from a nearby district were chosen by a school official from among a self-selected applicant pool. The teachers were given an overview of Goal-Based Scenarios and a demo of IDLE-Tool, were assigned a mentor, and worked in pairs half-time over a six-week period to build an application that would provide roughly thirty minutes of instruction. Four Goal-Based Scenarios were created using the tool (Table 1). The most obvious difference between these GBSs and those generated by the graduate students was that, in general, the teachers' GBSs were qualitatively better from an instructional perspective. That is, each of the teachers' GBSs possessed a well-defined set of pedagogical goals which the scenario addressed in a coherent way.

Figure 4. Startup screen from GBS authored in the first trial

All four teams reported that they liked IDLE-Tool, found it useful as a design aid, but had difficulties with structuring the investigation. One team drew a flowchart and said that it helped them determine what information would be important to students. Another described having difficulty "zeroing in on (the investigation)". Figure 5 shows a startup screen from one of the GBSs created by the teachers in this trial.

Nine months from the conclusion of the second study, a third evaluation was conducted using first-year graduate students enrolled in a seminar. As part of the seminar, students were shown four GBS design tools (including IDLE-Tool), and asked to form into pairs and select one of the tools to use in creating a GBS that would provide roughly thirty minutes of instruction. Eight of the eighteen students elected to use IDLE-Tool. After three weeks of design work, each team demonstrated their completed GBSs (Figure 6 shows an example startup screen from this trial). The GBSs produced in this study all followed closely the Investigate & Decide model (Table 1). This was the most obvious contrast between this trial and the previous two. The most likely reason for this is that these groups selected IDLE-Tool from among four tools. They therefore chose this tool because it represented the best match between their preliminary designs and the various tools [2].

Figure 5. Startup screen from GBS authored in the second trial

3.3 Discussion: Lessons Learned

Table 1 summarizes the IDLE applications created in the three trials. Results from these three trials offered preliminary support for the IDLE-Tool as a useful authoring environment, based on the relative ease with which authors in all three trials constructed IDLE applications, the broad range of scenarios and target skills represented, and the short periods of time in which they executed their designs. Although time savings arising from using the tool versus conventional methods were not measured, we can say at a minimum that: (1) training time for use of the tool was brief (on the order of one to two hours); (2) developing an application took several weeks, most of which time was spent on developing the idea and on collecting and preparing the graphical and video material (both of which must be done irrespective of the authoring environment). What the tool provided was infrastructure that abstracted away the detailed mechanics of organizing and implementing a complex software application.

Table 1. GBSs created by subjects in the three trials

Title	Mission	Trial
Aztec, P.I.	advise curator about objects' authenticity	1
Cardiac Counselor	advise clients at risk for heart disease	1
Crash Course	determine driver at fault in traffic accident	1
Diver Down	help plan scuba dives	1
Environmental Decision Maker	take action at a polluted site	1
GBSex	counsel clients about contraception	1
Public Health Advisor	advise mayor about outbreak of illness	1
Rags to Riches	advise investors	1
Scandal!	draft news story about a scandal	1
Secret Caves of Ellora	find solution to archeological problem	1
Debt Buster	advise teens about personal financial management	2
Kid Counselor	help other kids resolve interpersonal conflicts	2
Lend a Hand	help disabled kids negotiate everyday activities	2
Arson Investigator	advise fire chief about causes of suspicious fires	2
Breast Cancer Counselor	test patients for Breast Cancer and explain treatments	3
Gem Detective	advise jeweler about identity of gem samples	3
Pollution Investigator	recommend action to reduce pollution in lake	3
Storm Watcher	advise theme park as to whether storm will hit park	3

Of course, subjects were not entirely satisfied with the tool. The most common reaction and the one with the most central implications is that the tool focuses too much on the details of the interface and too little on the underlying design principles. The guidance it provides is interface-oriented: the tool steps the designer through the process of specifying all elements of the interface called for by the model. While this model specifies in detail which objects must be defined, it does not specify much about the relationships among those objects or about the criteria for defining an object. A way to address this is to modify the tool to adopt a conceptual orientation to supplement its interface orientation. For IDLE-Tool, this means that the tool should be able to represent the elements of investigating and deciding so that the designer would be specifying, not only interface parameters, but conceptual elements such as the source to be analyzed, the device performing the analysis, what information is derived, and what the student should be deciding based on that information. In order to support the design of GBSs at this conceptual level, the tool must be augmented with specific knowledge about the tasks implicit in the model (i.e., how investigating and deciding tasks are structured and what elements are needed).

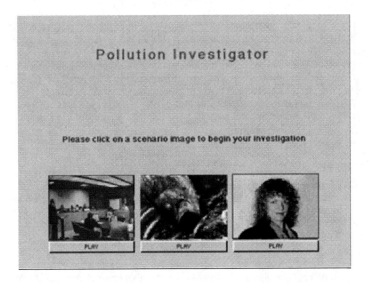

Figure 6. Startup screen from GBS authored in the third trial

4. RELATED APPROACHES TO AUTHORING TOOLS

4.1 From General-Purpose to Courseware Authoring

A number of sophisticated tools have emerged for creating interactive, multimedia software, including commercially available products such as IconAuthor and Authorware. These "general-purpose" tools serve a variety of functions, but offer little in the way of design constraints governing the kind of software which can be produced. The result is a tool which supports a broad range of possible applications, some of which may be good, and some of which are likely to be poorly executed, but none of which will have been created with much guidance from the tool itself.

For a more specialized purpose, for example, the creation of instructional software, tools can be constructed which are based on more specific models (Macmillan, Emme, & Berkowitz, 1988; Murray, this volume; Russell, Moran, & Jordan, 1988). The basic idea of these *ITS tools* is to enable non-programmers (e.g., a classroom teacher) to create instructional computer programs by setting values within some predefined template. Tools for the design of educational software, though going a long way toward a truly useful too, still aim to support the creation of any possible kind of instruction. In doing so, they base the interaction around general models of instruction, which unfortunately are too general to serve as a specification for a piece of educational software, and are too general to be of much help in guiding a designer in creating such software, for three reasons.

First, there may be a wide range of categories of instructional software; ITS tools have typically been based on prototypes in no more than a few of these categories, so understanding what a universal tool should do, exactly, is not yet possible. Second, the enormous range of potential activities which a general tool would need to support would require a detailed knowledge of the structure of activities and of the elements participating in these activities. Third, the guidance the tool provides would, by necessity, be in general terms so that the tool could offer help in any design context. The consequence here is that the value of the tool as an intelligent critic would be sacrificed in the name of generality.

4.2 From Courseware Authoring to Knowledge-Rich Tool

More recently, researchers have begun to address the need for authoring tools that possess specialized knowledge about their domain. Some approaches rely on an expert systems substrate (Reinhardt, 1997) or on a case-based reasoning engine (Goan, Stottler, & Henke, 1997; Ong & Noneman, 2000) for capturing and representing such knowledge. The knowledge itself is seen by some as a modular component in an authoring tool that can be assembled from appropriate parts (Ritter, Blessing, & Wheeler, this volume), though for some researchers, a modular architecture raises the concern mentioned previously that generality results in weak instructional models (Jona & Kass, 1997). A superior approach is to develop a suite of stand-alone specialized tools that collectively cover the same range of authoring needs (Ibid). Besides domain knowledge, researchers are also calling for pedagogical knowledge to be more explicitly incorporated into authoring environments (Ainsworth, *et al.*, this volume; Jona, 1995; Murray, this volume). The results reported in this chapter represent an attempt to accommodate the need for explicit pedagogies by supporting authors in creating a specific mode of instruction (Investigate & Decide Learning Environments). This work also recognizes the need for representation of domain knowledge. The ways in which these needs are addressed are discussed in the next section.

5. BLUEPRINT FOR A SMARTER TOOL

To transform IDLE-Tool into a more intelligent design aid, we must decide what aspects of investigation design we would like an enhanced tool to support. We need also to determine what knowledge would be required to supplement the tool. Finally, we must invent a representation that captures that knowledge.

5.1 The Internal Structure of an Investigation

Investigations can take many forms, but as used here, the term "investigation" takes on a specific meaning, namely, analyzing samples to derive data useful to support a particular hypothesis (Figure 7).

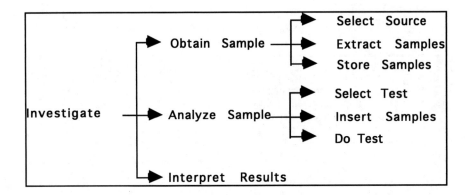

Figure 7. Investigation model for IDLE applications

The steps articulated in the model serve twin purposes. First, they provide a framework within which a designer can operationalize the design, by decomposing it into subtasks of the investigation. Second, they provide a default behavior for the way the program will execute. For example, any device specified by the designer in the Analyze Sample phase will accept a sample, and apply a default procedure to that sample when activated (*i.e.*, it instantiates a default device). These default behaviors have both a graphical component, specified as a set of images provided by the designer (*e.g.*, "the machine in its empty state; the machine with a blood sample",) and an executable component defined by the program (*e.g.*, when the on-switch is pressed, show the machine-with-sample picture and mark the sample "tested" by this device). Within the investigation activity, the student not only synthesizes knowledge, but also makes decisions regarding what sort of knowledge to construct and how to interpret it. Moreover, the results a student gathers must guide him toward making the decision around which the scenario is based. This means that a designer's specifications have an important semantic component extending beyond the investigation itself.

5.1.1 Example Interaction for Investigation Design

The context for the following example is a dialog between the (original) prototype tool and a designer in the process of creating an IDLE application called *Crime Lab*, in which students act as forensic investigators to establish whether lethal levels of toxic material are present in tissue samples collected in an autopsy [3]. The designer's objective is to implement a scenario in which an overdose of barbiturates is implicated. The tool asks the designer to specify various features of this scenario, eliciting text labels and graphics to be included in the screens comprising the investigation. The excerpts in Table 2 show, for a few representative elements of the Investigation, the way the tool prompts the designer.

352   B. BELL

Table 2. System prompts to the designer for scenario features

System Prompt	Author Input
Edit the button label for the source of the first sample	Take Liver Sample
Choose a picture of an empty container for the first sample	test-tube-empty.pict
Choose a picture for a full container for the first sample, which will appear after the student clicks on the extract sample movie.	test-tube-full.pict
Edit the button label for the first test. When the student clicks on this button, a graphic of the first test will appear.	Run Immunoassay Test

Figure 8 shows a screen resulting from the example dialog. The new Investigation reflects the parameters specified by the designer, supported by the default behavior of the executable GBS. Note, however, that the tool operates under the assumption that the designer possesses sufficient knowledge so that the resulting investigation is both internally consistent and relevant to the overall mission of the GBS. The tool enforces only syntactic constraints on which objects and labels are specifiable, and functional constraints on their run-time behavior.

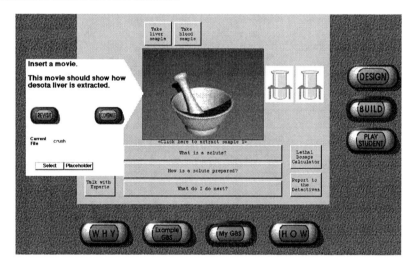

Figure 8. Investigation screen created from designer-supplied parameters

What the tool lacks is a representation of the designer's input choices. For example, the tool requires the designer to supply a label for the button which selects sample number one; the tool is also capable of processing clicks from that button. But the tool does not reason about the sample which that button selects; the designer's input here is treated simply as a text string. The decisions about which elements to include in an investigation are based on knowledge coming from the designer, not from the tool. The next section proposes a way to begin to classifying such knowledge.

5.1.2 Knowledge Applied in Creating an Investigation

Looking more closely at how a designer constructs an investigation, we can identify two categories of knowledge being applied: domain knowledge of the elements in the investigation and their relationships, and structural knowledge of how a coherent investigation should flow. Domain knowledge is exercised when a designer selects specific elements for inclusion in an investigation. In the example dialog, selecting Immunoassay as a test could be appropriate because it is useful in detecting the presence of various drugs, which is central to the scenario that the designer is implementing.

Liver tissue is useful because concentrations in the human liver at which various drugs are lethal are readily available. This kind of detailed knowledge represents a potential design obstacle. It is one thing to know the term "immunoassay", but something else altogether to understand that process well enough to fill in the details of an investigation employing this process.

Structural knowledge helps guide the application of domain knowledge. In selecting immunoassay (which measures concentrations of a target substance), the designer in the example recognized that the possible outcomes the student will be attempting to establish should be distinguishable on the basis of results derived from the available tests. The designer further recognized, perhaps implicitly, that tests (1) are useful insofar as they derive necessary information, and (2) must be consistent with the samples available to be tested. The connection between the information the student is ultimately deriving, and what his goal in the GBS is, can too easily be lost in the details of designing the investigation activities. Controlling the design by applying structural knowledge is another aspect of the design process.

The strategy here is to understand what it is designers know that enables them to create investigations. We have seen two kinds of knowledge that help a designer create an investigation: knowledge about the elements of a specific investigation, and knowledge about the structure of investigations in general. How is this distinction relevant to augmenting the capabilities of IDLE-Tool? Ideally, a tool would be able to critique a proposed investigation as well as offer suggestions for improving it. Identifying the structural and domain-specific aspects of investigation provides a starting point for considering what sort of knowledge is needed to move the prototype tool in this direction.

5.2 Investigation Knowledge in the Model

Now that we have a framework for analyzing investigation knowledge, we can revisit the knowledge implicit in the prototype tool. The following sections articulate what knowledge is there and consider where this knowledge is deficient in light of the previous discussion.

5.2.1 What the Tool Knows About Investigations

The IDLE model treats investigation as consisting of the Obtain Sample, Analyze Sample, and Interpret Results phases. Within each phase, the model directs the interaction with the designer by defining which features are to be elicited and in what order. In Analyze Sample, for instance, the sequence of design parameters elicited for a running a particular test is *test button label, test empty pict, test empty caption, start test pict, test full pict, test full caption*. The elements in this list, and their ordering, constitute the model's "knowledge" of the structure of investigations. While this model is sufficient for guiding the designer in supplying all required parameters, it obviously limits the program's ability to assist in creating the investigation, as discussed next.

5.2.2 Limitations of the Model

To understand the limits of the current model, we can look at two examples of design constraints that a designer would typically observe in creating an investigation. The first design constraint is that the available tests should be able to yield the desired results. If the student is supposed to determine whether a victim died from a drug overdose, for example, atomic absorption would be an inappropriate test, since it is effective for detecting elemental metals, but is not suitable for detecting barbiturates. The second constraint is that results obtained must relate to an outcome the student is investigating. If a student's mission in a GBS were to establish whether mercury poisoning were the cause of death, for instance, results from a pH test would be irrelevant, since the acidity of a sample does not indicate the level of metals it contains.

5.3 Representing Investigation Knowledge

We now see that IDLE-Tool needs two kinds of knowledge: domain knowledge of the parts of an investigation, and general knowledge of the structure of investigations. In this section I discuss how these types of knowledge can be represented in IDLE-Tool.

5.3.1 Domain Knowledge of Investigation Elements

Knowledge of the kinds of components likely to appear in investigations includes knowledge of the components themselves (*e.g.*, that a thermometer measures temperature), as well as knowledge of the relationships among them (*e.g.*, that atomic absorption detects the presence of elemental metals). Both of these kinds of information can be sufficiently represented using a taxonomic frame representation.

The top-most level of this taxonomy identifies four basic types of investigation elements: the samples to be examined, tests to analyze these samples, results which could potentially be found, and the possible outcomes a user could identify. Figure 9 shows an example class definition for a subclass of Test. The definition shown in Figure 9 indicates that an instance of the class "microscope" can provide information about the morphology of a cell. Note the "Results" slot, which identifies which features a test is capable of measuring. Results are also associated with particular sample classes. The results "cell-morphology" and "Hg-genotype", for example, are associated with the class "Blood-sample", as shown in Figure 10.

```
Class: Microscope
Superclass: Cellular-test
Results: (cell-morphology)
Default pict empty: micro-empty.pict
Default pict full: micro-full.pict
```

Figure 9. Example definition for subclass of TEST

```
Class: Blood-sample
Superclass: Circulatory-system-sample
Results: (cell-morphology Hg-genotype)
Default pict: blood-cells.pict
```

Figure 10. Example definition for subclass of SAMPLE

The results serve to identify the information derived from performing a given test on a given sample. For example, since the result "cell-morphology" appears in the definitions of "blood-sample" and "microscope", any microscopic analysis of a blood sample could yield information about the shape of the cells in that sample. The definition of this result class is given in Figure 11. The information supplied in these definitions is applied during the design process as explained later.

```
Class: Cell-morphology
Superclass: Cellular-property
```

Figure 11. Example definition for subclass of RESULT

The examples presented so far represent domain knowledge of specific investigation components. In the next section, I show how the second type of knowledge, that of the general structure of investigations, may be represented.

5.3.2 Capturing Structure via Investigation Templates

Investigations have a common sequence of scenes, partially captured by the phases of the Investigation in the current model. But the earlier discussion of how a designer builds an investigation implicated background knowledge beyond the Obtain-Analyze-Interpret phase definitions. For example, a designer looks for (1) samples possessing features which could be useful in arriving at an outcome, and (2) tests appropriate for uncovering such features from certain classes of samples. That is, certain default expectations regarding the elements of these scenes helped guide the designer in filling in the investigation.

The general knowledge which a designer applies to create an investigation, therefore, can be succinctly codified as a set of scenes and expectations, packaged by an investigation template. A template contains four elements: sample, test, result, and outcome. A complete template specifies that the outcome the student is attempting to support could in theory be established using the materials available, that is, it makes the assertion that "Sample W, when analyzed using Test X, yields Result Y, which supports Outcome Z."

Each template can be associated with specific scenarios. An investigation scenario supplies specific instances for the objects named in the template. If a template includes, for example, the outcome "cause of death", then a scenario for this template might contain the outcome "drug overdose". A scenario thus defines an explicit sequence of activity which a user of the resulting GBS would encounter.

To illustrate, consider the example template and scenarios in Figure 12. Verifying the constraints associated with the investigation sequence is straightforward because the knowledge needed to do so is basically syntactic. The second scenario in the figure, for example, is incomplete because no result has been specified. Verifying that a particular template satisfies the expectations associated with an investigation, though, requires semantic information about the items referred to in the template. The representation of such knowledge was introduced previously. Later, I describe a mechanism for applying this knowledge in helping a designer create a coherent investigation.

blood sample	immunoassay	concentration	cause of death
Angela blood	immunoassay	lethal dose arsenic	poison
Victor blood	immunoassay	<concentration>	overdose

Figure 12. Example investigation template and associated scenarios

5.3.3 Representational Issues for Investigation Knowledge

Three representational issues must be raised before proceeding. One issue is what leverage the investigation templates offer. The notion of packaging scenes and their default expectations within a structure is explained in detail by MOP theory (Schank, 1982). The MOP architecture provides a convenient structure for representing the internal configuration of investigations, and is well-suited to reasoning (part of Schank's intent), which is useful from the standpoint of creating a tool which can act as an intelligent assistant. Moreover, it supports the storage and retrieval of structures in memory, which offers the potential to support the design process with a well-indexed library of investigations.

A second issue is how broad the representation is, that is, what range of investigations the representation can cover. The purpose of extending the tool is to support the design of activity in Investigate & Decide GBSs, so the functional criterion here is whether investigations in the I&D context can be expressed in the vocabulary of the templates. One indication that the representation is sufficient would be its ability to capture the activities in the ten I&D GBSs that have been constructed to date.

Third, adopting a particular representation also raises the question of how a user would interact with the knowledge. In particular, we need some assurances that the representation is intuitive to a designer. A useful analogy to designing an investigation is creating an explanation (the outcome of an investigation is, in some sense, an explanation). In the course of generating an explanation, reasoners pose various explanation questions (Schank, 1986), for instance "what theory of physical causes explains this event?", or "what circumstances led to this event?". An investigation poses these same questions to the student, so the representation (in particular, the template's "outcome") mirrors the way a designer might think about the investigation. The remainder of the template is also structured around investigation questions that would naturally arise during design, namely, "what evidence would suggest this outcome?", "what analysis procedure could supply this evidence?", and "what source is subjected to this analysis?", corresponding respectively to the result, test, and sample.

5.4 Operationalizing Investigation Knowledge

The preceding analysis of investigation knowledge and how it may be represented sets the stage for an extension to IDLE-Tool, called the Investigation Map, or *IMap*. The IMap consists of an editor for adding elements to an investigation, an advisor, suggesting ways a designer might complete a partially-defined investigation, and a knowledge base for maintaining elements which designers may select for their investigations. A designer builds an IMap by creating an investigation template, and then defining scenarios which specify specific paths through the template. The input the designer provides to the IMap thus includes the samples, tests, results, and outcomes populating a particular investigation.

5.4.1 Defining an Investigation in IMap

To illustrate a typical interaction, let us consider an investigation in which the student must determine whether or not a lake has become polluted. The first step is to create a template which defines an appropriate type of investigation. In thinking through the investigation, it is important to consider first what the student will be deciding, that is, what purpose the investigation serves. In this example it is to determine "cause of change in ecosystem", which then becomes the "outcome" part of the investigation template. The next question to answer is how the student will make this determination, or put another way, what kind of results will help determine a cause of change in ecosystem. The designer in this example intends for the student to use the level of dissolved oxygen in the lake as a source for this kind of evidence, and thus the "result" part of the template is filled with "concentration dissolved gas". The designer can then select the type of device which can measure this concentration (in this case, "dissolved oxygen test"), and the type of samples which will be tested ("water sample"). The completed template occupies the top row of the table in Figure 3.

Once a template has been specified, the designer can instantiate different scenarios to be included in the GBS. To accommodate the case in which a region of the lake possesses a low level of dissolved oxygen, for example, the designer creates the scenario shown in the second row of the table in Figure 3. This process can be repeated for creating additional scenarios for this template. The designer can also define new templates, for example, one in which the student measures the pH of the water to look for high acidity.

There are two points to note in this example. First, the designer is operating at a conceptual level, selecting classes of objects to include in the investigation. In contrast, recall the emphasis on interface issues characteristic of the earlier IDLE-Tool prototype. Second, the knowledge which the tool encodes is applied in supplying object classes to the designer, in this case, "cause of change in ecosystem", "concentration dissolved gas", etc.

5.4.2 Template Guidance

As the designer creates the investigation IMap can offer suggestions about how to proceed. A suggestion contains two kinds of information. This first is syntactic advice, indicating which part of the template should next be defined (according to the outcome-driven order in which IMap elicits the investigation). The second is semantic, recommending specific kinds of objects which would be consistent with those already installed into the template. The suggestions which IMap offers at any point in the template construction are focused on the template item which IMap is currently expecting. For example, a designer who supplies an outcome and asks for help will be offered suggestions about which results might be appropriate (Figure 2). The suggestions IMap generates represent the choices which it knows to be compatible.

5.4.3 Class Compatibilities

Compatibility between two classes means that one class identifies another as being related in a particular way. A sample class and result class can be related via a *yields* link (line *a* in Figure 13). A test class and result class can also share a yields relation (line *b* in Figure 13). A result class and outcome class are linked via a *supports* relation (line *c* in Figure 13). A sample class and test class are implicitly consistent if they share a common result class (line *d* in Figure 13).

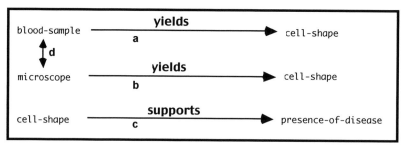

Figure 13. Link types among investigation classes

Links are dynamic structures which serve to support IMap's search for compatible classes, but are defined implicitly in the class descriptions within IMap's knowledge base. For links between a sample class and result class, for example, IMap would retrieve the sample class' definition and read the *results* slot. If sample class A possesses result B, the program asserts a yields link between sample class A and result class B. Appendix A defines the link types used in IMap's knowledge representation.

5.5 The Investigation Library

The architecture behind IMap calls for specific domain knowledge to be used in assisting a designer, so the baseline version of IMap must include a process for manipulating this knowledge, and some data to be manipulated. The initial library is aimed at investigations appropriate for scientific experiments in secondary physics, biology, and chemistry. The information within the libraries is aimed at helping the designer construct coherent investigations and at easing construction of the Investigation interface.

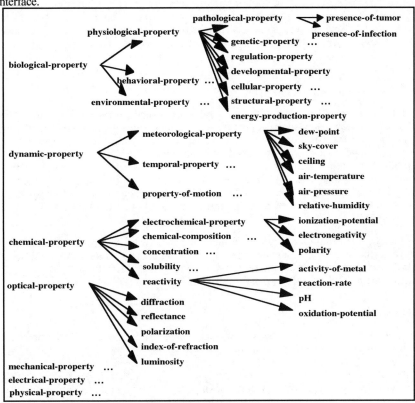

Figure 14. Partial hierarchy for result classes

5.5.1 Scope of the Baseline Knowledge Base

The investigation library defines several hundred classes of objects which typically appear in the kinds of investigations generally conducted in secondary science classrooms. At the top level, the classes are organized according to IMap's investigation model, as samples, tests, result, or outcomes. Within each category is a set of class definitions, organized hierarchically (example class definitions were illustrated in Figures 6 — 8). A portion of the hierarchy from one such category is shown in Figure 14; a more complete set of classes appears in Appendix B.

The hierarchical organization of the sample, test, result, and outcome categories serves two purposes. First, it imposes a structure to make it easier for a designer to browse each category for an appropriate selection, that is, the hierarchies serve an indexical purpose. For example, a designer looking for a test to measure an object's range and bearing could look under "dynamic test," and then within that category, under "range and bearing test," and from there could select "radar". Second, the hierarchies are a means for propagating information from each category to its specializations, that is, they supply an inheritance mechanism. For example, tissue samples are defined to possess a "cell-shape" feature, so specializations of tissue sample, such as liver sample or blood sample, need not have this attribute explicitly encoded.

5.5.2 Expanding the Knowledge Base

Since the tool should support as broad a range of investigations as is practical, the interface includes a knowledge acquisition mode which supports the addition of new definitions and modification of the existing knowledge. Adding a new class to the library is a matter of indicating its superclass, and identifying the classes to which this new class is related. Specifying a new class of outcome, for example, would involve identifying the superclass as well as the kind of results upon which this class of outcome is dependent. The example in Figure 15 shows a designer adding "temperature" to the dependencies (list of results) which are relevant to the new class "cause-of-change-in-ecosystem".

Modifying existing classes works in much the same way. Note that IMap enforces constraints regarding class compatibilities, by accepting defined classes as the only legal fillers for class-to-class relations (e.g., the designer must select from existing result classes in building the results slot in Figure 15).

5.6 A Rationale for IMap

IMap answers the question "how can we help someone design an investigation" by providing an explicit investigation model, by making domain knowledge available, and by following a procedure for helping a designer instantiate the model. The central question is whether IMap makes the designer's task easier. A secondary issue is whether IMap results in improved GBSs, without making the designer's task any more difficult.

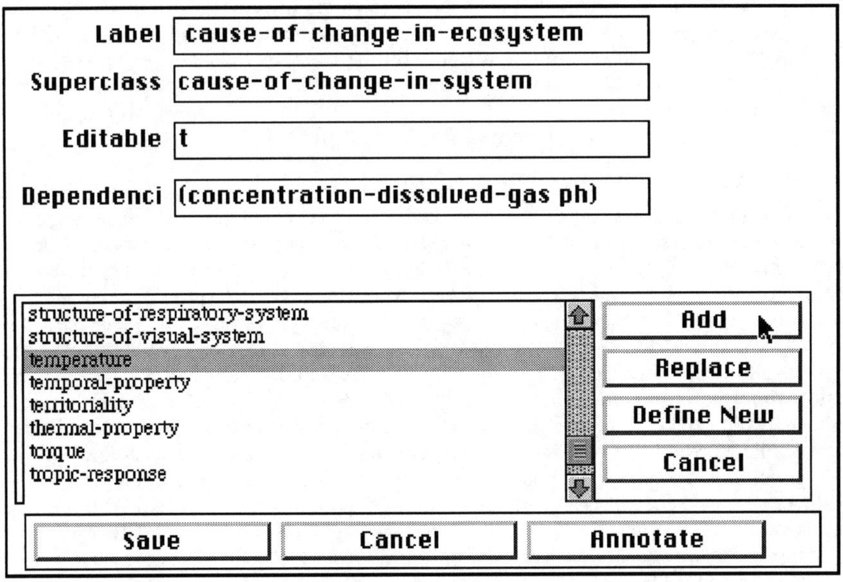

Figure 15. Defining a new test class

5.6.1 IMap and the Art of Investigation

At issue here is the extent to which IMap truly helps a designer create a GBS. People are more adept at imagining appropriate investigations than at conceiving of all the necessary details [4]. For example, a chemistry teacher may possess the requisite domain knowledge and a general design expressed as "students will learn about oxidation by being arson investigators, looking for clues by testing combusted materials." What is likely to pose more difficulty is turning that idea into a working system. IMap can assist designers who start with a broadly-framed idea by helping operationalize that idea as an investigation, turning the designer's general description into an explicit set of objects and sequence of interactions among those objects. The usefulness of IMap thus lies in helping a designer articulate an idea as a well-specified investigation.

5.6.2 IMap and the Science of Investigation

The issue of IMap's utility as a design aid is complementary to the question of IMap's role in creating better GBSs. In other words, even if IMap did not make life any easier for a designer, it would still be advantageous to IDLE-Tool if it contributed toward better GBSs without making life any harder for the designer.

A rough measure of how an investigation could make its GBS better or worse is external coherency, which here means that the overall purpose of the investigation contributes to the user's objectives in the scenario. In the absence of IMap, this question is never asked of the designer, since the conceptual information gained from the investigation has no direct interface analog and thus would not be considered by IDLE-Tool. IMap begins each design interaction with the question "what will your users be deciding?", thereby establishing the investigation as something which ought to leave the user with some conclusive outcome. IMap goes further by supplying a library of the kinds of outcomes which are appropriate for this kind of GBS.

A second measure of an investigation is its internal coherency, which here means how well the different parts of the investigation fit together. Without IMap, it is up to the designer to supply, for example, a test which does in fact yield evidence relevant to the outcome the user is meant to determine. IMap contributes to internal coherency in two ways. First, it encourages the designer to keep in mind how pieces of the investigation are related, by prompting for design parameters in a way which emphasizes these relationships. For example, a designer of who specified an "index of refraction" result would be prompted for a test with "What yields an index of refraction result?" Second, IMap can determine, for any piece of the investigation template, which choices from its library would be consistent with those already installed in the investigation.

The internal and external coherencies of an investigation design are thus left to the designer in the absence of IMap, and are guided by an explicit model with IMap. IMap can thus lead to a more effective GBS, by imposing constraints on the Investigation which, perhaps, force a designer to confront questions which had been left unanswered, but which enhance the contribution the investigation makes to the interaction.

5.6.3 Representational Tradeoffs

Table 3. Completed GBSs within the scope of IMap's knowledge base

Title	samples	tests	results	outcomes
Arson Investigator	textile	gas chromatography	presence	cause of fire
Breast Cancer Counselor	breast tissue	mammogram, biopsy	malignancy, presence of tumor	diagnosis
Cardiac Counselor	human, blood	EKG, reflotron	frequency, composition	risk assessment
Crime Lab	liver, blood	immunoassay, atomic absorption	concentration of toxin in tissue	cause of death
EPA Advisor	water	assay	presence	cause of change in ecosystem
Gem Detective	crystal	refractometer, microscope	structure, index of refraction	artifact type
Pollution Investigator	water	pH Meter, dissolved oxygen test	pH, concentration dissolved gas	cause of change in ecosystem
Public Health Administrator	water	pH, spectrometer	concentration in solution	cause of illness
Sickle Cell Counselor	blood	electrophoresis, microscope	genetic makeup	relative probabilities
Storm Watcher	air	radar, barometer	air pressure, range & bearing	predicted location

The sample-test-result-outcome representation admittedly excludes more complex notions of investigations, such as those involving multiple samples, iterations, and intermediate results. But the view of investigation adopted in IMap, while limiting, was abstracted from existing Investigate & Decide GBSs rather than being an *ad hoc* model adopted for convenience. And as Table 3 suggests, this basic model can support a reasonable range of potential applications.

Determining what, specifically, to include in IMap also relied in part on the GBSs which had been constructed using the tool. The investigation elements included in those applications formed the beginnings of the knowledge base, which was expanded by generalizing these elements to form broader categories until the top-level categories (sample, test, etc.) were reached. At the same time, a survey of the experimental activities typically included in high school science curricula was conducted to guide the evolution of the knowledge base. Science laboratory supplements were used from Biology (Brown, 1978; BSCS, 1968; BSCS, 1973a; BSCS, 1973b; BSCS, 1990; Edwards & Cimmino, 1975; Kroeber, Wolff & Weaver, 1965; Moore & Carlock, 1970), Chemistry (Ferguson, Schmuckler, Caro & Johnson, 1978; Garrett, Richardson & Montague, 1966; McGill, Bradbury, & Sigler, 1966; Metcalfe, Williams & Castka, 1982; Sutman, Harris & Greenstone, 1967; Vallarino, Quagliano & Kirkpatrick 1976; Weisbruch & Chewning, 1962), and Physics (Miner & Kelly, 1967; Stollberg & Hill, 1975; Taffel, Baumel & Landecker, 1970; Williams, Trinklein, Metcalfe & Lefler, 1973). These texts supplied information which shaped the sample, test, result, and outcome class hierarchies. The representation of investigation knowledge in IMap was thus derived in part from empirical judgments and in part from a review of secondary science education activities.

5.7 Extending the IMap: The Next Generation of IDLE-Tool

IMap was constructed in order to address the absence of semantic and structural knowledge of investigations in the original version of IDLE-Tool. This basic notion of developing a richer knowledge representation and then bringing that knowledge to bear to assist the developer was preserved in the successor to IDLE-Tool, called Indie, a tool for authoring Investigate and Decide applications (Dobson, 1998; Qiu, Riesbeck & Parsek, 2003). The extensions proposed below for IMap can thus also be viewed as design principles for related authoring environments (including Indie).

5.7.1 Reusing Investigation Maps

An important consideration is how we might adapt IMap to make previous investigations available to a designer, given that the task of creating an investigation is eased if a similar one were used as a starting point (Domeshek & Kolodner, 1991; Goel, 1989). IMap already stores the templates and scenarios which have been created for a particular GBS. We would simply augment the knowledge base with a collection of investigations (*i.e.*, templates and scenarios) from prior GBSs. A more challenging task is to allow IMap to retrieve the previous investigations most likely to be helpful to the designer. A straightforward scheme would be to use the outcome as the index, so that retrieval then becomes a simple matching process, possibly weighting each retrieved investigation according to how many elements it shares with the investigation currently being defined. A slightly richer variation on this theme is to use IMap's (existing) class-subclass relations to derive a similarity metric based on graphical distance between nodes. A variant on this approach is to allow some level of user control over the matching preferences (Figure 16).

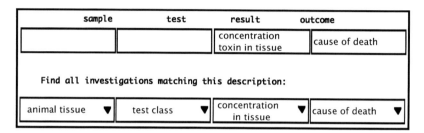

Figure 16. User-controlled match criteria for retrieving investigations

5.7.2 Acquiring Investigation Knowledge

The investigation libraries excerpted in Appendix B represent the object classes built into IMap. These libraries need to grow to accommodate a wider range of GBSs, and the information residing within these entries must be enhanced. A typical entry in the IMap library is designed to provide information that IMap can use to suggest compatible classes that could be used to create an internally consistent investigation. Although the current library possesses this data for only a few representative classes, IMap itself offers a simple mechanism for partially automating the knowledge acquisition process. While creating an IMap, a designer can define a new class of object, and can assign that class to a specific location within the appropriate taxonomy. To further facilitate knowledge acquisition, the IMap could at this point ask the designer questions to elicit the features that are critical to the program's ability to make suggestions. For example, if a designer were to create the class "dissolved oxygen test" as a subclass of concentration-test, the program could ask the designer to list the features which this test is capable of revealing. The obvious expectation is that the IMap libraries will grow more robust the more the tool gets used. But this sort of growth must be leveraged judiciously, so that the integrity and singularity of the IMap libraries is preserved despite the contributions and modifications of multiple designers. This remains an open issue.

5.7.3 A Better Model of Investigation

The sample-test-result-outcome model is sufficient for capturing the simplest investigations, but to support more realistic and interesting scenarios, IMap requires a deeper understanding of the structure of investigations. Four situations illustrate where a richer model would offer additional utility. First, results from one test can often influence a subsequent test, either by providing appropriate intermediate data, or by indicating which (if any) further tests to perform. Second, results from two tests may provide contradictory information. Third, determining a correct outcome may depend on multiple test results. Fourth, the results of a test are often simply to rule out, rather than confirm, an hypothesis.

To extend the IMap model so that the above aspects are accommodated, richer relationships among investigation elements are needed. For example, whereas an outcome in the current IMap is associated with one or more results, these associations would be elaborated to distinguish confirming from disconfirming results, or to indicate that a result may be necessary but not sufficient, or to point to a result that would rule out this outcome. An outcome could also be associated with competing outcomes. A consequence of this extended model of investigation is that the IMap would require additional heuristics for ensuring the integrity of an investigation: verifying the existence of at least one path to determining an outcome would rely on a grammar which included rules for each of the elaborated relationships mentioned above. For example, a rule might recursively encode that an outcome is reachable if (1) there are two results associated with it via "confirming" links, and (2) these links are AND'ed together, and (3) both results are reachable.

It may prove challenging to support the design of these richer investigations in the interview style of interaction employed in the current tool. This suggests that investigations instead be elicited in a less linear fashion. A possibility is to allow the designer to build a flow diagram of an investigation, with specialized connector nodes for representing more complex relationships like "supporting evidence", "rules out", and "necessary but not sufficient". An example diagram appears in Figure 17 that depicts an investigation sequence for a GBS called Crime Lab Chemist.

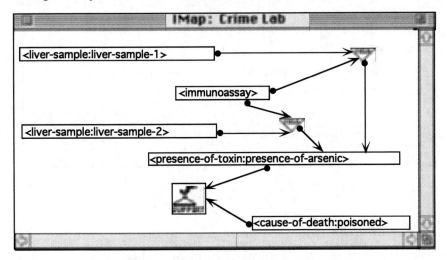

Figure 17: Graphically specifying an IMap

5.7.4 Toward an Intelligent Design Assistant

Given these extensions, the support IMap could lend a designer are illustrated in the hypothetical dialog depicted in Figure 18. In the dialog, IMap notices the absence of a conclusive sequence, suggests a test that closely matches the current IMap scenario, and applies a heuristic that less discriminating tests are generally run prior to more discriminating tests.

In your IMap, "poisoned" cannot be established by "presence of arsenic" alone. Should this be sufficient, or should we add another result?

ADD CONCENTRATION RESULT

What concentration result will help determine poisoned?

LETHAL DOSE

Are "presence of arsenic" and "lethal dose" sufficient for determining poisoned?

YES

How will the student determine lethal dose?

SUGGEST

I know of one investigation where chromatography yielded a concentration result to determine cause of death.

OK

Will results other than "lethal dose" be suggested by any chromatography testing (specify)?

NON-LETHAL DOSE

What sample will show "non-lethal dose" when tested via chromatography?

LIVER SAMPLE 2

I notice that "liver sample 1" and "liver sample 2" yield the same result after immunoassay testing, but different results after chromatography testing. I am guessing that your students should perform the immunoassay test prior to the chromatography test. Should I add this ordering to the IMap?

YES

Figure 18. Hypothetical dialog with a more intelligent IMap

5.7.5 Evaluating IMap

The major piece missing from this puzzle is a systematic evaluation of IMap. The IDLE-Tool (and its IMap extension) is a prototype meant to demonstrate an approach to building case-based design tools for Goal-Based Scenarios. At least as important as conducting a formal evaluation of this particular implementation is developing findings about the underlying methodology, because from this approach, a range of such design environments is likely to emerge. So one point is that, in considering evaluative data, it is important to distinguish between the authoring tool as an artifact and the tool as an instance of a general approach to design tools (Kass, 1998). The studies summarized at the beginning of this chapter (see also Bell, 1998) are a first step toward a more rigorous evaluation of the IDLE-Tool itself.

Two broad criteria that we can apply when evaluating a software design tool are its effectiveness as a design aid, and the overall quality of the applications that it helps produce. Although we cannot report findings that lend direct support to IMap's effectiveness in supporting investigation design, subjects' reactions to the original IDLE-Tool (regarding its emphasis on interface-level design and its lack of guidance at a conceptual level) were effectively remedied by the approach adopted in IMap (which was in fact created to address this problem). A teacher from the second study reported that "This (IMap) is nice. 'What do you do with these samples?' That's what I had trouble with." Another teacher from that study said that IMap "...cleared up some confusion I'd had about which were the samples and which were the tests."

If we consider more generally a class of tools based on this approach, it should not be too surprising that users would respond well to this mode of interaction. Two observations support this expectation. First, the design process typically makes extensive use of past experience (e.g., Domeshek & Kolodner, 1991). Second, skilled designers tend to possess an understanding (i.e., an internal model) which helps guide the application of past experiences (Goel, 1989). Since the IMap architecture supplies both an explicit model and access to cases, it is likely that users will be comfortable with the way in which the tool proceeds through the design cycle. This brief analysis is not meant as a substitute for rigorous evaluation. Although much work is needed in evaluation, some data has begun to emerge from studies with the successor to IDLE-Tool, called Indie, that offers support for this approach as an effective way to create Investigate & Decide learning environments (Dobson & Riesbeck, 1998).

A second aspect of the tool to consider is the value of what it can help produce. Although evaluations of Sickle Cell Counselor (Bell, Bareiss & Beckwith, 1994) offer preliminary indications of the efficacy of applications produced with the tool (since the underlying model is the same), studies should be done to evaluate each new learning environment produced with the tool, so that, over time, an empirical picture of the tool's educational worth can emerge. The Indie tool that succeeded the IMap/IDLE-Tool work has been used to develop dozens of applications (Dobson, 1998; Qiu & Riesbeck, 2002), several of which have been deployed and could be used to gather the data required for an evaluation of the principles implicit in the tool.

Finally, a truly intelligent tool should engender an improved grasp of the process to its user over time. In the case of IMap/IDLE-Tool, we would look for changes among the authors that reflected greater mastery over the domain of designing investigation-oriented GBSs, arising from a better internalized model of the investigate and decide process. This is an important outcome, though likely an elusive metric to measure [5].

6. CONCLUSION

IMap is an extension to IDLE-Tool for supporting the creation of investigations. The IMap tool is a knowledge-rich editor, allowing a designer to instantiate investigation elements, and also a help utility, able to make suggestions to ensure that the designer's investigation is consistent with its internal model. Motivating IMap is the obstacles typically faced in creating an investigation. The knowledge in IMap therefore comes from an analysis of the kinds of knowledge a designer applies to this process. This knowledge includes both a general component (a model of investigation), and specific knowledge about the elements within an investigation. IMap is useful as a design tool primarily because it enables designers possessing a general idea of the investigation they wish to create to define an explicit sequence of interactions, which are then operationalized as the Investigation in the GBS under construction. I have bounded the intended scope of IMap to support investigations appropriate for secondary science education, and have provided a rationale for why the knowledge built into the system is the right knowledge to include. Examples in the chapter have illustrated how such knowledge is brought to bear during interaction with a designer.

7. NOTES

[1] Smadar Kedar and the author led the design effort, with guidance from Roger Schank, Chris Riesbeck, Ray Bareiss, and Alex Kass. Steven Feist and Erica Dubach contributed their programming talents; Jaret Knyal supplied the interface artwork.

[2] The three other GBS tools available at the time supported the design of evidence-based reporting, script-based, and production planning GBSs respectively.

[3] Crime Lab was created by Smadar Kedar, Inna Mostovoy, Barbara Thorne, Mary Williamson, and the author.

[4] Chris Riesbeck was instrumental in helping develop this argument.

[5] My thanks go to an anonymous reviewer for suggesting this outcome.

8. REFERENCES

Ainsworth, S., Major, N., Grimshaw, S., Hayes, M., Underwood, J., Williams, B., and Wood, D. Redeem: Simple Intelligent Tutoring Systems From Usable Tools. This volume.
Bell, B.L. (1995). "Toward Modularity in Specifying Authoring Tools". In *Proceedings of the AI-ED '95 Workshop on Authoring Tools for Intelligent Tutoring Systems*, 9-17, Washington, D.C., 1995.
Bell, B.L. (1998). Investigate and Decide Learning Environments: Specializing Task Models for Authoring Tool Design. The *Journal of the Learning Sciences*, 7(1), 65-105.
Bell, B.L., Bareiss, R., and Beckwith, R. (1994). Sickle Cell Counselor: A Prototype Goal-Based Scenario for Instruction in a Museum Environment. The *Journal of the Learning Sciences*, 3(4), 347–386.
Brown, W.H. (1978). Concepts and Inquiries in Biology. Educational Methods.
BSCS (1968). High School Biology. Rand Mcnally: Chicago.
BSCS (1973a). Biological Science: an Inquiry into Life. Harcourt, Brace, Jovanovich: New York.
BSCS (1973b). Biological Science, Molecules to Man. Houghton Mifflin: Boston, MA.
BSCS (1990). Biological Science, a Molecular Approach. Heath & Company: Lexington, MA.
Dobson, W. (1998). Authoring Tools for Investigate-and-Decide Learning Environments. Ph.D. Dissertation, Northwestern University Department of Computer Science, Evanston, IL, June, 1998.
Dobson, W., and Riesbeck, C.K. (1998). "Tools for Incremental Development of Educational Software Interfaces". In *CHI '98. Conference Proceedings on Human Factors in Computing Systems*, 384-391.
Domeshek, E.A. and Kolodner, J.L. (1991). Toward a Case-Based Aid for Conceptual Design. *International Journal of Expert Systems Research and Applications*, 4, 201–220.

Edwards, G.I. and Cimmino, M. (1975). Laboratory Techniques for High Schools. Barron's Educational Series: Woodbury, NY.
Ferguson, H.W., Schmuckler, J.S., Caro, A.N., and Johnson, A. (1978). Laboratory Investigations in Chemistry. Silver Burdett: Morristown, N.J.
Garrett, A.B., Richardson, J.S., and Montague, E.J. (1966). Laboratory and Demonstration Problems for Chemistry. Ginn & Company.
Goan, T.L., Stottler, R.H., and Henke, A.L. (1997). Authoring Simulation-Based Intelligent Tutoring Systems. In *Intelligent Tutoring System Authoring Tools: Papers from the 1997 Fall Symposium*, Technical Report FS-97-01, AAAI, P. 25.
Goel, A. (1989). Integration of Case-Based Reasoning and Model-Based Reasoning for Adaptive Design Problem Solving. Ph.D. Dissertation, Ohio State University Department of Computer Science.
Jona, M.K. (1995). "Representing and Re-Using General Teaching Strategies: A Knowledge-Rich Approach to Building Authoring Tools for Tutoring Systems". In *Proceedings of the AI-ED '95 Workshop on Authoring Tools for Intelligent Tutoring Systems*, Washington, D.C., 1995.
Jona, M.K., and Kass, A.M. (1997). A Fully-Integrated Approach to Authoring Learning Environments: Case Studies and Lesson Learned. In *Intelligent Tutoring System Authoring Tools: Papers from the 1997 Fall Symposium*, Technical Report FS-97-01, AAAI, P. 39.
Kass, A.M. (1998). "Give Authors Freedom, But Only Within Ideological Boundaries". *Paper Presented at the Fourth International Conference on Intelligent Tutoring Systems, ITS '98*, San Antonio, TX.
Kroeber, E., Wolff, W.H., and Weaver, R.L. (1965). Biology. Heath & Company.
Macmillan, S., Emme, D., and Berkowitz, M. (1988). Instructional Planners: Lessons Learned. In Psotka, J., Massey, L.D., and Mutter, S.A. (Eds.), *Intelligent Tutoring Systems, Lessons Learned*. Lawrence Erlbaum: Hillsdale, NJ.
Major, M., Ainsworth, S., and Wood, D. (1997). REDEEM: Exploiting Symbiosis Between Psychology and Authoring Environments. In *International Journal of Artificial Intelligence in Education, 8*.
Mcgill, M.V., Bradbury, G.M., and Sigler, E.A. (1966). Chemistry Guide and Laboratory Activities. Lyons & Carnahan: Chicago.
Metcalfe, H.C., Williams, J.E., and Castka, J.F. (1982). Exercises and Experiments in Modern Chemistry. Holt, Rinehart, & Winston: New York.
Miner, T.D. and Kelly, W.C. (1967). Laboratory Experiments in Physics for High School. Ginn & Company.
Moore, H.A. and Carlock, J.R. (1970). In the Laboratory: the Spectrum of Life. Harper & Row: New York.
Murray, T. Eon: Knowledge Based Tutors Authoring Tools for Content, Instructional Strategy, Student Model, and Interface Design. This volume.
Ong, J., and Noneman, S. (2000). Intelligent Tutoring Systems for Procedural Task Training of Remote Payload Operations at NASA. In *Proceedings of the Industry/Interservice Training, Simulation and Education Conference* (I/ITSEC 2000).
Qiu, L., Riesbeck, C.K., and Parsek, M.R. (2003). The Design and Implementation of an Engine and Authoring Tool for Web-based Learn-by-doing Environments. In *Proceedings of World Conference on Educational Multimedia, Hypermedia & Telecommunications* (ED-MEDIA 2003). June 23-28, 2003, Honolulu, HA. AACE.
Qiu, L., and Riesbeck, C.K. (2002). Open Goal-Based Scenarios: An Architecture for Hybrid Learning Environments. In *Proceedings of World Conference on E-Learning in Corporate, Government, Healthcare, and Higher Education* (E-Learn 2002). Montreal, Canada, Oct. 15-19, 2002. AACE.
Reinhardt, B. (1997). Generating Case Oriented Intelligent Tutoring Systems. In *Intelligent Tutoring System Authoring Tools: Papers from the 1997 Fall Symposium*, Technical Report FS-97-01, AAAI, P. 79.
Riesbeck, C.K., and Dobson, W. (1998). "Authorable Critiquing for Intelligent Educational Systems". In *Proceedings of the 1998 International Conference on Intelligent User Interfaces*, January 6-9, 1998, San Francisco, CA.
Ritter, S., Blessing, S.B., and Wheeler, L. Authoring Tools for Component-Based Learning Environments. This volume.
Russell, D., Moran, T.P., and Jordan, D.S. (1988). The Instructional Design Environment. In Psotka, J., Massey, L.D., and Mutter, S.A. (Eds.), *Intelligent Tutoring Systems, Lessons Learned*. Lawrence Erlbaum: Hillsdale, NJ.
Schank, R.C. (1982). Dynamic Memory: A Theory of Reminding and Learning in Computers and People. Cambridge University Press: Cambridge, UK.
Schank, R.C. (1986). Explanation Patterns: Understanding Mechanically and Creatively. Lawrence Erlbaum: Hillsdale, N.J.

Schank, R.C., Fano, A., Bell, B.L., and Jona, M.Y. (1994). The Design of Goal Based Scenarios. The *Journal of the Learning Sciences*, 3(4), 305–345.

Schank, R.C., and Korcuska, M. (1996). Eight Goal-Based Scenario Tools. Technical Report 67, The Institute for the Learning Sciences, Northwestern University, Evanston, IL.

Schank, R.C., Berman, T.R., and Macpherson, K.A. (1999). Learning by Doing. In C. Reigeluth (Ed.), *Instructional Design Theories and Models* (pp. 161-181). Mahwah, NJ: Lawrence Erlbaum Associates.

Stollberg, R. and Hill, F.F. (1975). Physics Fundamentals and Frontiers. Houghton Mifflin: Boston, MA.

Sutman, F.X., Harris, S.P., and Greenstone, A.W. (1967). Concepts in Chemistry: Teacher's Manual and Answer Key. Harcourt, Brace & World.

Taffel, A., Baumel, A., and Landecker, L. (1970). Physics Laboratory Manual. Allyn & Bacon: Boston, MA.

Vallarino, L.M., Quagliano, J.V., and Kirkpatrick, J.W. (1976). Laboratory Manual to Accompany Chemistry; A Humanistic Approach. Mcgraw-Hill: New York.

Weisbruch, F.T. and Chewning, W.J. (1962). Semimicro Laboratory Exercises in High School Chemistry. Heath & Company: Boston, MA.

Williams, J.E., Trinklein, F.E., Metcalfe, H.C., and Lefler, R.W. (1973). Laboratory Experiments in Physics. Holt, Rinehart, & Winston: New York.

APPENDIX A: LINK CATEGORY DESCRIPTIONS

This appendix lists the category description for the link types encoded in the knowledge representation. The reasoning engine currently uses the "yields", "support", and "proves" link types only.

YIELDS: Indicates that the named instance of SAMPLE, when analyzed by the named instance of TEST, yields the specified RESULT.
Ex: «sample: blood_1» & «test: mass_spec» YIELDS «result: arsenic_neg»

Note that a simulation is specifiable as a collection of YIELDS links.

SUPPORTS: Identifies the named RESULT as one which supports the validity of the named CONCLUSION
Ex: «result: arsenic_pos» SUPPORTS «conclusion: arsenic_toxicity_pos»

WEAKENS: Inverse of SUPPORTS.
Ex: «result: arsenic_neg» WEAKENS «conclusion: arsenic_toxicity_pos»

PROVES: Similar to SUPPORTS, but stronger. Named RESULT is sufficient to prove named conclusion. If RESULT is a list, it means the conjunction of results proves the conclusion.
Ex: «result: arsenic_pos» (AND) «result: blood_toxic_pos» PROVES «conclusion: arsenic_toxicity»

DISPROVES: Inverse of PROVES.
Ex: «result: arsenic_neg» (AND) «result: blood_toxic_neg» DISPROVES «conclusion: arsenic_toxicity»

DERIVES: Not really a link instance, but an indication that the argument results will match an inference rule to produce the new result indicated.
Ex: «result: hg-type-aa» (AND) «result: hg-type-ss» DERIVES «result genetic-makeup-aa-ss»

APPENDIX B. EXCERPTS FROM THE INVESTIGATION LIBRARY FOR IMAP

sample-class
  organic
    animal
      animal-tissue
        regulatory-system
          liver
        excretory-system
          fecal
          urine
        external-animal-tissue
          hair
          <<...>>
        digestive-system
        sensorimotor-system
        circulatory-system
        <<...>>
        reproductive-system
        <<...>>
        skeletal
      animal-individual
        mammalian
          marine-mammalian
            <<...>>
          primate
            <<...>>
    plant
      plant-individual
      plant-tissue
    fungus
    simple-organism
  inorganic
      <<...>>

test-class
  electrical-test
    electrical-object-test
      electroscope

EDUCATIONAL SOFTWARE DESIGN WITH KNOWLEDGE-RICH TOOLS   373

    electrical-circuit-test
       voltmeter
       ammeter
       galvanometer
       potentiometer
       dry-cell
       galvanoscope
    electromagnetic-test
       compass
       magnet
physical-test
    <<...>>
thermal-test
    <<...>>
chemical-test
    <<...>>
point-motion-test
    <<...>>
biological-test
    <<...>>
optical-test
    <<...>>

result-class
   biological-property
     physiological-property
       pathological-property
         malignancy
       genetic-property
         pattern-of-inheritance
         phenotype
         phylogenetic-property
           biological-distance
           bio-classification
         genetic-makeup
         genotype-phenotype-link
         genotype
         sources-of-genetic-var
       regulation-property
         <<..>>
       developmental-property
         <<...>>
       respiration-property

            <<...>>
        cellular-property
            <<...>>
        immune-system-property
            <<...>>
        structural-property
          sensory-property
              <<...>>
          type-of-skeletal-system
          type-of-muscular-system
          pigmentation
        energy-product-property
            <<...>>
    behavioral-property
        <<...>>
    thermal-property
        <<...>>
    mechanical-property
        <<...>>
    dynamic-property
        <<...>>
    meteorological-property
        <<...>>
    electrical-property
        <<...>>
    chemical-property
        <<...>>
    physical-property
        <<...>>

outcome-class
  identification-outcome
    artifact-type
      artifact-behavior
        motion-outcome
          direction-outcome
          velocity-outcome
    artifact-property
      propagation
  artifact-outcome
    artifact-design-outcome
      system-design-outcome
        biological-system-design

```
                    pedigree
causal-outcome
   cause-of-event-outcome
      cause-catastrophic-event
         cause-of-fire
         cause-of-flood
         cause-of-explosion
      cause-physiological-event
         cause-of-death
   cause-of-change-outcome
      cause-change-in-artifact
      cause-of-change-in-system
         cause-chnge-ecosystem
   cause-of-state-outcome
optimal-choice-outcome
   optimal-treatment
   optimal-resource-allocation
   optimal-location
   optimal-route
classification-outcome
   diagnosis-outcome
predictive-outcome
   prognosis
   risk-analysis
      risk-assessment
      relative-probabilities
contributing-outcome
```

PETER BRUSILOVSKY

Chapter 13

DEVELOPING ADAPTIVE EDUCATIONAL HYPERMEDIA SYSTEMS:

From Design Models to Authoring Tools

Abstract. Adaptive hypermedia is a new area of research at the crossroads of hypermedia, adaptive systems, and intelligent tutoring systems. Educational hypermedia systems is currently the most popular kind of adaptive hypermedia. The goal of this paper is to uncover the secrets of authoring adaptive educational hypermedia. The paper provides a clear structured view on the process of adaptive hypermedia authoring starting from the early design stage. It also reviews a few modern adaptive hypermedia authoring systems that are oriented to educational practitioners.

1. INTRODUCTION

Adaptive hypermedia (AH) is an alternative to the traditional "one-size-fits-all" approach in the development of hypermedia systems. Adaptive hypermedia systems (AHS) build a model of the goals, preferences and knowledge of each individual user, and use this model throughout the interaction with the user, in order to adapt to the needs of that user (Brusilovsky, 1996). For example, a student in an adaptive educational hypermedia system will be given a presentation that is adapted specifically to his or her knowledge of the subject (De Bra, & Calvi, 1998), and a suggested set of most relevant links to proceed further (Brusilovsky, Eklund, & Schwarz, 1998b). An adaptive electronic encyclopedia will personalize the content of an article to augment the user's existing knowledge and interests (Milosavljevic, 1997). A virtual museum will adapt the presentation of every visited object to the user's individual path through the museum (Oberlander, O'Donell, Mellish, & Knott, 1998).

AH systems can be useful in any application area where users of a hypermedia system have essentially different goals and knowledge and where the hyperspace is reasonably large. Users with different goals and knowledge may be interested in different pieces of information presented on a hypermedia page and may use different links for navigation. AH tries to overcome this problem by using knowledge represented in the user model to adapt the information and links being presented to the given user. Adaptation can also assist the user in a navigational sense, which is particularly relevant for a large hyperspace. Knowing user goals and knowledge, AH systems can support users in their navigation by limiting browsing space, suggesting most relevant links to follow, or providing adaptive comments to visible links.

It is quite natural that educational hypermedia was one of the first application areas for AH. In educational context users with alternative learning goals and knowledge on the subjects require essentially different treatment. It is also in educational hypermedia where the problem of "being lost in hyperspace" is especially critical. A number of pioneer adaptive educational hypermedia systems were developed between 1990 and 1996. These systems can be roughly divided into two research streams. The systems of one of these streams were created by researchers in the area of intelligent tutoring systems (ITS) who were trying to extend traditional student modeling and adaptation approaches developed in this field to ITS with hypermedia components (Beaumont, 1994; Brusilovsky, Pesin, & Zyryanov, 1993; Gonschorek, & Herzog, 1995; Pérez, Gutiérrez, & Lopistéguy, 1995). The systems of another stream were developed by researchers working on educational hypermedia in an attempt to make their systems adapt to individual students (De Bra, 1996; de La Passardiere, & Dufresne, 1992; Hohl, Böcker, & Gunzenhäuser, 1996; Kay, & Kummerfeld, 1994).

Table 1. Design and authoring steps in the process of creating regular and adaptive educational hypermedia systems. The steps that are not essential for the whole process and can be skipped in special cases are shown in italics.

Regular educational hypermedia	*Adaptive educational hypermedia*
Design	
	Design and structure the knowledge space
	Design a generic user model
	Design a set of learning goals
Design and structure the hyperspace of educational material	Design and structure the hyperspace of educational material
	Design connections between the knowledge space and the hyperspace of educational material
Authoring	
Create page content	Create page content
Define links between pages	Define links between pages
	Create some description of each knowledge element
	Define links between knowledge elements
	Define links between knowledge elements and pages with educational material

The first adaptive educational hypermedia systems were relatively small with the hyperspace rarely exceeding 100 nodes. The focus of adaptive hypermedia research during the first 4-6 years was in developing innovative user modeling and adaptation technologies (Brusilovsky, 1996). As long as this field was moving to a more mature state with a good number of established and evaluated adaptation technologies, the researchers in the field of adaptive hypermedia attempted to build the systems with incrementally larger hyperspace. This trend was caused by both, availability of ready to be used technologies and by the growing needs of Web-based education. As a result, during the last 5 years the focus of research has gradually moved from creating more and more new AH technologies to the problems of design and authoring of AH systems. A number of design frameworks suitable for building large adaptive hypermedia systems were suggested (Brusilovsky, 1997; Grigoriadou, Papanikolaou, Kornilakis, & Magoulas, 2001; Neumann, & Zirvas, 1998; Steinacker, Seeberg, Rechenberger, Fischer, & Steinmetz, 1999; Stern, & Woolf, 2000; Süß, Kammerl, & Freitag, 2000) and a few authoring toolkits and systems were developed (Brusilovsky, et al., 1998b; De Bra, et al., 1998; Forcheri, Molfino, Moretti, & Quarati, 2001; Hockemeyer, Held, & Albert, 1998; Murray, 2001; Sanrach, & Grandbastien, 2000; Specht, & Oppermann, 1998; Weber, Kuhl, & Weibelzahl, 2001b).

This paper provides a summative review of the state of the art in adaptive hypermedia authoring. Instead of analyzing existing tools and frameworks one by one, I have attempted to provide a coherent unified view to the various aspects of AH authoring. The goal of this review is to help the potential authors of adaptive hypermedia systems to understand the variety of opportunities in this field and to select a framework or a tool that is most relevant to the needs of their subjects.

2. THE STRUCTURE OF THE REVIEW

The secret of adaptivity in all adaptive hypermedia systems is "knowledge behind pages". All adaptive educational hypermedia systems explicitly model the knowledge of the domain to be taught in the form of elementary knowledge elements or concepts that form a knowledge space. To let the adaptive system "know" what is presented on a particular page or page fragment author of an AH system has to specify the knowledge elements "behind" it thus creating links between the knowledge space and the hyperspace of educational material. As a result, the design and authoring of educational AHS is more complicated than the design of regular educational hypermedia. In addition to structuring the hyperspace and authoring the pages with educational content, the author of an adaptive hypermedia system need also to structure the knowledge space and define the connections between knowledge space and hyperspace of educational material. Table 1 shows the list of design and authoring stages for regular and adaptive educational hypermedia. As we see, there are a number of additional steps that have to be performed when creating adaptive educational hypermedia systems. Even though some steps (shown in italics) are not are not essential and can be skipped in some simpler systems, the job of creating an AH system is considerably harder than the job of creating a traditional hypermedia system with the same size of the hyperspace. This is the price of adaptivity.

I have structured this review according to the sequence of design and authoring steps to be performed when creating adaptive educational hypermedia systems. Two major parts of this paper correspond to two major stages – design and authoring. The subsections of the design part correspond to design and authoring steps. Each subsection presents a "universal approach" for this step and discusses known variations of this approach. The subsections in the authoring part correspond to major authoring approaches and explain how each of these approaches support main authoring steps. At the end I attempt to predict the future developments in the area of adaptive educational hypermedia authoring and clarifies his viewpoint on the design of adaptive hypermedia systems presented in this paper.

3. DESIGN STAGE: STRUCTURING THE INFORMATION

The information structure of a typical adaptive hypermedia system can be considered as two interconnected networks or "spaces" (Figure 1): a network of concepts (knowledge space) and a network of hypertext pages with educational material (traditional hyperspace). Accordingly, the design of an adaptive hypermedia system involves three key sub-steps: structuring the knowledge, structuring the hyperspace, and connecting the knowledge space and the hyperspace. On each step a developer of an AH system can choose from several known ways that are reviewed below. Also, in this part I review student model and learning goals design steps since they are to a large extent defined by a set of design choice made in structuring the domain information.

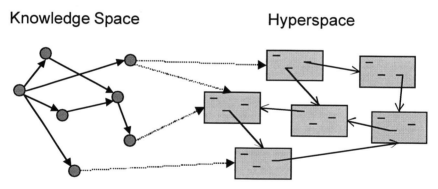

Figure 1. A typical structure of information space in an adaptive hypermedia system

3.1. Structuring the Knowledge

3.1.1. The Domain Model

The heart of the knowledge-based approach to developing adaptive hypermedia systems is a structured *domain model* that is composed of a set of small domain knowledge elements (DKE). Each DKE represents an elementary fragment of knowledge for the given domain. DKE concepts can be named differently in different systems—concepts, knowledge items, topics, knowledge elements, learning objectives, learning outcomes, but in all the cases they denote elementary fragments of domain knowledge. In this paper I will be calling DKE as *concepts*. Though this name is slightly misleading[1] it is currently the most popular way to name DKE. Depending on the domain, the application area, and the choice of the designer concepts can represent bigger or smaller pieces of domain knowledge. A set of domain concepts forms *a domain model*. More exactly, a set of independent concepts is the simplest form of domain model. I call it a *set model* or a *vector model* since the set of concepts has no internal structure. In a more advanced form of domain model concepts are related to each other thus forming a kind of semantic network. This network represents the structure of the domain covered by a hypermedia system. I call this kind of model a *network model* (Figure 2).

The structured domain model was inherited by adaptive educational hypermedia systems from the field of ITS where it was used mainly by systems with task sequencing, curriculum sequencing, and instructional planning functionality (Brusilovsky, 1992). The reason for that is that most of the early adaptive educational hypermedia systems had strong connection with ITS systems. In fact, a number of them were developed in an attempt to extend an ITS system with hypertext functionality (Beaumont, 1994; Brusilovsky, Schwarz, & Weber, 1996a; Brusilovsky, 1993; Gonschorek, et al., 1995; Pérez, et al., 1995). This model proved to be relatively simple and powerful and was later accepted as de-facto standard by almost all educational and many non-educational adaptive hypermedia systems.

---

[1] The name concepts can cause someone to think that concepts can only represent fragments of conceptual knowledge. However, a concept is a general name that can denote a fragment of knowledge of any kind, including procedural knowledge.

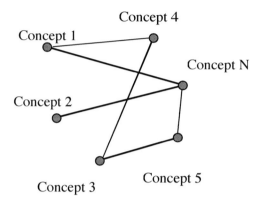

Figure 2. A network domain model

Domain models in adaptive hypermedia systems seriously differ in complexity. It could be surprising that some AHSs developed for teaching practical university courses employed simplest vector domain model (Brusilovsky, & Anderson, 1998a; De Bra, 1996). At the same time, several modern AHSs use networked models with several kinds of links that represent different kinds of relationships between concepts. The most popular kind of links in educational AHS is prerequisite links between concepts which represent the fact that one of the related concepts has to be learned before another. Prerequisite links are relatively easy to understand by authors of AHS and can support several adaptation and user modeling techniques. In many AHS prerequisite links is the only kind of links between concepts (Grigoriadou, et al., 2001; Henze, Naceur, Nejdl, & Wolpers, 1999a; Hockemeyer, et al., 1998; Neumann, et al., 1998; Pilar da Silva, Durm, Duval, & Olivié, 1998; Weber, et al., 2001b). Other kinds of links that are popular in many systems are classic semantic links "is-a" and "part-of" (De Bra, & Ruiter, 2001; Steinacker, et al., 1999; Vassileva, 1998).

Another difference in complexity is related with internal structure of concepts. For the majority of educational AHS the domain concepts are nothing more than names that denote fragments of domain knowledge. At the same time, some AH systems use a more advanced frame-like knowledge representation, i.e., represent an internal structure of each concept as a set of attributes (Beaumont, 1994; Hohl, et al., 1996; Weber, & Brusilovsky, 2001a).

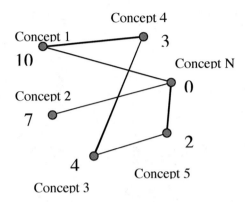

Figure 3. A simple overlay student model

3.1.2. The student model

One of the most important functions of the domain model is to provide a framework for representation of the user's domain knowledge. The majority of educational AHS use *overlay model* of user knowledge (known also as overlay student model). The overlay model was also inherited from the field of ITS (Wenger, 1987). The key principle of the overlay model is that for each domain model concept, individual user knowledge model stores some data that is an estimation of the user knowledge level on this concept. In the simplest (and oldest) form it is a binary value (known – not known) that enables the model to represent user's knowledge as an overlay of domain knowledge. While some successful educational AHS (De Bra, 1996) use this classic form of overlay model, the majority of systems uses a weighted overlay model that can distinguish several levels of user's knowledge of a concept using a qualitative value (Brusilovsky, et al., 1998a; Grigoriadou, et al., 2001) (for example, good-average-poor), an integer quantitative value (for example, from 0 to 100) like shown on Figure 3 (Brusilovsky, et al., 1998b; De Bra, et al., 2001), or a probability that the user knows the concept (Henze, & Nejdl, 1999b; Specht, & Klemke, 2001). A weighted overlay model of user knowledge can be represented as a set of pairs "concept–value", one pair for each domain concept. The overlay model is powerful and flexible because it can measure independently the user's knowledge of different concepts. Note that some versatile adaptive hypermedia systems that have integrated ITS components use more elaborate kind of overlay models to store multiple evidences about user level of knowledge separately (Brusilovsky, 1994; Weber, et al., 2001a).

In addition to concept-level overlay model, a number of AHS keep a page-level model also known as historic model. This model keeps some information about user visits to individual pages such as the number of visits or time spent on a page. While in some early adaptive hypermedia systems such as Manuel Excel (de La Passardiere, et al., 1992) the historic model was the only kind of student model used, modern AHS tend to ignore it or use it as a secondary source of adaptation. Still, ALE (Specht, Kravcik, Klemke, Pesin, & Hüttenhain, 2002), one of the most recent AH authoring systems has no concept overlay model and its adaptation bases solely on a historic model.

3.1.3. Modeling an educational goal

An ability to build a model of an educational goal is a very useful feature of an adaptive hypermedia system that extends its adaptivity and flexibility. This feature allows a teacher (or a student) to assign different educational goals to different students working with the same system. Using these individual goals, adaptive system can help different students to achieve different educational goals within the same course or set of knowledge. Currently the majority of educational AHS do not have a capability to model individual educational goals for students. In these systems all students have the same implicit educational goal - to learn all domain model concepts. In a few systems that support multiple educational goals (Brusilovsky, et al., 1998b; Grigoriadou, et al., 2001; Henze, et al., 1999a) the domain model offers a natural framework for goal modeling. This domain model-based approach to representing educational goals was also inherited by educational AHS from earlier works in the field of ITS (Brusilovsky, 1992; Elsom-Cook, & O'Malley, 1990; Vassileva, 1990). With this approach, an elementary educational goal is simply a target subset of domain concepts to be learned. This goal can be assigned to a student individually by the course author (Vassileva, & Deters, 1998), the teacher (Brusilovsky, et al., 1998b) or self-selected by the student (Brusilovsky, et al., 1998b; Grigoriadou, et al., 2001; Henze, et al., 1999a). In either case, with the goal mechanism in place, different students can pursue different educational goal within the same system. A natural way for the student to select an educational goal is to select a project, exercise, or other educational activity as a long-term goal (Henze, et al., 1999a) Then the prerequisite concepts of this activity form an individual educational goal. A more advanced elementary educational goal can be represented as a set of pairs: a concept and its target knowledge level. Elementary educational goals can be organized into more complex goals by being structured into sequences (goals have to be achieved one by one) or in trees (goals have to be achieved from leaves to the root). For example, in InterBook an individual learning goal was originally modeled as a sequence of sets (Figure 4) and later as stack of sets to enable a student to push a self-selected educational goal on the top of the stack (Schwarz, 1998). INSPIRE lets a student to pick up a structured educational goal for learning. This structured goal can be composed of a sequence of elementary sub-goals called layers each one composed as a set of concepts to be learned.

Figure 4. An individual educational goal can be modeled as a sequence of subsets of domain model concepts (shown as triangles).

3.2. Connecting knowledge with educational material

In Table 1, designing connections between the knowledge space and the hyperspace of educational material is listed as the last step in designing an educational AHS. We, however, review it before reviewing the hyperspace-structuring step since the approach to connecting "concepts and pages" significantly influence the hyperspace structure itself. The process of connecting domain knowledge with educational material is also known as indexing because specifying a set of underlying concepts for every page of educational material is very similar to indexing a page of content with a set of keywords. There are four aspects that are important to distinguish different indexing approaches: cardinality, granularity, navigation, and expressive power.

From the *cardinality* aspect, there are two essentially different cases: single concept indexing when each fragment of educational material is related to one and only one domain model concept and multi-concept indexing when each fragment can be related to many concepts. Single concept indexing is simpler and more intuitive for the authors. It has been applied in several AH authoring systems oriented to a non-expert user (Carmona, Bueno, EduardoGuzman, & Conejo, 2002; Vassileva, et al., 1998). Multi concept indexing is more powerful, but it makes the system more complex and requires more skilled authoring teams (Brusilovsky, et al., 1998b; De Bra, et al., 2001). It's probably a good idea to choose single concept indexing whenever it is meaningful from educational point of view (i.e., smaller systems and simpler domains). At the same time, in many cases using a multi concept indexing is imposed by the nature of the domain. For example, in programming and mathematics, elementary constructs and operators are often selected as domain model concepts. In that case a hypermedia system that needs to have a reasonably precise indexing has to use a multi-concept indexing approach since most of the examples and problems involve several constructs and operators.

Expressive power concerns the amount of information that the authors can associate with every link between a concept and a page. Of course, the most important information is the very presence of the link. This case could be named as flat indexing and it is used in the majority of existing systems. Still some systems with large hyperspace and advanced adaptation techniques want to associate more information with every link by using roles and/or weights. Assigning a role to a link helps distinguish several kinds of connections between concepts and pages. For example, some systems want to distinguish a case when a page provides an introduction, a core explanation or a summary of a concept and a case when it provides a core explanation of it (Brusilovsky, 2000). Other systems use *prerequisite* role to mark the case when the concept is not presented on a page, but instead required for understanding it (Brusilovsky, et al., 1998b). Another way to increase expressive power of indexing is to specify weight of a link between a concept and a page. The weight may specify, for example, the percentage of knowledge about a concept presented on this page (De Bra, et al., 2001; Pilar da Silva, et al., 1998).

Granularity concerns the precision of indexing. The two most popular cases are indexing of the whole hypertext page with concepts and indexing of page fragments with concepts. There are also a few cases where the whole cluster of connected pages is indexed with the same set of concepts (Pérez, et al., 1995).

Navigation aspect is important to distinguish a case where a link between a concept and a page exists only on a conceptual level and is used only by internal adaptation mechanisms of the system from the case when each link also define a navigation path. My own position is that any conceptual link should be also used by navigation. In all systems developed by our group every concept has an external representation as a real or virtual page in the hyperspace and every indexing link between a page and a concept defines a navigation path. Thus, from any page with educational material students can navigate to all concepts connected with it and from each concept to all pages indexed with this concept. This approach creates very rich navigation opportunities and supports special style of navigation that I call concept-based navigation (Brusilovsky, & Schwarz, 1997).

Existing AH systems suggest various ways of indexing that differ in all aspects listed above. However, all this variety can be described in terms of three basic approaches that are described in the remaining part of this section. Systems using the same indexing approach have similar hyperspace structure and share specific adaptation techniques that are based on this structure. Thus the indexing approach selected by developers to a large extent defines the functionality of an AH system.

3.2.1. Concept-Based Hyperspace

The simplest approach to organizing connections between knowledge space and hyperspace is known as *concept-based hyperspace*. This approach is naturally appearing in any AH system that uses single-concept indexing. I distinguish simple and enhanced concept-based hyperspace. *Simple concept-based hyperspace* is used in systems that have exactly one page of educational material for every concept. With this approach, the hyperspace is built as an exact replica of the domain model (Figure 5). Each concept of the domain model is represented by exactly one node of the hyperspace, while the links between the concepts constitute main paths between hyperspace nodes (Brusilovsky, & Pesin, 1994; Brusilovsky, et al., 1993; Hohl, et al., 1996). A very attractive feature of this approach is that the educational hyperspace become perfectly structured just by indexing and does not really require any additional hypertext structuring approach analyzed in the next section. The simple concept based approach was quite popular among early educational AHS that have their roots in the ITS field. For these systems the concept-based hyperspace was simply the easiest and the most natural way to produce a well-structured hyperspace. Currently it is rarely used in educational AHS in its pure form because it requires each page of the hyperspace to be devoted to exactly one concept. It is very appropriate for developing encyclopedically structured learning material such as encyclopedias (Milosavljevic, 1997), manuals (Brusilovsky, et al., 1994), and glossaries (Brusilovsky, et al., 1998b), but too restrictive for practical Web-based education where multiple pages of educational material can be created to teach the same domain model concept. The most typical use of this approach in modern educational AHS is to represent a part of the overall hyperspace such as glossary of concepts in InterBook (Brusilovsky, et al., 1998b) or glossary of Lisp functions in ELM-ART (Weber, et al., 2001a).

The educational AHS with rich content and single-concept indexing can use an *enhanced concept-based hyperspace* design approach. With this design approach multiple pages describing the same concept are connected to this concept in both information space and hyperspace. Each concept has a corresponding "hub" page in the hyperspace. The concept hub page is connected by links to all educational hypertext pages related to this concept. The links can be typed and weighted (Grigoriadou, et al., 2001; Pilar da Silva, et al., 1998), though it is not necessary for using the approach. The student can navigate between hub concept pages along conceptual links and from hub pages to the pages with educational material. This approach could be used for creating relatively large AHS with quite straightforward structure and allows for a number of adaptation techniques (Grigoriadou, et al., 2001; Steinacker, et al., 1999).

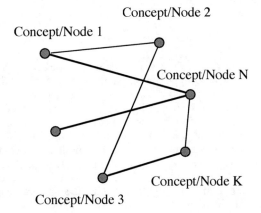

Figure 5. Simple concept-based hyperspace

The concept-based hyperspace design approach sets strong requirements to the domain model. It always requires a model with established links between concepts (preferably, several types of links) that will be used to establish hyperlinks. Another restriction is that this approach can hardly be used "post-hoc" to turn an existing traditional hypermedia system into an AH system. It has to be used from the early steps of a hypermedia system design (Weber, et al., 2001b). However, this approach is very powerful and provides excellent opportunities for adaptation. With concept-based approach, the system knows exactly the type and content of each page and the type of each link. This knowledge can be used by various adaptive navigation support techniques. Annotation is the most popular technology here. For example, ISIS-Tutor (Brusilovsky, et al., 1994), ELM-ART (Weber, et al., 2001a), InterBook (Brusilovsky, et al., 1998b), INSPIRE (Grigoriadou, et al., 2001) use different kinds of link annotation to show the current educational state of the concept (not known, known, well known). ISIS-Tutor, ELM-ART, and a number of other systems use annotation to show that a concept page is not ready to be learned (i.e., its prerequisite concepts are not learned yet). Systems that support individual educational goals can use annotation to mark links to concept pages that belong to the current goal (Brusilovsky, et al., 1994). Hiding technology can be used to hide links to concept pages with not yet learned prerequisites (Brusilovsky, et al., 1994; Forcheri, et al., 2001) and concept pages that do not belong to the current educational goal (Brusilovsky, et al., 1994; Grigoriadou, et al., 2001).

Note that the concept-based hyperspace is just one of the possible design approaches for AHS with single concept indexing. There are a few known systems, especially among early AHS (Pérez, et al., 1995) with single concept indexing but without concept-based navigation. The concept-based hyperspace in these systems is not formed since concepts have no external hyperspace representation and/or links between concepts and pages are purely conceptual and not used for hyperspace navigation. However, once discovered, the concept-based hyperspace approach is becoming more and more popular and I recommend it to all developers of AHS who plan to use single-concept indexing.

3.2.2. Page Indexing

The most popular design approach for multi-concept indexing is page indexing. With this approach, the whole hypermedia page (node) is indexed with domain model concepts. In other words, links ate created between a page and each concepts that is related to the content of the page (Figure 6). The simplest indexing approach is flat content-based indexing when a concept is included in a page index if some part of this page presents the piece of knowledge designated by the concept (Brusilovsky, et al., 1994; Henze, et al., 1999a; Laroussi, & Benahmed, 1998). A more general but less often used way to index the pages is to add the role for each concept in the page index (role-based indexing). The most popular role is "prerequisite": a concept is included in a page index if a student has to know this concept to understand the content of the page (Brusilovsky, et al., 1998b; Brusilovsky, et al., 1996a; De Bra, et al., 1998). Other roles can be used to specify the kind of contribution that the page is provided to learning this concept (introduction, main presentation, example, etc). Weights also can be used in multi-concept page indexing to show how much the page contributes to learning the concept (De Bra, et al., 2001).

Page indexing is a relatively simple approach. It can be applied even with vector domain models with no links between concepts (De Bra, 1996; Laroussi, et al., 1998). At the same time, indexing is a very powerful mechanism, because it provides the system with knowledge about the content of its pages. It opens the way for several adaptation techniques. With content-based indexing, the system knows which concepts are presented on a page. It can be used by various direct guidance, annotation and hiding techniques. Index-based guidance was used in ISIS-Tutor, ELM-ART and InterBook to recommend the "next best" page. Annotation was used to show the educational state of the page. For example, ELM-ART and ISIS tutor introduced a traffic light metaphor for annotation to distinguish and annotate the following important cases: the page is not ready to be learned (contains concepts which have not yet learned prerequisite concepts, red traffic light), the page is recommended (ready to be learned, contains concepts which are a part of the current learning goal, green traffic light). Prerequisite links can also be used to support simple adaptive presentation. For example, when LISP-Critic (Fischer, Mastaglio, Reeves, & Rieman, 1990) presents a page which has unknown prerequisite concepts, it inserts explanations of all the unknown concepts before the main content of the page. In the same context, ELM-ART and InterBook insert a warning message/image before the start of the page.

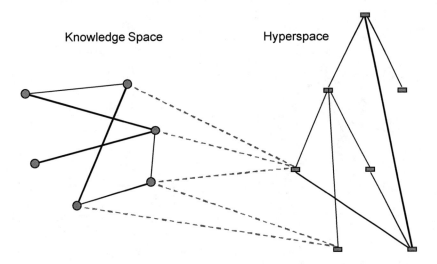

Figure 6. Multi-concept page indexing

3.2.3. Fragment Indexing

Fragment indexing is not a very popular indexing approach yet, but it is the most precise one. The idea of the approach is to divide the content of the hypermedia page into a set of fragments and to index some (or even all) of these fragments with domain model concepts which are related to the content of this fragment (Figure 7). Similarly to the page indexing approach it can be used even with a unstructured vector domain models. The difference is that indexing is done on a more fine-grained level. Generally, multi-concept indexing is used, though with smaller fragments it is often possible to use exactly one concept to index a fragment. In both cases the fragment indexing approach gives the system a more fine-grained knowledge about the content of the page: the system knows what is presented in each indexed fragment. This knowledge can be effectively used for advanced adaptive presentation. Depending on the level of user knowledge about the concepts presented in a particular fragment, the system can hide the fragment from the user (Boyle, & Encarnacion, 1994; De Bra, et al., 1998; Kobsa, Müller, & Nill, 1994; Stern, et al., 2000), shade it (Hothi, Hall, & Sly, 2000) or use an alternative way to present this fragment (Beaumont, 1994). Advanced adaptive presentation, of course, has its price – a more precise and more time-consuming indexing.

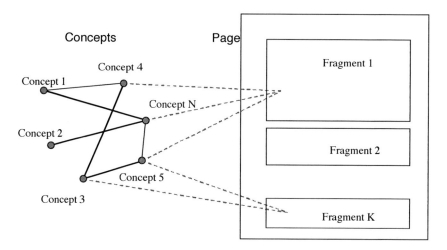

Figure 7. Fragment indexing approach

A good example is provided by MetaDoc (Boyle, et al., 1994), the first system that implements this approach. MetaDoc not only indexes some text fragments with related concepts, but also distinguishes three types of fragments: general text, additional explanations, and low-level details. The system decides whether to present the text fragment to the user or to hide it depending on the user's level of knowledge of the indexing concepts. A user with good knowledge of a particular concept will always get additional explanations of this concept (which can be boring for that user) hidden and all low level details presented. On the contrary, the user with poor knowledge of a concept will always get additional explanations of this concept and all low-level details (too complicated for that user) will be hidden. The user with medium level knowledge will see both kinds of text fragments.

At the moment only three AH authoring systems - AHA (De Bra, et al., 1998; De Bra, et al., 2001), WHURLE (Brailsford, Stewart, Zakaria, & Moore, 2002), and ALE (Specht, et al., 2002) support an author in composing a page from indexed fragments. AHA and WHURLE support adaptive hiding of fragments and ALE also supports adaptive page structuring that is based on student learning styles.

3.2.4. Mixing the Approaches

The three above approaches are the basic ones for the organization of hyperspace in AH systems. These approaches, however, do not contradict each other. Moreover, they are really complimentary because they are based on the same domain and user models. Using more than one approach opens the way to use more adaptation techniques because each approach supports its own set of techniques. For example, ISIS-Tutor (Brusilovsky, et al., 1994) uses a knowledge-based approach to build a part of the hyperspace representing the concepts of a programming language. Another part of the hyperspace (where the pages are problems and examples) is organized by indexing pages with concepts. This organization lets ISIS-Tutor to use the adaptation techniques from two corresponding groups. InterBook (Brusilovsky, et al., 1998b) which is based on the same ideas as ISIS-Tutor also uses a combination of knowledge-based and page indexing approaches.

3.3. Structuring the Hyperspace

An important step in designing an educational AHS is structuring the hyperspace. The hyperspace is formed by content pages connected by navigation links. The topology of connection between pages is usually referred to as hyperspace structure. In modern educational AHS hyperspace structuring is a separate design step that is independent (in the sense of choosing the design approach) from the knowledge structuring step. This section reviews several known hyperspace structuring approaches.

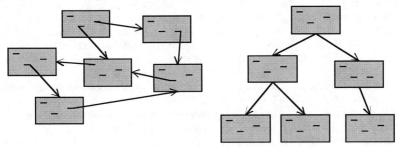

Figure 8. Unstructured hyperspace (left) and hierarchically structured hyperspace (right)

The first approach is *unstructured approach*, i.e. the case when this design step is skipped. It was the predominant "approach" in early educational AHS and it is still probably the most popular one. There are two reasons for that. First, concept-based hyperspace approach that is used in many education AHS produces quite rich and well-structured hyperspace that does not necessary require any other organization. Second, even in the systems that do not use concept-based approach the hyperspace is structured in some sense, since every page in it is connected to some other pages by classic hypertext reference links (Figure 8, left). There are educational AHS that use neither concept-based approach nor explicit hyperspace structure (De Bra, 1996; Pérez, et al., 1995) and even some design frameworks that impose no specific structuring requirements to the hyperspace and can work with an arbitrary structured hypertext (De Bra, et al., 1998). However, if no special strategy was used at the hyperspace design time, the resulting hyperspace may have a chaotic opportunistic structure that creates navigation and orientation problems to hypermedia users. It is not surprising that the vast majority of AH systems either use a concept-based approach or require the author to follow some explicit approach to structuring a hyperspace. Some recent systems oriented to Web-based education use both ways to obtain a rich well-structured hyperspace (Henze, et al., 1999a; Steinacker, et al., 1999).

The currently most popular approach to structuring the hyperspace is the hierarchical approach. ELM-ART (Brusilovsky, et al., 1996a) was the first adaptive hypermedia system that used a hierarchically structured hyperspace. This approach stimulated by the idea of an electronic book has been refined in InterBook (Brusilovsky, et al., 1998b) and later used in many educational AHS. With the hierarchical approach the hyperspace resembles a hierarchical structure of a textbook - with chapters, sections, and subsection (Figure 8). The hierarchy sets natural navigational paths from every node down to all descendant nodes and up to the ancestor node. Sequential "depth first" as well as "breadth first" navigational choices are usually also offered. One of the known benefits of a hierarchically structured hypertext is better navigation and orientation support in a hierarchy. This benefit of a hierarchical organization is especially important for categories of users that have navigation and orientation problems (Lin, 2003).

Another efficient approach to hyperspace structuring is "ASK" approach originally presented in (Bareiss, & Osgood, 1993). The goal of ASK approach is to build a "conversational" hyperspace with rhetorical links. With this approach a designer tries to anticipate a number of follow-up questions that the user may ask after visiting a page and provides links (each link is associated with a question) from the page to other pages in the hyperspace that may give answers to the questions. A generalization of this approach that uses a larger variety of rhetorical relationships is applied in MetaLinks (Murray, 2002) and Multibook (Steinacker, et al., 1999). We think that this promising approach will become more popular in the coming future.

Finally an interesting object-oriented approach to hyperspace structuring is used in KBS-Hyperbook system (Henze, et al., 1999a). The idea here is to build every page in the hyperspace as an external representation of some object. With this approach the hyperspace is turned into a network of objects that allows to use a standard object-oriented design approach and tools (such as UML) for hyperspace design. KBS-Hyperbook uses a good variety of objects of different level, such as chapter, lectures, examples, etc.

It is important to stress again that some of modern educational AHS often use a combination of several approaches to provide a better-structured hyperspace. In some cases, different approaches are used to structure different subspaces of the hyperspace. For example, in InterBook the set of glossary pages is structured as a concept-based hyperspace, while the remaining part of the hyperspace is formed by several hierarchically organized textbooks. In other cases two approaches can be used to "double-link" the same set of pages. For example, MetaLinks (Murray, 2002) uses a combination of the hierarchical and ASK approaches on the same set of textbook pages. Essentially, each of the structuring approaches allows the hyperspace designer to define a coherent set of links between pages. Thus the use of two approaches in parallel provides an opportunity to develop a more tightly interconnected hyperspace.

A special place should be devoted to the AHA! (De Bra, et al., 1998; De Bra, et al., 2001) structuring approach. The goal of this architecture is to model the information structure and functionality provided by a variety of adaptive hypermedia systems. To maintain the necessary level of generality, most recent versions of AHA completely blur the difference between pages and concepts. In AHA! both pages and concepts are modeled by AHA! pages/concepts (AHA! simply names them concepts). It allows the same mechanisms to be used for creating both content pages and domain concepts and the same linking and weight propagation mechanism to be used for defining the domain model, the hyperspace, and for linking these parts together. This generalized information model serves as a basis for a similarly generalized student model. Each page/concept may have any number of numeric properties (such as knowledge, interest, or simply number of visits) that can be propagated along different kinds of links (De Bra, Aerts, & Rousseau, 2002a; De Bra, Aerts, Smits, & Stash, 2002b). This generalized model can effectively simulate most known overlay and historic models while keeping enough potential for future development.

4. AUTHORING STAGE: HOW TO GET IT ALL INSIDE THE COMPUTER

Adaptive educational hypermedia is a reasonably mature field. Ten years of development brought to life dozens of experimental and practical systems and a good number of design approaches. Still, the field is probably too young to produce a good number of authoring tools, i.e., toolkits, systems, or shells that can be used by non-programming authors to develop an educational AHS. Two hands are still enough to count existing authoring systems (Table 2). The reason for that is reasonably clear. Before producing a real authoring tool, a research group has to develop an explicit design approach that usually requires developing one or more educational AHS. As shown on Table 2, existing authoring systems were produced by research groups that had some previous experience in developing AHS. In addition to that, there are several systems that were created as design frameworks such as CAMELEON (Laroussi, et al., 1998), PaKMaS (Süß, et al., 2000) RATH (Hockemeyer, et al., 1998), SKILL (Neumann, et al., 1998), ITMS (Mitsuhara, Kurose, Ochi, & Yano, 2001). These frameworks are application-independent and can be applied by their authors to rapid development of educational AHS in different domains. These design frameworks, however, have not yet reached the level of real tools that can be used by non-programming users outside of the original design team.

Generally, the basic steps of creating an educational AHS are not entirely different from steps in creating a regular hypertext system. In both cases the developer has to author the content objects and to specify the links between them. As in the case of generic hypertext and Web authoring, there are two major approaches used by authoring tools: the markup approach and GUI approach. In the markup approach the content of the pages and links between pages and concepts are authored in a regular word processor with the help of special markup language. With GUI (graphic user interface) approach they are created using special authoring user interface. In general, it could be a command-based, form-based or a direct manipulation interface, but all existing AHS authoring tools use form-based GUI.

Table 2. Authoring systems for developing adaptive educational hypermedia

Authoring tool	Earlier systems by the same authors
InterBook (Brusilovsky, et al., 1998b)	ITEM/PG (Brusilovsky, et al., 1993), ISIS-Tutor (Brusilovsky, et al., 1994), ELM-ART (Brusilovsky, et al., 1996a)
Web DCG (Vassileva, et al., 1998) and DCG+GTE (Vassileva, 1998)	TOBIE (Vassileva, 1992), DCG (Diessel, Lehmann, & Vassileva, 1994)
AHA! (De Bra, et al., 2001) and AHA! 2.0 (De Bra, et al., 2002b)	2L670 (De Bra, 1996)
ACE (Specht, et al., 1998) and ALE (Specht, et al., 2002)	AST (Specht, Weber, Heitmeyer, & Schöch, 1997), ELM-ART II (Weber, & Specht, 1997), ADI (Schöch, Specht, & Weber, 1998)
NetCoach/ART-WEB (Weber, et al., 2001b)	ELM-ART (Brusilovsky, et al., 1996a), AST (Specht, et al., 1997), ELM-ART II (Weber, et al., 1997), ADI (Schöch, et al., 1998), ELM-ART III (Weber, et al., 2001a)
ECSAIWeb (Sanrach, et al., 2000)	ESCA (Grandbastien, & Gavignet, 1994)
MetaLinks (Murray, 2002)	Tectonica Interactive (Murray, Condit, & Haugsjaa, 1998)
SIGUE (Carmona, et al., 2002)	(Trella, Conejo, & Guzmán, 2000)

The final product of both markup and GUI approaches is the same: the internal representation of knowledge and information in a some special form – a set of specially structured files or, more often, a database. This internal representation is used in the runtime by the AH engine to serve an AHS to the user. So, the authoring process is a bridge between the design and runtime stages, a process of getting the design inside the computer. The markup and GUI approaches provide two very different ways to achieve this goal. Since the difference between these two approaches is larger and more essential than the difference between ways to support the authoring steps listed in table 1, the following review of authoring tools is structured not by steps as the previous part, but by the authoring approaches.

4.1. Markup-based authoring tools

In many application areas markup approach precedes the GUI approach. InterBook (Brusilovsky, Schwarz, & Weber, 1996b), the first known system for developing AHS used the markup approach. More exactly, InterBook applied a rather unusual kind of markup approach that was inherited from earlier ELM-ART system (Brusilovsky, et al., 1996a). An author can create an adaptive textbook completely in Microsoft Word . Each textbook page or *section* in terms of InterBook was authored simply as a section in a Word document with a header on the top. All sections can reside in the same file or can be split in several Word files. The hierarchical structure of the hyperspace was defined as it is usually done in Word when creating hierarchical documents: by positioning descendant sections right after the ancestor section and assigning proper heading types to section headings. *Heading 1* was used for the top-level nodes in the tree, *Heading 2* for the second level nodes, and so on. The concept index for every section is authored in a special format with the use of a special font (Figure 9, top part). The index is divided into the prerequisite part (prefaced with *pre* tag on Figure 9) and the outcome part (prefaced *out* tag). Within each part, the concepts are simply listed by name. By using a few style conventions, we made Word work for the authors of an adaptive hyperbook as a kind of GUI. Different font types and styles work as markup operators. Since InterBook used a concept-based hyperspace approach, every concept may have an external representation as a glossary page. Glossary pages are created by the author as special subsections inside the last first-level section of the book named Glossary.

After the Word file with a textbook is created, it is saved in RTF format and converted to a real markup representation in the form of extended HTML (Figure 9, bottom part). What was expressed in Word with styles and fonts, is now expressed by markup commands. Since the markup commands had the form of specially structured HTML comments, the extended HTML file was still syntactically correct HTML and can be further edited/viewed using regular HTML tools. The extended HTML can be read directly by the InterBook runtime system that is based on Common LISP http server and converted to a LISP-based frame-styled internal representation.

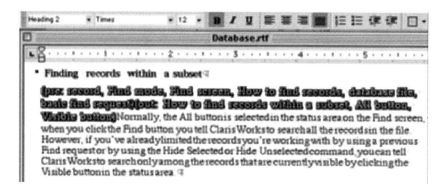

Figure 9. Authoring an adaptive hypertextbook in InterBook system. Top: Microsoft Word view. Bottom: Extended HTML view. On both parts "pre" starts the list of prerequisite concepts and "out" – the list of outcome concepts.

Using unusual markup approaches was rather typical in the early "before XML" days of Web-based educational (WBE) systems. Other (non-adaptive) WBE authoring tools also applied various extensions of HTML to author structured educational hypertext and to extend it with metadata (Owen, & Makedon, 1997). Nowadays XML offers a standard way of markup-based authoring supported by various XML editors and parsers.

A good example of XML markup-based authoring is AHA! (De Bra, et al., 1998; De Bra, et al., 2001). AHA! uses a multi-concept weighted indexing approach. Every page may have several prerequisite and several outcome concepts. Link weights can specify the contribution this page can provide for learning of each outcome concepts or a degree of user interest in some concepts. Each page is created as an XML file that includes specially tagged index part and a page content. The page content is created in HTML format with XML extensions that are used to author conditional fragments (fragment indexing). In addition to that, a special XML file defines domain concepts and connections between them. AHA! doesn't use concept-based hyperspace approach. Concepts are nothing but names and there is no content associated with them. However, the concepts can be connected by non-typed weight-propagating relationships. These relationships can be used to represent several kinds of semantic relationships. For example, it is possible to model is-a relationship when demonstrated knowledge of lower concepts contribute to the knowledge of higher level concepts (e.g., knowledge about Belgian chocolate contributes to the knowledge about Belgian food). The domain model XML file lets the author to specify these relationships between concepts. The runtime engine of AHA! based on Java servlets reads the authored XML files, converts it into internal object representation and maintains the adaptive interaction with the user. As was mentioned above, AHA! Version 2.0 (De Bra, Brusilovsky, & Conejo, 2002c) extends this flexible approach even further by removing the difference between concepts and pages and allowing an arbitrary number of weight-propagating relationships between them. Yet, the XML-based authoring in the new AHA! is very similar to the older versions of AHA! (De Bra, et al., 1998; De Bra, et al., 2001). In fact, it is the use of the flexible XML approach that allows AHA! to evolve so rapidly.

The markup-based authoring approach is certainly very attractive because of the combination of low cost and expressive power. The presence of XML with a wide range of supporting tools makes is especially easy for the developers to get their design inside the computer. XML-based markup languages are used in several design frameworks such as PaKMaS (Süß, et al., 2000) with its Learning Material Markup Language (LMML), WHURLE (Brailsford, et al., 2002) with a different XML-based language, and a number of recent small AHS (Bonfigli, Casadei, & Salomoni, 2000; Forcheri, et al., 2001; Kurhila, & Sutinen, 2000). The problem with this approach is that it provides too much freedom and too little support for the authors. It does not really matter for domain-oriented systems made by professional members of the design teams, but it is a serious problem for teachers and domain experts who are the target users of authoring tools. Even with using syntax-driven XML editors or other approaches (like the one used in InterBook) when the author does not require to write all XML tags, there are too many chances to make hard-to-find errors. A good example is indexing pages with concepts that in any markup-based approach will imply writing a list of concept names somewhere inside the markup-based page description. If the user will make a small typo in the concept name, the system will consider it as a different concept and the indexing will be wrong. In InterBook it was the most typical error of non-programming authors. Thus, in addition to XML editors, a variety of checking tools has to be provided with a markup-based authoring system to open it to non-programming authors

4.2. Form-based authoring tools

GUI-based authoring tools are harder to develop, so they usually follow markup-based tools. As already mentioned, all existing GUI-based tools use form-based interface. This kind of interface provides very good support for the non-professionals. The most obvious way to use a form-based interface for authoring educational AHS is to provide one input form for entering information about a concept and another form for entering information about a page. Text boxes on this form will provide a simple way to enter text content and pop-up menus with concept or page names supporting authoring links between pages and concepts. In some cases only one form may be required. For example, MetaLinks (Murray, 2002) uses the concept-based hyperspace approach where every page uses only one form. In other cases a separate form may be required for authoring different types of educational material. For example, KnowledgeTree authoring system (Brusilovsky, & Nijhawan, 2002) we use separate form for questions and examples that are special kinds of pages with learning material. ALE (Specht, et al., 2002) uses different forms to author learning material of different media types. The form based interface explicitly prompt the user what should be entered in each textbox and solves the problem of invalid input (i.e., typo in the concept name) by using menus and other form elements.

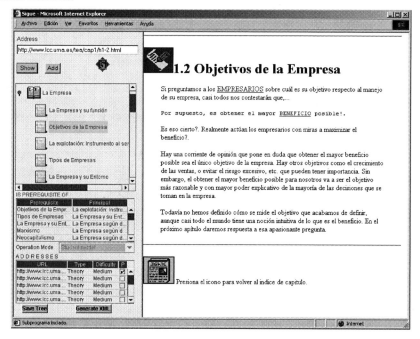

Figure 10. A form-based authoring interface in SIGUE system

A simple and straightforward example of practical form-based authoring is provided by SIGUE (Carmona, et al., 2002). SIGUE is an open corpus AHS - it relies exclusively on external Web-based educational content. SUGUE allows an author to organize and adaptively serve already existing content along the conceptual structure of the course. The core of a SIGUE course is a tree of concepts. The concepts are connected by prerequisite links that allow SIGUE to determine when each concept is ready to be learned and adaptively annotate links to the concept in ELM-ART/InterBook style. SIGUE uses a single-concept indexing paradigm: each external page is simply attached to one of the domain concepts. This straightforward organization requires a relatively simple authoring interface (Figure 10). Each

DEVELOPING ADAPTIVE EDUCATIONAL HYPERMEDIA 399

domain concept can be authored in just three simple steps: (a) creating a new concept in a proper place within the concept three; (b) defining prerequisite links; (c) attaching external educational content.

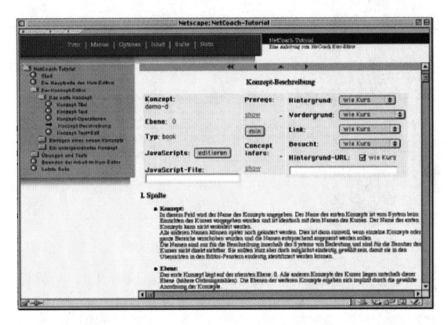

Figure 11. A form-based page/concept authoring interface in NetCoach system

A more complex example of a form-based interface is provided by NetCoach (Weber, et al., 2001b), the first commercially available tool for developing adaptive educational Web-based systems. NetCoach uses a concept-based hyperspace approach and supports both concept design and authoring and page authoring. As a results, its authoring interface is more complicated than in SIGUE. Pages/concepts in NetCoach also form a hierarchy, however links between concepts are more advanced than in SIGUE and include both prerequisite and inference (knowledge propagation) links. The form shown on (Figure 11) allows the author to provide page content (in HTML) as well as some presentation parameters, such as page background (*Hintergrund* in German) and behavior (in JavaScript). Other forms connected by links to the page/concept authoring form allow the author to specify prerequisite and inference links between the given page and other concept pages. The author can select an existing page to edit from an expandable menu (left side) or create a new descendant page of the current page. There are also separate forms for creating questions.

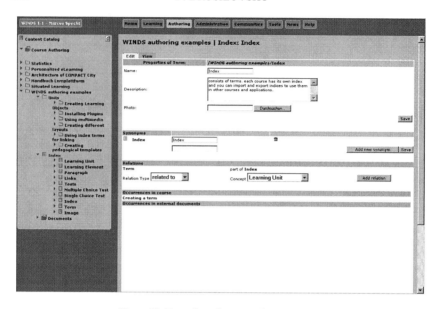

Figure 12. Form-based term authoring in ALE

The currently most advanced form-based interface is offered by ALE (Specht, et al., 2002). ALE strives to provide a complete courseware management system for practical courses. To compete with other state-of-the art systems, it provides an extensive content authoring interface that supports object-reuse and various multimedia formats. This is a rather unusual for AH authoring systems that typically provide a limited to none support to content authoring. From AH point of view, however, ALE is straightforward since it supports a relatively low level of adaptivity. Similarly to InterBook, an information space in ALE is formed by a network of index terms (representing knowledge about the domain) and a tree of content pages. Pages can be composed from reusable fragments. They are indexed by terms using simple multi-concept approach. A form for term authoring (Figure 12) allows specifying links, a brief description, and synonyms. A group of page-authoring forms allows inserting a new page in any place within a hierarchy and composing it from multiple fragments of different media types. An interesting feature of ALE is automatic page indexing. Since every concept in ALE is simply a set of synonym terms, their presence in content pages can be discovered by a simple text analysis. Automatic page indexing is avoided in modern AHS due to its low precision. However, as we have mentioned above, ALE does not maintain concept-level user model and uses very simple adaptation mechanisms. In this context the possibly low precision of indexing does not influence the adaptation.

As demonstrated by the above examples, nearly every AHS feature can be authored using a form-based interface, but it comes for a price. What requires just another tag in markup-based tools may require several interface widgets and overhead of positioning all these widgets in the main form and its sub-forms. While simple solutions can be authored with a relatively simple interface, an interface for

DEVELOPING ADAPTIVE EDUCATIONAL HYPERMEDIA

the systems with rich and competitively looking content or rich information structure tend to be complicated and expensive to develop.

To avoid problems with developing a more advanced content, early AH authoring systems attempted to rely on existing external tools. For example, InterBook authors were expected to use Microsoft Word formatting capability. MetaLinks (Murray, 2002) has used creatively a form-based authoring interface of Macintosh *Filemaker Pro* database. Most recent authoring systems such SIGUE tend to ignore the issue of content development completely. Indeed, it's just makes no sense to compete with modern Web content authoring tools such as *Macromedia Dreamweaver* or *Adobe GoLive*. Even ALE with its most advanced content authoring interface supports the use of externally authored content elements.

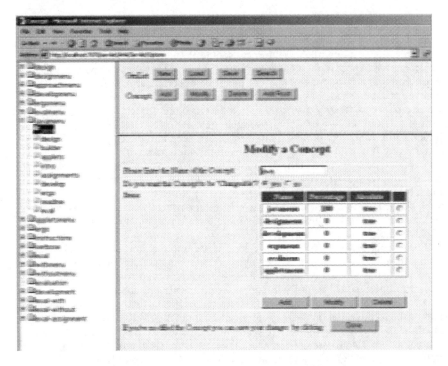

Figure 13. Domain model authoring in ALE.

Unfortunately, there are no form-based external tools that can help adaptive hypermedia authors to develop rich information structures. Here AH authoring tools have to provide full support. While simple structures can be successfully supported by a form-based interface as demonstrated by the systems above, more advanced structures still can't avoid a markup-based approach. In this context, a combination of a markup-based interface and a form-based interface can provide a good compromise between development cost and level of author's support. Some components of the target system where support and error prevention is essential can be created with a form-based interface, while the rest is authored with a markup approach. This combined interface will suite well an intermediate-level author: not completely computer-naive, but not one of the original tool developers either. AHA! (De Bra, et al., 1998) provides a good example. While the full power of AHA! (especially Version 2.0) is only available through the XML-based markup language, the system now also provide some form-based authoring tools (Figure 13) for the development of domain model (De Bra, et al., 2001). The authoring interface shown in Figure 13 allows an author to define new concepts, links between them, and weight propagation along the links. As it should be in the combined interface, the form-based editor produces a domain model description in the system's markup language that can be further extended by more demanding users.

5. A VIEW TO THE FUTURE

The previous sections of the review presented the current state of AH authoring. What can we expect in the next five years? I think that we may expect a splash of work in the area. The mature state of adaptive hypermedia as a field with a good number of established techniques and the need for more adaptive systems for Web-based education clearly serve as two major driving forces. These forces have brought many new teams in the area of adaptive Web-based educational hypermedia. A number of new frameworks have been introduced just within the last three years. It's natural to expect that several frameworks will be elaborated to the level of end-user oriented authoring tools just in a few years. The experience of the few existing authoring tools will help to shape out new tools and new generations of old tools. We may expect better markup-based and form-based tools.

I also expect the appearance of a new kind of "really graphic" user interface design tools. It's a definite contradiction that there is no graphic interface for getting highly graphical results of AHS design into the computer. The first graphic authoring tool that we will see really soon is a graphic editor of concept networks. With this editor the designer will be able to design and author connections between concepts just by placing concepts on a working window and connecting with a drag-and-drop interface. This tool will support both the design and authoring stages. A number of similar network editors exist currently in the field of concept-mapping and business presentation design, but all these tools are useful only with relatively small maps (under 50 nodes) and the main result of the work is the visual presentation of the network. As a result, these tools now can only be used during the design stage and for developing small networks. Future concept network editing tools will be very similar, but their main product will be an internal representation of the network in a database or XML markup form[2]. Gradually, they will also handle networks of 100 and more concepts. After concept editors we may expect the appearance of similar graphic tools for structuring the hyperspace and for indexing pages or fragments with domain model concepts.

---

[2] This prediction turned reality sooner than the author expected. While this book was in the process of publication, the first concept-network authoring tool for adaptive hypermedia system has been reported in (De Bra, et al., 2002a).

I also expect a gradual merge between two close approaches to authoring educational material. The one (reviewed in this paper) concerns authoring for adaptive Web-based educational systems. The other is the "new wave" in Web-based courseware authoring centered on learning objects, courseware reuse, metadata and standards. The authoring paradigm of this approach is quite similar to the one of adaptive systems. It is based on creating pools of learning objects of different level and indexing it with metadata. A Web/hypertext page with educational material is a typical learning object. One of the important kinds of metadata are learning objectives that are very similar to domain concepts from indexing point of view (they also can be used as outcomes or prerequisites of an educational object). Thus concept-indexed pages with educational material are not different from other reusable content objects indexed with metadata. With several adopted or coming standards in the area of metadata and metadata-enabled material (AICC, IEEE LTSC, IMS, SCORM) the metadata-based courseware re-use is reaching its maturity. More and more standard-compliant authoring tools are becoming available. We may expect that a number of authoring tools created for metadata-based courseware reuse approach will be quite useful for the authors of educational AHS. For example, there are some graphic tools for topic map editing in the courseware reuse field that are almost ready to be used as concept network editors (Coffey, & Cañas, 2001; Steinacker, et al., 2001). There are also some very good indexing tools that are almost ready to be used as concept indexers (Verhoeven, Cardinaels, Van Durm, Duval, & Olivié, 2001).

From the authoring and storage side adaptive hypermedia and courseware reuse approaches are quite similar. The difference is how the indexed material is used. In the courseware reuse approach the metadata are used by a search engine that helps a teacher to find and re-use educational material for his or her manually created course. An adaptive educational system uses it to decide whether a page of learning material is relevant in the current context and how to present the page and the links to it. There are no contractions between these goals so approaches may eventually use the same indexed educational material. There are already a few attempts to combine the adaptive hypermedia and metadata-based courseware re-use approaches in one framework (Brailsford, et al., 2002; Fischer, & Steinmetz, 2000; Specht, et al., 2001; Specht, et al., 2002; Steinacker, et al., 2001; Süß, et al., 2000). In the near future we should expect more powerful authoring systems and frameworks that combine adaptive hypermedia and courseware reusability ideas.

6. A VIEW TO THE PAST

This review is based on my personal (and probably subjective) view on AHS design based on my own work on adaptive hypermedia for about 10 years. Over these years my view on adaptive hypermedia and my understanding of it has broadened quite significantly. I was fortunate to work on adaptive hypermedia problems with several teams that were driven by different goals. I think, it has helped me to consider adaptive educational hypermedia from several prospects and to avoid a narrow and pragmatic view to it. To make my current prospect and viewpoint more clear to a reader, I risk to provide a brief history of my research on adaptive hypermedia. I hope, this section will explain how the change of projects and prospects has helped me to form the generalized view on adaptive hypermedia presented in this paper..

My research on adaptive educational hypermedia has started in 1991 at the Moscow State University with a group of students as an extension of my earlier work on curriculum sequencing in ITS (Brusilovsky, 1992). Our main focus was *adaptive navigation support,* currently one of the major AH technologies. We have developed two educational AH systems ITEM/PG (Brusilovsky, et al., 1993) and ISIS-Tutor (Brusilovsky, et al., 1994) and explored several ways of adaptive navigation support: direct guidance in the form of "teach me" button, adaptive annotation, and adaptive link removal. Our vision was that adaptive navigation support in educational hypermedia is "best of both worlds". Choosing the next task in an ITS with sequencing is based on machine intelligence. Choosing the next task in traditional hypermedia is based on human intelligence. Adaptive navigation support is an interface that can integrate the power of machine and human intelligence: a user is free to make a choice while still seeing an opinion of an intelligent system. Following this vision we considered adaptive hypermedia as a necessary *component of every ITS* (Brusilovsky, et al., 1993) and developed a specific authoring approach and a toolkit for developing adaptive hypermedia components for ITS (Brusilovsky, 1997).

The work on ELM-ART (Brusilovsky, et al., 1996a; Weber, et al., 2001a), one of the first practical Web-based ITS helped me to extend and re-consider the original approach as well as to adopt it to the hypermedia-centered Web context. Our team has adopted a new *electronic textbook* vision for an adaptive educational hypermedia systems. This approach and this vision have been refined and extended during our subsequent work on InterBook system (Brusilovsky, et al., 1998b), the first authoring system for adaptive educational hypermedia.

Two years of practical work in Carnegie Technology Education, a company focused on Web-based education and several years of participation in IEEE Learning Technology Standardization committee helped me to understand and appreciate the problems of WBE from both academic and industrial prospects. While my understanding of "what can be adapted" in adaptive educational hypermedia has not been significantly changed, my understanding of what is an adaptive educational hypermedia system and how it can be designed was considerably broadened and affected by the needs of practical Web-based education. I now consider adaptive hypermedia as a generic way to organize and design any hypermedia-based educational resource. It includes our earlier paradigms such as hypermedia-based ITS and adaptive electronic textbooks as well as a number of other known paradigms such as adaptive Web-based courses, pools of re-usable educational objects and even distributed educational hypermedia. From my point of view, all known types of adaptive hypermedia systems, while looking different to a casual observer, are really very similar. They can be viewed as instantiations of the same "universal" design approach and use subsets of the same collection of AH techniques. This is the viewpoint that I have attempted to communicate in this paper.

7. CONCLUSIONS

The availability of authoring frameworks and tools is gradually changing the situation in the field of adaptive hypermedia. Just a few years ago designing an adaptive hypermedia system was a large time-consuming endeavor that could only be attempted by skilled teams with programming expertise. With design frameworks and tools at hand, a less prepared teams and even a single teacher can create a meaningful adaptive hypermedia system. The challenge for the authors is to be aware about the variety of available tools and pick the right tool for the work. We hope that the anatomy of educational AHS design and a survey of existing approaches and tools provided in this paper will be helpful for the researchers in the field of adaptive hypermedia and authors of practical educational AHS.

8. REFERENCES

Bareiss, R., & Osgood, R. (1993). Applying AI models to the design of exploratory hypermedia systems. *Proceedings of Fifth ACM Conference on Hypertext*, 1993. Seattle, WA, ACM. - pp. 94-105.

Beaumont, I. (1994). User modeling in the interactive anatomy tutoring system ANATOM-TUTOR. *User Modeling and User-Adapted Interaction*, 4 (1), 21-45.

Bonfigli, M. E., Casadei, G., & Salomoni, P. (2000). Adaptive Intelligent Hypermedia using XML. *Proceedings of ACM Symposium on Applied Computing*, March 19-21, 2000. Como, Italy, http://www.acm.org/conferences/sac/sac00/Proceed/FinalPapers/WW-06.

Boyle, C., & Encarnacion, A. O. (1994). MetaDoc: an adaptive hypertext reading system. *User Modeling and User-Adapted Interaction*, 4 (1), 1-19.

Brailsford, T. J., Stewart, C. D., Zakaria, M. R., & Moore, A. (2002). Autonavigation, links, and narrative in an adaptive Web-based integrated learning environment. *Proceedings of World Wide Web 2002 Conference*, May 7-11, 2002. Honolulu, HI, - pp. .

Brusilovsky, P. (1994). Student model centered architecture for intelligent learning environment. *Proceedings of Fourth International Conference on User Modeling*, 15-19 August 1994. Hyannis, MA, MITRE. - pp. 31-36, available online at http://www2.sis.pitt.edu/~peterb/papers/UM94.html.

Brusilovsky, P. (1996). Methods and techniques of adaptive hypermedia. *User Modeling and User-Adapted Interaction*, 6 (2-3), 87-129.

Brusilovsky, P. (1997). Integrating hypermedia and intelligent tutoring technologies: from systems to authoring tools. In P. Kommers, A. Dovgiallo, V. Petrushin, & P. Brusilovsky (Eds.), *New media and telematic technologies for education in Eastern European countries* (pp. 129-140). Enschede: Twente University Press.

Brusilovsky, P. (2000). Concept-based courseware engineering for large scale Web-based education. In G. Davies, & C. Owen (Eds.), *Proceedings of WebNet'2000, World Conference of the WWW and Internet*, Oct. 30 - Nov. 4, 2000. San Antonio, TX, AACE. - pp. 69-74.

Brusilovsky, P., & Anderson, J. (1998a). ACT-R electronic bookshelf: An adaptive system for learning cognitive psychology on the Web. In H. Maurer, & R. G. Olson (Eds.), *Proceedings of WebNet'98, World Conference of the WWW, Internet, and Intranet*, November 7-12, 1998. Orlando, FL, AACE. - pp. 92-97.

Brusilovsky, P., Eklund, J., & Schwarz, E. (1998b). Web-based education for all: A tool for developing adaptive courseware. *Computer Networks and ISDN Systems*, 30 (1-7), 291-300.

Brusilovsky, P., & Nijhawan, H. (2002). A Framework for Adaptive E-Learning Based on Distributed Re-usable Learning Activities. In M. Driscoll, & T. C. Reeves (Eds.), *Proceedings of World Conference on E-Learning, E-Learn 2002*, October 15-19, 2002. Montreal, Canada, AACE. - pp. 154-161.

Brusilovsky, P., & Pesin, L. (1994). An intelligent learning environment for CDS/ISIS users. In J. J. Levonen, & M. T. Tukianinen (Eds.), *Proceedings of The interdisciplinary workshop on complex learning in computer environments (CLCE94)*, May 16-19, 1994. Joensuu, Finland, EIC. - pp. 29-33, available online at http://cs.joensuu.fi/~mtuki/www_clce.270296/Brusilov.html.

Brusilovsky, P., Pesin, L., & Zyryanov, M. (1993). Towards an adaptive hypermedia component for an intelligent learning environment. In L. J. Bass, J. Gornostaev, & C. Unger (Ed.), *3rd International Conference on Human-Computer Interaction, EWHCI'93* (Vol. 753, pp. 348-358). Berlin: Springer-Verlag.

Brusilovsky, P., & Schwarz, E. (1997). Concept-based navigation in educational hypermedia and its implementation on WWW. In T. Müldner, & T. C. Reeves (Eds.), Educational Multimedia/Hypermedia and Telecommunications, 1997, *Proceedings of ED-MEDIA/ED-TELECOM'97 - World Conference on Educational Multimedia/Hypermedia and World Conference on Educational Telecommunications*, June 14-19, 1997. Calgary, Canada, AACE. - pp. 112-117.

Brusilovsky, P., Schwarz, E., & Weber, G. (1996a). ELM-ART: An intelligent tutoring system on World Wide Web. In C. Frasson, G. Gauthier, & A. Lesgold (Ed.), *Third International Conference on Intelligent Tutoring Systems, ITS-96* (pp. 261-269). Berlin: Springer Verlag, available online at http://www.contrib.andrew.cmu.edu/~plb/ITS96.html.

Brusilovsky, P., Schwarz, E., & Weber, G. (1996b). A tool for developing adaptive electronic textbooks on WWW. In H. Maurer (Eds.), *Proceedings of WebNet'96, World Conference of the Web Society*, October 15-19, 1996. San Francisco, CA, AACE. - pp. 64-69, available online at http://www.contrib.andrew.cmu.edu/~plb/WebNet96.html.

Brusilovsky, P. L. (1992). A framework for intelligent knowledge sequencing and task sequencing. In C. Frasson, G. Gauthier, & G. I. McCalla (Ed.), *Second International Conference on Intelligent Tutoring Systems, ITS'92* (pp. 499-506). Berlin: Springer-Verlag.

Brusilovsky, P. L. (1993). Towards an intelligent environment for learning introductory programming. In G. Dettori, B. du Boulay, & E. Lemut (Eds.), *Cognitive Models and Intelligent Environments for Learning Programming* (pp. 114-124). Berlin: Springer-Verlag.

Carmona, C., Bueno, D., EduardoGuzman, & Conejo, R. (2002). SIGUE: Making Web Courses Adaptive. In P. De Bra, P. Brusilovsky, & R. Conejo (Eds.), *Proceedings of Second International Conference on Adaptive Hypermedia and Adaptive Web-Based Systems (AH'2002)*, May 29-31, 2002. Málaga, Spain, - pp. 376-379.

Coffey, J. W., & Cañas, A. J. (2001). Tools to Foster Course and Content Reuse in Online Instructional Systems. In W. Fowler, & J. Hasebrook (Eds.), *Proceedings of WebNet'2001, World Conference of the WWW and Internet*, October 23-27, 2001. Orlando, FL, AACE. - pp. 207-213.

De Bra, P., Aerts, A., & Rousseau, B. (2002a). Concept Relationship Types for AHA! 2.0. In M. Driscoll, & T. C. Reeves (Eds.), *Proceedings of World Conference on E-Learning, E-Learn 2002*, October 15-19, 2002. Montreal, Canada, AACE. - pp. 1386-1389.

De Bra, P., Aerts, A., Smits, D., & Stash, N. (2002b). AHA! Version 2.0: More Adaptation Flexibility for Authors. In M. Driscoll, & T. C. Reeves (Eds.), *Proceedings of World Conference on E-Learning, E-Learn 2002*, October 15-19, 2002. Montreal, Canada, AACE. - pp. 240-246.

De Bra, P., Brusilovsky, P., & Conejo, R. (Ed.). (2002c). *Adaptive Hypermedia and Adaptive Web-based Systems, AH2002*. Berlin: Springer-Verlag.

De Bra, P., & Calvi, L. (1998). AHA! An open Adaptive Hypermedia Architecture. *The New Review of Hypermedia and Multimedia*, 4 115-139.

De Bra, P., & Ruiter, J.-P. (2001). AHA! Adaptive hypermedia for all. In W. Fowler, & J. Hasebrook (Eds.), *Proceedings of WebNet'2001, World Conference of the WWW and Internet*, October 23-27, 2001. Orlando, FL, AACE. - pp. 262-268.

De Bra, P. M. E. (1996). Teaching Hypertext and Hypermedia through the Web. *Journal of Universal Computer Science*, 2 (12), 797-804, available online at http://www.iicm.edu/jucs_2_12/teaching_hypertext_and_hypermedia.

de La Passardiere, B., & Dufresne, A. (1992). Adaptive navigational tools for educational hypermedia. In I. Tomek (Ed.), *ICCAL'92, 4-th International Conference on Computers and Learning* (pp. 555-567). Berlin: Springer-Verlag.

Diessel, T., Lehmann, A., & Vassileva, J. (1994). Individualised course generation: A marriage between CAL and ICAL. *Computers and Education*, 22 (1/2), 57-64.

Elsom-Cook, M. T., & O'Malley, C. (1990). ECAL: Bridging the gap between CAL and intelligent tutoring systems. *Computers and Education*, 15 (1), 69-81.

Fischer, G., Mastaglio, T., Reeves, B., & Rieman, J. (1990). Minimalist explanations in knowledge-based systems. *Proceedings of 23-th Annual Hawaii International Conference on System Sciences*, January 2-5, 1990. Kailua-Kona, HI, IEEE. - pp. 309-317.

Fischer, S., & Steinmetz, R. (2000). Automatic creation of exercises in adaptive hypermedia learning systems. *Proceedings of Eleventh ACM Conference on Hypertext and hypermedia (Hypertext 2000)*, May 30 - June 3, 2000. San Antonio, TX, ACM Press. - pp. 49-55.

Forcheri, P., Molfino, M. T., Moretti, S., & Quarati, A. (2001). An Approach to the Development of Re-Usable and Adaptive Web Based Courses. In W. Fowler, & J. Hasebrook (Eds.), *Proceedings of WebNet'2001, World Conference of the WWW and Internet*, October 23-27, 2001. Orlando, FL, AACE. - pp. 1043-1048.

Gonschorek, M., & Herzog, C. (1995). Using hypertext for an adaptive helpsystem in an intelligent tutoring system. In J. Greer (Eds.), Artificial Intelligence in Education, *Proceedings of AI-ED'95, 7th World Conference on Artificial Intelligence in Education*, 16-19 August 1995. Washington, DC, AACE. - pp. 274-281.

Grandbastien, M., & Gavignet, E. (1994). ESCA: An environment to design and instantiate learning material. In T. de Jong, & L. Sarti (Eds.), *Design and production of multimedia and simulation-based learning material* (pp. 31-44). Dordrecht: Kluwer Academic Publishers.

Grigoriadou, M., Papanikolaou, K., Kornilakis, H., & Magoulas, G. (2001). INSPIRE: An INtelligent System for Personalized Instruction in a Remote Environment. In P. D. Bra, P. Brusilovsky, & A. Kobsa (Eds.), *Proceedings of Third workshop on Adaptive Hypertext and Hypermedia*, July 14, 2001. Sonthofen, Germany, Technical University Eindhoven. - pp. 13-24.

Henze, N., Nacuer, K., Nejdl, W., & Wolpers, M. (1999a). Adaptive hyperbooks for constructivist teaching. *Künstliche Intelligenz*, (4), 26-31.

Henze, N., & Nejdl, W. (1999b). *Student modeling for KBS Hyperbook system using Bayesian networks* (Report # . University of Hannover, available online at http://www.kbs.uni-hannover.de/paper/99/adaptivity.html.

Hockemeyer, C., Held, T., & Albert, D. (1998). RATH - A relational adaptive tutoring hypertext WWW-environment based on knowledge space theory. In C. Alvegård (Ed.), *Proceedings of CALISCE'98, 4th International conference on Computer Aided Learning and Instruction in Science and Engineering*, June 15-17, 1998. Göteborg, Sweden, - pp. 417-423.

Hohl, H., Böcker, H.-D., & Gunzenhäuser, R. (1996). Hypadapter: An adaptive hypertext system for exploratory learning and programming. *User Modeling and User-Adapted Interaction*, 6 (2-3), 131-156.

Hothi, J., Hall, W., & Sly, T. (2000). A study comparing the use of shaded text and adaptive navigation support in adaptive hypermedia. In P. Brusilovsky, O. Stock, & C. Strapparava (Ed.), *Adaptive Hypermedia and Adaptive Web-based systens* (pp. 335-342). Berlin: Springer-Verlag.

Kay, J., & Kummerfeld, R. J. (1994). An individualised course for the C programming language. *Proceedings of Second International WWW Conference*, 17-20 October, 1994. Chicago, IL, - pp. , available online at http://www.ncsa.uiuc.edu/SDG/IT94/Proceedings/Educ/kummerfeld/kummerfeld.html.

Kobsa, A., Müller, D., & Nill, A. (1994). KN-AHS: An adaptive hypertext client of the user modeling system BGP-MS. *Proceedings of Fourth International Conference on User Modeling*, 15-19 August 1994. Hyannis, MA, MITRE. - pp. 31-36.

Kurhila, J., & Sutinen, E. (2000). From intelligent tutoring systems to intelligent learning materials. In J. Bordeau, & R. Heller (Eds.), Educational Multimedia, Hypermedia and Telecommunications, 2000, *Proceedings of ED-MEDIA'2000 - World Conference on Educational Multimedia, Hypermedia and Telecommunications*, June 26 - July 1, 2000. Montréal, Canada, AACE. - pp. 511-516.

Laroussi, M., & Benahmed, M. (1998). Providing an adaptive learning through the Web case of CAMELEON: Computer Aided MEdium for LEarning on Networks. In C. Alvegård (Eds.), *Proceedings of CALISCE'98, 4th International conference on Computer Aided Learning and Instruction in Science and Engineering*, June 15-17, 1998. Göteborg, Sweden, - pp. 411-416.

Lin, D.-Y. M. (2003). Hypertext for the aged: effects of text topologies. *Computers in Human Behavior*, 19 (2003), 201-209.

Milosavljevic, M. (1997). Augmenting the user's knowledge via comparison. In A. Jameson, C. Paris, & C. Tasso (Ed.), *6th International Conference on User Modeling, UM97* (pp. 119-130). Wien: SpringerWienNewYork.

Mitsuhara, H., Kurose, Y., Ochi, Y., & Yano, Y. (2001). ITMS: Individualized Teaching Material System-adaptive integration of web pages distributed in some servers. *Proceedings of ED-MEDIA'2001 - World Conference on Educational Multimedia, Hypermedia and Telecommunications*, June 25-30, 2001. Tampere, Finland, AACE. - pp. 1333-1338.

Murray, T. (2001). Characteristics and Affordances of Adaptive Hyperbooks. In W. Fowler, & J. Hasebrook (Eds.), *Proceedings of WebNet'2001, World Conference of the WWW and Internet*, October 23-27, 2001. Orlando, FL, AACE. - pp. 899-904.

Murray, T. (2002). MetaLinks: Authoring and affordances for conceptual and narrative flow in adaptive hyperbooks. *International Journal of Artificial Intelligence in Education*, **13** (1), To appear.

Murray, T., Condit, C., & Haugsjaa, E. (1998). MetaLinks: A preliminary framework for concept-based adaptive hypermedia. *Proceedings of Workshop "WWW-Based Tutoring" at 4th International Conference on Intelligent Tutoring Systems (ITS'98)*, August 16-19, 1998. San Antonio, TX, - pp. , available online at http://www-aml.cs.umass.edu/~stern/webits/itsworkshop/murray.html.

Neumann, G., & Zirvas, J. (1998). SKILL - A scallable internet-based teaching and learning system. In H. Maurer, & R. G. Olson (Eds.), *Proceedings of WebNet'98, World Conference of the WWW, Internet, and Intranet*, November 7-12, 1998. Orlando, FL, AACE. - pp. 688-693, available online at http://nestroy.wi-inf.uni-essen.de/Forschung/Publikationen/skill-webnet98.ps.

Oberlander, J., O'Donell, M., Mellish, C., & Knott, A. (1998). Conversation in the museum: experiments in dynamic hypermedia with the intelligent labeling explorer. *The New Review of Multimedia and Hypermedia*, **4** 11-32.

Owen, C. B., & Makedon, F. (1997). ASML: Web authoring by site, not by hidnsight. In T. Müldner, & T. C. Reeves (Eds.), Educational Multimedia/Hypermedia and Telecommunications, 1997, *Proceedings of ED-MEDIA/ED-TELECOM'97 - World Conference on Educational Multimedia/Hypermedia and World Conference on Educational Telecommunications*, June 14-19, 1997. Calgary, Canada, AACE. - pp. 677-682.

Pérez, T., Gutiérrez, J., & Lopistéguy, P. (1995). An adaptive hypermedia system. In J. Greer (Eds.), Artificial Intelligence in Education, *Proceedings of AI-ED'95, 7th World Conference on Artificial Intelligence in Education*, 16-19 August 1995. Washington, DC, AACE. - pp. 351-358.

Pilar da Silva, D., Durm, R. V., Duval, E., & Olivié, H. (1998). *Concepts and documents for adaptive educational hypermedia: a model and a prototype*. Computing Science Reports, Eindhoven: Eindhoven University of Technology, 35-43.

Sanrach, C., & Grandbastien, M. (2000). ECSAIWeb: A Web-based authoring system to create adaptive learning systems. In P. Brusilovsky, O. Stock, & C. Strapparava (Ed.), *Adaptive Hypermedia and Adaptive Web-based Systems, AH2000* (pp. 214-226). Berlin: Springer-Verlag.

Schöch, V., Specht, M., & Weber, G. (1998). "ADI" - an empirical evaluation of a tutorial agent. In T. Ottmann, & I. Tomek (Eds.), Educational Multimedia/Hypermedia and Telecommunications, 1998, *Proceedings of ED-MEDIA/ED-TELECOM'98 - 10th World Conference on Educational Multimedia and Hypermedia and World Conference on Educational Telecommunications*, June, 20-25, 1998. Freiburg, Germany, AACE. - pp. 1242-1247.

Schwarz, E. (1998). Self-organized goal-oriented tutoring in adaptive hypermedia environments. In B. P. Goettl, H. M. Halff, C. L. Redfield, & V. J. Shute (Ed.), *4th International Conference, ITS-98* (pp. 294-303). Berlin: Springer-Verlag.

Specht, M., & Klemke, R. (2001). ALE - Adaptive Learning Environment. In W. Fowler, & J. Hasebrook (Eds.), *Proceedings of WebNet'2001, World Conference of the WWW and Internet*, October 23-27, 2001. Orlando, FL, AACE. - pp. 1155-1160.

Specht, M., Kravcik, M., Klemke, R., Pesin, L., & Hüttenhain, R. (2002). Adaptive Learning Environment (ALE) for Teaching and Learning in WINDS. In *Second International Conference on Adaptive Hypermedia and Adaptive Web-Based Systems (AH'2002)* (Vol. 2347, pp. 572-581). Berlin: Springer-Verlag.

Specht, M., & Oppermann, R. (1998). ACE - Adaptive Courseware Environment. *The New Review of Hypermedia and Multimedia*, **4** 141-161.

Specht, M., Weber, G., Heitmeyer, S., & Schöch, V. (1997). AST: Adaptive WWW-Courseware for Statistics. In P. Brusilovsky, J. Fink, & J. Kay (Eds.), *Proceedings of Workshop "Adaptive Systems and User Modeling on the World Wide Web" at 6th International Conference on User Modeling, UM97*, June 2, 1997. Chia Laguna, Sardinia, Italy, Carnegie Mellon Online. - pp. 91-95, available online at http://www.contrib.andrew.cmu.edu/~plb/UM97_workshop/Specht.html.

Steinacker, A., Faatz, A., Seeberg, C., Rimac, I., Hörmann, S., Saddik, A. E., & Steinmetz, R. (2001). MediBook: Combining semantic networks with metadata for learning resources to build a Web based learning system. *Proceedings of ED-MEDIA'2001 - World Conference on Educational Multimedia, Hypermedia and Telecommunications*, June 25-30, 2001. Tampere, Finland, AACE. - pp. 1790-1795.

Steinacker, A., Seeberg, C., Rechenberger, K., Fischer, S., & Steinmetz, R. (1999). Dynamically generated tables of contents as guided tours in adaptive hypermedia systems.Educational

Multimedia/Hypermedia and Telecommunications, 1998, *Proceedings of ED-MEDIA/ED-TELECOM'99 - 11th World Conference on Educational Multimedia and Hypermedia and World Conference on Educational Telecommunications,* Seattle, WA, AACE. - pp. .

Stern, M. K., & Woolf, B. P. (2000). Adaptive content in an online lecture system. In P. Brusilovsky, O. Stock, & C. Strapparava (Ed.), *Adaptive Hypermedia and Adaptive Web-based systens* (pp. 225-238). Berlin: Springer-Verlag.

Süß, C., Kammerl, R., & Freitag, B. (2000). A teachware management framework for multiple teaching strategies. In J. Bordeau, & R. Heller (Eds.), Educational Multimedia/Hypermedia and Telecommunications, 1998, *Proceedings of ED-MEDIA'2000 - World Conference on Educational Multimedia, Hypermedia and Telecommunications,* June 26 - July 1, 2000. Montréal, Canada, AACE. - pp. ??

Trella, M., Conejo, R., & Guzmán, E. (2000). A Web-based socratic tutor for trees recognition. In P. Brusilovsky, O. Stock, & C. Strapparava (Ed.), *Adaptive Hypermedia and Adaptive Web-based Systems, AH2000* (pp. 239-249). Berlin: Springer-Verlag.

Vassileva, J. (1990). An architecture and methodology for creating a domain-independent, plan-based intelligent tutoring system. *Educational and Training Technology International,* 27 (4), 386-397.

Vassileva, J. (1992). Dynamic CAL-courseware generation within an ITS-shell architecture. In I. Tomek (Ed.), *4th International Conference, ICCAL'92* (Vol. 602, pp. 581-591). Berlin: Springer-Verlag.

Vassileva, J. (1998). DCG + GTE: Dynamic Courseware Generation with Teaching Expertise. *Instructional Science,* 26 (3/4), 317-332.

Vassileva, J., & Deters, R. (1998). Dynamic courseware generation on the WWW. *British Journal of Educational Technology,* 29 (1), 5-14.

Verhoeven, B., Cardinaels, K., Van Durm, R., Duval, E., & Olivié, H. (2001). Experiences with the ARIADNE pedagogical document repository. *Proceedings of ED-MEDIA'2001 - World Conference on Educational Multimedia, Hypermedia and Telecommunications,* June 25-30, 2001. Tampere, Finland, AACE. - pp. 1949-1954.

Weber, G., & Brusilovsky, P. (2001a). ELM-ART: An adaptive versatile system for Web-based instruction. *International Journal of Artificial Intelligence in Education,* 12 (4), 351-384, available online at http://cbl.leeds.ac.uk/ijaied/abstracts/Vol_12/weber.html.

Weber, G., Kuhl, H.-C., & Weibelzahl, S. (2001b). Developing adaptive internet based courses with the authoring system NetCoach. In P. D. Bra, P. Brusilovsky, & A. Kobsa (Eds.), *Proceedings of Third workshop on Adaptive Hypertext and Hypermedia,* July 14, 2001. Sonthofen, Germany, Technical University Eindhoven. - pp. 35-48, available online at http://wwwis.win.tue.nl/ah2001/papers/GWeber-UM01.pdf.

Weber, G., & Specht, M. (1997). User modeling and adaptive navigation support in WWW-based tutoring systems. In A. Jameson, C. Paris, & C. Tasso (Ed.), *6th International Conference on User Modeling* (pp. 289-300). Wien: SpringerWienNewYork, available online at http://www.psychologie.uni-trier.de:8000/projects/ELM/Papers/UM97-WEBER.html.

Wenger, E. (1987). *Artificial intelligence and tutoring systems. Computational approaches to the communication of knowledge.* Los Altos: Morgan Kaufmann.

RANDALL SPARKS, SCOTT DOOLEY, LORI MEISKEY &
RICK BLUMENTHAL

Chapter 14

THE LEAP AUTHORING TOOL:

Supporting Complex Courseware Authoring Through Reuse, Rapid Prototyping, and Interactive Visualizations

Abstract. An important goal of current work in computer-based learning environments is to develop systems that combine the richness and effectiveness of an individually crafted intelligent tutoring system (ITS) with the generality and flexibility of a computer-assisted instruction (CAI) authoring tool. Our effort to achieve this goal is demonstrated in the Learn, Explore and Practice (LEAP^{sm}) ITS shell and its courseware development component, The LEAP Authoring Tool (LAT).[1] The LAT was developed for use by non-programmer subject matter experts to create courseware for use in the LEAP system, which was used to train telephone company customer service representatives to handle customer requests over the telephone while interacting with several computer-based database systems. In this paper we will provide a brief description of LEAP and then describe the goals, design, implementation, and evaluation of the LAT, and discuss the process we followed in the development of the LAT and some of the lessons we learned along the way.

1. INTRODUCTION

LEAP is designed around the tenet that the learning of a complex task is best achieved in a rich "apprenticeship environment", in which skills and knowledge are acquired through realistic exercises conducted in a realistic context (Collins, Brown & Newman, 1989; Lave & Wenger, 1991; Lesgold et al., 1992). The primary goals of the LEAP and LAT development efforts were to: (1) create this type of apprenticeship environment for users learning a certain type of complex task and (2) support low-cost authoring of high-quality (effective) courseware by subject matter experts without computer programming experience.

The specific task undertaken by the LEAP development team was to build a system to teach customer contact employees (CCEs), such as customer service representatives, the knowledge and skills they need to respond effectively to customer requests and problems. This includes knowledge of company products and services, appropriate conversational style, consultative sales skills, and the ability to find and use customer information and enter work orders, etc. LEAP simulates the CCEs' work environment, in which they are expected to carry on a dialogue with customers over the telephone while simultaneously interacting with database systems for entering service orders and obtaining information about customers, their accounts, etc. LEAP also provides: (1) an Instruction Manager that selects and recommends an appropriate scenario (simulated conversation) for a learning session; (2) coaching assistance to guide learners as they are engaged in the scenario; (3) an opportunity for learners to review and receive feedback on their performance at the completion of the scenario; and (4) conclusions about the skill levels the learner has achieved in the various areas of the domain. The LEAP ITS is described in detail in Bloom et al. (1995).

LEAP was designed as an ITS shell, but one centered around the task of interacting with customers and computer systems in a telephone-based dialogue.[2] The content of the dialogues, the domain courseware, is independent of the learning environment. This allows the rich learning environment of LEAP to be used for learning a relatively wide variety of particular skills and knowledge, even while focused on the general task of interacting with customers and related computer applications.

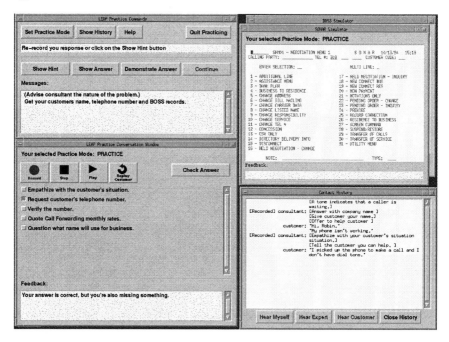

Figure 1. The LEAP Practice Environment

2. OVERVIEW OF LEAP

2.1. The LEAP Training Environment

The LEAP training environment is shown in Figure 1. At the top left is the LEAP Practice Commands window. This is where the trainee interacts with LEAP as a tutoring system, performing such actions as selecting a practice mode, reviewing the history of a practiced conversation, getting help on how to use the system, and quitting a practice session. The Set Practice Mode button allows the trainee to select one of three practice modes: (1) observe, (2) practice, and (3) focused practice. In observe mode, the trainee observes LEAP as it simulates an expert CCE handling a conversation using audio recordings, animated data entry into the database system simulators, etc. In practice mode, trainees practice performing the actions of a CCE within a simulated conversation. That is, the role of the customer is simulated by LEAP using audio recordings, while the trainee records his or her own replies and uses the database system simulators to perform appropriate actions on behalf of the customer. Coaching is available at any time from the system in the form of hints, explanations of appropriate actions, and observable simulations of appropriate actions (as in observe mode). In focused practice mode, LEAP uses its model of the student's progress to alternate between observe and practice modes, as well as skipping certain parts of the conversation, in order to focus practice on those actions on which the particular trainee appears to need the most work.

In addition, the Practice Commands window is where the trainee can receive certain types of coaching and other guidance from LEAP. Below the first row of buttons in the Practice Commands window is a prompt telling the trainee how to proceed through the conversation, such as by clicking the Continue button or recording a response to the recorded statement by the simulated customer. Below the prompt are buttons that allow the trainee to request that LEAP show a hint on how to proceed, show the best answer, demonstrate the best answer in the current situation, or, when appropriate, continue to the next step in the conversation. The Continue button most commonly results in the playing of the next statement by the simulated customer. The space below these buttons is used to display the requested hints, answers, etc.

Below the Practice Commands window is the Practice Conversation window. This window contains tape recorder-like controls that allow the trainee to re-play the last customer statement as well as record and listen to his or her own response. In practice mode, trainees are also asked to indicate what action or actions they are taking at this step in the conversation using a multiple-choice mechanism, and to check their answer against the courseware author's definition of appropriate actions. This is accomplished by clicking the Check Answer button, with feedback appearing at the bottom of the Practice Conversation window.

At the top right of the practice environment are two database application simulators. These allow the same operations as the real systems they simulate, but can also demonstrate user interactions with the databases by highlighting relevant regions of the screen and showing an animation of appropriate data being entered.

The simulators also provide immediate feedback on trainee actions, such as indicating that a certain action is correct, not appropriate at this time, etc.

At the bottom right of the practice environment is the Contact History window. Trainees can open this window in order to review what has occurred so far in the practice conversation. The history displays the actions for each turn in the conversation. Trainees can highlight a turn in the conversation by clicking on it and then on one of the buttons below in order to hear the customer's statement, his or her own recorded response, and the pre-recorded expert CCE response. This allows trainees to compare how they actually sound to the recorded expert CCE.

2.2. LEAP Courseware

The courseware component of a LEAP tutoring application combines features from the domain model and expert model components of a traditional ITS, although the knowledge is less explicit than in most ITSs. The courseware consists of a set of learning modules. Each learning module is essentially a conversation grammar (a kind of task model), augmented with domain and expert behavior information. Representing the knowledge in this way allows authors to concentrate on concrete examples of behavior that the learner will be coached toward. The authors do not have to build an abstract set of rules or other expert model representations.

A LEAP conversation grammar, in its simplest form, is a collection of separate conversations, each consisting primarily of a series of conversational turns taken by the CCE and the simulated customer. When a learner uses LEAP, the role of the CCE is played by either the learner or the simulated expert CCE, depending on whether practice or observation is the emphasis of the current learning mode. The LEAP "coach" may also interact with the learner during his or her turn. Audio recordings are used to simulate the customer and the expert CCE, and for learners to record and listen to themselves. Pertinent database systems are simulated and their use linked to particular steps in the LEAP conversation grammar. This allows the learner to practice performing actions such as entering and retrieving data and then receiving feedback on his or her performance, or to observe animated sequences showing the simulated expert CCE performing these steps.

The transcript in Figure 2 shows an example portion of a conversation in LEAP. The CCE's statements are preceded with the label "Rep" (for customer service representative). The CCE is talking on the phone with a customer, whose statements are similarly indicated.

Each turn in the conversation consists of a set of actions that one of the actors performs. For the learner, the author can specify constraints pertaining to the ordering, co-occurrence, and optionality of the actions in each turn. More flexibility can be introduced by adding branches to the conversations, thus introducing multiple solution paths. The example conversation in Figure 2 shows an example of 2-way branching. The author can also abstract high-level sub-tasks from the conversations, which we refer to as "subdialogues" (e.g., opening the conversation). Subdialogues can be shared by different conversations, thus allowing authors to efficiently reuse material.

In addition to the conversation grammar, a LEAP learning module requires a topic hierarchy. The topic hierarchy and the associations specified between topics and individual learner actions help define the domain. These allow LEAP to determine learner skill levels for each topic, based on the learner's exposure to and performance of the actions associated with that topic.

CONVERSATION BEGINS	
Rep:	U S WEST Communications. This is Sean. How can I help you?
Customer:	Hi. My call forwarding isn't working.
Rep:	I'm sorry to hear that. Can I have your telephone number?
Customer:	Sure, it's 303, 111, 2345
Rep:	That was 303, 111, 2345? [*Rep types number into application*] Is this Mr. Anderson?
Customer:	Yes.

BRANCH 1	BRANCH 2
Rep: I think I see what the problem is.	**Rep**: Could you please hold while I check into the problem?
	Customer: Sure.
	Rep: [*Retrieves customer service record; notices the problem.*] Mr. Anderson?
	Customer: Yes?
	Rep: I think I've found the problem.

BRANCHES COME BACK TOGETHER	
Customer:	Oh, great!
Rep:	[Rep explains the problem and negotiates a solution acceptable to the customer.]

Figure 2. A conversation with two branches.

Other components of a learning module include the hints that the author provides for each learner action and the expert CCE examples (demonstrations using text, audio, and screen animation) for each action. The various components of LEAP courseware—especially the conversation grammar and the power afforded by its flexibility—combine to make the author's task of creating one or more learning modules potentially very complex. In the following sections we discuss the ways in which we have attempted to support the author in accomplishing this task through the LAT and what we consider to be some of our successes, failures, and lessons we have learned along the way.

3. DESIGN OF THE LEAP AUTHORING TOOL

As described above, the goal of providing cost-effective, high-quality training for the types of skills needed by CCEs led us to the rich, apprenticeship learning environment of LEAP. However, the richness and complexity of this environment poses a significant challenge for the authoring process. Authors must create courseware that includes potentially complex conversation grammars, a description of all the individual actions that the actors in the conversation may take, a hierarchy of topics and links from the actions to these topics, hints for each step of the conversation, audio recordings and textual representations of customer and expert CCE actions, etc. In order to meet the requirement of cost-effectiveness without sacrificing the quality of training provided by a rich environment, we knew it would be necessary to provide courseware authors with a sophisticated, easy-to-use authoring tool to support and guide the authoring process.

We identified this requirement for the LAT on the basis of our experience working with the three subject matter experts initially assigned to the LEAP project: one expert CCE and two CCE training experts. These experts had to develop courseware for LEAP while it was under development using basic text editing tools. Their requirements for quality training led us to the rich, relatively realistic learning environment of LEAP and its associated complexities in the structure of the courseware. Their struggles to work effectively with these complexities and their suggestions on what would be most helpful to them led us to the particular design goals we set for the LAT and the ways in which we addressed these goals during its development.

3.1. Design Goals

The design of the LAT was guided by two types of constraints. First, the design had to accommodate the authoring of the particular structures and objects required for a LEAP courseware module, i.e., topics, actions, transitions between steps in a conversation, definition of subdialogue, hints, etc. (We will discuss these objects further in the discussion below.) Second, the design was also constrained by the expected skill set of the targeted authoring community, namely subject matter experts (i.e., expert CCEs and CCE trainers). These constraints led us to set the following goals for the design of the authoring tool: (1) ease of use, (2) rapid prototyping and iterative development, (3) reuse of courseware components, (4) multiple representations and input mechanisms, and (5) interactive visualizations of the courseware structure and content.

3.1.1. Ease of Use

Although it may have become somewhat commonplace to include ease-of-use as a design goal, one lesson we learned during our development effort was that it was extremely important to maintain an emphasis on ease-of-use throughout the design and development process. The possibility of including new, powerful features constantly had to be weighed against the need to maintain simplicity for the majority of use cases. For us, ease-of-use meant both easy to learn (new users from our targeted author community should be able to learn to use the tool to build runnable courseware within a couple of days) and easy and efficient for experienced users to maintain and extend an existing body of courseware.

3.1.2. Rapid Prototyping and Iterative Development

Based on the experiences of the subject matter experts involved in the development of LEAP and its initial body of courseware (developed without the LAT), it was apparent that authors would benefit substantially from the ability to see, right from the beginning, how the conversations they were authoring would actually be experienced by learners. This meant that they needed to "run" the courseware before it was complete, i.e., sketch out and run a skeletal, prototype version of their courseware in LEAP, then iteratively refine and complete it. The LAT was designed to support this style of development through the inclusion of several features, including usable default values for unspecified information, full integration with run-time LEAP so that changes can immediately be tested, an agenda mechanism to help authors keep track of any incomplete authoring tasks, and the provision of several alternative methods for entering courseware information (see section 3.1.4 on multiple representations below).

3.1.3. Reuse

To minimize the cost of developing new courseware, we made reuse of courseware components a key design goal for the LAT. Because there are many similarities among different conversations, both within a courseware module for a given domain and across modules, there is an opportunity to reuse portions of existing conversations to build new ones. For example, most, if not all conversations in a given body of courseware may begin with the same initial opening or greeting. In the initial set of LEAP courseware that our subject matter experts developed, all conversations begin with the telephone ringing. This is followed by the CCE answering by stating the company name and their own name, and then offering to help the customer. (See the example in Figure 2 above.) The authors took advantage of this by defining this segment of conversation as a reusable chunk, or subdialogue, to be used in all the conversations in this courseware module.

Re-using parts of conversations helps authors by: (1) reducing the amount of work involved in creating a new set of conversations, (2) reducing the maintenance effort required for updates such as changes in prices, policies, or procedures, and (3) making it easier to maintain consistency across a large number of conversations.

However, one lesson that we learned through our effort to support reuse was that it is relatively easy to underestimate the costs of adding this sort of "power" feature to a complex system such as an ITS authoring tool. We knew that reuse had the potential to save authors of relatively large bodies of courseware a great deal of effort in maintaining and extending their LEAP grammars. Yet, at the same time, supporting reuse may have considerable costs in terms of system complexity and ease-of-use.

In our case, supporting reuse required additional complexity, both in (1) the LEAP grammar representations and processing mechanisms and (2) the LAT user interface. The technical challenges this posed for the LEAP grammar itself proved to be manageable. Furthermore, we feel that we were able to leverage the capabilities of good GUI design to develop relatively sophisticated tools for helping authors handle the complexities of reuse. However, the experience we have had with users suggests that they may not be attracted to the advantages of reuse enough to be willing to deal with its associated complexities, at least not to the extent that we had anticipated. Reuse in the LAT thus constitutes one case in which power can be traded off against ease-of-use. It appears in this case that we may have underestimated the impact that adding this type of power to LEAP and the LAT would have on ease-of-use for authors. On the other hand, our experience with LEAP courseware authors was rather limited. We did not see the LAT used extensively enough for authors to have faced the need to maintain a relatively large body of courseware, which is the use case for which reuse offers the most significant advantage.

3.1.4. Multiple Representations and Input Mechanisms

Our experiences with the subject matter experts who served as courseware authors during the development of LEAP led us to the conclusion that different authors would have different individual authoring styles and different starting points for the authoring process. For example, some authors may be adapting existing training materials while others are starting from scratch. For this reason, we felt it was important to design the LAT to accommodate some of these different approaches to courseware development.

One significant difference in authoring approaches is that some authors prefer to work in a "bottom-up" manner and others in a "top-down" manner. Those who work in a bottom-up fashion begin by entering a "script" of a conversation. After the conversation has been scripted, they then divide it up into relevant subdialogues and, perhaps, elaborate this into several distinct conversations. Authors who work top-down begin by creating a conversation in terms of its high-level major subdialogues (such as "Greeting the customer", "Determining the customer's need", "Providing a response", and "Closing the call"). These authors then move to a more detailed level by defining the structure of each of these subdialogues, and continue in this fashion until each individual step of each subdialogue has been defined.

Another way that the LAT accommodates different authoring techniques is that a script of a conversation may initially be prepared in a word processor or text editor.

This script can then be read into the LAT as a structured text file and converted into a valid internal LEAP representation of a conversation. After importing the script, the author can test the conversation in LEAP and continue to develop it.

Finally, the LAT also accommodates different authoring styles by providing two distinct primary visualizations of the courseware content. These are discussed in the next section.

3.1.5. Interactive visualizations

As mentioned above, some authors may write new courseware by first creating scripts of conversations, then elaborating them into complete courseware modules. We also expect that all authors will find it helpful on occasion to be able to view a transcript-like representation of a particular conversation, i.e., a listing of what is said in each turn by each actor in the conversation, unencumbered by branching, hints, topics, associated audio files and other information associated with every step of the conversation. This is helpful, for instance, in determining that the flow of the defined conversation is coherent and natural. For these reasons, the LAT includes a "script editor" that provides such a view of a conversation and allows editing of the conversation within this view. The script editor is described in more detail below in section 4.1.

As mentioned above, other authors prefer to work primarily in a top-down fashion, defining a hierarchy of subdialogues before fleshing out the details. We also expect all authors to find it helpful to be able to view the subdialogue structure of their conversations. This is helpful, for example, in understanding branches in conversations or identifying which conversations share a particular subdialogue. For these reasons, the LAT includes a "subdialogue graph editor" that provides a node-and-link representation of the structure of a subdialogue and also allows editing from within this view. This editor is also discussed in more detail below in section 4.2.

In addition to the script and subdialogue views, a third visualization is provided for the transitions between nodes in the conversation grammar. The nodes in the grammar represent the state of a conversation being run in LEAP. That is, at any given moment, the current state of the simulated conversation is defined by the currently active node or nodes. The transitions define groups of actions available at a given node, i.e., that are available to the learner at any given point in the conversation. Transitions are potentially complex, as they may include many different combinations of operators for defining ordering, optionality, co-occurrence, and other relationships among available actions. The transition editor and the structure of transitions are discussed below in section 4.3.

4. USING THE LEAP AUTHORING TOOL

In this section, we will describe how the LAT is used for the creation of LEAP courseware, including descriptions and examples of the use of the script, subdialogue graph, and transition editors and other editing tools and how these tools address the design goals mentioned above.

4.1. Scripting Conversations with the Script Editor

The script editor is a text-based tool that provides a visualization of a single path of conversation through a LEAP grammar. We refer to this visualization as a "script view" or simply a "script". This visualization is analogous to the script of a play, although there are a number of additional elements in the display that allow the conversation to be edited in the ways required for creating a complete LEAP grammar. The script view provides a clear and concise description of who is performing which actions, speaking which parts of the dialogue, and the order (or the multiple possible orders) in which these actions may take place.

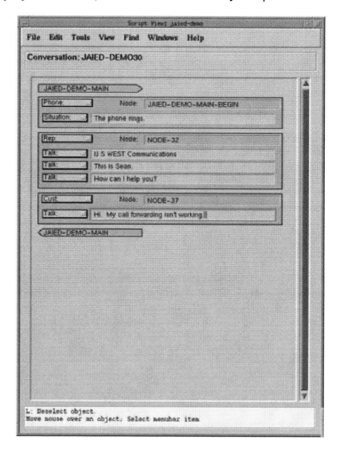

Figure 3. The Script Editor, showing the beginning of a conversation.

One primary purpose of the script editor is to allow a user to quickly and easily create a single conversation path (i.e., a script). To do this, a LEAP author (a subject matter expert) enters a script much as a playwright might create a play using a word processor. Using the script editor, the author can simply type in the text of the dialogue that takes place among the "players". However, because the script is not going to be performed by human actors, but rather executed by the LEAP tutoring system, it is important to provide the author with some guidance as to how to create a script that can run successfully in LEAP and meet the training goals for the courseware being developed.

Let's start with an example. We assume a use case in which the author is initially creating a new conversation and begin our discussion just after the author has entered the script editor. The author has previously informed the LAT that we are creating a new conversation, so the script editor is initialized to display a single first node of the conversation. The node appears as a box, surrounded above and below by "subdialogue bars". These indicate which subdialogue the current sequence of nodes is contained within. Figure 3 shows this first node (after two additional nodes have been created) as the top rectangular box, labeled with the name JAIED-DEMO-MAIN-BEGIN.

In the upper right-hand corner of the node box is an editable text field labeled "Node" in which the author can specify the name of the node, JAIED-DEMO-MAIN-BEGIN in this example. To the left of the node name is a pop-up menu that allows the author to select the actor who is responsible for performing the actions associated with this node. In this example, the "Phone" actor is selected. Because a telephone conversation typically starts with the phone ringing, this is the default configuration with which the LAT begins a script. Other actors in the conversation may include the trainee, the customer calling in, and a couple of special cases, such as the "coach", an actor that can be used by authors to provide direct coaching of the learner at any point in simulated conversation. In our example, the trainee appears as the CCE (the customer service representative, or "Rep", actor), as this is the role being tutored. The other human participant being scripted is the "Customer" role.

Below the actor and node name fields are specifications for one or more rows of actions contained within the node. The first node in Figure 3 has only one row with a single action for ringing the telephone. The pop-up menu on the left side of the actions specification allows the author to select the type of action being specified, in this case a "Situation" action. To the right of the selected action type is a text field. The purpose of this text depends on the type of action. This area is most frequently used to specify the spoken text of "Talk" actions.

At this point, we have a script that consists of the telephone ringing. To continue, the author adds a new node by selecting "New Node" from the Edit menu or pressing a key. The script editor adds a new node to the display and populates it with defaults for its name, actor, and action type. The default information is based on heuristic knowledge of how the conversation flows. In this case, the ringing of the telephone is typically followed by the Rep answering the phone. Thus, the new node shows the Rep as the actor and a Talk action in which the Rep will say something to the caller, such as "Hello".

With these defaults, the author only has to type in the text associated with the first Talk action. In our example, the author has chosen to have the Rep answer the phone by saying "U S WEST Communications. This is Sean. How can I help you." and to represent this as a sequence of three actions. The Rep's entire statement could be represented as a single Talk action. However, for the purpose of relating actions to instructional topics and for detailed modeling of learner performance, it is typically useful to divide statements of this type into several separate actions. So, after entering the text "U S WEST Communications" for the first Talk action, the author presses a key to create another action, enters "This is Sean", and repeats this for the third action. The result is the Rep node (the second rectangular box) shown in Figure 3, containing a sequence of the three "Talk" actions that make up the Rep's initial turn in the conversation.

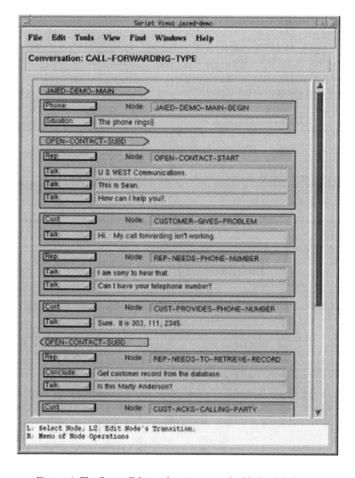

Figure 4. The Script Editor, showing an embedded subdialogue.

Next, the author creates another new node. This time, the actor supplied by the script editor defaults to "Customer", as the calling party is expected to say something next. The author may now fill in the spoken text for this turn in the dialogue, as above, or edit the actor, action type, or other information about the node. In Figure 3, the author has the customer respond by saying "Hi. My call forwarding isn't working." Creating a conversation in the script editor proceeds in this way—much like writing the script of a play, but with all of the additional editing capabilities needed to create the tutorial courseware close at hand.

Of course, the default information provided will not always be what the author intends. The script editor provides several mechanisms for allowing the author to easily change the default information. The actor and action menus can be used to specify a new selection, in which case the LAT keeps track of the implications of these changes behind the scenes. In addition, the script editor allows the user to invoke other components of the LAT. Each of the visual objects in the script editor corresponds to a LEAP grammar object. The appropriate editor for each of these objects can easily be invoked from within the script editor by selecting the object with the mouse and invoking an edit command.

Before continuing with our example, we describe two additional aspects of the visualization presented by the script editor: branching and subdialogues. LEAP conversation grammars are partitioned by authors into "subdialogues", each representing a relatively coherent chunk of the larger dialogue centered on a particular local topic. Knowing which subdialogues contain a particular node plays a vital role in the development of the grammars. The script editor displays this information with "subdialogue bars" that mark the beginning and end of subdialogues within the conversation. For example, as shown in Figure 4, the conversation begins with the JAIED-DEMO-MAIN subdialogue, indicated by the labeled subdialogue bar pointing to the right. After the node representing the telephone ringing, the embedded subdialogue OPEN-CONTACT-SUBD begins with the OPEN-CONTACT-START node. It ends four nodes later, as indicated by the labeled subdialogue bar pointing to the left.

Branching represents places in the grammar where two conversational paths diverge. This may represent either a choice of two different possible paths for the learner to follow within a single conversation or a point at which two or more conversations that had been sharing a sequence of nodes now diverge. Because branching may be difficult for authors to keep track of, it is important to represent branching information visually. The presence of branches at a node is depicted by visual "tabs" on the bottom of the node, as shown on the node REP-INVESTIGATES-OR-UNDERSTANDS in Figure 5. The author can click on one of these tabs to select which branch of the conversation is displayed below the tab in the editor. An alternative view shows the conversation and its various branches as a graph, as shown in Figure 6.

Returning to our example conversation as shown in Figure 4, the author has now created several nodes and their associated actions by entering the text of these actions and allowing other information to default to the values supplied by the LAT. At this point, the author may wish to invoke the LAT's ability to run the grammar under development in LEAP to see how the learner will experience the courseware as defined up to this point. This can be done seamlessly from within the LAT, because the LAT includes full LEAP run-time functionality and maintains an executable representation of the grammar objects being edited at all times. Of course, if grammar elements such as hints or recorded audio have not yet been authored, these will not be present when the grammar is run. For example, you would only see the written text for spoken actions rather than hearing them. By using useful default and place-holder information, the LAT allows authors to work with courseware that is runnable under LEAP right from the beginning of the authoring process. In our user testing, this proved to be a useful feature for the authoring process, as it allows an iterative write-and-test development cycle that lends itself to rapid prototyping of new courseware.

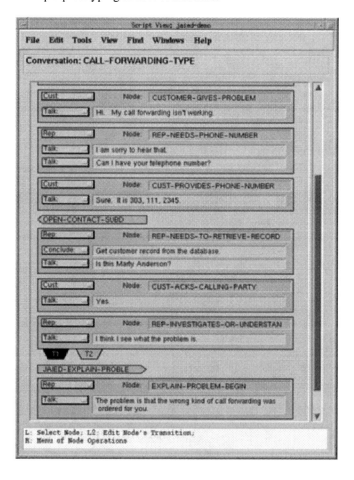

Figure 5. The Script Editor, showing a branching node.

4.2. Subdialogue Graph Editor

The subdialogue graph editor is the LAT component best suited for giving the author an overview of the courseware being working on. Figure 6 shows how the editor looks for the simple conversation in our example. The graph shown represents the top level subdialogue for the set of conversations in the conversation grammar.

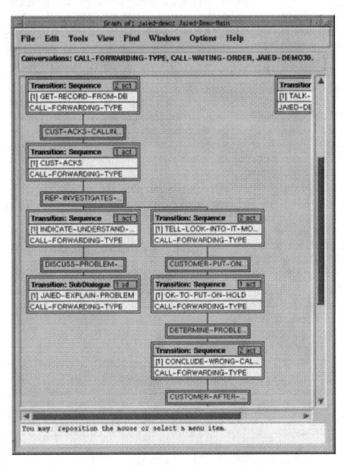

Figure 6. The Subdialogue Graph Editor.

Each of the smaller rectangles (with labels in all capitals) in the figure represents a node, and the larger, compound rectangles represent transitions between nodes. As previously noted, a transition is the set of actions to be performed by the learner, simulated customer, or some other agent to move from one point in time (a node) to the next. In addition to a simple set of actions, a transition can consist, instead, of a set of one or more subdialogues. This is how nesting of subdialogues is accomplished. In our example, the last transition on the left-most branch in the figure represents a single subdialogue, as indicated by the label "Transition: Subdialogue". The name of the subdialogue is shown as JAIED-EXPLAIN-PROBLEM.

In addition to displaying a graphical representation for a dialogue, the subdialogue graph editor also allows the creation of nodes and transitions. This is done by highlighting the appropriate node and choosing menu items to add or transitions to remove from it. Nodes and transitions are created with basic, default information that can then be modified.

The subdialogue graph editor is a structured graph editor. As items are added and deleted from the subdialogue graph, the other items automatically reposition themselves appropriately. This ensures that the graph maintains readability and removes this burden from the user. In future versions we would like to add the ability for the author to reposition items manually if he or she desires. This would require keeping positioning information so that the user's version of a graph could be restored as well as adding the mechanism to handle dragging items with the mouse.

In addition to creating and deleting new graph elements, the author can get to any of the appropriate editors for a component by highlighting it and either double-clicking or choosing an appropriate menu item. For example, from a transition component the author can go to the transition editor (see section 4.3) to see the ordering restrictions on the actions, or he or she can go directly to an editor for a component of the transition. This could include an action editor, a new subdialogue graph, a subdialogue information editor, or a conversation information editor. Additionally, by double-clicking a node or by choosing the appropriate menu item, the author can edit the name and other information for any node in the graph.

4.3. Transition Editor

The LEAP grammar formalism allows for a great deal of flexibility in how a conversation may unfold. For example, at a given point in a conversation, the author may allow the learner to follow only a single path or may define multiple acceptable paths by which the conversation may move forward. This feature allows learners using LEAP to experience relatively realistic simulated conversational interactions. However, the price to be paid for this flexibility is a corresponding degree of complexity in the LEAP grammar. The transition editor was designed to provide authors with a powerful, directly manipulable visualization of the transitions between the nodes in the grammar. The progression of a conversation from one step to the next is defined in a LEAP grammar in "transitions" between nodes. Transitions are LEAP grammar objects that define, for any given node, which nodes can come next and what actions can be performed to reach each of these possible next nodes. They are displayed in the transition editor in a way that quickly conveys which actions are available at a given node and the relationships among them. The relationships that may pertain among actions are those of ordering, co-occurrence, and optionality.

In some situations, actions must be taken in a certain order. For example, the actions Give-Company-Name, Give-Self-Name, and Ask-How-Can-Help in the OPEN-CONTACT-START node shown in Figure 7 are to be performed in this order. This is specified by combining the actions with the "Sequence" operator, as shown in the figure.

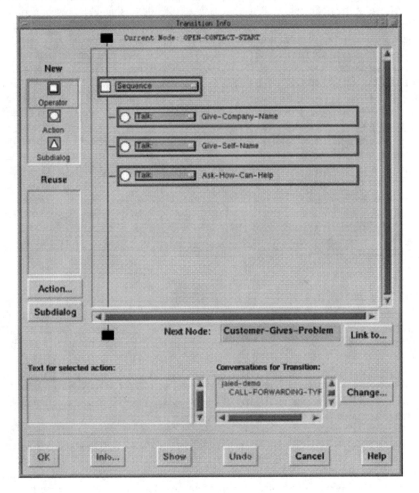

Figure 7. The Transition Editor.

In other situations, it may be appropriate to perform one action or another, but not both. In this case, there is a co-occurrence restriction between the two actions. This can be specified in the transition editor with the "xor" (exclusive or) operator. Finally, there are situations in which some actions are required while others are optional, which can be specified by other operators. Still other transition operators are used for combining subdialogues, rather than actions.

As shown in Figure 7, the main component of the transition editor is a large panel that displays graphically the current specification of the transition. A "flow line" runs down the left side of this panel that indicates how the transition links the node above to the node below. The visual objects inside this panel represent actions, subdialogues, and the transition operators used to combine them. The actions or subdialogues combined by an operator are referred to as its operands.

Most operators appear as short rectangles in the display and are marked with a small square icon. Operands are more elongated and are marked with a circle (for actions) or a triangle (for subdialogues). In Figure 7, the operator is "Sequence" and the action objects "Give-Company-Name", "Give-Self-Name", and "Ask-How-Can-Help" are its operands. Both operators and operands have associated pop-up menus that allow an author to quickly change their type.

As a transition is essentially a recursive specification of operators and operands, only one operator is allowed on the flow line at the left of the panel. All other operands and operators are nested within this top-level operator. Authors may use the mouse to drag and drop operator and operand objects to specify the structure of the transition.

On the left side of the transition editor is a palette from which the author may create new transition objects. Existing grammar objects can be reused in the current transition by selecting them from a list, then dragging and dropping them at the desired location in the transition being edited.

4.4. The Agenda

Although the conversation in the example we have been using can be run directly in LEAP as it is, the courseware is not complete and suitable for tutoring purposes until several additional authoring steps have been completed. Most obviously, perhaps, authors will want to create audio recordings for all spoken actions. After these recordings have been made and saved, these audio files need to be associated with their corresponding actions. The current version of the LAT does not provide its own facilities for recording audio, so authors must use other tools to create the audio files, and then associate them with actions using the LAT.

Authors will also want to engage in the other authoring steps, such as defining topics and associating actions with them, grouping sequences of conversation nodes into subdialogues, creating appropriate hints for each action and subdialogue, replacing the default names for nodes and actions with more helpful names, defining branches in conversations, etc. To help authors keep track of what authoring activities remain to be done to have a complete (as opposed to minimally runnable) LEAP grammar definition, the LAT provides authors with an agenda mechanism.

Complete LEAP grammars are complex, and in building all but the simplest conversations, it is difficult to keep track of all relevant aspects of the current state of the grammar. To help authors keep track of where they are in the authoring process, the agenda mechanism keeps track of the state of the grammar in relation to the authoring process. The various LAT editors communicate with the agenda in a manner that allows the agenda to watch authors as they construct the grammar. At any time, the author can call upon the agenda to provide assistance as to what remains to be completed.

The agenda contains a model of what information is needed to complete a LEAP grammar. By observing the author's activities, the agenda knows what information, if any, is still required before the grammar is complete. There are two categories of information that must be complete. The first includes missing information that is required for the grammar to run properly in LEAP. Without first supplying this information, the courseware may not run as the user expects. For example, a conversation might reach a point where it abruptly ends (i.e., the graph representing the grammar has unconnected pieces).

The second category consists of information for which the LAT has supplied default values. For example, the LAT keeps track of whether a recorded audio file has been specified for Talk actions. LEAP will display the text associated with the action if this action is executed without an associated recording, but the recordings are needed for effective use of LEAP for tutoring.

4.5. Refining and Completing LEAP Grammars with the LAT Editors

To fully specify a LEAP grammar and make it ready for learners to use, an author needs to use additional form-style editors for each of the LEAP grammar objects. These editors allow the author to provide additional information not needed for initial prototyping but important to a fully functioning LEAP grammar. Six such editors are included in LAT; one each for modules, conversations, subdialogues, nodes, actions, and topics.

4.5.1. Node Editor

Figure 8 shows the node editor with a node representing a state in which the learner is expected either to recognize the customer's problem or to ask the customer to wait on hold for a short time while he/she figures out the problem. This information, as described in the comment field of the node, indicates the types of transitions the author has created that can be taken to move to the next node. For more information on transitions and the transition editor see section 4.3.

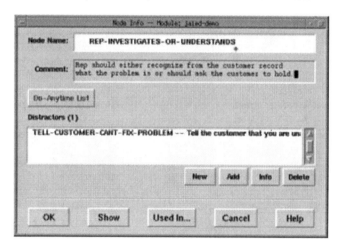

Figure 8. The Node Editor.

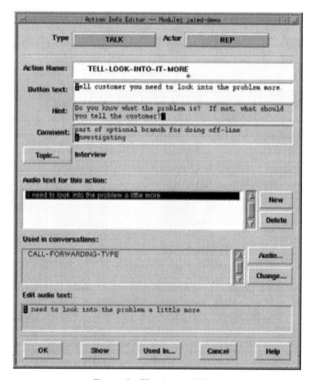

Figure 9. The Action Editor.

One optional field that an author may specify from the node editor is the distractor field. Distractors are used in LEAP in much the same way as they are in multiple-choice tests. They are included with the set of correct steps for a given situation (node) for a learner to choose from. LEAP distractors are actually action instances, and the author can create actions specifically as distractors for a given node, choose existing actions (that are correct in other contexts), or let LEAP choose the distractors to be used for a node.

4.5.2. Action Editor

The most complex object type, in terms of the number of fields, is the LEAP action. Actions of various types can be created. "Talk" actions, such as saying "hello" to the customer and the customer telling the learner that she has a problem with her service, are the most common type of action. Figure 9 shows the action editor for a talk action. Another action type is the "Conclude" action. These are used by an author when the learner does not need to perform any observable action, but rather needs to make an appropriate inference based on the current situation.

For actions in which the learner (referred to in Figure 9 as "Rep") is the actor, the author needs to specify the "button text". This text should briefly describe the action. It will appear for the learner using LEAP next to a checkbox in a list of choices of steps that may be appropriate to take in a given situation. An optional but recommended learner action field is the hint. When the learner requests a hint in a specific situation, the hint field values for the correct actions for that situation are displayed. Another important field for learner actions is the topic field. By associating an action with a topic, the author allows the LEAP tutoring module a way to group actions and determine mastery levels for topics by analyzing the learner's performance on the actions associated with the topic.

Even with the fields discussed above fully specified, an action created in the action editor is still generic in the sense that it is independent of any particular conversation. In other words, it is not yet really being used. What remains to be done is the application of the action to one or more conversations. The author does this by specifying the audio text (transcript) for talk actions, or a detailed description for other action types, for each specific conversation in which the action is to be included. Actually, this is exactly what an author does when he or she uses the script editor to type in what is to be said or done in a particular conversation. The action editor also provides a way to create or edit the audio text. It also provides a concise description of the applications of an action in specific conversations, whereas the script editor shows the action's audio text for just one conversation (although, as described earlier, it provides an excellent mechanism for creating and checking the flow of that conversation.) Figure 9 shows that the action TELL-LOOK-INTO-IT-MORE is used in just one conversation: CALL-FORWARDING-TYPE.

4.5.3. The Other LAT Editors

The topic hierarchy editor, shown in Figure 10, lets the author specify the topics that the learner needs to master and their hierarchical relationship. It is used to specify the topic name and a short description of the topic, which is displayed each time a learner highlights the topic, which is the first step in practicing a conversation focusing on the topic.

Other secondary editors allow editing of such information as the author's estimated complexity of a conversation (used as a factor in suggesting conversations to practice by the LEAP tutoring module) and the description of a learning module that the user sees when he or she is choosing which module to practice.

5. DESIGN PROCESS

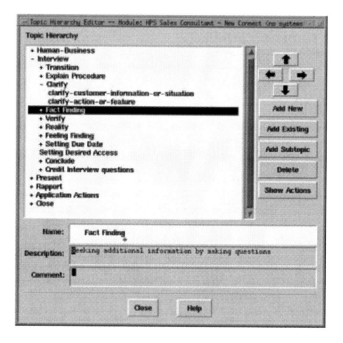

Figure 10. The Topic Hierarchy Editor

The LAT was built using a collaborative design process that included potential users, subject matter experts (in the initially targeted courseware domain of consultative skills), human factors experts, and programmers. (See Muller et al. 1995). Because the purpose of the LAT is to support the authoring of courseware to be run as a tutoring session in LEAP, the design of the LAT began with a specification of the functionality required to build working LEAP grammars. This part of the design process primarily involved the LEAP developers and took a relatively short amount of time. The bulk of the design process involved the specification of the user interface for the LAT. This phase involved numerous design meetings, building user interface mock-ups and paper simulations, and testing a small set of users with these simulated systems.

5.1. Use Cases for the LAT

The interface design phase began with a determination of a set of expected "use cases" for the tool. These use cases included such information as what background an author likely would have (in using computers, developing training materials, building other LEAP courseware, etc.), what an author's starting point would be (e.g., whether other types of training materials for the targeted domain were available), and what individual preferences and working styles should be considered. We used these use cases to determine the structure and content of the tools various components and the relationships among them, to recommend methods for use of the tool, and to test the tool's ability to support the required authoring activities.

We outlined three general use cases for the tool along the two dimensions of (1) the author's experience in using the tool and (2) the author's preferred approach to building courseware. The first use case involved a novice LEAP courseware author. We assumed that a novice would probably start by building scripts, and then introduce more complex structures as he or she progressed. This would allow the novice author to get started without having to learn too much about the use of the tool and its more complex features. We also expected it to be easier for most authors start with the more familiar representation formalism of a script of a conversation.

A second use case involved an author maintaining existing courseware. The tool must support authors in the tasks of revising, repairing, and extending the courseware content. This use case required search tools and good visualizations so that the author could easily find the piece of courseware that needed to be changed and edit it.

A third use case involved the reuse of courseware objects to build new courseware or to extend existing courseware. Because building good courseware is a time-consuming effort, the tool was designed to support the reuse of courseware components for building new material. This use case also required good search tools and the ability to insert courseware components designed for other modules into the current module.

The design process we followed turned out to be a mixture of a sequential design-code-test approach and a more iterative design-as-you-code approach. Design team members tended to fall into one of two groups, depending on which approach they favored. One group wanted to follow a more traditional design process, where the design was documented up-front, after which the tools were coded to this design and then tested. The benefit of this approach is that the design is thought out ahead of time and documented for all members to agree on and work towards.

The other group of design team members wanted to work out the design as various components were implemented. The motivation for this approach was that it was difficult and time-consuming to map out all of the aspects of and interactions among different tool components in detail before beginning any implementation. In addition, designs sometimes led to dead ends that were only found when a use case was tried on an implemented system component. Once a component had been implemented, users could try it out. This typically exposed problems in the existing design and suggested possible improvements that could then be made. On the other hand, in some cases, the implementer's understanding of the goals for a component did not completely match that of the other team members.

There was also some tension between the two groups over control of the design. The developers could control the design either through the design meetings or by coding the tool in a particular way. Most of the developers favored a "design as you go" approach. The user interface experts, on the other hand, could only control the design by having a formal design document that was followed. Therefore, this group favored the design-code-test approach. The actual design occurred through a combination of both methods. The design of the main components of the tool was documented and followed, whereas details of the tool and some subsidiary components were designed as they were coded.

One lesson learned from our design process was that the diversity of backgrounds on the design team both aided and complicated the design process. We often found it difficult to find common ground, and some members of the team felt less empowered than others. (The programmers had the power to actually produce the interfaces, and thus had the most power). Our desire to support multiple authoring styles also caused difficulties, since different members of the team focused on different styles or use cases, sometimes producing conflicts over the importance of specific user interface strategies. However, the development of the LAT involved a complex set of goals and many different system components, and it was difficult for any one person to keep all of the goals and constraints in consideration and in balance. Multiple perspectives on the design kept us honest and struggling, so that we didn't forget or minimize any particular authoring style or use case. In the end, we found that our particular set of compromises between the two basic design strategies worked pretty well, though it did involve a considerable degree of frustration for different team members at different times.

5.2. Design Strategies

Throughout the design process, the team used analogies to existing systems and tools whenever possible. This aided our thinking about the LAT, and we expected at least some of these analogies to be helpful for new users of the LAT, as well. For example, in order to visualize how the script editor should work, we used two analogies: word processors and scripts for plays. Although LEAP grammars are networks of interconnected subdialogues, the result of engaging in a LEAP session is a linear sequence of interactions. In order for authors to test their courseware, they needed to be able to see the conversations that resulted from the courseware. These conversations are very similar to the script of a play. In a printed play script, the lines each character says are shown, preceded by the character's name. Other stage directions are marked in the script in the order in which they need to occur. Since scripts are a relatively well-known way to represent dialogues, we thought it would be useful to present LEAP conversations in this way. However, authors also need to be able to edit these scripts. Therefore, we combined the structure of a script with the editing capabilities of a word processor (e.g., cutting and pasting text), which are also familiar to our target users.

Another way we tried to leverage users' familiarity with other tools was to include a facility for importing scripts composed as simple texts. Users can write a script in a word processor, save it as a simple text file, then import it for use in LEAP. As long as the file follows the simple formatting convention of lines of text preceded by the actor's name, the LAT will read the script file and transform it into the data structures required by LEAP. A simple, working LEAP grammar can be created this way, although authors will always want to use the LAT further to complete the conversation with hints, topics, audio, etc.

Similarly, we hoped to leverage authors' potential familiarity with graphics programs to enhance the usability of the graphical components of the LAT, especially the subdialogue graph and transition editors. Although our direct experience with authors during the design of the LAT was limited to three potential users, our conclusion is that most of our targeted author community would not have a great deal of familiarity with the kinds of graphical tools that would best transfer to using the LAT. For example, the graphical class browsers often included in object-oriented programming environments have a number of similarities to the LAT's editors, but we expect few of our targeted authors to be familiar with this or similar types of graphical editor. Rather, many of them may be more familiar with such graphics applications as draw and paint programs. These, however, bear only a superficial resemblance to the LAT's graphical components. (For example, typical drawing programs give the user a great deal of control over the layout and appearance of objects, whereas the LAT's graphical editors impose a much greater degree of constraint over the appearance of a given structure—mostly, we believe, to the benefit of typical authors.)

So, although in retrospect we don't believe the LAT design has been able to leverage users' prior familiarity with similar graphical programs to the extent we had hoped, the graphical representations used have still proved successful in their goal of enabling authors to conceptualize and manipulate the complex structures of LEAP grammar representations. The three authors who have both written LEAP courseware by hand and used the LAT all found the LAT's graphical representations superior to the alternative textual representations and were able to learn the LAT graphical conventions and manipulations relatively easily.

6. EVALUATION OF THE LEAP AUTHORING TOOL

After determining the main components that would be needed for the LAT, based on our chosen set of use cases, we conducted participatory design sessions. Participants included several representatives of the actual community of potential LEAP authors, a CCE training expert, as well as the LAT software developers and human factors experts. These sessions resulted in both paper and interactive computer-based mockups of the various LAT user interface components. These designs were then tested with potential authors and several others. Based on the results of these tests, we made appropriate revisions to the design and began development of the LAT software.

After an initial (alpha-level) version of the LAT was built, we conducted a focused user test with one novice author. This evaluation focused on the following questions: (1) Can the user create a simple module easily?, (2) Does the flow of use of the tools seem "natural" to the author?, (3) Is the method of presenting the grammar (script, graph, and information windows) clear and helpful?, (4) Are the concepts of conversations, subdialogues, transitions, and reuse clear?, and (5) Did the user have any trouble finding and using specific windows, commands, or operations?

After completing less than one day on instruction and a tutorial, the author was able to build a simple module easily. The author found the tool simple to work with and was able to use all of the components of the LAT successfully to produce a working body of courseware within three days (Meiskey, Root, & Somers, 1996).

We attribute the successful results of this user test (and of the design of the tool) to the following factors. First, our method for training the novice user was to move from building simple to more complex courseware. The tool was specifically designed to accommodate this transition. Second, in the design of the LAT, we had used analogies to other tools that were familiar to the user, including word processors and graphics programs. In fact, the user was annoyed when the tool didn't follow some of the conventions of other tools (e.g., she couldn't drag and drop objects in the graph editor).

The LAT was also used by two other authors for maintaining the large body of courseware initially developed in parallel with the LEAP system for training CCEs. These authors found the LAT to be a great improvement over their previous method for developing courseware: editing grammar files as text, an extremely difficult and error-prone method. The authors were able to take a large LEAP grammar and create several new ones from it by reusing subdialogues, adding new "coaching" actions, and making other relatively minor changes.

7. SUMMARY & CONCLUSION

LEAP is an ITS that provides a rich, apprenticeship environment for people learning CCE skills. The LEAP Authoring Tool provides LEAP courseware authors with a powerful, yet relatively easy-to-use tool for developing the kind of high-quality and sophisticated courseware needed for such a rich learning environment in a cost-effective and, we think, enjoyable manner. The LAT was designed to achieve this through a number of features that support rapid prototyping of new courseware material, reuse of existing material, and multiple, interactive visualizations for creating and manipulating courseware structures and components.

One valuable lesson that we learned through the experience of designing and developing LEAP and the LAT is that it is important to maintain a focus on ease-of-use throughout the design and development process. In the end, we felt that we had probably erred somewhat in the direction of including power features that would be of use primarily to more experienced users because this also added complexity and therefore some difficulty for less experienced users. We believe we missed the best possible balance between power and ease-of-use primarily because we over-estimated the level of experience that would be achieved by typical LEAP authors, but also because the development effort was somewhat experimental in nature, and we felt it important to explore new possibilities and approaches to solving the challenges of authoring complex courseware.

We believe that much of the success of the LAT design was due to the fact that we had the participation of appropriate subject matter experts (potential authors) and human factors experts from the beginning of the project. The requirements and recommendations of our initial LEAP courseware authors provided direction at the key decision points in the design of the LAT. We also learned a great deal about how to design some of the LAT components simply by watching the authors struggle with the task of writing courseware. In this sense, it was quite valuable to have the working LEAP system with (hand-coded) courseware already running before we began the design of the LAT. The requirements of the existing LEAP system and the experiences of the original courseware authors provided a great deal of valuable constraint on the design of the LAT.

It also proved important to use a participatory design process that captured the input and expertise of the different categories of team members: subject matter experts (in our case, both expert CCE trainers and expert CCEs themselves), human factors and user interface experts, and software developers. Many conflicts among team members and their points of view had to be resolved to achieve the best results. We also profited from an iterative design process that included early user evaluations of our designs (e.g., using paper or computerized mockups).

Finally, we believe that our experience developing the LAT has also taught us the importance of (1) providing authoring tool users with multiple ways of accomplishing the primary tasks involved in courseware development, (2) providing multiple, well-designed, and manipulable visualizations of courseware structure, (3) accommodating different authors' individual preferences, work styles, and starting points for authoring, and (4) supporting rapid, incremental courseware development that allows authors to test what they have created so far throughout the development process.

The LEAP system has so far been used by a few hundred learners, and user evaluations have confirmed its value as a tool for training CCEs (Bloom, Linton, & Bell 1993). However, it was not deployed as widely as we would have liked and, as a result, the LAT has not been widely used. This is due in part to the fact that the requirements for the delivery of LEAP training changed so as to focus delivery of LEAP training over a corporate intranet.

10. REFERENCES

Bloom, C. P., Linton, F., & Bell, B. (1993). An Evaluation of the Learn, Explore and Practice Intelligent Tutoring Systems Platform. U S WEST Advanced Technologies, Technical Report AT-09_10-002817-00.01.

Bloom, C. P., Bell, B., Meiskey, L., Sparks, R., Dooley, S., & Linton, F. (1995). Putting intelligent tutoring systems technology into practice: A study in technology extension and transfer. Machine Mediated Learning, 5, 13-41.

Blumenthal, R., Meiskey, L., Dooley, S., Sparks, R. (1996). Reducing Development Costs With Intelligent Tutoring System Shells. Position Paper for ITS'96 Workshop on Architectures and Methods for Designing Cost-Effective and Reusable ITSs, Montreal, June 10, 1996.

Collins, A., Brown, J. S., & Newman, S. E. (1989). Cognitive apprenticeship: Teaching the crafts of reading, writing, and mathematics. In L. B. Resnick (Ed.), Knowing, learning, and instruction: Essays in honor of Robert Glaser (pp. 453-494). Hillsdale NJ: Erlbaum.

Dooley, S. A., Meiskey, L., Blumenthal, R., Sparks, R. (1995). Developing Usable Intelligent Tutoring System Shells. Workshop on Authoring Shells for Intelligent Tutoring Systems, 7th World Conference on Artificial Intelligence in Education (AI-ED '95).

Lave, J., and Wenger, E. (1991). Situated learning: Legitimate peripheral participation. Cambridge: Cambridge University Press.

Lesgold, A., Lajoie, S., Bunzo, M., & Eggan, G. (1992). SHERLOCK: A coached practice environment for an electronics troubleshooting job. In J. Larkin & R. Chabay (eds.), Computer-assisted instruction and intelligent tutoring systems. Hillsdale, NJ: Lawrence Erlbaum Associates, pp. 201-238.

Meiskey, L., Root, R., Somers, P. (1996). LEAP Authoring Tool User Test Phase 1 Results. U S WEST Advanced Technologies, Technical Report No. T-09_04-005638-01.00.

Muller, M. J., McClard A., Bell B., Dooley, S., Meiskey L., Meskill, J. A., Sparks R., & Tellam, D. (1995). Validating an extension to participatory heuristic evaluation: Quality of work and quality of work life. Proceedings of the 1995 ACM Conference on Human Factors in Computing Systems (CHI '95), 115-116. Denver, Colorado.

10. NOTES

[1] LEAP and the LAT were developed at U S WEST Advanced Technologies in Boulder, CO. LEAP is a service mark of U S WEST (Qwest). This paper appeared previously in the *International Journal of Artificial Intelligence in Education*, Vol. 10, Num. 1 (1999).

[2] Although most of the training situations targeted by LEAP that we know of involve telephone-based conversations, we expect that LEAP would also be appropriate for training face-to-face interactive tasks, as well. For example, one inquiry that we received regarding a possible use for LEAP was for preparing legal testimony.

TOM MURRAY

Chapter 15

PRINCIPLES FOR PEDAGOGY-ORIENTED KNOWLEDGE BASED TUTOR AUTHORING SYSTEMS:

Lessons Learned and a Design Meta-Model

Abstract. While intelligent tutoring systems (ITSs), also called knowledge based tutors, are becoming more common and proving to be increasingly effective, each one must still be built from scratch at a significant cost. This paper discusses a number of design issues and design tradeoffs that are involved in building ITS authoring tools, and discuss knowledge acquisition and representation "lesson learned" in our work. A generic framework or "reference model" called KBT-MM (knowledge based tutor meta-model) for knowledge based tutor authoring tools is described. The reference model articulates a minimal but necessary set of features for knowledge based authoring tools that aim for scope, depth, learnability, and productivity.

1. INTRODUCTION

Intelligent tutoring systems. Intelligent Tutoring Systems (ITSs), also called knowledge-based tutors, are computer-based instructional systems that have separate data bases, or knowledge bases, for instructional content (specifying what to teach) and teaching strategies (specifying how to teach), and attempt to use inferences about a student's mastery of topics to dynamically adapt instruction. ITS design is founded on two fundamental assumptions about learning. First, that individualized instruction by a competent tutor is far superior to classroom style learning because both the content and style of the instruction can be continuously adapted to best meet the needs of the situation (Bloom 1956). Second, that students learn better in situations which more closely approximate the situations in which they will use their knowledge, i.e. they "learn by doing," learn via their mistakes, and learn by constructing knowledge in a very individualized way (Bruner 1966, Ginsburg & Opper 1979). Individually paced instruction and frame-based computer aided instruction (CAI) comprised early attempts to provide adaptive instruction, and, though successful for some types of learning, fell short because their learning environments were too contrived and their ability to adapt was limited to branching between static screens. ITSs use techniques that allow automated instruction to come closer to the ideal, by more closely simulating realistic situations, and by incorporating computational models (knowledge bases) of the content, the teaching process, and the student's learning state (Wenger 1987).

The need for ITS authoring tools. In the last decade ITSs have moved out of the lab and into classrooms and workplaces where some have proven to be highly effective as learning aides (see Chapter 17 in this volume). While intelligent tutoring systems are becoming more common and proving to be increasingly effective, each one must still be built from scratch at a significant cost. Little is available in terms of authoring tools for these systems. Authoring systems are commercially available for traditional CAI and multimedia-based training, but these authoring systems lack the sophistication required to build intelligent tutors. Commercial off-the-shelf (COTS) authoring systems excel in giving the instructional designer tools to produce visually appealing and interactive screens, but behind the presentation screens is a shallow representation of content and pedagogy.

Pedagogy-oriented tutors. A fundamental aspect of intelligent tutors is that knowledge about the domain and knowledge about how to teach is stored in modular components that can be combined, visualized and edited in the process of tutor creation. I use the term "knowledge based tutors" to highlight this aspect. In Chapter 17 I claim that intelligent tutors can be categorised into two broad groups, pedagogy-oriented and performance-oriented (though some systems fall in a grey area between these two):

> Pedagogy-oriented systems focus on how to sequence and teach relatively canned content. Most of them pay special attention to the representation of teaching strategies and tactics. Performance-oriented systems focus on providing rich learning environments in which students can learn skills by practicing them and receiving feedback. Most of them pay special attention to the representation of human problem solving skills or domain-specific processes or systems (either man made ones such as electrical components, or natural ones such as the meteorology). In general, performance-oriented systems focus on feedback and guidance at the level of individual skills and procedural steps, while pedagogy-oriented systems pay more attention to guidance and planning at a more global level, looking at the sequence of topics and the need for prerequisite topics.

This paper focuses on pedagogy-oriented tutoring systems. The suggestions presented in this paper apply to performance-oriented tutors also, but will be useful only to the extent that they model the conceptual structure of a domain, represent curriculum, and/or incorporate teaching strategies (as do most pedagogy-oriented systems). In Chapter 11 I describe the Eon knowledge based tutor authoring system. This Chapter summarizes some lessons learned from our experiences in the Eon project, and describes a generic framework or "reference model[1]" called KBT-MM (knowledge based tutor meta-model) for knowledge based tutor authoring tools.[2] The reference model proposes a minimal but necessary set of features for knowledge based authoring tools that aim for high generality, usability, flexibility, and power (see Chapter 17 for a discussion of these terms). It specifies representational and authoring features that systems should have, but not how these features should be implemented.

The Chapter begins by discussing some general issues that characterize knowledge based tutors in comparison with traditional CAI systems. I characterize this difference as an evolution from a story-board metaphor to a knowledge based metaphor for representing instructional content. I explain that an important characteristic of knowledge based tutors is that they are designed using building blocks at a higher more expressive level of abstraction. I call this "designing at the pedagogical level" (vs. at the media level).

The Chapter then describes the KBT-MM, beginning with a conceptual model of the primary objects needed in the pedagogical domain model (including topics, lessons, and contents), their attributes and how they relate to and interact with each other. This model is called the "five layered decision architecture." Then we describe general features of student models and teaching models within the KBT-MM framework. Next, I discuss how Ontology objects are used to specify the domain-specific details of a tutor and allow for the development of special purpose authoring systems. Finally I will discuss lessons learned and some of the problematic areas of representing pedagogical knowledge in knowledge based tutors.

2. FROM COMPUTER-BASED TO KNOWLEDGE-BASED INSTRUCTION

How an authoring tool is designed depends critically on who the intended user audience is. I begin by clarifying our target authoring audience and design team model, and then describe the types of design paradigm shifts needed to build ITSs.

2.1 Who Are the Users of ITS Authoring Tools?

In Chapter 17 Section 5.3 is a discussion of what skills are needed for using authoring tools of different types. As discussed in that Chapter, many ITS authoring systems simplify the authoring process by either making some aspects of the ITS non-authorable, or by constraining the type of ITSs that can be produced. For this Chapter our goal is support the authoring of all aspects of an ITS: domain model, teaching model, student model, and interface. The skill set needed to do this dictates that an ITS will usually be built by a team rather than an individual. The software

---

[1] Our term meta-model is similar to "reference model/reference architecture" mentioned in Schoening & Weeler (1997) and Betz et al. (1997).

[2] The reader may read either Chapter first, depending on whether one finds it most perspicuous to learn about generalities or a particular example first.

we are picturing has a complexity on the order of magnitude of Photoshop, AutoCAD, or FileMaker, i.e. it would take more skill or training than is usually associated with tools like word processors and PowerPoint. Building an ITS from scratch in this way requires a significant time commitment on the part of a teacher or domain expert. The "master" teachers or trainers who become ITS authors will have to be able to invest significant time building the systems and invest additional start-up time on the learning curve for these sophisticated tools. Our goal here is not to lower the skill threshold so far that the average classroom teacher can author an ITS (but they may be able to customize the ITS, see Section 3.7) but lower it to a point where every company and every school district could have at least one team capable of ITS authoring. These teams could work with teachers, subject matter experts, and graphical artists to rapidly produce ITSs.

By providing visualizations of key concepts and components in the ITS, authoring tools could make ITS authoring accessible to hundreds of thousands of individuals rather than a few hundred. We will call the lead person on an ITSs design team, the one who synthesizes knowledge of the domain, teaching strategies, and the requirements of the authoring system, the "instructional designer." The goal of the KBT-MM framework is to facilitate cost-effective ITS production by these instructional designers, as well as by those who have traditionally built ITSs from scratch (primarily those in academic and industrial research labs).

2.2 From Story Boards To Knowledge Bases

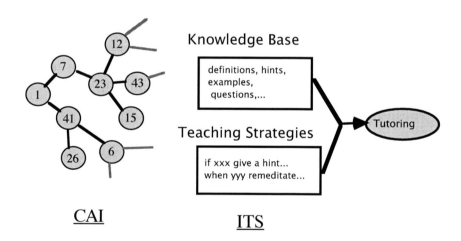

Figure 1: CAI story board vs. ITS knowledge base

Though there are few ITS instructional designers, there are many CAI instructional designers. Empowering these users to build more powerful instructional systems requires new tools *and* a shift in the way many of them conceptualize instructional systems. Specifically, it is proposed that moving from CAI authoring to ITS authoring involves a fundamental paradigm shift from "story board" representations of instructional material to more powerful and flexible "knowledge based" representations. The basic concept is not new; in fact, it is fundamental to all AI work. Our contribution is in fleshing out how the knowledge based paradigm can be best presented to empower instructional designers.

Commercially available authoring systems assume and support a representation of instructional content and instructional flow that is explicit, non-modular, and fairly linear. At a conceptual level, the instruction is specified like this (see Figure 1): "Bring up screen # 41; If the user clicks on button A, then go to screen # 26." Though branching is allowed, each branch must be explicitly specified. Adding a new topic or question involves explicitly encoding the branches to this content. Designing new content requires a duplication of efforts. I call this paradigm for designing instructional systems "story boarding" because it is based on enumerating all of the screens and the explicit links from each screen to the next. In contrast, in a knowledge based tutor the instructional content is separated from the specifications of how and when that content is presented to the student, so that the content can be used and re-used in multiple ways. Specifying how and when the content is to be presented is done with generic, reusable teaching strategies. For example, a CAI system may be programmed to give two hints for wrong answers to exercises. If the author later realizes that 3 hints are necessary, she has to go back and change every link associated with giving hints. In contrast, in the knowledge based model, there is one strategy specifying how and when hints are given, so that changing from 2 to 3 hints is a matter of making one change.

Designing at the Pedagogical Level. In traditional CAI instructional actions are encoded using building blocks at the level of the media: text, pictures, button clicks, etc. In contrast, knowledge based tutors can facilitate the design of instructional actions using pedagogically relevant building blocks. For example: "give a hint," or "teach the prerequisites". Designing instruction using building blocks such as "hint," "prerequisite," "if-confused," "mastered," "explanation," and "summarize" is much more powerful than designing instruction at the level of "show video," "present picture" or "wait for the button click" The instructor can conceptualize the curriculum at a more appropriate and powerful level of abstraction. An instructional strategy in the intelligent tutor might be: "if the current topic is conceptual and the student is doing poorly, give several examples." Alternate strategies can be created, so that the appropriate strategy can be used according to the needs of the student (e.g. learning style or mastery of the current topic) or the pedagogical characteristics of the content being taught (e.g. whether it is procedural or conceptual information).

Benefits of knowledge based tutoring. Designing tutoring systems in this way has many advantages over the traditional CAI design paradigm:

1) The behavior of the tutor can be **easily modified**. As shown above, to change when hints are given, only a single "give hint" strategy needs to be

changed and this effects how hints are given through the entire curriculum. This is true for the author making this change and also for a "meta-strategy" that sets this parameter during run time.

2) The content of the knowledge base is modular and can be **used for several purposes**. For example, a "topic" object in the knowledge base can contain information about how to teach itself, summarize itself, give examples of itself, introduce itself, and test the student's knowledge of itself. The same topic can then be used in many parts of the tutorial, for example, giving a summary at some point and teaching itself later on.

3) Systems designed in this way can be more **adaptive** to the needs of the student.

4) Instruction can be much more **learner-centered**, since modularization allows students to navigate to the topics they want to learn, and to ask for hints, examples, etc.

5) Because the content is modularised, authoring tools can be built to provide multiple and abstracted views of the instructional content. This facilitates instructors in being able to **easily view, inspect and navigate through the knowledge bases**.

3. A KNOWLEDGE-BASED TUTOR META-MODEL

3.1 Focussing on the Representation of Pedagogical Knowledge

Authoring tools can be described in terms of two aspects: an underlying representational framework (conceptual model), and a user interface (the authoring "tools") that reify this framework for the user, allowing her to create, visualize, and modify the elements of an ITS. Thus, the end usability and power of an authoring tool depends on both the power and fidelity of the underlying conceptual model and also on the usability of the interface tools. The conceptual model is of primary importance because if it is insufficient the best that the interface can do is to skillfully reify a weak model. Therefore, one goal of this Chapter is to define a conceptual model for knowledge based tutor authoring tools that aims for high power, generality, flexibility, and usability, based on what we see in a variety of other ITS authoring systems. The architecture is a "reference architecture" that illustrates the key distinctions necessary for a knowledge based tutor, but is not meant to constrain how these distinctions are implemented in a system. Rather than specify a particular design, KBT-MM prescribes properties that we think all knowledge-based authoring tools should have. It is a base-line model that contains a minimal but necessary set of features and elements, rather than (a baroque) model that tries to include most of the features seen elsewhere. In some instances it describes *innovations* to what is found in most ITS authoring tools, but in most aspects it is a systematic *synthesis* and abstraction of the important elements found in other systems. The Eon authoring system, described in Chapter 11, is one example of many possible implementations that conform fully with our description of the KBT-MM.

As is commonly done, we can describe the knowledge encoded in an ITS as being either domain knowledge or teaching knowledge. However, some of the knowledge in an ITS is in both categories. For example, hints and prerequisite relationships are usually considered part of the domain knowledge base, yet they are relevant only to the teaching of a subject (not to performance in the subject). As shown in Figure 2, I define a domain's "pedagogical knowledge" (sometimes called propeadutic information) as information specific to a domain that is relevant to teaching about the domain. As shown in the figure, some domain knowledge is relevant to performance but not necessarily used in instructional decisions. This "performance expertise" usually comprises the expert system rules (or production rules or procedures) in performance-oriented systems. Teaching knowledge can also be categorized as either teaching strategies, the (usually) domain independent strategies indicating how to teach; and pedagogical knowledge, the domain dependent declarative knowledge mentioned above. Performance-oriented systems tend to have non-existent or degenerating teaching strategies, and pedagogy-oriented systems tend to have non-existent or degenerative performance expertise.

The purpose for clarifying these distinctions is that KBT-MM focuses on the representation of pedagogical knowledge. Pedagogical knowledge is declarative information (whether "canned" or generated) such as examples, hints, explanations, definitions, problem descriptions, and problem answers. It includes the definition of topics and their relationships (e.g. prerequisite, generalization) that are needed to sequence instructional units. It also includes the classification of knowledge (or topics) according to knowledge type (e.g. fact, concept, principle) for the purpose of instruction.

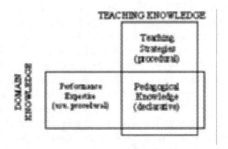

Figure 2. Teaching and Domain Knowledge

Traditionally, ITSs are described as having four major components or functions (Wenger 1987): a domain model, a teaching model, a student model, and an interface. Above I have mentioned the domain and teaching models. KBT-MM has less to say about the representation of the teaching strategies. This is because there is significant overlap and agreement (though nothing approaching consensus) among numerous ITSs, ITS authoring tools, and instructional design theories, on how content and curriculum knowledge should be conceptualised, while there is very little agreement on how to represent teaching strategies. As indicated above, the representation of expert problem solving knowledge is outside the scope of KBT-MM. KBT-MM does not specify details about a general framework for student modelling. This is because, at the knowledge representation level, student models are a rather straightforward "overlay" assignment of student knowledge values (or user history or performance metrics) to elements in the domain model. The algorithmic method of *inferring* the student state from student behavior is much more complex and idiosyncratic. The representation of the student model follows in a straightforward way from the representation of the domain model, plus a consideration of the data types needed to store the outputs of these inference methods. For example, a system that uses Bayesian inferencing methods will have a student model representational formalism tailored specifically to this method. Inferencing methods whose calculations use the number of hints given in each problem will of course have to store this information for each problem solved.

3.2 Abstract Topic Objects

Intelligent tutors make inferences about what knowledge or skills the student has. As such they differ fundamentally from traditional CAI in that they deal with abstract entities assumed to exist in the minds of students, in addition to the concrete content presented to the student. We call these entities "topics." They are called "instructional units," "domain knowledge elements," "knowledge units," "cognitive rules" etc. in other systems. Expository content, stored as text or media, is "presented," and inquisitory content (such as questions and tests) can be "correct," "answered," "passed" etc. In contrast, topics are "known," "understood," etc. In KBT-MM instructional units of any grain size are represented by Topics. Brusilovsky (in this Volume) notes that in hypermedia authoring there is a parallel distinction between the knowledge space and the hypermedia content space. Topics have a **Topic Type** that allows them to be categorized. Topics can have **Topic Properties**, such as difficulty and importance, as needed. **Topic links** define directed relationships between topics. Since one can define different types of topics and create arbitrary relationships between topics, this single object suffices for many representational schemes. That is, the topic object can be used to represent different types of units (such as concepts and facts) and can be used to represent different hierarchical or containment levels of units--what might be called chapters, sections, or sub-topics.

For a given tutor the vocabulary of topic types and link types is defined in an "Ontology" (see Section 4.5). Customizable link types allow the representation of a wide variety of topic networks, including component hierarchies, skill lattices, concept networks, etc. Each knowledge type defined in the Ontology has its allowed properties, allowed link types it can connect to, and allowed topic levels. Buggy Knowledge can be represented as topics of type Misconception, Procedure Bug, etc., depending on the type of knowledge that is in error.

3.3 A Layered Curriculum Object Framework

As I have mentioned, our goal is for KBT-MM to have a minimal but necessary set of features for KBT-authoring tools that promotes power, usability, generality and flexibility. From an informal analysis of pedagogy-oriented ITSs and ITS authoring tools, I propose a five layered "decision architecture," illustrated in Figure 3, as a general framework or reference architecture that illustrates common pedagogical components of these systems. The architecture specifies, at a conceptual level, the five main types of pedagogical objects and shows how control is mediated among them as a simple and necessary result of their nature. The Topic, Presentation Contents, and Events layers are common to all knowledge based tutors (though they may be called different things and implemented in various ways). The Lesson and Topic Level layers are less common and are included to satisfy the requirements of power and generality. Next I describe the five layers in an order that facilitates explanation of their purpose.

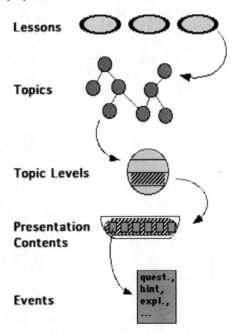

Figure 3: Five-Layer Decision Architecture

Events. Events are the low level interactions between the student and tutor, such as a student clicking a button, or the tutor giving a hint, several of which will occur while a Content is running.

Presentation Contents. The Presentation Contents layer contains the specific concrete contents that the student will see and manipulate (text, graphics, buttons, interactive screens, etc., or the templates or algorithms for generating this content). Contents are expository or inquisitory interactions.

Topic Levels. As mentioned above, topics are related to each other via topic links to form hierarchies or networks. Having only the semantic network formalism to represent all aspects of curriculum structure was found to be inadequate. In some domains the most perspicuous structure for representing aspects of the content may be a table rather than a network. In our Eon system we found that Levels within topics allowed us to represent multiple levels of performance (e.g. memorizing vs. using knowledge), mastery (novice to expert), and pedagogical purpose (summary, motivation, example, evaluation, etc.) for each topic. This layer of the architecture allows for a structural layer within each topic object. As shown in the Figure, Presentation Contents are referenced from inside the topic levels. (Section 5.4 describes uses of topic levels in more detail.)**Topics.** Topics were defined above. They are specialized according to Topic Types, specified with Topic Properties, and related with Topic Links. Topic networks do not specify any ordering or starting point for learning sessions, and are independent of the instructional purpose of particular sessions.

Lessons. Lesson objects are used to specify instructional goals and learning/tutoring styles for a particular group of students or learning session. Nominally, the Lesson lists a one or more starting or goal topics, and specifies a default teaching strategy. The teaching strategy then determines how the topic network will be traversed, causing other topics to be taught, to satisfy the goal of learning the goal knowledge.

The nature of the objects in the Decision Architecture implies the following general control structure: running a Lesson runs a number of Topics, each of which runs some of its Topic Levels, each of which contains a number of Presentation Contents, each of which leads to a number of Events. In the next Section we discuss how previous research and theory informs the KBT-MM model as described so far.

3.4 Previous Work in Representing Pedagogical Knowledge

This Section focuses on what we have learned about representing pedagogical domain knowledge, including elements from various instructional theories and authoring tools, and use this as evidence for the validity and generality KBT-MM described above. We will make reference to the following authoring tool systems, references to which can be found in Chapter 17: XAIDA, REDEEM, Eon, DNA, Expert CML, Instructional Simulator, IDLE, IRIS, CREAM, SimQuest, and Eon.

A. Modular abstract knowledge units. As mentioned in Section 3.2, intelligent tutors represent units of knowledge to be learned, which we call topics, as modular units separate from content and instructional strategy. All of the principles and theories mentioned below implicitly or explicitly assume that content can be modularized to organize the learning. (However, in Section 6.3 I discuss some problems inherent in knowledge modularization.) Of the authoring tools described in the Overview Chapter (Chapter 17), every one of them uses modular knowledge units, except for a couple of special purpose authoring systems for tutors that do not reason about what to teach next. Authoring tools use different schemes and use different names for instructional units. REDEEM has pages and sections. Expert CML organizes domain knowledge in a hierarchy of objects including Departments, Programs, Courses, Topics, Subtopics, Modules, SubModules, Objectives, and Activities.

B. Types of Knowledge. Researchers in computer science, psychology and educational theory have developed many schemes for classifying knowledge. VanLehn (1987, pg.60), speaking from an AI perspective, says that the popular procedural/declarative distinction is "notorious...as a fuzzy, seldom useful differentiation." It is recommend that the procedural/declarative distinction be abandoned for classifying knowledge in instructional systems (except in contexts where it has a precise meaning, as in the ACT* theory of cognition (Anderson 1983)) and that more descriptive and precise schemes be used.

Bloom (1956) and Gagne (1985) were among the first to develop clear classifications of knowledge and learned behavior, and assert that different types of knowledge require different types of learning or instructional methods. Other knowledge typing schemes were later developed which are better grounded in modern cognitive theory and are more operational and concrete for the purposes of computational representation. For example, Merrill's Component Display Theory (Merrill 1983) classifies learning objectives (content types) as facts, concepts, procedures, or principles. In contrast to the hierarchical typing schemes of Bloom and Gagne, Merrill's content types are organized into a matrix along with performance types (explained later). Kyllonen and Shute (1988) propose a more complex multidimensional model which distinguishes knowledge types in a hierarchy which illustrates cognitive complexity, and organizes these types in relation to the level of autonomy of learning and the processing speed needed to perform the task. Reigeluth's Elaboration Theory of Instruction (1983) is another complex knowledge typing scheme. It builds upon Merrill's theory for how to teach individual units of knowledge of different types, and goes further to proposes a theory of how these units can be organized and taught within entire domains, which require knowledge of many types.

Topics ("basic learning units") in IRIS use Merrill's typing scheme: facts concepts, procedures, principles. DNA organizes topics ("curriculum elements") into facts (symbolic and episodic knowledge), procedures, and concepts. CREAM uses Gagne's system: verbal information, intellectual skills, cognitive strategies, motor skills, attitudes.

C. Hierarchies. latices, and networks. A number of educational theories mention the hierarchical nature of knowledge. For example, Ausubel's "subsumption theory" of learning (Ausubel 1960) focuses on the hierarchical organization of concepts in disciplines. He proposes that abstract knowledge (further up in the hierarchy) is more meaningful and useful, and preferred to more specific or rote learning. His Advanced Organizer model prescribes that new information must relate to previous information, and that effective learning paths through the hierarchy of knowledge will differ for each student. Web teaching (Halff 1988) similarly requires that knowledge networks be annotated with information about the relatedness of topics (e.g. prefer more closely related topics) and generality (e.g. give generalities before specifics). The subsumption relationship is valid for conceptual learning, but pedagogical knowledge for procedural or skill learning can require a different treatment. Burton and Brown's BUGGY tutor (1982) uses a skill lattice to represent subtraction subskills. The NEOMYCIN system (Clancey 1982) uses an and/or lattice to represent medical diagnostic procedures. The BIP-II programming tutor (Westcourt et. al 1977) uses a network of subskills related by four links: analogous, harder than, same difficulty, prerequisite. Knowledge is often messier than can be represented in a simple hierarchy or lattice and network representations are needed. Cognitive science has shown that cognition has network-like aspects (Collins & Loftus 1975). Goldstein's (1982) ITS uses a Genetic Graph with relationships among procedural rules which represent the way knowledge evolves while a student learns how to master a maze exploration game. The relationships include explanation, generalization, analogy, and refinement, and show how learning can follow knowledge pathways from abstract (simple) to more refined, from deviation to correction, and from specialization to generalization.

Most of the authoring systems incorporate hierarchical or network-like topic representations. They differ in the types of topics and topic relationships used. Brusilovsky (this Volume) says that most adaptive hypermedia systems use "is-a" and/or "part-of" relationships. LAT, REDEEM, and RIDES use simple hierarchical representations with one of two relationship types. "Instructional units" in RIDES are in a hierarchy of sub-tasks. XAIDA has associative information (facts) related as "subparts" in the "Physical Characteristics" shell; casual reasoning relationships in its "Theory of Operation" shell, linked procedural steps in its "Procedures" shell, and a discrimination net (fault tree) in its 'Troubleshooting" shell. Within the Physical characteristics shell parts are related using: part-of, function, location, and connected-to. DNA incorporates hybrid network structure that borrows from classic semantic networks and GOMS production rule networks to represent several knowledge types and relationships in a unifying formalism (it also seems to be the only system that has strengths or weights associated with its topic links). Its relationship types include: procedural-part, next-step, conditional-step, causes, and part-of. IRIS uses these relationships between its learning units: prerequisite, procedural (next-step, if/then decision), conceptual (is-a and part-of); theoretical (cause-effect) and precondition. CREAM uses separate networks for three classes of objects. "Capabilities" (similar to our "topics") are related with these relationships: analogy, generalization, abstraction, aggregation, and deviation. "Objectives" are related using: mandatory prerequisite, desirable prerequisite, supporting (or "pretext"), and aggregation. Resources are related using: analogy, abstraction, case, utilization, assistant, and equivalence.

Our goal in KBT-MM is to have a meta-level system that is compatible with all of the above, not a specific system that incorporates all of the topic types and link types.

D. Representing buggy knowledge. Many of the theories and instructional systems mentioned above include some representation of buggy knowledge and a method for remediating it. Buggy knowledge, such as misconceptions and buggy skills or rules, is usually represented in a form similar to its corresponding performance knowledge, but with additional properties and relationships that allow the buggy knowledge to be diagnosed and remedied.

Relatively few authoring systems seem to incorporate misconceptions and bugs. XAIDA stores "misconception" facts. Ontologies developed for the Eon system use misconceptions, procedural bugs, and erroneous facts. Model Tracing Tutors (see Ritter et al. in the Volume) store buggy procedural rules.

E. Beyond networks to more structured knowledge. Above we argued for the need to include an additional level of (or levels) of structure beyond network representations. We proposed Topic Levels as such a structure, but there are many possibilities (the Topic Level idea is an inclusive and general framework, but some systems use schemes too complex to be incorporated into Topic Levels.). Topic Levels allow the tutorial to distinguish particular levels, methods, or modes of teaching within the topic. We describe two uses for Topic Levels seen in authoring tools: task levels and behavioral objective levels.

To distinguish task levels IDLE breaks a an inquiry topic or problem into these steps: learning the problem context, gathering information from sources, gathering data from instruments, abstracting and manipulating data, drawing conclusions, and communicating conclusions. SimQuest allows for several 'assignment types:" performance, investigation/explaination, specification, and optimization. Instructional Simulator has templates specifying different types of patterned exercises: describe parts, identify and locate parts, demonstrate ("Simon sys" method), practice, and perform. XAIDA has 11 such exercise templates, and RIDES has 25.

Several systems (IRIS, DNA, CREAM, Eon, Instructional Simulator, and XAIDA) incorporate an important principle from instructional design theory: that a subject matter can be learned at several levels corresponding to different types of behavioral objectives. For example consider the procedure for starting a car. We can distinguish at least three types of objectives: the procedural steps can be memorized, the procedural skill can be mastered, and the purpose and causal relationships of its components can be understood. We can distinguish "topics" such as "starting a car" from the types of objectives. For example, Merrill's content matrix (Merrill 1983) incorporates "performance levels" called remember, apply, and create. This is handled in different ways by different authoring systems, but overall it calls for an additional level of structure beyond the network. In CREAM concepts can be identified, recognized, classified, and generalized. IRIS uses the levels defined by Bloom as described above.

Again, our goal is to propose an overall structure (Topic Levels) that is compatible with most (but not all) of the schemes described. In KBT-MM Presentation Contents are assigned to the Topic Levels within each topic, not directly to the topics. This is compatible with the authoring systems mentioned above.

F. Knowledge attributes. Several theories point to the need to assign pedagogically relevant attributes to topics, such as importance and difficulty. Bruner's (1966) theory of learning focuses on how we form new concepts, categories, and rules by induction from examples or cases along with the analysis of key features. This indicates that not only knowledge chunks and their relationships, but also their pedagogically relevant properties, need to be represented. Case-based tutors, such as some of the Goal-Based Scenarios described in (Schank et al. 1994), which use knowledge bases of example objects or situations, search the knowledge base for appropriate cases based on case attributes. Many ITSs incorporate topic attributes into tutoring strategy decisions. Adding attributes to topics gives them internal structure like "frames" or "schemes" in AI knowledge representation.

Brusilovsky (in this Volume) notes how frame-like knowledge representations are used in many adaptive hypermedia systems to represent internal topic structure. The components or parts in Instructional Simulator, RIDES, and XAIDA have properties associated with them. REDEEM and other systems include topic difficulty levels.

G. Lessons and instructional objectives. Lesgold (1988) points out that the concept of prerequisite is often inadequate, since whether one topic is a prerequisite of another may be a function of the learning goal of a particular session, rather than a static relationship between topics. He proposes a goal lattice structure that captures the different "viewpoints" of a curriculum structure that result from different instructional goals (or perspectives).

Leinhardt and Greeno (1986) distinguish lesson structure and subject matter as the two fundamental systems of knowledge needed for teaching, where subject matter knowledge is used by the lesson structure, the later being in charge of tailoring a session for an individual student.

For most systems, including adaptive hypermedia systems, the learning goals are a sub-set of the topic or concept network. RIDES and Eon store goals in lesson objects. IRIS, and CREAM represent learning objectives in terms of behavioral objectives, and described above. Van Marcke's (1992) GTE framework makes a similar distinction between content and instructional goals.

The above principles support the following prescriptions which are used in the KBT-MM framework. Separate "what to teach" into *modular units* independent of how to teach it (item A above). Use *network formalisms* for knowledge units with directed links allows for the creation of hierarchies and lattices and less canonical frameworks (C). Include a number of different *types of nodes and links* (B). Knowledge units should have *pedagogically relevant properties* associated with them (F). *Learning goals* for a tutorial session should be represented separately from instructional content (G). ITSs should be able to distinguish among different *types of knowledge* (B), and also represent *buggy knowledge* (D), so that teaching strategies can be predicated on knowledge classes. There is an indication that exclusive use of a network formalism does not provide enough knowledge structuring complexity, and that *more complex data structures* (such as Topic levels) will often be needed to support multiple levels or modes of instruction for each topic (E).

3.5 Student Model and Teaching Strategies in KBT-MM

Theories from instructional design and cognitive psychology have much to say about the declarative organization of content and knowledge, and this has influenced ITS design. In contrast, though there are many prescriptions for how and when to present content, there is little agreement nor general understanding of how procedural teaching strategies should be formally represented or implemented.

The inference method used by the student model is left unspecified in KBT-MM, but the Decision Architecture does suggest some constraints on what types of information the student model should represent. The student model can include values for objects at all five layers of the architecture (as in Eon's student model). That is, it can store an overlay value for lessons, topics, each level within a topic, presentations, and events. A given implementation can opt out of including some layers in the Student model, for example, the simplest models will include only Topic values (and perhaps will also save the history of all user interactions at the Event layer). For the objects in each layer the student model can have one or more values, for example: mastery, confidence level, was-attempted, was-shown-to-the-student, number-given, etc. KBT-MM specifies the five layers, but leaves the particular vocabulary of value types for each object to the Ontology. The value of objects at each level is a function of the values at the next lower level. For example, a Topic's values are a function of the values of its topic levels.

Teaching strategies are part of the "control structure" of an ITS-- the algorithms or rules that determine how the ITS will behave and respond to the student. Embedded in this control structure will be numerous individual decisions related to deciding what, when, and how to teach. KBT-MM leaves it up to the implementation whether the control structure is, for instance, blackboard-based or production rule based. In any case, at an conceptual level we can say that there are many decisions to be made in the form of "IF X then Y" rules. The antecedents inspect internal states, which must be about the student (e.g. IF the student understands the current topic...), the history of the session (e.g. IF greater than 6 hints have been given for the previous three activities...), or the nature of the current content (e.g. IF the current topic is a difficult fact...). The bulk of the consequents are tutorial actions (e.g. ...THEN give a hint, THEN begin the next topic, THEN show the topic summary) or student model inferences (e.g. THEN increase student model confidence for mastery of the current topic level).

Thus, the vocabulary of terms used in the antecedents and consequences of teaching strategies come from the decision architecture. The vocabularies for student model values and domain model details that are defined in the Ontology. It is possible and preferable to design authoring tools such that tutoring strategies reference these and only these pedagogical building blocks. I.E. no new objects or terms need to be introduced beyond the framework described in the Sections above.

3.6 Ontology Objects

As explained in Chapter 17, the goals of usability, flexibility, and power are often at odds with each other, since systems tailored for specific domains can include powerful non-generic representational and instructional methods. Attempting to create a single ITS framework that includes the capabilities of many existing systems would, at the least, result in a very complex and obscure system. In contrast, we have tried to identify a minimum underlying framework that is neutral regarding domain or instructional theory. KBT-MM includes a highly generic, yet underspecified, Layered Decision Architecture that has many aspects left open to particular implementations. Ontology objects specify the remaining complexity for each implementation. The decision architecture specifies the structure of objects and control. Ontologies in KBT-MM are simply sets of terms that specify the types, levels, or attributes that are allowed for the objects in a particular incarnation of the KBT-MM.

In general, an ontology is a particular way of describing the world (or some domain); it is a scheme for conceptualizing the objects and relationships in a domain (Gruber 1993).[3] I use the term "ontology object" for a data object which defines a conceptual vocabulary for the system. Relating this to the Decision Architecture above, an ontology could specify the following: lesson properties, topic types, topic link types, topic properties, and topic levels. The ontology could also specify the types of values used by the student model, as described above. As an example of Ontology use, consider the ontology that was created for the Eon Statics Tutor. It defined topic types Fact, Concept, Procedure, and Misconception, and topic links Prerequisite, Generalization, and SubConcept. A (fictitious) tutor for Manufacturing Equipment might have topic types Safety, Maintenance, Operation, Theory, and Common Failures, and topic links SubPart and SimilarPart. Ontologies can be generic and reusable, for example, an ontology developed for one science tutor should be usable (perhaps with slight modifications) for other tutors with similar pedagogical characteristics (e.g. instruction at a predominantly conceptual level).

Most tutoring systems fall into one of a number of loose classes, each addressing specific types of cognitive skills or knowledge types. Example domain classes include: conceptual information, factual information, problem solving skills, design skills, procedural skills (such as maintenance), inquiry and experimentation skills, equipment diagnostic skills, customer contact (and other interpersonal) skills, sensory-motor skills, association and pattern recognition skills, and argumentation/hypothesis generation skills. Ontology objects may be reused across tutors within a domain class. Reigeluth (1983) prescribes that each domain be assigned an "organizing content type:" conceptual, theoretical (principle-like), or procedural, that best fits the characteristics of the domain and the instructional goals. His "elaboration theory of instruction" specifies methods for selecting and sequencing content according to the organizing content type. Others have categorized domains according to whether their structure is predominantly

---

[3]The ARPA Knowledge Sharing Effort (KSE) described in (Gruber 1993) is exploring the use of standardized ontologies for sharing knowledge in knowledge-based systems. Our work is related, but currently we are focusing on ontologies that support knowledge authoring rather than sharing, and we focus on pedagogical knowledge, where the KSE deals with performance knowledge.

procedural, historical, structural, causal, teleological, inferential, etc. Domain types have characteristic links between topics, for example analogy, physical-part, a-kind-of, etc.[4] Classifying domains according to organizing content type, and creating ontology objects for each organizing content type, would help bootstrap ITS construction.

Several other ITS projects address ontologies. Some of these, for example (e.g. (Mizoguchi et a. 1996) and (Van Marcke 1992)) have a goal to define a generic conceptual vocabulary that can be used do describe describing all of the objects, attributes, and methods needed to design a tutor. The scheme usually includes hierarchical sets of ontologies, with a core ontology defining terms generic to all instruction, and set of domain-specific ontologies (for example, for mathematics or automobile maintenance) to be loaded on top of the core ontology. Some projects also include authoring tools for developing and extending these ontologies, Our use of ontologies is different than, yet compatible with, these efforts. In KBT-MM the Ontology is an open structure that allows the designer to define a vocabulary for a particular tutor. The goal of these other projects is to define a complete vocabulary that is independent of any specific implementation--it is almost a conversational vocabulary defining the concepts needed to define or describe an ITS and its behavior. In the case of KBT-MM the Ontology framework is tied closely to the architectural framework, as its purpose is to allow the author to specify implementation-specific attributes of the primary objects defined by the architecture (topics, presentations, student models, etc.). The two methods are compatible because, once other research teams successfully define vocabularies, elements of these vocabularies can and should be used for KBT-MM Ontologies (especially if the vocabularies are standardized or in common use).

Moving the discussion from representational frameworks to authoring tools, an authoring tool that conforms to KBT-MM needs a tool for defining the ontology. In authoring an ITS an ontology must be defined first, and then the authoring tools must adapt to the specifics of the ontology. For example, if the ontology specifies that the allowed knowledge types for the tutor are Facts and Principles, then the tool for creating topics should only allow these two types of topics to be created.

3.7 Meta-Authoring Special Purpose Authoring Systems

Even with tools that are relatively generic, powerful, and usable, the process of starting from scratch to build an ITS is still a formidable one. Not surprisingly, in our research with the Eon system we consistently ran up against the classic knowledge acquisition bottleneck (Hoffman 1987). Domain experts are usually good at sketching out student interactions, lessons to teach particular topics, and responses to specific student behaviors, but articulating knowledge at a more abstract or generic level is difficult. The following ITS knowledge representation tasks were inherently difficult for most subject matter experts:

---

[4](Wenger 1987, pg. 331) describes several "justification types," such as structure, functionality, and constraints, that could be used as topic links.

1. **Ontology design.** Defining the types of topics, topic links, and topic levels for the Topic Ontology, and also defining the ontology of allowable values for the student model.
   2. **Curriculum representation.** Breaking the instructional material and goals up into discrete components (topics) and providing relationships between these components (topic links);
   3. **Strategy and diagnostic procedure representations.** Representing teaching strategies and procedures in a general way (e.g. how do we recognize that a student is confused, and what is a reasonable general response to student confusion?);
   4. **Student model definition.** Defining rules that express when a student knows a topic, and labeling or characterizing the student's level of knowledge.

In our experience, it takes a knowledge engineer, a person skilled in the elicitation and representation of these types of knowledge, to work with the subject matter expert (the teacher) to build these aspects of the system. Highly usable authoring tools help, since they help the teacher visualize the information and participate more intimately in design process, once the knowledge engineer has broken the ice and explained things once or twice.

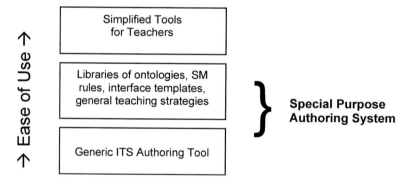

Figure 4: Three Tiered Suite of Authoring Tools

One solution to the knowledge acquisition problem is creating special purpose authoring tools, for example authoring tools for building ITSs that teach anatomy, foreign policy, or verb conjugation. Authoring shells which are used to build tutors for specific task types (Jona 1995, Sparks et al. in this Volume, and Bell in this Volume) can, in principle, build tutors with more fidelity and depth than general purpose tools. The depth vs. breadth tradeoff seems to imply that you can have one but not the other, that 1) ITS authoring tools that can build powerful tutors that closely match the pedagogical needs of a domain must have a narrow scope, and that 2) an all-purpose ITS shell, by necessity, must have a shallow knowledge representation and the learning environment it creates will have little conceptual fidelity (in comparison to special purpose tools).

Our approach is to build special purpose authoring systems on top of the generic authoring system, so that the authoring tool becomes a "meta-authoring tool." This would involve constructing libraries of pre-built components such as ontologies, student model rules, and interface screens. Since some teaching knowledge is general in nature (Van Marcke 1992, Jona 1995), default teaching strategies and meta-strategies could also be provided. We could then provide sets of these components tailored to facilitate building tutors for classes of domains or tasks. For example, ITS authoring shells could be produced for science concepts, human service/customer contact skills, language arts, and equipment maintenance procedures. Instructional designers could immediately start constructing tutors in an environment that supports and helps structure the knowledge acquisition process.

By using a meta-authoring approach, we hope to achieve a fair degree of fidelity and depth, while maintaining usability and generality. Figure 4 illustrates the potential for a three-tiered suite of authoring tools, using the Eon system as the example base authoring system. At the first tier is a general purpose ITS authoring system that requires moderate knowledge engineering and instructional design expertise to use. At the second tier are special purpose ITS authoring systems (built on top of the first tier system) that require minimal knowledge engineering and instructional design expertise. The third tier involves tools for the average teacher using an ITS in her class. At the third tier are a simplified subset of the authoring tools, so that once an ITS is built, *any* teacher can customize it for a particular class or group. For example, by modifying a hint's text, replacing a picture with a more recent version, making a teaching strategy more verbose, or by changing a prerequisite relationship between topics. This is important because some teachers will be reluctant to use instructional systems that they can't understand or adapt.

4. SUMMARY OF KBT-MM

Below I will summarize our recommendations for the design and use of knowledge based authoring tools using the KBT-MM conceptual model.

4.1 Domain and Curriculum Model

The fundamental conceptual entities in an ITS are the curriculum objects. The representational framework should allow for, and the authoring tools should reify, these objects in accordance with the following principles:

- Represent instructional (teaching) **strategies separately** from domain knowledge (i.e. use a "knowledge based paradigm").
- Design for **modularity** and re-usability of content. I.E. whenever possible content should be independent of the way it is used, and be able to be used in multiple contexts.
- Provide a representational formalism that is **customizable and extensible**. The vocabulary of properties and building blocks used to conceptualize and

build a tutor should reflect the structures and assumptions inherent to the particular domain and/or instructional style. KBT-MM does this through the **Ontology** object. Below when the specification calls for customizability, the tutor-specific aspects are intended to be specified in the Ontology of that tutor.

- Explicitly represent abstract pedagogical entities-- referring the knowledge to be learned--from the concrete media which the student will see, read, hear, and manipulate. In KBT-MM we call the knowledge units "**topics**" and the concrete media "**contents.**"
- Provide separate data objects to store the individual user (and tutor) events that happen during presentations, for example: "hint given", "correct answer" "poured water into the flask." KBT-MM calls these objects "**events**".
- Represent topics and their relationships in a semantic network, which we call a "topic network." Allow for a customizable vocabulary of **topic types and link types**.
- Provide methods for assigning **pedagogically relevant attributes**, such as difficulty, importance, and is-qualitative, to topics. The vocabulary of these attributes should be customizable.
- Provide a method for an **additional level of structure** inside of topic objects, as this will facilitate knowledge representation in most domain. In KBT-MM we do this by allowing topic to have any number of "**topic levels**" within them. The number and names of the topic levels should be customizable. Example topic levels are: introduction, examples, easy-level, practice, review.
- Provide methods for associating domain knowledge objects and media content objects to instructionally relevant categories or purposes, e.g. "explanation," "summary," "hint," "difficulty," so that teaching strategies can be designed using building blocks at the **pedagogical level** of abstraction. The KBT-MM design does this through a number of features, including customizable topic levels.
- Provide a method for defining the **objectives and context** of particular tutorial sessions. In KBT-MM we do this with **Lesson** objects, which, at the minimum, specify goal topics and the default teaching strategy for a particular assignment of the ITS to a group of students.
- KBT-MM specifies a "five **layered decision model**" that shows the logical and control relationships between the major objects in the curriculum model: Lessons, Topics, Topic Levels, Presentations, and Events.

4.2 Student Model

The KBT-MM specifies the following for the Student Model representational framework:

- The student model is an **overlay** on the five types of objects in the decision architecture. The types of values that can be assigned to each object (e.g. mastery, number of times given, certainty) is customizable.
- KBT-MM does not constrain the **inference methods** that are used to assign values to curriculum overlay objects, but specifies that the value of objects at each level is a function of the values at the next lower level.
- Define topic types for **buggy knowledge** or misconceptions to allow these to be recognized, diagnosed, and dealt with. The student model accumulates evidence for this "incorrect" knowledge using methods parallel to its regular topic diagnostic methods.

4.3 Teaching Model

The KBT-MM specifies the following for the Teaching Model representational framework:

- Allow the representation of instructional content and instructional **strategies separately**.
- Allow content to be generated and **sequenced dynamically**.
- Allow authors to create generic and **reusable teaching strategies** that can be used with different instructional content.
- Allow instructional strategies to be predicated upon **pedagogically relevant characteristics** of the content (e.g. whether a topic is a fact or a concept; whether a topic level is difficult or easy).
- Instruction decisions, if conceptualized as **rules**, have the objects, properties, and ontology vocabulary as described above available for their **consequents** (for example, running, showing, of "giving" a topic, lesson, presentation, hint, etc.). Similarly, the properties of the student model and of the curriculum model are available for rule **antecedents** (for example, predicating a tutorial action on mastery of a topic, the type of topic, or how many hints were given).

4.4 Authoring Tools

Finally, I summarize our recommendations regarding authoring tools that reify the KBT-MM representational framework.

- Provide **visual reification** for the concepts and structure of the underlying representational framework. This relieves working memory load and assists long term memory by providing memory cues. As a general rule, if some aspect of the representational framework is too complex to create clear visualization, then the framework may be too complex to expect non-programmers to be authors. Multiple views or multiple representations of the same structure are often needed to convey the full form and function of a feature.

- Provide tools that make it easy to **browse, search for, and reference all content** objects. Include tools that make it easy to navigate among the objects and tools.
- Anchor usability on **familiar authoring paradigms**, and facilitate evolution to more powerful paradigms. It is useful to have a look and feel similar to off-the shelf CAI authoring tools, and to provide features which allow a smooth transition from traditional authoring paradigms to authoring more powerful intelligent tutors. (For example, Eon's interaction editor and flowline editor have many surface similarities to off-the-shelf multimedia authoring tools.)
- Provide features powerful enough to author **generative content** and to create new presentations on the fly based on parameters of the current state. Similarly, provide productivity tools that capitalize on repetitive or **template-like content** (as in Eon's Presentation Content Editor). Other useful features include scripting languages, the ability to assign interface component attributes to methods or expressions, and the ability to have attribute values reference each other.
- Provide **WYSIWYG tools** that allow easy movement between authoring content and test-running the tutorial to facilitate rapid build-and-test iterations. If interface template screens are used, the tools need to help the author comprehend the distinction between the fixed items of a tutorial screen and the database-driven variable items.
- Facilitate an **opportunistic design** process. ITS authoring tools should allow for top down (starting with the abstract curriculum structure), bottom up (starting with specific screens and content), and opportunistic (switching between top down and bottom up as needed) design of ITSs.
- Allow for **interface extensibility**. Little is said in this paper about how authoring tools should support the design of ITS interfaces, but regardless of the method used, it is recommend that the system allow plug-ins or APIs such that interfaces of arbitrary complexity can be incorporated, and the author is not limited to building all learning environments from scratch using the primitive graphical objects available in the authoring tool. (An example is the "custom widgets" feature in Eon.)
- Provide tools to create the Ontology first, and subsequently the interface should **reify the Ontology**. Once the Ontology for a tutor is defined, the forms, menu selections, etc. of the authoring tool should reflect the vocabulary of the ontology. For example, if the Ontology defines the types of relationships allowed between topics then the tool that allows topics to be linked together should show exactly this list of relationships.
- Create **special purpose authoring** tools for increased usability and productivity. Generic authoring tools having Ontology objects can be used as "meta-authoring tools" to build special purpose authoring tools for particular classes of intelligent tutors.

5. ISSUES AND LESSONS LEARNED IN REPRESENTING PEDAGOGICAL KNOWLEDGE

This Section covers important issues that we have encountered when working with instructors trying to explicitly represent pedagogical knowledge for intelligent tutors. Human knowledge does not exist in neatly defined, clearly named packages---it is inherently complex, densely connected, fuzzy, and ambiguous. Yet to use knowledge in AI systems we try to represent it in individual units with definite structure and properties. The tension between the organic nature of knowledge and our need to modularize it leads to a number of unavoidable issues for ITS knowledge representation, which I discuss below, along with how we dealt with these issues in our research using the Eon system.

5.1 How Generic Can Teaching Strategies Be?

In Chapter 17 Section 5.3 I discuss limitations to what we can expect authors to be able to conceptualise and perform. In addition There are also limits to what we can reasonably expect in the level of sophistication of tutoring strategies. In our design for KBT-MM we are aiming for a particular level of generality in teaching strategies. To illustrated, consider the progression of hypothetical teaching strategies or rules from very specific to very general, where each item is intended to be an abstraction or reason encompassing the previous one:

1. If button #1 on screen #5 is pushed, then go to screen # 12.
2. If question-12 is answered wrong, then give explanation-5.
3. If the student gets a question wrong twice, then give a canned explanation.
4. If the student is very confused, then give an additional level of feedback.
5. Give students several opportunities to think about each situation so that they may learn from their mistakes, then scaffold feedback of increasing levels of specificity.
6. Learning happens through an active process of concept formation while trying to account for new information within in the context of previous knowledge.

This progression of hypothetical ITS tutoring rules goes from the trivial to the impossible. The first two items illustrate the low-level coupling of state testing and action found in (non-intelligent) CAI. The third item illustrates a type of tutorial reasoning that is typical of today's intelligent tutors. A tutor using this rule must keep a record of the student's behavior, but the reason why the rule is applicable is not explicit. The fourth item, though less common, is well within the state of the art for ITSs. A tutor using this rule must have abstract models of the student's mental state and the tutoring process. A diagnostic strategy must infer the level of "confusion" from student behavior (such as number of times asking for help), and the appropriate interpretation of "feedback" must be inferred based on the current state of the tutorial session. The fifth item states a pedagogical belief or strategy, and represents the principle behind the previous rule. It could be operationalized in a limited way but is not precise enough to be part of a robust ITS (with today's technology). The final item is based on a theory---a psychological assumption. It represents the reason for the previous principle and the purpose for the rule above it. Representing and using knowledge at this level of abstraction is clearly out of the reach of current technology.

5.2 Topic Modularity and Interdependence

When knowledge in a domain is organized into modular units, which are then sequenced flexibly according to instructional strategies, a number of unavoidable problems arise. First, it is difficult to encode the knowledge "between" the topics, which can be about how they are related to each other, or the emergent knowledge that comes from understanding topics together. Reigeluth (1983) and Lesgold (1988) refer to this as the "glue" in a curriculum (Lesgold also refers to this as "non-linearities" between topics).

The issue of curricular "glue" is not as much a natural property of the content, as an emergent phenomena that happens when instructional designers break up the content or domain knowledge into discrete chunks. In Eon we deal with this glue in several ways. First, Topics can have Topic Levels such as "Introduction" and "Conclusion," which address how the topic relates to other topics that are likely to precede or follow it in most curriculum paths. Second, Topic Types called Composites and Synthesizers can be used. A Composite topic is one that represents the whole which is more than the sum of its parts. For example, our Static Tutor's Linear Equilibrium (LE) topic had "sub-part" links to LE Intuition, LE Concept, and LE Principle. Knowing Linear Equilibrium involves knowing each of these parts, and also how the parts fit together in an understanding of static situations.

"Synthesizer" is a term used by Reigeluth (1983) for instructional components that interrelate and integrate instructional units. In Eon we can define a topic type called Synthesizer. One possible strategy using synthesizers relates two topics the student has learned: after a topic is taught check whether a synthesizer connects it with another mastered topic, and if so, teach the synthesis material. Another possible strategy connects new information with existing information before the new information is presented: before a topic is taught, check whether a synthesizer connects it with an already known topic and, if so, present the synthesis material.

Lesson objects are another mechanism for dealing with curricular "glue". Since Lesson objects can specify a sequence of goal topics, they can also be used to insure that certain information is presented between topics, to compare and contrast them.

The second modularity problem is that topics are often interdependent. For example, in our Statics tutor, the student has to know something about Gravity to fully understand Linear Equilibrium, yet some understanding of Linear Equilibrium is prerequisite to learning about Gravity. Topic Levels organized by mastery, combined with levels of prerequisites, allow us to deal with this in Eon. We can assign content to topics at various levels (e.g. easy, moderate, and difficult) and allow prerequisite links such as Familiarity, Easy Prerequisite, and Moderate Prerequisite. Thus we can specify that the easy level of Linear Equilibrium should precede learning the difficult level of Gravity, and that the easy level of Gravity should precede the difficult level of Linear Equilibrium. This method simulates spiral teaching, in which the same topics are taught from successively more difficult perspectives (see (Murray & Woolf 1992) for more discussion of spiral teaching).

5.3 Knowledge Structure and Complexity

In order to create structured and purposeful instruction the instructional designer organizes her understanding of a domain into common "epistemic forms" (Collins & Ferguson 1993) such as hierarchies, tables, networks, scripts, and schemas, and as complex nested constructs using these basic forms. Halff (1988) notes that "the sequence of exercises and examples should reflect the structure of the (knowledge) being taught and should thereby help the student induce the target (knowledge)". ITS authoring must be supported with tools that allow clear visualization of the knowledge structures, and more esoteric or complex structures are difficult to comprehend and author. In KBT-MM we have devised a system that accommodates many but not all possibilities.

Having Topic Levels within the topics allows a significant increase in representational power over strictly network representations, without a large increase in complexity. For example, we have simulated Merrill's Performance Content Matrix (Merrill 1983) by assigning content types to Topic Types (fact, procedure, skill, etc.), and performance levels to Topic Levels within each topic (remember, use, apply, create, and meta-knowledge). If we tried to do this with topic networks without Topic Levels, there would be a confusing proliferation of related Topics, one for each level of each Topic, i.e. we would need topics called Gravity-memorize, Gravity-use, etc. Levels of mastery (e.g. easy, difficult) can be encoded using topic levels, as can different pedagogical functions for a topic. For example, a teaching strategy can tell a topic to "teach" itself, "summarize" itself, "define" itself, and "test" for its knowledge if the Ontology defines these topic levels.

Additional analysis of a domain seems to always lead to additional complexity. For example, in our study of authoring the Statics Tutor we discovered numerous different perspectives on the material (Murray 1991 pg. 218), most of which we did not attempt to implement. For example, Newton's' Third Law can be taught by presenting questions which progress from existence (does a force exist here?), to direction (what direction is the force?), to relative magnitude, to quantitative questions. This material can also be taught by showing a progression of example situations using different surface features, e.g. with objects hanging, falling, rolling, colliding, etc. It can also be taught by dealing with first horizontal forces, then vertical, then both, then rotational forces. Each of these methods has some instructional merit. Some are within the capacity of the topic-network and topic-level to represent, and some would require a more complex scheme if the representational formalism is to clearly reflect the structure of the domain knowledge.

5.4 Non-Independence of Content and Strategies

Unfortunately, it would seem that little in ITS authoring is as simple "as advertised." One of the fundamental characteristics of ITSs, and what characterizes ITS authoring tools from CAI authoring tools, is the separation of content from teaching strategies--the separate representation of what to teach/present from how and when to teach/present it. However, it turns out that it is epistemologically impossible to completely separate them. In fact, the *meaning* of most of the conceptual objects used to define content depends inextricably on the strategy that is implemented to use those objects. For instance: what is the meaning of "prerequisite?" At a vague level the term specifies that one thing should be known before another is taught. But at a more precise level, for a particular ITS, the meaning is most strongly related to what a prerequisite relationship causes to happen. Are prerequisites always taught first? Are the parts of a subtopic also prerequisites of the topic? If you have to "know" all prerequisites before being taught a topic, do you have to know them completely, or only at an introductory level? The answers to these questions are found in the teaching strategies (and perhaps in the student model rules). One *might* be able to design the content knowledge base without making any assumptions about teaching strategies, but more likely, the decision about whether one topic should really be called a "prerequisite" of another will depend on knowing the answer to these types of questions. As another example, consider the decision of whether to classify a topic as a "concept". At a vague level we may have a meaning for "concept," but at a deeper level whether we classify a topic as a concept or something else is closely related to how the system will behave as a result of that categorization.

All this does not change our vision for effective authoring tools, but is offered as a note of caution to designers. Content can still be authored to be flexible and reusable. But every ITS design group must engage in an ongoing process of grounding the meaning of the objects and terms that they use. An authoring tool, by its very nature or through accompanying documentation, can suggest meanings or ranges of interpretation for these terms, but this does not alleviate the necessity of meaning-grounding within each design team. It means that designing content ontologies and tutoring strategies may need to be an iterative process, and that when decisions are made about ITS conceptual building blocks, that the designer should note what this reveals about assumptions related to teaching strategies.

6. CONCLUSIONS

Authoring tools can have a variety of purposes and intended users, and their design must account for tradeoffs among four overall goals: usability, power, flexibility, and generality. This paper describes a reference model or generic framework (KBT-MM), plus a set of guidelines and lessons learned, with the goal of supporting the creation and use of ITS authoring tools that maximize among these four goals (especially for pedagogy-oriented tutors). KBT-MM is in a sense an attempt to answer the question: is there a common underlying framework that could be used to describe all or most ITSs or ITS authoring systems? In terms of the systems described in this book it does so with only moderate success, because of the diversity of systems represented. However I believe that it does capture the essential or fundamental elements of the systems that fall within our definition of knowledge-based tutors. If compared to any particular knowledge based tutor authoring tool one might say that KBT-MM is fine as far as it goes, but leaves out all of the most interesting parts. This is precisely because what one find most interesting about a particular system are the parts that are particularly innovative or distinctive. The KBT-MM is offered as a reference model which could be used to compare systems and as a starting point for the design of new systems.

The issues involved in building an ITS can be subtle, and a trained knowledge engineer may always be needed on the ITS design team. But with appropriate representational formalisms and tools that visually reify the conceptual structures involved, learning how to be a good ITS knowledge engineer can be made accessible to many more people, not just to computer programmers and AI scientists. Also, once a trained person gets the primary structures set up, an instructional designer with much less training can continue to fill in the content.

Future plans for this line of work include working with researchers who work in the area of performance-oriented systems, especially model-tracing tutors, to extend or combine the principles outlined in this paper to that domain. I have also applied many of these principles to the design of an authoring tool for adaptive hypermedia, as described in (Murray 2002).

7. REFERENCES

Anderson, J. (1983). The Architecture of Cognition. Harvard Univ. Press: Cambridge, MA.
Ausubel, D.P. (1960).The use of advanced organizers in the learning and retentions of meaningful verbal material. J. of Educational Psychology 51, 267-272.
Betz, F. Suthers, D., Wheeler, T. (1997). Architecture Abstraction Hierarchy Reference Model. IEEE Learning Technology Standards Committee draft document.
Bloom, B. (1956). Taxonomy of Educational Objectives, Vol. 1. David McKay Co., New York.
Bruner, J. (1966). *Toward a Theory of Instruction.* Harvard Univ. Press, Cambridge, MA.
Burton, R. R., & Brown, J. S. (1982). An Investigation of Computer Coaching for Informal Learning Activities. In Sleeman & Brown (Eds.), Intelligent Tutoring Systems. New York, NY: Academic Press.
Clancey, W. (1982). Tutoring rules for guiding a case method dialogue. In Intelligent Tutoring Systems, D. Sleeman & J. Brown (Eds.), Academic Press 1982, pp. 201-225.
Collins, A. & Ferguson, W. (1993). Epistemic Forms and Epistemic Games: Structures and Strategies to Guide Inquiry. Educational Psychologist, 28(1), 25-42.Collins, A.M. & Loftus, E.F. (1975). A spreading activation theory of semantic processing. Psychological Review 82(6), 407-428.
Gagne, R. (1985). *The Conditions of Learning and Theory of Instruction.* Holt, Rinehard, and Winston. New York.
Ginsburg, H. & Opper, S. (1979). *Piaget's Theory of Intellectual Development.* Prentice-Hall: Englewood Cliffs, NJ.
Goldstein, I. P. (1982). The Genetic Graph: A Representation of the Evolution of Procedural Knowledge. In Sleeman & Brown (Eds.), *Intelligent Tutoring Systems.* New York, NY: Academic Press.
Gruber, T. (1993). Toward Principles for the Design of Ontologies Used for Knowledge Sharing. In *Formal Ontology in Conceptual Analysis and Knowledge Representation*, Guarino & Poli (Eds.). Kluwer Academic Publishers.
Halff, H. (1988). Curriculum and Instruction in Automated Tutors. In *Foundations of Intelligent Tutoring Systems*, Polson & Richardson (Eds.). Lawrence Erlbaum Assoc., Hillsdale, NJ.

Hoffman, R. (1987). "The Problem of Extracting the Knowledge of Experts From the Perspective of Experimental Psychology." *AI Magazine*, pp. 53-67, Summer 1987.

Jona, M. (1995). Representing and re-using general teaching strategies: A knowledge-rich approach to building authoring tools for tutoring systems. In AIED-95 workshop papers for Authoring Shells for Intelligent Tutoring Systems.

Kyllonen & Shute (1988). "A Taxonomy of Learning Skills." Brooks Air Force Base, TX: AFHRL Report No. TP-87-39.

Leinhardt, G., & Greeno, J. (1986). The Cognitive Skill of Teaching. In *Journal of Educational Psychology*, Vol. 78 No. 2, 75-95.

Lesgold, A. (1988). Toward a Theory of Curriculum for Use in Designing Instructional Systems. In Mandl & Lesgold (Eds.), *Learning Issues for Intelligent Tutoring Systems*, Springer-Verlag, New York.

Merrill, M.D. (1983). Component Display Theory. In *Instructional-design theories and models: An overview of their current status*, pp. 279 - 333. C.M. Reigeluth. (Ed), Lawrence Erlbaum Associates, London.

Mizoguchi, R., Sinitsa, K., Ikeda, M. (1996). Knowledge Engineering of Educational Systems for Authoring System Design. In *Proceedings. of EuroAIED-96*, pp. 593-600. Lisbon.

Murray, T. (1991). *Facilitating Teacher Participation in Intelligent Computer Tutor Design: Tools and Design Methods*. Ed.D. Dissertation, Univ. of Massachusetts, Computer Science Tech. Report 91-95.

Murray, T. (2002). MetaLinks: Authoring and Affordances for Conceptual and Narrative Flow in Adaptive Hyperbooks. International Journal of Artificial Intelligence in Education, Vol. 13.

Murray, T. & Woolf, B. (1992). Tools for Teacher Participation in ITS Design. In Frasson, Gauthier, & McCalla (Eds.) Intelligent Tutoring Systems, Second Int. Conf., Springer Verlag, New York, pp. 593-600.

Reigeluth, C. (1983). The Elaboration Theory of Instruction. In Reigeluth (Ed.), *Instructional Design Theories and Models*,. Lawrence Erlbaum Assoc., Hillsdale, NJ.

Schank, R., Fano, A. Bell, B. & Jona, M. (1994). The Design of Goal-Based Scenarios. *Journal of the Learning Sciences*, Vol. 3 No. 4.

Schoening, J. & Wheeler, T. (1997). Standards--The key to educational reform. IEEE Computer, March 1997, pp. 116-117.

Van Marcke, K. (1992). Instructional Expertise. In Frasson, C., Gauthier, G., & McCalla, G.I. (Eds.) *Procs. of Intelligent Tutoring Systems '92*. Springer Verlag, Berlin.

VanLehn, K. (1987). "Learning One Subprocedure per Lesson," *Artificial Intelligence*, Vol. 31.

Wenger, E. (1987). *Artificial Intelligence and Tutoring Systems*. Los Altos, CA: Morgan Kaufmann.

Westcourt, K., Beard, M. & Gould, L. (1977). Knowledge-based adaptive curriculum sequencing for CAI: application of a network representation. *Proceedings of the National ACM Conference*, Seattle, Washington, pp. 234-240.

Winne P.H., 1991. Project DOCENT: Design for a Teacher's Consultant. In Goodyear (Ed.), *Teaching Knowledge and Intelligent Tutoring*. Norwood, NJ: Ablex.

ACKNOWLEDGMENTS

This material is based upon work supported by the National Science Foundation and the Advance Research Projects Agency under Cooperative Agreement No. CDA-940860.

STEVEN RITTER, STEPHEN B. BLESSING &
LESLIE WHEELER

Chapter 16

AUTHORING TOOLS FOR COMPONENT–BASED LEARNING ENVIRONMENTS

Abstract. We argue that a focus on building an authoring tool for a complete learning environment is misplaced. An analysis of the task of authoring a commercial educational system reveals it to be best accomplished through authoring separate components. For some of these components, authoring tools already exist and need not be duplicated for use in educational systems. Connecting the various components together is a separate authoring task, and parts of this task are different for educational systems than for typical component-based software. The last part of this paper describes the current way in which our model–tracing ITSs are constructed.

1. INTRODUCTION

Intelligent tutoring systems have proven to be remarkably effective instructional tools (Koedinger, Anderson, Hadley and Mark, 1997; Person, Bautista, Graesser, Mathews, The Tutoring Research Group, 2001; Rosé, et al., 2001), but the cost of developing them has been a major obstacle to their commercial success. As a result, there has recently been a strong emphasis on developing authoring tools that simplify the task of creating such systems. An authoring tool is usually considered to be responsible for the creation of all elements of the learning environment, including the student model, domain knowledge, user interface, and the evaluation and reporting facilities. Some authoring tools (e.g. the Tutor Development Kit or TDK described in Anderson & Pelletier, 1991) treat the authoring process as a programming task. They provide a collection of tools that make it easy for programmers to construct an intelligent tutoring system. Other authoring tools (the tools discussed in this volume) have a more ambitious goal. They allow domain experts who are not programmers to create complete intelligent tutoring systems by demonstrating correct (and incorrect) solutions to a set of tasks.

We argue that neither approach is likely to provide a general solution to the authoring problem. While both approaches are successful on their own terms, a task analysis reveals that the authoring task is multi-faceted and unlikely to be solved within a single system. The goal of building commercial-quality learning environments is ill-served by monolithic authoring systems. However, if we consider learning environments to be composed of several different components, we can imagine separate authoring tools directed at each component. These components often overlap with components of other systems, so good authoring tools already exist. There are, however, some special needs of component-based educational systems. In particular the goal of creating an environment which acts as a problem-solving environment, either independent of or in conjunction with an instructional agent requires a different kind of communication between the components. In the last part of this paper, we describe how we have addressed this issue. We turn now to discussing an architecture for intelligent tutoring systems based on separate components and the challenges of authoring the different parts.

2. THE AUTHORING PROBLEM

It is widely accepted that a good task analysis is an essential element in creating an effective learning system. We describe below the components of a prototypical intelligent tutoring system and provide a tentative account of the skills involved in creating each element of the system.

2.1. Intelligent Tutoring System Design Overview

In this section, we describe the conceptual architecture of a fairly complete intelligent tutoring system. This provides us with a way of describing the functions and goals of the system. Our intention is not to describe the architecture of any existing system, but to cover the most important aspects that must be possessed by any commercial-quality intelligent tutoring system.

We have tried to frame this architecture in a general way that will accommodate many different approaches to teaching and learning. While we have strong beliefs and evidence about the effectiveness of certain teaching methods, we do not believe that our architecture should be limited only to such systems. Although our examples come from our own experiences, our architecture does not assume, for example, that the tutor agent is a model-tracing production system that gives immediate feedback to students when they make mistakes. At the architecture level, we can simply treat the tutor agent as a black box which interacts with the rest of the system whenever and in whatever way it sees fit. Still, the architecture we assume is most appropriate under certain circumstances:

• *Learn by Doing*. We assume that the learning environment primarily encourages users to learn by performing tasks. Although learning environments may contain declarative instruction, such as text, movies and audio, or multiple-choice questions, our reference architecture is best suited to environments where the student's primary activity (or, at least, the primary learning activity) involves accomplishing a task using computer-based tools.
• *Guided Learning*. We assume that the learning environment provides students with some guidance in accomplishing the task. This guidance may be (but does not have to be) in the form of unsolicited assistance (where the student does not explicitly request feedback). In contrast, the system may provide assistance only when requested to do so. We make no assumptions about the content or timing of the assistance. This assumption does exclude pure discovery learning systems, which would have no use for a tutor agent.

• *Computer-based Activity.* Many learning environments involve significant learning and problem-solving activities that do not take place at a computer or other computer-observable device. Since the tutor agent will not be able to receive information about these kinds of activities, this architecture will be less relevant to such learning systems. Further, we assume that the tutor agent can benefit from the kind of detailed, protocol-like information that is communicated in the client/tutor architecture.

Given these three issues, this approach may be more amenable to certain types of tutors than others. Using Murray's (this volume) classification, this approach is probably less useful to Intelligent/Adaptive Hypermedia, where the emphasis is on declarative learning and navigating through a knowledge space, and more useful to Domain Expert Systems, with their emphasis on procedural learning. Other classifications (e.g., Curriculum Sequencing and Planning) may apply to only part of our architecture, while Device Simulations and Equipment Training (e.g., RIDES & XAIDA, this volume) could (and do, to at least some extent) make use of separating out the interface from the underlying data representation of the domain. The underlying idea with this approach is to allow the individuals who create ITSs to concentrate on the part in which they have expertise.

At a broad level, an intelligent tutoring system consists of four classes of components: tools, tutor agents, curriculum organizers and administrative facilities (see Figure 1). We do not see this as a better or even substantially different way of describing a typical ITS, but just one that emphasizes the component nature of ITSs.

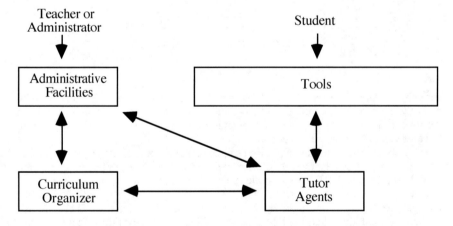

Figure 1: General component architecture

2.1.1. Tools

The tools consist of the graphical and textual elements that the user sees and manipulates. We refer to these parts as "tools" (following Ritter & Koedinger, 1996) rather than "interfaces" because they can comprise much more than simple user interfaces. They may interact with the user and can be quite sophisticated in their own right. An example of a simple tool is a window for displaying text and diagrams. More complex tools could include spreadsheets or simulations. Some tools are designed to be used outside of a learning environment. That is, they are not created with the intention of teaching; they simply exist to help users accomplish some task. Other tools are developed specifically for use in a learning environment. Still other tools (for example, simulations and on-line textbooks) are created for educational purposes but do not have a model of the student's current knowledge state. They have no sense of a level of knowledge which a student is to achieve or of the student's progress towards achieving that knowledge. While tools help the user to accomplish some task, they have little or no understanding of the user's task goals and they are unable to assist the user in achieving those goals, beyond assistance in using the tool itself. A

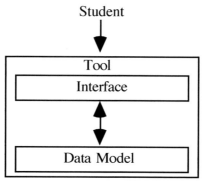

Figure 2: Substructure of the tool component

spreadsheet tool, for example, might be able to offer help to the student on how to enter the appropriate formula to add the values of several cells, but it could not assist the user in determining that adding the value of a set of cells is an appropriate step towards achieving a higher-level goal.

Tools are an extremely varied lot, covering most of the range of computer programs. A tool may be thought of as containing an interface component and a data model (see Figure 2). The data model stores the state of the application, and the interface component displays that state and allows the user to change it. In most applications, this is a conceptual distinction only. That is, the interface is closely tied to the data model, so that manipulating something in the user interface necessarily causes a change in the data model. For example, moving a shape from one position to another in a drawing program is closely linked to changing the underlying numbers that specify the position of that shape.

Closely linking the interface to the data model can provide consistency between the two, but it leads to a lack of flexibility. Making changes to the program's interface usually requires corresponding changes in the data model. In addition, such programs are frequently more difficult to develop and maintain for multiple platforms. To some extent, interfaces tend to be specific to a hardware platform. Cross–platform environments like Java reduce but typically do not eliminate this problem. The data model, on the other hand, consists of standard data structures that could be portable to any platform. Even with the advance of Java and other cross–platform tools, the decoupling of the actual interface from its data model has advantages. Changes can be more readily made to interface (for example, the use of buttons over pop–up menus) if the two are not intimately tied. Moreover, the skills for creating these two pieces may reside in different people—a designer for the interface and a programmer for the data structures. Another concern is in running over the internet. The separation of interface and data model allows the possibility of running the interface on the client side of the connection and the data model on the server.

These considerations lead to an architecture where the interface and data model are implemented as separate components which communicate through a fixed protocol. Such separation is sometimes called "factoring" the application. Factoring the application makes it easier to implement different interfaces to the data model. Factoring also provides a consistent way to describe changes to the data model. For example, a word processor may allow you to change the currently-selected text to boldface by either pressing the "B" icon on a toolbar or by pressing the key combination command-shift-B. Each of these actions in the interface can result in an identical message being sent to the data model: "set the textface of the current selection to bold." Factoring may also allow an agent (such as an instructional agent) to "peek" into the processing within the tool.

In order to allow independence of the interface from the data model, it is important that this communication protocol express events in terms of their semantics, rather than their user-interface implementation. That is, the user's action could be described as either "click on the bold icon" or "set the textface of the current selection to bold." The latter allows a single message to be sent for either of the user-interface actions, greatly simplifying the communication. The choice of a description in terms of the data model also has implications for the ability of the instructional agent to interpret user actions, as we will discuss below.

Factored applications which provide an external language for describing these changes to the data model are called "scriptable" applications. With such applications, it is possible (at least in principle) to develop new interfaces to the data model. For example, in such an application, you might be able to construct a menu item which results in the script "set the textface of the current selection to bold" being sent to the data model. Choosing that menu item would be identical in function to choosing the "B" icon or pressing the command-shift-B key combination.

Many scriptable applications also provide commands to access the data model itself. For example, a word processor might allow the interface (or another application) to "get the textface of the current selection." Applications which support these kinds of queries are termed "inspectable." One advantage of inspectable tools is that they provide the possibility of enhancing the tool with representations that are not natively provided by the tool. For example, a graphing tool might be able to query a spreadsheet for some data and then construct a graph of that data in a format not provided by the spreadsheet.

One use of scriptable and inspectable applications in learning environments is that they allow alternative interfaces to be created. Such interfaces can be added to existing applications to increase their educational value or their appropriateness to a particular age group. The ESSCOTS system (McArthur, Lewis, & Bishay, 1995) is an example of an educational system which takes advantage of this approach. The real power of this approach can be seen if the tutor agent can automatically adjust the interface to adapt to the user's skill level. Fox, Grunst and Quast (1994) describe such a system.

Factored applications have an additional advantage that makes them especially useful for inclusion in learning environments. If interface actions result in messages being sent from the interface to the data model, and if it is possible for an external application to "watch" those messages, then it is possible to learn what actions a user is taking in the tool, in the terms of the data model. If these conditions are satisfied, then the application is termed "recordable."

Since information about changes to an application's data model can be easily mapped to semantic information about the steps in accomplishing a task, recordable applications are especially suited to use as tools in an intelligent learning environment. Ritter and Koedinger (1996) describe several systems built using this principle.

It is important to emphasize that information about changes to the data model is not available unless the application provides that information. The operating system may be able to provide information about primitive interface actions, but it is extremely difficult to determine data model changes from interface actions. For example, if the only information available were that a user had pressed the mouse button at one position in a word processing application, moved the pointer and then let go of the button at another position, there are many possible interpretations of this action in terms of the data model. Depending on the exact positions of the mouse-down and mouse-up actions, the result might be moving a window, resizing a window, selecting some text, moving some text, scrolling a window, etc. In general, the ability to infer changes in the data model from user-interface actions requires complete knowledge of every aspect of the interface. The computation required to perform this mapping approaches the complexity of the application itself.

2.1.2. Tutor Agents

The tutor agent is an intelligent agent which should (ideally) act as a human tutor acts. The presence of tutor agents transforms a tool into a guided learning environment. A tutor agent understands the student's goals and the tasks which the student can complete as a way of accomplishing those goals. The tutor agent tracks the student's progress towards these goals and can provide the student with assistance in achieving them.

The tutor agent is a complex object, but it basically provides three functions (see Figure 3). It gives help in response to a request; it provides unsolicited feedback and it evaluates the student's progress based on the student's actions. In a TDK-like model-tracing tutor, all three of these functions are subsumed by the same expert system. Solicited and unsolicited feedback are generated as the direct result of firing certain productions in the production system. Evaluative information consists of ratings of the student's skill on various dimensions, each of which corresponds to one or more production rules.

In our conceptual architecture, we have separated out these components. The help generation system is responsible for constructing appropriate feedback in response to a direct request from the user. The student action analysis component is responsible for updating the student model whenever the student performs an action. In some cases, it may generate unsolicited feedback for the user. The student action analysis component also generates evaluative information about the student which is passed to the curriculum organizer (so that the curriculum organizer can use that

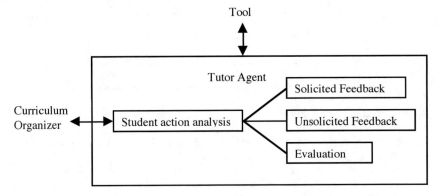

Figure 3: Substructure of the tutor agent

information to select tasks). The student action analysis component may contain further sub-components. For example, in a model-tracing tutor, this component would contain an expert model and a student model. For our current purposes, the substructures at this level are unimportant.

2.1.3. Curriculum Organizer

The curriculum organizer (see Figure 4) is responsible for presenting appropriate tasks and instruction to the student. In many systems, tasks are pre-defined. Other systems generate problems on-the-fly to reflect the student's progress towards educational goals. The decision to choose or generate a particular task or piece of instruction can be as simple as picking the next problem on a pre-set list or can be as complex as generating a task which emphasizes skills deemed to be incompletely mastered by the student.

The curriculum component is responsible for knowledge tracing, or tracking a student's progress across tasks. This requires storing information about individual students in a student database. The curriculum component also needs to have access to a curriculum database. This database indicates the range of tasks available and a pedagogical strategy for ordering those tasks

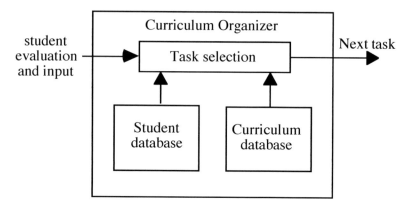

Figure 4: Substructure of the curriculum component

for presentation to the student. The use of the term "database" may be slightly misleading: the curriculum database may generate tasks, rather than store them, but the rest of the system should be able to act as if the task were drawn from a collection in the database.

The task selection module is the subcomponent which takes evaluative information about the student and combines this with information from the student and curriculum databases to suggest the next task. In some systems, the evaluative information may be augmented by the student or teacher's direct instructions or stated preferences. This information is conveyed to the curriculum component through administrative tools.

2.1.4. Administrative Facilities

Administrative facilities are used by teachers, curriculum administrators, and students to examine the system itself. Such tools might provide the ability to inspect the system's assessment of a student or to modify the system's assessment of a group of students. In addition, most systems include reporting tools, which output information about the progress of a class or an individual student. In some systems, there is a facility to assign a password to a student or specify a particular curriculum for a class of students.

Administrative facilities are often ignored in the description of learning environments because they often hold little research interest. In fact, many intelligent tutoring systems omit these tools completely. We include these systems as a major component of learning environments for three reasons. First, they are essential to the commercial success of any system. Second, the assumption that such facilities exist puts constraints on the rest of the system. For example, the assumption that there are reporting tools creates a requirement that the student model maintained by the tutor agent be inspectable in some way. Finally, the skills required for the creation of these tools differ substantially from those required for the creation of other parts of the system. Such differences may warrant the use of different authoring tools for their creation.

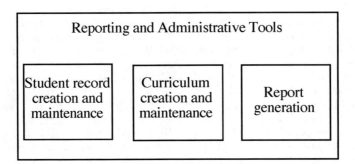

Figure 5: Substructure of the reporting and administrative tools

The reporting and administrative tools provide a way to view and, if necessary, modify the student and curriculum databases. There are three major subcomponents involved (see Figure 5). First, there is a module which is concerned with creating and maintaining student records. This module allows a teacher or system administrator to set student passwords, assign students to a particular curriculum and override knowledge tracing by moving a student to a different part of the curriculum than is suggested by the tutor. The curriculum creation and maintenance facility allows a curriculum developer to add, delete, reorder and restructure tasks. Some existing systems (e.g., Ainsworth's REDEEM, this volume) have concentrated on this aspect of curriculum and have developed a finely-tuned way for this interaction to occur. Finally, the report generation facility allows the teacher or student to view their progress.

3. CLIENT–SERVER VERSUS CLIENT–TUTOR

For the most part, the overall learning system architecture just described follows a standard client/server model. The different components must request information from each other, and in some cases, must be able to be partly controlled by a different component. For example, suppose a teacher wants to advance a student from lesson 1 to lesson 2. The teacher would call up an administrative facility and direct it to send a message to the curriculum component. The message would roughly correspond to "Change Student A's lesson to 2." In the transmission of this message, the administrative facility acts as a client and treats the curriculum component as a server; the client makes a request, and the server services it.

In order for client/server communication to work, three conditions must be satisfied. First, the client must know about the server and about the services that the server provides. Second, the server must know that is should expect to receive requests for services from the client. Third, the client and server must agree on a protocol for expressing requests and responses to requests. These requirements seem logical and may even seem necessary, but it is important to recognize that the tool and tutor agent have a fundamentally different relationship which cannot be expected to fulfill these requirements (Cheikes, 1995b makes a similar point).

One requirement of the tutor agent is that it be unobtrusive. For the most part, the tutor agent should just silently watch the student perform the task without interference. When a mistake is made or help is required, however, the tutor should make its presence known (at the appropriate time and in an appropriate manner, depending on the type of tutoring being done). We like to think of the tutor agent as watching over the student's shoulder. Besides being unobtrusive to the student, the tutor agent needs to be unobtrusive to the tool. The tool is used to accomplish a task, and a knowledgeable user can accomplish that task using the tool without the assistance of a tutor agent. In short, the tool doesn't need the tutor agent (though the user might). In a client/server system, the client needs the server. The server accomplishes a task for the client that the client could not accomplish without it. In the tool/tutor agent system, the tool accomplishes its task with or without the tutor agent. Since the tool doesn't need the tutor agent, it is unreasonable to expect tool authors to add features specifically to support the possible existence of a tutor agent. This poses a problem, since the tutor agent still needs to observe the student's use of the tool.

This distinction between client/tutor and client/server is analogous to one made in cognitive psychology when a participant in an experiment is asked to give a verbal protocol. There are two main types of reporting procedures for verbal protocols: concurrent and retrospective (Ericsson & Simon, 1993). In concurrent verbal protocol reports, participants are constantly talking while performing the experimental task, saying aloud the things which are going through their minds. In contrast, a retrospective report has participants remember, after the experiment has already taken place, what went through their minds. Depending upon the experiment and the way the protocols are to be used, one reporting method may be better than the other. Concurrent protocols are immediate and not open to interpretation by the participant, but may influence the way the participant does the task. Retrospective reports will not influence the way the participant does the task, but the participant may interpret their memory in response to the way the experimenter probes for the protocol.

For our purposes, the crucial distinction is not timing but the fact that retrospective reports are elicited by the experimenter. Most reporting aspects of the overall learning system architecture operate in a manner similar to a retrospective report: one part of the system asks for information from another part, and the information that is sent back can be specialized (i.e., "interpreted") for the requester. However, in the special relationship between the tool and the tutor agent, the ideal situation would have the tool providing something like a concurrent verbal protocol. That is, the tool should be sending out, for whoever wants to listen, a stream of information corresponding to the user's actions within that tool. The tutor agents which are monitoring that stream can then interpret that information in whatever way they are programmed. Concurrent verbal protocols are useful to psychologists precisely because the subject giving the protocol does not (or, at least, should not) filter anything out. The protocol-giver does not need to make any decision about what information is more or less important to report. In the same way, a tool should not make this decision: it merely reports every action the user takes, leaving it to the tutor agent to judge the appropriateness of the action.

Since the tool and the tutor agent are not as tightly coupled as in a typical client/server relationship, there may be a need for a mediator or translator between the two components. Later in this paper, we discuss solutions to this problem.

5. TASK ANALYSIS OF AUTHORING AN INTELLIGENT TUTORING SYSTEM

Now that we have described the learning environment, we can specify the skills needed to create such components and link them together.

5.1. Authoring the Tools

The designer of a tool needs to understand the range of tasks to be performed with the tool and be able to design an interface which allows the user (both students and teachers) to efficiently accomplish tasks which make appropriate use of the tool. The skills involved in building a tool vary, depending on the tool-building tools that the implementor chooses to use. Currently, there is a wide range of traditional programming languages and several visual programming environments to choose from. There are specialized visual programming systems that would be appropriate for tools that are heavily database- and report-oriented and others that emphasize multimedia content. If the tool is not very complex and fits well into a standard category, creation of the tool may not involve programming at all. In other cases, it may be possible to incorporate a pre-existing, off-the-shelf tool into the learning system.

In short, if a tool is to be built (as opposed to purchased in pre-existing form), the skills involved in building the tool match the skill set required to create any standard computer program. This set may, but does not have to, involve programming and graphic design.

A more important set of skills for the tool designer involves understanding the tasks to be performed with the tool well enough to design an effective tool. There is a range of generality that must be considered. A general-purpose spreadsheet can be used for either accounting or data analysis, but there are also specialized tools that can only be used for one or the other of these tasks. Typically, generality of the tool trades off with ease-of-use. At the extreme, a tool could be built to complete all of the tasks expected to be presented in the learning environment with little (or no) interaction from the user. In this case, of course, the user would learn nothing. An appropriate tool for a learning environment should always be general enough that it is useful for performing tasks which are not in the student's curriculum. This perspective emphasizes the fact that the tool developer need not know about the intended curriculum for the learning environment. For more general tools, like spreadsheets, the tool developer may not even know the nature of the tasks to be performed in the curriculum (for example, a spreadsheet developer need not know whether the spreadsheet will be used in a learning environment for accountants or statisticians).

5.2. Authoring the Tutor Agent

Now, consider the set of skills involved in developing a tutor agent. For programming skills, the situation is similar to that faced by the tool developer. In some cases (as when using the Tutor Development Kit), creating a tutor agent is a programming task. In other cases, high-level visual programming tools may exist (e.g. Blessing, this volume). Beyond these considerations, the tutor agent developer must have a very different set of skills. Primary in this task is the ability to analyze a domain and extract the features relevant to working through tasks in the domain. In addition, the tutor agent developer needs to carefully analyze the particular steps involved in moving from the initial task state to the final state. In most tutor agents, the developer must also anticipate common errors along the way to task solution. This sort of information is gathered by careful study of experts performing the task and of novices learning to perform the task. The skills involved here are generally those related to task analysis. The resulting task description must then be converted into an implementation as a computer program. Thus, the cognitive scientist performing the task analysis must additionally be able to communicate this analysis in sufficient detail to a programmer (or to program the system him or herself).

Another important skill required for developing a tutor agent is the ability to construct and present feedback in an appropriate manner for the target students. McKendree (1990) found that careful tailoring of help messages had a dramatic effect on learning results. In our work with the PAT algebra tutor (Koedinger, et. al., 1997), we have found that the best feedback messages are generated by the teachers, not the programmers or cognitive scientists. Teachers appear more likely to use vocabulary, phrasing and examples appropriate to the target audience.

5.3. Authoring the Curriculum Organizer

The curriculum organizer is primarily a database application. As such, it requires database creation and design skills. Creating an appropriate curriculum for a task requires knowledge not only about the task but about the goals of the teachers, students and society. A high school mathematics curriculum created to prepare students for calculus will be quite different from a curriculum directed at students of the same age who want the basic mathematics needed for computer programming or business. Once the general decision about curriculum content has been made, the specific nature of tasks and the ordering of lessons in the curriculum still need to be decided. Koedinger and Anderson (1993) describe the case of an educational system which, though an effective learning environment, proved less successful in implementation due to changes in the school's curricular goals. The lesson, we believe, is to work closely with teachers and school administrators from the beginning (Anderson, Corbett, Koedinger and Pelletier, 1995; Schofield, Evans-Rhodes and Huber, 1990).

5.4. Authoring Administrative and Reporting Tools

The administrative and reporting tools are essentially database tools as well. Providing usable tools in this area depends on working closely with teachers and students to determine their needs and desires.

6. LESSONS OF THE TASK ANALYSIS

Developing a commercial-quality educational environment is a large task, involving a varied set of skills. By breaking the task down into components, we can see that the skill sets form natural groups. While programming skill may be involved in developing any of the components, graphic design skill is needed only for developing the tools and administrative facilities. Knowledge of a school's and teacher's curricular goals is most needed in developing the curriculum organizer and tutor agents. Database skills are needed for the curriculum organizer and administrative facilities. Although there are some people who may possess all of the skills needed to develop the entire system, a more likely scenario is that the system be developed by a team. The team should, at minimum, consist of the following roles: curriculum expert (usually a teacher or curriculum administrator), cognitive scientist or knowledge engineer, programmer and database designer. The team approach allows the various components of the ITS to be developed in parallel. If off-the-shelf components can be found (or the authoring tools use embody already some of the knowledge contained within these roles), of course, members of this team could be omitted.

This component architecture also allows appropriate authoring tools to be focused on each of the major system components. Depending on the task domain, there may be several choices for authoring the tools, or the possibility exists that the tools can be bought as off-the-shelf components. The administrative and reporting tools and programming aspects of the curriculum component are best authored with database tools. Curriculum content is best authored by someone experienced in the target domain. The tutor agent is the heart of the system, and it can require several different sets of skills. Authoring tools do exist for this task, but, we would argue, better authoring tools would concentrate on the creation of this part of the system only. There is no reason to incorporate multimedia authoring tools or database authoring tools into an authoring environment targeted towards creating intelligent tutoring systems. Good tools already exist for this purpose, and we suggest that the developers of intelligent tutoring systems make use of them. Similarly, good tools exist to maintain and author reports from a database. Why not use them to develop the administrative facilities?

Before proceeding, we need to address the concern that this approach to authoring an intelligent learning environment generates much additional work (i.e., authoring four separate tutor components as opposed to authoring only one tutor) for perhaps little added benefit. There are two responses to this concern. First, by using authoring tools specialized for the creation for a particular component, the creation of these separable parts has been much enhanced. Using a database tool for the administrative facilities or a visual programming language for the interface allows for more rapid creation of those pieces, over just using a general-purpose programming language for the design of the whole thing. Secondly, once these separate components have been created, they can be more easily swapped around with other learning environments. It is very hard to take a piece of code from an integrated tutor and transplant it into another, no matter how similar the tutors are. However, when the pieces are actually separate components which know how to communicate with one another, transplanting the tutor agent from one tutor to another is an easily-done operation. And, as was pointed out before, it opens up the possibility of using off–the–shelf software for the tools the student will use, saving time and encouraging transfer to a real-world environment.

This component-based approach suggests that authoring tools should be focused on creating individual components of the overall system, but it requires that we provide a way to connect the various components together. In particular, if we intend to build a system in which the tutor agent is truly a separate component from the tools, we must have a component that knows how to translate user actions in the tool into a format understood by the tutor agent. The action recoding module shown in Figure 6 serves that purpose. In addition, we need to translate the desires of the tutor agent into a form that is available to the student. The feedback presentation component shown in Figure 6 serves this purpose. This remainder of this section considers these subsystems in greater detail.

The action recoding module ensures that user actions in the tool are communicated clearly to the tutor agent. Since the tool is developed as an application independent of the learning environment, the language that the tool uses to talk about user actions may differ from the language of the tutor agent. For example, one graphing tool might create an object called "y–axis label" for each graph. The "y–axis label" object might have a property called "text." When the user labels the y–axis, this action would be described as "set the text of the y–axis label of the graph" to some value. In another graphing tool, there might be a "y–axis label" property of the graph. In this tool, the same user action would be described as "set the y–axis label of the graph" to some value. The results are the same, but the applications differ in the way that they describe actions, since their data models differ. The tutor agent may or may not consider the y–axis label to be a separate object. Its representation is not dependent on the tool's data model representation.

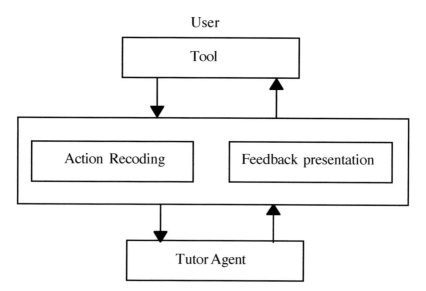

Figure 6: Substructure of the translator

The feedback presentation system is responsible for determining the way in which feedback is presented to the student. The simplest form of feedback is text, but other kinds of feedback may be used. For example, the system might want to point to some element of the display for emphasis or the system might want to present a picture, video clip or sound. The feedback presentation system is the part of the tutor agent which knows about the tool that the student is using. It is able to translate the tutor agent's desires into actions in that tool. For example, if the tool were a spreadsheet, the tutor agent might indicate that it wants to highlight a particular cell. The tutor agent could communicate that information as a message saying, for example, "highlight cell R1C1". But the tutor agent does not know the specific capabilities of the tool. It is up to the feedback presentation system to decide how, exactly, to highlight the cell. One possibility is to set the background color of the cell to red. Another might be to change the border around the cell to a thick line. The decision about which of these specific highlighting methods to use is dependent on the capabilities of the tool, the operating system and the hardware. For example, changing the background color of the cell to red might be a good solution if the spreadsheet tool allows it, but this would be a poor choice if the student does not have a color monitor. Our system architecture allows the tutor agent to specify when a message should be given and what it should say, but the specific method by which the message is communicated is up to the feedback presentation system.

We might think that, if a team is building a tool and a tutor agent together, it makes sense for them to agree on a language to describe the objects in the system. But even in this case, it pays to decouple the tutor agent from the tool. This decoupling allows the tutor agent to be retargeted to different tools, which may use different languages. Decoupling also allows the range of use of the tool and/or tutor agent to be more easily expanded. Indeed, for some of our current tutors, the tool is in Java and the tutor agent is in LISP. Such changes typically involve changes to the data model. By decoupling the two elements, changes in one do not affect changes in the other. In addition, the fact that the tool is typically developed to be useful for a wider range of tasks than the tutor agent suggests that there might be natural differences in the data models of the two components.

7. CURRENT PRACTICES

Since the first publication of this paper, our tutors and curriculum have started to sell as commercial products. They are in use in over 700 schools well over 2000 teachers have been trained. Given this success, we would like to describe the current way our tutors are architected in relation to the vision described above and our current thoughts on those ideas. (The original version of this paper described at this point a tool called the Visual Translator. While this tool is not used to author any part of our commercial systems, the details of our current practices match closely to what was previously discussed.)

7.1. Our Component Architecture

Figure 7 displays the high–level picture of the architecture of our current system. As can be seen, it differs little from the original conceptualization (Figure 1).

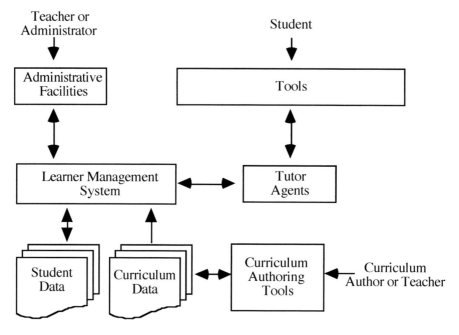

Figure 7. Our current component architecture

The major modification is a clearer definition of the Curriculum Organizing component. This component has been re-christened the Learner Management System (LMS), and it controls and coordinates access to both curriculum and student data by both the tutor agent and the administrative tools. The LMS handles requests by the tutor agent to save and retrieve student data, and to retrieve curriculum data (e.g., problem scenarios and unit specifications). The LMS is also used by our administrative facilities in order to set up and manage class rosters and to generate student reports (see below). In these roles, then, it is largely a database application. It also, however, performs the knowledge tracing function, in that it is responsible for picking the next problem for students to work on, given their current position within the curriculum and their current skill set. This function is common across many different tutor agents and many different curricula, and it makes sense to centralize it into the module that is also doing curriculum and student data management. As a point of reference it took between 12 and 15 person months to create the current version of LMS.

7.2. Communication between Tool and Tutor

Our general approach in tool–tutor communication (as stated above and also in Ritter & Koedinger, 1996; Ritter & Blessing, 1998) has been to regard the tool and tutor agent components of an intelligent tutoring system as separate components.

Our Cognitive Tutors adopt such a stance. Technically, this allows different people to work on the two parts—programmers and people skilled in HCI for the tool, and cognitive scientists for the tutor. Pedagogically, this arises from a specific approach to what a well-written intelligent tutoring system is doing. We have come to regard such systems as promoting "learning by doing" by presenting students with a problem and a set of tools to solve that problem. From this perspective the tutor agent is not a crucial part of the system at all. In fact, if the student is progressing without problems, there is no reason for the tutor agent to show itself at all.

In retrospect, we have found the pedagogical reason to separate tool and tutor agent to be more compelling than the technical reason, and this has led us to regard the tool and tutor agent components to be a collaboration between a tool designed for education purposes and a tutor agent, rather than communication between a more generic "productivity application" and an external tutor agent.

Although separation of these software components allows different development teams to work on different aspects of the system, we have usually needed closer communication between these different developers than we had initially envisioned. In part, this is a recognition that educational tools are different from tools constructed for other purposes. Educational tools require students to perform actions that would be nonsensical in another application of the tool. For example, our graphing tool sometimes asks students to plot points on the graph, even though the data for those points are already available in a table within the system. In statistical software, where the goal is to produce a graph of data already in a table (and where we can assume that the user understands the relationship between these two representations), asking the user to plot points would be strange. Similarly, our symbolic mathematical tool sometimes preserves less-expert representations. It is perfectly acceptable (and common) for students to enter numbers like 2/4, and it would be inappropriate for the system to automatically convert 2/4 into 1/2 or 0.5. In a system for more advanced users, however, that conversion would be acceptable and, perhaps desirable. These kinds of considerations result from constructing tools that are specifically targeted to specific kinds of users (who, in this case, are educational users). There still may be a role for commercial off-the-shelf software in intelligent tutoring systems, but it is probably in peripheral tools or in systems whose role is to train users in the use of the tool itself (e.g. Cheikes et al., 1999).

A second consideration dampens the prospect for the use of generic tools in intelligent tutoring systems. In order for the tutor agent to "look over the shoulder" of the student, it needs to be able to observe the students actions in a fair amount of detail. To this point, authors of productivity software not intended for educational use have not provided the hooks to allow a tutor agent (or other agent) to observe user activity at the appropriate level of detail. In part, this may be because there was little incentive for such developers to do so, since few agents are available to take advantage of such hooks. Efforts to standardize this communication (e.g. IEEE P1484.7) may help this process in the future. We do still believe that a general-purpose protocol for communication between educational tools and tutor agents is an achievable goal and do not believe that inferring semantic actions from user-interface events is a robust and general-purpose solution to this problem.

7.2.1. Tool Agent Communication Protocol

In Figure 6, we emphasized the role of the communication between the tool and the tutor agent. We would like to provide some explanation about how our tools and tutor agents do this. Our most recent tutors use a proprietary scripting communication protocol called Dormin, which closely follows the communication semantics described in Ritter and Koedinger (1996). As a point of reference, it took about 3 person months to create the first version of Dormin. While details of the syntax of the system are beyond the scope of this article, an illustration of the kind of interaction that Dormin allows should suffice to explain the general action of the system.

In a typical problem in our Cognitive Tutor Algebra I system, the student is presented with a problem scenario and is asked to create a spreadsheet-like table, graph and equations which describe the scenario. For example, the scenario might state that you have saved $550 and are saving $175 per month. The student uses tables, graphs and equations to model this situation. The first step in the modeling is for the student to label the columns on the table. One student might label them "time" and "amount of money saved".

Now, consider what happens when the student types "time" into the top-left cell in the table. The table tool echoes the student's input as it is typed. When the student hits "return" (or clicks on a different cell), a Dormin message is transmitted from the table tool to the tutor:

```
NotePropertySet:
        Object=Cell named R1C1 in Worksheet number 1 in Application number 1
        Property=value
        Value=time
```

This message identifies the kind of event that has taken place. From the perspective of the tool's data model, the student has set the property of some object. The property is named "value" and that property belongs to the object called "Cell named R1C1 in Worksheet number 1 in Application number 1".

In response, the tutor sends the following messages to the tool:

```
SetProperty:
        Object=Cell named R1C1 in Worksheet number 1 in Application number 1
        Property=foregroundcolor
        Value=(0,0,0)
SetProperty:
        Object=Cell named R1C1 in Worksheet number 1 in Application number 1
        Property=isEditable
        Value=false
SetProperty:
        Object=Cell named R1C1 in Worksheet number 1 in Application number 1
        Property=fontstyle
        Value=plain
```

These messages sets the cell to be locked and to display its contents in a black (RGB values of 0,0,0), plain font. In contrast, the following messages would be sent in response to an incorrect action (typing "foobar" in the same cell):

TOOLS FOR COMPONENT–BASED LEARNING ENVIRONMENTS 485

```
SetProperty:
        Object=Cell named R1C1 in Worksheet number 1 in Application
number 1
        Property=foregroundcolor
        Value=(255,0,0)
SetProperty:
        Object=Cell named R1C1 in Worksheet number 1 in Application
number 1
        Property=fontstyle
        Value=italic
```

The details of this kind of feedback are unimportant, but the general concept is. The tool provides messages which describe the student's actions at a high level. The tutor agent has a set of very general and powerful mechanisms for altering the tool's data model. The tool does not know (or need to know) the semantics of the messages that it receives. That is, it doesn't know that turning the font of a cell red and italic means that the user entered an erroneous value. It simply publishes a set of properties that make sense it its data model. In addition, the tool runs asynchronously with respect to the tutor. That is, the tool does not wait for a response from the tutor before allowing the student to proceed.

7.2.2. Communication between LMS and Tutor Agent

The communication between LMS and the Tutor Agent is XML based, and different in form from Dormin. LMS is essentially acting as a "stateless server", which means that all requests are initiated by the Tutor Agent, and that the Tutor Agent sends as part of the message all of the information about the student that LMS will need to know in order to provide a response. The LMS-Tutor Agent communication is also synchronous; the Tutor Agent waits for a response from LMS before proceeding with another request to LMS, or with messages to the tools. The Tutor Agent sends a sequence of messages requesting that LMS retrieve the current problem for the student, and provide the current problem information. The responses to these messages include all of the information needed to run the particular problem. The tutor agent parses these responses and sends a series of messages to the tool, including:

```
SetProperty:
        Object=Application number 1
        Property=problemName
        Value=Bh1t17
Create:
        Object=Application number 1
        ObjectType=Worksheet
        PropertyNames=numberOfRows, numberOfColumns, name
        PropertyValues=6,3,Worksheet
SetProperty:
        Object=Cell named R1C1 in Worksheet number 1 in Application
number 1
        Property=horizontalAlignment
        Value=middle
```

The first of these messages informs the tool application of the name of the problem (so that it can be displayed). The second creates a "worksheet" (our spreadsheet-like table) with 6 rows and 3 columns. The third message is one of a series of messages that set various properties of the cells in the worksheet. This one says that the cell should center its input.

This kind of interaction is used to restore a student's problem state, if the student logs off the system before completing a problem. The student's state is represented by a set of Dormin messages that define the state of the tools that the student is using. Restoring that state amounts to replaying the Dormin messages.

7.3. Our Administrative Facilities

We would like to again emphasize the importance of good administrative facilities. For any ITS to be of commercial quality, its administrative facilities must be approachable by the average teacher. For some, these facilities will be their first exposure to the system as they begin to set up their classes and students. A screen shot from our administrative program, called Teacher's Toolkit, is shown in Figure 8.

From within Teacher's Toolkit, a teacher can:

• Create new class rosters at the beginning of a term, create new student datafiles and assign students to a curriculum.
• Track student progress as they work through the tutor curriculum and print class summary or individual progress reports.
• Maintain class rosters by changing student names, transferring students to different classes, or removing students.
• Restart a problem, skip to the next problem, or change the placement within the curriculum for a student.

All of these tasks are accomplished by Teacher's Toolkit communicating with the LMS (via a XML–based protocol), which in turn retrieves or writes the appropriate information from the curriculum and student data. It took about 6 person months to create Teacher's Toolkit.

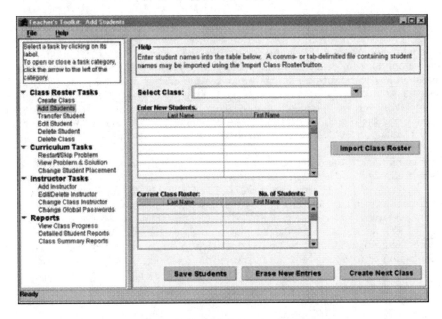

Figure 8. Our Administrative Facilities

7.4. Other Changes

In comparing Figure 7 to Figure 1, there are only two other changes. One is the removal of an arrow between the Tutor Agents and the Administrative Facilities. In practice, this communication channel is not needed, particularly given that LMS can serve as an intermediary. The second, bigger change, is the separating out of the curriculum authoring tools from the administrative tools. From a technical standpoint, there is no need for the curriculum authoring tools to communicate with LMS—any additions or modifications to the curriculum can be made directly to the curriculum data. From a task analysis standpoint, the people who interact with the administrative tools (teachers), except in a few cases, are not the same people who interact with the curriculum authoring tools (curriculum designers). Currently, our curriculum authoring tools are rudimentary. Changes to the curriculum must be done in–house and there is no real user–interface.

8. CONCLUSION

This component approach to authoring systems still has not been widely embraced by those creating ITSs (and indeed, nor has it in the wider domain of software design). In order for it to succeed, it takes a committed group of people coming from disparate backgrounds to engage in dialogue over an extended period (over 10 years in our case). It obviously takes some amount of capital to sustain such an enterprise, and a willingness by the participants to learn from one another. Just getting started, then, is not easy. However, despite these obstacles, we remain optimistic about the outlook of component architectures for Intelligent Tutoring Systems. This optimism stems from our confidence that component-based systems are feasible now and that this approach to authoring ultimately reduces the cost of bringing these types of systems to market, and our success at having done so. Several component architectures for intelligent tutoring systems have been proposed (e.g. Cheikes, 1995a), and these architectures appear to be converging on a common standard. Such a standard would allow components of different systems to work together. As the other systems discussed in this volume mature and receive wider dissemination, their commonalities and the ways in which they complement each other will be discovered, hopefully helping to foster this component–based view. Indeed, some of the systems already have a component–based feel, either by having the author make multiple passes in the authoring (e.g., IRIS, described in this volume) or by having separate networks and tools (e.g., CREAM, also in this volume).

Our analysis of the skills required to develop a commercial-quality learning environment suggests that the proper approach to authoring systems is to use a combination of authoring tools, each specialized for a particular component of the overall system. Instead of a single, monolithic authoring tool, we suggest a suite of authoring tools, each specialized for a specific component of the overall system. These architectures also allow for the possibility of using off-the-shelf components (e.g., REDEEM's use of ToolBook; see also Woods & Warren, 1995).

The relationship between the tool and tutor agent portions of the architecture is special. Unlike in most component relationships, the two components in the system cannot assume anything of each other. In fact, we argue, the tool should not assume that the tutor component even exists. Under such constraints, it becomes necessary to think about a different way to define the interaction between those components. In our current tutors, we use a lingua franca called Dormin. This allows for one team to work on the tools (with primarily programming and HCI skill) and another to work on the tutor agents (with primarily cognitive science skill). In fact, the tools and the tutor agents can be (and are, in our released systems) in different programming languages. Dormin allows for the tool to communicate to the tutor agent concerning the student's actions, and for the tutor agent to direct the tool to present any feedback to the student.

Our solution, then, to the authoring problem comes in two parts. One part requires the development of standards for communication between the components of learning environments. The other part, as yet unrealized in our commercial systems, lies in developing specialized authoring tools, like Visual Translator (Ritter & Blessing, 1998), that embody these communication standards. With both of these parts in place, we can build learning environments that can be continually updated to take advantage of the best components available. Only when we have learned to avoid the investment of resources required to reproduce components that are specific to only one context will we see intelligent tutoring systems enjoy success in the marketplace equal to the success they have had in the research lab.

9. REFERENCES

Anderson, J. R., Corbett, A. T., Koedinger, K. R., & Pelletier, R. (1995). Cognitive tutors: Lessons learned. *The Journal of the Learning Sciences, 4* (2) 167-207.

Anderson, J. R., & Pelletier, R. (1991). A development system for model–tracing tutors. In *Proceedings of the International Conference of the Learning Sciences* (pp. 1–8). Evanston, IL.

Cheikes, B. A. (1995a) GIA: An Agent-Based Architecture for Intelligent Tutoring Systems. In *Proceedings of the CIKM'95 Workshop on Intelligent Information Agents.*

Cheikes, B. A. (1995b). Should ITS designers be looking for a few good agents? In *Proceedings of the AI-ED'95 Workshop on Authoring Shells for Intelligent Tutoring Systems.* Major, N., Murray, T., and Bloom, C. (eds.).

Cheikes, B. A., Geier, M., Hyland, R., Linton, F., Riffe, A. S., Rodi, L. L., & Schaefer, H. (1999). Embedded Training for Complex Information Systems. International Journal of Artificial Intelligence in Education (1999), 10, 314-334.

Ericsson, K. A., & Simon, H. A. (1993). *Protocol Analysis.* Cambridge, MA: MIT Press.

Fox, T., Grunst, G. and Quast, K. (1994). HyPLAN: A context-sensitive hypermedia help system. In R. Oppermann, (Ed.), *Adaptive User Support* (pp. 126-193). Hillsdale, NJ: Lawrence Erlbaum Associates.

Koedinger, K. R. & Anderson, J. R. (1993). Effective use of intelligent software in high school math classrooms. In *Proceedings of the Sixth World Conference on Artificial Intelligence in Education,* (pp. 241-248). Charlottesville, VA: Association for the Advancement of Computing in Education.

Koedinger, K. R., Anderson, J. R., Hadley, W. H., & Mark, M. A. (1997). Intelligent tutoring goes to school in the big city. *International Journal of Artificial Intelligence in Education,* 8, 30–43.

McArthur, D., Lewis, M. W. and Bishay, M. (1996). ESSCOTS for Learning: Transforming Commerical Software into Powerful Educational Tools. *Journal of Artificial Intelligence in Education,* 6(1), 3-33.

McKendree, J. E. (1990). Effective feedback content for tutoring complex skills. *Human-Computer Interaction,* 5, 381-414.

Person, N. K., Bautista, L., Graesser, A. C., Mathews, E. & The Tutoring Research Group (2001). Evaluating student learning gains in two versions of AutoTutor. In J. D. Moore, C. L Redfield, & W. L. Johnson (Eds), *Artificial Intelligence in Education: AI–ED in the Wired and Wireless Future* (pp. 286–293). Amsterdam: IOS Press.

Ritter, S. & Blessing, S. B. (1998). Authoring tools for component–based learning environments. *The Journal of the Learning Sciences,* 7(1), 107-132.

Ritter, S. & Koedinger, K. R. (1996). An architecture for plug-in tutor agents. *Journal of Artificial Intelligence in Education,* 7, 315-347.

Rosé, C. P., Jordan, P., Ringenberg, M., Siler, S., VanLehn, K., & Weinstein, A. (2001). Interactive conceptual tutoring in Atlas–Andes. In J. D. Moore, C. L Redfield, & W. L. Johnson (Eds.), *Artificial Intelligence in Education: AI–ED in the Wired and Wireless Future* (pp. 256–266). Amsterdam: IOS Press.

Schofield, J. W., Evans-Rhodes, D., & Huber, B. R. (1990). Artificial intelligence in the classroom: The impact of a computer-based tutor on teachers and students. *Social Science Computer Review,* 8:1, 24-41.

Woods, P. J., & Warren, J. R. (1995). Rapid Prototyping of an Intelligent Tutorial System. In *Proceedings of ASCILITE95* (pp. 557–563). Melbourne: University of Melbourne.

10. ACKNOWLEDGEMENTS

This paper previously appeared in *The Journal of the Learning Sciences,* volume 7 (1), pages 107 – 132.

TOM MURRAY

Chapter 17

AN OVERVIEW OF INTELLIGENT TUTORING SYSTEM AUTHORING TOOLS:

Updated Analysis of the State of the Art

Abstract. This paper consists of an in-depth summary and analysis of the research and development state of the art for intelligent tutoring system (ITS) authoring systems. A seven-part categorization of two dozen authoring systems is given, followed by a characterization of the authoring tools and the types of ITSs that are built for each category. An overview of the knowledge acquisition and authoring techniques used in these systems is given. A characterization of the design tradeoffs involved in building an ITS authoring system is given. Next the pragmatic questions of real use, productivity findings, and evaluation are discussed. Finally, I summarize the major unknowns and bottlenecks to having widespread use of ITS authoring tools.

1. INTRODUCTION

Intelligent Tutoring Systems (ITSs) are computer-based instructional systems with models of instructional content that specify *what* to teach, and teaching strategies that specify *how* to teach (Wenger 1987, Ohlsson 1987, Shute & Psotka 1996). They make inferences about a student's mastery of topics or tasks in order to dynamically adapt the content or style of instruction. Content models (or knowledge bases, or expert systems, or simulations) give ITSs depth so that students can "learn by doing" in realistic and meaningful contexts. Models allow for content to be generated in real time. ITSs allow "mixed-initiative" tutorial interactions, where students can ask questions and have more control over their learning. Instructional models allow the computer tutor to more closely approach the benefits of individualized instruction by a competent pedagogue. In recent years ITSs have moved out of the lab and into classrooms and workplaces where some have been shown to be highly effective (Shute and Regian 1990; Koedinger et al. 1997; Mark & Greer 1991; Person et al. 2001; Rosé, et al. 2001). While intelligent tutors are becoming more common and proving to be increasingly effective they are difficult and expensive to build. Authoring systems are commercially available for traditional computer aided instruction (CAI) and multimedia-based training, but these authoring systems lack the sophistication required to build intelligent tutors. Commercial multimedia authoring systems excel in giving the instructional designer tools to produce visually appealing and interactive screens, but behind the screens is a shallow representation of content and pedagogy. Researchers have been investigating ITS authoring tools almost since the beginning of ITS research, and over two dozen very diverse authoring systems have been built. This paper summarizes the contributions of these systems and describes the state of the art for ITS authoring tools.

This article is written for two types of readers. First are research and development personnel who are building ITS and/or ITS authoring tools. They might ask the question "what methods and designs have been used, and how successful have they been?" in their efforts to build the next generation of systems. The second type of reader is the developer or purchaser of instructional software (intelligent or otherwise) who might ask the question: "what is really available (or soon to be available) to make ITS authoring cost effective?" I hope both readers will find this article informative. For those needing an "executive level summary": 1) In the last few years there has been significant progress in the development of ITS authoring tools and in the understanding of the key issues involved. 2) The development efforts to date represent many diverse approaches, and it is still too early to get a sense for which approaches will prove to be the most useful (or marketable). 3) In general, ITS authoring tools are still research vehicles which have demonstrated significant success in limited cases, yet have not been made robust enough to be placed and supported in production contexts or commercial markets. However, it is encouraging that several systems have been released as products or are approaching productization, and some relatively large scale evaluations have taken place. Significant progress has been made since this first version of this paper was published in 1999.

The paper is organized according to four broad questions that readers might have concerning ITS authoring tools:

- What types of tutors can be built with existing authoring tools?
- What features and methods do the tools use to facilitate authoring?
- Have the tools been used in realistic situations; have they been evaluated; are they available?
- What have researchers learned about the process of authoring and the tradeoffs involved in designing an authoring tool?

The Sections of this paper are sequenced to answer these questions. I first describe the types of ITSs that have been built with ITS authoring tools. Next I describe the interface, knowledge representation, and knowledge acquisition techniques that have been used to allow non-programmers to build ITSs using authoring tools. Then I report on the pragmatic aspects of ITS authoring in order to locate current work in the research-to-application spectrum. Finally I discuss a number of general issues and lessons learned (for example "who should author ITSs?"), and discuss tradeoffs between power, usability, and fidelity among authoring tools.

2. A CLASSIFICATION ACCORDING TO TASKS AND TUTORS

Any discussion about authoring tools would be too abstract without some context describing the tutors that they have been used to build. ITS authoring tools have been used to build tutors in a wide range of domains, including customer service, mathematics, equipment maintenance, and public policy. These tutors have been targeted toward a wide range of students, from grade school children to corporate trainees. However, the key differences among ITS authoring systems are not related to specific domains or student populations, but to the domain-independent capabilities that the authored ITSs have. In this Section I present a classification of authoring tools based on these capabilities. But before describing a number of ITS authoring tools I need to mention a related area of work that will not be directly addressed.

Shells vs. tools. An ITS "shell" is a generalized framework for building ITSs, while an ITS "authoring system" (or authoring tool) is an ITS shell along with a user interface that allows non-programmers to formalize and visualize their knowledge. Inspired by goals of elegance, parsimony, and/or cost effectiveness, software designers seem naturally driven to write software that is general and reusable. Thus there have been many papers published describing ITS "shells" that consist of software architectures, code libraries, or conceptual frameworks that make ITS construction more efficient for programmers. Though some of these systems include form-based data entry to support authoring tasks, most of them are either content acquisition shells or instructional planning shells. For examples, see Goodkovsky et al., 1994 (Pop ITS shell), Ikeda & Mizoguchi, 1994 (FITS), McCalla & Greer, 1988 (SCENT-3), Goodyear & Johnson, 1990 (TOSKA), Anderson & Pelliteri, 1991 (TDK), McMillan et al., 1980 (SIPP), Wasson, 1992 (PEPE), Winne & Kramer, 1989 (DOCENT), Jona & Kass, 1997 (GBS architectures). This paper focuses on authoring tools only.

A bags of tricks vs. a shelf of tools. Over two dozen ITS authoring systems have been built. They differ by the types of domains and tasks they are suited for, by the degree to which they make authoring more easy or efficient, and by the depth and fidelity employed to represent the knowledge or skill being taught. Not all of the designers of these systems would describe their systems as being "ITS authoring systems." But I include computer-based instruction authoring systems that use AI representation techniques such as rules and semantic networks, and those that include models of content and/or teaching strategies. These systems seem to populate the space of authoring tool features almost uniformly, making it difficult to cluster them into discrete groups in an effort to summarize the field. In fact, every system I will describe in one category has important elements from at least one other category. Since the field is still in a formative stage, this paper is intended to help the reader envision the next generation of authoring tools, more than to select an existing one to use. Therefore its organization is more like the description of a "bag of tricks" that can be mixed and matched to create an authoring tool than a description of a shelf of completed authoring tools.

Early ITS authoring systems fell into two broad categories: those based on a traditional curriculum (or courseware) metaphor and those geared toward device simulation and embodying a "learning environments" instructional metaphor. The majority of current authoring tools fall similarly into two broad categories: pedagogy-oriented and performance-oriented (Murray 1997). Pedagogy-oriented systems (categories 1, 2, 5, and 7 in Table 1) focus on how to sequence and teach relatively canned content. Most of them pay special attention to the representation of teaching strategies and tactics. Performance-oriented systems (categories 3, 4, 6, and sometimes 5, in Table 1) focus on providing rich learning environments in which students can learn skills by practicing them and receiving feedback. Most of them pay special attention to the representation of human problem solving skills or domain-specific processes or systems (either man made ones such as electrical components, or natural ones such as the meteorology). In general, performance-oriented systems focus on feedback and guidance at the level of individual skills and procedural steps, while pedagogy-oriented systems pay more attention to guidance and planning at a more global level, looking at the sequence of topics and the need for prerequisite topics. Some systems have elements of both categories, but those that do tend not to have very complete or deep representational systems for both pedagogy and domain processes. Though it is possible to create a system with full capabilities in both areas, none yet exists. This is probably due to a combination of the fact that supporting each type of authoring is difficult (and each project has limited recourses to spend) and supporting each type of authoring requires a very different kind of expertise.

Table 1: ITS Authoring Tools by Category ([brackets] refer to Chapter numbers)

CATEGORY	AUTHORING SYSTEMS
1. Curriculum Sequencing and Planning	Swift/DOCENT, IDE, ISD Expert, Expert CML
2. Tutoring Strategies	REDEEM (& COCA) [8], Eon [11], GTE
3. Simulation-Based Learning	SIMQUEST [1], XAIDA [2], RIDES[3], DIAG [5], Instructional Simulator [7]
4. Domain Expert System	Demonstr8 [4], DIAG [5], D3 Trainer, Training Express
5. Multiple Knowledge Types	XAIDA [2], DNA [6], Instructional Simulator & IDVisualizer [7], ID-Expert, IRIS [9], CREAM-Tools [10], ,
6. Special Purpose	IDLE-Tool/Imap/Indie [12], LAT [14], BioWorld Case Builder, WEAR
7. Intelligent/Adaptive Hypermedia	InterBook [13], MetaLinks, CALAT, GETMAS, TANGOW, ECSAIWeb

Table 2: ITS Authoring Tool Strengths and Limitations by Category

CATEGORY	STRENGTHS	LIMITS	VARIATIONS
Curriculum Sequencing and Planning	Rules, constraints, or strategies for sequencing courses, modules, presentations	Low fidelity from student's perspective; shallow skill representation	Whether sequencing rules are fixed or authorable; scaffolding of the authoring process
Tutoring Strategies	Micro-level tutoring strategies; sophisticated set of instructional primitives; multiple tutoring strategies	(same as above for most systems)	Strategy representation method; source of instructional expertise
Device Simulation and Equipment Training	Authoring and tutoring matched to device component identification, operation, and troubleshooting	Limited instructional strategies; limited student modeling; mostly for procedural skills	Fidelity of the simulation; ease of authoring
Domain Expert System	Runnable (deeper) model of domain expertise; fine grained student diagnosis and modeling; buggy and novice rules included	Building the expert system is difficult; limited to procedural and problem solving expertise; limited instructional strategies	Cognitive vs. performance models of expertise
Multiple Knowledge Types	Differential pre-defined knowl. representation and instructional methods for facts, concepts, and procedures, etc.	Limited to relatively simple fact, concepts, and procedures; pre-defined tutoring strategies	Inclusion of intelligent curriculum sequencing; types of knowledge/tasks supported
Special Purpose	Template-based systems provide strong authoring guidance; fixed design or pedagogical principles can be enforced	Each tool limited to a specific type of tutor; inflexibility of representation and pedagogy	Degree of flexibility
Intelligent/ Adaptive Hypermedia	WWW has accessibility & UI uniformity; adaptive selection and annotation of hyperlinks	Limited interactivity; limited student model bandwidth	Macro vs. micro level focus; degree of interactivity

Proponents of constructivist learning theories (e.g. Jonassen & Reeves 1996) often criticize pedagogy-oriented tutors and the instructional design theories behind them as being too "instructivist." Such critics contend that these systems ignore important aspects of learning such as intrinsic motivation, context realism, common misconceptions, and social learning contexts. Actually these factors are acknowledged by most instructional design theorists (Merrill 1983, Gagne 1985, Reigeluth 1983), but are either seen as not being as important or as being too complex or incompletely understood to incorporate into instructional planning and knowledge representation.[1]

Table 1 enumerates seven categories of ITS authoring systems, grouped according to the type of ITSs they produce.[2] Table 2 describes the strengths and limitations of each category, along with a summary of how systems within the category differ. The categories are described below in their particular sequence because some build upon concepts developed in previous categories.

2.1. Curriculum sequencing and planning

Authoring systems in the Curriculum and Course Sequencing category organize instructional units (IUs, or "curriculum elements") into a hierarchy of courses, modules, lessons, presentations, etc., which are related by prerequisite, part, and other relationships. The instructional units typically have instructional objectives. Some systems include IUs that address misconceptions or remedial material. The content is stored in canned text and graphics. These systems are seen as tools to help instructional designers and teachers design courses and manage computer based learning.

Intelligent sequencing of IUs (or content, or topics) is at the core of these systems. To the student, tutoring systems built with these tools may seem identical to traditional computer-based instruction. Screens of canned text and pictures are presented, and interactions tend to be limited to multiple choice, fill-in, etc. Of course, the difference is that the sequencing of the content is being determined dynamically based on the student's performance, the lesson objectives, and the relationships between course modules. Because domain knowledge is not represented in a very "deep" fashion, any arbitrary domain can be tutored (just as a textbook can be about any domain). But the depth of diagnosis and feedback in tutors built with these authoring tools is limited by the shallowness of their domain knowledge representation. This makes them more appropriate for building tutors

---

[1] Historically, instructional design theories were ignored by most ITS researchers in favor of cognitive learning theories, but in the realm of ITS authoring tools instructional design was a primary basis for the early systems. Thus I believe the authoring tools research community was instrumental in promoting the more balanced merger of instructional design and cognitive theories that we increasing see in recent years.

[2] In the case of two relatively large-scale ITS authoring system projects, MITT-Writer and ICAT, there was insufficient published material for me to include them in my analysis (these systems are mentioned in an overview of US government sponsored ITS research (Youngblut 1995)).

that teach conceptual, declarative, and episodic types of knowledge, and less pedagogically powerful for building tutors that teach procedural or problem solving skills. Authoring systems in the Curriculum Sequencing category are, generally speaking, the most "basic," or minimally functional (though each system in this category has certain very evolved signature features or capabilities). All of the systems in this category except Swift are "historical" in that they were early examples that inspired other projects. In particular, the systems in categories 2 and 5 build upon the functionalities of category 1 systems. Swift is a commercial product that calls itself an authoring tool for "minimalist" ITSs.

2.2. Tutoring strategies

Systems in this category excel at representing diverse teaching strategies. They tend to be similar to the Curriculum Sequencing systems described above, in that content is stored in canned text and graphics and domain knowledge representation is shallow. Systems in this category go beyond Curriculum Sequencing systems to encode fine-grained strategies used by teachers and instructional experts. Systems in the Curriculum Sequencing category tend to focus on the "macro" level of instruction--i.e. the sequencing of topics or modules, while systems in this category also address the "micro" level of instruction. Instructional decisions at the micro level include when and how to give explanations, summaries, examples, and analogies; what type of hinting and feedback to give; and what type of questions and exercises to offer the student. Systems in the Tutoring Strategies category have the most sophisticated set of primitive tutorial actions, compared with systems in other categories. In addition some systems in this category represent multiple tutoring strategies and "meta-strategies" that select the appropriate tutoring strategy for a given situation (e.g. REDEEM and Eon). The availability and intelligent interjection of small grain sized components such as explanations, multiple levels of hints, and analogies can make the tutor appear quite responsive, at times even conversational (as in Socratic strategies).

In GTE and COCA authors create instructional rules. In Eon teaching strategies are defined using procedural flow lines. In REDEEM authors specify strategy parameters using sliders.

2.3. Simulation-based learning

For tutors built by authoring tools in this category, instruction centers around a simulation of a man-made process or phenomena. In RIDES, XAIDA, DIAG, and Instructional Simulator the student is shown a piece of equipment and is asked to identify its components, perform operating steps, perform maintenance steps, or diagnose faulty device behavior and fix or replace the implicated parts. These authoring tools have been used to build instructional simulations of mechanical, electrical, and hydraulic systems. These types of skills are relatively widespread and generic, so authoring tools that specialize in this area should be widely usable. The expert knowledge for component locations and operational scripts is straightforward

498   T. MURRAY

to model. Performance monitoring and instructional feedback is also straightforward (e.g. "That is not the Termination Switch," and "You should have checked the safety valve as your next step"). Thus authoring tools can be built which closely match the needs of the author (and student).[3] The most difficult authoring task with these systems is building the simulation. But once the simulation is authored, much of the instructional specification comes "for free." Component location and device behavior "what if" activities can be generated automatically. However, the device operation procedures must be authored. The four systems mentioned differ in the complexity of the simulation models that they can author. While these systems focus mostly on learning procedural skills, SimQuest focuses more on conceptual knowledge and physical principles. It has features for providing explanations of phenomena, exploratory and hypothesis generation learning activities, and instructional sequences based on a "model evolution" paradigm (White & Frederiksen 1995). SimQuest simulations are based on a set of equations which constitute a model of a physical process. Though they are not covered in this paper, there are other simulation-based and model-based educational software projects that incorporate authoring tools for building models (see a brief summary in Murray, et al. 2001).

In contrast to the previous two categories of authoring tools, students using tutors built with tools in this category will be "learning by doing." It is usually assumed that students have a basic familiarity with important concepts and procedures in the domain before using the tutor and students immediately start to practice skills. Specific feedback is given for each skill step, and task difficulty is increased as students progress.

A major differentiating factor among systems in this category is the depth and fidelity of the simulation. Authoring tools range from those supporting static expression-based relationships between device components (XAIDA, which also supports domains other than device simulation, see the Multiple Knowledge Types category), to those supporting runnable but shallow simulation models (RIDES), to those supporting deeper, more causative or cognitive models of how the device works (SIMQUEST).

2.4. Expert systems and cognitive tutors

An important class of intelligent tutors are those that include rule-based cognitive models of problem solving expertise. Such tutors, often called model tracing tutors (Anderson & Pelletier 1991), observe student behavior and build a fine-grained cognitive model of the student's knowledge that can be compared with the expert model. Authoring tools have been prototyped for such tutors. I also include in this category authoring tools which use traditional expert systems (built to solve problems, not to teach) and produce "value added" instruction for the encoded

---

[3] Equipment diagnosis tasks ("troubleshooting") are more complicated, less standard among types of equipment, and thus more difficult task to model and teach than operation and maintenance steps.

expertise. These systems are similar to model tracing systems, except the expert system is based on performance competency, rather than cognitive processes. Some systems include buggy or novice-level rules that capture common mistakes, allowing the tutorial to give feedback specific to those errors.

Students using these systems usually solve problems and associated sub-problems within a goal space, and receive feedback when their behavior diverges from that of the expert model. Unlike most other systems described above, these systems have a relatively deep model of expertise, and thus the student, when stuck, can ask the tutor to perform the next step or to complete the solution to the entire problem. Authoring an expert system is a particularly difficult and time-intensive task, and only certain tasks can be modeled in this manner.

Demonstr8 allows authors to build an expert problem solver through demonstration of an example problem solution. D3 trainer and Training Express add a tutorial component onto an existing expert system (authored with an expert system shell). DIAG includes an expert model of fault diagnosis strategies.

2.5. Multiple knowledge types

Instructional design theories classify knowledge and tasks into discrete categories, and prescribe instructional methods for each category. They tend to be limited to types of knowledge that can be easily defined, such as facts, concepts, and procedures. Though the knowledge types and instructional methods vary for different theories, they typically prescribe instruction similar to the following. Facts are taught with repetitive practice and mnemonic devices; concepts are taught using analogies and positive and negative examples progressing from easy prototypical ones to more difficult borderline cases; procedures are taught one step at a time, with particular attention payed to branching decision steps. Instruction for these knowledge types includes both expository presentations of the knowledge, and inquisitory exercises that allow for practice and feedback. Straight-forward instructional strategies for how to sequence content and exercises, and how to provide feedback, are defined separately for each knowledge type (for example see Merrill 1983). The pre-defined nature of the knowledge and the instructional strategies is both the strength and the weakness of these systems. Domain knowledge for each knowledge type can be easily represented for authors, who fill in templates for examples, steps, definitions, etc. (depending on the knowledge type). The tools support the decomposition of complex skills into elementary knowledge components. Links between knowledge components can be authored and used in instruction (e.g. the concepts or facts that support a procedure or a concept that helps explain another concept). Since instructional strategies are fixed and based on knowledge types they do not have to be authored. Of course, not all instruction fits neatly into this framework, but it has significantly wide applicability (problem solving and other higher order cognitive skills can not be represented in this way).

Authoring systems in the Multiple Knowledge Types category are diverse in many respects, but they all use a knowledge/skill classification scheme and represent and instruct differentially based on knowledge type. Also, they all cite classic instructional design literature as part of the basis for their pedagogical approach. For the student, tutors built with these systems are similar in character to those in the Multiple Teaching Strategies category. The main difference is for the authors, whose task is more constrained, and thus both easier and less flexible.

2.6. Special purpose systems

In this category are authoring tools that specialize in particular tasks or domains. Systems in the Device Simulation and Multiple Knowledge Types categories are also for particular types of tasks, but systems in the Special Purpose category focus on more specific, less general tasks. There is a rough principle that authoring tools tailored for specific tasks or instructional situations can better support the needs of the student and author for those situations. Systems in this category were designed by starting with a particular intelligent tutor design, and generalizing it to create a framework for authoring similar tutors. Authoring is much more template-like than in other categories of authoring tools. One potential problem with special purpose authoring is that once a task and its instructional approach have been codified enough to become a template, the resulting system reflects a very particular approach to representing and teaching that task; one that may only appeal to a limited authoring audience. On the other hand, preferred design and pedagogical principles can be strictly enforced, since the author has no influence over these aspects. Bell (this volume) calls this approach using a "strong task model" to build "knowledge rich" authoring tools.

Since the only thing that systems in this category have in common is that they support particular types of tasks or domains, we can not say anything in general about the types of tutors built or about students' experience using the tutors. The IDLE-Tool/Imap/Indie systems build tutors for "investigate and decide" GBS (goal based scenario) learning environments. LAT builds tutors to train customer service representatives how to answer product questions. Both of the above mentioned projects involve learning by doing in role playing environments. BioWorld is a learning environment for promoting scientific reasoning in the medical domain. Its authoring tool is a template-based tool allowing teachers to create new medical cases. WEAR builds tutors in algebra-related domains.

2.7. Intelligent/adaptive hypermedia

As adaptive hypermedia systems and web-based tutors become more sophisticated, they increasingly incorporate methods and models from the field of intelligent tutoring. Since these systems and their authoring tools are becoming more predominant, I have created a separate category for them. The functions of these systems overlap with those from the Curriculum Sequencing and Tutoring Strategies categories above (depending on whether the focus is on instruction at the macro or micro level). The level of interactivity and fidelity available to the student is low for tutors built with these authoring tools. They are HTML-based, and do not yet incorporate highly interactive features available through programming languages such as Java and Flash. Unlike systems in the other categories, these systems must manage the hyperlinks between units of content as well as the form and sequencing of the content itself. The links available to the student can be intelligently filtered, sorted, and annotated based on a student model or profile (Brusilovsky 1998). Link filtering can be based on prerequisites, cognitive load, topic appropriateness, difficulty, etc. Brusilovsky's Chapter 13 in this Volume has a more complete overview or adaptive hypermedia authoring tools.

3. HOW ARE THE PARTS OF AN ITS AUTHORED?

Having described ITS authoring tools in the concrete terms of what types of tutors they can build, I will move on to describe features of the authoring tools themselves. ITSs are often described as having four main components: the student interface, the domain model, the teaching model, and the student model. Though this categorization is not always sufficient to describe an ITS, the functionality of ITS authoring tools can best be described in terms of authoring these four components.

3.1 Authoring the interface

Interface design is the one area where traditional multimedia authoring tools excel over ITS authoring tools. This is probably because building an interface construction kit is quite time consuming. Since basic graphics authoring is a "solved problem" most ITS authoring researchers have not prioritized the effort need to build full graphics construction tools. However, the experience of our research team has indicated that customizing the tutorial's interface is a priority for authors (Murray 1998). Also, constraining the student interface to pre-defined screens and layouts severely constrains the types of tasks and interactions that an ITS can have with the student.

Three of the authoring systems, RIDES, SIMQUEST, and Eon, allow authors to construct the tutoring system's interface completely from scratch, using interface objects such as buttons, text, sliders, imported graphics, movies, and low level "drawing" objects. The interface objects in these systems are "live," in that they can be scripted to respond to user and program generated events, and their properties (color, position, etc.) can be set to depend on other values in the tutor. With the RIDES system the author can define components, sub-components, and physical connections such as wires and pipes. In the Eon system authors define graphical screen 'templates' and the system automatically creates a database for holding the template contents. For instance if a screen containing a movie, a question, and an explanation was authored, the author could use a data entry tool to easily fill in the text and movie names for dozens of these interactive screens.

Features that actively assist the author in designing an ITS interface, for example by analyzing the interface design for clarity and usability, have not yet been included in ITS authoring systems. The vast majority of authoring systems assure reasonable interface designs simply by pre-defining the student interface--i.e. by not providing interface design features at all.

Authoring the interface, though more flexible, has the negative side effects of freeing authors to design poor interfaces, and adding to the list of skills that an author must have. Building the interface for "user friendly" software can take from 50% to 90% of the entire project resources. The MetaLinks system addresses this trade-off by allowing the author to customize the layout by selecting from two menus. The first menu lists purposes of the page (e.g. glossary, explanation, chapter introduction, etc.) and second menu lists layout types (e.g. pictures in upper right; first picture above the main text with other pictures half size at the bottom, etc.). MetaLinks combines these two parameters to determine the overall layout and look and feel of the page. The REDEEM system allows users to import interactive screen created with an off-the-shelf multimedia authoring tool (ToolBook).

Systems in the Intelligent Hypermedia category offload the job of displaying the interface to the web browser. Though no interface authoring is allowed (or needed) for these systems, the layout capabilities of web browsers make it easy to generate web pages with a fair degree of adaptability with little effort.

3.2 Authoring the domain model

ITSs contain representations of curriculum knowledge, simulation models, and problem solving expertise. Authoring tools have been built for each of these domain model categories, as described below.

Models of curriculum knowledge and structures. Several authoring systems include tools for visualizing and authoring content networks (including IDE, Eon, RIDES, and CREAM-Tools). These tools help the author visualize the relationships between curriculum elements (such as topics, courses, concepts, and procedures) and allow a bird's eye view of the subject matter. Some tools are limited to strict hierarchical representations of courses, modules, lessons, topics, etc., but most allow more free-formed network representations.

Curriculum knowledge can include knowledge about the pedagogically relevant properties of topics, such as their importance and difficulty. Almost all of the authoring tools in the Curriculum Sequencing, Tutoring strategies, and Multiple Knowledge Types categories include the ability to author topic properties. Several systems (including IDE, IRIS, and Cream-Tools) provide tools for authoring instructional objectives separately from topics.

Simulations and models and of the world. The level of fidelity of a simulation is constrained by the representational formalism used for domain modeling. Among the systems we have mentioned, SimQuest has the "Deepest" modeling framework. It models continuous physical processes using systems of algebraic equations and differential equations that can interact as "functional blocks." The next most sophisticated is the RIDES system which models device component behaviour determined using event-based based methods (e.g. when the user performs some event on the interface an action is triggered) and constraint-based methods (the value of an object property is determined by a mathematical expression). Next in sophistication are state-based simulation models, as used by XAIDA and Instructional Simulator. Components have different states depicted graphically and simple branching procedures are used to determine what state a component is in. Instructional Simulator uses a PEAnet (processes, entity, activity network) representation which includes a simple rule base describing how properties and events affect elements of a simulated process. This allows authors to easily build simple cause-and effect simulations.

RIDES and SIMQUEST include sophisticated WYSIWYG tools for building models of devices and other physical phenomena. In RIDES authors combine atomic components, such as switches, levers, pipes, electronic black boxes, etc., each of which have properties (such as color, voltage, on/off state) and the ability to connect with other components (via input and output connections). Components are joined to form larger components. Rules and constraints are authored to specify how each component affects others (e.g. how a pressure meter value effects a pneumatic valve position).

While simulations in RIDES are based on device components (and properties) and their connections, simulations in SIMQUEST are based on an authored model, i.e. a set of equations. Devices and other physical phenomena are constructed in SIMQUEST using simple graphical objects, and the properties (size, location, color, etc.) of these objects are linked to variables in the model. While SIMQUEST is more cumbersome that RIDES for authoring devices with many parts, SIMQUEST can more easily model natural phenomena such as in physics and meteorology.

Models of domain expertise. Domain expertise can include several types of knowledge, including problem solving expertise, procedural skills, concepts, and facts. Authoring systems in the Curriculum Sequencing, Tutoring Strategies, and Multiple Knowledge Types categories allow authors to represent simple facts, relationships, and procedures. Facts and relationships are stored as associations (e.g. the color of X is Y, A is the capital of B). Simple procedures are stored as a sequence of steps, and some systems have the ability to author sub-procedures. Most systems that use content networks incorporate domain information into the model of curriculum structures. For example, a topic network can relate concepts to sub-concepts (with Is-a links) and procedures to sub-procedures. This type of information is both content (i.e. the student should learn the sub-steps of a maintenance procedure, and the fact that a mushroom Is-a type of fungus) and curriculum specification (since the teaching strategy may teach about siblings before parents and sub-steps before general steps).

Procedural expertise for device operation and other procedures is represented using simple script-like representations with steps, sub-steps, and limited decision branches. More complicated procedural skills and problem solving skills require the production-rule-based representation used in expert systems (or a similarly complex formalism, such as constraints). The PUPS and Demonstr8 systems facilitate the authoring of production rules (Demonstr8 uses an example-based method described later). D3 Trainer re-uses the production system rules authored using the D3 expert system shell (Training Express uses a similar method). Both of these systems provide authoring support for associating hints and explanations with each production rule. LEAP allows users to author dialog grammars, which are similar in complexity to production rules.

As is the case with other AI systems, the authoring of facts, relationships, and simple procedures is relatively straightforward. For domain expertise modeled with rules, grammars, or constraints, the authoring is much more demanding. Authoring tools for these types of representations require programming or knowledge engineering skills. (Knowledge engineering is the skill of formalizing knowledge or procedures into computationally-relevant forms.)

Domain Knowledge Types. As mentioned above, systems in the Multiple Knowledge Types category distinguish different knowledge types and have different knowledge representation schemes and different teaching strategies for each knowledge type. This structure guides and constrains authoring. The DNA system is used to author symbolic (factual), conceptual, and procedural knowledge. These knowledge types are related by "what, how, and why" links. For example, an author creating a curriculum unit for "standard deviation" is prompted to create additional content describing "how" to calculate it (procedure), "why" it is important (concept), and "what" it is used for (fact). DNA uses a single representational framework for its three types (symbolic, procedural, and conceptual): a semantic network that includes GOMS (goals, operators, methods, and selection rules) inspired link types to represent procedural and rule-like information as well as more common is-a, part-of, and causal relationships between knowledge elements.

XAIDA provides maintenance training in four areas: the physical characteristics of a device, its theory of operation, operating and maintenance procedures, and troubleshooting. Tools for the last two categories are only partially complete. Semantic networks are used to represent physical characteristics and operation/maintenance procedures; causal reasoning schemes are used to represent theory of operation, and fault trees are used to represent troubleshooting expertise. CREAM-Tools and IRIS use more elaborate systems. CREAM-Tools use different vocabularies for learned capabilities vs. behavioral objectives. It uses Gagne's five categories of learned capabilities, Bloom's six-level classification of learning objectives (further divided into 31 terms), and a large vocabulary of relationships between these elements. IRIS uses different vocabularies for the pedagogical description of domain knowledge vs. the performance specification of domain knowledge. It also uses both Gagne's and Bloom's descriptive vocabularies.

3.3 Authoring the tutoring model

Tutoring strategies specify how content is sequenced, what type of feedback to give, when and how to coach, explain, remediate, summarize, give a problem, etc. A variety of representational methods are used to model tutoring expertise, including procedures, plans, constraints, and rules. However, the vast majority of ITS authoring tools include a fixed, i.e. non-authorable, tutoring model. Eon, COCA, REDEEM, IDE, and GTE allow authoring of the pedagogical model. COCA uses a rule-based representational method, and the author uses pull-down menus to specify the right and left-hand components of IF-THEN rules. Eon uses a flowline-based graphical programming language that allows the user to author arbitrary instructional procedures. For both of these systems the flexibility comes at the price of ease of use, and no guidance is given to help the author create effective tutoring strategies. REDEEM has a fixed rule set defining the pedagogical behaviour, but authors can define their own "teaching strategies," which are settings for key pedagogical parameters such as "amount of student choice," "preference for specific (vs. general) informationfirst," and "amount of help." For example, a strategy called "Advanced learners " might have high student choice, start with general information before teachingspecific information, and help only available on error.

Plan-based systems. Several systems (including IRIS, GTE, IDE, and REDEEM) include plan-based mechanisms with multi level hierarchical representation of instructional objectives, strategies, and tasks (various other terms are used such as goals, events, and actions). For example, the IRIS framework includes three levels: cognitive processes, instructional events, and instructional actions. IDE is unique in allowing authors to specify rationales for each planning rule, so that each rule can be justified by a specific pedagogical theory. The plan rules in some systems are fixed but IDE and GTE allow authors to type in plan rules that define a hierarchy of sub-tasks. For example: "To Teach Functions => 1: Present Function, 2: Teach Linked Processes, 3: Teach Sub-Functions, 4. Present Summary." The item "Teach Linked Processes" may be further defined using another rule. The authoring and visualization tools provided for such systems are minimal, however, and the authoring task requires significant programming or knowledge engineering skills.

Multiple strategies. Some systems include multiple teaching strategies and dynamically choose the appropriate strategy based on content and user characteristics. Systems in the Multiple Knowledge Types and Simulation categories have a handful of relatively simple teaching strategies, one for each type of task or knowledge recognized by the system. For example, a different strategy would be used to teach facts, procedures, and concepts. There is no strategy authoring for these systems. The REDEEM and Eon systems allow authors to define multiple strategies and "meta-strategies" for dynamically selecting among multiple strategies.

Meta-strategies in REDEEM are easily authored. They are defined via a set of sliders that set key pedagogical parameters (such as the depth of hints, and whether prerequisites are required). REDEEM steps authors through a set of multiple-choice questions which determine the conditions under which each defined teaching strategy is used. For example, for the "Advanced Learner" strategy above the author would select the conditions (or triggers) for using this strategy, e.g. when the student is doing well, when the material was previously summarized, and when the content is not very difficult. Eon meta-strategies combine the authoring of meta-strategy triggers, as in REDEEM's meta-strategies, with parameterization values, as in

REDEEM's strategy authoring, with the added flexibility of allowing the author to define which variables appear in the sliders.[4]

Tutorial action vocabularies. Those developing systems in the Tutoring Strategies category (and many ITS "shells") have developed elaborate vocabularies for describing instructional methods. Tutoring strategies or rules are then used to determine the type of action needed at any given time. Example tutorial actions include hint, explain, remediate, summarize, practice, select-a-topic, and reflect-on-exercise. Most such systems have a layered vocabulary in which some actions expand into other actions (e.g. active-prior-knowledge expands into recall-prior-knowledge and/or use-prior-knowledge). The GTE system, for example, has several hundred items in its library of instructional tasks and methods. (See Mizoguchi et a. 1996, Van Marcke 1992, and Murray 1996b for example vocabularies, ans see Section 5.6 on ontologies.)

3.4 Authoring the student model

Almost all of the systems mentioned in this paper use "overlay" student models; i.e. topics or procedural steps are assigned a value based on student performance. XAIDA and Eon allow the author to define misconceptions as well as topics, so that the tutor can evaluate and remediate common errors. Demonstr8 seems to be the only system using a "runnable" student model (i.e. one that can be used to predict and simulate student behavior). Various AI modeling techniques have been incorporated into ITS student models, including fuzzy logic (Goodkovsky et al. 1994) and Bayesian networks (Collins et al. 1996), but none have been incorporated in to ITS authoring systems yet. Eon seems to be the only system that allows the student model to be authored, i.e. it allows the author to specify how the values of topics are calculated based on student responses and actions. A "layered overlay" student model is used, which includes overlay values at several layers: interface events, presentations, topic levels, topics, and lessons (in contrast to other systems that have only one layer for topics). The author specifies simple expressions at each level that define how the overlay values at one level are calculated based on the next lower level.

Some systems use user modelling in unique ways. With RIDES authors can create prototype student models for tutorial testing. The WEAR system contains a model of the *teachers* goals, expertise level, interests, preferences for tool settings, and teaching methods (e.g. a preference for quizzes to be given regularly to students). It uses this model to customize the authoring session by giving the teacher context-sensitive feedback during authoring.

---

[4] Not all of REDEEMs meta-strategy capability has been implemented and tested with users.

4. WHAT AUTHORING AND KNOWLEDGE ACQUISITION METHODS HAVE BEEN USED?

Next I will discuss general methods used by authoring systems to simplify and automate authoring and knowledge acquisition. These methods are general, in that they could be used to improve authoring for any of the four main parts of an ITS described above, and could be used in an authoring tool for any of the seven categories of authoring tools described earlier.

Authoring tool goals. Before enumerating the authoring methods used, I will summarize the overall goals that motivate these methods. Generally speaking, authoring tools have these goals, in rough order of importance or predominance:

- Decrease the effort (time, cost, and/or other resources) for making intelligent tutors;
- Decrease the skill threshold for building intelligent tutors (i.e. allow more people to take part in the design process);
- Help the designer/author articulate or organize her domain or pedagogical knowledge;
- Support (i.e. structure, recommend, or enforce) good design principles (in pedagogy, user interface, etc.);
- Enable rapid prototyping of intelligent tutor designs (i.e. allow quick design/evaluation cycles of prototype software).
- Another goal is to use the rapid prototyping capability of authoring tools to evaluate alternate instructional methods and add to our inadequate body of understanding of how to match instructional methods with learning scenarios.[5]

Scaffolding knowledge articulation with models
Embedded knowledge and default knowledge
Knowledge management
Knowledge visualization
Knowledge elicitation and work flow management
Knowledge and design validation
Knowledge re-use
Automated knowledge creation

Authoring tools achieve these goals using a number of methods or features. Most of the methods address several of the above goals (for example, a feature that helps the designer articulate a teaching strategy will also decrease the effort and skill

---

[5] Yet another possible goal is helping the author *learn* something about pedagogy, instructional design, or knowledge representation, and thus become a better author as they use the system.

threshold of building a tutor). I describe eight methods in detail, listed in the box below, and then briefly mention several other methods or capabilities seen in authoring tools.

4.1. Scaffolding knowledge articulation with models

ITS Authoring is both a design process and a process of knowledge articulation. The most significant method that authoring tools employ to allow non-programmers to build tutors is to scaffold the task by incorporating a particular model or framework. Simplification by restricting the universe of what can be built is a somewhat obvious method since that is what all software applications do (e.g. an electronic address book is easier to use than a database application). Providing authors with clear frameworks or templates helps them organize and structure the authored information. Though obvious, it is worth highlighting because one of the major differences between authoring tools is the degree to which their models constrain the product (see the later Section on design tradeoffs).

A significant part of authoring an ITS (or any instructional system) is the systematic decomposition of the subject matter into a set of related elements (usually a hierarchy). Each authoring system provides tools or cues which assist the author in this (usually top-down) process of breaking down and elaborating the content to the necessary level of detail according to a particular model of instructional elements and their relationships. Such "content analysis" can be distinguished from "task analysis" and "cognitive task analysis." Content analysis tools help authors decompose their declarative knowledge of facts, concepts, procedures, and principles. The DNA Chapter (6) describes a system for doing content analysis of factual, conceptual, and (simple) procedural knowledge. Task analysis tools help authors articulate procedures and action sequences. For example tools in Demonstr8, Instructional Simulator, and RIDES allow domain experts to demonstrate a procedure which is then generalized. Cognitive task analysis tools help experts articulate problem solving and other thinking skills. For performance-oriented tutors, the most significant task is in articulating and representing expert performance. Ritter et al. (in this volume) say that "good task analysis is essential in creating an effective learning system [yet] little effort has gone into authoring systems for task analysis." Ritter et al. describe efforts to do cognitive task analysis for model tracing tutors.

Some systems, particularly in the adaptive hypermedia category, minimize the use of authoring tools by allowing authors to enter content using a standard word processing application and a "mark-up" system or language. Characteristics of content such as its place in a content hierarchy, its prerequisites, its difficulty, etc. can be typed into a word processor and tagged in one of two ways (see Brusilovsky in this Volume). The first method is to mark the text (in Microsoft Word) using styles, as is done in the InterBook project. The second method is to mark the text with special symbols (e.g. "<<*difficulty-topic*>>") as is done in the AHA system. This method has the benefit of being simple and no new tools have to be developed or used. It has disadvantages including the need to memorize the mark-up language and being susceptible to typographical errors in the mark-up.

4.2. Embedded knowledge and default knowledge

One way to make authoring easier and more powerful is to embed knowledge right into the system. "Embedded knowledge" means knowledge that is pre-wired and non-authorable. This knowledge can be passive or active. Passive knowledge is knowledge that is implied as part of the structure or constraints imposed by an authoring system. For instance the systems in the Multiple Knowledge Types category have instructional design principles embedded into their structure (e.g. that concepts have necessary and sufficient attributes). Authoring systems that highly constrain ITS design, such as those in the Special Purpose category, contain substantial passive embedded knowledge. (And see the discussion in Section 4.7 on knowledge re-use, which is similar to embedded and default knowledge.)

Active embedded knowledge is runnable and produces some result. For example, REDEEM contains a sophisticated rule-based instructional strategy that the author can effect through the use of strategy parameters, but otherwise can not alter. XAIDA uses embedded expertise to generate 19 different types of practice questions for procedural knowledge. The author can specify when to use each type for a particular instructional module.

Special Purpose systems and several others (including XAIDA and REDEEM) make use of reasonable default values that allow the author to postpone entering some information but still be able to test-run the tutor. Default values in templates can also provide examples of the type of information to be entered, and thus be informative as well as functional. In REDEEM even though the author can modify the teaching strategy, the system has a robust default tutoring method so that a tutor can be authored and run without ever defining teaching strategies. IDLE-Tool scaffolds authoring using a "guided case adaptation" method. Associated with every data-entry template screen is sample input from a prototypical IDLE tutor. Thus authoring is then more like adapting a similar case to fit the needs of a new tutor than starting from scratch. The system, as a special purpose authoring tool, also contains a specific model of the investigate-and-decide task (for example, the investigate task is composed of parts: decide on what sample to take, obtain the sample, determine the analysis method, do the test, interpret the results) and a detailed domain-specific taxonomy of types of samples, tests, and results to help guide the authoring process.

4.3. Knowledge management

ITSs are elaborate systems and authoring them involves managing a large amount of complex information. A number of common user interface techniques are used by authoring systems to assist with knowledge management and organization. Simplifying input through the use of templates, data entry forms, and pop-up menus is quite common. Whenever the range of possible input values can be limited to a finite set, tools should be provided to allow authors to choose rather than type.

ITSs are particularly difficult to author because of the many diverse and interconnected types of information they contain. A primary tenet of ITS design is to have separate representations of content (what to teach) and tutoring strategy (how to teach it), but these can not be made completely independent. Even if a system successfully encapsulates certain aspects in independent modules there are still complex conceptual relationships that the author must be aware of. For example, the structure of the student model depends on the structure of the domain model; the form of the teaching strategies depends on the structure of the domain model; the actions in the teaching strategies depend on the form of the tutor's student interface. Navigation aides that let authors move between various related pieces of information and different representations of the same information have been implemented. For example, if different parts of a tutoring strategy refer to topics, student model rules, and interface components, the author should be able to click on the associated item in the strategy authoring tool and be brought directly to the topic authoring tool, student model authoring tool, or interface authoring tool(this is done in Eon and CREAM-Tools).

Tools that allow authors to zoom in and out between the details and the big picture can help manage large information spaces. Object browsers, which allow authors to scroll through all of the objects of one type and inspect properties and/or relationships with other objects are available in several of the systems (as exist in RIDES, D3 Trainer, IRIS, Eon, SimQuest, and CREAM-Tools). Tools for managing evolving software components and versions are important to most off-the-shelf software engineering design environments, but these features have not yet been incorporated into ITS authoring tools.

4.4. Knowledge visualization

Perhaps the most powerful way to help authors understand and comprehend the large amounts of complexly interconnected knowledge is with powerful visualization tools. Unfortunately, building the user interface is usually far and away the most labor-intensive part of programming any interactive software. The level of interactivity and visualization in ITS authoring tools is still quite primitive as compared with off-the-shelf productivity software (with the exception of RIDES and Eon, which have fairly sophisticated interface design tools).

LAT has tools that help authors visualize conversational grammars. LAT's grammars, which represent how a customer contact employee should respond to service calls of various types, are composed of individual scripts that define the possible actions (things to say to a customer) and decisions points of a thematic unit in the conversation (such as "processing a discounted sales order"). Each script can invoke other scripts. A relatively simple set of scripts can result in a large and complex set of possible conversational scenarios. LAT provides visualization tools that allow the author to see both the static structure of the scripts and the run-time dynamics that simulate possible tutorial scenarios. LAT designers also stress the importance of providing multiple views of authored content.

Topic or curriculum network tools are the most common knowledge visualization tools in ITS authoring. Little currently exists to allow authors to visualize teaching strategies. Eon uses a highly visual flow-line metaphor for authoring tutoring strategies. Strategy authoring in REDEEM consists of setting parameters, so strategies can be easily visualized with a screen of sliders and radio buttons.

4.5. Knowledge elicitation and work-flow management

Knowledge acquisition is widely acknowledged as the limiting factor or bottleneck in building AI systems. A number of techniques have been used for extracting knowledge from experts, most of which are "manual" methods that involve a knowledge engineer interviewing or observing the expert (Hoffman 1987). Software tools have been developed to scaffold or automate some knowledge acquisition (Boose 1988; Shaw & Gaines 1986). Many of the automated techniques use contrived tasks such as sorting or ranking to find conceptual dependencies, logical entailments, or other patterns in the data, which are not generally applicable to acquiring domain or teaching knowledge for ITSs. However, the method of interactive elicitation of knowledge to fill in a pre-structured knowledge base *has* been used in ITS authoring, as described below. As mentioned previously, using an authoring tool to build an ITS involves both knowledge acquisition and design processes. Authors need to be supported not only in filling in a knowledge base, but in the overall ITS design *process*. This includes designing the interface, domain model, and teaching strategies; conceptualizing the interaction among *several* knowledge bases; and the iterative process of user testing and refinement. Interactive prompts and dialogs can help with work-flow management (or "performance support"), as well as knowledge elicitation.

ISD-Expert (an early precursor to Instructional Simulator) led the author through a sometimes excruciatingly long dialog to create an entire course in a top-down manner. The dialog started with general questions such as "what is the title of the module?" and "what is the average motivation for the target audience?" Then a series of questions fleshed out the content and behavioral objectives in a top down fashion, and included questions for each content unit such as "which of the following describes what the student will learn: a. What is it? b. How to do it; c. How does it work?" The potential benefit of this system was that, since the authoring involves responding to specific prompts, the author did not have to make any high-level design decisions (only low level and concrete decisions). But there were two serious drawbacks to the system. First, authors felt too constrained by the fixed sequence of data entry. The design of complex systems usually requires a mixture of top down and bottom up design (i.e. "opportunistic" design). The second problem with such highly constrained dialogs is that the more a system constrains data entry the more essential it is that the underlying model be accurate and complete. But instructional theories are neither entirely accurate nor entirely complete, and each author may have her own style or preferences. It is often better for a system to offer suggestions but allow the author to override the default design decisions. REDEEM's meta-strategy authoring tool uses an automated knowledge elicitation dialog that is less restrictive. First, the dialog is limited to defining the meta-strategy parameters for a particular strategy, and the author chooses when to initiate this dialog. Second, the dialog consists of a series of screens rather than a series of text-based questions. Each screen has a data entry form for several parameters, and includes default choices for these parameters. REDEEM includes an agenda mechanism that keeps track of incomplete authoring tasks and prompts the user to complete them.

DNA uses a semi-structured interactive dialog to elicit domain knowledge from a SME (subject matter expert) (a process called cognitive task analysis). As mentioned earlier, DNA can elicit curriculum elements of three interrelated types: factual ("symbolic knowledge"), procedural, and conceptual. Thus, as the SME is defining a curriculum element he is prompted for the existence of related facts, concepts, and procedures. Questions such as "What is the definition of [a term used in a procedure]" and "Why is [some fact] important" prompt the SME to continue to flesh out the content to include all three knowledge types. The process is called "semi-structured" elicitation because the questions are presented as options on the design screen, allowing the author to choose which one to answer next (and which ones to ignore).

Expert-CML is designed to scaffold the instructional design process by providing advice that is sufficient for the novice user but does not hinder the expert user. A rule-base of over 100 rules provides advice in two forms. The first suggests what to do next (similar to DNA above) and the second points out possible errors in the tutor (as discussed in the next Section). The advice is shown in a status bar at the bottom of the screen, where the author can use it or choose to ignore it. Also, the author can turn off certain instructional design rules to permanently override the system's suggestions.

4.6. Knowledge and design validation and verification

Each authoring system makes different compromises along the spectrum of free-form design to constrained design. More open-ended systems allow for more flexibility in both the form of the content and the sequence of steps taken to design the tutor. However, the more flexibility given to the author the higher the probability that they will enter something inconsistent, inaccurate, or something that is at odds with the principles of good instructional design. Special purpose authoring tools can ensure content validity by tightly constraining what is entered. One way to allow flexible authoring while maintaining quality is to allow the author to enter what she wants in the way that she wants, but to include mechanisms that check the authored information for accuracy, consistency, completeness, and effectiveness. As mentioned above, the Expert-CML system includes an expert system that offers this type of content evaluation. For example, rules exist that inform the author of the following: when the author's estimate of the time to complete a lesson is at odds with the accumulated times given for the component parts; when a summary or introduction might be needed to break up a long sequence of new material; when the objectives of a lesson are not adequately covered by the lesson's instructional components; and when a lesson's general cognitive level (according to Bloom's Taxonomy) does not match with the cognitive levels of the lesson's objectives.

The DNA system deals with content accuracy and completeness by facilitating the process of having several SMEs review the knowledge structures authored by the primary author/SME. The reviewing SMEs can edit and comment on the original knowledge base. The ECSAIWeb system allows authors to simulate learning paths to check the validity of the curriculum model. D3-Trainer is the only system that validates authored information by matching it with a case base of previously authored examples.

Inconsistencies in authored information that manifest at run time might be invisible during authoring. By allowing teachers to match teaching strategies to prototypical student attributes, REDEEM supports teachers in understanding the consequences of the teaching strategies. RIDES includes a consistency checker and an integrated debugger/stepper that allows authors to run and debug their device simulations. It also lets authors create prototype student models for validation testing.

4.7. Knowledge re-use

Authoring tools have the potential to increase the efficiency of building ITSs through re-use of common elements. To date most ITS authoring tools have not been used to build enough ITSs to experience this benefit. Realizing re-use would require a resource library structure, where authored topics, activities, strategies, interface components, and/or domain knowledge could be stored independently from a tutor, and loaded from this library into any tutor. Sparks et al (1999--- the LAT system) discuss the implications of object libraries for work reduction, reduced maintenance effort; and increased consistency among tutors. However, they note that supporting re-use may have considerable costs in terms of system complexity and ease of use.

REDEEM is built to take advantage of courseware libraries. The content and interactive screens of a REDEEM ITS are not authored using REDEEM, but are authored in either html or. ToolBook, an off-the-shelf multimedia authoring tool. This authored content is exported to a library and from there it is imported by REDEEM. Component libraries in SIMQUEST included reusable interface components as well as reusable content objects. D3 Trainer keeps a library of actual cases for re-use, and SimQuest has a library of content from past authors (also see Section 5.7 on interoperability and re-use).

4.8. Automated knowledge creation

Some ITS authoring systems infer or create new knowledge or information from scratch, saving the author from having to derive, articulate, and enter this information. RIDES and Demonstr8 use example-based programming techniques to infer general procedures from specific examples given by the author. RIDES creates a device's operational procedure by recording the author's actions as he uses the device simulation to illustrate the procedure. Demonstr8's method, which generalizes the elements of the authors actions to produce expert system production rules, is more powerful but potentially has more limited application. The DIAG system infers a large body of device fault diagnosis information from a relatively small number of failure consequences it captures by analyzing the device model prepared by the author.

Systems in the Device Simulation and Expert System categories are sophisticated enough to generate new problems and their solutions from general principles or rules, thus saving the author from having to enter every problem and its solution.

4.9 General Authoring Features

Though the authoring systems described in this paper have a variety of features, a number of features have emerged as being generally important to robust usability, as described below.

1. WYSIWIG editing and rapid testing. Authors should be able to easily see and test both the static visual elements of the tutor and the dynamic run-time behavior of a tutor. Easy movement back and forth from editing to test-run modes facilitates rapid prototyping.

2. Flexible, opportunistic design. ITS authoring tools should be designed to work best for those who have had some training. Features that make it easy for a first-time user to get to work should not get in the way of serious longer term use. Tools should allow for a mixture of top down (starting with the abstract curriculum structure) and bottom up (starting with specific screens and content) authoring for different design styles.

3. Visual reification. The conceptual and structural elements of a representational formalism should be portrayed graphically with high visual fidelity if ITS Authoring systems are to be used by non-programmers. Such user interfaces relieve working memory load by reifying the underlying structures, and assist long term memory by providing reminders of this structure. Also, multiple views (visual perspectives) of information are often needed.

4. Content modularity and re-usability. Instructional content should be represented and authored modularly so that it can be used for multiple instructional purposes. Include library structures for saving reusable components. Provide productivity tools that capitalize on repetitive or template-like content. Provide tools that make it easy to browse, search for, and reference content objects.

5. Customization, extensibility, and scriptabilty. A tool cannot anticipate everything a designer will want. All modern design and authoring software provides for extensibility and scripting. Scripting allows authors with moderate skills to create "generative" ITSs that construct problems, explanation, hint, etc. on the fly.

6. Undo! Mundane features such as Undo, Copy/Paste, and Find can be extremely time consuming to build into complex design software such as authoring tools, yet such features are essential components of all robust usable software.

7. Administrative features. Only a few of the authoring tools (including RIDES and SimQuest) have administrative facilities for such things as class rostering, grade analysis and statistics, and generating progress reports, such features may be essential to the eventual adoption of ITSs into mainstream education. CREAM Tools is the only system so far to support collaborative authoring with rights management and access security features.

To the above list I will add the following which, though not as generally accepted, I believe to be important for building authoring tools that are both usable and powerful (these items are discussed in more detail in Chapter 15 Section 5.4):

8. Include customizable representational formalisms. An authoring system will be based on some underlying representational formalism, and any such formalism will satisfy the needs of authoring some types of tutors yet not be appropriate for authoring other tutors. To achieve greater flexibility, authoring tools should include the ability to customize the representational formalism (see Section 5.6 on ontologies and meta-authoring).

9. Anchor usability on familiar authoring paradigms, and facilitate evolution to more powerful paradigms. For those used to building traditional computer-based instruction, building intelligent tutors requires a conceptual shift from "story board" representations of content to more modular knowledge based representations (Murray 1996). It is useful to have some ITS authoring tools have a look and feel similar to common off-the-shelf CAI authoring tools, and to provide features which allow a smooth transition from traditional authoring paradigms to authoring more powerful intelligent tutors.

10. Facilitate design at a pedagogically relevant level of abstraction. Provide tools which allow subject matter experts to author using primitives at the "pedagogical level" as well as the media level (Murray 1996). Media level primitive are "graphic," "button," mouse click, etc. Objects at the pedagogical level have instructional meaning, for example "hint," "explanation," "topic," "prerequisite," and "mastered."

The commercially available and heavily used systems tend to have more of these features. For example, RIDES has multiple levels of undo/redo, copy/pasting, Find, a consistency checker, and an integrated debugger that lets authors step through a simulation execution to evaluate run time bugs. It also includes an instructor administrator module. SimQuest has an online help manual, a context sensitive advice tool (a hypertext on-line manual), authoring Wizards (step by step procedural help), a content re-use library, a scripting language, and administrative reporting features.

5. HOW ARE AUTHORING SYSTEMS BUILT? -- DESIGN PRINCIPLES

In the previous Sections I have characterized the range of tools and methods used by ITS authoring systems. The wide variation among these systems should be evident to the reader. The differences are in part due to different theories and models of knowledge and instruction, but in large part can be attributed to different priorities and design tradeoffs. If one were in the (unrealistic) position of choosing among all of these authoring tools for a specific job, or in the position of intending to design a new ITS authoring tool from scratch, how would one decide which of the tools, methods, and features were most important? Trying to build an authoring tool that incorporates the "the whole enchilada" is practically impossible, not only because of the prohibitive cost and complexity, but because the design decisions these systems are based on are at odds with each other. For instance, increasing the flexibility/power of a system comes at the cost of usability.

5.1 A space of design tradeoffs

Figure 1 illustrates the space of factors leading to design tradeoffs for ITS authoring systems, including breadth, depth, learnability, productivity, fidelity, and cost.[6]

		Domain Model	Tutoring Strategy	Student Model	Learning Envrnmnt.
Power/ Flexibility	Breadth				
	Depth	[The design space has 24 (6x4) independent dimensions or axes.]			
Usability	Learnability				
	Productivity				
	Fidelity				
	Cost				

Figure 1: ITS Authoring Tool Design Tradeoffs

Overall, Power/flexibility and Usability are usually at odds with each other, since simplicity tends to correlate with usability. As shown in the Table, power/flexibility has two aspects: breadth (scope) and depth of knowledge. Breadth is how general the framework is for building tutors for diverse subject areas and instructional approaches. Knowledge depth is the depth to which a system can reason about and teach the knowledge, and the depth to which it can infer a student's knowledge and

---

[6] The important metric of "instructional effectiveness" is not included in our metrics, because this depends very much on how the authoring tool is used to produce a tutor. However it is also true that the design of an authoring tool can have a tremendous effect on the instructional effectiveness of the systems it is used to build.

respond accordingly. Breadth and Depth are often at odds, because one must often limit the generality of a system to be able to represent deep causal knowledge. Usability also has two aspects: learnability and productivity. Learnability is how easy a system is to learn how to use. Productivity is how quickly a trained user can enter information and produce a tutoring system. Learnability and productivity are often at odds, since a system that is designed to be picked up quickly by novices may not provide the powerful features that experienced users need to efficiently produce large systems. Fidelity is the degree to which a tutor perceptually and operationally matches its target domain.[7] A 3-D immersive environment has more visual fidelity than a 2D simulation. A learning environments that allows the student to directly practice a task has more fidelity than one that merely describes and asks questions about the task. Fidelity can be closely related to depth, since deeper knowledge facilitates more realistic interactions, but it is possible for a system to have shallow knowledge and high fidelity. Cost refers to the amount of resources needed to build the authoring system (for this discussion the availability of personnel, expertise, and time are included in this category). I will not say more about cost except to note the obvious fact that the resources available to a software project greatly effect design decisions. Figure 1 illustrates that all of the design factors mentioned above come into play for each ITS component separately---domain model, tutoring strategy, student model, and learning environment. For example, an authoring system can have a highly usable tool for authoring shallow student models and a not so usable tool for authoring deep teaching strategies. Additional evaluation criterion have been proposed. Ainsworth (Chapter 8 in this Volume) adds: 1) the ability of an authoring tool to successfully represent an expert's teaching strategies (and, by extension, domain knowledge), 2) the effectiveness of the resulting ITSs, and 3) the ability of the tools (through the authoring process) to help educators reflect on, share, and expand their own knowledge of how to teach in their subject area.

The design space for ITS authoring tools is indeed huge. There is rough consensus on the nature of the tradeoffs involved, but not on how to balance those tradeoffs to produce the most effective and usable authoring systems. Questions that must be addressed include:

- How much should the author be constrained to a particular (favored) pedagogical model?
- Who are the prototypical authors who will use the system?
- What types of knowledge and skills should be modeled by the system?
- What is the source of the teaching and domain expertise?

These questions must be answered to make the design decisions and compromises involved in building an ITS authoring tool. Each authoring tool, no matter how general, will embody particular assumptions and models and thus be more

---

[7] Fidelity, depth, and cost are qualities of the *tutor* that an authoring system produces, while all of the other design factors are about the authoring system itself.

appropriate for building certain types of ITSs than others. Before designing an ITS authoring tool it is best to be as explicit as possible about the nature of the ITSs to be built. I discuss some of the design decisions in more detail in the following Sections.

5.2 General or special purpose authoring systems?

One of the most active areas of disagreement among the authoring tool research community concerns the appropriate degree of generality for an authoring system. For example, the LAT system is designed to only produce tutors to train customer service personnel how to respond to customer inquiries. It is a general tool in that it can be used to create a customer service ITS for a variety of products. An authoring tool that specializes in producing a very particular type of ITS has many benefits. In principle, by severely constraining the universe of what can be designed, an authoring system can have higher usability, higher fidelity, more depth, and be more efficient. More constrained systems make it less likely for authors to enter incorrect, inconsistent, or pedagogically poor content or teaching methods.

IDLE-Tool is designed to build tutors for "Investigate and Decide" learning environments. Bell (1998, and Jona & Kass 1997) proposes a suite of special purpose authoring tools, each for learning a particular type of complex task, such as Investigate and Decide, Run an Organization, and Evidence Based Reporting. In Investigate and Decide environments learners are supported in gathering data about a realistic case or scenario (such as a medical diagnosis), interpreting the data, taking some action based on their hypothesis (such as prescribing medication), and receiving feedback about their action (such as whether it helped the patient). The IDLE authoring tool provides the author with a fixed template for representing the outcomes, feedback, reference informant, and graphics. The task structure and the pedagogy for teaching about the task are predefined based on (presumably) sound instructional principles. A formative study found the tool to be too constraining. Its fill-in-the blanks style did not support the kind of "big picture" view of the instructional scenario that can be important in designing instructional scenarios. Bell and others are continuing to work toward authoring tools that tightly constrain the authoring process but include adequate flexibility.

There are several issues related to tool generality. First, although "Investigate and Decide" seems to be a very general type of task, the authoring system embodies a very specific interpretation of that task and a fixed pedagogical model. Assuming there are a large number of educators (mostly science and technology educators) who would be interested in building (or using) an Investigate and Decide tutor for some topic, it is not clear how many of these would find IDLE-Tool's specific model agreeable. Bell's formative study will lead to more flexible and customizable systems, such as IMAP, which will inevitably require more skilled authors. We can't yet say where the most appropriate generality vs. usability line should be drawn for these types of systems, but every new data point will help.

The LAT system paints a slightly clearer picture. Its conversational grammar approach to customer service training seems more certain to be widely usable than

IDLE-Tool's template-based approach to Investigate and Decide types of inquiry learning. This is partly because LAT has a deeper and more general representation of the task. But it is also because the customer contact task is more easily defined. I think that special purpose authoring tools will find much wider appeal in "training" applications than "educational" applications. With training applications there is wider agreement on the nature of the task and what the behavioral objectives are, but in educational applications (which tend to address higher order thinking and skills) there is much less agreement over exactly what and how to teach. The authoring tools in the device simulation category are a good case in point. The task of training someone how to operate and understand (at a basic level) how a piece of machinery works is very general and there is a fair degree of agreement concerning effective training approaches. Consequently, the RIDES system has seen the widest application of any of the authoring tools.

Research with XAIDA is pushing the generality vs. usability issue in interesting directions. Its target user is much less sophisticated than RIDES', which also teaches about device operation and maintenance. This has lead to a number of design simplifications aimed at usability. For instance, RIDES represents component interdependencies in terms of constraints and event results, while XAIDA uses a less powerful but more felicitous cause-effect framework. Compared to RIDES and the systems in the Domain Expert System category, XAIDA has a relatively shallow knowledge representation (but it is still runnable or executable knowledge---i.e. the system has limited "understanding" of what it is teaching). If looked at separately each of XAIDA's four knowledge types (physical characteristics, theory of operation, operating and maintenance procedures, and troubleshooting) has a relatively shallow representation. Yet its incorporation of four different knowledge types adds a degree of power and generality. Thus XAIDA has been used to prototype tutors in a number of domains, including several that are quite distant from the originally intended domain of equipment operation and maintenance. These domains include algebra, medicine, computer literacy, and biology.

DNA and Instructional Trainer rely on a similar combination of relatively shallow knowledge representation and distinct knowledge types to achieve a high level of generality. The preliminary successes of these systems indicate that the correct level of abstraction for distinguishing different types of authoring tools may be more at the cognitive level of knowledge types (such as concepts vs. procedures) than at the more surface level of task types (such as investigate vs. advise).[8]

Up to this point I have shown how usability is at odds with the power/flexibility of an authoring tool. The only method mentioned thus far that results in both powerful and usable authoring tools is to limit them to particular domains or knowledge types. Another method, that of creating "meta-authoring" environments, is described in a Section 5.6.

---

[8] It is also possible that an appropriate level of abstraction will similar to the "generic tasks" proposed in the context of expert systems research (Chandrasekaran, B. 1986).

5.3 Who are the authors? --an authoring skills analysis

The main goal of an ITS authoring system is to make the process of building an ITS easier. This ease translates into reduced cost and a decrease in the skill threshold for potential authors. The design specifications of a piece of software are highly dependent on the assumptions made about the intended prototypical user. In the case of ITS authoring tools we must ask:

- What is the assumed skill level in: knowledge engineering?
- In multimedia creation and interface design?
- In instructional design and instructional theories?
- In testing or evaluating educational software?
- In the particular subject matter domain of the tutor?
- How much time does the user have available for training?
- For design and development of the tutor?
- How well does the author know the characteristics of the target student audience?

As this list of questions implies, it will usually require a team of people with different knowledge and skills to author an ITS. But how fast and easy can authoring an ITS be? Of course, in part, the answer to this question depends on what is meant by "an ITS"-- some fairly simple instructional systems have been built that still qualify as adaptive or intelligent. It also depends on how similar are the ITSs that we want to build with the tool, as was discussed in the Tradeoffs Section. Another way to phrase the overall question is: how much of the design process can be scaffolded or automated? If we identify hard limitations in the answer to this question, then this will imply constraints on the amount of a) skill, and b) time required to author an ITS. Below I use a analysis of authoring task complexity to help address this issue. Four levels of task complexity are defined 1) templates, 2) relationships, 3) modelling, and 4) behaviors. For now we ignore tasks that clearly require the skills of a software designer, such as building a plug-in learning environment interface or creating a complex algorithm needed in student model diagnosis.

    1. **Templates and forms**. The easiest types of authoring task are filling in template information, selecting items from pre-defined lists, and answering prompted questions. Aspects of an authoring tool that clearly reify the main objects of an ITS and their editable properties through fill-in-the-blanks forms could be accessible to designers and teachers at all skill levels.

    2. **Defining object relationships and structures**. Though this task seems easy, defining relationships between objects is a significant conceptual jump over specifying object properties in templates. Some types of relationships are straightforward to create, such as connecting an explanation object with a graphic object, or specifying that the "engine" component is "a part of" an "automobile"

component. But creating object links at more abstract levels is more difficult. The primary example of this is the creation of the topic network. It may be easy for most users to create a concept network that illustrates their informal ideas about how topics are related. But to design a good topic network, one that expresses the important pedagogical relationships in a domain and, when traversed according to some teaching strategy, will result in reasonable and expected tutorial behavior, is difficult and subtle. One inevitably runs into questions about subtle distinctions such as whether one topic is a part-of, a-kind-of, or a prerequisite-of another topic. Questions such as the following arise: are the sub-topics of a topic's prerequisites also the topic's prerequisites? Reasoning through these situations often requires the skills attributed to knowledge engineers. The complexity of the task is compounded by content-strategy interactions, as described in Chapter 15 Section 6. Also, as the complexity of a system of relationships increases, the task looks more like modelling. Software designers have learned that building robust models requires such techniques as data and procedural abstraction, encapsulation, and indirection--concepts they are difficult for many non-programmers to exploit.

3. **Modelling**. I believe that it is not possible to author an ITS without considering the big picture. This includes conceptualizing the intended audience and their needs; reconceputalizing instruction so that it can be delivered flexibly for each student; and decomposing content in a way that maintains coherence and consistence when it is dynamically reconstructed for a student---i.e. ITS authoring will usually involve modeling. It has been said that building explicit models of expertise is at the heart of AI work (Clancey 1986). Questions about building explicit models are also at the heart of ITS authoring. ITSs are complex systems containing embedded models of several types (roughly characterized as domain, teaching, and student models). Understanding ITS authoring requires a conceptual separation of content from instructional method--a reconceptualization of content as flexible and modular. This is very different from designing the screens that a student will see and enumerating the possible paths a student can take, as is done in designing traditional educational software. Building an explicit model of anything is not an easy task, and requires analysis, synthesis, and abstraction skills along with a healthy dose of creativity. Even though an authoring tool might be able to reduce the process to a long sequence of simple atomic steps done in isolation, some degree of holistic understanding and abstract thinking will eventually have to come into play. Authoring tools can significantly decrease the cognitive load involved in various design steps, but it is difficult to reduce the entire design task to low-level decisions.

4. **Defining behavior**. ITSs are user-oriented software systems that behave. Designing good ones involves iterative test trials to make sure they work as intended. Testing software implies that it will be fixed or debugged. This means that the designer has to understand the relationship between non-optimal runtime behavior and information inside the system. Defining and debugging some behaviors is relatively straightforward, for example: "when this button is pushed highlight the hint text," and "if the student gets over 80% of the answers correct, assign mastery to the topic." However, defining control structures, rules, or algorithms proves to be more difficult, even when authoring tools are provided to

make the task easier and at a higher level of abstraction (as is done in LAT and Eon). When the task includes specifying looping/repeating or conditional structures (including IF/THEN rules) the complexity increases dramatically. This is not because it is so difficult for users to understand the meaning and local effects of these structures, but because the emergent global behavior of control structures is complex. No matter how easy we make it, such tasks are essentially "programming tasks" and the skills associated with programming are needed. The main difficulty comes when, inevitably, the system behaves in some way that does not meet the author's expectations, either do to a bug in the algorithm or an unforeseen consequence of the interaction of parts. The task then is one of diagnosing and debugging an algorithm, which takes a programmer's skill. This level of programming skill is usually part of the skill set of knowledge engineers, who may not be skilled enough to write, say, a Java application, but do understand the basics of computer data structures an algorithms.

As mentioned, most ITS authoring will require a team effort. Graphics and multimedia skills will be needed if the multimedia resources are not already available. Interface design skills are not necessary for most authoring tools, because they do not allow the user to design the interface from scratch. As discussed in the XAIDA Chapter (2) and the DNA Chapter (6), the standard model for creating training materials in industry assumes separate roles for subject matter expert and instructional designer. But to simplify our discussion we can temporarily assume that there is one instructor on the team who has both of these skill sets. We will also temporarily ignore the skills needed to formatively evaluate the ITS to ensure that it works as expected. Chapter 15 Section 4.6 describes how the following tasks are particularly difficult for non-knowledge engineers: curriculum representation, strategy representation, ontology design, and student model definition. We can ignore the last two of these as they apply only to very high level authoring situations. Thus we can narrow down the discussion to one primary question: how much knowledge engineering skill is needed? I.E. under what situations can a "regular" instructor or teacher do the bulk of the work in creating the content of an ITS, and when is a trained knowledge engineer needed on the team? In terms of the task complexity levels defined above, we can say the following.

Tasks in level 1 are accessible to most teachers and "laypersons" who are comfortable using computer applications. Tasks at level 2 are already moving beyond what can be expected of most instructors without substantial training, and tasks at levels 3 and 4 require significant training or help from a knowledge engineer. When authoring tools have been empirically evaluated with many users the lessons learned indicate that completing tasks levels above level 1 require significant (initially unexpected) levels of training and skill. Van Jolingen (in this Volume) notes "though SimQuest can take away much of the burden of the authoring process, the conceptual part of authoring in itself requires considerable training for the author [and] training and support are necessary." Ainsworth et al. (this volume) report that in evaluations of REDEEM teachers had the most difficulty in decomposing the material into modular units. Though the benefits of ITSs come in large part by supporting a knowledge-based, as opposed to a storyboard metaphor for content (see Chapter 15 Section 2.2), REDEEM authors tended to create storyboard-like tutors. Ainsworth et al. note that the studies have contributed to our understanding of how the average teacher conceptualizes content by highlighting the important role that narrative plays for them. In numerous evaluations of XAIDA researchers noted a reluctance of some trainers to reconceptualize their model of instruction from a linear lesson plan to the more modular one used in the knowledge-based approach. In formative evaluations of the LAT system researchers concluded that they overestimated the level of experience that would be achieved by typical authors. Findings compatible with all of the above studies were found in evaluations of SimQuest and IDLE-Tool. Until an authoring system has been evaluated or used by many users who are not affiliated with the originating research team we should be cautious about claims for its usability.

Some systems, such as XAIDA, and REDEEM, are aimed at authors with very little training (on the order of several hours), so that any instructor could, theoretically, built an ITS. This level of skill is on the order of an intermediate level user of a word processor or spreadsheet program. Other systems, such as RIDES and Eon, assume that the author will be more skilled. My own belief is that, in general, ITSs are complex systems and we should expect authors to have a reasonable degree of training in how to author them, corresponding with a skill level on the order of database applications, CAD software, 3-D modeling, or scripting in Excel or Lingo. This does not raise the bar unrealistically high, since this level of knowledge and creative/analytical skill is used for many common jobs. There are many thousands of people with proficient levels of these skills, as compared to the small number who know how to program an ITS from scratch, so having ITS authoring tools aimed at this level of usability is a substantial improvement. Each company or school could have one person trained in using an ITS authoring tool. Fortunately, it is often reasonable to expect an untrained SME or teacher to enter the bulk of the authored information, and then hand the system over to a more highly trained person for completion. In the case of the XAIDA project and the D3 Trainer project, the goal was to allow SMEs to create tutors by authoring domain knowledge (in XAIDA by describing physical artefacts and demonstrating how they operate, and in D3 Trainer by defining expert system rules). The instructional knowledge is contained within these systems, so instructional designers and teachers may not be needed in the authoring process.

But this design picture is not shared by all. Several Chapters in this volume show evidence that regular instructors can create tutors with very little training (see XAIDA, REDEEM, and Instructional Simulator). Such "easy authoring" seems possible in several situations: 1) when the resulting tutor and content are very simple; 2) for special purpose authoring systems that are highly tailored a particular domain and teaching strategy, and 3) for situations in which the author is essentially customizing an existing tutor, rather than designing one from scratch (and see the discussion of meta-authoring in Section 5.6).

Most of the highly usable authoring systems simplify authoring by providing a fixed and relatively uncomplicated model of the domain that can be authored through templates. We will look at the most usable systems: XAIDA, DNA, Instructional Simulator, IDLE-Tool, and REDEEM. XAIDA, IDLE-Tool, and

DNA contain fairly simple (instructor-friendly) domain models and fixed (non-authoreable) teaching strategies. In XAIDA and Instructional Simulator the domain is composed of parts, their name and location, their sub-components, etc. In DNA the content is described as answering what (facts), how (procedures), and why (concepts and principles) questions. In IDLE-Tool the learning task is divided in to fixed steps: obtain data, analyze data, and interpret results. In all of these cases the system has a fixed teaching strategy. REDEEM takes a different tact. It has essentially no domain model and has a CBT-like open yet shallow content model--just multimedia pages as in a book. But it allows authors to modify the tutoring strategy. It simplifies strategy definition by reducing it to parameter settings (as described above). This puts specifying tutorial behavior at the complexity level of "templates and forms" (reminiscent of the Swift system's "minimalist ITS approach").

The question of how easy authoring can be made, and thus what set of skills is needed by an author is still an open question. We have seen that the amount of knowledge engineering skill needed can be minimized in constrained situations, potentially allowing any teacher or trainer to create or customize an ITS.

I should mention that another important class of potential users are educational theorists. ITS authoring tools should allow theorists to rapidly prototype ITSs and easily modify their teaching strategies and content to experiment with alternative curricula and instructional methods (Winne 1991). Evaluations of SimQuest and REEDEM have included such experimental comparisons of alternate teaching methods or styles.

Finally, another class of authoring tool users is students. In the SimQuest project teachers have created learning experiences for students that involve using authoring domain models and tutors for each other. Arroyo et al. (2001) created an authoring interface for the AnimalWatch tutor that was specifically for students to be able to author arithmetic word problems for each other. Initial trials indicate that this task was quite easy and motivating for them.

5.4 Collaborative authoring

If an ITS is to be created by a team, then the tools should support collaboration. Several authoring projects have directly addressed collaborative authoring. The IDE project supported collaboration by having authors enter the design rationale for each instructional element and decision in the system. Ritter et al.'s vision of tutor agent components (in this volume) is mean to support collaboration among curriculum experts (teachers), cognitive scientists/knowledge engineers, and programmers/database designer s. The DNA project provides tools for a subject-matter expert to work with several domain experts in developing content and check for overlap and differences in what they produce. The WEAR system allows teachers to search for pre-authored problems according to topic and difficulty level. It monitors the creation of a new problem and notifies the instructor if a similar one already exists in the database. In the REEDEM project teachers were observed sharing and critiquing each others tutoring strategies. As mentioned above,

CREAM Tools supports collaborative authoring with rights management and access security features.

5.5 Where do the teaching strategies come from?

Another area of active disagreement in the research community is the appropriate source of instructional expertise. The question regards both embedded, fixed tutoring expertise and authored tutoring expertise. There is very little agreement on this front, and the arguments sometimes sound more religious than analytical. Below I present a somewhat hyperbolic characterization of the arguments.

Some emphasize that the power to determine an ITS's teaching strategy should rest with the practicing **teacher** (for example see Chapter 8 on REDEEEM). After all, they are ones working "in the trenches" (the XAIDA project adopted training strategies observed "in the wild"). But others argue that practicing teachers are, first, not very pedagogically adept on the average, and second, not very good at articulating their knowledge. Systems in the Multiple Knowledge Types category rely on **instructional design theories**. ID theories, though primarily prescriptive and lacking in rigorous experimental verification, have stood the test of time in countless on- and off-line industry and government training programs. Though their theories include the most practical and operational prescriptions, some critique instructional design theorists as being "arm-chair" researchers and systems thinkers. Some say that instruction via computers is too new to be able to rely on existing theories, and that we need to rely on empirical evidence from **educational psychologists** to determine which teaching strategies are most appropriate under various conditions. But educational researchers are sometimes criticized for having amassed decades worth of data which has lead to very few generally agreed upon operational principles. Perhaps instructional settings are just too complex to hope for definitive data and analysis. Still others maintain that traditional educational theory and research are based on outmoded behaviorist theories that do not take into account the constructivist and situated nature of learning, and that **cognitive science** might come to the rescue and show our ITSs how to teach. After all, they know how the mind works (!). And finally there are some research groups who simply have the right answer, and reference only their own **home-grown theories** of learning and instruction, ignoring outside empirical or theoretical work.

It is too early to ignore any of the sources of inspiration for ITS teaching strategies: practicing teachers, instructional designers, educational theorists, cognitive scientists, and innovative mavericks. The best models will most probably come from a synthesis of theories from several of these areas.

5.6 Meta-level authoring and Flexible Ontologies

As mentioned above, one method for maintaining both depth and usability in an ITS authoring system is to forgo breadth, i.e. specialize the authoring tool for a specific type of domain or task. Another approach, which has the potential of maintaining depth, breadth *and* usability, is meta-authoring (discussed in more detail in Chapter

15 Section 4.6). By a meta-authoring system I mean a general purpose authoring system is used to build or configure special-purpose authoring systems. For example, ITS authoring shells could be produced for science concepts, human service/customer contact skills, language arts, and equipment maintenance instruction. One problem with current special purpose authoring systems is that so many of them would have to be built to cover a reasonable diversity of tasks or domains. A proliferation of special purpose tools, each with different underlying frameworks and user interface conventions, will be hard to learn. Meta-authoring allows for the proliferation of special-purpose shells with a common underlying structure, so that inter-domain commonalties can be exploited in both content creation and in training the authors. A meta-authoring system requires a relatively high level of skill to use, but relatively few authors would use it. Most ITS authors would be using the more usable special purpose authoring systems that were built with the meta-authoring tools.

Current special purpose systems were programmed from scratch. Yet there are many common features among the diverse authoring tools described in this paper. A topic or curriculum network authoring tool would be useful to almost any authoring tool, as would a highly usable authoring tool for procedures or instructional strategies. Though very few of the authoring systems have tools for constructing the user interface, an interface building tool would be of use to all of them. Eon was designed as a meta-authoring tool, (as well as an authoring tool) but this use has not been realized yet. Jona and Kass (1997) describe an approach similar to meta-authoring, but in the context of ITS shells (architectures) rather than authoring tools.

An important aspect of meta-authoring is the ability to customize the conceptual vocabulary or ontology used to represent knowledge. An ontology is shared vocabulary describing key components, concepts, and properties, along with axioms that define relationships and constraints for these items (Gruber 1991). Many authoring systems use a semantic network representation of content but they differ on the types of nodes and links used. A more flexible approach is to let the author define this vocabulary. Expert-CML has a variety of common taxonomies for knowledge and learning objectives that the author can choose from. The Eon system allows the user to customize the vocabulary of node and link types in its topic network, the topic properties (such as importance and difficulty), and the vocabularies used in the student model and strategy editors.

Mizoguchi, Ikeda, and associates (Yayashi et al. 2000, Ikeda et al. 1997, Mizoguchi & Bourdeau 2000).have been developing ontologies. Mizoguchi et al. have developed such terminological building blocks for describing instructional strategies and actions, curriculum and task components, and learner states. Smart-Trainer is an ITS shell that has been implemented in the domain of electric power systems. It uses and "ontology-aware" approach that allows authors to build a high-level conceptual model of a domain and tutoring system before implementing the details. The system uses the axioms in its ontology in an authoring verification phase to identify discrepancies in the authored model.

5.7 Toward interoperability and re-use

Many have called for more interoperability and reusability in educational software applications and educational e-content. ITSs and ITS authoring tools tend to be monolithic pieces of code that can not communicate with each other (Roschelle et al. (1998) calls them "application islands"). Roschelle et al. (pg. 9) observe that the educational technology community's increasing sophistication in regards to a wide spectrum of teaching and learning theories has lead to the "unforeseen consequence [of] fragmentation of the authoring community around particular tools (rather than learning objectives), with limited ability to share innovation across different authoring tools." There is considerable redundancy in the design of many of these systems. Also, it tends to be difficult to extend to new domains or scale up to large courses. In the best of worlds a project should be able to re-use components of another project in a "plug-in" fashion. For example, the best Bayesian student modeler or the most fully functional graphing tool could be re-used by many ITS or ITS authoring tool design teams. Hodgins & Masie (2002) have identified a set of related issues, which I list below with additions from Roschelle et al. (1998) and Ritter et al. (in this volume). Authoring tools should support:

- **Interoperatability** -- can the system work with other systems? The trend is away from centralized client-server architectures toward more decentralized agent-based architectures. Ritter et al. (this volume) note that for applications to interoperate they need to, at the very least, be "inspectable" -- i.e. one application can ask another for specific types of information. A higher level of interoperability involves "record-ability", in which an application is broadcasting data (for example student behaviors) to any application that cares to notice (for example a feedback agent). A further level of interoperability involves "script-ability" which allows one application to control another, for example a tutorial agent invoking a weather simulator with specific constraints on the simulation.
- **Manageability** -- can the overall system track information about the learner and learning session? One method for this is record-ability, as mentioned above. But there are many ways to address this issue.
- **Re-usability** -- can courseware (learning objects) be re-used by applications and by developers different from the context for it was originally designed?
- **Durability and scalability** -- will the item remain usable as technology and standards evolve? Designing software so that it is extensible is one approach. Extensibility can be achieved by using open source coding or by having a plug-in architecture. Authoring tools that work with medium sized-domains or (in the case of on-line systems) with a few users, can experience performance problems when scaled up to large domains or many simultaneous users. Integration with off-the-shelf components such as robust database applications can alleviate this problem.

- **Accessibility** -- can the learner or content developer locate and download the material in a reasonable time? Content repositories, mentioned below, are addressing this issue.

In order to accomplish any of these objectives common standards are needed. In the area of application interoperability, several component software architectures have been developed including OpenDoc (no longer supported by Apple), Active X, and JavaBeans. Though these architectures may make interoperability a reality, so far there have been only a few attempts. Roschelle et al. (1998) describe the EduObject project in which four research groups used OpenDoc to share components of their learning environments. Koedinger et al. (1998) describe a project in which three independently developed educational applications were combined using the "MOO communications protocol" as a communication infrastructure. The applications were Active Illustrations Lab, an open-ended simulation environment (Forbus & Falkenhainer 1995); Belvedere, an environment supporting scientific dialoging and argumentation (Suthers et al. 1997); and a model tracing Tutor Agent that was able to give feedback to students (Ritter & Koedinger 1997). These two projects were feasibility demonstrations that did not see extensive use. Others are working on large scale in-house component based systems (e.g. Cheikes 1995), but a major bottleneck to interoperability of educational components is the lack of shared open standards. As stated in Ritter et al. (this volume) an interoperability framework needs "separate interface and data models which communicate through a fixed protocol [that] should express events in terms of their semantics, rather than user-interface implementation."

Several groups have been working toward and using an emerging set of educational software and learning management system interoperability standards (including IMS & IEEE LOM (Schoeneing & Wheeler 1997) and ARIADNE (Forte et al 1997)). The standards address content meta meta-data, content sequencing, question and test interoperability, learner profiles, and run-time interaction (see Hodgins & Masei 2002). SCORM (sharable content object reference model) is becoming a de-facto reference model for integrating the various standards. There are still many unsolved issues, including how to handle intellectual property rights in an environment of highly shared components and content, and how to include more pedagogically descriptive attributes in the standards (see Suthers 2000, Murray 1998).

Many efforts are underway to develop web-based repositories and catalogues that give educators and learners easy access to a wide range of educational materials (including EDUTELLA (Nejdg et al. 2002); OCW & OKI (Kumar & Long 2002); GEM (Fitzgerald 2001); MERLOT (Wetzel 2001)). These projects have begun to use meta-data standards to converge on common methods for describing generic attributes of learning objects. However, this software is currently designed to facilitates humans searching for educational material. The industry and the research communities are still far from having repositories of interoperable components that can be automatically retrieved and used by intelligent tutoring systems shells or authoring tools.

6. ITS AUTHORING SYSTEM "REALITY-CHECK" -- USE AND EVALUATION

In this Section I address the pragmatic questions of use, evaluation, throughput, and availability of ITS authoring tools. Availability is easy to describe. Several of the systems described here have become commercial products: Electronic Trainer (a simplified cousin of ID-Expert), and SIMQUEST. Neither of these have seen widespread purchasing or use in real educational situations as of yet. In addition some systems have been used by several groups other than the research group that developed the system and may be available through special arrangement.

6.1 Authoring tool use

One measure of the viability of an authoring tool is the number and variety of tutors it has been used to build, and the degree to which the system has been used independent of the lab in which it was developed. Of course, the fact that a system has not seen much use does not indicate that its design is not viable. But, since making usable software requires design iterations based on feedback from user and field tests, it is reasonable to assume that systems that have not been widely used will require significant additional work to become robust. It is also important to note that some systems are the latest in a series of efforts by a particular research group, so a relatively new and untested system may be built with the cumulative expertise from previous generations. For example RIDES, DIAG, and Instructional Simulator are third or fourth generation systems, and REDEEM, SimQuest, and Eon are second generation systems.

Several of the systems are commercial products, mentioned next. SimQuest is in use in a number of school systems. Electronic Textbook has been commercialised as IDXelerator (along with its sister product Instructional simulator, commercialised as IDVisualizer). A simplified version of CREAM-Tools is available under the name "Training Office," which has been adopted by a number of companies. Swift is commercial product, but there is no literature as yet describing its level of use. The D3 authoring tools has been used to produce three commercial training systems in the medical sector. Ritter et al. (in this Volume) describe tools used build Cognitive Tutors, several of which are commercial products being used in over 700 schools.

Table 3 shows a rough estimation of the degree to which various systems have been used. (The significant changes in this table since the original version of this paper in 1995 gives a striking picture of now far the field has progressed.) Category 1 is for early prototypes that are not fully functional authoring systems, and have been tested on a small number of "toy domains." Category 2 contains prototype systems that are complete authoring tools, most of which have been used to build several complete tutors, but the tutors were not used in authentic learning or training contexts. Category 3 systems are a bit more robust or have seen more use than those in category 2, and most have been used outside of the lab where they were built. Category 4 systems have been used to build a dozen or more tutors, have built tutors that have been used in real training situations, and have reached a stage of maturity in robustness and user documentation where they have been used relatively independently of the authoring tool designers.

Table 3: Degree of use of ITS authoring tools

1. Early prototypes and proofs of concept	Demonstr8, Expert-CML, IRIS, Training Express, BioWorld Case Builder, WEAR
2. Evaluated or used prototypes	DNA, Eon, IDLE-Tool, LAT, GTE, MetaLinks, ISD-Expert
3. Moderately evaluated or used	Electronic Trainer, REDEEM, XAIDA, D3 Trainer, DIAG, CREAM-Tools, Interbook, Swift
4. Heavily used (relatively)	RIDES, SIMQUEST, IDE[9], CALAT

- SimQuest has been used to create over 20 applications. including physics (collisions, electricity), biology, chemistry, economics, and geography. These tutors have been used in middle school and high school physics and chemistry classes. SMISLE (SimQuest's predecessor) has been used to author half a dozen systems in various introductory science domains.
- REDEEM has been used to build a Genetics tutor consisting of 12 hours of on-line content, which was used in a high school classroom. It was also used to develop an 8-hour tutorial on "understanding shapes" for 7-11 year old children. and a seven chapter Navy training course on communication and information systems principles.
- CALAT has been used to build over 300 web-based "courseware packages" which are being used for in-house training at NTT, where CALAT was developed.
- RIDES has been used to develop tutors or components of tutors in a number of research efforts, most of which involved exporting the technology to another lab. As well as producing tutors for a variety of types of equipment, these efforts are investigating such issues as immersive VR training, real-time collaborative environments, diagnostic expert systems, and web-based delivery.
- DIAG has been used to create training applications for electronic fault diagnosis for a eight devices including a power supplies, a radio receiver, and a warning system.
- CREAM-Tools have been used in a university biology course and a university mathematics course, and to create tutors in the domains of Baxter pump manipulation, Traffic regulations, problem solving strategies, intensive care unit, and Excel spread sheets.

---

[9] Though IDE was one of the most heavily used systems, it was also one of the earliest. IDE is now a "legacy system," since it runs on obsolete software (NoteCards) and does not incorporate multimedia capabilities that are now de rigueur.

- As mentioned above, XAIDA has been used to develop tutors in diverse domains, including algebra, medicine, computer literacy, and biology, as well as device operation and maintenance.
- Instructional Trainer has been used to build tutors for HP 5S1 printer operation (this tutorial is distributed commercially with the physical product), ethnographic methods, simple canal theory of operation, and customer service in the telecommunications industry.
- The three commercially available tutorials produced using D3 Trainer have been evaluated via field tests for 4 years. It has been used to build case-based classification tutors in medical domains such as Rheumatology and in other domains such as Flower Classification.
- IDLE-Tool underwent three informal trials: 21 graduate students produced 10 goal-based scenario (GBS) tutors during a six week graduate seminar; 8 primary school teachers produced four GBS tutors over a six week period; and eight graduate students produced GBS tutors in another seminar over a three week period. The INDIE tool has been used to produce 8 goal based scenario tutors, including: Immunology Consultant, Is it a Rembrandt, Volcano Investigator, and Nutrition Clinician.
- Eon has been used to build five prototype tutors covering a wide range of domain types and instructional methods, including: a tutor that incorporates a Socratic teaching strategy to remediate common misconceptions in science; a tutor that teaches a part of Japanese language called "honorifics;" an open-ended learning-by-doing chemistry workbench environment, and a tutor that uses a spiral teaching method to teach introductory physics concepts.
- IRIS has been used to create tutors for power plant operator training, computer program specification, concepts in human resources, and mathematical symbolic differentiation.

6.2 Authoring tool productivity

ITS authoring tools have the potential for decreasing the effort it takes to build instructional systems or, with the same effort, increasing the adaptivity, depth, and effectiveness of instructional systems. A very rough estimate of 300 hours of development time per hour of on-line instruction is commonly used for the development time of traditional CAI. We have indications of the development ratios for some ITS authoring tools. These numbers are very hard to interpret, but give us hope that cost-effective ITS authoring is possible. One reason it is hard to interpret these results is that they usually do not include the time for creating graphics or pre-planning the curriculum design. But what we can say is that there is a strong indication that authoring tools change coding the domain and/or expert knowledge in a tutor from the most labor intensive part of the process to the least labor intensive (as compared with media creation and off-line design analysis)

Many hope to see ITS development times that are an order of magnitude less than the 300:1 CAI productivity ratio. ID-Expert's goal is a 30:1 ratio. The

Instructional Simulator reduced the time to create a simulation from 100s of hours (if programmed from scratch) to a few hours. An informal analysis of Demonstr8 describes a model tracing multi-column addition or subtraction tutor being built in less than 20 minutes. XAIDA's goal is for a 10:1 productivity ratio. Formative evaluations to date indicate that in some situations a first-time XAIDA user can develop a 1-2 hour lesson in 3-4 days, including training.

In three separate studies productivity metrics for the REDEEM system showed authoring to tutorial time ratios between 2:1 and 3:1 for authoring courses that were 8 to 20 hours in length.

A sixteen month case study of three educators using KAFITS, the precursor to Eon, to build a 41 topic tutor for high school Statics (representing about six hours of on-line instruction) resulted in a 100:1 effort ratio. Analysis of time vs. development task and development role yielded the following: 47% effort by the SME, 40 % by the "knowledge based managers", and 13% by the knowledge engineer. Also, design constituted about 15% of the total time, and implementation the other 85%. A similar breakdown of authoring tasks for use of the CALAT system yielded these estimates: planning 10%, design 50%, multimedia material creation 30%, and testing and evaluation 10% of the total time. It was estimated that development time for CALAT tutors was about the same as traditional, non-adaptive instructional systems.

The DNA system supports cognitive task analysis, which usually involves extensive interviews with experts and transcription and analysis of the protocols. This process usually requires a knowledge engineer working with domain experts over many months. DNA attempts to "streamline the bulk of the interview, transcription, and [information] organization process." In evaluations of the DNA system a collaborative authoring process yielded over 50% of the knowledge base in a tiny fraction of the development time.

For authoring tools that build tutors with deeper knowledge, much more time is typically needed. It tool 4 to 9 weeks to use DIAG to build tutors simulating complex electronic systems of up to 150 components. The problems posed by the resulting tutorials are solved on the order of 10 minutes each. Some tools have been developed to make Cognitive Tutors more cost effective but it still takes many man-years to build a cognitive tutor. However, these are among the very few intelligent tutors built to date that cover content from a significant percentage of an entire course.

6.3 Authoring tool evaluation

Because ITS authoring tools are still relatively new, summative evaluations, which ostensibly prove that an entire system "works," may be less valuable than formative evaluations, which give indications of what parts of a system do and don't work and why. A number of qualitative and formative evaluation methods can be used (Murray 1993). In Section 5.3 we mentioned how results from evaluations of SimQuest, REDEEM, XAIDA, IDLE-Tool, and LAT. In Section 6.2 we mentioned system evaluations that had implications for authoring productivity (XAIDA,

KAFITS, CALAT, DNA, and DIAG). A summary of other authoring tool evaluations follows (we do not discuss evaluations of the tutoring systems built by the authoring tools--in fact very few of these have been done).

REDEEM and XAIDA are (by far) the most heavily evaluated authoring systems. REDEEM'S predecessor COCA underwent several evaluations. Ten teachers each using COCA for 2 to 3 hours to build a tutor for the American Revolution. Teachers' attitudes regarding the ability of AI technology to simulate reasonable teaching strategies changed from noncommittal to positive. However, many of the systems features were too complex for teachers, and these problems lead to the design of REDEEM.

REDEEM has been used in 4 major studies (and several minor studies not discussed in Ainsworth et al.). Two studies involved an 8-hour tutorial on "understanding shapes" for 7-11 year old children. One study involved 12-hour secondary school tutorial in genetics, and the final study involved a seven chapter Navy training course on communication and information systems principles.

In two of the studies that looked at how instructors can customize intelligent tutors a novel evaluation method was used. Subjects were given vignettes describing a number of "virtual students," including descriptions of how they performed in the subject area over the previous semester. The author's task was, first, to group the virtual students into similarity classes, and second, to design a tutoring strategy that met the needs of each of these groups (the REDEEM tools directly support such student grouping, strategy creation, and assignment of student groups to strategies). The above method was the primary one used to evaluate the authoring process. To evaluate student learning Ainsworth et al. designed studies that compared learning on a REDEEM-delivered intelligent tutor to leaning with the original non-intelligent courseware d ("vanilla CBT") which served as the content basis for the intelligent tutor.\

In an analysis of usability, two of the studies found that instructors with no prior experience with computer-based learning were able to express, represent, and assess their teaching strategies after only one to 2 hours of training. We mentioned the REDEEM productivity analysis above.

A "virtual student" study of primary school teachers found strong inter-author difference in how they grouped virtual students for differential instructional treatments, and in how they designed teaching strategies for each of these groups. In contrast, the group of Navy training personnel showed mush less differentiation among virtual students and teaching strategies. In both situations authors who used REDEEM to tailor the instructional strategies of tutorial reported more satisfaction than those who did not. When the tutorial was run these authors recognized the existence of their personal classroom-based teaching strategies and styles in the behavior of the tutorial that they authored.

Five separate evaluation studies looked at the effectiveness of REDEEM-authored ITSs, in comparison to similar CBT tutorials. In the first study 86 15 year old students used a Genetics tutor in a laboratory setting. There were no significant difference in outcomes for either high or low achieving students. However, a very similar study done in a classroom context showed significant differences. REDEEM-tutored students improved 16% vs. an 8% improvement for vanilla-CBT-tutored students. An effect size analysis showed that REDEEM led to an average 0.82 sigma improvement in learning outcomes compared to CBT. In a study using the Navy-built tutor REDEEM was again significantly better than the vanilla CBT. REDEEM lead to a 32% pre-to-post test improvement, as compared with a 19% improvement with the vanilla CBT (effect size 0.76 sigmas).

The other extensively evaluated ITS authoring tool is XAIDA.[10] Formative data was taken as XAIDA was used in eight authoring field studies with an average of about 10 participants (mostly military training personnel) in each study. As mentioned, one result was that a 1-2 hour lesson can be developed in 3-4 days. The framework was found appropriate for a wide variety of domains, as mentioned above. In addition to formative evaluations of the authoring tools, there have been 13 studies of students using tutors built with XAIDA. These have indicated that tutors built with the XAIDA framework successfully promote mastery of a wide range of subjects, and that students acquire robust cognitive structures if they are motivated learners. Finally, researchers conducted an in-depth study of 17 participants' attitudes and skills as they learned to use XAIDA (only the physical characteristics shell). Several types of data were gathered, including usability comments, attitudes, productivity metrics, and knowledge base structural analyses. Results indicate that the tool can be used to author ITSs rapidly. However, the training and evaluation focussed on low level authoring skills, and it was unclear how limitations in higher level design and content analysis skills would effect authoring and the adoption of such authoring tools by instructors.

Below we briefly describe other authoring tool evaluation studies:

- In evaluations of IDLE-Tool, conclusions included the need for a higher level view of the curriculum and more conceptually oriented help (as opposed to interface or task oriented help). Practicing teachers using the system differed from the graduate students in their higher pedagogical competence and willingness to work within the limits of the template-based authoring. All users found the example-based help feature very helpful.
- A formative evaluation of LEAP consisted of user participatory design sessions with three authors from a population of target users. The users built a working body of courseware from scratch, and maintained a large body of pre-existing courseware. Anecdotal usability data indicated that the authoring tool was much easier and less error prone than previous text-based methods used for knowledge elicitation.
- A preliminary evaluation of DNA compared the knowledge base of a "measures of central tendency" (statistics) tutor, built using DNA's automated knowledge elicitation, with the knowledge base of a benchmark ITS for the same domain. The benchmark tutor was build from scratch using a lengthy hand-coded cognitive task analysis, which took several months and resulted in 78

---

[10] Note however that for the most part, only the simplest of XAIDAs four knowledge types was authored in these trials, i.e. physical characteristics.

"curriculum units" (topics). Three subjects used DNA to elicit their knowledge about this domain, and the three resulting knowledge bases were compared with each other and with the benchmark. Analysis of the results showed that the three authors had 25%, 49%, and 23% coverage of the 78 curriculum units, with a combined coverage of 62% over the total of nine hours that the three experts used the system. That a collaborative authoring effort that took nine hours resulted in 62% coverage of a knowledge base that took several months to code by hand indicated that the DNA framework is viable.

Above I mentioned that authoring tools are of significant advantage in evaluating alternate instructional strategies. In addition to REDEEM, this type of studies was done with Instructional simulator and SimQuest.

- Instructional Simulator underwent a series of studies (Mills, Lawless, Drake, and Merrill in press) with elementary students using the canal boat simulation described in Chapter 7. One test evaluated three variations of explanation: at every step, only when a user action resulted in no simulation change, and no explanation at all. The study showed a significant long term retention improvement when either explanation method was included. A second study compared three variations on how simulation instructional demonstrations were given: "Simon says" demonstrations, free exploration demonstrations, and no demonstrations. Students using to the Simon Says mode outperformed the other two conditions.
- The SimQuest system has been used to conduct a number of studies on alternate teaching strategies. The studies looked at variations in learning environments configuration. Variations in the following aspects of the learning environment were evaluated in separate studies (see Chapter 1): model progression, assignment type, and intelligent feedback.

7. FUTURE DIRECTIONS

In 1995 A large scale review of US government-sponsored research and development in intelligent tutoring systems, looking at 47 funded projects, found that one third of the total expenditure was on the 11% of the projects developing authoring tools (Youngblut, 1995). The review concluded that this level of funding might be premature because there were many basic research issues in ITS needing to be resolved before authoring systems were generally applicable. However, ITS authoring tools have matured substantially in the last decade. Several are at or near commercial quality. Though there are of course many unanswered questions in this relatively new research area, it seems that there are three related major unknowns. The first is the extent to which the difficult task of modeling can be scaffolded, as discussed above. The second question, representing the other side of the coin, is the degree to which we can identify instructional situations that can be embodied in special purpose authoring shells that are both specific enough to make authoring template-based, yet general enough to be attractive to many educators. Third is the larger question of whether intelligent tutoring systems will ever be in demand enough to warrant the effort of building authoring tools for them. Those in the authoring tools community see this as a chicken-egg problem, since the demand for ITSs depends in part on their cost, and in part on their perceived effectiveness. Authoring tools certainly reduce the cost, and they also will make it possible to build enough systems so that formal and anecdotal evidence will accumulate regarding ITS effectiveness.

Much more research and development is needed in the field of ITS authoring. We need more empirical testing using multiple authors and domains; more research on authoring student models; more complete and standardized ontologies and meta-data standards; more research on the differential effectiveness of various computationally explicit instructional strategies; and more exploration of open component-based architectures. The future of ITS authoring, like the future of ITSs, depends in part on supply and demand forces. Innovations in software interoperability, web-based applications, and ubiquitous computing provide a "technology-push." Increasing demand for scalability, accountability, personalization, easy access, and cost-effectiveness in computer-based instruction should provide a sufficient "pull" to bring more of these systems into schools and market places.

8. REFERENCES

The references and citations to articles describing authoring systems are in a non-standard format in this Chapter. Citations to the major authoring tool projects are give by the tool name (e.g. RIDES) rather than the author of a paper (e.g. Munro et al. 1997). References are listed in an Appendix table grouped according to the authoring system.

Arroyo, I., Schapira, A. & Woolf, B. (2001). Authoring and sharing worked problems with AWE. *Proc. of Artificial Intelligence in Education* (Moore et al. Eds), pp. 527-529.
Bloom, B. S. (1956). *Taxonomy of Educational Objectives, Vol. 1*. New York: David McKay Co.
Boose, J. H. (1988). "A Survey of Knowledge Acquisition Techniques and Tools." 3rd AAAI-Sponsored Knowledge Acquisition for Knowledge-Based Systems Workshop, November 1988, pg. 3.1-3.23. Banff, Canada.
Brusilovsky, P. (1998). Methods and Techniques of Adaptive Hypermedia. In P. Brusilovsky, A. Kobsa, and J. Vassileva, editors, *Adaptive Hypertext and Hypermedia*, Chapter 1, pp. 1-44, Kluwer Academic Publishers, The Netherlands, 1998.
Chandrasekaran,B. (1986). Generic tasks in knowledge based reasoning: high-level building blocks for expert system design. IEEE Expert, 1(3), pp. 23-30.
Cheikes, B. (1995). Should ITS Designers be Looking for a Few Good Agents? In AIED-95 workshop papers for Authoring Shells for Intelligent Tutoring Systems.
Clancey, W. J. (1986). "Qualitative Student Models." In Annual Review of Computer Science, pp. 381-450: Palo Alto, CA.
Collins, J.A., Greer, J.E., & Huang, S.H. "Adaptive assessment using granularity hierarchies and Bayesian nets." *Proceedings of the Third International Conference: ITS '96*. Frasson, Gautheir & Lesgold (Eds). Springer, pp. 569-577.
Fitzgerald, M (2001). The Gateway to Educational Materials: An evaluation Study: Year 2. ERIC Clearinghouse technical report.
Forbus, K & Falkenhainer, B. (1995). Scaling up Self-Explanatory Simulators: Polynomial-time Compilation. *Proceedings of IJCCAI-95*, Montreal, Canada.

Forte, E., Wentland, M. & Duval, E. (1997). The ARIADNE Project: Knowledge Pools for Computer-based and Telematics-supported Classical, Open, and Distance Learning. European Journal of Engineering Education 22(1).

Gagne, R. (1985). *The Conditions of Learning and Theory of Instruction.* New York: Holt, Rinehard, and Winston.

Goodkovsky, V.A., Kirjutin, E.V. & Bulekov, A.A. (1994). Shell, tool, and technology for Pop Class ITS production. In P. Brusilovsky, S. Dikareve, J.Greer & V. Pertrushin (Eds). Proc. of East-West International Conference on Computer Technology in Education. Part 1, pp. 87-92. Crimea, Ukraine.

Goodyear, P. & Johnson, R. (1990). Knowledge-based authoring of knowledge-based courseware. In Proc. of ICTE-7, Brussels:CEP Consultants LTD.

Hodgins, W. & Massie, E. (2002). Making Sense of Learning Specifications and Standards: A decision makers guide to their adoption. MASIE Center technical report, Saratogy Springs, NS.

Hodgins, W. et al. (2002). Making Sense of Learning Specifications & Standards: A Decision Maker's Guide to their Adoption. Industry Report by the MASIE Center: Saratoga Springs, NY.

Hoffman, R. (1987). "The Problem of Extracting the Knowledge of Experts From the Perspective of Experimental Psychology." *AI Magazine,* pp. 53-67, Summer 1987.

Jonassen, D.H. & Reeves, T.C (1996). Learning with Technology: Using Computers as Cognitive Tools. In D.H. Jonassen, (Ed.) Handbook of Research on Educational Communications and Technology. New York: Scholastic Press, Chapter 25.

Koediner, K.R, Suthers, D.D., Forbus, K.D. (1998). Component-based construction of a science learning space. In the *Proceedings of Intelligent Tutoring Systems 4th International Conference*, Goettl, Half, Redfield, & Shute (Eds), 166-175.

Koedinger, K., & Anderson, J. (1995). Intelligent tutoring goes to the big city. *Int. J. of Artificial Intellignece in Education,* 8, 30-43.

Kumar, M.S.V. & Long , P. (2002) MITs Open Courseware Initiative (OCW) and Open Knowledge Initiative (OKI). At www.cren.net/know/techtalk/mit.html.

Mark, M.A. & Greer, J.E. (1991). The VCR Tutor: Evaluating instructional effectiveness. In Hammond, & Gentern (Eds.) Proceedings of the 13th Annual Conference of the Cognitive Science Society, Lawrence Erlbaum Asso., Hillsdale, NJ., 564-569.

McCalla, G. & Greer, J. (1988). "Intelligent Advising in Problem Solving Domains: The SCENT-3 Architecture." Proceedings of ITS-88, pp. 124-131. June, 1988, Montreal, Canada.

McMillan, S., Emme, D., & Berkowitz, M. (1980). Instructional Planners: Lessons Learned. In Psotka, Massey, & Mutter (Eds.), *Intelligent Tutoring Systems, Lessons Learned.* Hillsdale, NJ: Lawrence Erlbaum, pp. 229-256.

Merrill, M.D. (1983). Component Display Theory. In *Instructional-design theories and models: An overview of their current status,.* C.M. Reigeluth. (Ed.). Hillsdale, NJ: Lawrence Erlbaum, pp. 279 - 333.

Murray, T (1998). A Model for Distributed Curriculum on the World Wide Web. J. of Interactive Media in Education 98(5). On-line journal at http://www-jime.open.ac.uk/.

Murray, T. (1993). Formative Qualitative Evaluation for "Exploratory" ITS research. *J. of AI in Education.* 4(2/3), pp. 179-207.

Murray, T. (1996b). Toward a Conceptual Vocabulary for Intelligent Tutoring Systems. Working Paper.

Murray, T. (1997) Expanding the knowledge acquisition bottleneck for intelligent tutoring systems. *International J. of Artificial Intelligence in Education.* Vol. 8 , No. 3-4, pp. 222-232.

Murray, T., Winship, L., Bellin, R. & Cornell, M. (2001). "Toward Glass Box Educational Simulations: Reifying Models for Inspection and Design." In workshop proceedings for External Representations in AIED at AIED-2001. May 2001, San Antonio, TX.

Nejdl, W., Wold, B., Staab, S., & Tane, J. (2002). EDUTELLA: Searching and Annotating Resources within and RDF-based P2P Network. White paper at edutella.jxta.org.

Ohlsson, S. (1987). Some Principles of Intelligent Tutoring. In Lawler & Yazdani (Eds.), *Artificial Intelligence and Education, Volume 1.* Ablex: Norwood, NJ, pp. 203-238.

Person, N. K., Bautista, L., Graesser, A. C., Mathews, E. & The Tutoring Research Group (2001). Evaluating student learning gains in two versions of AutoTutor. In J. D. Moore, C. L Redfield, & W. L. Johnson (Eds.), *Artificial Intelligence in Education: AI–ED in the Wired and Wireless Future* (pp. 286–293). Amsterdam: IOS Press.

Reigeluth, C. (1983). The Elaboration Theory of Instruction. In Reigeluth (Ed.), *Instructional Design Theories and Models.* Hillsdale, NJ: Lawrence Erlbaum.

Ritter, S. & Blessing, S. (1998). Authoring tools for component-based learning environments. *Journal of the Learning Sciences,.* 7(1) pp. 107-132.

Ritter, S. & Koedinger, K.R. (1997). An architecture for plug-in tutoring agents. In *J. of Artificial Intelligence in Education,* 7 (3/4) 315-347.

Roschelle, J., Kaput, J., Stroup, W. & Kahn, T.M. (1998). Scaleable integration of educational software: Exploring the promise of component architectures. *J. of Interactive Media in Education,* 98 (6). [www-jime.open.ac.uk/96/6]

Rosé, C. P., Jordan, P., Ringenberg, M., Siler, S., VanLehn, K., & Weinstein, A. (2001). Interactive conceptual tutoring in Atlas–Andes. In J. D. Moore, C. L Redfield, & W. L. Johnson (Eds.), *Artificial Intelligence in Education: AI–ED in the Wired and Wireless Future* (pp. 256–266). Amsterdam: IOS Press.

Schoening, J. & Wheeler, T. (1997). Standards--The key to educational reform. In IEEE Computer, March 1997.

Shaw, M. L. G. & Gaines, B. R. (1986). "Advances in Interactive Knowledge Engineering." Submitted to Expert Systems '86. University of Calgary, Alberta, CANADA: Dept. of Computer Science.

Shute, V. J., and Psotka, J., (1996). Intelligent tutoring systems: Past, present, and future. In D. Jonassen (Ed.), Handbook of Research for Educational Communications and Technology (pp. 570-600). New York, NY: Macmillan.

Shute, V.J. and Regian, J.W. (1990). Rose Garden Promises of Intelligent Tutoring Systems: Blossom or Thorn? Presented at Space Operations, Automation and Robotics Conference, June 1990, Albuquerque, NM.

Suthers, D. (2000). Using learning object meta-data in a database of primary and secondary school resources. *Proc. of International Conf. on Computer in Education,* November 2000, Taipei, Taiwan.

Suthers, D., Toth, E., 7 Weiner, A. (1997). An integrated approach to implementing collaborative inquiry in the classroom. *Computer Supported Collaborative Learning (CSCL-97),* Toronto, December, 1997.

Wasson, B. (1992) PEPE: A computational framework for a content planner. In S.A. Dijkstra, H.P.M. Krammer & J.J.G. van Merrienboer (Eds), Instructional Models in Computer-Based Learning Environments. NATO ASI Series F. Vol. 104 (pp. 153-170). New York: Sringer-Verlag.

Wenger, E. (1987). *Artificial Intelligence and Tutoring Systems.* Los Altos, CA: Morgan Kaufmann.

Wetzel, M., & Hanley, G. (2001). Evaluation of MERLOT Tools, Processes, and Accomplishments. Center for Usability in Design and Assessment: Long Beach CA.

White, B. & Frederiksen, J. (1995). Developing Metacognitive Knowledge and Processes: The Key to Making Scientific Inquiry and Modeling Accessible to All Students. Technical Report No CM-95-04. Berkeley, CA: School of Education, University of California at Berkeley.

Youngblut, C., 1995. Government-Sponsored Research and Development Efforts in the Area of Intelligent Tutoring Systems: Summary Report. Inst. for Defense Analyses Paper No. P-3058, Alexandra VA.

APPENDIX

Below is a table of the ITS authoring tools discussed in this paper, with selected references for each.

BioWorld-Case Builder	Lajoie, S., Faremo, S. & Wiseman, J. (2001). A knowledge-based approach to designing authoring tools: From tutor to author. In *Proc. of Artificial Intelligent in Education*, J.D. Moore C. Redfield, L.W. Johnson (Eds). ISO Press, pp77-86.
CALAT (& CAIRNEY)	Kiyama, M., Ishiuchi, S., Ikeda, K., Tsujimoto, M. & Fukuhara, Y. (1997). Authoring Methods for the Web-Based Intelligent CAI System CALAT and its Application to Telecommunications Service. In the *Proceedings of AAAI-97*, Providence, RI.
CREAM-TOOLS	See Chapter 10 in this volume. Frasson, C., Nkambou, R., Gauthier, G., Rouane, K. (1998). An authoring model and tools for curriculum development in intelligent tutoring systems. Working Paper available from the authors. Nkambou, R., Gauthier, R., & Frasson, M.C. (1996). CREAM-Tools: an authoring environment for curriculum and course building in an ITS. In *Proceedings of the Third International Conference on Computer Aided Learning and Instructional Science and Engineering*. New York: Springer-Verlag.
D3-TRAINER	Schewe, S., Reinhardt, B., Bestz, C. (1999). Experiences with a Knowledge Based Tutoring System for Student Education in Rheumatology. In *XPS-99: Knowledge Based Systems: Survey and Future Direction, 5th Biannual German Conference* on Knowledge Based Systems, Lecture Notes in Artificial Intelligence 1570, Springer. Puppe, F., Reinhardt, B. (1996). Generating Case-oriented training from Diagnostic Expert Systems. In *Machine Mediated Learning* 5 (3&4), 199-219. Reinhardt, B. (1997). Generating Case-oriented Intelligent tutoring systems. *In Proc. of AAAI Fall Symposium, ITS Authoring Systems*, November 1997.

DEMONSTR8 (& TDK, PUPS)	See Chapter 4 in this volume. Blessing, S.B. (1997). A programming by demonstration authoring tool for model tracing tutors. *Int. J. of Artificial Intelligence in Education.* Vol. 8 , No. 3-4, pp 233-261. Anderson, J. R. & Pelletier, R. (1991). A development system for model tracing tutors. In *Proc. of the International Conference on the Learning Sciences*, Evanston, IL, 1-8. Anderson, J. & Skwarecki, E. (1986). The Automated Tutoring of Introductory Computer Programming. *Communications of the ACM*, Vol. 29 No. 9. pp. 842-849.
DIAG (& ReAct, DM3)	See Chapter 5 in this volume. Towne, D.M. (1997). Approximate reasoning techniques for intelligent diagnostic instruction. *International J. of Artificial Intelligence in Education.* Vol. 8 , No. 3-4, pp. 262-283. Towne, D.M. (2002). Advanced Techniques for IETM Development and Delivery, Proceedings Human Factors and Ergonomics Society, 46th Annual Meeting, Baltimore, MD, October 3, 2002.
DNA/SMART	See Chapter 6 in this volume. Shute, V.J. (1998). DNA - Uncorking the bottleneck in knowledge elicitation and organization. *Proceedings of ITS-98*, San Antonio, TX, pp. 146-155. Shute, V. J., Torreano, L. A., and Willis, R. E. (2000). Tools to aid cognitive task analysis. In S. Chipman, V. Shalin, & J. Schraagen (Eds.),Cognitive Task Analysis. Hillsdale, NJ: Erlbaum Associates. . Shute, V. J. & Torreano, L., & Willis, R. (2000). DNA: Towards an automated knowledge elicitation and organization tool. In S. P. Lajoie (Ed.) *Computers as Cognitive Tools, Volume 2.* Hillsdale, NJ: Lawrence Erlbaum Associates, pp. 309-335.
ECSAIWeb	Sanrach, C. & Grandbasien, M. (2000). ECSAIWeb: A Web-based authoring system to create adaptive learning systems. *In Proceedings of Adaptive Hypermedia 2000.*
EON (& KAFITS)	See Chapter 11 in this volume. Murray, T. (1998). Authoring knowledge-based tutors: Tools for content, instructional strategy, student model, and interface design. *J. of the Learning Sciences*, Vol. 7. No. 1, pp. 5-64. Murray, T. (1996). Special Purpose Ontologies and the Representation of Pedagogical Knowledge. *In Proceedings of the International Conference on the Learning Sciences,* (ICLS-96), Evanston, IL, 1996. Charlottesville, VA: AACE. Murray, T. (1996). From Story Boards to Knowledge Bases: The First Paradigm Shift in Making CAI "Intelligent.". Proceedings of the ED-Media 96 Conference, Boston, MA, June 1996, pp. 509-514.

EXPERT-CML	Jones, M. & Wipond, K. (1991). Intelligent Environments for Curriculum and Course Development. In Goodyear (Ed.), *Teaching Knowledge and Intelligent Tutoring*. Norwood, NJ: Ablex.
GETMAS	Wong, W.K. & Chan, T.W. (1997). A Multimedia authoring system for crafting topic hierarchy, learning strategies, and intelligent models. *International J. of Artificial Intelligence in Education*, Vol. 8, No 1, pp. 71-96.
GTE	Van Marcke, K. (1998). GTE: An epistemological approach to instructional modeling. *Instructional Science*, Vol. 26, pp 147-191. Van Marcke, K. (1992). Instructional Expertise. In Frasson, C., Gauthier, G., & McCalla, G.I. (Eds.) *Procs. of Intelligent Tutoring Systems '92*. New York: Springer-Verlag.
Instructional Simulator (&Electronic Textbook, IDVisualizer, IDXelerator, ID-EXPERT, Electronic Trainer, ISD-Expert)	See Chapter 7 in this volume. Merrill, M.D., & ID2 Research Group (1998). ID Expert: A Second generation instructional development system. *Instructional Science*, Vol. 26, pp. 243-262. Merrill, M. D. (2001). Components of instruction: toward a theoretical tool for instructional design. *Instructional Science*. 29(4/5), 291-310. Mills, R. J., Lawless, K. A., Drake, L., & Merrill, M. D. (in press). Procedural knowledge in a computerized learning environment.
IDE (& IDE Interpreter)	Russell, D. (1988). "IDE: The Interpreter." In Psotka, Massey, &Mutter (Eds.), *Intelligent Tutoring Systems, Lessons Learned*. Hillsdale, NJ:Lawrence Erlbaum. Russell, D., Moran, T. & Jordan, D. (1988). The Instructional Design Environment. In Psotka, Massey, & Mutter (Eds.), *Intelligent Tutoring Systems, Lessons Learned*. Hillsdale, NJ: Lawrence Erlbaum.

IDLE-Tool (& IMAP, INDIE, GBS-architectures)	See Chapter 12 in this volume. Bell, B. (1998). Investigate and decide learning environments: Specializing task models for authoring tools design. *J. of the Learning Sciences*, Vol. 7. No. 1. Jona, M. & Kass, A. (1997). A Fully-Integrated Approach to Authoring Learning Environments: Case Studies and Lessons Learned. In the *Collected Papers from AAAI-97 Fall Symposium workshop Intelligent Tutoring System Authoring Tools*. AAAI-Press. Dobson, W.D. & Riesbeck, C.K. (1998). Tools for incremental development of educational software interfaces. In *Proceedings of CHI-98*. Qiu, L., Riesbeck, C.K., and Parsek, M.R. (2003). The Design and Implementation of an Engine and Authoring Tool for Web-based Learn-by-doing Environments. *Proc. of World Conf. on Educational Multimedia, Hypermedia & Telecommunications* (ED-MEDIA 2003). June 23-28, 2003, Honolulu, HA. AACE.
InterBook (& ELM-Art, NetCaoch)	See Chapter 13 in this volume. Brusilovsky, P., Schwartz, E., & Weber, G. (1996). A Tool for Developing Adaptive Electronic Textbooks on WWW. *Proc. of WebNet-96*, AACE. Brusilovsky, P, Schwartz, E. & Weber, G. (1996). ELM-ART: An Intelligent Tutoring System on the Work Wide Web. *In Proceedings of ITS-96*, Frasson, Gauthier, Lesgold (Eds.), Springer: Berlin, 1996. pp. 261-269.
IRIS	See Chapter 9 in this volume. Arruarte, A., Fernandez-Castro, I., Ferrero, B. & Greer, J. (1997). The IRIS shell: How to build ITSs from pedagogical and design requisites. *International J. of Artificial Intelligence in Education*. Vol. 8, No. 3-4, pp. 341-381.
LAT (LEAP Authoring Tool)	See Chapter 14 in this volume. Sparks, R. Dooley, S., Meiskey, L. & Blumenthal, R. (1999). The LEAP authoring tool: supporting complex courseware authoring through reuse, rapid prototyping, and interactive visualizations. *Int. J. of Artificial Intelligence in Education*. Dooley, S., Meiskey, L., Blumenthal, R., & Sparks, R. (1995). Developing reusable intelligent tutoring system shells. In AIED-95 workshop papers for Authoring Shells for Intelligent Tutoring Systems.
MetaLinks	Murray, T., Condit, C., & Haaugsjaa, E. (1998). MetaLinks: A Preliminary Framework for Concept-based Adaptive Hypermedia. *Workshop Proceedings from ITS-98 WWW-Based Tutoring Workshop.*, San Antonio, Texas, 1998.
REDEEM (& COCA)	See Chapter 8 in this volume. Major, N., Ainsworth, S. & Wood, D. (1997). REDEEM: Exploiting symbiosis between psychology and authoring environments. *International J. of Artificial Intelligence in Education*. Vol. 8, No. 3-4, pp. 317-340. Major, N. (1995). Modeling Teaching Strategies. *J. of AI in*

	Education, 6(2/3), pp. 117-152. Major, N.P. & Reichgelt, H (1992). COCA - A shell for intelligent tutoring systems. In Frasson, C., Gauthier, G., & McCalla, G.I. (Eds.) *Procs. of Intelligent Tutoring Systems '92.* New York: Springer-Verlag.
RIDES (& IMTS, RAPIDS, and see DIAG)	See Chapter 3 in this volume. Munro, A., Johnson, M.C., Pizzini, Q.A., Surmon, D.S., Towne, D.M, & Wogulis, J.L. (1997). Authoring simulation-centered tutors with RIDES. *International J. of Artificial Intelligence in Education.* Vol. 8 , No. 3-4, pp. 284-316. Towne, D.M., Munro, A., (1988). The Intelligent Maintenance Training System. In Psotka, Massey, & Mutter (Eds.), *Intelligent Tutoring Systems, Lessons Learned.* Hillsdale, NJ: Lawrence Erlbaum.
SIMQUEST (& SMISLE)	See Chapter 1 in this volume. Jong, T. de & vanJoolingen, W.R. (1998). Scientific discovery learning with computer simulations of conceptual domains. *Review of Educational Research*, Vol. 68 No. 2, pp. 179-201. Van Joolingen, W.R. & Jong, T. de (1996). Design and implementation of simulation-based discovery environments: The SMISLE solution. *Int. J. of Artificial Intelligence in Education* 7(3/4). pp. 253-276.
Smart Trainer (& FITS, ontology-based tools)	Ikeda, M. & Mizoguchi, R. (1994). FITS: A Framework for ITS--A computational model of tutoring. J. of Artificial Intelligence in Education 5(3) pp. 319-348. Mizoguchi, R., Sinitsa, K., Ikeda, M. (1996). Knowledge Engineering of Educational Systems for Authoring System Design. In Proceedings. of EuroAIED-96, Lisbon, pp. 593-600. Ikeda, M., Seta, K. & Mizoguchi, R. (1997). Task ontology makes it easier to use authoring tools. Proc. of IJCAI-97, Nagoya, Japan. Mizoguchi, R. & Bourdeau, J. (2000). Using ontological engineering to overcome common AI-ED problems Int. J. of Artificial Intelligence and Education, Vol. 11. pp 107-121. Yayashi, Y., Ideda, M., Seta, K., Kakusho, O. & Mizoguchi, R. (2000). Is what you write what you get?: An operational model of training scenario. Proc. of Intelligent Tutoring Systems 2000.
Swift (& DOCENT, Study)	Winne P.H. (1991). Project DOCENT: Design for a Teacher's Consultant. In Goodyear (Ed.), *Teaching Knowledge and Intelligent Tutoring.* Norwood, NJ: Ablex. Winne, P. & Kramer, L. (1988). "Representing and Inferencing with Knowledge about Teaching: DOCENT." *Proceedings of ITS-88.* June 1988,Montreal, Canada.
TANGOW	Carro, R.M., Pulido, E.., Rodriquies, P. (2002). *An authoring tool that automates the process of developing task-based adaptive courses on the web.* J. of AI and Education.

TRAINING EXPRESS	Clancey, W. & Joerger, K. (1988). "A Practical Authoring Shell for Apprenticeship Learning." *Proceedings of ITS-88*, 67-74. June 1988, Montreal.
WEAR	Virvou, M & Moundridou, M. (2001). Adding an instructor modeling component to the architecture of ITS authoring tools. *Int. J. of Artificial Intelligence in Education* 12(2), pp 185-211.
XAIDA	See Chapter 2 in this volume. Hsieh, P., Halff, H, Redfield, C. (1999). Four easy pieces: Developing systems for knowledge-based generative instruction. *Int. J. of Artificial Intelligence in Education.* Wenzel, B., Dirnberger, M., Hsieh, P., Chudanov, T., & Halff, H. (1998). Evaluating Subject Matter Experts' Learning and Use of an ITS Authoring Tool. *Proceedings of ITS-98*, San Antonio, TX, pp. 156-165. Redfield, C.L., (1996). "Demonstration of the experimental advanced instructional design advisor." In the *Third International Conference on Intelligent Tutoring Systems*, Montreal, Quebec, Canada, June 12-14, 1996

Author Index

A

Ainsworth, 2, 206, 222, 223, 224, 225, 226, 227, 228, 311, 332, 350, 477, 519, 525
Almond, 151
Anderson, 151, 152, 205, 245, 260, 274, 315, 331, 382, 415, 449, 469, 480, 495, 500, 542, 93, 94, 95, 97, 112, 116, 118
Aroyo, 300
Arroyo, 526
Arruarte, 233, 234, 243, 244, 248, 255, 256, 257, 259, 270, 544
Ausubel, 449

B

Bailey, 50
Balacheff, 274
Bareiss, 369, 393
Barnard, 243
Barr, 271
Beaumont, 378, 381, 382, 390
Bell, 117, 207, 343, 344, 345, 368, 369, 438, 456, 502, 520, 544
Betz, 441
Blessing, 114, 117, 206, 260, 350, 469, 480, 485, 490, 542
Bloom, 205, 238, 239, 245, 272, 274, 276, 280, 281, 299, 412, 438, 439, 449, 451, 506, 515
Blumenthal, 411, 544
Bonfigli, 398
Boose, 513
Boring, 34
Borning, 69
Bourdeau,, 528, 545
Boyle, 390, 391, 93, 116
Brailsford, 391, 398, 404
Breuker, 243
Brown, 110, 150, 229, 364, 411, 450
Bruner, 212, 439, 451
Brusilovsky, 377, 378, 379, 381, 382, 383, 384, 385, 386, 388, 389, 391, 393, 395, 397, 398, 405, 446, 450, 452, 503, 510, 544
Burton, 110, 450

C

Carbonell, 52, 54, 55, 56
Carlsen, 2
Carmona, 385, 395, 399

Carr, 241
Carro, 545
Casaus, 48
Chandrasekaran, 521
Cheikes, 331, 478, 486, 490, 530
Chipman, 149, 542
Clancey, 309 450, 523, 546
Coffey, 404
Cohen, 205
Coller, 63
Collins, 151, 41, 411, 450, 463, 508
Corbett, 245, 480, 93, 94
Cypher, 93, 101

D

Derry, 150, 269, 271
Di Eugenio, 144
Diaz de Ilarraza, 243
Diessel, 394
Dobson, 344, 365, 369, 544
Dodds, 55
Domeshek, 365, 369
Dooley, 411, 544

E

Edwards, 364
Elsom-Cook, 63, 241, 339, 384
Ericsson, 478
Evertsz, 240

F

Ferguson, 364, 463
Fernández-Castro, 233, 237, 250, 261
Ferrero, 233, 245, 250, 544
Finch, 269
Fitzgerald, 530
Forbus, 124, 530, 63
Forte, 530
Fox, 474, 48, 51
Forcheri, 379, 388, 397
Frasson, 269, 274, 277, 285, 288, 299, 541, 543, 544
Fuller, 86

G

Gagné, 168, 238, 271, 272, 273, 274, 276, 281, 298, 299, 300, 304, 34, 35, 57
Garrett, 364
Gavignet, 249, 395
Gellevij, 21, 30
Gettman, 35
Gijlers, 30
Ginsburg, 439
Goan, 350
Goel, 365, 369
Goldstein, 241, 249, 450
Gonschorek, 378, 381
Goodkovsky, 495, 508
Goodyear, 495, 543, 545
Gordon, 157, 165
Graesser, 206, 234, 469
Grandbastien, 379, 394
Grigoriadou, 379, 382, 383, 384, 387, 388
Gruber, 331, 454, 528
Gutiérrez, 233, 237, 240, 261, 378

H

Halff, 33, 34, 35, 37, 38, 40, 48, 49, 52, 55, 93, 202, 206, 269, 311, 450, 463
Hall, 390, 50
Hartley, 269, 271, 272
Henze, 382, 383, 384, 388, 392
Hickey, 35
Hill, 364, 85
Hockemeyer, 379, 382, 394
Hodgins, 529, 530
Hoffman, 455, 513
Hohl, 378, 382, 386
Hollan, 52, 55, 62
Holt, 240
Hothi, 390
Hsieh, 33, 34, 37, 38, 40, 47, 48, 49, 546
Hubert, 172

I

Ikeda, 258, 495, 528, 541, 545

J

Johnson, 123, 125, 127, 205, 364, 495, 541, 545, 80
Johnson-Laird, 154
Jona, 343, 350, 456, 457, 495, 520, 528, 544
Jonassen, 498
Jones, 270, 543
de Jong, 1, 2, 3, 5, 7, 9, 12, 19, 20, 25, 26, 30, 112, 207, 545, 63
van Joolingen, 1, 3, 5, 9, 12, 19, 25, 26, 29, 63, 112, 207
Jorgensen, 86

K

Kass, 350, 368, 495, 520, 528, 544
Kay, 300, 378
Khuwaja, 234
Kiyama, 541
Klahr, 5
Klausmeier, 272, 276, 279
Kobsa, 390
Kok, 240
Kosko, 132
Kroeber, 364
Krueger, 255
Kumar, 530
Kurhila, 398
Kuyper, 30
Kyllonen, 449

L

Lajoie, 122, 150, 205, 541, 542
Laroussi, 389, 394
Larrañaga, 260
Lave, 411
Lefebvre, 274, 277, 283, 289
Leinhardt, 452
Lesgold, 122, 205, 269, 271, 272, 339, 411, 452, 462
Lesser, 331
Lewis, 474, 93, 112
Limbach, 20, 30
Lin, 393
Löhner, 10, 30

M

Macmillan, 349
Mager, 282
Major, 206, 217, 223, 243, 257, 259, 273, 331, 544
Mark, 205, 261, 262, 469, 493, 93
McArthur, 474
McCalla, 269, 270, 495, 543, 544
McKendree, 480
McMillan, 495
Meij, 21, 30
Meiskey, 411, 437, 544
Merrill, 151, 168, 181, 186, 201, 202, 237, 270, 274, 276, 279, 298, 299, 300, 311,
    35, 37, 40, 47, 52, 449, 451, 463, 498, 501, 537, 543
Metcalfe, 364
Mills, 201, 537, 543
Milosavljevic, 377, 387
Miner, 364
Minstrell, 154
Mislevy, 151, 166
Mitrovic, 245
Mitsuhara, 394
Mizoguchi, 258, 270, 300, 455, 495, 508, 528, 545
Moore, 364, 391, 541
Muller, 433
Munro, 123, 127, 207, 25, 259, 273, 315, 323, 47, 545, 61, 63, 68, 74, 78, 80
Murray, 167, 168, 181, 202, 206, 207, 221, 223, 229, 233, 256, 258, 259, 26, 27,
    28, 29, 270, 272, 273, 298, 300, 309, 331, 336, 349, 350, 379, 393, 395, 398,
    402, 439, 463, 465, 471, 493, 496, 500, 503, 508, 517, 530, 534, 542, 544,
    54, 93
Myers, 93

N

Nardi, 101
Nejdl, 382, 383
Neumann, 379, 382, 394
Neves, 115, 116
Newell, 115
Njoo, 5, 7
Nkambou, 258, 269, 274, 277, 283, 285, 288, 289, 299, 541

O

Oberlander, 377
Ohlsson, 217, 245, 332, 493

Ong, 350
Owen, 397

P

Paquette, 298, 300, 38, 40
Passardiere, 378, 383
Pérez, 378, 381, 386, 388, 392
Person, 469, 493
Pilar da Silva, 382, 386, 387
Pirolli, 298
Pizzini, 123, 128, 545
Pizzini, 63, 78, 80
Polson, 150, 271, 34, 37, 53
Puppe, 541

Q

Qiu, 344, 365, 369, 544

R

Rainey, 86
Redfield, 33, 34, 37, 38, 541, 546
Reigeluth, 239, 299, 37, 449, 454, 462, 498
Reinhardt, 350, 541
Reye, 234
Richardson, 150, 364, 48
Riesbeck, 344, 365, 369, 544
Ritter, 350, 451, 469, 472, 474, 485, 486, 490, 510, 526, 529, 530, 531, 87, 94, 114
Roschelle, 529, 530
Rosé, 469, 493
Rueda, 254
Russell, 206, 256, 273, 298, 331, 349, 543

S

Saab, 30
Salvucci, 97
Sanrach, 379, 395, 542
Scandura, 237
Schank, 154, 343, 356, 357, 370, 452
Schewe, 541
Schöch, 395
Schoening, 441

Schofield, 480
Schvaneveldt, 50, 52
Schwarz, 377, 381, 384, 386, 395
Self, 240, 66
Shaw, 513
Shraagen, 166
Shute, 118, 149, 150, 151, 155, 156, 166, 167, 169, 170, 205, 222, 449, 493, 542
Sleeman, 150
Smith, 101
Soloway, 205
Sparks, 229, 411, 456, 515, 544
Specht, 379, 383, 384, 391, 395, 398, 401, 404
Spector, 271, 34, 35, 38, 40
Spensley, 332, 63
Srisetamil, 234
Steinacker, 379, 382, 387, 393, 404
Stern, 379, 390
Stevens, 237, 240, 62
Stiles, 79, 80
Stollberg, 364
Süß, 379, 394, 398, 404
Suthers, 530
Sutman, 364
Swaak, 30

T

Taffel, 364
Tennyson, 298, 299, 305, 37, 53
Towne, 123, 124, 125, 128, 142, 207, 273, 315, 35, 542, 545, 63, 74, 86
Trella, 395

U

Underwood, 221, 223, 225, 228, 229
Urretavizcaya, 233, 245

V

Vadillo, 243
Vallarino, 364
Van Marcke, 207, 234, 257, 273, 331, 332, 452, 455, 457, 508, 543
VanLehn, 152, 449
Vassileva, 234, 382, 384, 385, 395
Veermans, 30

Verdejo, 240, 245
Verhoeven, 404
Virvou, 229, 263, 546

W

Wasson, 249, 495
Weber, 379, 381, 382, 383, 387, 388, 394, 395, 399, 404
Webster, 280
Weisbruch, 364
Wenger, 240, 261, 327, 383, 411, 440, 445, 455, 493
Wenzel, 33, 34, 38, 48, 49, 51, 546
Westcourt, 450
Wetzel, 530
White, 154, 500, 7
Wiederholt, 123
Williams, 169, 223, 225, 364, 62
Winne, 495, 526, 545
Wong, 543
Woods, 490
Woolf, 206, 298, 310, 379, 463, 93

Y

Yayashi, 528, 545
Youngblut, 498, 537

Z

Zadeh, 132

Subject Index

A

adaptive hypermedia, 450, 452, 466, 503, 511, (and see Chapter 13)
AHA, 391, 394, 395, 397, 403, 407, 408, 512
AICC, 404
ALE, 384, 391, 395, 399, 401, 402, 410
annotation, 388, 389, 405, 497
ASK, 393

B

BioWorld-Case Builder, 496, 502, 532, 541

C

CAIRNEY, 541
CALAT, 496, 532, 534, 535, 541
CAMELEON, 394, 409
CLAI Model, 234, 244, 258, 265, 266
COCA, 206, 217, 231, 257, 258, 267, 339, 496, 500, 508, 536, 546
Component Display Theory, 237, 267, 449, 467, 540
CREAM-Tools, 260, 268, 496, 505, 507, 513, 532, 533, 534, 543, (and see Chapter 10)

D

D3-TRAINER, 541
Demonstr8, 206, 257, (and see Chapter 4)
DETECTive, 246, 247, 251, 261, 263
DIAG, 86, 89, 273, 496, 499, 501, 516, 531, 532, 533, 534, 535, 542, 545, (and see Chapter 5)
diagnosis, 121, 122, 124, 142, 146, 155, 207, 234, 237, 240, 246, 249, 252, 253, 260, 261, 263, 273, 278, 333, 364, 497, 499, 501, 502, 517, 521, 523, 534 (and see student model)
DNA, 496, 506, 510, 514, 515, 521, 524, 526, 532, 534, 535, 537, 542, 448, 449, 450, 451, (and see Chapter 6)
domain model, 149, 150, 169, 170, 176, 205, 224, 240, 25, 273, 309, 314, 315, 381, 382, 383, 384, 385, 386, 388, 389, 390, 394, 398, 403, 404, 414, 441, 445, 454, 504, 505, 506, 513, 514, 527, 64

E

ECSAIWeb, 395, 409, 496, 516, 544
ELM-ART, 387, 388, 389, 393, 395, 396, 400, 405, 407, 410
Eon, 207, 258, 273, 496, 499, 503, 504, 507, 508, 512, 513, 524, 525, 528, 531, 532, 533, 534, 542, (and see Chapters 11, 15)
EXPERT-CML, 543

F

FITS, 259, 267, 495, 547
form-based interface, 398, 400, 401, 402, 403
free exploration, 236, 245, 538
Frogalan, 263, 264

G

GETMAS, 496, 543
glossaries, 387
granularity, 212, 385, 540
GTE, 207, 256, 257, 258, 273, 332, 394, 452, 496, 499, 507, 508, 532, 543

H

hypermedia, 377, 378, 379, 380, 381, 385, 388, 389, 390, 393, 394, 395, 403, 404, 405, 406, 407, 408, 409, 446, 491, 504, (and see Chapter 13)
hyperspace, 377, 378, 379, 380, 385, 386, 387, 388, 389, 391, 392, 393, 394, 396, 398, 399, 400, 404
hypertext, 20, 518, (and see hypermedia)

I

IDE, 257, 258, 268, 273, 298, 496, 505, 508, 527, 533, 545
IMTS, 63, 123, 124, 137, 145, 545
IMS, 168, 305, 404, 531
INSPIRE, 384, 388, 408
instructional design, 157, 164, 166, 168, 169, 170, 173, 177, 202, 204, 232, 259, 260, 264, 268, 269, 271, 286, 291, 299, 303, 304, 305, 311, 33, 34, 35, 36, 37, 38, 40, 53, 54, 55, 56, 57, 58, 59, 344, 4, 22, 26, 30, 31, 440, 442, 443, 446, 451, 453, 457, 463, 464, 466, 493, 499, 503, 510, 512, 515, 523, 525, 526, 528, 529, 545, 548
instructional objectives, 121, 240, 247, 248, 249, 255, 265, 272, 280, 283, 284, 292, 293, 297, 304, 40, 47, 452, 499, 505, 508, 69, 80

InterBook, 384, 387, 388, 389, 392, 393, 395, 396, 397, 398, 400, 401, 402, 405, 496, 512, 546
INTZA, 233, 237, 240, 241, 267
IRIS, 306, 448, 449, 450, 451, 452, 490, 496, 505, 507, 508, 513, 533, 534, 546, (and see Chapter 9)
ISIS-Tutor, 388, 389, 391, 395, 405

K

KAFITS, 20, 298, 309, 338, 534, 535, 542
KBS-Hyperbook, 393

L

LEAP Authoring Tool (LAT), 450, 496, 502, 512, 515, 520, 521, 524, 525, 532, 535, 544, (and see Chapter 14)
learner model, 234, 240, 241, 242, 256, 270, 272 (and see student model)
learning goal, 164, 265, 316, 378, 380, 384, 389, 452, 5, 66 (and see learning objective)
learning objective, 157, 164, 238, 260, 270, 271, 273, 280, 291, 381, 404, 449, 452, 507, 529, 530, 53, 55, 66
LISP-Critic, 389

M

Maisu, 236, 237, 238, 239, 240, 242, 244, 247, 248, 251, 255, 256, 257, 262, 264
markup approach, 394, 396, 397, 403
metadata, 299, 397, 404, 410
MetaDoc, 391, 406
MetaLinks, 393, 395, 399, 402, 409, 467, 496, 505, 533, 546
Model-Directed Diagnosi, 251
model-tracing, 246, 261, 339, 466, 470, 474, 475
motivation, 236, 237, 244, 245, 247, 256, 266, 434, 448, 499, 514
Multibook, 393
multiple teaching styles, 234

O

overlay model, 219, 383 (and see student model)

P

page indexing, 389, 390, 392, 401
PaKMaS, 394, 398
pedagogic knowledge, 244, 250, 261

pedagogy oriented system, 257
performance oriented system, 257, 260
prerequisite, 208, 210, 240, 245, 254, 257, 271, 283, 284, 289, 297, 299, 311, 315, 316, 318, 327, 382, 384, 386, 388, 389, 396, 397, 399, 400, 440, 443, 445, 450, 452, 458, 463, 465, 496, 499, 518
procedural contents, 234

R

RAPIDS, 63, 75, 545
RATH, 394, 408
REDEEM, 259, 273, 306, 333, 371, 448, 449, 450, 452, 477, 490, 496, 500, 505, 508, 509, 512, 514, 515, 516, 526, 527, 532, 533, 535, 536, 537, 538, 546, (and see Chapter 8)
RIDES, 25, 127, 202, 207, 256, 259, 273, 323, 450, 451, 452, 47, 57, 471, 496, 499, 500, 503, 504, 505, 508, 510, 512, 515, 516, 517, 521, 525, 531, 532, 545, (and see Chapter 3)
RTF, 396 (and see XML)

S

SCORM, 168, 300, 305, 404, 531, 57
SIGUE, 395, 399, 400, 402, 407
SIMQUEST, 207, 496, 500, 503, 505, 515, 531, 532, 545, (and see Chapter 1)
SKILL, 394, 409
SMISLE, 25, 63, , 532, 545
standards, 130, 156, 172, 179, 19, 27, 205, 207, 213, 260, 263, 297, 381, 393, 397, 473, 477, 479, 490, 501, 507, 511, 525, 76, 86, 87 (and see SCORM)
student model, 149, 150, 152, 154, 155, 156, 213, 218, 219, 241, 258, 269, 270, 272, 274, 277, 278, 283, 288, 289, 291, 306, 309, 314, 319, 328, 329, 333, 340, 378, 380, 383, 384, 394, 44, 47, 441, 445, 453, 454, 455, 456, 457, 459, 460, 465, 469, 475, 476, 497, 504, 509, 513, 516, 520, 523, 524, 525, 530, 539, 544, 67, 69, 84, 87, (and see user model)
student modeling, 154, 155, 156, 274, 277, 278, 291, 329, 378, 497 (and see student model)
symbolic differentiation, 236, 237, 248, 534

T

taxonomy of teaching objectives, 238
TANGOW, 496, 545
teaching styles, 221, 222
THuman, 262, 264
TRAINING EXPRESS, 546

U

user model, 377, 378, 379, 382, 391, 401, 409, 509, (and see student model)

X

XAIDA, 448, 450, 451, 452, 471, 496, 499, 500, 505, 506, 508, 511, 521, 524, 525, 526, 527, 532, 533, 534, 535, 536, 546, (and see Chapter 2)
XML, 299, 397, 398, 404, 406, 487